THE NAMES OF YEMENITE JEWRY
A SOCIAL AND CULTURAL HISTORY

In appreciation
to the esteemed
brothers Reuven (Ronald) and Ya'akov (Jay) Domb
Manhattan, New York

Descendants of the Dayyan Rabbi Aharon ben Shalom Hakohen
Ṣan'a, Yemen

May the Lord bless their offspring and enjoy their deeds.

STUDIES AND TEXTS IN
JEWISH HISTORY AND CULTURE
The Joseph and Rebecca Meyerhoff Center for Jewish Studies
University of Maryland
XXVII

THE NAMES OF YEMENITE JEWRY

A SOCIAL AND CULTURAL HISTORY

by
Aharon Gaimani

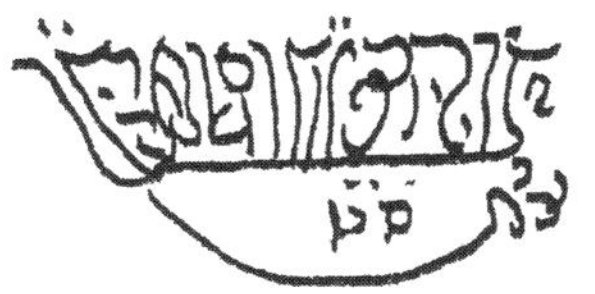

University Press of Maryland
Bethesda, Maryland
2017

LIBRARY OF CONGRESS CATALOGING-IN-PUBLICATION DATA

Names: Gimani, Aharon, author.
Title: The names of Yemenite Jewry : a social and cultural history / by Aharon Gaimani.
Description: Bethesda, Maryland : University Press of Maryland, 2017. | Series: Studies and texts in Jewish history and culture ; XXVII
Identifiers: LCCN 2015048919 | ISBN 9781934309582
Subjects: LCSH: Names, Personal—Jewish—Yemen (Republic) | Jews—Yemen (Republic)—Genealogy. | Jews—Yemen (Republic)—Social life and customs. | Yemen (Republic)—Ethnic relations.
Classification: LCC CS3010.Z9 Y465 2017 | DDC 929.4089/9240533—dc2

Cover photograph: Lineage of the Qoraḥ Family in a manuscript of the Mishnah, Tractate Avot, copied by Rabbi Yosef Qoraḥ, 20th century; in the possession of Pinḥas Qoraḥ, Bnei Brak.

ISBN 9781934309582

Studies in Jewish Onomastics

The Project for the Study of Jewish Names

Israel and Golda Koschitsky Department
of Jewish History and Contemporary Jewry
Bar Ilan University Ramat-Gan, Israel

JEWISH NAMES שמות

Aaron Demsky, Series Editor

Volume 1
Pleasant Are Their Names: Jewish Names in the Sephardi Diaspora
Aaron Demsky ed.
ISBN 9781934309247

Volume 2
The Names of Yemenite Jewry: A Social and Cultural History
Aharon Gaimani
ISBN 9781934309582

TABLE OF CONTENTS

PART III: ADDITIONAL ASPECTS

PREFACE

The name given to a person has deep significance; it is a window onto one's society. It carries the weight of the family's past and the parents' wishes for the newborn; it expresses values, feelings, and aspirations.

Thus far, no in-depth study has been made of the names of Yemenite Jewry. For this present work, I gathered a great deal of material on the various Jewish communities of Yemen and analyzed the characteristics and uniqueness of the names in comparison to those of other Jewish communities. In this study, I relied upon a range of documents and certificates from Yemen, among them religious-court record books (*pinkas* Bet Din), marriage (*ketubbah*) and divorce (*get*) documents, and manuscript colophons, as well as works by Yemenite rabbis, mainly volumes of responsa and *halakha*. I also availed myself of the writings of emissaries and travelers to Yemen. Further assistance came from the writings of rabbis and scholars in the diaspora who have dealt with the issue of naming.

An important source was information gleaned from questionnaires containing twenty-six questions relating to naming conventions originating in Yemen. This data, as well as information from distinguished rabbis who graciously took the time to reply at length to my queries, have been extremely valuable for research into the customs of Yemenite Jewry on this topic.

In this study, I have focused on the uniqueness of Yemenite Jews, which is expressed in ancient traditions, such as calling a father and his son or a mother and her daughter by the same name. I have examined the characteristics of the personal names, the frequency of their usage, the translations or equivalences of names from the earliest time, and the influence of Islamic culture. I have also included in this study issues such as giving certain names as a *segula* (blessing for life), changing a name, encoding names in poems and works by poets and rabbis of Yemen, lineages in Yemen, and the custom of giving names in the synagogue. I conclude this work by examining the changes in naming conventions that occurred after the mass immigration of Yemenite Jews to Israel in the middle of the twentieth century.

I express my gratitude to Prof. Aaron Demsky, the leading figure in the research into Jewish names. He encouraged me to study of the names of Yemenite Jewry and participate in the international conferences he organized and subsequent scholarly publications, including the series, *And These Are the Names*, which he edited. May he enjoy a good, long life and pleasant years, and see the fruits of all his endeavors.

I thank my friend R. Itamar Ḥayim Cohen, who is closely involved in the spiritual heritage of Yemenite Jewry, for reading my manuscript and sharing his reactions with me.

I am grateful to Avraham Ben Amitai for his advice and insight into arranging the chapters in the book and for his incisive comments on all facets of this volume. I would like to express my appreciation and thanks to the translator, Fern Seckbach, for her meticulous work and for bringing the volume to press. I wish to express my gratitude to Prof. Bernard Cooperman for including this volume within the framework of the series.

A special blessing to the distinguished Domb family, to the father Shalom (Sam) and the children Reuven (Ronald), Ya'akov (Jay), and Michal (Michelle), of Manhattan, New York, who supported me in my research into the heritage of Yemenite Jewry. This book is dedicated to them and for *ilui nishmat* of their mother, Sarah née Sirri, a great-granddaughter of the *dayyan*, R. Aharon ben Shalom Hakohen (Yemen 1841–1934), one of the most outstanding and esteemed rabbis of Yemen in the first third of the twentieth century. I wish to bless them with the blessing of Moses to the Children of Israel (Deut. 1:11): "May the Lord, the God of your fathers, increase your numbers a thousandfold, and bless you as He promised you."

To my parents, who were privileged to emigrate from Yemen to Israel after two thousand years of exile and who raised their eleven children under difficult circumstances with loving-kindness and mercy and who passed away at advanced ages. May we be comforted in the ingathering of the exiles and the building of Jerusalem.

I conclude with appreciation to my wife Beruria, whose name is beautiful and deeds pleasant, as stated in Midrash Genesis Rabbah (71:3), "Said Rabbi Yose bar Hanina, 'Names [of people] fall into four categories . . .some have fair names and their deeds are fair." To my children, who were given names of righteous people and men of action, as stated in Midrash Tanḥuma (*parashat Ha'azinu*, section 7): "One should take care to call his son a name that is worthy of someone who is righteous, since sometimes the name brings about good." To my sons Amitai and Aviran, Amihai and my daughter-in-law Odelia, and my daughter Shani and my son-in-law Doron, and to my grandchildren Shiraz, Amit, and Sharon, may it be God's will that we shall see them grow to be a source of pride for the Jewish people. I fervently pray to the Creator for my children who devote themselves to the building up of the nation and the Land: "They were swifter than eagles, they were stronger than lions." May there be peace among our children, serenity in our homes.

Aharon Gaimani
January 2017

Note to the Reader:

The Arabic names presented in this volume come from various periods and different areas of Yemen, which results in variant spellings and makes total consistency difficult to achieve. Pronunciation of the same name often differed in the various regions of Yemen, and this is reflected in the listings. The same applies to place names. For instance, there is variance between *g* and *q*, even when orthographically they are indistinguishable. In general, initial *alef* is not indicated. Short and long vowels are indicated (*ā*; *ī*; *ū*) as found in the spelling of names (they are not indicated for Hebrew names). The women's names as listed in this volume reflect the orthography, such as the *h* (ה) or alef (′) at the end of a name.

Arabic transcription

ا *alif a*	ض *ḍad ḍ*
ب *ba b*	ط *ṭa ṭ*
ت *ta t*	ظ *ẓa z*
ث *tha th*	ع *'ayn '*
ج *jim j*	غ *ghayn gh*
ح *ḥal ḥ*	ف f
خ *khal kh*	ق *qaf q* (also g)
د *dal d*	ك *kaf k*
ذ *dhal dh*	ل *lam l*
ر *ra r*	م *mim m*
ز *zay z*	ن *nun n*
س *sin s*	ه *hey h*
ش *shin sh*	و *waw w*

ABBREVIATIONS

AM	Anno Mundi: Year After Creation
OBM	Of Blessed Memory, equivalent of *zal*
SEL	Seleucid year
TB	Babylonian Talmud
TP	Palestinian Talmud

'ky"r	*amen ken yehi raṣon*	Amen, may it be His will
'"m	*adoni mori*	My master, my teacher
'm"v	*avi mori ve-rabbi*	My father my teacher and my rabbi
"mv"r	*adoni avi mori ve-rabbi*	My revered father, lit. My master, my father, my teacher and rabbi
hy"v	*Hashem yishmerehu veyeḥayyehu*	May the Lord protect and sustain him
kh"r	*kevod ha-rav rabbi*	The honorable rav, rabbi
kmh"r	*kevod morenu ha-rav*	Our honorable teacher and rav, rabbi
kmhr"r	*kevod morenu ha-rav rabbi*	Our honorable teacher and rav, rabbi
m"w	*morenu ve-rabbenu*	Our teacher and rabbi
mv; mmvr	*mi-mori ve-rabbi*	My teacher and rabbi
mv"z	*mori u-zeqeni*	My teacher and grandfather
n"'	*nuḥo 'eden*	May he rest in Eden
n'"g	*nuḥo 'eden gan*	May he rest in the Garden of Eden

ng"'	*nuḥo gan 'eden*	May he rest in the Garden of Eden
nrv	*niṣaro ram ve-nisa*	May the Lord protect and redeem him
s"ṭ	*sin ve-tin*	Mire and mud (an expression of humbleness)
tanṣebah	*tihye nishmato ṣerurah bi-ṣror ha-ḥayim*	May his soul be bound in the bond of life
yshl	*yenon shemo la'ad*	May his name last forever
yṣ"v	*yishmerehu ṣuro veyoṣero*	May His Rock and Redeemer [or Creator] protect him
zal	*zikhrono li-vrakhah*	Of blessed memory; OBM
zaṣal	*zekher ṣaddiq li-vrakhah*	Blessed be the memory of the true righteous man
zaṣuqal	*zekher qaddish ve-ṣaddiq li-vrakah*	May the memory of the righteous and saintly be a blessing
zlhh	*zikhrono le-ḥayyei ha-'olam ha-ba*	May his memory be everlasting

INTRODUCTION

Yemen is located at the southwestern tip of the Arabian Peninsula. The highlands of Yemen, which traverse the entire length of the country from the north to the south, is a highly fertile mountainous region, in the past referred to as Arabia Felix (Happy Arabia). Most of the population dwells in the highlands, where the major cities are located: Ṣa'dah, Ḥajjah, Ṣan'a, Radā', Dhamār, Yarīm, and Ibb.

The Jewish community of Yemen is ancient and, according to legend, the initial settling of Jews there took place at the time of the First Temple. On the tradition held by the Yemenite Jews as to their arrival in the country, R. Shelomo 'Adani, one of the expellees from Yemen who immigrated to the Land of Israel in the sixteenth century, wrote: "From the aforementioned parental home of my father, I have a tradition that there were Yemenite cities that were redeemed from the first exile, for he had read as it is written at the end of the Book of Kings 'and he set them (biblical text: placed them) in Halah, and in Habor, on the river of Gozan, and in the cities of the Medes' (2 Kings 17:6), it speaks also of us."[1] We have proof after the destruction of the Second Temple,

1. Introduction to the commentary on the Mishnah *Melekhet Shelomo*, printed in the introductions to part one of the series. The verse cited by R. Shlomo 'Adani refers to the expulsion of the Ten Tribes from the Land of Israel by the king of Assyria, an event that took place 135 years before the destruction of the First Temple. For extensive coverage of the event, see 2 Kings 17. For a discussion of the various traditions, see Aharon Gaimani, *Temurot be-Moreshet Yahadut Teiman: be-Hashpa'at ha-Shulḥan 'Arukh ve-Qabalat ha-Ari* (Ramat Gan: Bar-Ilan University, 2005), pp. 15–16; Yehudah Ratzaby, *"Ezra ha-Sofer ve-Golei Teiman,"* in his *Be-Ma'agalot Teiman* (Tel Aviv, 1948), pp. 1–5; Joseph Tobi, *'Iyyunim bi-Megillat Teiman* (Jerusalem, 1986), pp. 57–63.

from the period of the Mishna onward. Found in a mosque in the village of Bayt al-Ḥāḏer, near Ṣan'a, was a stone with a Hebrew inscription containing a partial list of the Priestly Divisions.[2] According to Efraim Elimelech Urbach, this is evidence that priests were among those exiled from the Land of Israel to Yemen after the destruction.[3]

We lack the information needed to estimate the number of Jews living in Yemen during various historical periods, but, according to an assessment in the first half of the twentieth century, the Jews of Yemen then numbered around 80,000. The vast majority, about 85 percent, lived in villages and were scattered over 1,100 settlements. The large Jewish communities were in the middle of Ṣan'a, the capital; in the northern part of the city of Ṣa'dah; south of Ṣan'a in the cities Radā', Dhamār, and Yarīm; and at the southern end, in the coastal city of Aden.[4] During the early months of the Hebrew year 5642 (October 1881), groups of Yemenite Jews began to emigrate to the Land of Israel, and this *aliyah* continued almost incessantly until the mass emigration of 1949–1950, known as *'Al Kanfei Nesharim*, "On the Wings of Eagles," thereby ending almost entirely the Yemenite Diaspora.[5]

Geographically, Yemen is distant, and thus somewhat isolated, from other Jewish communities, a fact that enabled Yemenite Jews to preserve ancient customs that were forgotten over the course of centuries elsewhere. The spiritual heritage of the Jews of Yemen contains more ancient traditions and customs than does any other Jewish community.[6] This phenomenon has stimulated researchers to become

2. Discovered and photographed by Dr. Walter W. Mueller, a member of the German archaeological mission that went to Yemen in 1970. See Reiner Diegan, *"Ketovet mi-Teiman al 24 Mishmerot Kehuna," Tarbiẓ* 42 (1973): 302.

3. See E. E. Urbach, *"Mishmarot u-Ma'amadot," Tarbiẓ* 42 (1973): 308–27. For additional evidence, see Gaimani, *Temurot be-Moreshet*, 15–16 n. 1.

4. On the number of communities and their distribution throughout Yemen, see Moshe Gavra, *Enṣiqlopedya le-Qehilot ha-Yehudiyyot be-Teiman*, I, introduction (Bnei Brak, 2005), pp. 25–36.

5. Until the founding of Israel, some 25,000 people immigrated to the land, and "On the Wings of Eagles" brought some 50,000 to the country. Remaining today in northern Yemen are a few hundred Jews, and the government does not prevent them from leaving. See Aharon Gaimani, *"Ha-Hanhaga ha-Yehudit be-Ṣan'a 'im Ḥissul Golat Teiman" (Sanaa's Jewish Leadership and Communal Self-Liquidation), Miqqedem Umiyyam* 7 (2000): 196–200. Owing to a lack of statistics in Yemen, the numbers are estimations. On the different assessments, see Gavra, *Enṣiqlopedya le-Qehilot be-Teiman*, pp. 26–27.

6. For a comprehensive discussion of this topic, see Gaimani, *Temurot be-Moreshet*.

familiar with the culture and spiritual heritage of Yemenite Jews. The most prominent of the twentieth-century scholars were Abraham Zevi Idelsohn, who did research on Yemenite poetry;[7] Erich Brauer, who studied the ethnology of the Jews of Yemen;[8] and Shlomo Dov Goitein, the well-known scholar of the Cairo Geniza, who published a number of studies on Yemenite Jews.[9]

Sources

In many Jewish communities, the rabbis discussed the halakhic and social aspects of names. As far as we know, the Yemenite sages did not. The essential information that I draw upon for my research is based on written documents and oral communication. I have also used comments and documents written by emissaries and rabbis who came in contact with the Jews of Yemen. Below I specify the main sources.

I had at my disposal photographs of 1,506 *ketubbot* (marriage contracts) and 175 *gittin* (writs of divorce) from 570 locations throughout Yemen from the sixteenth century to the end of the twentieth century, the overwhelming majority from the years 1700 to 1950.[10] *Ketubbot* and *gittin* have been an untapped treasure for research into names. Listed alongside the names of the couple marrying or divorcing are the names of the father of the groom and the father of the bride. Sometimes *ketubbot* contain extensive lineages. In addition, family names and occasionally an additional byname are listed. Moreover, the witnesses signed their names and those of their fathers in the margins of the documents. Owing to the halakhic meticulousness demanded for this aspect of *ketubbot* and particularly of *gittin*, these documents serve as an authoritative source for the study of names.

I examined a listing of 684 colophons from Yemenite manuscripts dating from the twelfth century to the middle of the twentieth in which the name of the copyist and of the person commissioning the copy are registered; these documents sometimes include family trees.[11]

7. Avraham Zevi Idelsohn and N. H. Torczyner, *Shirei Teiman* (Cincinnati, 1931).
8. Erich Brauer, *Ethnologie der Jemenitischen Juden* (Heidelberg: 1934).
9. The studies by Goitein were anthologized in *Sefer ha-Teimanim – Mivḥar Meḥkarim*, edited by Menahem Ben-Sasson (Jerusalem, 1983).
10. I collected the majority of the *ketubbot* from private sources. Most of the *gittin* are from the Y. L. Nahum Collection, Project of Unveiling the Treasures of Yemen, Holon.
11. I copied the vast majority of the colophons from the Institute of Microfilmed Manuscripts in the National Library of Israel (henceforth IMHM).

I drew from bibliographical sources of names written down by scholars. The main sources are (1) the Registry of the Rabbinical Court that met in Ṣan'a in the eighteenth and nineteenth centuries, which contains 1,372 listings of renderings and court sessions;[12] (2) the log of the mission of the emissary R. Shlomo Naddāf, which includes registration of contributors from the entire country. His list covers 350 locations, constituting some one-third of all the Jewish settlements in Yemen;[13] (3) a list of 1,704 family names from northern Yemen cited in the book *Bet ha-Even* by R. Dr. Aharon Ben David;[14] (4) family registration of some 200 births and deaths written by Yemenite Jews on empty pages of books they had at hand.[15]

The main source for a large group of family names is the registration of immigrants to Israel that was made by R. Shalom Gamliel, who immigrated to Israel in 1944. In 1949, at the time of the mass immigration after the establishment of the State of Israel, he went to the "Geulah" camp in Aden on behalf of the Ministry of Religions and the Immigration Department of the Jewish Agency in order to assist in organizing the immigrants. In his book *Ha-Naḥshonim al Kanfei Nesharim mi-Teiman* (The Vanguard on the Wings of Eagles from Yemen),[16] he listed the family names of the immigrants whom he had registered during his mission to Aden. The list contains 330 locations, and under each appear the main family names; it is estimated that this list covers about a third of the immigrants from Yemen.

12. The two-volume Registry of the Rabbinical Court is called *musawwada* in Arabic. Its call number in the National Library of Israel in Jerusalem is Heb 80 3281/1–2. Volume one covers the years 1765–1776 and numbers 352 pages; volume two covers the years 1786–1867 and has 557 pages. The copy of volume two was made by rabbinic judge Hayyim Hūbara in Ṣan'a in 1936 at the invitation of Prof. Yehudah Ratzaby. Other volumes of Rabbinic Court verdicts exist but at present they cannot be precisely located. See Yehdua Ratazby, *Toratan she-li-Vnei Teiman* (Qiryat Ono 1994), p. 250. Volume one has been printed; see Yehudah Nini, *Al-Misawwadeh, Bēth-Dīn (Court) Records of the San'ānī Jewish Community in the Eighteenth Century* (Tel Aviv, 2001).

13. I wish to thank R. Aviran Yitzhak Halevi of Bnei Brak, who gave R. Shlomo Naddāf's notebook to me; it is about to be published in the book by R. Aviran Yitzhak Halevi, *Ish Yemini: Sefer Zikkaron le-Rav Yiḥye' Yiṣhak Halevi* (Bnei Brak, 2011).

14. Aharon Ben David, *Bet ha-Even, Hilkhot Yehudei Ṣefon Teiman*)[Qiryat Eqron], 2008), pp. 672–717.

15. I received the great majority of the listings from private sources.

16. Jerusalem, 1996. A list of places appears in the index at the beginning of the book. The Yemenite Jews, as noted, lived in over a thousand locations. In many settlements there lived only a few Jewish families.

I utilized responses to questionnaires that had 26 questions on issues such as name selection, identical names, name changes, family names, and nicknames. Those responding came from various Yemenite communities, and among them were immigrants who left Yemen at the end of the twentieth century or at the beginning of the twenty-first, and who now live in Israel, London, and New York. Among those providing information were R. Raṣon Arussi, chief rabbi of Qiryat Ono, a scion of the Ṣan'a community; R. Avraham Arye, rabbi of the Bet Midrash Torah ve-Hora'a in New York, whose parents immigrated to Israel from the Maḥwīt community; R. Azaryah Basis, chief rabbi of Rosh HaAyin, from the Radā' community; R. Itamar Hayyim Kohen, chairman of the Or Israel Institute, whose parents emigrated from the Ṣan'a community; R. Shelomo Maḥfud, head of the Badatz (Court of Justice) Yore De'ah and neighborhood rabbi in Bnei Brak, who emigrated from the village of Masyab in central Yemen; R. Pinḥas Qoraḥ, rabbi of the Bet Midrash Sha'arei Halakhah in Bnei Brak, from the Ṣan'a community; R. Shlomo Qoraḥ, chief rabbi of Bnei Brak, from the Ṣan'a community; R. Yiṣḥaq Raṣābi, head of the *kollel* Pe'ulat Ṣaddiq in Bnei Brak, whose parents immigrated to Israel from the Raṣāba community; R. Ovadya Ya'beṣ, who had served in the position of the last chief rabbi of the Ṣa'dah community in northern Yemen. I turned to some of the informants on the basis of personal acquaintance; other informants replied to my questions through the intercession of interviewers.

I made use of names as written by researchers and travelers in their books, books of documentation and memorial volumes, as well as works by Yemenite rabbis, parts of which have not been published as yet.

Lastly, one of the most important sources found in every country for documenting names from the past are tombstones. However, tombstones are absent from Yemen (except Aden), since it was not customary there to erect such markers.

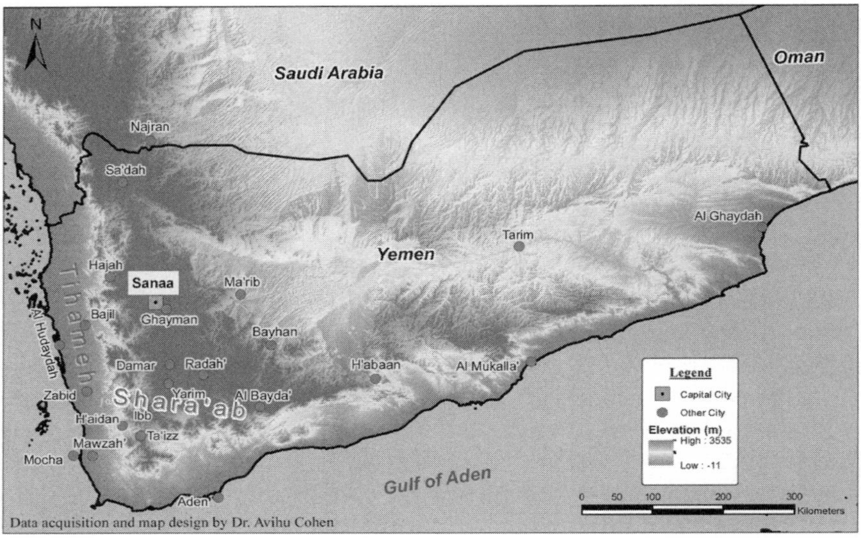

Settlements in Yemen

PART I
PERSONAL NAMES

CHAPTER ONE
GIVING A NAME

Sages throughout the Jewish world wrote of the right of the husband or wife to select their child's name, as well as the proper time for giving the name. However, Yemenite sages have left no such writings, the one exception being naming at the time of circumcision. The following analysis is based upon responses by Yemenite rabbinical scholars living in Israel, familiar with the customs of their communities in Yemen, and by informants from' the different communities in Yemen. Other information is available as a result of the Yemenite Jews' custom of registering the names of the newborns and the departed in private books.

1. WHO CHOOSES THE NAME?

The custom prevalent among Sephardi and Ashkenazi Jews is that the father and mother alternate in giving names to the children, but for Sephardim the privilege of being first is given to the father, while among Ashkenazim, to the mother.[1] S. D. Goitein wrote about the custom of naming daughters as seen in the Cairo Geniza: "Not necessarily the mother, but the senior woman in the family, in this case an aunt, determined the name."[2]

R. Solomon b. R. Shimon Duran (Algeria, 15th c.) came from a family stemming from Spain. On his mother's side he was the sixth gener-

1. Avishai Teherani, *Keter Shem Tov,* I (Jerusalem, 2000), section 3, 1–3, pp. 42–45; Yosef David Weisberg, *Oṣar ha-Berit, Enṣiklopeya le-Inyanei Milah,* I (Jerusalem, 1993), ch. 6, section 3, 1–7, pp. 335–37.
2. Shelomo Dov Goitein, *Sidrei Ḥinnukh bi-Ymei ha-Ge'onim u-Bet ha-Rambam: Meqorot Ḥadashim min ha-Geniza* (Jerusalem, 1962), p. 26.

ation from Nachmanides. From a question he answered about his family's lineage, we learn about the priority in choosing a name, as was customary in his time and place. Under discussion was the naming of Nachmanides' grandson, who was also the grandson of Rabbenu Jonah Gerondi, who died the same year when the child was born:

> And you inquired, about my grandfather Nachmanides, OBM (of blessed memory; *zal*), and also about Rabbenu Jonah bar Abraham, OBM. Know that the daughter of Rabbenu Jonah bar Abraham, OBM, was married to Solomon the son of Nachmanides, OBM. And when Rabbenu Jonah passed away in Toledo his daughter was pregnant. And when she gave birth, it was to a son, and he should have been called Moses after the name of his [the father's] father. Nachmanides, OBM, said that even though he should have been called by my name, I want him to be called Jonah on the name of his grandfather, the father of his mother because the sun rises and the sun sets (Eccl. 1:5), before the sun of this one set, the sun of the other rose,[3] and so it was that he had a great man as offspring and he became a great rabbi among the Jews, and his son's name was Solomon and he was the father of the father of my mother, R. Jonah de Maestre, *zaṣal* (*zekher ṣaddiq li-vrakhah*; Blessed be the memory of the righteous man). This is the family tree: Jonah bar Solomon bar Jonah b. R. Solomon b. Nachmanides, OBM.[4]

From his statements, we see that back in his time the Sephardim customarily gave the son the name of the father's father and the mother's father while they were still alive, as is still done today in some communities of eastern Jewry. Moreover, they call the first daughter by the name of the father's mother, and the second by the name of the mother's mother. We are also informed that even though preference is given in this case to the mother, priority of choice was given to the father and afterwards to the mother. It was in the spirit of this reply and in that of the solution noted that R. Ovadia Yosef wrote a responsum concerning priority in the naming of the firstborn son, when the husband and the wife each wanted to name the child after his or her father, who was then still alive. In his answer, he wrote, "So it is only right for the husband to call the first son by the name of his father, for he has the rights of the

3. TB Yoma 38b; Kiddushin 72b: "Before the sun of Eli set, the sun of Samuel of Ramathaim rose."
4. R. Shlomo ben ha-Rashbaṣ Duran, *Shut ha-Rashbash*, ed. R. Moshe Sobel (Jerusalem, 1998), Section 291, p. 239. See also *Shem ha-Gedolim of the Ḥida* (Jerusalem, 1992), section *Ma'arekhet Gedolim*, entry "Rabbenu Jonah the Hasid from Gerona," p. 86.

firstborn, and only the second son should be called by the name of the wife's father."[5] And in the summation of his reply, he stated:

> The rule discerned is that one should take care to call the first son by the name of the father of the husband, unless he has relinquished his honor in favor of the wife's father. And if the father of the husband is alive, but the father of the wife has passed on it is worthy to name the first son for the wife's father so that his name be perpetuated among the Jews. And this is the custom. [6]

R. Abraham b. R. Samuel Meyuḥas (Israel, 18th c.) was asked about a man who had become the father of a firstborn son and who wanted to name him for his father in line with accepted custom. However, his wife wanted to name him for her father. For the sake of domestic harmony, the husband agreed, but his conscience sorely troubled him, lest his concession to his wife would be considered disrespectful of the honor due his father. From R. Meyuḥas's reply, we learn that the custom among the Sephardim was that the right to name the firstborn was given to the father to call him by the name of his father, and for the second son to the mother to name him for her father. Whoever deviated from the existing custom detracted in some way from the father's dignity. He further explained "lest he will not be blessed with a second son, and it will turn out that no one among the Jews was called by the name of his father, for giving a name is a highly important issue.[7]" R. Yosef Chaim (Baghdad, 20th c.) also discussed this issue, "In a place where they usually called the firstborn son by the name of his [the father's] father, and his mother wanted to call by the name of her father, the husband cannot follow the wish of his wife in this instance, but must first of all call the firstborn by his father's name and the second will be named for her father."[8]

As noted above, the Ashkenazi custom is to give preference to the mother to choose the name of the firstborn child, the father the name of the second, and so on alternately. R. Ezekiel Shraga Halberstam (Poland, 19th c.), in a letter from 1895, underscored the custom of the Ash-

5. R. Ovadia Yosef, *Shut Yabi'a Omer*, part 5 (Jerusalem, 1969), *Yoreh De'ah*, Section 21, p. 225.
6. Ibid., p. 227.
7. R. Avraham b. R. Shemu'el Meyuhas, *Shut Sedeh ha-Areṣ*, pt. 3 (Salonika, 1797), *Yoreh De'ah*, sect. 22, p. 43a.
8. Yosef Chaim, *Ben Ish Ḥai*, *Halakhot*, second year (Jerusalem, 1952), *parshat* Shoftim, par. 27.

kenazi Jews, "And the custom is to call the first child by a name from the mother's family, and the second for the father's family, and so on, calling all the children in order, one in the name of her family, then one in the name of his family."[9] In his statements, R. Halberstam took care to write "a name from the mother's family" and not like the Sephardi Ḥakhamim who write "father of the mother," since Ashkenazi custom was not to name for a grandfather while he was still alive. Generally, when a grandson was born and the grandfather was still living, the infant was named after a deceased relative, such as the great-grandfather.

On this issue, R. Jacob Moses Freiberg queried R. Katriel Ephraim Tscursh (Israel, 20th c.), and the Ashkenazi custom finds expression both in the question and the response. In his question, R. Freiberg included citations from Torah scholars who had discussed this issue. He wrote about the Ashkenazi custom: "Indeed, this custom has already taken root among the women and even among many men, and they feel and think that only the mother's family has the initial right to give the name."[10] R. Tscursh, who also quoted sources for this custom in his response, agreed with the Ashkenazi custom and even wrote a *sevara* (explanation by halakhic logic) for this custom: since in marriage a woman leaves her parents' home, then, so as to not interrupt the link between them, they gave her precedence to call her first child by a name related to her parents' home.[11] Among the writings of the Ashkenazi sages, we find additional explanations for the custom: owing to the distress of birth that the woman undergoes,[12] and also in honor of her parental home, which pledged, following their custom, to provide for the young couple during the early years of their marriage.[13]

In the State of Israel the Names Law (1956) was enacted: "A forename is given to a child by his/her parents soon after the birth. When the parents do not agree, each one of them is permitted to give the child a forename."[14] The meaning of the law is that the child's personal name registered on the birth certificate is determined by agreement between the parents, and in the case of lack of accord, each parent is permitted

9. R. Yehezkel Shraga Halberstam, *Divrei Yeḥezqel he-Ḥadash, Kitvei Qodesh* (Ramat Gan, 1986), Response 9, p. 62.
10. R. Katriel Fishel Tscursh, *Keter Efrayim* (Tel Aviv, 1967), sect. 38, p. 405.
11. Ibid., pp. 406–407.
12. Teherani, *Keter Shem Tov,* I, sect. 3, 3, p. 43.
13. Is. Zusya Wilhelm, *Ziv haShemot* (New York, 1987), ch. 1, 7 n. 12, p. 27.
14. *Sefer ha-Ḥukim shel Medinat Yisra'el* 207, 26 Av 5716 (3 Aug 1956), no. 54, p. 94.

to give the child a name and both names will be registered on the birth certificate, and this is his/her name for the Interior Ministry for all purposes.

1.1 The Custom in Yemen

Owing to the lack of reference to this issue in the writings of the Yemenite sages, information was retrieved from the testimonies of informants about the custom of the Jews in the large communities and various districts in Yemen. Through the replies, which at time complement each other, we can draw conclusions and reconstruct the custom of Yemenite Jews. I cite the responses I received from the Yemenite sages in Israel about the customs of their communities in Yemen, and then the other answers, which include the accounts from informants.

R. Ya'aqov Shar'abi said that the names of the sons were usually chosen by the father, though sometimes the father and the mother would agree on the name. The names of the girls were generally selected by the mother and her mother-in-law.

1.1.1 Central Yemen

R. Shelomo Qoraḥ, R. Pinḥas Qoraḥ, and R. Raṣon 'Arusi, all born in Ṣan'a, the capital of Yemen, reported on the custom of the Jewish community of Ṣan'a. R. Shelomo Qoraḥ said that the father generally determined the name, but there were many instances in which a daughter's name was chosen by her mother.[15] R. 'Arusi informed me that usually the husband chose the name in consultation with his wife. To be sure, the husband was the dominant party, though the issue is not the right to choose but rather consensus, and at times, other factors influenced the selection of a name. For example, many couples visited the grave site of R. Shalom Shabazi to pray for children. When their prayers were answered, if it was a boy, some called him Sālem and if it was a girl, they called her Sham'ah, the name of R. Shabazi's daughter.[16] R. Pinḥas Qoraḥ wrote:

> Usually, the husband decided upon the name that would be given to the newborn, and this was often in agreement with his wife's wishes or in consideration of the desire of the grandfather and grandmother,

15. In a personal correspondence dated May 2010.
16. In a personal correspondence dated 26 Apr 2010. R. 'Arusi's statements are based upon an interview with Mori Shim'on Dhahbani, aged 90, who immigrated from Ṣan'a and lives in Qiryat Gat.

> who had expressed the wish to propose a name for the baby. Most often, this was the name of a family relative, or of a parent who had died, or of the husband as a charm to ensure the well-being of the newborn. My uncle, R. Slaymān al-Qārah, was named for his father who was still alive. And I heard that it once happened that a husband and wife could not decide what name should be given to their son, so they decided that the child would be named for the first guest to arrive for the celebratory meal at the circumcision, and it happened that the name of the first guest was the same name as the father, so the father and son were called by the identical name.[17]

R. Shelomo Maḥfud, from the village of Masyab in central Yemen wrote: "(1) Selection of a name for a boy is usually done by the father, and for a daughter by the mother. (2) The right to choose names was given exclusively only to the two parents. (3) They selected the names of relatives who had died or according to a topic in the weekly portion, or the names of parents who were still alive."[18]

R. Avraham Arye, whose parents were from Maḥwīt, wrote that names of sons were usually chosen by the father and names of daughters by the mother, and they were named either for a relative, living or deceased, or according to an issue alluded to in the weekly portion.[19]

R. Almog Shelomo Akhlufi wrote about the customs of his father's family, who lived in the villages of Bayt Sālem and Yafīd in central Yemen, and of his mother's family, who lived in the villages of Maḥaṣer and Jerāf, also in central Yemen—north of Ṣan'a—where generally the husband chose the children's names in consultation with his wife, with the husband taking precedence. Some followed a custom whereby, on the whole, the husband had priority. Still others usually had the sons' names chosen by the father and the girls' names by the mother. He wrote further about the selecting of names:

> And sometimes the name was given according to the season of birth. For instance, my [paternal] grandfather R. Dawid called his daughter, who was born close to Purim, by the name Malkah (queen), for the name of Queen Esther. His brother R. Shelomo called his son, who was born in the month of Menaḥem Av, by the name Menaḥem. And my [maternal] grandfather called his daughter (my mother), who was

17. In a personal correspondence dated April 2010. On calling the newborn the name of the first guest to arrive at the circumcision, see below end of par. 3.1.
18. In a personal correspondence dated 12 Apr 2010.
19. In a personal correspondence dated 7 May 2010.

born on Rosh Hashanah eve, Ṭovah, with the blessing that we should granted a good (*ṭovah*) year. Some people gave a name linked to the weekly portion.[20]

Naomi Badiḥi from the Ṣan'a community said that in her family the parents also included the paternal grandfather and grandmother in name-giving. She noted that in one of the births at which she was also the midwife, she called one of her granddaughters Zoharah after a star that was shining brightly.[21] Shim'on and Roma Ṣadoq, from the Manākhe community, related that the father chose the names of the sons whereas the mother named the daughters.[22] Neḥemyah Radā'i, whose parents also came from Manākhe, said that the names were picked by the father, the grandfather, or the rabbi.[23] Zekharyah 'Aṣmi, from the Madīd community, located northeast of Ṣan'a, noted that the father was the one who determined the name, although at times his wife would offer her opinion. The grandfather and grandmother usually did not become involved in name-giving.[24] Ezra 'Aṭari, from a family originating in the 'Athār community in the Arḥab district, said that generally the father chose the sons' names and the mother the daughters' names.[25] Shalom Sa'ad, whose parents came from Kafr Nābāth, said that the choice of name was, for the most part, made by the father in consultation with the grandfather.[26] Shoshana Basha, whose parents were from the community of Ḍūwāle', which lies north of Ṣan'a, told that the children's names were chosen solely by the husband or the grandfather, but if one of the relatives of the mother had died and the mother wanted the baby to be named after that relative, they usually agreed to it.[27] Sarah Nissim, from the village of Bane Hajāj in the Ḥaymeh district, related that usually the husband and wife chose the names together, but the husband always took priority in making the selection. The names they chose could be those of living or deceased family members, though usually deceased.[28]

20. In a personal correspondence dated 16 Feb 2011.
21. Interview conducted by her granddaughter Michal Badiḥi of Givatayim.
22. Interview conducted by her granddaughter Vardit Yonati of Qiryat Ono.
23. Interview conducted by his grandson Avihai Jarafi of Pardes Hanna.
24. Interview conducted by R. Gilad Ṣadoq of Bnei Berak.
25. Interview conducted by Yossi Atari of Rosh HaAyin.
26. Interview conducted by Yehonatan Levi of Rosh HaAyin.
27. Interview conducted by her granddaughter Einat Basha of Yavneh.
28. Interview conducted by her granddaughter Lirit Zindani of Rehovot.

R. Yiṣḥaq Raṣābi wrote in his book Shulḥan *'Arukh ha-Mequṣar*, "As for the custom among the Ashkenazim that the right to the name of the firstborn child belongs to the mother, and the second to the father and so on, this is not the custom among us, but rather both of them together decide and agree what they want and how they want it, and the father always takes precedence because each man rules in his home."[29] In a similar manner, he reported on the customs of the Raṣāba community and its environs: in general names were determined jointly, by the husband and the wife, but if there was a difference of opinion, it would be according to the husband's decision. As to how they chose the name, whether according to an event that had occurred or the time of the birth or in memory of a relative, R. Raṣabi cites examples:

> I, for instance, was called Yiṣḥaq, because my circumcision took place on Rosh Hashanah, on which the Patriarch Yiṣḥaq, may peace be upon him, was born, so I was told by *"mv"r* (*adoni avi mori ve-rabbi;* My master, my father, my teacher and rabbi), OBM (and it seems to me that something such as this is found in *Leket Yosher* in the name of *Terumat ha-Deshen*, that whosoever was born on Rosh Hashanah should be called Yiṣḥaq in honor of Yiṣḥaq our Patriarch, OBM). Upon the birth of my firstborn son, Moshe, I called him thus for he was born on the Sabbath of the weekly portion of Yitro, and through him we received our holy Torah. Afterward, I was asked by one of my revered father's friends, "Why didn't you call him Yisra'el after your deceased uncle? For it is written (Ps. 49:12), 'They call their lands after their own names.'" The question also went unanswered by my revered father, who was present on that occasion. Then, I had a second son and I called him Shelomo, on the name of one of my forefathers, Ha-Rav ha-Gaon Shelomo ben Ya'aqov, *zaṣuqal*. Indeed, I did call my third son by the name Yisra'el after my uncle, but since that uncle died young, may it never befall you,[30] I incorporated another intention, namely the name of the author of *Ḥafeṣ Ḥayim*, may the memory of the righteous and saintly be a blessing (but not after the name of our Patriarch Yisra'el, since some say not to give the names of the Patriarchs and the Matriarchs, as I think it is mentioned in *Ta'amei ha-Minhagim*).[31]

29. R. Yiṣḥaq Raṣabi, *Shulḥan Arukh ha-Mequṣar*, vol. 5 (Bnei Brak, 1989), section 159, 10, *Zion* 43, p. 14.
30. That such a misfortune should not happen to you. Compare Lam. 1:12: "May it never befall you, all who pass along the road—look about and see: is there any agony like mine." See also Yehudah Ratzaby, *Oṣar Leshon ha-Qodesh she-li-Vnei Teiman* (Tel Aviv, 1978), p. 138, entry *"Lo aleikhem."*
31. In personal correspondence dated 22 Apr 2010.

R. Azaryah Basis, originating from the Radā' community, the second largest Jewish community in Yemen, wrote me:

> As to choosing a name, on the whole the husband selected the names, and at times he consulted with his parents, who on occasion wanted to perpetuate their parents. And in our city, Radā', the wife usually relied upon her husband, and he would consider whether there was a request from his wife to commemorate a parent of hers by calling their child by the name of her father or her mother. A name was chosen at times according to a certain event that had occurred, such as, if there had been an occasion for mourning in the family and a son was born afterwards, they would call him Menaḥem or Neḥemyah; if he were born in the month of Av, they would call him Menaḥem; and sometimes the name would be taken from the weekly Torah portion, such as if he were born in the week of chapter Lekh Lekha, he would be called Avraham, and so on.[32]

Aharon Yehudah, from the Ra'ūḍah community, related that the husband and wife jointly chose their children's names, but there were no rules governing this.[33]

R. Nissim ben Nissim Ṭayri, a native of the Radā' community, wrote, "The custom in Yemen was that whoever was born on Hanukkah would be called Nissim, in commemoration of the miracles and wonders performed for our forefathers by the Hasmoneans, so they called me 'Nissim' (miracles). It turns out that my revered father was born on Hanukkah, and he, too, was called by that name."[34]

R. Shim'on Mal'akhi, from the Dhamār community, the third-largest Jewish community in Yemen, wrote that generally the father was the one who decided upon the name, but if his wife or a grandfather had a request it was usually accepted. Moreover, he wrote that his parents had made the pilgrimage to the grave of R. Shalom Shabazi and so when he was born, they named him Shim'on, the name of one of R. Shabazi's sons.[35]

1.1.2 Southern Yemen

Tov Osheri, from one of the communities in Qaryat al-Mi'rāḍ[36] in the Yarīm district, said that the name was usually determined by the

32. In a personal correspondence dated 8 Mar 2010.
33. Interview conducted by Idan Yehudah of Petah Tikva.
34. R. Nissim Ṭayri, *Bi-Tela'ot ha-Galut ve-ha-Ge'ulah* (Ramat Gan, 1998), p. 13.
35. In a personal correspondence dated Sep 2010.
36. Qaryat al-Ma'arad is a name covering fourteen villages.

father, whereas girls' names were usually chosen by the mother or grandmother. The name given the infant was either that of a parent during his or her lifetime or of a grandparent, whether living or deceased.[37] Zekharyah 'Iṭwār, from the community of Jubān in the Radā' district, related that there were no strict rules for name-giving: the name was often chosen by the father, but if the mother wanted to name the child after her deceased parent, the father usually agreed.[38] Shelomo 'Adani, a descendant of the Ḍāli' community, said that, on the whole, the husband was the one who selected the children's names.[39] Shelomo Raṣhabi, from the Raḍa'i community, said that in most cases the husband chose the children's names, though sometimes the parents jointly decided upon the name. Sometimes the name was chosen by the mother, when she wanted to name someone after a deceased relative, though she would consult with her husband first; at other times she might choose the name of the grandfather or grandmother, particularly if they had asked that someone be named after them so that they would be remembered.[40] Sarah Gafni, whose parents emigrated from the village of Saḥban, related that the decision was made by the husband, who chose whatever he deemed fit.[41] Se'īdah Aharon, from the village of Adūfa in the Shar'ab district, said that names were given by the father or grandfather by opening to a page in a book by a person adept at this practice.[42] Ḥannah Ḥofi, from the village of Qūrana, said that the right to choose names belonged to the husband, but if at times the wife would suggest a name, the husband would consider her proposal. The same occurred if the wife's parents proposed a name; the husband would take it under consideration out of respect for them.[43] Menashe Ṣubari, from the Bayḍa community in southeastern Yemen, stated that the husband was usually the one who selected the children's names; the wife never intervened. There were also those who consulted their father to ask if a certain name was good. Sometimes the mother would suggest a name for her newborn daughter, generally the name of her mother, that is, the maternal grandmother. In cases in which the husband was uncer-

37. Interview conducted by his son Yoel Osheri of Tel Aviv.
38. Interview conducted by his son Yirmiyahu 'Itwar of Rishon Lezion.
39. Interview conducted by R. Gilad Ṣadoq of Bnei Berak.
40. Interview conducted by R. Gilad Ṣadoq of Bnei Berak.
41. Interview conducted by her granddaughter 'Einat Basha of Yavneh.
42. Interview conducted by Ya'ir Shunam of Rosh HaAyin.
43. Interview conducted by Shemu'el Ḥofi of New York.

tain, he would go to the rabbi, who often selected a name by opening to a page in a book[44] or, mainly in southern Yemen, would determine the name through astrological calculations.[45]

1.1.3 Northern Yemen

On the customs of the Jews of northern Yemen, R. Ovadya Ya'beṣ, who served as the last chief rabbi of the Ṣa'dah community, reported: "In my hometown Ṣa'dah, northern Yemen, I knew that children's names were chosen by the father, and [an exception was made] only if there was a reason, such as the mother was asking to perpetuate the name of one of the female members of the family with the agreement of the husband, but the sons' names were determined solely by the father."[46]

R. Dr. Aharon ben Dawid, from the Waṭan al-Maqāsh in north Yemen, reported:

1. In most cases, a daughter's name was chosen by important women among the female members of the extended family on both sides. A boy's name was decided upon by the father and, most often, in consultation with the eldest in the family, while a girl's name was usually initiated by the mother, in consultation with her mother or her grandmother and, of course, with the agreement of her husband. When a male was born, the boy's father would inform the family elder, and he would immediately propose a name; his suggestion was accepted without question. Upon the birth of the son of Da'ūd ben Yosef, a person from Bet ha-Even (the stone house),[47] he informed his grandfather, Mori Slaymān ben Yosef, and owing to his great joy declared decidedly Hārūn Ghadqah,[48] meaning

44. This is referring to the method of clarifying certain questions through a person who owns a special astrological book for resolution of queries. Interview conducted by R. Gilad Ṣadoq of Bnei Berak.

45. On astrological consideration for changing the name of a bride prior to marriage, see below part 3, chap. 4, sec. 2.

46. In a personal correspondence dated 4 Mar 2010. R. Ovadya died on 17 Jan 2011.

47. The stone house was the edifice in which the writer's family lived in North Yemen. The seven-story building was given this name for its having been built on a large rock. See Aharon Ben David, *Bet ha-Even, Hilkhot Yehudei Ṣefon Teiman* ([Qiryat Eqron], 2008), pp. 5–6.

48. R. Aharon Ben David wrote to me about the meaning of this word in a personal correspondence dated 15 Adar 5771 (21 Mar 2011), "The meaning of the word '*ghadqah*' as understood by the name-giver, namely, Mori layman ben Yosef, is 'a

'Hārūn who is entirely good.' Of course, everyone called him Hārūn, but the relatives knew of the additional Ghadqah. And when Da'ūd ben Yosef's daughter was born, his second son, Se'īd, was present and he ran to tell his grandfather, Mori Yosef Slaymān and inform him that "Bardaqūshah" (an aromatic herb) had been born, and that was how her name was decided upon by her mother, Hawīdah, with the agreement of her husband, Da'ūd.

2. The right to choose a name belonged to the husband and he was the arbiter. The mother had the right to suggest a name for a daughter (the wife usually did not become involved in selecting a name for a son), but the ultimate decision was the father's. And one must say that though this was the accepted way, no rules were set about it. Moreover, the final decision was, as said, made by the husband, but if the wife was a strong, dominant person, she had great influence on the selection of the name.
3. The choice of a name was usually made from among the names of relatives in the extended family who were considered important as devoted, Torah-observing Jews or as personages of standing. The name was also selected from those of important family members who had already passed away. There was no instance in which a name was given by chance; each name was picked with definite intention. Even when a biblical name was selected, there was purpose in its choice, and the biblical name was given in the name's translation into Arabic, such as Mūsa (Moshe), Brāhīm (Avraham), Ya'aqūb (Ya'aqov), and so on.
4. All the foregoing encompasses all areas of North Yemen.
5. On the whole, the name for a girl was chosen from among the important women in the extended family.[49]

2. WHY GIVE A CERTAIN NAME?

There are various Yemenite traditions as to selecting a particular name for the child. Information can be ascertained from questionnaires. In addition, lists of newborns, written on empty pages of a book, can inform us of the reason for selecting a particular name.[50] Prof. Goitein, when

plenitude of good.' Thus, Harūn who heralds a plenitude of good will be called Harūn Ghadqah, that is, 'Harūn who is a plenitude of good, who heralds good things, who brings good luck."

49. In a personal correspondence dated 27 Tevet 5770 (13 Jan 2010).

50. On the registration of newborns in Yemen, see below section 4.

dealing with the range of women's names in the Cairo Geniza, did not find biblical names, which is the opposite of what is customary among the other Jewish communities. He found a phenomenon similar to that of the Geniza among the Jews of Yemen, noting, "As we know, also among the Yemenites, 'the most authentic among all the Jews,' it was not the custom to give girls biblical names."[51]

2.1 Weekly Torah portion or haftara:

Ḥannah Ḥofi said that they chose biblical names, such as those in the weekly Torah reading or the *haftara*, as well as naming for deceased relatives.[52] Zakharyah 'Aṣmi told that names were determined by the weekly Torah portion or in memory of deceased relatives as well as names of a grandfather or a grandmother, whether alive or deceased, or the name of the husband or the wife.[53] Neḥemyah Radā'i noted that he was called Neḥemyah because he was born on the Sabbath of the weekly portion of Va-Ethḥanan, soon after the Ninth of Av, which is known as Shabbat Naḥamu.[54]

One list of newborns, informs us: "Born was the good flower, Yehudah b. Se'īd b. Yiḥye b. Yiḥye al-'Idwi in the year 2224 SEL [Seleucian years][55] in the month of Kislev, the 20th day [5673 Anno Mundi (AM)/ 5 Dec 1912]."[56] The birth took place in the week of Genesis chapter Mi-Qeṣ and the circumcision on the Sabbath of chapter Va-Yigash. The

51. Shelomo Dov Goitein, *Sidrei Ḥinnukh bi-Ymei ha-Ge'onim u-Bet ha-Rambam: Meqorot Ḥadashim min ha-Geniza* (Jerusalem, 1962) p. 26; see also, idem, *A Mediterranean Society*, vol. 3 (Berkeley, Calif., 1978), p. 315.
52. Interview conducted by her son, Shemu'el Ḥofi of New York.
53. Interview conducted by R. Gilad Ṣadoq of Bnei Berak.
54. Interview conducted by his grandson Aviḥai Jarafi of Pardes Ḥannah.
55. The use of the *minyan sheṭarot* (dating used for legal documents) was common in the Geonic period and the one that followed it. This system counts from the beginning of the Seleucid reign. Three Macedonian generals fought to take rule over the Macedonian Empire. Seleucus I Nicator, who was the satrap of Babylon and the ally of Ptolemy, ruler of Egypt, defeated Demetrius Poliocretes, who commanded the army of his father Antigonus I, a Macedonian general, in the battle of Gaza in 312 B.C.E. After his victory in the battle of Gaza, Seleucus returned to Babylon, recaptured it, and founded his kingdom in it. The event of his return to Babylon was marked as the beginning of a new era for counting. It occurred on 7 December 312 B.C.E. in the Macedonian calendar and on 3 April 311 B.C.E. in the Babylonian calendar. Apparently, the Jews began the dating from 311 B.C.E. See *Encyclopaedia Judaica*, 14:1123, s.v. "Seleucid Era"; 16:1264, s.v. "Chronology". See also Avraham A. Akiva, *The Calendar and Its Use*, pp. 60–61 [in Hebrew].
56. On the title page of a manuscript containing three scrolls, Nissim 'Idwi, Holon.

name Yehudah was chosen owing to the dominant figure of Yehudah in these chapters.

2.2 Living parent or family member:

Shalom Sa'ad told of naming boys for their father who was still alive because of the belief that thereby the infant would be blessed and protected from dying from disease, or of giving the name of a relative, even if he was still alive. Girls were named for grandmothers or from among a wide range of names common in the area.[57] 'Ezra 'Aṭari stated that the names were for the parents who were still alive, as well as in memory of venerated relatives. For example, the grandfather Slayman called his grandson Slayman, the same as his own name.[58]

2.3 Traditional family name:

Shelomo 'Adani related that the selection of names was made according to names handed down in the family or in memory of relatives who had died. Some sons were called by the name of their father, while other children were given the name of the grandfather or grandmother. For example, a girl was called Kādhiyyah the daughter of Miryam the daughter of Kādhiyyah.[59]

2.4 Event at the time of birth:

Shelomo Raṣhabi related that if the children died, the couple would vow to make a pilgrimage to the grave of R. Shalom Shabazi so as to be graced with offspring, and when their plea was accepted and they had a child, if it were a boy they called him Sālem and if it were a girl they called her Sham'ah, the name of R. Sālem Shabazi's daughter.[60] Some, mainly in southern Yemen, would go to the local rabbi, and he would determine the name through astrological calculations.[61] Naomi Badiḥi from the Ṣan'a community noted that in one of the births at which she was also the midwife, she called one of her granddaughters Zoharah after a star that was shining brightly.[62] The following inscription also documents name selection based on an event:

57. Interview conducted by Yehonatan Levi of Rosh HaAyin.
58. Interview conducted by Yossi 'Atari of Rosh HaAyin.
59. Interview conducted by R. Gilad Ṣadoq of Bnei Berak.
60. Interview conducted by R. Gilad Ṣadoq of Bnei Berak.
61. On astrological consideration for changing the name of a bride prior to marriage, see below part 3, chap. 4, sec. 2.
62. Interview conducted by her granddaughter Michal Badiḥi of Givatayim.

> Born to me was the good flower, resembling a moist tree, on Monday, a son whose name is Binyamin, the 8th of the month of Ḥeshwān,[63] and his mother was called above on the 16th, in the year 2230 [SEL = 5679/22 Oct 1918]. May the Lord make him prosper in His service and awe, *'ky"r* (*amen ken yehi raṣon*; Amen, May it be His will), never ceasing (*neṣaḥ, sela', wa'ed*).[64]

The mother died after the birth, on the ninth day, which was the day of her son's circumcision. One may reasonably assume that the name Binyamin, which the father gave his son, alluded to the biblical figure Jacob naming his newborn son Binyamin after the death of his beloved Rachel.

2.5 Calendar:

Zekharyah 'Iṭwār related that if the child was born in the month of Adar, they would call him Mordekhai, and if in the month of Elul, Raḥamim, as the month is called by Yemenite Jews. Tov Osheri said that if a boy's birth took place during Hanukkah, the child was called Nissim; on Purim, Mordekhai; during the month of Av, Menaḥem; in Elul, Raḥamim. If a daughter was born during Sukkot, she was named Tiranjah (in Hebrew, Etrogit), after the *etrog*, the citrus used on the festival of Sukkot. He noted further that he had been called Ṭov, a name alluding to the month in which he was born, Tevet.[65]

The following listing alludes to the name of the month:

> "A good name is better than fragrant oil" (Eccl. 7:1). Born was the good child, who resembles a moist tree, may the Lord give the good, Menaḥem ibn Raḍa', Friday night, the first hour, the hour of the moon, the sixth of the month, [the week of] the chapter of Mas'ot,[66] in the month of Menaḥem, the year 2221 SEL [5670 creation AM/12 Aug 1910]. And may there be fulfilled through him the passage stating "[My words] shall not be absent from your mouth, nor from the mouth of your children, nor from the mouth of your children's children ... from now on, for all time" (Isa. 59:21)].[67]

63. In daily life, Yemenite Jews pronounce this month as Meraḥshewān. This pronunciation reflects the original Akkadian name, *waraḥ shamnun*, that is, the eighth month. In oral Torah study, the Yemenite Jews customarily pronounced the month's names as Meraḥshewān. See *Ha-Tiklal ha-Mevu'ar*, ed. and proofread under the direction of R. Pinḥas Qoraḥ (Bnei Brak, 5766), p. 301.
64. In a printed book, *Kesher Gadol* by R. Ḥayim Yosef David Azulai, Livorno 1842, in the possession of Yosef Ma'bari.
65. Interview conducted by his son Yo'el Osheri of Tel Aviv.
66. Alludes to *parashat* Mas'ei, read the previous Sabbath.
67. The listing is found in a printed book owned by Nira Yahav, Holon.

The child was called Menaḥem after the name of the month in which he was born, the month of Av, which is called by Yemenite Jews Menaḥem (and in Jewish tradition in general is known as Menaḥem Av). Some twenty-three years later this Menaḥem registered the birth of his son as follows:

> The good child, reminiscent of a moist tree, and like a tree planted by streams of water sending forth its roots by a stream (Jer. 17:8),[68] Da'ud ben Menaḥem, the evening of the end of Sabbath, the hour of Mars, 26th day of the month of Menaḥem in the year 2230 SEL [5693 AM/ 19 Aug 1933], *parshat* Re'eh. And may He fulfill the verse as it is written "Recite it day and night" (Josh. 1:8). Ha-Makom, blessed be He, will protect him and sustain him in life, and see that he reaches fulfillment of Torah and his wedding and his good deed [should be "deeds"], *'ky"r*. And he will ful[fill] through him the verse as it is written, "Recite it day and night" (Josh. 1:8).[69] [My words I have placed in your mouth] to him [should be "No"] shall not be absent from your mouth, [nor from the mouth of your children,] nor from the mouth of your children's children from now and forever (Isa. 59:21).[70]

It is reasonable to assume that the father, Menaḥem, called his son who was born in Av David, with a name that somehow symbolized redemption. The following is a listing for a child born in Adar:

> The good child was born, Efrayim ibn Pinḥas Ḥasan, *yṣ"v* (*yishmerehu ṣuro ve-yoṣero*; May His Rock and Redeemer [or Creator] protect him), 23 Adar 2, Sunday night, at [ ][71] o'clock, in the year 5687 AM [27 Mar 1927], and he was called after the *mazal* of the month that produces fish. May the Holy one blessed be He make his parents worthy to see his Torah, marriage, and good deeds, may it be His will.[72]

A number of factors are involved in giving the name Efrayim to a child born in Adar. First, the name Efrayim alludes to fertility, as Joseph explained the naming of his son Efrayim: "God has made me fertile in the land of my affliction" (Gen. 41:52). Similarly, Jacob blessed Joseph's sons, Menashe and Efrayim, with a blessing to be as fertile as fish (*dagim*): "And may they be teeming (*vayidgu*) multitudes upon the

68. This verse does not contain the word "streams"; the error intruded owing to similarity to the verse in Psalms 1:3.
69. Seemingly the verse was repeated by mistake.
70. This registration is found in the book mentioned above.
71. Empty spot.
72. The listing was written in a printed Zohar. In the possession of Yo'el Osheri, Tel Aviv.

earth" (Gen. 48:16). Rashi on that verse explains *vayidgu* "just like fish, which multiply and increase, and no evil eye has power over them."[73] Thus, fish symbolize fertility, and the zodiac sign for Adar is Pisces, "the fish."

2.6 To express a wish:

Tov and Rumiyah Ṣadoq of the Manākhe community in central Yemen, called their daughter Bekhorah, as an allusion to the wish that she would be the eldest of other daughters they would have, but she was their only daughter.[74] Yosef and Esther 'Ūzayri, of the Dhamār community, had a daughter after two sons, and the mother called the daughter Mazal (good luck). When her father-in-law, Grandfather Se'īd, who dealt in commerce, heard this, he asked that they call the newborn girl Berakhah (blessing), because, he said, "Good luck—thank the Lord—I have, and I want a blessing upon the family, and his suggestion was accepted.[75] Yiḥye' and Zoharah Ṣubara of Ḥaymeh in central Yemen, had a girl in 5709 (1949), during one of the first nine days of Av, in which festive occasions are limited. They called her Ghane', which means song or joy, an expression of happiness, and the aim in giving this name was to express a meaning contrasting with the time during which she was born.[76]

Some intended the name to be an expression of their heart's desire. R. Shalom (Arabic: Sālem) 'Ūzayri from the Manākhe community in central Yemen, wrote for his first two children, who were born in Yemen:

> The good flower was born, Tuesday, 28 Shevat 2245 SEL [5694 AM/ 13 February 1934], in the weekly chapter Oil for Lighting (Ex. 25:6),[77] and I have called him Neḥemyah, *hy"v* (*Hashem yishmerehu veyeḥayyehu*; May the Lord protect and sustain him), and console me for my sorrow and suffering, and tell them "enough." And the same way He has graced me with having him enter the covenant, so shall He

73. After Genesis Rabbah 97:3: "Just as these fish have no evil eye with power over them, so your sons have no evil eye with power over them."
74. As told by Tov Ṣadoq of Qiryat Ono. On the name Bekhorahh, see also below, ch. 5, section 2. Tov is the brother of Bekhorah, and he bears the same name as his father. See below, part 3, chap. 4, sect. 1.
75. As related by Berakhah Bore of Bat Yam. Berakhah is the daughter spoken about, and she told me the story of the change of her name on 22 Shevat 5772 (15 Feb 2012).
76. As told by Lirit Zindani. Ghane' is the informant's mother.
77. An allusion to a verse from the weekly reading, *parashat* Terumah.

> grace me with seeing that he will reach fulfillment of Torah and commandments and marriage and good deeds, may it be His will. And later, his name was changed to Ḥayim, *hy"v* [father's signature], the hum[ble] Sālem ibn Avr[aham] al-'Ūzayri, may the Lord protect and sustain him, the lowliest of the low.
>
> And then his sister was born, Friday, 28 Tevet 2248 SEL [5697 AM/8 January 1937],[78] in the weekly chapter Va-Era,[79] and she was given the name Esther, for they will hide my iniquities [*yisteru*] and forgive them. And I have been graced, thank the Lord, to have fulfilled the commandment of be fruitful and multiply, as it is written male and female He created them and He blessed them (Gen. 1:28).[80] And may He grace me to have more sons and daughters, who obey the commandments and study Torah, and give me the privilege to see them marry soon after their proper time comes, as our sages commanded, may it be His will. [father's signature] The hum[ble] Sālem ibn Avr[aham] al-'Ūzayri, *hy"v*.[81]

Perhaps he called his daughter Esther because she was born close to the month of Adar. In addition to the wishes expressed by R. 'Ūzayri upon the births of his children, he stressed that through the birth of his son and his daughter he had fulfilled the commandment to be fruitful and multiply.

2.7 First guest at the circumcision

The custom of naming the child for the first guest to arrive at the circumcision was little practiced in Yemen,[82] though below are comments that do inform us about this phenomenon occasionally occurring there. Azaryah Basis, from the Radā' community, reported on this custom in another community in Yemen, inferring that the custom was not followed in Radā':

> And know that I heard from *mmv"r* (*mi-mori ve-rabbi*; my teacher and master) Shelomoh 'Adani, *zaṣal*, that in the town of Ṣa'fān, in the Ḥarāz district, there was a custom to give the circumcised son the name of whoever came first to the circumcision ceremony, whether a relative

78. The birth was three years after that of the son that was listed in the previous paragraph, and this coincides with the situation among most of the women in Yemen, who gave birth once in three years, since they nursed for two years.
79. This alludes to the first verse in the Torah reading of the week, *parashat* Va'era.
80. The precise citation is "male and female he created them. God blessed them…."
81. R. Shalom 'Uzayri, *Sefer Iqvei Shalom*, ed. by author's family ([Tel Aviv], 2006), p. 24.
82. Ibid., Sect. 43, p. 15.

or a neighbor. Perhaps this was an impetus for the commandment of circumcision, similar to the Passover sacrifice for which one says to his sons "I will slaughter the Passover-offering for whosoever of you shall come up first to Jerusalem," which is explained in the Mishnah, tractate Pesaḥim 8:3, with the intention of urging them on, so that each will act quickly to be the first, as one can see in the commentaries on it.[83]

I was told by Aharon Amram, the greatest singer of the repertoire of Yemenite Jews, who was born in Ṣan'a, that he was named for the *dayyan* R. Aharon ben Shalom Hakohen, who was the first guest at his circumcision ceremony.[84] I was also told that 'Azri ben ha-Rav Ḥayim ben ha-Dayyan Aharon Hakohen, who was born in Ṣan'a,[85] was named for 'Azri ben Slaymān Shar'abi, who was the first guest to arrive at his circumcision.[86]

2.8 Summary

Yemenite communities did not have set, written rules for selecting a name. One may say that a son's name was chosen by the husband and the daughter's generally by the wife. The mother or father determined the name with prior consultation, sometimes with members of the extended family, such as a grandfather or a grandmother. The right to choose belonged to the husband, since he made the decisions in every facet of life, including family matters, as befit a patriarchal society. Often, however, there were opportunities for the wife, mainly to keep domestic harmony. Sometimes even the midwife or a relative such as a grandmother or an aunt picked the name.[87]

Among Yemenite Jews, a name was usually chosen from among names of relatives, deceased or living. At times names were given based on the weekly Torah reading, the month, a holiday, an event associated with the birth, or to express a wish.

83. In a personal correspondence dated 8 Mar 2010.

84. As related by R. Ṣefaniah Shar'abi of Qiryat Sefer, from the family of R. Aharon Hakohen, as well as from Aharon 'Amram of Petah Tikva, who told me about the name given him. See also Aharon 'Amram, *Keter, Taj, Ve-zot ha-Torah* ([Petaḥ Tikvah], 2004), dedication pages in the closing pages of the book.

85. He lives in Ramat Gan.

86. As related by R. Ṣefaniah Shar'abi of Qiryat Sefer. For another instance, see above section 1.b.1 in the remarks of R. Pinḥas Qoraḥ.

87. Some Jewish communities refrained from having one of the relatives give the name. See Yosef Hakohen Oppenheimer, *Va-Yikra Shemo be-Yisra'el* (Buenos Aires, 1975), pp. 17–19.

3. THE TIME FOR NAME-GIVING AND DISSEMINATION OF THE NAME

3.1 Naming a son

In the Babylonian and Jerusalem Talmuds, as well as in Maimonides' writings and in the Shulḥan Arukh, there is no mention of naming the newly circumcised child at the time of the ceremony, as is customary today. Moreover, there is no mention of prayers for the circumcised child and his parents.[88] Perhaps, these prayers were not included by Maimonides and the Shulḥan Arukh because they relied upon the prayer books, where these prayers were readily accessible. For example, the prayer that begins *tishtalaḥ asuta* ("May a remedy be sent"), preserved only by Yemenite Jewry, appears in the *siddur* of Rav 'Amram Gaon and the *siddur* of Rav Sa'adyah Gaon.[89]

Sources inform us that there were places where the infant was named before the circumcision ceremony,[90] though others waited until

---

88. See TB Shabbat 137b; TP Berakhot 9, 3; Maimonides, *Hilkhot Milah* 3, 1–3; *Shulḥan Arukh, Yore De'ah,* sect. 265 a–b.

89. See *Seder Rav 'Amram* (Jerusalem, 1972), pp. 179–80; See *Siddur Rav Sa'adyah Ga'on,* eds. I. Davidson, S. Assaf, and B. I. Joel (Jerusalem, 1985), p. 98. See also Gaimani, "Rav Sa'adyah," p. 44. R. Yihye Badīḥi brought in the name of *Sefer Sharvit ha-Zahav* by R. David Lida (Ashkenaz, 17th c.): "I found in the Jerusalem Talmud, that some used to pray in the synagogue for the circumcised child and his mother, according to the version *tishtalaḥ* etc." The prayer opening with the words *tishtalaḥ asuta* does not appear in the TP we have at hand, but it is cited by a number of the Ashkenazic Rishonim, such as Ravyah (R. Eliezer ben Yoel ha-Levi, Mainz, 12th c.) in his book *Avi ha-'Ezri,* Shabbat, sect. 289; *Or Zaru'a* by R. Yiṣhaq ben Moshe (Vienna, 13th c.), *Hilkhot Milah,* sect. 107. This shows us that the formulation of this prayer is ancient. See R. Yiḥye' Badīḥi, *'Im Ḥen Ṭov, Ḥenah shel Torah,* with annotations, notes, and commentaries by R. Itamar Ḥayim Kohen (Bnei Brak, 2008), p. 91 n. 34.

90. From the words of R. Yehudah ha-Ḥasid (Ashkenaz, 12th c.), one may learn that they gave the name to the infant at the time they put him in the cradle. As he put it, "This is the record of Adam's line (Gen. 5:1), this is an allusion that when they place the child in the cradle and call him a name, they put a copy of Leviticus at his head (*Sefer Hasidim,* section 1540). If this refers to the cradle used at circumcision, then one cannot learn from here about a difference from what is customary today when giving the name during the circumcision ceremony. R. Ya'aqov ben ha-Rosh (Ashkenaz and Spain, 14th c.) cites in the name of R. Yiṣhaq b. Abba Mori (France, 12th c.), author of *Sefer ha-'Ittur,* the text of a prayer that perhaps informs us that they gave the name to the child before fulfilling the commandment of circumcision, "[A]nd the author of *Ha-'Ittur* wrote, and it is a custom to put wine in the infant's mouth after the blessing over the wine and after performing the circumcision, and to say, 'preserve this child for his father and mother, and his name in Israel *has been*

the ceremony itself.[91] The custom prevalent among the different Jewish communities today, and which has been handed down from previous generations, is to announce the infant's name at the circumcision ceremony, after he has been circumcised.[92] The question is as what stage in the ceremony is it customary to proclaim the name and whether it is only his personal name that is mentioned or also that of his father.

The circumcision ceremony includes blessings and a prayer for the infant and his parents. The well-known custom is that after the blessing over the circumcision, the father of the child recites two blessings: one which concludes with the words "enter into the covenant of Abraham our father" and the other, *she-heḥeyanu* ("who has sustained us"). These are followed by additional blessings. According to Sephardi custom, three blessings are recited in the following order: (1) a blessing over fragrant spices, such as the blessing for "fragrant trees" over myrtle; (2) the blessing "creates fruit of the vine" over a cup of wine; and (3) "who

called ...'" (Tur, Yoreh De'ah, sect. 265; emphasis mine, A.G.). Similar statements were written by R. David Abudirham (Spain, 14th c.) in a prayer formulation recited to the circumcised infant and his parents, "Our God and God of our fathers, preserves this child for his father and mother, *who name has been called* X, for many miracles and wonders were performed for him when he was born (*Abudirham ha-Shalem, Milah,* ch. 9, p. 351; emphasis mine–AG). See also Sarah Munitz, "*Shemot Benei Adam—Minhag ve-Halakhah*" (PhD diss., Bar-Ilan University, 1989), pp. 4–12; Ratzabi, *Shulḥan 'Arukh ha-Mequṣar*, 5, sect. 109, 10, par. 44, p. 15.

91. R. Jacob Hagozer (Ashkenaz, 13th c.) wrote, "Why was it determined to give a name to the child immediately upon circumcision? Because until then, before the circumcision he had a name of impurity and shame, a name of the uncircumcised; but now that he is circumcised and has fulfilled the commandment of circumcision, he name must be changed to [one of] praise, a holy, pure name like the name of his forefathers, Abraham, Isaac, and Jacob ... ("*Kelalei ha-Milah le-R. Ya'aqov Hagozer,*" the laws for giving a name to a child, in R. Ya'aqov Glasberg, *Sefer Zikkaron Berit la-Rishonim* [Berlin, 1892], pp. 94–95).

92. See, for example, the statements of R. Shem Tov Gagin (England, 20th c.), who wrote, "And it is certainly clear that they did not have the custom we follow today to call him a name precisely at the time of circumcision (R. Shem Tov Gagin, *Keter Shem Tov: Yalqut Minhagei Qehilot ha-Sefardim u-Meqoroteihem* [Jerusalem, 1998], par. 1909, p. 480). R. Yosef Weisberg (Israel, 2oth c.) wrote "It is customary to give a name to a male [infant] after he has entered the covenant of our Patriarch Abraham, *OBM*, within a prayer for his welfare after the blessing 'who sanctified the beloved one from the womb'" (Weisberg, *Oṣar ha-Berit*, 1, ch. 6, sect. 2, 2). R. Avishai Teherani (Israel, 20th c.) wrote, "The time for giving the name is immediately after the circumcision and not earlier, for after the child has been circumcised there is power in the commandment of circumcision for the acceptance of the prayer, and a person's name is a prayer for his future (Teherani, *Keter Shem Tov*, I, sect 4, 1, p. 46).

has sanctified the beloved one from the womb." According to the Yemenite rite, the blessing over the cup of wine comes first, while the Ashkenazi custom forgoes the blessing over fragrant spices.

After these blessings, the prayer for the infant and his parents is recited, and in that prayer the name of the child is mentioned for the first time, in the jussive form of "Let his name be called in Israel" (Ruth 4:14), and in this prayer the child's name occurs twice. The prayer begins with the words "Our God and the God of our fathers, preserve this child to his father and to his mother and let his name be called in Israel," citing the name of the circumcised infant, and in Ashkenazi rite also his father's name. It continues "May his father rejoice in his offspring ..." and concludes with an additional mention only of the name of the infant, finishing with "the Lord shall make the small infant great. Just as he has entered the Covenant, so may he enter into Torah and commandments, into marriage, and into good deeds." Added to the Ashkenazi version is the recitation of *Mi she-berakh* ("May He who blessed"), in which are mentioned the name of the infant and of his father.[93]

Writing about customs of Yemenite Jews, R. Yiḥye' Ṣāliḥ (Mahariṣ), one of the greatest Yemenite *poseqim* (decisors) of the eighteenth century, stated that after the circumcision blessing the boy's father would recite two blessings, as noted above: a blessing concluding with the words "enter into the covenant of Abraham our father" and the *she-heḥeyanu*. At this point he notes the instruction for giving the name: "Then the father of the circumcised child shall recite the *she-heḥeyanu* prayer, and he shall call him by a name that he loves, and he shall say, 'Come enter the covenant, ____.'" Following that are three more blessings: "Who creates the fruit of the vine" over a cup of wine; a blessing over spices, such as the blessing for "fragrant trees" over the myrtle; and the blessing "who has sanctified the beloved one from the womb." After these three blessings are pronounced, three prayers are recited. Two of them begin *tishtalaḥ asuta*, one for the infant in which his name and that of his father are cited, and the other for the mother of the circumcised infant.[94] The third prayer is for the infant and his parents, as noted above, and in it the infant's name occurs twice.[95]

93. See, for example, the Ashkenazi custom, Weisberg, *Oṣar ha-Berit*, 1, chp. 8, pp. 494–95; Oriental Jewry, ibid., pp. 500–501; Yemenite tradition, pp. 502–4.

94. See *Seder Rav 'Amram*, pp. 179–80. In *Siddur Rav Sa'adyah Ga'on*, the prayer beginning with the words *tishtalaḥ asuta* appears only once, and it is a blessing for the circumcised infant. The introductory line to the blessing states, "Then he prays for him and calls out a name for him in the prayer," *Siddur Rav Sa'adyah Ga'on*, p.

From the foregoing, the custom of the Eastern Jewish communities is to mention the name of the infant twice at the circumcision ceremony by the person reciting the prayer opening with the words "Our God and the God of our fathers, preserve this child to his father and to his mother and let his name be called in Israel," while in Ashkenazi custom, once, when reciting "May He who blessed." In the Yemenite custom, however, the name of the circumcised child is noted four times: after the *sheheḥeyanu* blessing, the father of the infant announces the name with the formula "Come enter the covenant, ___," which means join the covenant of Torah,[96] or you shall enter the covenant of the Jewish people with the Holy One blessed be He with this name.[97] Another time, the names of the infant and his father occur in the blessing that begins with the words *tishtalaḥ asuta*, which is recited for the circumcised child; and two more times, as in the custom of the Jewish communities, in the prayer concluding the ceremony, which begins "Our God and God of our fathers, preserve this child to his mother and his father, and let his name be called in Israel ...."

The widespread custom in recent generations among Yemenite Jews is that when the father of the infant declares his name with the formula, "Come enter the covenant, ___," the assembled repeat the words "Come enter the covenant, ___."[98] So, it turns out that, according to Yemenite custom, the name of the infant is mentioned five times in the circumcision ceremony: once by the father; three times by the person reciting the prayer, and once by the congregation.[99]

99). See also Gaimani, *Rav Sa'adyah*, p. 44. In the twelfth-century *Siddur Rabbenu Shelomoh ben Natan*, the prayer is found only once, as in *Siddur Rav Sa'adyah Ga'on*. See *Siddur R. Shelomoh ben Natan*, p. 142.

95. See Mahariṣ, *Tiklal Eṣ Ḥayim*, vol. 1, pp. 287a–287b; Mahariṣ, *Tiklal Eṣ Ḥayim*, ed. Ḥ. Ḥovav (Jerusalem, 1962), pp. 177b–180a. Cf. *Tiklal Eṣ Ḥayim*, ms. in the possession of R. Eliyahu Yiṣḥak Halevi (Qaḍi), New York, pp. 180b–183a. See also Manṣura, *Qunteres Hilkhot Milah*, ch. 15, p. 110.

96. Avraham Shalom Shaqi, *Heikhal Avodat Hashem*, vol. 4 (Bnei Brak, 1981), vol. 4, p. 142.

97. Raṣabi, *Shulḥan Arukh ha-Mequṣar*, vol. 5, sec. 159, 10, par. 44, p. 15.

98. Raṣabi, ibid.; Yosef Qāfiḥ, *Halikhot Teiman* (Jerusalem, 1961), p. 168; Yosef Ṣubayri, *Siddur Keneset ha-Gedolah*, vol. 1 (Tel Aviv–Jerusalem, 1976), p. 670; idem, *Va-yiṣbor Yosef Bar*, vol. 4 (Jerusalem, 2000), pp. 29–30.

99. Cf. the widely distributed prayer books in the Yemenite rite which cite the formula and the order somewhat differently from what the Mahariṣ wrote, according to the custom of recent generations. See, for example, Ṣubayri, *Siddur Keneset Gedolah*, vol. 1, pp. 668–74; *Ha-Tiklal ha-Mevu'ar*, pp. 556–63; *Tiklal Torat Avot ke-Minhag Q"Q*

Mahariṣ wrote about the importance of giving the name at the time of the circumcision in his commentary *Eṣ Ḥayim*, in the name of R. Azulai:

> R. Ḥesed le-Avraham w[rote] that the name the father declares at the circumcision is the true name of the soul, and the Holy Spirit engulfs the father and he calls him by the name determined for him, and this is the hidden meaning of "they called their names on earth" (Ps. 49:12). This means that same set name for the soul is what they call him on earth.[100]

Thus, at the hour of circumcision, the father is surrounded by the Holy Spirit, which guides him in giving the infant his name, the name connected to the root of his soul.

Yemenite Jews in Israel today maintain the custom of Yemen, as R. Yiṣḥaq Raṣabi relates, reiterating the above observations of the Mahariṣ:

> And this is the order of the circumcision [ceremony] according to our custom ... who has sanctified us with his commandments and ordered to [carry out] the circumcision ... and while the *mohel* (circumciser) is dealing with *peri'ah*, the father of the boy gives him a blessing for entering the covenant of our Patriarch Avraham ... and the father also recites the *she-heḥeyanu* prayer ... and then he calls him a name that he likes (the Holy Spirit enwraps the father to call the set name for that soul) in the formula, "Enter the covenant, ___." And the assembly

---

Teiman Nusaḥ Baladi, ed. R. Netanel Alsheikh (Bnei Brak, 1996), vol. 1, pp. 332–35. A custom among a portion of the Jews of Shar'ab in southern Yemen is to say a prayer opening with the words *Yequm purqana min shemaya* in which the name of the infant and the father are mentioned. This prayer is recited after the prayer beginning with the words *tishtalaḥ asuta,* which is said for the circumcised child. See R. Sa'adya Ḥozeh, *Toledot ha-Rav Shalom Shabazi u-Minhagei Yahadut Shar'ab be-Teiman,* 1 (Jerusalem, 1973), p. 100.

100. See Mahariṣ, *Tiklal Eṣ Hayim*, vol. 1, pp. 288b, and cf. the statement by R. Avraham Azulai: "And for this [reason], they customarily did not call him a name until after the circumcision, since after that the foreskin had already been removed and the impurity, so then, of course, the secret of the spirit will rest upon him, that is, the spirit of the soul. So thereby the name of a Jewish person shall be given, Shi 'on, Re'uven, and so on, if so, it is understood that a Jew is named through the circumcision commandment, and that is what I wished to explain" (*Ḥesed le-Avraham* of R. Avraham Azulai [Bnei Brak, 1997], ma'yan 2, nehar 52, *Be-Ma'alat Miṣvat ha-Milah*, p. 69). R. Yehezkel Shraga Halberstam, who in his letter of 1894 on a question asked about giving a name, wrote: "And as to what he asked of me concerning expressing my opinion on the name they should call him, I verily heard that the Amor, the holy rabbi, our teacher the rabbi Shalom of Belz, *zṣl*, said that from the heavens they tell the father of the son the name he should call him" (Halberstam, *Divrei Yeḥezqel he-Ḥadash, Kitvei Qodesh,* Response 8, p. 62).

> repeats after him, Enter the covenant, ___... and then they bring a cup of wine and fragrant herbs ... they recite the blessing over wine, "creates fruit of the vine." And then he recites a prayer over fragrant herbs ... and then the blessing "who has sanctified the beloved one from the womb" and so on ... and he still does not drink or even taste it until he recites over the cup the phrase *tishtalaḥ asuta* and so on, for the circumcised child, and after that, for the mother, and he also recites the formula "preserve this child" and so on.[101]

It may have been, however, in Yemen that they usually named the child immediately upon the circumcision, since, the foreskin having been removed, the child is now in a state of special holiness, having entered the covenant of Abraham, and this would be the earliest suitable time for naming him. For the custom, attested but a few times in Yemen, of naming of the child for the first guest to arrive at the circumcision, see above.

3.2 Naming a Girl

For naming a boy there is a delaying as well as a summoning factor. The delaying factor is the foreskin and the summoning factor is the circumcision ceremony, so the custom became widespread to wait for the day of the ceremony to announce the name of a son. For a daughter these factors are absent, so various customs developed among the different Jewish communities in the world, both Ashkenazi and Sephardi.[102]

R. Eliezer Waldenberg (Jerusalem, 20th c.) says that the custom among the Ashkenazim is to name newborn girls on the Monday, Thursday, or Sabbath soon after the birth.[103] These are the days of Torah reading in the synagogue and during the reading it was customary to say "May He who blessed" for those called to the Torah. To publicize the announcement the father is called to the Torah and after his portion is read, "May He who blessed" is said for the woman who gave birth and for the infant girl, and the child's name is declared. Some people were meticulous about giving a name only five days after the birth, and

101. Raṣabi, *Shulḥan Arukh ha-Mequṣar*, vol. 5, chap. 159, 10–11, pp. 8–16.

102. For sources discussing this topic, see Oppenheimer, *Va-Yikra Shemo be-Yisra'el*, pp. 23–24; Munitz, *Shemot Benei Adam*, pp. 13–20; R. Aharon Katz, *Zeman Netinat Shem la-Ben u-la-Bat*, *Sefunot* 6 (1990): 41–45; R. Binyamin Shlomo Hamburger, *Shorshei Minhag Ashkenaz*, 1 (Benei Brak, 1995), pp. 433–41; Teherani, *Keter Shem Tov*, 1, sec. 5, pp. 60–71.

103. R. Eliezer Yehudah Waldenberg, *Ṣiṣ Eliezer* (Jerusalem, 1978), part 13, section 20, par. 6.

apparently this refers to the day on which the Torah is read immediately following the passage of five days.

David Zakkut of Modena (Italy, 19th c.) wrote that it was customary where he lived to name a girl when called to the Torah, noting that "some give the name on the day of birth."[104] On the custom of giving the name at the first opportunity of a Torah reading, we are informed from the responsa of R. Moshe Feinstein (U.S., 20th c.): "And girls are sometimes named at the first Torah reading day that occurs after the birth, which may also be the day after the birth."[105] Some took care to declare the name only after five days, as cited above in the response of R. Waldenberg.

In Iraq and Kurdistan, the girl's name was given at a special ceremony held on the Friday evening after the birth at the home of the woman who had given birth. The declaration of the name by the midwife took place during the ceremony with the accompaniment of clapping and cries of "*mazal tov.*"[106]

Some wait as long as thirty days, like the cycle of the moon, to which a woman is compared,[107] or because upon completion of this period the

104. R. David Zakkut of Modena, "*Zekher David,*" Torah Encyclopedia (Jerusalem, 2001), section 1, ch. 81, p. 580.

105. R. Moshe Feinstein, *Igrot Moshe, Even ha-'Ezer,* part 3 (New York, 1973), sec. 35, p. 480.

106. David Solomon Sassoon, *A History of The Jews in Baghdad* (Letchworth, 1949), p. 138; idem, *Massa Bavel* (Jerusalem, 1955), p. 200; Avraham Ben Ya'akov, *Minhagei Yahadut Bavel,* 2 (Jerusalem, 1993), p. 30; Erich Brauer, "*Milah ve-Yaldut eṣel Yehudei Kurdistan,*" *Edot,* 1 (1946): 131; Zev Hirsch, "*Ha-Sefardim be-Mizraḥ ha-Raḥoq,*" *Sinai,* 50 (1962): 469. Some Iraqi Jews used to have a festive meal on the Friday night after the birth of a daughter, and at the ceremony, the oldest of those gathered would hold the girl, who was dressed in embroidered clothing and jewelry, and recite "May He who blessed" in combination with a blessing for the infant girl phrased as "He shall bless this pleasant girl." See Teherani, *Keter Shem Tov,* vol. 2, pp. 416–19.

107. R. David Zakkut of Modena wrote: "And I saw in a *Sefer Ot Brit* manuscript, ch. 11, that he wrote concerning the name of girls, and it was as follows 'And it is a wise custom to name girls at the end of their [first] month, since the woman is compared to the moon, and when she has lived a period as the days of the cycle of the moon, she is called a name,' see there. And what is the reason that the R. Torat Ḥayim wrote according to his system for Sanhedrin 42, that the Lord set precisely the New Moons as a holiday for women and not another day, for it all stems from women being similar to the moon that is renewed every month, so the women are renewed every month by their menstrual period, since most women have a cycle of thirty days one from the other (Zakkut of Modena, *Zekher David,* chap. 1, sub-chapter 81, p. 581).

newborn is out of neonatal peril;[108] there were others who wait forty days.[109]

There were cases in which naming a girl was not subject to any fixed period following birth, depending instead on other factors. For instance, some waited until the mother had fully recuperated, so she could go to the synagogue where they would name the girl.[110] Some delayed even longer if the father was away on business; in the meantime, the girl was assigned a temporary name related to the family name:

108. In the sixteenth century, R. Eli'ezer Mordekhai wrote: "That it is customary now in our generations on the thirtieth day, when the woman who has given birth has left her bed and the newborn is no longer [in danger of] neonatal death, that the woman makes a meal with friends for the son or daughter. And she makes a donation to charity, or her husband [makes it] for her. And the young men give a name to that son, or the virgins to that daughter. And they call that Sabbath *vollkreis* [full circle]. And even though they gave the son a name on the day of circumcision, in any event, sometimes they give the son a byname that is not written in the Torah, and that byname is given to him on the thirtieth day. And they make a meal with friends and distribute fruit to the children" (Avraham Naftali Sevi Rut, *"Al ha-Ho"l Qraysh," Yeda Am* 7 [1962]: 68). R. Ya'aqov Emden wrote that in case the woman who gave birth cannot walk to the synagogue on the Sabbath, the father or someone else gives a name to the daughter at the end of four weeks, since then the child is almost free of fear of neonatal death. See Emden, *Migdal Oz* (Warsaw, 1882), *shoqet* 2, 17, p. 22.
109. R. Avraham Azulai compared the waiting of 40 days for a girl to circumcision: "And know that a Jewish boy is not worthy of being called a name until he is circumcised. For through circumcision Avraham's masculinity was corrected to be right and proper to join the community to beget sons. And likewise, a daughter is not worthy of being called a name until there be created for her the root of the womb, which takes place forty days after her birth, as from then on she is worthy of joining the community, for we have found that Sarah's womb was not created until she was called Sarah. This is an allusion to the main aim of creation being none other than for having sex to be fruitful and multiply" (Azulai, *Ba'alei Berit Avram* [Jerusalem, 1964], *parashat Tazri'a,* beginning "when a woman at childbirth"). On this R. Binyamin Shlomo Hamburger commented: "Anatomically it is difficult to understand the meaning of the creation of the womb a number of weeks after the birth, for isn't this organ formed in the embryo while still in the mother's womb?" (Hamburger, *Shorshei Minhag Ashkenaz,* p. 437). One may assume that R. Avraham Azulai was not speaking about the physical organ but about its spirituality, and this is apparently what he meant by writing "the root of the womb," and the word "root" is meant to express a spiritual connotation.
110. R. Shem Tov Gagin wrote: "And customarily after the girl's mother has recuperated, she carries her daughter to the synagogue in her arms and there the prayer leader declares her name" (Gagin, *Keter Shem Tov,* p. 581, sect. 39).

> In some families, when the mother gave birth to a girl and the father was not in the city, no name was given to the girl until her father returned; in the interim she was called by the family name. If the family name was Ahuvi, she was called Ahuva, and so on. And when the father came, she would receive her actual name: Sarah or Rivqah and the like.[111]

From the foregoing we learn that there were various customs as to the time for announcing a girl's name. The common time for doing so among the Jewish communities is in the synagogue on the Sabbath, in conjunction with the recitation of "May He who blessed" when the father is called up to the Torah, or on Monday or Thursday, the other two days on which the Torah is read.[112]

In some congregations, it is customary for the new mother to go to the synagogue on one of the Sabbaths after the birth for the naming ceremony. R. Ya'aqov Emden (Germany, 18th c.) wrote: "On the holy Sabbath day, a woman who had given birth to a daughter would go to the synagogue, [where they would] make a 'May He who blessed' for the child and give her her Jewish name."[113] The name of a girl was incorporated into a special event at which sweets were distributed; sometimes there was even a meal. R. Emden wrote about the Sabbath in which the mother would go to the synagogue:

> On that Sabbath, there would be some festiveness by giving out roasted seeds and nuts to the children visiting the newborn and reading verses of blessing at her crib; and there is no straightforward, set custom among the Ashkenazim, and this was not written in a book. Among Sephardi customs, however, I have seen *zeved ha-bat*.[114]

In the Sephardi communities there is a widespread special ceremony called *zeved ha-bat* in which the name of a girl is announced, selected verses in praise of the woman are read, and a *se'udat mișvah* (obligatory festive meal) is held. On the manner in which the *zeved ha-bat* ceremony is conducted R. Gagin wrote:

> The custom in London is that when giving a name to a girl they usually say the verse: "O my dove, in the cranny of the rocks" (Song of Sol. 2:14), and if she is the first daughter, he says: "Only one is my dove, my perfect one" (ibid. 6:9), and they make a "May He who blessed"

111. Alfandari, *Yad Aharon, Even ha-'Ezer*, Laws of Gittin, par. 129, 62, p. 57b.
112. Hamburger, *Shorshei Minhag Ashkenaz*, pp. 440–41.
113. R. Ya'aqov Emden, *Sefer Birat Migdal Oz* (Warsaw, 1882), Shoqet 2, 16, p. 22.
114. Ibid., 19, pp. 22–23.

for her as written in the London daily prayer book, and the formula mentioned is called *zeved ha-bat*.[115]

Among some Sephardi communities, to this ceremony, which was also held on weekdays, attendees brought gifts for the mother, while others offered greetings and congratulations, and it may be that because of this it is called *zeved ha-bat*, as an allusion to the gifts[116] given at the time of the ceremony held for a daughter.[117]

In Persian Jewish communities it was customary to announce a daughter's name on the seventh night after the birth. On that night, a joyous meal would be held for the relatives and the infant would be dressed festively. The rabbi would take the girl from her father's arms and announce the name chosen for her, along with reciting the verse "O my dove, in the cranny of the rocks ..." In Israel, the Persian immigrants usually hold this ceremony on the Sabbath, in the afternoon.[118]

In the Moroccan communities, they generally announced the name on the Sabbath after the birth. Some held the ceremony *zeved ha-bat* ceremony, accompanied by the recitation of a blessing, such as reciting the verse "O my dove, in the cranny of the rocks ..."[119]

The following are Yemenite customs concerning the naming of baby girls.

3.2.1Central Yemen

Of Ṣan'a, R. Pinḥas Qoraḥ wrote: "No ceremony at all was held for giving a name to a daughter, rather the parents would decide between themselves the daughter's name. They would also not widely announce the birth of a girl. And when once I was asked by someone why we didn't know about the birth of a girl in the family, he answered me quite distinctly, 'With us we do not announce it, for it is written "Her voice could not be heard"' (I Sam. 1:13)."[120]

In contrast, we do find written that in Ṣan'a announcing the name of a daughter was accompanied by a party called *Yawm al-'Aṣīṭ* (*'aṣīṭ* is a thick porridge made of flour), which was held during the first week

115. Gagin, *Keter Shem Tov*, p. 581, sect. 39.
116. *Zeved* means gift.
117. Munitz, *Shemot Benei Adam*, pp. 18–19.
118. H. Mizrahi, *Yehudei Paras* (Tel Aviv, 1959), p. 74.
119. David Ovadya, *Kehillat Sefrou*, vol. 3 (Jerusalem, 1976), vol. 3, p. 87; Eliezer Bashan, *Yahadut Maroqo: 'Avarah ve-Tarbutah* (Tel Aviv, 2000), pp. 219–20.
120. In a personal correspondence he sent to me in April 2010.

after the birth; some people observed it on the eighth day. The invitees or the children were served a meal of *'aṣīṭ* with *samna* (boiled, herb butter) or soup for the celebration. The infant would be dressed in beautiful garments and ululations of joy (in Arabic: *yehjaru*) would be heard; and then the name would we announced.[121]

Mori Shim'on Dhahbāni of the Ṣan'a community said that for a girl the name was given upon birth with no ceremony.[122] What he meant was that even though they would make a party in honor of the birth of a daughter, for men and women attendees (separately), as was the custom in the Ṣan'a community, the girl's name was given at the women's ceremony.[123]

Naomi Badiḥi of the Ṣan'a community said that a daughter's name was given about two weeks after her birth, at a party when women would come to the home of the mother to bring her joy.[124]

R. 'Azaryah Basis, formerly of Radā', wrote: "Some would name a daughter in the week she was born. Usually on the Sabbath with a *ja'ale* (roasted items in the language of the Jews of Yemen),[125] the father of the girl would hold her in his hands and say "O my dove, in the cranny of the rocks ...," as appearing in *Siddur Tefillat ha-Ḥodesh*, and say "May He who blessed," "And "let her name be called in Israel ..."[126]

Shelomoh Raṣabi, from Radā', said that generally the name for a girl was given during the first week, and no ceremony was made for the name-giving.[127]

Shim'on and Raḥel Maḥfud, who immigrated to Israel from Dhamār, relate that on the second day after the birth of a daughter they would give her a name at a ceremony called *sumayt al-benaye* (naming a girl), which was held in the mother's home. At this event, they would make

121. Yehudah Ratzaby, "*Darda'im* (*Minhagim ve-Takkanot*)," *Edot* 1 (1946): 173; Erich Brauer, *Ethnologie*, pp. 188–91.

122. Interview conducted by R. Raṣon 'Arusi of Qiryat Ono.

123. On the party that Ṣan'a Jews customarily held for the birth of a daughter, see Qāfiḥ, *Halikhot Teiman*, pp. 178–82; Naḥum, *Mi-Ṣefunot*, pp. 145–46.

124. Interview conducted by her granddaughter Michal Badiḥi of Givatayim.

125. This refers to a gathering of family members or friends at which they usually eat fruit and roasted seeds. See the articles by R. Qāfiḥ, *Gha'ala*; A. I. Kohen, *Oṣrot Teiman*, pp. 187–94.

126. In a personal correspondence dated 8 Mar 2010.

127. Interview conducted by R. Gilad Sadoq of Bnei Brak.

lasīs, a kind of cooked lentils or scalded seeds, and distribute them to the attendees.[128]

In the Tan'em community, they used to announce the name on the third day. On that day, they would decorate the infant girl with beauty marks on her face, blue near her eyes, and a drawing of the Star of David on her forehead, and they would conduct a meal for the immediate family in the study hall where the children learned, along with the children who studied in the *ḥeder*, who were also decorated at this party.[129]

R. Yiṣḥaq Raṣābi wrote me about the customs of the Raṣāba community and its environs in which a name was given to a girl immediately after birth and without any ceremony.[130]

R. Shelomo Maḥfud and R. Avraham Arye informed me about the custom in a number of Central Yemen communities: the name of a daughter was given in the first few days after birth, and no special ceremony was held.[131]

R. Almog Shelomo Akhlufi wrote to me about the customs in his father's family that lived in the villages Bayt Sālem and Yafīd, and the customs of his mother's family that lived in Mahaṣer and Jerāf, also in Central Yemen north of Ṣan'a, in which they usually gave a name soon after birth, with no special ceremony.[132]

Shoshana Basha, whose parents emigrated from Ḍūwāle', which lies north of Ṣan'a, said that a girl's name was given at the time she was born, without any special ceremony.[133]

3.2.2 Southern Yemen

Shelomo 'Adani, a descendant of the Ḍāli' community, stated that a girl's name was given on the day of birth or the following one, but no later than a week after, and no special ceremony was held for the birth of a daughter.[134]

Se'īdah Aharon, from the village of Adūfa in the Shar'ab district, related that a daughter's name was given on Sabbath morning after the

128. Interview conducted by their grandson, Shlomi Maḥfud of Einav.

129. As told by Rumiyah Abahr of Ashekelon.

130. In a personal correspondence dated 22 Apr 2010.

131. A personal correspondence dated 12 Apr 2010 from R. Shelomo Maḥfud , and that of R. Avraham Arye 7 May 2010.

132. In a personal correspondence dated 16 Feb 2011.

133. Interview conducted by her granddaughter Einat Basha of Yavneh.

134. Interview conducted by R. Gilad Ṣadoq of Bnei Brak.

second Sabbath meal, and refreshments were offered, consisting of kinds of fruits and roasted items (*ja'al*e).[135]

Ḥannah Ḥofi, from the village of Qūrana, in the district of Shar'ab, told that a daughter's name was given on the day of birth or a few days later, and on the following Sabbath a party was held for all the relatives.[136]

Sarah Gafni, whose parents were from the village of Saḥban, related that they gave the girl her name upon birth or a few days later, without any special ceremony.[137]

Sarah Nissim, from the village of Bane Hajāj in the Ḥaymeh district, said there was no special ceremony for naming a girl but rather an informal gathering. On the Sabbath after the birth, people would come to the home of the mother, and on that occasion the infant's parents would give her a name. Refreshments were offered, and they mixed water with tumeric and spread it on the child's hand and beneath her dress as a perfume.[138]

Aharon Yehudah, of the Ra'ūḍah community, told that for naming a girl there was no special ceremony.[139]

Tov Oshri, from one of the communities in Qaryat al-Mi'rāḍ in the Yarim district, related that the mother or grandmother would choose the name and invite the women neighbors to come to a meal, where they served a dish called *lasis* (a kind of cooked lentils or scalded seeds), and *laḥuḥ*[140] and a drink called *qishr*.[141]

Moshe Ben David and Shalom Lahav are from Bayḥān. Moshe Ben David wrote that names for girls were given at birth, without any special ceremony.[142] In contrast, Shalom Lahav wrote that in their community the announcement of the name was made on the Tuesday after birth. That day they would pierce the infant's ears, insert a thread through them, and proclaim the name that had been given to her after the birth.[143]

135. Interview conducted by Ya'ir Shunam of Rosh HaAyin.
136. Interview conducted by her son, Shmu'el Ḥofi of New York.
137. Interview conducted by Einat Basha of Yavneh.
138. Interview conducted by her granddaughter, Lirit Zindani of Rehovot.
139. Interview conducted by Yehudah 'Idan of Petah Tikvah.
140. A kind of porous pancake made out of a thin batter and cooked in a frying pan.
141. Qishr is the peel of coffee beans. Yemenite Jews used to prepare a hot drink (*qahwa*) from this peel. Interview conducted by his son, Yo'el Osheri, Tel Aviv.
142. In the interview with Moshe Ben David, who lives in Nes Zionah.
143. In a personal correspondence Shalom Lahav sent me in 1998.

Menashe Ṣubari, from the Bayḍa' community in southeastern Yemen, told that generally they would name the girl two or three days after birth. About a month later the mother would invite her relatives to a meal, a kind of thanksgiving repast, at which the women would bless the mother and her daughter.[144]

In Ḥabbān is southeastern Yemen, they would name a girl on the day of birth or the following day.[145]

3.2.3 Northern Yemen

R. Ovadya Ya'beṣ wrote that at Ṣa'dah: "A name for a boy was determined on the day of circumcision, and for a girl, on the thirty-first day after her birth in the presence of the families of the husband and wife, without any ceremony."[146]

R. Dr. Aharon Ben David wrote to me about the customs of the Jews in northern Yemen: "The name was given a few days after birth but no later than the fortieth day, the day on which the sequestered woman first went out of her house into public territory."[147]

3.2.4 Summary

There were no set rules and sometimes within the same community there were different customs. At times, the name was given on the day of birth or a few days after, and other times even later. The naming of a girl usually took place within a family framework without any special ceremony. Contrary to customs outside Yemen, it was not customary in Yemen for the father to be called up to the Torah to declare the name; nor did anyone recite a "May He who blessed" for the mother who had just given birth.[148]

---

144. Interview conducted by R. Gilad Ṣadoq of Bnei Brak.
145. Tuvya Ashkenazi, *"Yehudei Derom 'Arav," Sinai* 22 (1980): 252.
146. In a personal correspondence dated 4 Apr 2010.
147. In a personal correspondence dated 13 Jan 2010. See also Aharon Ben David, *"Shemot Yehudim bi-Ṣefon Teiman al pi ha-Sefer 'Beit ha-Even'," Mesora le-Yosef* 6 (2009): 445.
148. Raṣabi, *Shulḥan Arukh ha-Mequṣar*, vol. 2, sect. 60, par. 89, p. 123; ibid., vol. 5, sect. 159, par. 43, p. 14. In the Yemenite synagogues, usually no special "May He who blessed" was said for the woman nor was her name mentioned in the "May He who blessed" for her husband, and this stemmed from modesty. For example, when they had to say a "May He who blessed" for an ill woman, they would recite it for a man and add a blessing in the form of "May He send complete healing to the oasis of his house," and the like.

Common among the Yemenite Jews was a custom that the woman did not leave her home for the first thirty days after giving birth. After a month had passed, it was customary to hold a ceremony with the accompaniment of incense and the distribution of lasis for the children learning in *ḥeder*. Then the mother with the young infant would exit her home for the first time. This ceremony was aimed against harmful spirits so they should not do damage to the mother and child.[149]

The ceremonies held by the Yemenite communities to mark the birth of a daughter, which were typified by the distribution of sweets, or with the accompaniment of a meal such as *yawm al-'aṣiṭ*, are a kind of *zeved ha-bat*;[150] but there was no recitation of biblical verses or a "May He who blessed," as found in Sephardi prayer books, except for a few communities such as Radā'.[151]

4. REGISTERING THE NAMES OF THE NEWBORNS AND THE DECEASED

Some Jews in Yemen customarily made lists of births and deaths in their families on the empty page of a book in their possession. In formulating the registration of the births and deaths, some people went to great lengths and others wrote briefly. On the whole, included in the listing of a birth were the date and good wishes that the newborn would have a good, long life, while in the registration of a death the date and an expression of sorrow at the passing were recorded.

With the lack of birth and death registrations in Yemen by authorized agencies, such as the community or the government, and with the lack of inscriptions on tombstones, the registrations in books are highly important. For example, at the end of a *Tiklal* manuscript appear 17 listings of births and deaths from one famous Ṣan'a family: the Sāliḥ family.[152] At the start of the list, one of the grandsons wrote the dates of death for his grandfather and father. For his grandfather, the greatest religious decisor in Yemen, R. Yiḥye' Sāliḥ (Mahariṣ), he wrote: "Departed *mv"z* (*mori zeqeni morenu*; my teacher, my grandfather, our teacher) R. Yiḥye' Sāliḥ, may his memory be everlasting, on the Sabbath

149. Ratzaby, *'Darda'im,'* pp. 173–74; Qāfiḥ, *Halikhot Teiman*, pp. 181–82.
150. Ratzaby, *'Darda'im,'* p. 173; Qāfiḥ, *Halikhot Teiman*, p. 180 n. 66.
151. Raṣabi, *Shulḥan Arukh ha-Mequṣar*, vol. 5, sect. 159, par. 43, p. 14.
152. Shocken Library MS 12824 (IMM 45361). For a photograph of a page from the manuscript and a discussion of the list, see Moshe Gavra, *Mahariṣ* (Bnei Brak, 1994) pp. 7–10, 210–11.

in the afternoon, 28 Nisan 2116 SEL [5565 AM/23 Aug 1805], in the ch[apter] Kedoshim."[153] The date of the death of his father, the *dayyan* R. Avraham the son of Mahariṣ, was phrased in the following pattern: "Departed *'m"v* (*avi mori ve-rabbi*; my father my teacher and my rabbi) Avraham, *ng'* (*nuḥo gan 'eden*; may he rest in the Garden of Eden), in the year 2220 SEL, on Sunday, which is the last day of the Intermediate Days of Sukkot [5669 AM/9 Oct 1808]." Registered on the title page of *Tiklal Eṣ Ḥayim* by his father, R. Yiḥye', who was the chief rabbi and ḥakham bashi, is the date of birth of R. Shalom Yiṣḥaq Halevi, according to the following formula: "Shining and glowing a dear child, a sweet son, my firstborn Sālem [Shalom], of Monday night, at the hour of one, the 21st of Heshvan in the year 5651 AM. May He from whom all emanates make me worthy and the Creator give me life [the initials of the four Hebrew words spell out God] to see sons and grandsons occupied with Torah and commandments. May it be His will."[154]

At the end of a printed book, the birth of the esteemed Prof. Yehudah Ratzaby was registered by his father, R. Yiḥye', as follows: "Born to me was the good flower, resembling a moist tree, may the Lord also give him good, and good character, his name is Yuda' (יודא)[155] ben Yiḥye' called Raṣābi. The Lord will establish him as His holy people (after Deut. 28:9) ... Tuesday, the 19th of Iyar, 2227 SEL [5676 AM/11 May 1916]."[156]

In a manuscript of the Qāfiḥ family, one of the most famous families in Yemen, are 21 listings of births and deaths. The date of birth of R. Yosef Qāfiḥ was registered in the following formulation: "Born was Yosef ibn David, Tuesday, sixth hour, 12 Kislev 2229 [SEL], 5678 [27 Nov 1917]."[157] The date of the death of his grandfather, R. Yiḥye', founder of the Dor De'ah movement in Yemen, was written as follows: "Today is a day of waste and desolation, a day of darkness and gloominess, a day of clouds and thick darkness, the day of the taking of the ark of the Lord, *kmhr"r* (*kevod morenu ha-rav rabbi*; our honorable teacher and rab-

153. That is, the chapter Kedoshim (Holy) they read that Sabbath, and an allusion that also the deceased was holy.

154. *Sefer Zikkaron le-Rav Yiḥye' Yiṣḥaq Halevi*, vol. 3, p. 461.

155. He wrote יודא and not יהודה so as to avoid writing approximating הוי"ה, the tetragrammaton.

156. *Sefer Maqor Ḥayim*, in the possession of the Raṣabi family.

157. For a photo of the manuscript page, see Avivit Levy, *Holekh Tamim: Morashto, Ḥayyav u-Po'alo shel ha-Rav Yosef Qafiḥ* (Jerusalem, 2003). p. 29.

bi), Yiḥye' ben Slaymān al Qāfiḥ, *tanṣeba"h* [*tihye nishmato ṣerurah bi-ṣror ha-Ḥayim*; may his soul be bound in the bond of life], and the day of rising to the heavens was on the holy Sabbath at the end of the ninth hour 17 Kislev 5692, 2243 [SEL / 27 Nov 1931]." The list also includes the date of death of R. Yiḥye' Abyaḍ, who served as the chief rabbi of Yemenite Jewry from 1932 until his death: "He went up to God as *kmhr"r* R. Yiḥye' ben Shalom Abyaḍ, at the end of the holy Sabbath, at the time of 2:30, 26 Sivan 5695, 2246 SEL [4 Nov 1934]."

Below I present several registration lists in chronological order.

4.1 Guide of the Perplexed, MS London - British Library, Arabic MS I.O. 3379 (IMM 49332)[158]

The manuscript was copied in 1380 in the Ṭawīlah community. On the final page of the manuscript appear three listings of births: Sa'adyah, Yehudah, and Yesha', who are the sons of the owner of the manuscript David ben Se'īd.

1. The good flower was born, Sa'adyah ben David, Monday which is the twenty-second[159] day in the month of Kislev in the year 1697 SEL [5146 AM/27 Nov 1385]. May God give him a good, long life and pleasant years, Amen Neṣaḥ Sela. And fulfill for him as written in biblical verses "The Lord bless and protect you, the Lord make his face shine to you…[160] and deal graciously with you, the Lord lift up his countenance to you and grant you peace" (Num. 6:24– 26).
2. The good flower was born, Yehudah ben David, 8 Shevat in the year 1712 SEL [5162 AM/12 Jan 1402]. May God give him a good, long life and pleasant years. And fulfill for him as written in biblical verse "For a child has been born to us, a son has been given us …"[161] He has been named *Pele yo'eṣ El gibbor* [the Mighty God is planning grace; the Eternal Father, a peaceable ruler] (Isa. 9:5). And also fulfill for him, "The Lord bless and protect you, the Lord make his face shine to you and deal graciously with you, the Lord lift up his countenance to you and grant you peace." Amen, may it be the will of heaven.

158. On the manuscript, see Aharon Gaimani, *"Ha'ataqah Qedumah mi-Teiman le-*Moreh Nevukhim *le-ha-Rambam," Tehuda* 14 (1994): 15–20.
159. Monday fell on 23 Kislev.
160. Missing in the manuscript.
161. Missing in the manuscript.

3. The good flower was born, Yesha' son of R[av] Sa'adyah on the tenth day of the month of Av in the year 1724 SEL [5173 AM/9 July 1413]. May God give him a good, long life and pleasant years. And He will fulfill for him the verse as written "The smallest shall become a clan and the l[east], a mi[ghty] nation, I the Lord shall s[peed it] in due t[ime]" (Isa. 60:22). And also fulfill for him, "The Lord bless and protect you, the Lord make his face shine to you and deal graciously with you, the Lord lift up his countenance to you and grant you peace."

4.2 Tiklal, MS London 2227 (IMM 6061)[162]

The manuscript was copied in the early sixteenth century in Ṣan'a. At its end the births of two sons, Sa'adyah and Shalom, are listed:

1. As a good sign and blessing. Born was the good flower, like a moist tree, also God will give him the good, Sa'adyah ben Yehudah ben Shelomo ben Yosef[163] al-Ladāni, in 1828 SEL [5277 AM/1516/17]. May the Lord make him a good sign and blessing from now and forever, and protect him and keep him in life for his father and his mother and happiness is in the land, and He will fulfill for him the bibli[cal verse] as it is writ[ten], "For a child has been born to us, a son has been given us, and authority has settled on his shoulders; he has been named the Mighty God is planning grace, the Eternal Father, a peaceable ruler" (Isa. 9:5). "The Lord bless and protect you, the Lord make his face shine to you and deal graciously with you, the Lord lift up his countenance to you and grant you peace" (Num. 6:24– 26).
2. A good sign and a blessing. Born is the good flower, resembling a moist tree, may God also give him the good, Shalom ben Yehudah ben Shelomoh ben Yosef[164] al-Ladāni, in the month of Av in the year 1843 SEL [5293 AM/1533], in Wadi Dhahabān. May the Lord sustain him and protect him for his father and his mother,

162. Margaliot Catalogue, serial no. 711, pp. 396–402.
163. Written above the name Sa'adyah is ש"צ [protect him], above the name Yehudah יש"ל [May his name endure forever], above the name Shelomoh, רי"ת [the spirit of the Lord will rest upon him, and above the name Yosef is תנצב"ה [May his soul be bound up in the bond of eternal life]. For a discussion of the ornateness of signatures, see below part 3, chap. 2, sect. 2.
164. Written above the name Shalom is יש"ל; above the name Shelomoh, ש"צ; above the name Yosef, תנצב"ה.

and fulfill for him the biblical verse as it is writ[ten], "The [smallest] shall become a clan and the least, a mighty nation, I the Lord shall speed it in due time" (Isa. 60:22). And may He fulfill for him the biblical verse as it is writ[ten], "The angel who has redeemed me from all [harm]—Bles[s] the lad[s]. In the[m] [m]y name shall be recal[led] and the names of my fathe[rs] Avra[ham] and Yiṣḥaq, and may they be teem[ing] multitude[s] up[on] the earth" (Gen. 48:16). "The Lord bless and protect you, the Lord make his face shine to you and deal graciously with you, the Lord lift up his countenance to you and grant you peace" (Num 6:24– 26). Salvation He will bring on nigh, joy will be sweet.

4.3 Printed Book, Responsa of Ridbaz, in the Possession of R. Yosef Qāfiḥ, Jerusalem

R. Shalom al-Manṣūra listed three deaths in his family in Ṣan'a in the nineteenth century. He wrote down the deaths of his father and mother on the title page, and the passing of his son on the approbation page.

1. My honorable father and master, Yehudah ibn Shalom al-Manṣūrah, *ng'*, was called to the Court on High, on Tuesday of which it is sa[id] twice that it is good, 14 in the month of Kislev in 2146 SEL [5595 AM/16 Dec 1834] to the judgment of God (Ps. 76:10). The weekly portion of "And Jacob journeyed on to Succoth, and built a house for himself" (Gen. 33:17), his virtue will protect me and the members of my household and my sons forever. [Regular signature] the humble Sālem son of " [my master, my father] Yuda' Manṣūrah, His rock and redeemer should guard him.
2. And my esteemed mother, Naḍrah daughter of Yiḥye' al-Ṭayri, was called to her eternal home, Friday Sabbath eve on the 17 of the month of Shevat in 2120 SEL [5569 AM/3 Feb 1809], in the weekly portion "Honor your father and your mother [אמ"ך]" (Ex. 20:11; Deut. 5:15). End of *alef, peh,* and the end of *mem, mem,* that come to 120, and the *kaf,* in of *imekha,* in small number is two, comes to 2120 [SEL].[165]

165. Elsewhere in a collection on different issues in the possession of R. Yosef Ṣubayri, R. Shalom Manṣūrah wrote down the deaths of his parents. Apparently, R. Manṣūrah copied the deaths of his parents another time from the listing below in responsa of Ridbaz. There are few differences and in the following listing the name of his mother is Esther, and apparently her previous name had been Naḍrah. About his mother's death he wrote: "*Ḥay* my mother Mrs. Esther bat Yiḥye' al-Ṭayri was

3. The complete, honest, pleasant, divine sage, my master, my lovely son, Shlomo, his resting place in paradise, for our many iniquities, was called on Monday, 6 Tammuz 2170 SEL [5619 AM/1859] when Shelomo obeyed me and kept my charge,[166] happy is his lot, *tanṣeba"h*. And the world became dark for me, for he was my enjoyment out of all my wealth (Eccl. 2:10), and he was like Shelomo, a new being with no defect, and he never angered me nor rebelled, and he never ceased learning Torah. He was meticulous in prayer and humility. Woe is me for my loss. [regular signature] the humble Sālem ben *adoni avi* Yuda' Manṣura, may the Lord protect and sustain him.

Owing to the lack of orderly registration by the community or the authorities, the family listings of names of the newborns and the deceased, which some of the Yemenite Jews used to write in their books, assist us as we have seen above (section 1) in the study of names, such as choosing a name in commemoration of events in the annual cycle and expressing personal wishes when giving a name. Similarly, they are of help with important notations of dates of birth and death of famous people who were active in the Yemenite communities. These listings are of further benefit to us in the study of naming customs among the Yemenite communities, such as identical names for father and son, or grandfather and grandson during the lifetime of the grandfather or after his passing, as we shall see in the next chapter, as well as in learning about rare names and appellations given as a charm, as we shall see in the following chapters.

taken to her eternal home owing to our many transgressions, on Friday, 17 of the month of Shevat in 2120 [SEL = 5569/3 Feb 1809], of the weekly portion, "So Yitro, Moshe's father-in-law took Ṣippora, Moshe's wife, after she had been sent home." May the blessed Lord remember me in her honor and her righteousness forever, may it be His will, Amen. The humble Shalom." About the death of his father, he wrote: "My honorable Abba Mori, my glory and crown, Yudah ben Shalom Manṣūrah, *ng'*, departed on Tuesday, 14 Kislev in 2146 [SEL = 5595/16 Dec 1834] was called to the judgment of God. The weekly portion of "Deliver me, I pray, from the hand of my brother Esau … and Ya'aqov journeyed on to Succoth and built a house for himself and made stalls for his cattle" (Gen. 33:17). [Ornamental signature] The humble Sālem son of son of my master, my father Yuda' Manṣūrah, His rock and redeemer should guard him, the most humble.

166. After Gen. 26:5.

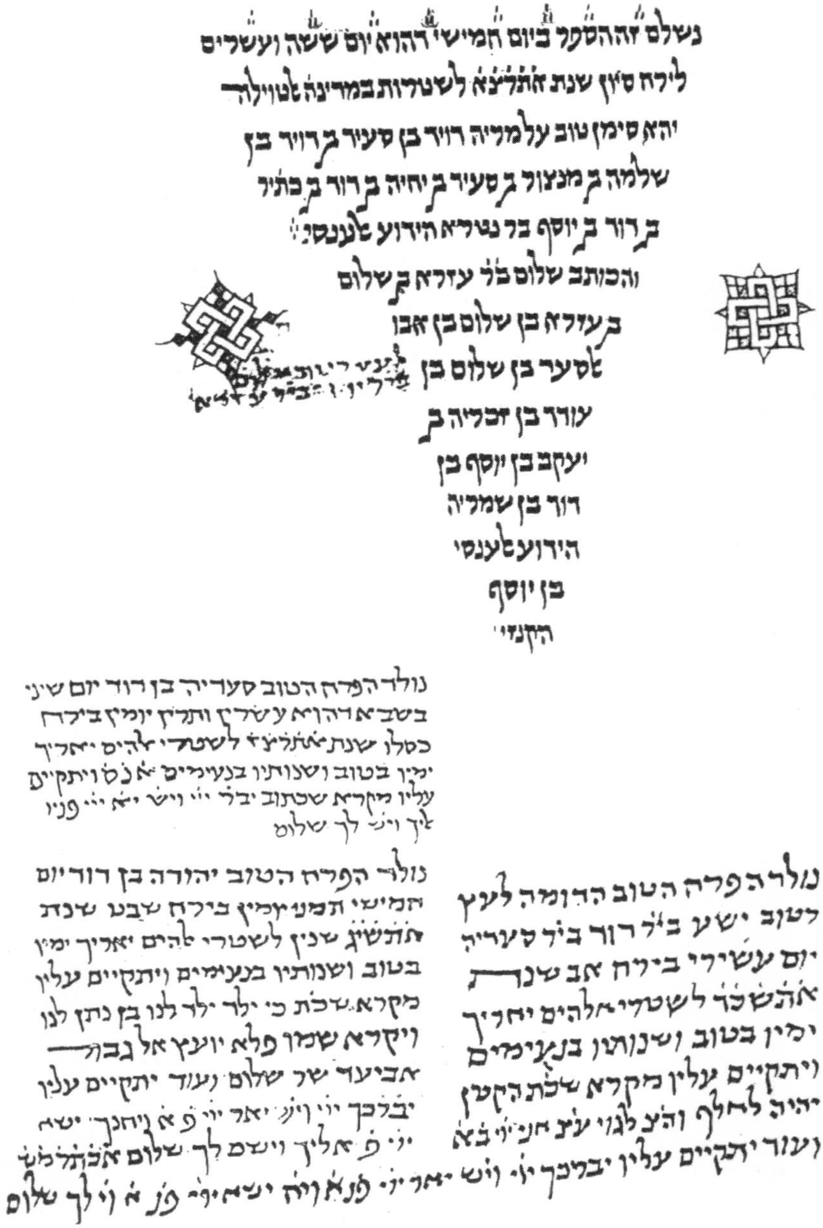

Registration of births in one of the families in the 13th–14th centuries.
Guide of the Perplexed, MS London - British Library, Arabic MS I.O. 3379.

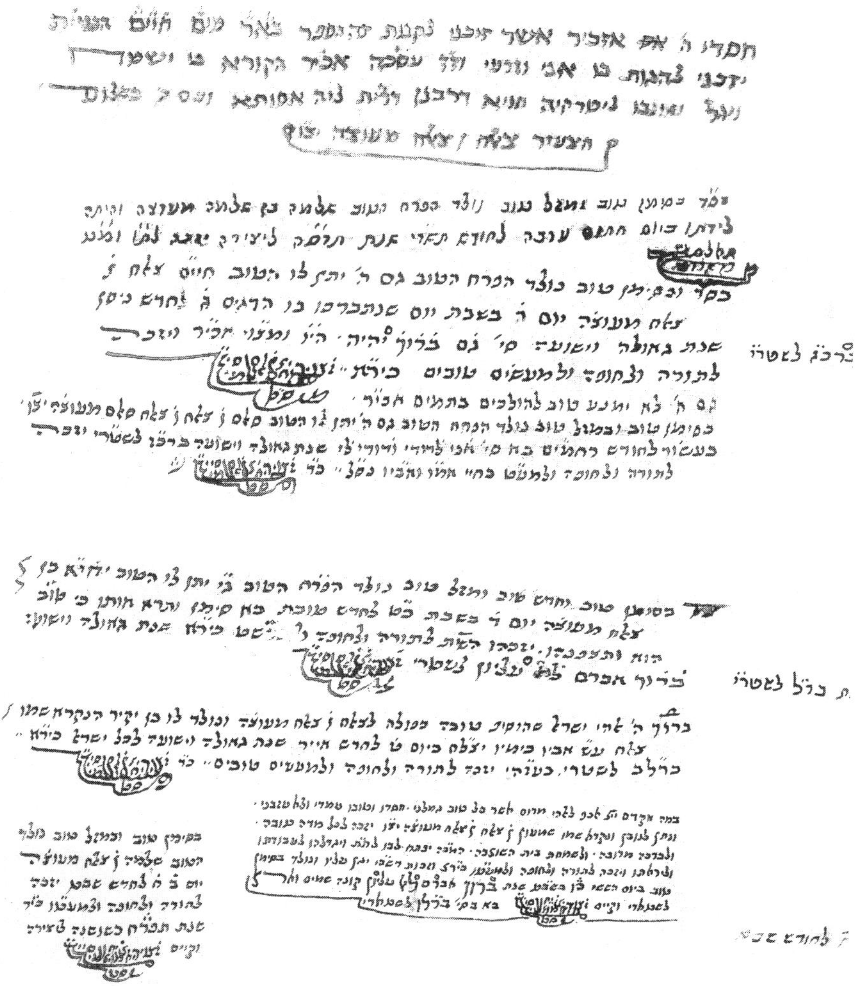

List of births in the Ma'ūḍa family of the Radā' community, first half of the 20th century. In a printed book, Leviticus, Lemberg 5634, Shelomoh Amihud, Bat Yam.

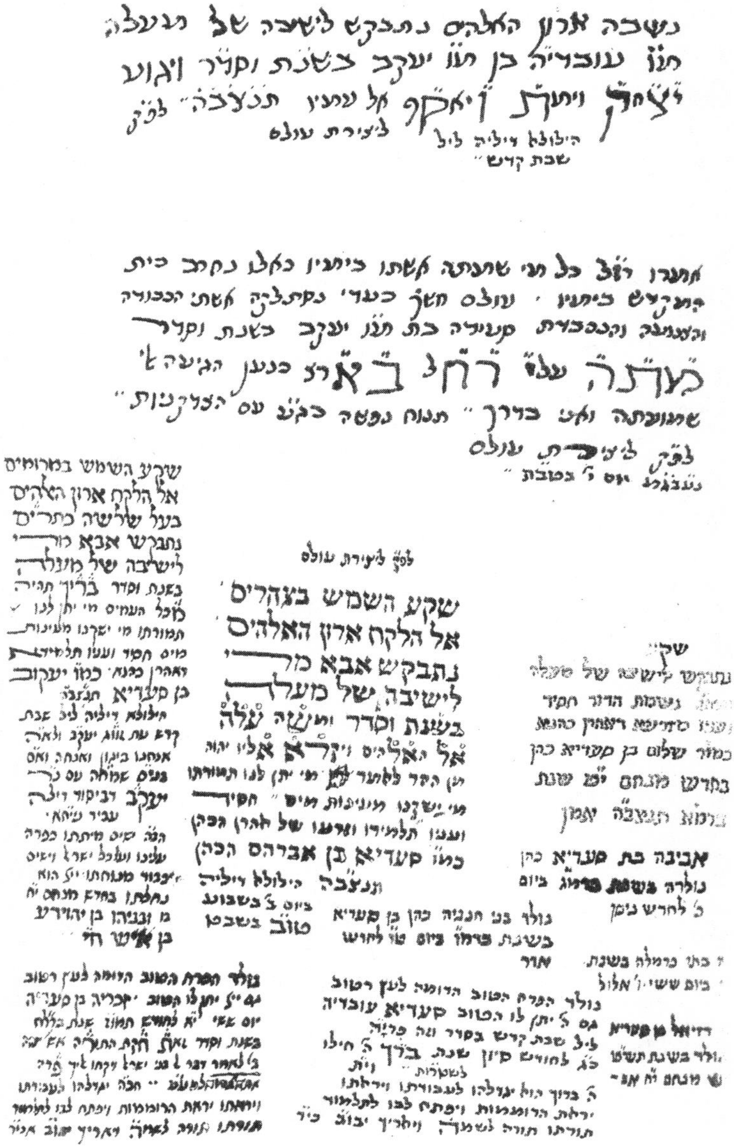
שקע השמש בצהרים
אל הלקח ארון האלהים
נתבקש אבא מרי
לישיבה של מעלה

Lists of births and deaths of one of the families in the Ṣa'dah community. In a printed edition of Ashmoret ha-Boqer, *Salonika 5602, Zekharyah Kohen, Rehovot*

CHAPTER TWO

NAMES WITHIN THE FAMILY CIRCLE

In the ethical will of R. Yehudah Heḥasid, one of the early sages of Ashkenaz, are a number of restrictions about the giving and using of names. They include the restriction that a man should not marry a woman with the same name as his mother's name, or whose father's name is the same as his; also, names should not be given for the living, only for the dead. Some communities were meticulous in carrying out the directives of the will, mainly among the Jews of Ashkenaz, while others were not careful to maintain them even though they were familiar with the restrictions, and those were mainly among the Jews in Muslim countries. Rabbis discussed these issues and registered the customs of their communities, and there were sages who were asked about these customs and, in reply, wrote the reasons for the custom. The Yemenite sages did not deal with these matters at all, though they could be discerned from documents, such as *ketubbot* (marriage contracts), *gittin* (divorce documents), colophons, the Rabbinic Court registry for the Ṣan'a community, as well as from the replies of the Yemenite rabbis in Israel.

1. IDENTICAL NAMES FOR GRANDFATHER AND GRANDSON

As early as the rabbinic period, the custom of fathers naming their sons after their own fathers became widespread; thus we find identical names for a grandson and a son (paponymy).[1] On the difference in nam-

1. For a discussion on this, see Yosef Hakohen Oppenheimer, *Va-Yikra Shemo be-Yisra'el* (Buenos Aires, 1975), pp. 32–33; Avraham Zifroni, *"Minhagim Qedumim," Mizraḥ u-Ma'arav* 1 (1929): 38–39., pp. 38–39; S. Klein, *"Le-Ḥeqer ha-Shemot ve-ha-Kinnuyim," Leshonenu* 1 (1929): 327–29; Sarah Munitz, *"Shemot Benei Adam—Minhag ve-Halakhah"* (MA diss., Bar-Ilan University, 1989), pp. 34–39. A rare instance in the

ing between the biblical and rabbinic periods, the Midrash states about the verse in Genesis (10:25) "Two sons were born to Eber: the name of the first was Peleg, for in his days the earth was divided (*niflegah*)":

> R. Jose said: The ancients, since they knew their genealogy, named themselves in reference to the events [of their days]. But we who do not know our genealogy name ourselves by our fathers. R. Simeon b. Gamaliel said: The ancients, because they could avail themselves of the Holy Spirit, named themselves in reference to [forthcoming] events, but we who cannot avail ourselves of the Holy Spirit are named after our fathers.[2]

In the case at hand, the name that was given is for a future event, as it is written in the continuation of the midrash, "R. Jose b. R. Halafta said: Ever must have been a great prophet, seeing that he named his child in reference to a [future] incident."[3] Below are examples of fathers naming their sons for their own fathers.

In the following examples, the names recur after skipping one generation: "R. 'Uzziel, the grandson of the elder R. 'Uzziel" (Mo'ed Qatan 5a); "R. Parta the son of R. El'azar b. Parta and the grandson of the great R. Parta" (Gittin 33b); "R. Hyrkanos the son of R. Eliezer b. Hyrkanos" (Menaḥot 35a). Also in the lineage of the *nesi'im* given below, one may see the phenomenon mentioned: "The last Hillel was the son of R. Yehudah Nesi'ah (the third), son of R. Gamali'el, son of Yehudah Nesi'ah (the second), son of R. Gamali'el, son of R. Yehudah HaNasi (editor of the Mishnah), son of R. Shim'on (known as Rashbag de-Usha), son of Gamali'el (of Yavneh), son of Shim'on (known by the name Rashag ha-Neherag [killed]), son of Rabban Gamali'el (the elder), son of Shim'on son of Hillel Ha-Zaqen."[4]

The phenomena mentioned are found among the various Jewish communities with certain differences. The Ashkenazi custom is to

---

Bible of calling the son by the name of his grandfather is Naḥor ben Terah ben Naḥor (Gen. 11:25–26). Another case in which a daughter was named for her grandmother is Ma'akah bat Avshalom ben Ma'akah (2 Sam. 3:3; 2 Chron. 11:25–26).

2. Gen. Rabbah 37:7.

3. This was the attitude adopted by R. Israel Lifschitz (19th c.) in his commentary *Tiferet Yisra'el* on Mishnah Sheqalim 6:1, in which are explained the names of kings on the basis of what was going to occur in their times and apparently assumes that they were given their name by a prophet.

4. R. Reuven Margaliot, *Le-Ḥeqer Shemot ve-Kinnuyim ba-Talmud* (Jerusalem, 1960), p. 58 n. 4.

name a son for his grandfather only after the latter has passed away, while among Sephardi Jews a child was named for his grandfather even if he was still alive.

1.1 Ashkenazi Custom

R. Asher Anshil Greenwald (Hungary, 20th c.) commented on the custom in past periods and on the contemporary difference between the Sephardi and the Ashkenazi customs:

> And in the past among the Jews, [customarily children] were named after grandfathers, as we have seen in the genealogy of Hillel ha-Nasi and in many similar cases. And they would name their sons with the name of their grandfathers who were still alive. But in our country, we take meticulous care about this and only name for the deceased, to perpetuate their name. And rabbinic works tell us that this is of benefit for the soul if we are naming for him.[5]

From R. Greenwald's statements we understand that among the Ashkenazim it was considered an honor for the soul of the deceased if the grandchildren were named for grandfathers and grandmothers after they had died. Another reason for this custom among the Ashkenazim was cited by Baruch ha-Levi Epstein (Lithuania, 19th–20th centuries) in his commentary *Torah Temimah*, namely, to remember the family's genealogy, "since we wander about in the Galut it is worthwhile for us to remember the sequence of the family lineage, by having the fathers name their sons with the names of the departed fathers [of the fathers], and as we do now in this time, we find this custom also in the Talmud in a number of places."[6]

In the early circles of Ḥasidei Ashkenaz, active in the twelfth and thirteenth centuries, Jews refrained from naming the newborn after someone still living. In *Sefer Ḥasidim* by R. Yehudah Heḥasid (d. 1217) it is written: "There is nothing in the non-Jews calling their children the name of their fathers, and the Jews are meticulous about that. And there are places where they do not give names for the living but rather only after they have died."[7] Apparently the custom among Ashkenazi Jews stems from this, and they were afraid, owing to the statements of R. Ye-

5. R. Asher Anshil Greenwald, *Zokher ha-Berit* (Uzhhorod-Ungvár, 1931; (photocopy [Tel Aviv], 1964 section 24, 3).
6. R. Baruch HaLevi Epstein, *Ḥumash Torah Temimah* (Vilna 5664 (1904)), Gen. 32:11, and see below this chapter, sect. 4.
7. *Sefer Ḥasidim*, sect. 470, p. 315.

hudah Heḥasid, that if they would name someone for a living grandfather, he would now be in danger since there was now someone else in his stead. This fear is also expressed by R. Avraham Elazar Hershovitz, "And so they should not call a grandson by the name of his grandfather (*zayde*)[8] or his grandmother (*bobbe*)[9] while they are alive, even if they live in a different city, for now in our times they call the newborns only after their deceased grandparents, and [if they do so] he may be endangered, and a danger is more serious than a prohibition (Ḥullin 6)."[10]

We are informed of an interesting source for the Ashkenazi custom by the listing of the grandchildren of R. Shelomo Yiṣḥaqi (Rashi) from his daughter Yokheved. In a detailed biographical note in Rashi's commentary to Job 40:27, we find:

> From here on comments his grandson Rabbenu Shemu'el the elder [Rashbam], the brother of Rabbenu Ya'aqov [Rabbenu Tam], brother of Rabbenu Yiṣḥaq, of R. Shelomo, the grammarian, the sons of Rabbenu Me'ir the elder son of the *ḥaver* Rabbenu Shemu'el, may the memory of the righteous be a blessing. And the name of their mother, the pious Lady Yokheved daughter of Rabbenu Shelomo, may the memory of the righteous be a blessing.[11]

The grandson Shelomo was named for his grandfather on his mother's side, Rashi, while the grandson Shemu'el for his grandfather on his father's side.

1.2 Sephardi/Eastern Jews Custom

Some with origins in Islamic countries name their children after a grandfather or grandmother while he or she is still alive.[12] R. Ḥayim Ben Attar, author of *Or ha-Ḥayim*, was born in the Salé, Morocco, in 1696, and his father, R. Moshe, named him Ḥayim after his father. The son, R. Ḥayim, gained most of his Torah knowledge from his grandfather, R. Ḥayim.[13] The act of naming was a way of expressing honor for

8. A Yiddish term for grandfather.
9. A Yiddish term for grandmother.
10. Avraham Elazar Hershovitz, *Oṣar Kol Minhagei Yeshurun* (Lvov, 1930).
11. Sarah Japhet and Robert B. Saulters, *The Commentary of R. Samuel ben Meir, Rashbam, on Qoheleth* (Jerusalem, 1985), p. 11 n. 2.
12. Avraham Ben Ya'akov, *Minhagei Yahdut Bavel*, 2 (Jerusalem, 1993), p. 30.
13. See R. Reuven Margaliot, *Toldot Or ha-Ḥayyim* (Beersheba, 2005), p. 4, 60. On his studying with R. Ḥayim, he wrote, "And I sat to study Torah before *mmv"r*, the

elders and pleased them by having their name perpetuated while they were still among the living.[14]

Below is an example from the family of my wife, Beruriah, whose parents originated from Iraq.[15] My father-in-law, Ya'aqov Dali, called his eldest son Shelomo, after the name of his father, and one of his daughters, Avivah, by his mother's name, Ḥavivah.[16] My mother-in-law, Juliette, called her youngest daughter Ayyalah (in Arabic, Ghazāla), after her mother.[17] Each of my father-in-law's brothers, Yosef, Menashe, and Danny, called one of their sons Shelomo, and two of them, Menashe and Danny, named one of their daughters Avivah.

Customary though it was among Sephardi Jews to name a child for a grandfather who was still alive, at times a son was named for his father who was alive. R. Shabtai Lifschitz wrote about the custom of the Sephardim in Jerusalem, and from his statements we learn of the difference between the Ashkenazi and Sephardi customs:

> Among our co-religionists, the people in Jerusalem stemming from Spain, it is accepted (for attaining) long life for the father that a son should be named for him while he is alive. And sometimes they do the same for the child's paternal grandfather, calling him by the name of his grandfather who is still alive, as a *segulah* [benevolent charm] that he should live for a long time. Perhaps the reason the custom has

---

famous rabbi, my master my grandfather my teacher whose glorious reputation is known publicly, the pious teacher R. Ḥayim Ben Attar, may his memory be for the World to Come, whose waters I drank as a living well, and upon whose knees I grew, and in whose bosom I dwelled from the day I was able to draw upon his good ways" (R. Ḥaim Ben Attar, *Ḥefeṣ Hashem, Tractates Berakhot, Shabbat, Horayot, and Ḥullin* [Jerusalem, 1995], Introduction).

14. See, for example, Farija Zuarez, "*Mi-Minhagei Yahadut Luv,*" in A. Wasserteil (ed.), *Yalqut Minhagim* (Jerusalem, 1980), p. 217; Farija Zuarez et al. (eds.), "*Havai u-Minhagim,*" in *Yahadut Luv* (Tel Aviv, 1960), p. 390.
15. My father-in-law was born in Hillah in the region of Baghdad and my mother-in-law in Mosul in northern Iraq; they married in Israel in 1957.
16. In the Land of Israel, it was not customary to use the name Ḥabība (Heb., beloved), just as it is not common to use names that were widespread among the Jewish communities, such as Zalman, Kalman, or Mendel in Europe, Makhluf, Mas'ūd, or Sultana in Morocco, Yiḥye', Sa'id, or Ḥamamah in Yemen, so they gave the name *Avivah,* which has a ring similar to *Ḥavivah.*
17. My mother-in-law told me that when her oldest son was born she wanted to call him by the name of her father, but her family did not recommend that because among them priority for giving the father's name goes to a son, that is, it was her brother's right.

> become widespread, that newborns are named for their deceased father or grandfather, and perhaps this memorialization of his name, which was determined for him from the heavens will, heaven forfend, cause a hastening of his death, so they do it earlier, and call the child by his name while he is still alive. And once, I was in a home at a circumcision, and I saw that they did this and I was astonished since this is not our custom (from the rabbi the *gaon*, our teacher the rabbi) Shelomo Aharon Wertheimer from the Holy City of Jerusalem, may it be built and established soon.[18]

These remarks inform us that the Sephardi custom of naming a grandchild for a grandfather is considered a charm to ensure a long life for the grandfather. In addition, the custom of naming after a living grandfather and not after his death involves the belief that if his name is perpetuated after his demise, it may cause the newborn to have a short life. Among Ashkenazi Jews, however, the custom of naming a child for one of the deceased grandfathers is a charm for a long life for the baby,[19] as well as for the remembrance of the family lineage.[20]

S. D. Goitein found in his research into the Cairo Geniza that in Jewish society a son was called by the name of his paternal grandfather, even if there were other grandchildren named for him. For example, he pointed out a merchant who had four sons, and each one of them called one of their sons by his name, so that there were four grandsons named for him. Goitein observes that there is a difference between this custom and that followed by the Jews in Christian Europe, where they named children for their grandfather only after his death. This is the opposite of what he found in the Geniza, namely, that children were called by their grandfather's name while he was still alive. He explained the custom of naming for the grandfather in that the grandfather always took

18. Shabtai Lifschitz, *Sharvit ha-Zahav he-Ḥadash Nikra Berit Avot* (Mukachevo, [5674] 1924), section 8, 16.
19. R. Yehezkel Shraga Halberstam wrote in a letter in 1894 that "the *admor*, the holy rabbi, our teacher the rabbi, Shalom of Belz, OBM, said ... I have also heard that he said it is advantageous for a long life to give a name from the family." In an 1895 letter, he stated, "And what he asked for advice for a name for the child, I have heard in the name of the *admor*, our teacher and rabbi, the holy rabbi of Belz, may the memory of the righteous be a blessing for the World to Come, that it is good for a long life to name from within the family after a father or a mother" (Yehezkel Shraga Halberstam, *Divrei Yehezkel he-Ḥadash, Kitvei Kodesh*, 8–9 (Ramat-Gan, 1986), pp. 61–62).
20. See the statements by R. Baruch Halevi Epstein in his commentary *Torah Temimah*, below, section 4.

an interest in the education of his grandchild, in light of biblical verses: Deuteronomy (4:9), "And make them known to your children and to your children's children" and Psalms (128:6) "And see your children's children." He also noted regarding the naming customs mentioned that in biblical times there was no custom to name after the grandfather, and this should be attributed to external influence. For example, the Hellenistic rulers named their sons after themselves or their fathers as did the Hasmonean kings and the *nesi'im* in the Second Temple period, while the custom to call their sons after themselves was uncommon.[21]

1.3 Yemenite Custom

It was common among Yemenite Jews to name a grandson after his grandfather, either during his life or after his death. R. Ya'aqov Shar'abi wrote regarding the customs of the community of Ṣan'a and the center:

> Usually children are named after a deceased relative, and some even during their lifetime to grant them perpetuation in the world. The result of this custom was that many times certain names recurred in a family for ten generations or more, until there were five men or women in the family whose names and family names were identical, and they are cousins or remote cousins, and all of them were named for one of their forefathers. As an example, I cite the lineage in my family: Ya'aqov b. Avraham b. Ya'aqov b. Ḥayim b. Ya'aqov b. Ḥayim b. Ya'aqov.[22]

R. Shar'abi further wrote that this use of identical personal names within a family resulted in having some people called by their name and their father's name instead of the family name. For example, Ḥayim ben Matanyah Badiḥi was called Ḥayim Matanyah, since there were other relatives called Ḥayim Badiḥi. In the same manner there were Yiḥye' Sālem (Badiḥi), Yiḥye' Slaymān (Badiḥi), Sālem Yehudah ('Irāqi), and Ḥayim Sakhar ('Irāqi).

R. Almog Shelomo Akhlufi provided examples of naming a grandson after his grandfather from his father's family, which lived in Bayt Sālem and Yafīd in Central Yemen, and from his mother's side, which lived in Mahaṣer and Jerāf, also in Central Yemen, north of Ṣan'a. He told as follows:

> Sons were often named for the family's forefathers. For example, my father's grandfather, R. Gaon Yiḥye' ben R. Slaymān ben R. David ben

21. Shlomo Dov Goitein, *A Mediterranean Society*, vol. 3 (Berkeley, Calif., 1978), 3:6–8.
22. In a personal correspondence dated 2 Dec 2010.

> Our Distinguished Teacher and R. Yosef, may his memory be a blessing for the World to Come, named three of his sons by the names David (my grandfather), Slaymān, and Yosef for the three forebears noted. And his sons behaved the same way: My grandfather R. David called two of his sons Shelomo and Zekharyah (which is Yiḥye' in Arabic) on the names of his noted forefathers, and another son, who is my father, teacher, and rabbi Yesh'ayahu, on the name of his father in law, Ya'īsh Sālem Akhlufi. And the elder brother of my grandfather, the rav R. Shemu'el, also named one of his sons Yiḥye' for his father and this was in the father's lifetime, and his daughter Badrah for his mother. Moreover, the younger brother, R. Shelomo, called one of his sons Zekharyah for his father R. Yiḥye'. And my grandfather, my mother's father, acted in the same way, calling his son Shelomo after his grandfather, R. Shelomo.[23]

In the lineage of R. Aharon Hakohen, who was active in Ṣan'a in the first third of the twentieth century, there are recurring names for those called by his name after his death. His grandsons from his sons Meshullam and Shemu'el were named Aharon. The great-grandson of his son R. Avraham was named Aharon, and two of the great-grandsons of R. Ḥayim were named Aharon.[24]

Some birth registrations indicate that a boy was named for his grandfather. For instance, in the list of the Ḥatūkah family from Radā', the following formulation was written for the first child:

> As a good sign and good luck, born is the good flower, may the Lord give him [all] good, and he merit a good, pleasant life, a long life. And his birth [was] on Sunday of the year 5698 in the month of Shevat [AM/1938]. May God, blessed be He, grant him good deeds. And his name was called Sālem ben 'Awad Sālem Ḥatūkah, may the Lord protect and redeem him, *'ky"r*.[25]

The name of the son Sālem was after his grandfather who was alive, since the grandfather's name was accompanied by the expression "May the Merciful protect him and save," written for a living person. In the

23. In a personal correspondence dated 16 Feb 2011.
24. I wish to thank his great-grandson Aharon ben Yehudah ben R. Ḥayim son of the Dayyan, R. Aharon Hakohen of Bnei Brak, who provided me with the lineage of his great-grandfather, the *dayyan* R. Aharon Hakohen.
25. In the first pages of printed books, Genesis, Exodus, Deuteronomy with Masorah and Ein ha-sofer, Lemberg 563[4] (1873). With the permission of Ilana Jaraydi, Yehud.

list for the Ṣāliḥ family in Ṣan'a,[26] the birth of one of the sons was listed as follows:

> My son, my firstborn, was born on Tuesday, 11 Marheshvan 2127 SEL [5576 AM/14 Nov 1815]; *and I have named him Avraham like the name of my grand[father]*,[27] in the *sid*[*ra*] for "I shall make you the father of a multitude of nations" (Gen. 17:5).[28] May it be His will that he will merit Torah and commandments and the marriage canopy and to grandchildren, during his lifetime. *'ky"r.*

The son Avraham was named for the *dayyan* R. Avraham, the son of R. Yiḥye' Ṣalih (Mahariṣ), who died on 18 Tishri 5669 (9 Oct 1808). Upon the birth of another son into the Ṣalih family, who was also named for the grandfather, it was written:

> My son, my firstborn, was born on Friday, 15 Av 2090 SEL [5539 AM/ 26 July 1839], *and he was named for his father Yosef like the name of his grandfather*, may it be His will that he shall merit Torah, commandments, and the marriage canopy and grandchildren and the grandfathers may live to see this, *'ky"r.*

Upon the birth of another boy in the Ṣāliḥ family, who was also named for the grandfather, it was written:

> The good flower was born, like a moist tree, may the Lord also give him good, and make his portion good, Sunday [...] Tevet. *And I called his name Dawid like the name of my father*, blessed be the memory of righteous and holy man for the life of the world to come. May it be His will to sustain him for a long life of Torah and divine service, during his lifetime, and he should merit the marriage canopy, *'ky"r.*

From an examination of 1,506 *ketubbot* documents ranging from the sixteenth to the twentieth centuries, 64 identical names for grandfathers and grandsons were found. The following names occurred: Yiḥye' (15 times), Sālem (6 times), Yosef (5 times), Ibrāhim (5 times), Slaymān (5 times), Hārūn (3 times), Ḥayim (3 times), Se'īd (3 times), 'Awād (2 times), Mūsa (2 times), and once each, Da'ūd, Ḥasan, Yehudah, Ya'īsh, Ya'aqov, Yiṣḥaq, Moshe, Naḥum, Nissim, Netan'el, 'Oded, Ṣevi, Shukr, Shalom, Shim'on.

---

26. MS Schocken Library 12824. For a photograph of a page from the manuscript and a discussion of the list, see Gavra, Mahariṣ, pp. 7–10, 210–11.
27. Emphasis here and below is mine [A.G.].
28. This verse alludes to the weekly Torah reading, Vayera, in which the child was born.

Colophons reveal instances of the naming of a son after a grandfather. In a copy of Maimonides' *Guide for the Perplexed* made in 1380 in the Ṭawīlah community, the copyist of the manuscript indicated the lineage of his family: Shalom ben R. 'Ezra b. Shalom b. 'Ezra b. Shalom ben Abu al-Sa'd ben Shalom ben 'Oded ben Zekharyah ben Ya'aqov ben Yosef ben Dawid ben Shemaryah known as al-'Ansi ben Yosef the Qenazi."[29] In the first part of the lineage, we see the skipping of the names by generation in this family. In a manuscript of the Taj, which was copied in Ṣan'a in 1498, the person who ordered the copy named one of his sons for his father, Amram, and one of his grandsons was called by his own name, Aharon.[30] In a copy of the books *Mada'* and *Ahava* from Maimonides's *Mishneh Torah* from 1507, in the village of Bayt An'am, the copyist indicated his name: "Sa'adyah ben Avraham ben Sa'adyah ben Avraham ben Sa'adyah ben Me'oded Halevi."[31] In a 1695 copy of the *Shulḥan Arukh* by R. Yosef Qaro, made in Radā', the copyist wrote down his name: "Me'oded ben Sa'adya' son of *kmhr"r* Me'oded, may he rest in honor, ben Sa'adya' ben Yonah ben Gad, *tanṣeba"h*, known as al-Ḥamāmi al-Fatīḥi."[32]

R. Yiḥye' Bashīri, one of the outstanding seventeenth-century rabbis, listed his family's lineage in three manuscripts: Ḥayim son of our honorable rabbi and teacher Avraham *beirav* Sa'adyah *beirav* Avraham *beirav* Sa'adyah ben Shemaryah al-Bashīri (Yiḥye' Bashīri).[33] While copying a collection of laws of ritual slaughter in the eighteenth century, in the village of Barāqish, the copyist registered his name, "Sa'adya' ben Shalom ben *adonenu morenu* [our master our teacher] Sa'adyah ben Shalom Sharārah called al-'Uzayri."[34] While copying Genesis-Exodus

29. British Library, London, Arabic MS I. O. 3679 (IMHM 49322). For a description of the manuscript, see Aharon Gaimani, "*Ha'ataqah Qedumah mi-Teiman le-*Moreh Nevukhim *le-ha-Rambam,*" *Tehuda* 14 (1994): 15–20. See also below, part 1, chap. 3, sect. 3.

30. See below part 3, chap. 5, sect. 1.

31. MS Sasoon 1011 (IMHM 9800); Sasson, *Ohel David Catalogue*, 2, p. 699.

32. MS of Yehudah Mu'allim, Aḥihud; Aharon Gaimani, *Temurot be-Moreshet Yahadut Teiman: be-Hashpa'at ha- Shulḥan 'Arukh ve-Qabalat ha-Ari* (Ramat Gan, 2005), p. 294, photo of the manuscript's colophon, p. 295.

33. *Qoveṣ be-Qabbalah*, MS JTS, New York, Mic. 1767/8 (IMHM 10865); *Seder ha-Yom* by Moses ben Makhir, ms R. Shim'on Ṣālih, Bnei Brak; Taj, ms Zekharyah Samina, Elyakhin. See Gaimani, *Temurot be-Moreshet*, pp. 282–83; idem, *Ḥavaṣelet ha-Sharon by R. Yiḥye' Bashiri*, (Jerusalem, 2008), pp. 12 n. 19 and p. 14.

34. MS Bill Gross, Tel Aviv, no. 190 (IMHM 47250).

with Rashi's comments, in 1831, in the village of Bayt Sālem, the copyist listed in the colophon: "And the writer, the humblest of all and the dust at the feet of the sages, Yosef ben Aharon ben Yosef ben Aharon ben Tudah[35] called al-'Akhlufi."[36] When copying three scrolls in 1784, the copyist wrote in the colophon: "And the writer, the humblest of all and the dust at the feet of the scribes, Dawid ben *'m"v* Aharon ben Shalom ben Aharon ben Shalom."[37]

An examination of the names from northern Yemen shows that there was a custom of naming a grandson for his grandfather. We find, for example, Da'ūd ben Hārūn ben Da'ūd Qa'ṭabi;[38] Da'ūd ben Yiḥye' ben Da'ūd Jamīl;[39] Da'ūd ben Mūsa ben Da'ūd ben Ya'īsh ben Se'īd ben Hārūn al-Ḥarizi;[40] Da'ūd ben Sālem ben Da'ūd ben Slaymān Zindāni;[41] Yiḥye' ben 'Īḍah ben Yiḥye' ben 'Īḍah Yemani;[42] Salāmah bint Yosef ben Slaymān Jāhli ben Yosef ben Slaymān;[43] Se'īd ben Mūsa ben Se'īd Najjār.[44]

In the listing of twelve generations of a family lineage written by the son of the poet R. Yosef ben Yisra'el in southern Yemen in 1605 the names Yisra'el and Yosef appear four times skipping generations: "The humblest of scribes, *beirav* Abba Yosef, may God protect him, *beirav* Abba Mori Yisra'el, *beirav* Abba Mori Yosef ..."[45]

35. Todah is the name Yehudah which in Arabic is called Shukr. On the name and its translation, see below part 3, sect. 1.
36. MS Yehuda Levi Naḥum, *"Hasifat Genuzim mi-Teiman"* Project, no. 7; Yehuda Levi Naḥum, *Ṣohar le-Ḥasifat Ginzei Teiman* (Tel Aviv, 1986), pp. 3–4, serial no. 12.
37. MS Shlomo Yiṣḥaq Halevi, Bnei Brak.
38. Aharon Ben David, *Bet ha-Even, Hilkhot Yehudei Tzefon Teiman* (Qiryat Eqron, 2008), p. 676, no. 158.
39. Ibid., p. 676, no. 166.
40. Ibid., p. 676, no. 171.
41. Ibid., p. 677, no. 177.
42. Ibid., p. 688, no. 596.
43. Ibid., p. 703, no. 1151.
44. Ibid., p. 707, no. 1322. See also ibid, p. 682, no. 390; p. 683, nos. 409, 436–37; p. 700, no. 1073; p. 701, no. 1113; p. 702, no. 1138, p. 706, nos. 1282, 1296; p. 708, no. 1344; p. 711, no. 1484.
45. *Sefer ha-Haftariyyot*, ms Ratson Halevi, Tel Aviv. For a photo of the colophon, see the introduction of R. Yosef Ṣubari to the *Tiklal Mashta Shabazi*, photo edition, published by Binyamin Oded-Yefet (Jerusalem, 1986). See also Yehudah 'Amir, "The Poetry of Yosef ben Yisra'el" (doctoral dissertation, Bar-Ilan University 2001), p. 80. See also below, part 3, chap. 5, sect. 1.

Appearing in a thirteen-generation family lineage registration for the family of R. Yosef Qāfiḥ, which was written in Jerusalem in 1968, the names Slaymān and Yiḥye' appear seven times skipping generations: "Slaymān, son of R. Sālem, ben R. Slaymān, ben R. Yiḥye' the rabbi, ben R. Slaymān, ben R. Yiḥye', ben R. Slaymān the rabbis, ben R. Yiḥye' ..."[46]

In the lineage of the Shar'abi family, the names Ya'aqov and Ḥayim, which belonged to the family forefathers, recur with generations skipped. For example, "Ya'aqov ben Yosef ben Ya'aqov ben Slaymān ben Ya'aqov ben Se'īd ben Ya'aqov ben ha-Rav Sālem al-Shar'abi the Elder"; Ya'aqov and Ḥayim sons of Avraham ben Ya'aqov ben Ḥayim ben Ya'aqov ben Ḥayim by Ya'aqov ben ha-Rav Sālem al-Shar'abi the Elder."[47]

2. IDENTICAL NAMES FOR FATHER AND SON

In the rabbinic period, there are cases in which the father's name is identical to that of his son (patronymy).[48] Found in Babatha's archive were the names Ela'zar ben Ela'zar ben Ḥita, Yeshu'a ben Yeshu'a the orphan.[49] In an Aramaic marriage contract from 134 CE appear the names Ela'zar bar Ela'zar, Yehudah bar Yehudah.[50] In the cemetery of Bet She'arim the name Yosef occurs from father to son and even from grandfather to grandson.[51]

In the Babylonian and Jerusalem Talmuds there are cases in which the name of the father is identical to that of the son, such as R. Aḥa son of R. Aḥa (TB Sabbath 101a), R. Ḥiyya son of R. Ḥiyya (TB Avoda Zarah 31a), R. Yose be Yose (TB Menaḥot 6b), R. Ba son of Ba son of Memel (TP Peah 8, 5), R. Lezar son of R. Lezer ha-Qappar (TP Beṣah 1, 3). For some of these names there is evidence that the fathers were living when

46. Maimonides, Commentary on the Mishnah [Qāfiḥ], Tohorot, the end, n. 79. See also below, part 3, chap. 5, sect. 2.

47. R. Ṣefanya Shar'abi, *Bet al-Shar'abi, Quntres odot "Yeshivat Bet al-Shar'abi"*... (Qiryat Sefer, 2002), p. 20.

48. Rachel Hakhlili, *"Shemot ve-Kinnuyim eṣel Yehudim bi-Tkufat ha-Bayit ha-Sheni," Ereṣ Israel* 17 (1984): 192–4; R. Reuven Margaliot, *Toldot Or ha-Ḥayyim* (Beersheba, 2005), pp. 60–61.

49. Yigael Yadin, *"Maḥaneh 4—Me'arat ha-Iggerot," Yedi'ot be-Ḥaqirat Eretz Yisra'el ve-'Atikoteha* 26 (1962), p. 228, doc. 44; idem, *Ha-Ḥippusim aḥar Bar Kokhba* (Jerusalem, 1971), pp. 176, 178, 233–34, 240, 249.

50. J. T. Milik, "Un contrat juif de l`an 134 apres J.-C.," *Revue Biblique* 61 (1954), p. 183.

51. Moshe Shuva and Baruch Lifschitz, *Bet She'arim*, vol. 2 (Jerusalem, 1967), p. 7.

they called their sons by these appellations. We find in the JT, "It is told of R. Ḥananiah ben Ḥananiah whose father had excluded him as a *nazir* and brought him before Rabban Gamliel ..." (TP Nazir 4, 6).[52]

The TB tells of a dialogue Samuel had [with the dead] in a cemetery: "I am looking for Abba. They said to him: There are many Abbas here. I want Abba b. Abba, he said. They replied: There are also several Abbas b. Abba here" (Berakhot 18b). The explanation is that Samuel was looking for his father, whose name was "Abba." They told him that there were many there by that name. Then he said I am looking for "Abba son of Abba." They replied that here, too, there are many men named "Abba son of Abba." This informs us that it is highly unlikely that all of those called "Abba son of Abba" were born after the death of their father, while it is more certain that in those times a son was called by the name of his father when the latter was still living. Another example cited from the TB:

> Bonias son of Bonias once visited Rabbi. "Make room," Rabbi called out, "for the owner of a hundred maneh [in honor of his being wealthy]." Another person entered, as he called out, "Make room for the owner of two hundred maneh." "Master," said R. Ishmael son of R. Yose, "the father of this man [Bonias] owns a thousand ships on the sea and the same number of towns on land." "When you meet his father," was the reply, "tell him not to send him to me wearing such clothes." (Eruvin 85b–86a).[53]

From what is written at the end of the story, "When you meet his father," we learn that the father gave his son the name identical to his.

However, neither Ashkenazi Jews nor Sephardi Jews usually named a son for a father who was still living.[54] R. Ḥayim Yosef David Azulai (the Ḥida; Land of Israel and Italy, 18th c.) noted in his commentary *Berit Olami* on *Sefer Ḥasidim* about naming a son with the same name as the father:

52. Cf. Tosefta, Nidah 5, 6.

53. For additional versions of the name Bunyis ben Bunyis, see *Masoret ha-Shas, Eruvin*, ibid.; *Gittin* 59a; R. Raphael Nathan Neta Rabinovitch, *Dikduqei Sofrim, Eruvin* (Jerusalem, 1960), 169a, annotation to: "And according to this, he is called Bunyis ben Bunyis and as he is mentioned in *Gittin* 59a, and in both places equally, and as it is in Rashi and also as the Or Zaru'a copied it...."

54. See Ovadia Yosef, *Shut Yabi'a Omer*, part 5 (Jerusalem, 1969), part 8, *Yoreh De'ah*, sect. 21, letter *bet*.

> There are places where names are not given for the living....And they gave a sign, "They called their lands after their own names" (Ps. 49:12). And by all customs, a man does not call his son by his own name. Yet, I did see in one place, by way of example, that a Jewish man was named Mordechai, and he called his son Mordecai, and this was quite strange to me.[55]

Concerning the reason for refraining from calling father and son by an identical name R. Shabtai Lifschitz wrote:

> And the reason for meticulousness in this seems to me to be according to what Maimonides, OBM, ruled in *Hilkhot Mamrim*, ch. 6,[56] and in *Hilkhot Talmud Torah*, ch. 5,[57] that if the name of his father was like other names, they change their name, since it is forbidden to call others by the name of his father. See Shulḥan Arukh, *Yore De'ah*, par. 240,[58] and in *Siftei Kohen*, ibid.[59] Therefore, for this reason they did not usually have a father and son called by the same name, for it would be prohibited to the other sons to call his brother[60] by his name, so I think. And many years later, I found something like this in *Yad Shaul*, sect. 240, and in the responsa *Devar Moshe*, sect. 58.[61]

The basis, as explained above, is that out of respect for one's father it is forbidden to call others by the father's name. For this reason a father will not give his son the same name as his, for, if he did, the son's brothers would not be able to call their brother by his name out of respect for their father.

Yemenite Jews, more than those of any other Jewish community, were influenced by the rulings of Maimonides and thus it is important to understand Maimonides' position on naming.[62] Statements by Maimonides in *Hilkhot Talmud Torah* and *Hilkhot Mamrim*, according to the printed edition, as well as the Yemenite manuscript, inform us about the giving of names.

---

55. *Berit 'Olam*, printed within *Sefer Ḥasidim*, p. 315.
56. Law 3.
57. Law 5.
58. Par. 2.
59. Sub-par. 3.
60. Should be "their brother."
61. R. Shabtai Lifschitz, *Sharvit ha-Zahav*, sect. 8, 11.
62. On Maimonides' influence on the Jews of Yemen, see Gaimani, *Temurot be-Moreshet*, pp. 28–41.

The printed version of *Hilkhot Talmud Torah* 5:5 states:

> It is forbidden for a student to refer to his teacher by name, even outside his presence. He should not mention his name in his presence, even when referring to others with the same name as his teacher's—as he does with the name of his father. Rather, he should refer to them with different names, even after their death.

The printed version of *Hilkhot Mamrim* 6:3 states:

> And he should not call him by his name, neither when alive nor when dead, but he should say Abba Mori. If the name of his father or the name of his teacher is like others' name, he should change their name. It seems to be that one is not careful about this other than for a "Pele" [uncommon] name that is not frequently used. But names usually given by people, such as Avraham, Yiṣḥaq, Ya'aqov, Moshe, and the like, in every language and in all times, others refer to them [by name] when they are not present and that means nothing.

The law in *Hilkhot Talmud Torah* concerning use of the personal name of one's rabbi or father contradicts that in *Hilkhot Mamrim*. Many scholars have remarked on this, among them R. Yosef Qaro in his commentary *Kesef Mishneh* on Maimonides, and R. Abraham di Boton in his commentary *Leḥem Mishneh* on Maimonides. This contradiction arises since, according to Maimonides' statement in *Hilkhot Talmud Torah*, that on all occasions it is forbidden for a person to mention the personal name of another person whose name is identical to that of his teacher or father, since the listeners may think that he is mentioning the name of his teacher or father and is thereby liable to think that he is degrading the honor of his teacher or father. He must, therefore, refer to them differently.[63] According to *Hilhot Mamrim*, one is supposed to do so only

63. As for the prohibition against a student calling his teacher by name, TB Sanhedrin 100a states: "Epikoros … R. Naḥman said is one who calls his master by name, for R. Yoḥanan said, Why was Gehazi punished? Because, he called his master by name, as it is written, 'And Gehazi said, "My lord, O King, this is the woman, and this is her son, whom Elisha restored to life' (2 Kings 8:5)." Rashi explicates the passage beginning "by his name": "For he says 'Ploni' and does not say my teacher, my rabbi 'Ploni." Further cited there in the name of the geonim was that the personal name of Abaye was Naḥmani, and owing to respect for his father, for this name was a rare one, Rava changed the name of his disciple and nephew and called him Abaye, as an allusion that his name was the same as his father, and that is how the name Abaye was formed, and in Aramaic it stems from the term Abba. See *Sefer ha-'Arukh*, entry Abaye. See also TB Gittin 34b, Rashi's commentary, passage beginning *ve-hilkheta ke-naḥmani.*

if the name is uncommon.[64] If the name is common, one is permitted to use the personal name of someone whose name is identical to that of his teacher or father.[65]

A review of the version in the Yemenite manuscripts shows that there is no contradiction with Maimonides. The Yemenite version of *Hilkhot Talmud Torah* 5:5 states:

> And it is forbidden for a student to call his teacher by his name, and even not in his presence. He also should not mention his name when before him or even call others whose name is the same as his teacher in the same way he behaves regarding his father. But he should change their name even after their death. And it should be the name 'Pele' so that whoever hears it knows he is "Ploni"

The difference from the printed version is that the phrase "And it should be the name 'Pele' so that whoever hears it knows he is 'Ploni'," occurs at the end of the passage. This informs us that the only prohibition is the mention of a rare personal name of another person whose name is identical to that of his teacher or father, but other names are permitted; and thus there is harmony between Maimonides' statements in both sources. R. Ḥayim Kisār and R. Yosef Qāfiḥ commented on the printed editions in light of the Yemenite manuscript in *Hilkhot Talmud Torah*. R. Ḥayim Kisār wrote "and with this formulation the wonderment of the commentators, OBM, dissipated, and the statements of our rabbi here and in *Hilkhot Mamrim* agree with each other."[66] R. Yosef Qāfiḥ wrote "And many debated at length over this seeming contradiction, and they came up with different solutions ... and in any event our rabbi's words are uniformly clear in their source here and in *Hilkhot Mamrim*."[67]

R. Yosef Qaro wrote in the *Shulḥan Arukh*: "And they should not call him by his name, neither in his lifetime nor after his death, but should say Abba Mori. If his father's name is the same as others' name, he should change their name if it is a name that is 'Pele' that people do not

64. According to what is written in Jud. 13:18, "And it is unknowable," that is, wondrous and different from the other names that people are called and the intent is to a rare name.

65. TB Ketubbot 103b tells that Rabbi said before his expiring, "My son Simon is wise," even though that was also his father's name. He acted in this manner because this name is one of the common ones.

66. Maimonides, *Mishneh Torah* [Shem Tov], *Talmud Torah* 5:5.

67. Maimonides, *Mishneh Torah* [Qāfiḥ], *Talmud Torah* 5, par. 15, p. 207.

usually call him by."[68] The Rama added in his explanatory note to this law: "But a name that is common may be used to denote others when not in his presence."

Yemenite Jews seem to have followed Maimonides' manuscript version, namely, that this law applies only in the case of unusual names, not common ones.

Rav Sa'adyah Gaon (Babylonia, 10th c.) noted this phenomenon of identical names for father and son, writing in his commentary to Ex. 31:2: "See, I have singled out by name": "Possibly the name of the king of Tyre was Hiram son of Hiram, in the way that people today give the name Yehudah ben Yehudah."[69]

As for the custom of the Yemenite Jews, the phenomenon of identical names for a father and son, and sometimes also a grandson, did occur. On the commentary of Sa'adyah Gaon cited above, Yehudah Ratzaby noted that "the custom of calling a son by the father's name was accepted in talmudic times, and among Yemenite Jews it continues to this day."[70] Similarly, in *Midrash ha-Gadol* by R. David 'Adani, a thirteenth-century Yemenite rabbi, on the verse "And Joseph was the vizier" (Gen. 42:6), he wrote: "they said that very day three decrees ... that a person should not enter until he has written his name, his father's name, and the name of his grandfather."[71]

R. Yisra'el Hakohen, a seventeenth-century Yemenite sage, wrote in his work *Segulat Yisra'el* about the statement of R. David 'Adani "Since for most people their name and the name of their ancestors are equal,"[72] by which he meant that many peoples' names are identical to those of their father. R. Yiṣḥaq Raṣabi wrote about the custom of Yemenite Jewry:

> And many in our community customarily called one of their sons by their own name, that is, by the name of the infant's father, even though his father was still alive. Quite the contrary, this was considered an honor for them. And also the mother, that is, the one who has given birth ... and many among us as well were in the habit of calling a

68. *Yoreh De'ah*, par. 240, 2.
69. R. Sa'adyah Gaon, *Perush le-Sefer Shemot*, edited by Y. Ratzaby (Jerusalem, 1998), pp. 186–87.
70. Ibid., n. 13.
71. R. David 'Adani, *Midrash ha-Gadol, Bereishit* (Jerusalem, 1947), p. 723.
72. Yisra'el Hakohen, *Midrash Segulat Yisra'el* (Jerusalem, 1994), 1:246.

> grandson by the name of his grandfather even during his lifetime, and it was considered an honor.[73]

In a letter to me, R. Raṣabi cited an example in his family:

> And according to what I heard both the Jews and the non-Jews were not meticulous about this. Just the opposite, a father would give a beloved son his own name. My master, my father, my teacher, and my rabbi, OBM, was called Nissim, the name of his father, and this was after some twenty years when his mother gave birth to no sons but only to daughters. My grandfather, R. Nissim ben R. Shalom asked her to [let him] marry another woman, and she agreed wholeheartedly, but she requested of him that the name Nissim be kept for a son she would give birth to, and so it was.[74]

This custom of Yemenite Jewry astounded the Admor of Munkacz, R. Chaim Elazar Shapira. During his thirteen-day trip in 1930 to the Land of Israel, he chose to attend a circumcision ceremony of Yemenite immigrants who lived in the Mahanaim neighborhood of Jerusalem. He was very impressed by the rite and commented about the giving of the name: "And when reciting 'Let his name be called in Israel,' they gave the child the same name as his father (even though the father was present at this, since they are not meticulous about this according to their custom), and this was something new for us."[75]

R. Yaacov Sappir wrote of his visit to the Jirwāḥ community in central Yemen in 1859, in the home of the congregation's leader, R. Yosef ben Sa'adyah: "He has three wives, but does not have many sons, except for one from his third wife, and he was named Yosef after him (this is their custom for good luck, anyone whose sons will not perpetuate him, God forbid, will name his son for himself in his lifetime. And remember this, for it is necessary!)."[76] Sappir's intention by saying that Yosef had three wives was to hint that the reason for his polygamy was that the first two wives had not given birth to boys. By the words "And remember this,

73. R. Yiṣḥaq Raṣabi, *Shulḥan Arukh ha-Mequṣar*, vol. 5 (Bnei Brak, 1989), sect. 159, 10, par. 43, p. 14.

74. In a personal correspondence dated 22 Apr 2010.

75. Moshe Goldstein, *Mas'ot Yerushalayim: Mas'o shel ha-Admor Ḥayim El'azar Shapira be- Eretz Yisra'el* (Jerusalem, 2004), pp. 83–84.

76. Yaacov Sappir, *Even Sappir* 1 (Lyck, 1866), p. 51a. On the instance about which the disciples of the Besht related, that a father, son, and grandson were called the same name as a charm for life, see the book *Derekh ha-Emunah u-Ma'aseh Rav*, published by Yeḥi'el Yosef Gutman (Warsaw, 1897) on the matter of giving names, pp. 88–89.

for it is necessary," he meant to say that the reader should remember this so as not to be surprised when he will read in the continuation of the book about people whose name is the same as their father.

R. Avraham 'Afāri, one of the Yemenite sages, who lived in Ḍū-wāle', two days distant from Ṣan'a, remarked about the phenomenon of identical names for parents and children: "In one village there were two families. One's byname was Zaydi and the other's, al-Qūri. And in both families were people with the name Yosef ben Yosef. Now, one came to divorce his wife, and in the *get* we wrote Yosef al-Quri." While at the wedding of the divorcing man on 4 Tevet 5691 (24 Dec 1930), his name was written in the *ketubbah* as Yosef ben Yosef ben Yosef al-Quri. Also, from my discussions with the elders from Yemen, I received the impression that it was customary for a father to name a son for himself.

R. Almog Shelomo Akhlufi wrote about the customs in his mother's and father's families in central Yemen. He also noted R. Aharon and his wife Zihrah Jamīl from the town of Qaryat Wād'ah, who had only two children, a son and a daughter. The father named his son Aharon, the same as his, and the mother named her daughter Zihrah, the same as hers. He wrote:

> As to the issue of identical names for a father and son, while the father is alive this is a common occurrence. For example, the father of the mother of my grandfather, R. David, was named R. Yiḥye' Se'īd from the village of Masyab, and he called his son Yiḥye' like his own name. And the father of my grandfather on my maternal side, R. Aharon, called his only son Aharon like his own name; also the mother of my grandmother, Zihrah, named her only daughter Zihrah. Also the father of my grandmother, R. Yosef named his firstborn son Yosef like his own name. Also the great-grandfather of the grandmother I mentioned, R. Mas'ūd, named his son Mas'ūd (in time he was the *av bet din* of the religious court of 'Aram), the same as his name. This phenomenon was also common regarding daughters but not as frequent as for sons.[77]

Shelomo Raṣhabi, from the Raḍa'i community in southern Yemen, related that there were instances in his community of identical names for father and son, and he gave the example of his uncle Yiḥye' who named his son Yiḥye' too.[78] Zekharyah 'Aṣmi, from the Madīd commu-

77. In a personal correspondence dated 16 Feb 2011. He sent further information on the name Zihrah in a personal correspondence dated 24 Jan 2012.

78. Interview conducted by R. Gilad Ṣadoq of Bnei Brak.

nity, situated northeast of Ṣan'a, told that there were cases in his community of identical names for father and son, and he gave as an example the name Mori 'Awāḍ ben 'Awāḍ Baydani, who was given that name during his father's lifetime.[79] Lirit Zindāni tells that her paternal great-grandfather, Yiḥye', who lived in the town of Rajūzah in northern Yemen, named his son Yiḥye' and her great-grandfather's brother Ībrahīm named his son Ībrahīm.[80] Shemu'el Ḥofi tells of his uncle who was called Sālem ben Sālem, his father's cousin who was named Ya'aqov ben Ya'aqov, another relative who was named Yiḥye' ben Yiḥye', and a female relative named Se'īdah bat Se'īdah.[81] Ṣāliḥ Drāmi of the Radā' community named his second son the same name as his, Ṣāliḥ.[82] Aviva Himoff, whose parents emigrated from Ṣan'a, tells that her grandfather Yosef Sham'e called his son Yosef.[83]

In the Ṣan'a community Rabbinical Court record, there is the case of the division of property of the father Mūsa by his sons Mūsa and Avraham, which shows that his father called his son by his own name. The ruling reads as follows:

> Mūsa and Avraham, sons of Mūsa Sālem al-Jarashi, bought, obliging themselves to pay twenty qirsh to Yiḥye', their brother, by Rosh ha-Shana 2082 SEL [5531 AM/1770]. And Mūsa and Avraham had a part in the house in the estate of their deceased father. According to this document, it is father's debt, a *sheṭar* in the sum of 23 qirsh. And he gave his brother a discount of 3 qirsh. And for that which Mūsa will pay the rates, he will have that percentage of the house according to what he pays. And what Avraham—he will have the percentage of what he will pay. And Avraham will continue to live in the room until they will divide the house between them. Tuesday, 10 Tammuz 2081 SEL [5530 AM/3 July 1770].[84]

In thirteen letters sent by the false messiah Shukr Kuhayl II, in the third quarter of the nineteenth century, to the leaders of the Rubū' in central Yemen, we find among the recipients a father and son both named Slaymān, both of whom were still living.[85]

79. Interview conducted by R. Gilad Ṣadoq of Bnei Brak.
80. In the questionnaire she turned in to me in July 2010.
81. In the questionnaire given to me in Dec 2010.
82. The Deromi family, p. 20.
83. Aviva Himoff lives in Manhattan, New York City.
84. *Misawwadeh*, 1, אות 279, p. 111.
85. Shukr Kuhayl II was active in the period 1868–1875. His messianic activity was

Here are the openings of three of the letters: "They shall approach and come to the brother more pleasant than gold and better than refined gold, for whom discernment is the basis and wisdom fundamental, being our rabbi, R. Slay[mān] al-Mughmi, *yṣ"v*, and last, but not least, the son of the holy ones, namely, the son Slay[mān], *yṣ"v*"; "Greetings to you by the thousands / from the small person / to he who has a good name / a perfect pearl, a great, distinguished person, fulfilling Torah and commandments, wholeheartedly, for he is the outstanding rabbi, my teacher and master, Slaymān al-Mūghmi, *yṣ"v*, and last, but not least, the good flower, the son of the holy ones, stock of the elderly, amazingly wise, faithful scion, Slaymān, son of our teacher and master, the R. Slaymān mentioned, may the Lord protect and sustain him"; "Great, precious *shalom* / from the supreme God / shalom for the honorable throne / and *shalom* from the Lord of the universe / *shalom* from the three holy patriarchs / and many *shlomot* / to thousands and tens of thousands / from before the dweller in *aravot* [one of the heavens] / the Lord of the patriarchs / they will approach and come to the good brother / like a moist tree / the Lord will also give him good / he is my teacher Slaymān, *yṣ"v*, and last, but not least, your son Slaymān, You, O Lord will keep them (Ps. 12:8), encompassing him with favor like a shield (after Ps. 5:13)."[86]

In the emissary Shelomo Naddāf's notebook on his mission to the Yemenite communities in the first half of the twentieth century are 23 instances of identical names for father and son:[87] Yiḥye' ben Yiḥye' (11

halted with his exile in 1875 to Istanbul by the Turks, who ruled Yemen. A short while later he was returned to Ṣan'a, and he stayed there until his death in 1877 or 1878. On his activity, see Eraqi-Klorman, *Meshiḥiyyut u-Meshiḥim* (Tel Aviv, 1995), pp. 77–112; idem, *"Iggeret ha-Mashi'aḥ Shukr Kuhayl II li-Yhudei Ḥidān," Peamim,* 64 (5755): 103–7; Aharon Gaimani, "The Messianism of Shukr Kuhayl II: Two New Letters," *Jewish Quarterly Review*, 92 (2002): 347–58.

86. Gaimani, *"Shukr Kuhayl*, letters 1, 3, 6.

87. The journal of his mission is in the possession of R. Meir Naddaf, Jerusalem. A photocopy of the journal was given to me by R. Aviran Yitzhaq Halevi, Bnei Brak. R. Shlomo ben Avraham Naddaf was born c. 1867 in Kafr Hijre, west of Ṣan'a, the capital. In 1875, when he was about eight, the family immigrated to the Land of Israel and settled in Jerusalem. Around 1910, upon the advice of Avraham Naddaf, one of the leaders of the Yemenite community in Jerusalem, he left for Yemen as an emissary on behalf of the community to collect donations for the community's *kollel*. His mission lasted quite a while, in the second and third decades of the twentieth century. The chief rabbi, R. Yiḥye' Yiṣḥaq Halevi, who lived in Ṣan'a, supervised his activity concerning the contributions and transferred them to his

times), Se'īd ben Se'īd (4 times), Sālem ben Sālem (3 times), Yosef ben Yosef (3 times), Ibrāhim ben Ibrāhim (2 times). In Rūḍa lived Se'īd ben Se'īd ben Se'īd. There are three instances of donors who appear in the mission journal of the emissary R. Shelomo Naddāf, from which we learn that they had sons whose names were the same as theirs. In one case, the father gave his son his name, and in two cases the father called two of his sons by his name: in Rūḍa there were donations from "Se'īd ben Se'īd al-Zabīb—rial, and his sons Se'īd and Ḥayim—2 rial," that is, three generations with the identical name; in 'Ar Baydar contributions came from "Salīm al-Sāhi and his so[ns] Salīm and Salīm," that is, both sons had the same name as the father, and so it was in Qarn al-Duhūr: "Yosef Hā[rūn] and his so[ns] Yosef and Yosef."

An examination of 1,506 *ketubbot* from the sixteenth to the twentieth centuries revealed 82 instances of identical names for father and son: Yiḥye' ben Yiḥye' (28 times), Salīm ben Salīm (22 times), Yosef ben Yosef (9 times), Ibrāhim ben Ibrāhim (4 times), Ḥasan ben Ḥasan (4 times), Se'īd ben Se'īd (4 times), Hārūn ben Hārūn (2 times), Slaymān ben Slaymān (2 times), Ṣāliḥ ben Ṣāliḥ (2 times), Da'ūd ben Da'ūd, Wahab ben Wahab, Mūsa ben Mūsa, Menaḥem ben Menaḥem, Shelomo ben Shelomo. In a *ketubbah* from 1890, one finds Yiḥye' ibn Yiḥye' ibn Yiḥye'; in a *ketubbah* from 1931, Yosef ben Yosef ben Yosef; and in a *ketubbah* written in 1948, Salīm ben Salīm ben Salīm. In the following marriage contracts, identical names appear in the lineages of the groom and bride, which inform us of the widespread custom in Yemenite communities of the father and son having the same name. In a *ketubbah* from the 'Arām community, 26 Sivan 5672 (11 June 1912), the name of the groom Yiḥye' ben *morenu ve-rabbenu* Yiḥye' Moshe Alkhayyaṭ, and the name of the bride, Ḥamāmah bint *morenu ve-rabbenu* Yiḥye' ben *morenu ve-rabbenu* Yiḥye' ben *morenu ve-rabbenu* Yiḥye' Alḥadād; and in a *ketubbah* from the Manākhe community, dated 5 Tevet 5709 (6 June 1949),

friend, R. Avraham Naddaf, in Jerusalem. In the mission journal that Shlomo Naddaf kept, he listed the place of the donation, the names of the donors, and the sum contributed. The list includes some 350 places throughout Yemen, which is about one-third of all the Jewish settlements in the country, so the journal is an important source in the study of the names of Yemenite Jews. On his mission, see Yehudah Ratzaby, *"Golat Teiman,"* ed. idem, *Bo'i Teiman: Meḥqarim u-Te'udot be-Tarbut Yehudei Teiman* (Tel Aviv, 1967), pp. 187–229, pp. 215–17; Zekharyah Gluska, *Lema'an Yehudei Teiman* (Jerusalem, 1974), p. 420; Yosef Tobi, *Ha-Qehilah ha-Teimanit bi-Yrushalyaim, 5641–5681 (1881–1921)* (Jerusalem, 1994), pp. 24–25, 130–32, 145; Aharon Gaimani, *"'Maggid Ṣedeq'—al Batei Keneset she-be-Ṣan'a,"* *Kenishta* 3 (2007): 92.

the name of groom is written as Ḥayim b. Ḥayim b. Ḥayim Ṣāliḥ, and the name of the bride, Ḍobyah bint Ibrāhim b. Ibrāhim al-Yamani.

An examination of the names in the list of Jews in north Yemen uncovers 27 instances of identical names for father and son: Yiḥye' b. Yiḥye' (15 times),[88] Se'īd b. Se'īd (4 times),[89] Harūn b. Harūn, (3 times),[90] Sālem b. Sālem (3 times),[91] Yosef b. Yosef;[92] Pinḥas b. Pinḥas.[93]

In the Radā' community, Ṣāliḥ ben Ṣāliḥ Ma'ūḍa gave one of his sons his name, that is, three generations with the very same name. This is how his father-in-law, R. Yiḥye' Ūmaysi, who was also a *mohel*, registered the marking of the birth:

> Blessed is the Lord, God of Israel, who has added double good to Ṣāliḥ ibn Ṣāliḥ Ma'ūḍa, and a precious boy has been born to him whose name was called Ṣāliḥ after his father, who was still alive, on 9 Iyyar in the year of Redemption and Salvation for all Israel, may it be His will, Amen, 2232 SEL [5681 AM/ 17 May 1921], may he merit Torah, marriage, and good deeds. Stated by [signature with exotic flourishes]: the humble Yiḥye' ben Sālem 'Ūmaysi, the most unworthy.[94]

Likewise, in the 1940s, an immigrant to Israel from Yemen listed the birth of his son with a name identical to his, as follows: "The good flower was born, may the Lord also give him the good, Shalom ben Shalom Naḥum, may his Creator protect and sustain him, may the Lord grant him a good year, and much Torah, born on the eve of Rosh Hashanah 5705 (1944), may God educate my son and He will save him from all trouble and distress."[95]

R. Avraham Arye, whose parents emigrated from the Maḥwīt community, detailed his family lineage, which goes back eight generations,

88. Ben David, "*Bet ha-Even*," p. 686, nos. 536–545; p. 692, no. 731; p. 693, no. 814; p. 696, no. 922; p. 714, no. 1586; p. 696, no. 896.
89. Ibid., p. 708, nos. 1340–1343.
90. Ibid., p. 678, nos. 220–222.
91. Ibid., p. 701, nos. 1105–1106; p. 685, no. 486.
92. Ibid., p. 683, no. 407.
93. Ibid., p. 709, no. 1377.
94. On the back of the title page of a printed Leviticus, Lemberg 1934, in the possession of Shelomo 'Amihud, Bat Yam. For a photo of the list of births in the Ma'ūḍah family in the Rada' community, see above, chap. 1, sect. 3.
95. On the back of the title page of the Yemenite version of *Siddur Tefillat Kol Peh* for the High Holidays, owned by R. Shlomo Almog, Jerusalem. For the registration of the birth of another son of Shalom Naḥum, see below part 3, chap. 7, sect. 1.

and it includes two instances of identical names for father and son: "Avraham ben Avraham ben ha-Rav Yosef b. R. Yehudah b. R. Yiḥye' ben ha-Rav Slaymān b. ha-Rav Slaymān al-Kabīr (the great) ben ha-Rav Se'īd."[96]

The listings of births of the 'Adwi family of the Thila community contained: "A good flower has been born, Yiḥye' ibn Se'īd ibn Yiḥye' ibn Yiḥye' al-'Īdwi, the year 2226 SEL, the month of Tevet, 21st day [5675/7 AM; Jan. 1915]." In this lineage, one finds "Yiḥye' ben Se'īd ben Yiḥye' ben Yiḥye'," with identical names for father and son, as well as for grandfather and grandson.[97]

In the lineage of the Dayyan R. Aharon Hakohen, there are identical names for son and father, grandson and grandfather, and the fathers-in-law as well. At a marriage in Ṣan'a on 9 Kislev 5624 (20 Nov. 1863), the name of the groom in the *ketubbah* was written as Hārūn ibn Sālem ibn Sālem Alkohen. The name of the bride was given as Ghazāl bint Sālem ibn Sālem ibn Yusuf al-Qindīl. From what we know of the groom's lineage, he is Aharon ben Sālem ben Sālem ben Moshe ben Sālem Hakohen. From the listing of the lineage of the groom and bride in the *ketubbah*, we see identical names for son and father, who are also the fathers-in-law. In the groom's lineage there are also identical names for a grandson and grandfather.[98]

R. Itamar Ḥayim Cohen told me in the name of R. Yiṣḥaq Raṣabi: One of the Yemenites came to Rosh HaAyin in the early years after the "On the Wings of Eagles" immigration and asked where his relative Yiḥye' ibn Yiḥye' lived. They told him that there are many so named. He asked where does Yiḥye' ibn Yiḥye' ibn Yiḥye' live? They told him there are three of them. Which one are you looking for?

This phenomenon applied also to women. Here are a few examples: Rūmiyah Ḍur'āni, from the Maḥwīt community, called her daughter by her own name in Israel, and to differentiate between them, people would call the mother Rūmiyah kabira (the big) and the daughter Rūmiyah zaghira (the small).[99] The sister of R. Shalom Efrayim Cohen, from the Ṣan'a community, is called Ni'māh, after her paternal grandmother who died before she was born, even though her mother's name

96. For part of this lineage, see R. Avraham Arye, *Ohel Yosef* (Be'er Yaakov, 1973), p. 6.

97. On the title page of three Megillot, Nisim Adwi, Holon.

98. See below, section 4 in this chapter.

99. In a personal correspondence dated 7 May 2010 by R. Avraham Arye. See also below, beginning of section 3.

was also Ni'māh.[100] Simḥah Ḥayyaṭ, from the Dhamār community, had the same name as her mother, Simḥah. She named one of her daughters Simḥah, since Grandmother Simḥah died at the time of the delivery.[101] Yiḥye' Manṣūra, from the 'Imrān community, told me that his grandmother Ḥamāmah called his mother by her own name, and his mother even called her daughter Ḥamāmah, by her own name.[102] In the list of names of Jews in northern Yemen is an identical name for mother and daughter: Ṣīniyyah bat Ṣīniyyah of the Marḥabi family from the village of Qarḥaw.[103]

The examples cited above reveal that in Yemen there was no stringency about not calling children by the name of their parents while they were still alive, and this accords with Jewish custom in former times. There were also some who customarily named the child after a living or deceased grandparent. In her study on names in the Second Temple period, Rachel Hakhlili wrote:

> We have seen, therefore, that the two customs widespread to this day among the Jews, to name a grandson for his grandfather and a son for his father (today, mainly in the Sephardi communities), began to spread at the beginning of the Second Temple period, and they are characteristic of family's with distinguished lineages. Naming a son for his father was particularly common among the aristocratic families and the priests (but it may be also among the "simple folk," though we do not have enough sources about this). The custom was so common that any deviation from it aroused astonishment.[104]

3. ADDING A BYNAME TO IDENTICAL NAMES

The Babylonian Talmud tells of the two sons of R. Ḥisda, Mar Qashisha and Mar Yanuqa.[105] Rashi and Tosafot write about the meaning of the names. Rashi writes: "R. Ḥisda had two sons and they had the same name. But the older was called Mar Qashisha and the younger, Mar Yanuqa."[106] The authors of the Tosafot write: "Mar Yanuqa. He is the

100. From R. Itamar Ḥayim Cohen, son of R. Shalom Efrayim Cohen noted.
101. From her children, Malkah Ḥayyat-Zaiden and Shim'on Ḥayyat of Netanyah.
102. Yiḥye' Manṣura of Giv'at Sha'ul. Died in 5770/2010.
103. Ben David, *Bet ha-Even*, p. 713, no. 1595. For other examples, see part 3, chap. 4, sect. A [4].
104. Hakhlili, *"Shemot ve-Kinnuyim,"* p. 194.
105. TB Ketubbot 89b; Bava Batra 7b.
106. Rashi on TB Ketubbot 89b, beginning "Mar Qashisha and Mar Yanuqa."

older one, and the reference is that he was born when R. Ḥisda was in his youth, so they called him Mar Yanuqa, while Mar Qashisha is the younger and was born in R. Ḥisda's old age."[107] Thus, according to Rashi the two boys had one name. A similar phenomenon of calling two children by the same name—and bynames to distinguish between them—is found among the Yemenite Jews.

Yom Tov Tzemach, the Alliance Israélite Universelle emissary who visited Yemen in 1910, noted the phenomenon of two sons with the same name who were differentiated by calling the older by the byname *al-kabir*, that is, the big one: "Frequently, they call a father and son, and sometimes the father and two of his sons, by the same name. It is not difficult to come across brothers who are called Slaymān ibn Slaymān. To know which is which, they add to the name of the older one *al-kabir*."[108]

In the Ṣan'a community, apparently, the phenomenon of identical names was less frequent than among other Yemenite communities. R. Pinḥas Qoraḥ wrote to me about this:

> It was unusual to call two sons by the same name, and see *Midrash ha-Gadol, parashat Bemidbar* on the verse about the number of names (Num. 1:2): "that there not be two with equal names and people become confused about them."[109] And I have heard that there were two brothers given the identical name, the older one was called Yiḥye' al-Kabir, and the other, Yiḥye' al-Zaghir.[110]

R. Ya'aqov Shar'abi wrote to me about the custom of the Ṣan'a community in central Yemen:

> When there were two cousins with the same name, some would dub them Ploni al-Kabir and Ploni al-Zaghir, as was done with one of my relatives, 'Azar ben Menaḥem Ḥibshūsh, who was called 'Azar al-kabir, and his cousin, 'Azar ben Hārūn Ḥibshūsh, who was called 'Azar al-zaghir, who was several years younger than he.[111]

107. Tosafot on TB Bava Batra 7b, beginning "Mar Yanuqa."
108. Abraham Elmaleh (trans.), "*Massa Yom Tov Ṣemaḥ le-Teiman,*" in eds. Y. Yeshayahu and A. Tzadok, *Shevut Teiman* (Tel Aviv, 1945), p. 313.
109. 'Adani, *Midrash ha-Gadol, Bamidbar*, p. 8. See also Shabazi, *Ḥemdat Yamim, parshat Bamidbar* (Jerusalem, 1977), p. 115.
110. In a personal correspondence dated April 2010.
111. In a personal correspondence dated 2 Dec 2010.

R. Shar'abi wrote to me about another phenomenon with identical names, among the children of the great rabbis who were called by their first names with the addition of the descriptor "Mori." For instance, Moshe ben Mori, which refers to Moshe the son of Mori Yiḥye' Yiṣḥaq Halevi, who was the chief rabbi of Yemen; 'Azri ben Mori, referring to 'Azri the son of Mori Yiḥye' Abyaḍ, who was chief rabbi after the passing of R. Yiḥye' Yiṣḥaq Halevi; Dawid ben Mori, referring to Dawid, the son of R. Yiḥye' Qāfiḥ, one of the outstanding Yemenite rabbis in the first third of the twentieth century.

R. Avraham Arye reported of the phenomenon of identical names in the Maḥwīt community, and he noted as an example two brothers and two sisters in one family with identical names:

> There were brothers with an identical name. One was called *the big one* and the other *the small one*. A cousin of my master, my father, my teacher, and my rabbi (his mother's brother) from the Qarawāni family from Ḍūbr al-Maḥwīt[112] was called Shelomo Kebir (big), and his younger brother, Shelomo Zaghir (small). Likewise, these brothers had two sisters with the same name, one was Zihrah Kebira (big), and the younger Zihrah Zaghira (small).[113]

In the Radā' community, two uncles of R. 'Azaryah Basis' mother were called Yiḥye', and to differentiate them, they were called Yiḥye' al-Kabir, the larger, and Yiḥye' al-Zaghir, that is, the small one;[114] also the two older sons of Manṣur 'Arami, of the Radā' community, were named Yiḥye' al-Kabir and Yiḥye' al-Zaghir.[115] In the Manākhe community were a father and two of his sons with identical names. The name of Shim'on Ṣadoq's grandfather was Ḥayim, and he named two of his sons Ḥayim, who were distinguished by adding the bynames *al-kabir* and *al-zaghir*.[116] In the al-Ma'araḍ community in the Yarīm district, in the family of Se'īd Wanneh were two brothers named Yiḥye': Yiḥye' Se'īd al-Kabir and Yiḥye' Se'īd al-Zaghir.[117]

112. A village near Maḥwīt. See Gavra, *Enṣiqlipedya le-Qehilot ha-Yehudiyyot be-Teiman*, 2 (Bnei Brak, 2005), pp. 468–69, entry Subar.
113. In a personal correspondence dated 23 Iyyar 5770 (7 May 2010) from R. Avraham Arye. See also, end of section 2 above.
114. In a personal correspondence dated 22 Adar 5770 (8 Mar 2010).
115. M. Yiṣhari, *Shim'on Drumi u-Mishpaḥto* (n.p. [Israel], 2004), p. 215.
116. The interview with Shim'on Ṣadoq was conducted by his granddaughter Vardit Yonati of Qiryat Ono.
117. As related by Tov Oshri of Hod ha-Sharon.

In the list of names of the Jews of northern Yemen an identical name appears for two brothers: Slaymān *al-awwal* (the first) and Slaymān *al-thāni* (the second), the sons of 'Īḍah ben Yiḥye' ben 'Īḍah.[118]

Included in the mission notebook of the emissary Shelomo Naddaf to the Yemenite communities in the first half of the twentieth century are six occurrences of donors who gave two or more of their children identical names. In two cases, the father called two of his sons by his own name. Contributing in the town of 'Ar Baydar was "Sālem al-Sāhi and his sons Sālem and Sālem," and in the village of Qarn al-Duhūr, "Yosef Hā[rūn] and his sons Yosef and Yosef." In one instance, the father gave two of his sons the identical name. In the town of Bane Aḥlas, a contributor was "Our teacher and rabbi, Yosef Serārah ... Sālem his brother, Sālem his brother the elder." In this case the adjective "the elder" was added to the older brother. In two cases the father gave the same name to two of his sons: one the Arabic name and the other, the Hebrew. Donating in the Dhamār community were "Yiḥye' Najjār and his sons Av[raham] and *Slaymān* and 'Awad and *Shelomo*." Donating in the Bayt al-Daja'a community were "Sālem Yiḥye' Jarārah and his sons *Moshe* and Mūsa." In another instance the father gave four of his sons the same name: In 'Ar Baydar contributed "Ḥayim Ṣefirah and his sons Slay[man] and Slay[man] and Slay[man] and Slay[man].

A similar phenomenon occurred among girls' names, and to distinguish between them they add *al-kabira* (the big one) for the older and *al-zaghira* (the small one) for the younger.

In the Ḍūlayme community in the Ḥabbūr district,[119] there were two sisters with the same first name, Ḥamāmah. The older was called Ḥamāmah al-kabira and the younger Ḥamāmah al-zaghira. Another method for distinguishing between two with the same name was to add to the first, *al-awlah* (the first) and for the second, *al-thāniyya* (the second). At times, they used to call two sisters by similar names, such as Ḥamāmah and Ḥamamiyah or Ni'māh and Ni'miyah.

Sa'dah Shunem of the Maḥwīt community tells that she had two sisters with the name Zihrah and, to distinguish between them, they call the older Zihrah al-kabira and the younger, Zihrah al-zaghira.[120] After

118. Ben David, *Bet ha-Even*, p. 704, nos. 1218–1219.

119. North of Ṣan'a. See Gavra, *Enṣiqlipedya le-Qehilot be-Teiman*, pp. 472–74, entry Ḍūlayme. The information is from Mrs. Naomi Gadis-Lowenstein, who emigrated from the Ḍūlayme community.

120. As related by Ya'ir Shunem of Rosh HaAyin.

their immigration to Israel, both changed their first names to Sarah, a Hebrew name with a similar ring.

Raḥel Maḥfud from the Dhamār region related that two of her mother's sisters were both called Zihrah and in order to tell them apart they called the older one Zihrah Kabira and the younger Zihrah Zaghira. After they came to Israel, both changed their names to Sarah.[121]

Some communities took care that a man should not marry a woman whose name was the same as that of his dead wife,[122] but in Yemen they were not meticulous about this. When Salāmah, the wife of R. Yehudah Ḍurāni of the Maḥwīt community, passed away, he married another woman whose name was identical to that of his deceased wife. To distinguish between them, some people called the first one Salāmah al-Kabira and the second Salāmah al-Zaghira.[123]

R. Almog Shelomo Akhlufi wrote to me that R. Shalom ben R. Se'īd Shalit of the Yafīd community married three women and all three were named Sham'ah; with the latter two he had children, even though this, too, is prohibited by the ethical will of R. Yehudah Heḥasid.[124]

Janāḥ ben Slaymān Halevi of the village 'Amīdah in northern Yemen had eight wives, and they were also called, as was the custom, by their family name.[125] Some of them had identical first names: two were called Ṣīniyyah: Ṣīniyyah Jubber and Ṣīniyyah Levi; and three had the name Kādhiyyah: Kādhiyyah Qa'ṭabiya, Kādhiyyah Ridiyah, and Kādhiyyah 'Azariyah.[126]

121. The information was given to me by the grandson Shlomi Maḥfud of Einav.

122. See Shmu'el Pinḥas Gelbard, *Oṣar Ta'amei ha-Minhagim* (Petaḥ Tiqvah, 1996), Marital status issues, par. 1005, p. 423.

123. As related by Menaḥem Ṣubayri of Herzliyya and more from R. Avraham Arye of Bnei Brak. R. Yehudah Ḍur'āni is the great-grandfather of R. Avraham Arye. The Ḥida's second wife was called Raḥel, the same as his first wife. See Meir Benayahu, *R. Ḥayim Yosef David Azulai* (Jerusalem, 1959), p. 472.

124. In a personal correspondence dated 16 Feb 2011.

125. See below, this chapter, sect. 5.

126. Ben David, *Bet ha-Even*, p. 676, no. 146. On the bynames for a woman after her marriage, see below sect. 5.

4. IDENTICAL NAMES FOR A SON-IN-LAW AND HIS FATHER-IN-LAW, FOR A DAUGHTER-IN-LAW AND HER MOTHER-IN-LAW, AND FOR IN-LAWS

In some Jewish communities care was taken not to match a man with a woman who had the same name as his mother or whose father's name was the same as his. Some even refrained from a match if the names of the in-laws were the same, since it would not portend well for the couple.

These customs were based on the ethical will of R. Yehudah Heḥasid, in which was written, "A man should not marry a woman whose name is the same as his mother's, or his name like his father-in-law's. And if he married her, the name of one of them should be changed, perhaps there will be hope."[127] He further wrote, "Two people whose names are the same should not make a match between their children, and there is a doubt whether he meant it for his descendants or for everyone."[128] There are a number of manuscripts of Yehudah Heḥasid's ethical will from which one may learn about the issue of whether what was stated in the will was intended for his family or for all Jewry. In one of the manuscripts the title of the will has "Some of them were commanded only to his descendants, and some of them were commanded to the entire Jewish people."[129] Written as a title in another manuscript, we find: "It is doubtful whether to the entire world or just his descendants, it seems to be the whole world, and one must take care."[130]

Yet, as we shall see in the ensuing, some people acted according to what was written in R. Yehudah Heḥasid's will owing to his distinguished standing, as well as fear that one who would not heed his warning would be whipped. R. Baruch Halevi Epstein, in his commentary *Torah Temimah*, elevated R. Yehudah Heḥasid's admonitions to the level of *din* [religious law]: "And many wanted to be lenient in this and produced the notion that R. Yehudah Heḥasid had ordered this only for his family and other similar ideas ... and many Aḥaronim have written various opinions on this. But I think that this is forbidden not out

127. The Ethical Will of Rabbenu Yehudah Heḥasid, par. 23, in *Sefer Ḥasidim*, ed. R. Margaliot (Jerusalem, 1957), p. 17–19.

128. Ibid., sec. 24, pp. 19–20.

129. Daniel Sperber, *Minhagei Yisra'el*, vol. 2, p. 11 (Jerusalem, 1989).

130. Ibid.

fear of a danger but from the heart of the *din*."[131] R. Epstein noted the prohibition, that if the names of the son-in-law and father-in-law are the same, the wife is forbidden to call her husband by his name, then if the names of the daughter-in-law and her mother-in-law are identical, the husband is prohibited from calling his wife by her name. We saw above[132] in the words of Maimonides according to the Yemenite manuscript that there is no legal prohibition about this, and thus the statements by R. Epstein do not follow the statements of Maimonides from whom he brings proof. At the end of his exposition, R. Epstein cites another reason. If the names of the son-in-law and father-in-law are the same, they cannot give the name of the father-in-law to a son after the grandfather's death, for then the name of the son will be the same as his father's, and it is Ashkenazi custom to be meticulous about a father not calling his son by his own name while he is still living. The same holds true for daughter-in-law and mother-in-law. This ruling, which means that they cannot give the names of one of the grandfathers or grandmothers after their deaths, bars proper remembrance of the family lineage and, as he puts it, "this matter causes the prevention of a precious pearl for the purpose of remembering our chain of lineage."[133]

Despite the foregoing, there were some who were not concerned by the statements of R. Yehuda Heḥasid and were not meticulous about this issue. R. Ezekiel Landau (Poland, 18th c.) was asked by one of his disciples about the match-making of his sister-in-law to a young man whose name had been changed owing to illness, and his new name was that of the father of the intended bride. In his response to his disciple, R. Landau wrote:

> My dear student, were it not for my love for you, I would not usually answer about such issues, things that have no root in the Talmud and *poseqim* (decisors), but my great love for you has shaken me out of complacency. You should know, dear disciple, and this should be etched in your heart to be remembered, the great rule, that no sage after the close of the Talmud has permission to say anything contrary

---

131. Epstein, *Torah Temimah*, Gen. 32:11.

132. Section 2 of this chapter.

133. See above section 1. In a personal correspondence dated 12 Adar 1 5771 (16.2.2011) from R. Almog Shelomo Akhlufi, he commented on R. Epstein's statement, and wrote about the custom of Yemenite Jews: "For us it is accepted and common that a father give his son the same name as his, and this applies to the mother as well, and if so, this precious pearl casts light and shines among us to this very generation."

to the Talmud, and whoever says anything contradicting the minutest detail of the Talmud text will not be considered a Jewish sage. To be sure, when we do find one of the sages of Israel who is undoubtedly devoted to Torah and fear of heaven, who wrote in a book something contradicting the Talmud's opinion, we must go to extremes to try to resolve it, not just a temporary solution or one for an individual family, for the words of the Talmud are for all society. And this applies to R. Yehudah Heḥasid in whose will are things we are almost forbidden to heed, for he says a man should not marry his niece,[134] and in the *gemara* it was said that this is a good deed (TB Sanh. 76b). It says that a father and his son should not marry two sisters,[135] and Rav Papa and his son married two daughters of Abba of Sura (Ket. 52b). He says

134. The Ethical Will of Rabbenu Yehudah Heḥasid, sect. 22, in *Sefer Ḥasidim* by Rabbenu Yehudah Heḥasid, ed. R. Margaliot (Jerusalem, 1957), p. 16. In Yemen, they did not pay close attention to this. R. Ḥayim Kisar, who immigrated to Israel from the Ṣan'a community and who was one of the greatest rabbis of Yemen in the twentieth century, married his niece. R. Shalom Abohar, who came to Israel from the Tan'em community in central Yemen and served as the rabbi of the Yemenite community in Ashkelon, married his niece, Rūmiyyah Tan'ami. In a personal correspondence dated 12 Adar 1 5771 (16 Feb 2011) from R. Almog Shelomo Akhlufi, he wrote that R. Shemu'el (the grandfather of my grandfather) ben Yiḥye' Se'īd from the village of Masyab married Sham'a the daughter of his sister Badrah.

135. The Ethical Will of Rabbenu Yehudah Heḥasid, sect. 27, in *Sefer Ḥasidim*, p. 20. In Yemen they were not meticulous about this. R. Yiḥye' Qarah and his son, R. Meir, of the Ṣan'a community, married two sisters who were the daughters of R. Shelomo Kisar. See Y. Qoraḥ, *Maskil Doresh 'al ha-Torah* (Tel Aviv, 1964), introduction, *Eshet Ḥaver*, p. 20. In a personal correspondence of Tishri 5771 (2010), Shim'on Mal'akhi, a member of the former Dhamār community, wrote me that the Av Bet Din (president of the rabbinical court) of Dhamār, R. Slaymān Mal'aḥi, and his son Shim'on married two sisters. R. Avraham Arye wrote to me in a personal correspondence dated 7 May 2010 that R. Shalom Mhāṣri and his father, Sa'adyah, of the Mhāṣr community (the father lived in Pardes Hana and the son in Bnei Brak) married two sisters. In a personal correspondence dated 16 Feb 2011 from R. Almog Shelomo Akhlufi, he stated that his great-grandfather, R. Yiḥye' from the village of Bayt Sālem, took as a wife in a second marriage Qurt the daughter of R. Yiṣḥaq Akhlufi, while his son Shlomo married Naḍrah, the sister of Qurt who was his father's wife. Michal Badihi of Givatayim wrote to me in April 2010 about the sisters of her great-grandmother from the Ṣan'a community, who married a father and son. Moshe Ben David, who immigrated to Israel from the community, told me in an interview that in his community Sālem Se'īd married Salamah, who was the sister of his daughter-in-law, and the reason they did not want to bring into the family a woman from a foreign family was so as to not lose family property. Interview conducted by Omri Portuguez of Nes Ṣiyyona.

two brothers should not marry two sisters,[136] while in the Talmud 80 pairs of brothers, all priests, married 80 pairs of sisters, all of the priestly family (Ber. 44a), and the two daughters of R. Hisda who were married to Rami b. Hama and to Mar 'Uqba b. Hama (Ber., ibid.). And

136. The Ethical Will of Rabbenu Yehudah Heḥasid, sect. 25, in *Sefer Ḥasidim*, p. 20. In Yemen, they were not meticulous about this and marriages between two brothers and two sisters were common. I have a *ketubbah* from Yemen for two brothers who married two sisters on the same day: on 18 Sivan 5706 (17 June 1946), in the village of Bayt Maqbili in southern Yemen, the brothers Ya'aqov and Ḥasan sons of Se'īd Methana married the sisters Ghaliyah and Tiranjah, daughters of Yiḥye' Sālem the father of R. Yiṣḥaq Raṣabi; R. Nissim Naḥum Raṣābi, and brother of R. Yisra'el of the Raṣaba community married two sisters. See Raṣābi, *Responsa 'Olat Yiṣḥaq*, 1 (Bnei Brak, 1989), sect. 166, par. *alef.* Tuvya Oshri of Hod ha-Sharon, who emigrated from the Yarīm community, told that in his family there were many instances of marriages of two brothers to two sisters, and he cited two examples: The brothers Ḥayim and Zekharyah Osheri, OBM, were married to the sisters Miriam and Zehava; the brothers Shelomo and Moshe were married to the sisters Ṣādqah and Zehava. Mori Se'īd Ṣabari, who came from the town of Madar in northern Yemen in 2009 and lives in Monsey, New York, told me that three brothers from the Jaradi family married three sisters from the Ṣabari family: Sālem married Fuḍah; Yiḥye', Rashushah; 'Amrān, Turkiyya. (On the family of Yiḥye' and Rashushah Jarādi, see below, part 3, chap. 7, sect. 4). Mori Faīz Jaradi is a rabbinical figure among the remnant of the Yemenite Jews, and he was also a leader on behalf of the government seated in Ṣan'a. He left the settlement in northern Yemen in 5767 (2007) and lives in Monsey, New York. He told me about Yiḥye' and Ḥayim, the sons of Ya'ish Qarni, who married two sisters of the Na'aṭi family, and two other sons of Mori Ya'ish, Yosef and Se'īd wedded two sisters from the Ṣabari family. In a personal correspondence dated 23 Iyyar 5770 (7 May 2010), R. Avraham Arye sent me on 23 Iyyar 5770 (7 May 2010), he wrote that three of his aunts (his mother's sisters) married the sons of Yosef: Yiḥye' married Ḥamāmah; Avraham, Ni'ma; Nissim, Simḥa. Also, three daughters of my aunt Ni'ma Najjar of Ra'anana—Henya, Malkah, and Dina—married three brothers from moshav Ge'ulim: 'Azri, Tziyyon, and Moshe from the Petaḥya family. The first two couples, Henya and 'Azri along with Malkah and Tziyyon were married the same evening 21 Av 5733 (19 Aug 1973), in the Nesi'im Hall in Tel Aviv; Dina and Moshe were married on 17 Sivan 5736 (15 June 1976). Two daughters of my maternal uncle, Shalom Raḥabi of moshav Zavdiel, Edna and Teshuva, married two brothers from Bnei Brak, Avino'am and Elazar of the Shlomi family. Two daughters of my brother, R. Shai of Bnei Brak, Shira and Meital, married two brothers from Bnei Brak, Shai and Uri'el of the Matari family. R. Pinḥas Qoraḥ and his brother, R. Ezra Qoraḥ of Bnei Brak, married two sisters from the Shar'abi family. On this R. Pinḥas Qoraḥ wrote to me in a personal correspondence he sent me in Iyyar 5770 (April 2010): "The frequency of the marriage of brothers to two sisters is especially known from small villages, and even marriages within the family circles, and in our family, too, there are marriages of brothers to two sisters and they did not take the ethical will of R. Yehudah Heḥasid into account at all.

> similarly in this ethical will. And if Heḥasid had directed this will to the entire Jewish people, he would be contradicting the statements of the Talmud, for he saw with divine spirit that his descendants would not succeed with such matches. Thereby, he was not going against the Talmud, for this is for everyone, while the words of Heḥasid are of the individual.[137]

In the continuation of his responsa, R. Landau noted that in the instance addressed to him, the subject is a fellow whose name was changed owing to illness, so that there is no trepidation even in the opinion of R. Yehudah Heḥasid, since the statement by R. Yehudah Heḥasid refers to a name given at circumcision. He concluded his responsa:

> And besides all this, according to your letter, your father-in-law wants to have a marriage with that *ṣurba de-rabbanan*[138] and observer of the commandment. And I am surprised that most people feel that giving their daughter to an uneducated Jew is a simple thing for them, and no one is afraid to refrain [from doing so], while this contradicts the opinion of the rabbis, who said that it "is as though he bound and laid her before a lion," while they are asking whether to marry a *ṣurba de-rabbanan* whose name is like theirs, and our perfect Torah should not be like an insignificant will. So, in my opinion, let your father-in-law conclude this match and may his deeds be for the sake of heaven.[139]

As R. Landau put it, though R. Yehudah Heḥasid's will applies only to his descendants, it does provide answers for other scholars. There are some rabbis who believe it was written for the entire Jewish people. Others, even if they accept the statements of Heḥasid, are lenient if a certain change was made, such as changing the name, or if the mother-in-law or father-in-law were no longer alive, or if the groom was over the age of twenty.[140]

An even more extreme position on R. Yehudah Heḥasid's ethical will was expressed by Rabbi Moses Provinciali (Italy, 16th c.). On the question of whether to fulfill what is stated in the will, even if it contradicts the sages' opinion, he replied:

---

137. Yehezkel Segal Landau, *Responsa Noda bi-Yehuda*, Tanina edition, *Even ha-Ezer*, (Jerusalem, 1998), par. 79.

138. A rabbinic scholar.

139. Landau, *Responsa Noda Bi-Yhudah, Even ha-Ezer*, par. 79.

140. For sources in which the rabbis discuss these issues, see Yishayahu Zussya Wilhelm, *Ziv haShemot* (New York, 1987), chaps. 38–38, pp. 116–22; Avishai Teherani, *Keter Shem Tov*, 1–2 (Jerusalem, 2000), sections 1–3, pp. 241–68; Munitz, "*Shemot Benei Adam*," pp. 106–25.

> I, for the name of the true Go[d] and his true Written and Oral Torah, did not know what to say, for those wills were not stated by Joshua from the mouth of the Lord and one should not believe them, let alone act according to them in contradiction to their tradition, OBM, and those who go against the words of the sages for them, I call them as those "who leave the paths of rectitude ..." (Prov. 2:13) and they "have forsaken me, the fount of living waters ..." (Jer. 2:13). And also not from the Lord that all came from the mouth of Heḥasid, but from the mouths of others and they attributed it to him, or they were found in his estate and they believed it was from him though it was not, in the way that Maimonides wrote in the first part of the *Guide* about foreign names in amulets, and this is certainly for one as incisive and wise as you.[141]

Rabbi Provinciali negated those sections of the will that contradicted the words of the sages. To support his statements, he cites proof from *Guide for the Perplexed*, where Maimonides comes out fiercely against the writers of amulets, calling them "the evil, ignorant men" whose product created false names of God. He further states that their writing came into the possession of sages whom he calls "the foolish, weak proper ones," who did not have sufficient knowledge to invalidate these names, and later the names were found in their estates, a situation which caused others to think that perhaps the names of God found in them are true.[142]

On the dissemination of R. Yehudah Heḥasid's will among Eastern communities who were not careful about these issues, we can learn from the comment by R. Rahamim Palagi (Izmir, 19th c.) in whose place of residence among the Izmir community they began to be careful about names because of a rabbi who gave a sermon to the congregation about the matters written in the ethical will of R. Yehudah Heḥasid.[143]

In 1950, R. Ovadiah Yosef, who was then chief rabbi of Egypt, discussed the prevalent situation of not paying any attention as to whether the name of the groom was the same as that of his father-in-law or the name of the bride was the same as her mother-in-law's. In his halachic ruling, he extensively reviewed the sources dealing with R. Yehudah Heḥasid's will, noting its influence on Sephardi and Eastern Jews. He

141. Responsa of R. Moshe Provinciali, chapter 9.

142. See *Guide for the Perplexed* 1, MS London, British Library, Arabic MS. I.O. 3379.

143. Rahamim Palagi, *Yafeh la-Lev*, (Izmir; photocopied edition, Brooklyn, 1992), part 6, *Even ha-Ezer*, par. *tav*, pp. 46b–47a.

included an additional topic, the Sephardi custom of naming sons with the names of their living grandfathers, in contrast to the statements of R. Yehudah Heḥasid. In his opinion, there was no need to make those statements known to the Egyptian communities.[144]

R. Yaakov Haim Sofer (Israel, 20th century), the grandson of R. Yaakov Haim Sofer who wrote *Kaf ha-Ḥaim*, discussed in depth the dissemination of R. Yehudah Heḥasid's ethical will. He cites rabbis of eastern communities who thought that one should follow what is written in the will, concluding that its warnings should be heeded.[145] We learn from his citations that in recent generations there were communities in Morocco and Tunisia that were very careful about matters discussed in the will of R. Yehudah Heḥasid.[146]

In the Talmudic period people were not meticulous in this matter, and we find instances in which the groom and his father-in-law had the same name. For example, Rami bar Tamari was the father-in-law of Rami bar Diqule,[147] and Shemu'el Sabba was the father-in-law of Shemu'el bar Ami.[148]

From reviewing various sources from the Yemenite Jews, one learns that they were not strict about this issue. In his first marriage, the chief rabbi, R. Yiḥye' Yiṣḥaq Halevi, took as his wife Sa'adah bat R. Yiḥye' Khameri, and was not affected by his name being the same as his father-in-law's.[149] In my Yemenite *ketubbot* collection, comprising some 1,600 marriage contracts from the sixteenth to the twentieth century, there are 124 cases in which the name of the groom and his father-in-law were identical. Below are a few examples from first marriages.

In a *ketubbah* dated 16 Shevat 5296 (9 Jan 1536), from the Ṣan'a community, the name of the groom is Ma'uḍa and the name of the bride, Shamsiyyah bint Ma'uḍa. In a *ketubbah* from 11 Tevet 5439 (16 Dec 1678), from the Faṣīrah community, the groom is called Yiḥye' b.

144. R. Ovadia Yosef, *Shut Yabi'a Omer*, pt. 2, *Even ha-Ezer*, par. 7.

145. Yaakov Haim Sofer (1), *Or Moshe*, Clarifications, Novellae and Annotations to Tractate *Kiddushin* (Jerusalem, 1990), sect. 1, pp. 3–21.

146. Ibid., pp. 13–14.

147. TB Menahot 29b; cf. TB Hullin 110a.

148. TB Sotah 10b. The author of *Seder ha-Dorot* remarked in the entry "Shemu'el Sabba": "And we see from this that they were not fastidious about the name of a father-in-law and his son-in-law, of which there was a warning in the will of R. Yehudah Heḥasid (Yehiel Heilprin, *Seder ha-Dorot* [Jerusalem, 1957], p. 177b).

149. From a personal correspondence dated 12 Oct 2010 of R. Aviran Yiṣḥaq Halevi.

Slaymān and the bride is Ghazāl bat Yiḥye' ben Naḥum Manṣur. In a marriage document dated 9 Shevat 5507 (9 Jan 1747), from the Radā' community, the groom is named Se'īd b. Ibrāhim b. Hassan al-'Arshi, while the bride's name is Qadriyyah bint Se'īd al-Qahari. A *ketubbah* from 5 Sivan 5583 (15 May 1823), from the community of Maru'agha, the name of the groom is Yosef ben Yiḥye' al-Kaw kabāne, and the bride's names is Badrah bint Yosef al-Shu'al. In a *ketubbah* from 12 Shevat 5704 (6 Feb. 1944), from the Mashhūr community, the groom's name is Yiṣḥaq ben 'Awāḍ and the bride's names is Shams bat Yiṣḥaq.

There are also similar cases with remarriage of a divorced couple and with second marriages, which also inform us that they were not particular about this issue and did not fear it would harm the relationship. For example, in a *ketubbah* dated 11 Iyyar 5687 (13 May 1927), from the Ṣan'a community, of a person remarrying his divorced spouse, the groom's name is Musa b. Sālem Melaḥiya and the bride's name is Badrah bint Musa Da'ūd al-'Usṭa. A marriage contract dated 11 Adar 5707 (3 Mar 1947), from the Fūqa community, the groom is Slaymān ben Maḥfuḍ ben Sālem Alḥadād, while the bride, a divorcee, is Miryam b. Slaymān ben Sālem al-'Arqabi.

In the registry of the Ṣan'a community religious court, in which the court's judgments were listed in brief, were 37 cases of a groom and his father-in-law with the same name. A few examples follow. In the ruling of 23 Marheshvan 5531 (31 Oct), the opening sentence states "Sālem ben Slaymān Se'īd Maḥrāz divorced his wife, Badrah b. Sālem Alḍarāb ...";[150] in a ruling from 24 Tevet 5532, the opening sentence notes "Yiḥye' b. Se'īd Kohen divorced his wife Mlāḥ b. Yiḥye' Alkohen;[151] in a decision from 13 Adar I 5532 (17 Feb 1772), we find in the beginning sentence "Yuda' b. Yosef Jamīl divorced his wife Rūmiyah, who is called Naḍrah, daughter of Yuda' Almu'alam."[152]

From a look at the list of Jews in northern Yemen, one sees that they were not careful on this matter. For example, Yiḥye' b. Slaymān Najjar married Ghazāl bat Yiḥye';[153] Da'ūd Slaymān married Ḥabība bat Da'ūd;[154] Yiḥye' b. Slaymān Jāhli married 'Āfiya b. Yiḥye' Jāhli;[155]

150. *Misawwadeh*, 1; par. 340, p. 136.
151. Ibid., par. 349, p. 139.
152. Ibid., par. 357, p. 141.
153. Ben David, *Bet ha-Even*, p. 675, no. 108.
154. Ibid., p. 681, no. 331.
155. Ibid., p. 687, no. 576.

Yiḥye' Damarmari married Simḥah b. Yiḥye' Maḍmūn;[156] Yiḥye' Sa'adi married Sa'adah b. Yiḥye' Baraṭi.[157]

Also regarding identical names of the fathers-in-law, whose children, according to R. Yehudah Heḥasid's will, should not marry, we find that in the Talmud they were not particular about this matter, such as "Rav Judah held a wedding feast for his son in the house of R. Judah b. Habībah" (Berakhot 42a). The Yemenite Jews were also not zealous on this issue. In my collection of Yemenite *ketubbot* are 144 cases of fathers-in-law with the same name. Below are a few examples.

In a *ketubbah* dated 9 Tevet 5538 (6 Feb 1778), from the Ṣan'a community, written by the greatest of the rabbinic decisors in Yemen, R. Yiḥye' Ṣāliḥ (Mahariṣ) for his son, the name of the groom was Ibrāhim b. Yiḥye' b. of our teacher and rabbi Yiḥye' b. Yosef b. R. Ṣāliḥ, may the memory of the saintly be a blessing, and the name of the bride was Ghazāl b. of our teacher and rabbi Yiḥye' b. of our teacher and rabbi Se'īd Al'uzayri. In a marriage contract from 15 Av 5650 (1 Aug 1890), from the Ṣan'a community, for the wedding of R. Amram Qoraḥ, who was the last rabbi of Yemenite Jewry in their Diaspora, the name of the groom is listed as Amram b. of our teacher and rabbi Yiḥye' b. of our teacher and rabbi Sālem Qoraḥ, and the bride is Ni'māh b. Yiḥye' b. Yiḥye' Shiryan.

There are three instances of identical names not only of in-laws but also of grandfathers. In a *ketubbah* dated 11 Tamuz 5751 (17 July 1891), from the Ṣan'a community, the name of the groom is written as Ya'aqub b. Yiḥye' b. Sālem Shim'on al-Levi, and the name of the bride as Salāmah b. Yiḥye' b. Sālem Khulayb; in a marriage contract from 22 Adar 5653 (10 Mar 1893), from the Ṣan'a community, the groom's name is listed as Ya'aqub ibn Sālem ben Yosef Ghiyāt, and the bride as, Sa'adah b. Sālem b. my teacher and master Yosef Ḥubārah; and in the *ketubbah* of the *dayyan* Aharon Hakohen, of the Ṣan'a community, dated 9 Kislev 5624 (20 Nov 1863), the groom's name is written as Harūn b. Sālem b. Sālem Alkohen, and the bride as Ghazāl b. Sālem b. Sālem b. Yosef al-Qindil.[158]

156. Ibid., p. 688, no. 612.

157. Ibid., p. 689, no. 644. See also p. 696, no. 920; p. 699, nos. 1003, 1006, 1018; p. 702, no. 1125; p. 703, no. 1164; p. 705, nos. 1236, 1245; p. 706, no. 1300; p. 709, nos. 1407–1408; p. 710, nos. 1448–1449; p. 713, nos. 1550, 1557, 1560; p. 716, nos. 1641, 1660; p. 717, no. 1698.

158. See above section 2.

There is one instance of three generations of fathers-in-law with the same names. In a *ketubbah* from 15 Av 5668 (13 Aug 1908), from the Ṣan'a community, for R. David Qāfiḥ, the son of R. Yiḥye' Qāfiḥ and father of R. Yosef Qāfiḥ, the groom's name is written as Da'ūd b. Yiḥye' b. Slaymān b. Sālem al-Qāfiḥ, and the name of the bride as Naḏrah daughter of our teacher and rabbi Yiḥye' b. our teacher and rabbi Slaymān b. Sālem Ṣāliḥ.

In the registry notebook of the Ṣan'a community *Bet Din*, 31 cases were found of fathers-in-law with identical names. Here are a few examples. In a decision from Monday, 24 Shevet 5526 (3 Feb 1766), the opening sentence states "Yosef b. Se'īd took as his wife Ghane' b. Se'īd al-'Irāqi";[159] in a decision of 18 Adar II 5527 (19 Mar 1767), the first sentence says "Sālem b. Se'īd Abu Se'īd divorced his wife Se'īdah b. Se'īd al-Raḥabi";[160] in a rendering from 29 Sivan 5531 (11 June 1771), the first sentence states "Yiḥye' b. our teacher and rabbi Se'īd Shadhrah";[161] in a decision of 23 Tevet 5572 (30 Dec 1771), the opening sentence has "Avraham b. Se'īd al-Quḥoṭa divorced his fiancée Salāmah b. Se'īd and was put under *ḥerem* with a Torah scroll, since he never had intercourse with her even once."[162]

A review of the list of Jews in northern Yemen shows us that they were not meticulous about this issue. For example, Berāhīm ben Yiḥye' Qa'ṭabi married Khadra' bint Yiḥye';[163] Sālem ben Yosef Jamil married Wardah bat Yosef Jāhli;[164] Yosef ben Sālem Zindani took as his wife Hinda bat Sālem Zindani;[165] Yosef ben Se'īd Najjar married Luluwa bat

159. *Misawwadeh*, I, par. 584, p. 213.

160. Ibid.

161. Ibid., par 338, p. 136.

162. Ibid., par. 348, pp. 138–39. In Yemen, until recent generations, it was customary to have a lengthy period separating the engagement from the wedding ceremonies, as in the Talmudic period. But in the first half of the twentieth century, it became customary in Ṣan'a and in a number of other places in Yemen to have the *kiddushin* (i.e., the engagement) right before the wedding, with the engagement at night and the wedding the following day. Yet, there were still a few who maintained a long separation between the engagement and the wedding. See Aharon Gaimani, "Marriage and Divorce Customs in Yemen and Eretz Yisrael," *Nashim*, 11 (2006):47–48.

163. Ben David, *Bet ha-Even*, p. 674, no. 81.

164. Ibid., p. 680, no. 316.

165. Ibid., p. 684, no. 440.

Se'īd Ḥashdi;[166] Yosef ben Se'īd 'Uzayri married Ṣīniyyah bat Se'īd 'Irji;[167] Da'ūd b. Yosef married Kādhiyyah bat Yosef.[168]

There are instances in which the names of the groom and his father-in-law were identical as well as those between fathers-in-law. On the list of names of Jews from northern Yemen, one find's the name "Yiḥye' b. Yiḥye' Ṣa'di, *zawj* (husband) of Sa'adah b. Yiḥye' Baraṭi";[169] and in the *Bet Din* registry notebook there is a case of an identical name of a groom and his father-in-law, as well as between the fathers-in-law: "Se'īd b. Se'īd Manṣur divorced his wife Ghazāl b. Se'īd with a *get shelihut* to their village Almadid through an emissary of our teacher and rabbi Se'īd b. our teacher and rabbi Slaymān. Wednesday, 20 Kislev 2087 SEL [5536 AM/ 13 Dec 1775].[170]

So too, the Jews of Yemen were not strict regarding identical names for a bride and her mother-in-law. The chief rabbi, Yiḥye' Yiṣḥaq Halevi, for his second marriage, married Rūmiyah b. R. Slaymān Ḥibshūsh, while his mother's name was Rūmiyah b. R. Shalom Manṣura;[171] Naomi (in Arabic, Ni'māh) Ḥubārah, who was born in Sūq al-'Ithnayn, married Yiḥye' Ḥubārah, whose mother was named Ni'māh;[172] Zihrah, the daughter of Sa'adah Shunem of the Maḥwīt community, wed Shalom Se'īd, whose mother was named Zihrah;[173] Se'īdah 'Adan, from the Ḥūṭaib community, in the district of Bane Bahlūl, relates that her mother-in-law's name was Se'īdah, the same as hers;[174] Raḥel Maḥfud, from the Dhamār region, tells that her mother-in-law was Raḥel, as she is called;[175] Michal Badiḥi wrote about her grandfather's sister, from the Ṣan'a community, whose name was Sham'ah, the same name as that of her mother-in-law;[176] Yocheved Gaimani told me about the identical

166. Ibid., p. 684, no. 459.

167. Ibid., p. 685, no. 484.

168. Ibid., p. 691, no. 705. See also ibid., p. 694, no. 823; p. 697, no. 953; p. 704, no. 1201; p. 705, no. 1241; p. 709, no. 1401; p. 715, no. 1609.

169. Ibid., p. 686, no. 545.

170. *Misawwadeh*, I, par. 605, p. 186.

171. In a personal correspondence dated Marheshvan 5771 (12 Oct 2010) from R. Aviran Yiṣḥaq Halevi.

172. See the memoirs of Naomi Ḥubārah, *Mi-Pe'ate Teiman* (Tel Aviv, 2010), pp. 53, 97.

173. Interview given to the grandson Yair Shunem of Rosh HaAyin.

174. As related by Rahamim Adan of Kfar Saba.

175. As related by her grandson Shlomi Maḥfud from Einav.

176. In a questionnaire I received from her in Iyyar 5770 (April 2010).

name of two brides and mothers-in-law in her grandmother's family. The grandmother, who was from one of the villages near Tan'em in central Yemen, was named Sham'ah and each of her two sons, Ya'aqov, who married in Yemen, and Levi, who married in Israel, had a wife named Sham'ah.[177]

Some people assume that when the will of R. Yehudah Heḥasid states, "Two people whose names are the same should not make matches between their children," this applies as well to mothers-in-law whose names are identical.[178] Yemenite Jews were not particular about this even though we do not have written evidence owing to the way names in a lineage list are given according to the father's name and not the mother's. Below is an instance taken from one of the questionnaires in which the mothers-in-law had the same name. Ya'aqov ben Miryam Ta'sa married Raḥel bat Miryam. They lived in the village of 'Abbar in the Ḥubeish district of southern Yemen. They called their eldest daughter, who was born prior to their immigration to Israel in 1949, Miryam, the name of both grandmothers.[179]

Sefer Ḥasidim further states about names related to matches:

> If a person took a wife named Rivqah or another name, and his son married a woman named Rivqah, and his grandson took a wife named Rivqah, they will not turn out well. One will see that this does not succeed for she is tripled or he is tripled, that the woman and the daughter and the daughter's daughter took three names, one finds that it will not succeed and there are many like this. Even though you shall not divine or augur and it did not say about this that "you must be wholehearted" (Deut. 18:13).[180]

The Yemenite Jews were undoubtedly not assiduous about this matter, even if we do not have testimony concerning it.

Of the influence of *Sefer Ḥasidim* and the will of R. Yehudah Heḥasid regarding names, we learn from the statements of a number of rabbis from communities in Yemen who responded to my questions on this topic. From reading their replies, we learn of the familiarity of the Ye-

177. Yocheved, the daughter of Sham'a and Levi Shunem is married to my brother Barukh, and Sham'a the wife of Ya'aqov Shunem is my mother's sister [A.G.].

178. See the Will of R. Yehudah Heḥasid, par. 24, in *Sefer Ḥasidim*, n. 36, p. 19.

179. In a questionnaire I received from Ami'el Ta'sa of Qiryat Ono, in Jan 2012. Ami'el interviewed his parents, Ya 'aqov and Ḥana.

180. *Sefer Ḥasidim*, par. 477, p. 323.

menite sages with the words of R. Yehudah Heḥasid and of the influence they had on Yemenite communities.

R. Raṣon 'Arusi clarified the influence of the R. Yehudah Heḥasid's ethical will among the elderly who came from various communities in Yemen:

> You asked me whether the Yemenite Jews were anxious about the wills of R. Yehudah Heḥasid. The answer to that is generally negative. They had no fear of the same name for in-laws or for a groom and his father-in-law or a bride and her mother-in-law. They had no hesitation about calling a son by his father's name, even when he was still alive. They had no fear of brothers living in the same city, and some even in the same courtyard. And a brother married his brother's daughter or his sister's daughter, and two brothers married two sisters, and so on. These are proven things, since there are still elderly men and women whose names are evidence of all the foregoing, as well as their familial relations, and from ancient *ketubbot* documents. Also from the testimony of the elderly men. Here one should note that I asked the elderly of Shar'ab, where they were anxious about the date of the wedding and arranged it according to those using *sifrei ḥefetz*, as well as coordination of the names of the couple toward their success, and even with all the foregoing, they were not afraid.[181]

R. Pinḥas Qoraḥ, from the Ṣan'a community, wrote to me at length about the will of R. Yehudah Heḥasid in Yemen. He noted that despite their broad familiarity with the writings of the other rabbis, they ignored what was written in the will, which informs us of its lack of acceptance in Yemen. As he puts it:

> As for the attention paid by Yemenite Jewry to the will of R. Yehudah Heḥasid regarding match-making and marriage, as far as I know there was no reference to it, and it was not mentioned anywhere in the writings of the Yemenite rabbis, and in any event they did not take it into consideration, and there were often marriages that ran counter to R. Yehudah Heḥasid's will. And even though R. Yehudah Heḥasid was one of the Medieval rabbis, at any rate, he is not mentioned in the books of the Yemenite rabbis like the other books of Rishonim that reached Yemen, and even in manuscripts, and even his being mentioned in the works of *poseqim* and responsa that made their way to Yemen did not move the Jews of Yemen from ignoring his will.

181. In a personal correspondence dated 26 Apr 2010.

As he went on, R. Qoraḥ noted the reservation of R. Yehezqel Landau in his *Noda bi-Yehudah* regarding what was written in the will, with which some of the *poseqim* do agree. He also wrote that there were warnings in the Talmud about doing this or that deed, and they were not heeded, so there is no preference for admonitions in the will of R. Yehudah Heḥasid over those in the Talmud. On the influence of the ethical will in Yemen, he wrote:

> And it seems, in order to support our statements, that the will of R. Yehudah Heḥasid did not reach Yemen, that is, it was not adhered to. For there are many customs and warnings of all kinds of behaviors and different beliefs that the Yemenite Jews were careful about, as we know, and these were given voice in the Yemenite literature; if so, why weren't specific admonitions in light of the will interspersed [in it], so you have to understand they did not adhere to it, meaning, it was not accepted by Yemenite Jewry.

At the end of his letter, R. Qoraḥ summarized his approach, writing: "In conclusion: the will of R. Yehudah Heḥasid was not given expression in the rabbinic literature of Yemen, both halakhically and practically, for it had no reflection at all in the behavior of Yemenite Jews, and even if someone did know about this will, in any event, he felt it applied only to the descendants of R. Yehudah Heḥasid."[182]

R. Avraham Arye, whose parents came from the Maḥwīt community, wrote: "As far as I know, one heard nothing in general and in our district in particular, in the great city of Maḥwīt, may it be built and established, and its environs that referred to the will of R. Yehudah Heḥasid ... and if they were aware of it, they did not pay attention to it, and in our place it was not to be found."[183] In the continuation of his response, R. Arye referred in detail to the sections of the will and based his statements on many examples from the Maḥwīt community:

A. As to what he wrote in the will in section 23 "One shall not marry a woman with the same name as his mother," many examples attest that they did not pay attention to this, and here is an example:

---

182. In a personal correspondence dated April 2010. In this letter, R. Pinḥas Qoraḥ wrote to me about the custom of Yemenite Jews regarding the admonitions in the will of R. Yehudah Heḥasid, that the name of the groom not be the same as is father-in-law nor of the bride like her mother-in-law: "And, at any rate, they were not at all careful about identical names, and they did not change names for the purpose of marriage as the teachers now do instruct [us]."

183. In a personal correspondence dated 7 May 2010.

my grandfather's father, R. Yehudah, OBM, had a sister named Salāmah, and one of her sons, who was called Moshe, married in his first match my cousin, the daughter of my great-grandfather, who was also called Salāmah, and in his second marriage he wed the daughter of his cousin (my grandfather R. Yosef) and her name was Salāmah.

B. As for the issue of what he wrote there "or his name like that of his father-in-law," here are two examples. (1) My grandfather, my father's father, R. Yosef married in his first match the daughter of R. Yosef Shukr Būsāni (on him, see *Sefer Ma'aseh Ish*, part Even ha-Ezer, section 11); (2) My grandfather Sālem (Shalem) took as a groom for his daughter Badrah a fellow named Sālem (Shalem) Sāliḥ.

C. As for what is written there, chapter 25, my three aunts (my mother's sisters), Ḥamāmah, Ni'māh, and Simḥah, daughters of my grandfather R. Sālem noted above, married three brothers, the sons of R. Yosef Qarawāni, who were named Yiḥye', Avraham, and Nissim.

D. Regarding what is written in *Sefer Ḥasidim*, section 460. They did name a son for his father when the father was alive, let alone for his grandfather. Here are six examples, as follows: (1) I am the youngest of one of them, whom my father called me by his own name, and I have already cited in my book a manuscript of the source of this custom. (2) The aforementioned R. Yosef Qarawāni named one of his sons for himself. (3) The father of my maternal grandmother, R. Avraham Mansūr, called his son by his own name. (4) My uncle who was married to my aunt (my mother's sister, Ḥamāmah), the person of good reputation, Yiḥye' Qarawāni, mentioned above, gave one of his sons his own name. (5) My uncle who was married to my aunt (my father's sister, Banayyah), the person of good reputation, Yiḥye' Būsāni, was called by his father with his own name, and he, too, gave one of his sons his name, that is, three generations with one name, and throughout all Yemen they were not meticulous about this. (6) In the book *Lekaḥ Ṭov* (photocopy of a manuscript), the author signed his name on the title page as: Se'īd ben our distinguished teacher, the rabbi Se'īd ben our distinguished teacher, the rabbi Se'īd ben Se'īd Būṭa,[184] that is, four generations with the same name.

184. R. Sa'adya Būṭa (1858–1910) lived in the village Gibr in central Yemen. On the title

R. Shelomo Maḥfūd, who came from the village of Masyab in central Yemen, wrote:

> As for the will of R. Yehudah Heḥasid, in the region of Ṣan'a and its environs, there was no apprehension at all about his admonitions, and they used to call their sons by the father's name even while the father was alive, and I have a brother who was called by the name of my father, OBM, during his life. Also regarding marrying one's niece, they married a niece, and also when the name of the woman was the same as her mother-in-law, or his name like his father-in-law's, and they had no fear of that; see Sotah 10b: "Shemu'el the elder, father-in-law of R. Shemu'el b. Ammi"'; and they understood that after the Talmud no sage has permission to say anything against the Talmud, and see *gemara* Sanhedrin and Yevamot 62b that it is a mitzvah to marry one's niece, and in *gemara* Berakhot 80 *kohanim* married 80 *kohanot*, or that they [meaning Jews of Yemen] follow what was commanded only to his descendants. As far as marriages of two brothers to two sisters, in the Qarawāni family three brothers were married to three sisters, and there were other families who were married to sisters ... the Jews of Yemen were familiar with the ethical will of R. Yehudah Heḥasid but did not act according to what was written in it.[185]

R. Azaryah Basis, from the Radā' community, the second-largest Jewish community in Yemen, wrote:

> Be aware that I have in my late father's estate the very old *Sefer Ḥasidim* ... this *Sefer Ḥasidim* was printed in Warsaw in 1879. I was also given a similar *Sefer Ḥasidim* from the Ḥaduqa family.[186] At the beginning of the book appears the will of R. Yehudah Heḥasid ... and thus even though they knew of this will of R. Yehudah Heḥasid, they were not affected at all.[187]

R. Shelomo Qoraḥ and R. Aviran Yitzhaq Halevi wrote about the custom of the Ṣan'a community, in which the sages of Ṣan'a, though acquainted with the will of R. Yehudah Heḥasid, did not cancel matches because of issues cited in the will.[188]

---

page of the manuscript, the author wrote: "In beseeching and pleading, hoping for the grace of God, the humble Se'īd ibn our honorable teacher and rabbi Se'īd ibn the honorable teacher R. Se'īd ibn Se'īd Buṭa, may he see descendants and a long life, Amen." (R. Se'īd ibn Se'īd Buṭa, *Sefer Lekaḥ Tov*, photocopied edition of ms (Jerusalem, 1968), introduction).

185. In a personal correspondence dated 12 Apr 2010.
186. This family also lived in the Radā' community.
187. In a personal correspondence dated 8 Mar 2010.

R. Yiṣḥaq Raṣabi wrote: "Seemingly, a few of the Yemenite rabbis knew of the wills of R. Yehudah Heḥasid, but actually it did not move them. I recall that I saw them copied in later manuscripts, and in any event, it might be that a very few of them were strict for themselves, but they did not publicize the matter."[189] In his books, he wrote in a similar vein: "And among the Yemenite communities his wills were not publicized, and they did not refrain from these things and others at all."[190]

R. Almog Shelomo Akhlufi wrote about this issue regarding his father's family, which lived in the villages of Bayt Sālem and Yafīd in central Yemen, and his mother's family, which lived in the villages of Mhāsr and Jerāf, also in central Yemen, north of Ṣan'a. His statement follows:

> They had no apprehensions at all from the will of R. Yehudah Heḥasid in our locations, and from what we have heard also in most of the holy communities of Yemenite Jews, so they had no fear if the name of groom was the same as his father-in-law's or if the name of the bride was like that of her mother-in-law. For instance, the father of my grandfather, the rabbi, the gaon, R. Yiḥye', his memory should live in eternity, had the same name as his father-in-law, R. Yiḥye' Se'īd, his memory should live in eternity.[191]

Another opinion about the influence of the will of R. Yehudah Heḥasid was given by R. Ovadyah Ya'beṣ, who inherited from his grandfather the office of the last chief rabbi of Ṣa'dah in northern Yemen, and thus he wrote about his grandfather:

> Respectful of the learning of my teacher and master, R. Zekharyah Ya'beṣ, may his merit protect us, Amen, he was the address also for name changes as needed according to his expertise in names through his holy books. The instructions of R. Yehudah Heḥasid, may his merit stand on our behalf, were given by him to the public in greatest strictness.[192]

---

188. In a personal correspondence dated May 2010 from R. Shelomo Qoraḥ; and in a personal correspondence dated 12 Oct 2010 from R. Aviran Yitshaq Halevi.
189. In a personal correspondence dated 22 Apr 2010.
190. Raṣabi, *Shulḥan Arukh ha-Mequṣar*, 6, sect. 205, 7, p. 348. See idem, *Shu"t Olat Yitzhaq*, 1, sect. 166 (Jerusalem, 1989), pp. 403–4.
191. In a personal correspondence dated 16 Feb 2011.
192. In a personal correspondence dated 4 Mar 2010.

Another conclusion can be drawn from a conversation with *mori* Faiz Jaradi, who was a rabbinic figure among the remnant of Jews in northern Yemen and leader on behalf of the Ṣan'a regime. He left the village of Raidah in northern Yemen in 2007 and lives in Monsey, New York. He told me that as far as he knows the Jews of northern Yemen had no apprehensions about what was written in the will of R. Yehudah Heḥasid, and he gave two examples in which the name of the groom was the same as his father-in-law's. Yiḥye' Qarni married the daughter of Yiḥye' Ya'aqov Ḥalle; the daughter of Sālem Aḥmar was divorced from Sālem Nahari and her second marriage was to Sālem Shaghdari. Likewise, there were some who named their sons with names identical to theirs, such as Sālem ben Sālem Nahari, Se'īd ben Se'īd Nā'ti, and Sālem ben Sālem Ḥabīb.[193]

Moreover, as previously noted, an examination of the list of names from the villages in northern Yemen during the first half of the twentieth century shows that they did not pay any attention to the instructions in R. Yehudah Heḥasid's ethical will. In a *ketubbah* from Ṣa'dah, dated 10 Adar II 5605 (19 Mar 1845), the groom's name was the same as his father's, Sālem ben Sālem. Apparently, one can consider the statements by R. Ovadyah Ya'vets about his grandfather being meticulous over these issues as personal influence that did not go beyond his place and time.

It is told of R. Aharon Maṣrafi, the leader of the Akamat Bane Manṣūr community in southern Yemen, that he was very careful that the name of the bride should not be the same as that of her mother-in-law; and for the marriage of his son, Ya'aqov, the name of the intended bride was Kādhiyyah, the same name as his wife's, so he changed the name of the bride to Ḥabība.[194] We do not hear, however, that R. Maṣrafi took special care about other issues cited in R. Yehudah Heḥasid's will, such as identical names for a groom and his father-in-law or identical names for in-laws. R. Maṣrafi's meticulousness apparently resulted from the influence of statements cited in the name of the Ari about identical names for the bride and her mother-in-law.[195] And perhaps R.

193. The meeting with *mori* Faiz Jaradi took place in Monsey, New York, in Dec 2010.

194. Shemu'el Maṣrafi, *"Toledot HaRav HaGaon R. Aharon Maṣrafi, zaṣal, Rabbah ha-Aḥaron shel Qehillat Akamat Bane Manṣūr ve-ha-Sevivah,"* in Gilad Ṣadoq, *Zikhron Teiman* (Bnei Brak, 2006), p. 216.

195. R. David Pardo wrote: "One must add the statements of warning by Maran ha-Ari"al, may his merit shield us, that there is nothing better for a man than to marry

Maṣrafi was exposed to this stringency owing to his dealings in Aden where Jews from other communities lived as well. Undoubtedly, R. Maṣrafi's activity teaches us only of his place and time, and we have not heard from the Yemenite rabbis over the generations any reference to the objections that appear in the ethical will of R. Yehudah Heḥasid about these issues. Even if they knew about them, we may reasonably assume that they did not relate to them at all.

To date, the ethical will of R. Yehudah Heḥasid is found in only one manuscript from Yemen, in a *Tiklal* (prayer book), which was copied in 1707,[196] informing us, as noted above, that R. Yehudah Heḥasid's ethical will had no influence in Yemen.

Aside from the reason that the Yemenite Jews were not anxious about the will of R. Yehudah Heḥasid, it seems that they felt it was difficult to fulfill, since most of them were called by the common names Yiḥye', Sālem (Heb.: Shalom), Yosef, Se'īd, Slaymān (Heb.: Shelomo), Avraham, Da'ūd (Heb.: David), Musa (Heb.: Moshe). Among the women as well there were a few names that were dominant statistically, such as Zihrah, Ḥamāmah, Sa'dah, Rūmiyah, Lūluwah, Badrah, and Sham'ah.[197] So it frequently occurred that a man was matched to a woman with the same name as his mother, or her father had the same name as the groom, or the fathers- or mothers-in-law had the identical name, as demonstrated by the many examples cited above in this section, from *ketubbot* and *gittin*, the Ṣan'a community religious court registry, and interviews.

---

a woman whose name is the same as his mother's (David Pardo, *Sefer Mizmor le-David*, photocopy of Livorno printing [Brooklyn 1991], par. 116, p. 110b). R. Yosef Ḥayim also cited the words of R. David Pardo noted, which he wrote in the name of the Ari and he noted: "The language of our rabbi, OBM, doesn't sound good ... it is a weak warning. One must say, it stems from someone's honor, and in any event, since this warning was written in the name of Ari, OBM, it would appropriate to be careful. But if he changes the name, it's also all right."

196. *Tiklal*, MS Jerusalem, Jewish National and University Library, Manuscript Department 4^0 949; Aharon Gaimani, *Temurot be-Moreshet*, p. 317, MS no. 14.

197. See below chap. 3, sect. 2.

5. NAMES AND BYNAMES FOR A WOMAN BASED ON HER MAIDEN NAME OR HER FATHER'S NAME

When a woman married in Yemen and moved into her husband's home, she was called by her family's name, or that of her father's lineage, or her husband's name. R. Pinḥas Qoraḥ wrote: "After [a woman] was married she was called by the name of her husband's family, but often she was identified by the name of her father's family, such as "bint al-Ṭayri" or "bint al-Shar'abi," or "bint al-Qeha'" and so on, and especially if she was a widow or divorcée."[198] In the Ṣan'a community, Rūmiyah from the Ḥubārah family was married to Sālem Meghori, and in her husband's home she was called Rūmiyah Ḥubārah marat [the wife of] Sālem Meghori. In the same manner, we find Badrah Ṣāliḥ marat Ya'īsh Ḥubarah.[199] Sarah Alsheikh, from the Ṣan'a community, related that after a woman married they called her by her previous family's name or by her father's personal name. For example, bint Ḥibshush according to the family name, or bint Se'īd after her father's first name.[200] Similarly, in northern Yemen, Hawīdah and Ḥabībah, who came from the Zindani family and married into the Slaymān family, would be called Hawīdah Zindaniya and Ḥabībah Zindaniya. The same applied to the sisters Se'īdah and Sham'ah Ḥale', who married members of other families, but were called Se'īdah Ḥal'iya and Sham'ah Ḥal'iya.[201] Similarly, Se'īdah of the Dhamāri family of Ṣa'dah, who married Harūn Jamīl from the village of Falla was called Se'īdah Dhamāriya,[202] Hawīdah from the Tharābān family, who married Yiḥye' Shukr, was called Hawīdah Tharābāna,[203] Ḍobyah of the Qahlāni family, who married Zāhir Dhamarmari, was called Ḍobyah Qahlāniya.[204] Ni'māh Qa'ṭabi, whose parents emigrated from the Baraṭ community in northern Yemen, wrote me that after a woman's marriage she was called according to her father's first name, such as bint Se'īd, bint Yosef.[205]

---

198. In a personal correspondence dated April 2010.
199. Yosef Shalom Ḥubarah, *Bi-Tla'ot Teiman vi-Yrushalayim* (Jerusalem, 1970), p. 38.
200. Interview conducted by David ben Shalom Qāfiḥ of Jerusalem.
201. In a personal correspondence dated 13 Jan 2010 from R. Dr. Aharon Ben David of Qiryat 'Eqron.
202. Ben David, *Bet ha-Even*, p. 678, no. 238.
203. Ibid., p. 680, no. 323.
204. Ibid., p. 680, no. 303. For additional examples, see above end of section 3.
205. In a personal correspondence dated April 2009.

Below are further attestations from a number of communities in northern Yemen. Yiḥye' Selus from the village of Amlaḥ took as his wife Miriam bat Mori Slaymān, and she was called according to her father's name, Miriam Slaymāna.[206] Yiḥye' Jerāfi from the town al-Miḥtawiya married Miriam the daughter of Harūn Jamīl, and she was called after her father's name Miriam Harūna.[207] Mūsa Jamīl of Falla married Se'īdah of the Dhamāri family from the Ṣa'dah community, and she was called Se'īdah Dhamāriyya.[208] Mas'ūd Ḥashdi of the village of Shara-māt took as his wife Se'īdah from the Hindi family, and after her marriage, she was called Se'īdah Hindiya.[209] Sālem Zindani from the town Rajūzah married Hawīdah from the 'Irji family, and after her marriage, she was called Se'īdah 'Irjiya.[210]

This phenomenon occurred in other places in Yemen where, in addition to the first name, after her marriage a woman was given a byname based on her family name. For example, Sa'dah Sheḥib, of the Tan'em community, was named for the family name, Sa'dah Sheḥiba; Yona Jerāfi, of the Qifla community, was called for her family name Yonah Jerāfiya. Similarly we find Marḥūma and Maḥfūḍah of the Radā' community were named after their families Marḥūm and Maḥfūḍ.[211] In the Ḥabbūr district, Tamniyyah 'Afāri was named 'Ifriya, just as we find Najāra of the Najjār family, Shirwiya and Sharāwa of the Shirwi family. In this district and in other places in Yemen, sometimes they called the woman a name based on her father's first name. For example, Ḥamāmah bat Mūsa was called Musaya; Sham'ah bat Sha'ul was called Sha'ula; Ḥayma bat Ḥayim. In the Ḥūtaib community in the Bane Bahlūl district in central Yemen, the first wife of Yosef 'Aden, was named Se'īdah Harūna, after her father's name, Harūn (Hebrew: Aharon).[212]

206. Ben David, *Bet ha-Even*, p. 698, nos. 968–969.

207. Ibid., p. 687, no. 589.

208. Ibid., p. 693, no. 811.

209. Ibid., p. 695, no. 864.

210. Ibid., p. 701, no. 1083.

211. For additional names, see Shlomo Amihud, *Pe'ulot Ṣaddiq—YbY'* [= Yiḥye' ben Yiḥye' 'Umaysi[(Hemed 5787 [1988]) pp. 220–21. See also the statement by R. Azaryah Basis below in this chapter, start of sect. 6.

212. As related by Raḥamim 'Adan of Kefar Saba.

Shlomo 'Adani, a descendant of the Ḍāle' community in southern Yemen, told that usually a married woman was called by the name of her father's family and sometimes in addition her family name or only her family's byname. Examples are Sham'ah bint Adujma and Salāmah bint Avraham al-Ḥaddad.[213]

Shi'tāle of the Ḍuwāle' community (north of Ṣan'a) was called by the temporary name *bint* when young.[214] When she grew up, she was give the name Shi'tāle, so as to preserve the family name Shi'tāl, after the seven children born before her had died. Her name is written in a *ketubbah* dated 11 Tammuz 5699 (28 June 1939), for the marriage of Ibrāhim ben Yiḥye' al-'Afāri, in the community of Bane 'Abd, as Shi'tāle bat Yūda Shi'tāl.[215] After her immigration to Israel, her name was changed to Shula, which sounds similar to her former name.[216]

6. WHAT A HUSBAND CALLS HIS WIFE AND WHAT A WIFE CALLS HER HUSBAND

In Eastern Jewry, customarily the couple does not call each other by their first names, though Ashkenazi Jews are not meticulous about this.[217] Radak commented on this phenomenon in his exegesis on the Torah:

> For the man calls his wife by her name, but not the woman to her husband, except by way of respect in the language of authority she does not call him by his name, for whosoever is of higher status over another, it is not fitting for the one lower than he to call him by his name, such as his father or his teacher or his masters … and so for the woman to her husband for he is her master, as He said, "And he shall rule over you" (Gen. 3:16), and also Sarah said, "my husband so old" (Gen. 18:12), and she did not say, and Abraham is old, while Abraham said "Can Sarah" (Gen. 17:17), and it is written through a story (Jud. 19:26) "entrance to the man's house where her husband was." Therefore he said to Abraham, you shall not call her Sarai, but he did not say the same to Sarah about Abraham, but He said "you shall no longer be called" (Gen. 17:5), meaning, among the people who call him by name.[218]

213. Interview conducted by R. Gilad Ṣadok of Bnei Brak.
214. On the name *bint* as a temporary name, see below part 3, chap. 4, sect. A [1].
215. In the possession of Netanela 'Uzayri of Pardes Hana.
216. As told by her son, R. Meir Afari of Herzliyya.
217. See Wilhelm, *Ziv ha-Shemot*, p. 113.
218. Commentary on Gen. 17:15, passage beginning *lo tikarei*.

Perhaps one may find some allusion to this topic in the words of the sages, "R. Jose said: I have never called my wife 'my wife' or my ox 'my ox,' but my wife [I called] 'my home,' and my ox 'my field'" (Shab. 118b; Gittin 52a).

R. Menashe ben Eliezer Ze'ev Klein noted after he cited the passage mentioned from the Gemara: "And this is what the books wrote, to not call his wife by her name, which as is known is a wonderful charm."[219]

In Yemen, spouses did not usually call each other by their personal names but through an allusion for reasons of respect and modesty. R. Azaryah Basis, a descendant of the Radā' community wrote:

So it was customary in all districts of Yemen for the husband to not call his wife by her name, and the wife, the husband, but the husband would say to her "Ya Mreh" or "Ya Banayyah" or "Ya hahah," and the woman would call to her husband, "Ya rajjāl" or if her husband was a *talmid ḥakham,* "Ya mori," or another hint. Some even called the woman by her family name, such as "bint al-Ṭayri" or Ṭayriyyah, Ḍāhari, 'Adaniyyah, or "Ya bint al-'Adani," even if they were male or female neighbors.[220]

R. Shelomo Qoraḥ wrote about the Ṣan'a community:

> The woman never calls her husband by his name. When she mentions him to others, she says: "He." But he says: "the woman." But when he calls to her, he says, "daughter of her family," that is, *bat ha-yiṣhari* (daughter of the Yiṣhar family), *bat ha-qehati*, and so on. And when she calls to him, she says "Hayyeh."[221] "And when she calls to him, she says 'Hayyeh'," is meant to hint to him that she wishes to speak to him. The husband, however, would call to his wife in Arabic, as in this quotation from the Ḍele' community in southern Yemen: "The husband does not call to his wife by name but through an allusion, then he calls her "Ya mara" (Oh, woman), and all of this for reasons of modesty.[222]

219. Menashe ben Eliezer Ze'ev Klein, *Mishneh Halakhot, Medor ha-Teshuvot* ... in the four parts of the Shulḥan Arukh and a number of topics in the Shas [Makhon Mishnah Halakhot Gedolot], part 9 (Brooklyn 1983), Responsa division, part 9, sect. 249.

220. In a personal correspondence dated 8 Mar 2010.

221. Shelomo Qoraḥ, *'Arikhat Shulḥan,* 1–3 (Bnei Brak, 1975–1985), 3, Laws of Modesty and Proper Behavior Followed by Jewish Women, 7, p. 219. Cf. Yehudah Levi Naḥum, *Mi-Ṣefunot Teiman* (Tel Aviv, 1987), pp. 75–76.

222. R. Gilad Ṣadoq, *Zikhron Teiman*, p. 272.

R. Pinḥas Qoraḥ wrote about the Ṣan'a community:

> Among us they never called, not a husband to his wife nor a wife to her husband, by their first names, out of respect and modesty. And when they wanted to call each other and tell the spouse something, the husband would address the wife by calling "bedisme'i," which means "Do you hear?" or by wife to husband, "bedisma,'" meaning, "Do you hear?" Or they would turn to each other after making some sound. And in this generation many have forsaken this custom.[223] And even when he would say something in the name of his wife or about his wife, he would not say her name but rather *"al-mara"* (the woman), and when she would say something in the name of her husband or about him, she would say *"al-rajjāl"* (the husband), or they would say *"ḥuqna"* (ours). Generally, they would use a byname of respect and modesty, as stated in *gemara* Shabbat, "R. Yose said, 'I never called my wife "my wife" but "my house."'"[224]

R. Avraham 'Arusi wrote in his work *Yore Ḥaṭa'im*: "The woman calls to her husband only through an allusion to his name. The same goes for him, should he call her, he will not do so by name, out of modesty because of 'to walk modestly with your God' [Micah 6:8]."[225]

R. Shelomo Maḥfūd, who came from central Yemen, wrote: "It was customary that the husband not call his wife by name, and similarly the wife, only through a hint, because of modesty."[226]

R. Avraham Arye, whose parents emigrated from the Maḥwīt community, wrote in his reply that a couple did not call each other by personal names, but rather the women hinted to her husband with the word *hei*, and the husband called to his wife with *"bint 'ammi"* (my uncle's daughter), and explained that they used to call a father-in-law *'ammi.*[227]

R. Ovadyah Ya'beṣ wrote about the custom in his locality of the Ṣa'dah community in northern Yemen: "A husband calls his wife by her name or the byname of Ya thayye, and the woman by his name or Yadha."[228]

223. In this sentence he means the generation of the children who live in the Land of Israel.

224. In a personal correspondence dated Iyyar 5770 (April 2010). R. Qoraḥ quoted from the passage in tractate Sabbath (118b) from memory. For the language of the Talmud, see the beginning of this section.

225. Yehudah Ratzaby, "*'Yore Ḥata'im' le-Rabbi Avraham 'Arusi,*" *Asufot*, 8 (1995): 416.

226. In a personal correspondence dated 12 Apr 2010.

227. In a personal correspondence dated 7. May 2010.

228. In a personal correspondence dated 4 Mar 2010.

R. Almog Shelomo Akhlufi, whose parents emigrated from central Yemen, wrote:

> It is commonly known that he turns to her only through a hint, and I have never heard from the elders that they addressed their wives by their first name but by the byname "Halleh" or "Mareh" or "Ya heh" and so on. While there were some who called her by her family name, such as *"bint al-kohen," "bint al-ḥubarah."* But also the opposite, she also does not turn to him by his first name, but as Hayyeh and the like. And if he is her uncle, she addresses him with the title *"'ammi"* (my uncle). And if he is a *talmid ḥakham*, she turns to him with the title *mori*, as I heard in the home of the Rav the Gaon R. Shalom Mhasri, his memory should live in eternity, and in the home of the Rav the Gaon R. Levi Qeshet, his memory should live in eternity.[229]

He noted further in his statements, that a man would not call his wife by her name by reason of good manners and modesty, while the wife would not call her husband by name owing to dignity and respect.

Moshe Ben David, of the Bayḥān community, relates that in his community husband and wife did not address each other by their first names but by using the sound *Eiheh* to draw their attention.[230]

Zekharyah 'Iṭwār, from the Jūban community in the Radā' district, told that spouses would call each other with a hint, using the word *hayei*, and the husband would call his wife *Banayya*, that is, "girl," and the wife would call her husband *Wulayd*, that is, "boy."[231]

Menashe Ṣubari, formerly of the Bayḍa' community in southeastern Yemen, related that the husband would call his wife by a hint, and vice versa. When the husband would call to his wife, he would say to her *Wiladey'* and when the wife called the husband she would say to him, *Weled."*[232]

Ezra 'Aṭari, a descendant of the 'Athār community in the Arḥab district, told that the husband called to his wife with a hint *hei* and the wife also called to her husband with an allusion, *rajal* (man).[233]

Shim'on and Raḥel Maḥfuḍ, who emigrated from the Dhamār region, tell that the woman called to her husband with the hint *'ana layk,*

229. In a personal correspondence dated 16 Feb 2011.
230. Interview conducted by Omri Portuguez of Nes Ṣiyyona.
231. Interview conducted by Yirmiyahu 'Iṭwār of Rishon Lezion.
232. Interview conducted by R. Gilad Tzadok of Bnei Brak.
233. Interview conducted by Yosi 'Attari of Rosh HaAyin.

which means "I am for you (masc.)," and the husband would call similarly to his wife, *'ana laysh,* meaning "I am for you (fem.)," or *Ya hei.*[234]

Shalom Sa'd, whose parents emigrated from Kafr Nābāth in central Yemen, told that the husband called to his wife by alluding to the name of her father's family, such as *bint 'anis,* or with the words *'ana laysh,* meaning "I am for you."[235]

Ni'māh Qa'ṭabi wrote to me about testimony she received from her mother, that they would call through allusions using nonsense words, *ashbesh* or *ashbeiq,* or the husband, on his part, would call to his wife "Ya mara" (Oh, woman), and the woman would call to her husband "Ya rajal" (Oh, man).[236]

Aharon Yehudah, who emigrated from the Ra'ūḍah community, related that he calls to his wife, Yonah, through a hint, *bint al-hizmi,* after the name of her family, and his wife calls him "Ibn Yehudah" after the name of his father.[237]

Shelomo Raṣhabi, who emigrated from the Raḍa' community in southern Yemen, told that a husband called to his wife with an allusion or by the name of her father: *bint Se'īd.*[238]

Ḥannah Ḥofi, from the village of Qūrana, in the Shar'ab district, related that in her community the husband never called his wife by name, and vice versa, but the husband called his wife "Ya mara" (woman), and the wife called the husband "Ya rajal" (man).[239]

Zekharyah 'Aṣmi, from the Madīd community, northeast of Ṣan'a, told that in his community the husband would call to his wife through the hint Hei, and the woman, after her marriage, was always called by the name of her father's family, even in her old age.[240]

Shoshana Basha, whose parents immigrated to Israel from Ḍūwāle', located in the center of Yemen north of Ṣan'a, related that a husband and wife called to each other only through a hint. The husband used "Ya bint," and the wife used "Ya walad."[241]

234. The information was given to me by their grandson, Shlomi Maḥfud, Einav.

235. Interview conducted by Yehonatan Levi of Rosh HaAyin.

236. In a personal correspondence dated April 2009.

237. Interview conducted by Idan Yehudah of Petah Tiqva.

238. Interview conducted by R. Gilad Ṣadoq of Bnei Brak.

239. Interview conducted by her son Shemu'el Ḥofi of New York.

240. The interview was conducted by R. Gilad Ṣadoq of Bnei Brak.

241. Interview conducted by her granddaughter 'Einat Basha of Yavneh.

Sarah Nissim, from the village of Bane Hajāj in the Ḥaymeh district, said that the husband and wife never called each other by name, but addressed one another with the exclamation *"Hei."*[242]

Mori Se'īd Ṣabari, who left Raidah in northern Yemen in 2009, told me that the husband and wife called to each other by allusion, and turned to one another through the utterance *"Ya he."* Sometimes the husband called his wife *"Ya mara,"* and the wife called him *"Ya rajal."*[243]

R. Yiṣḥaq Raṣabi wrote about the custom among Yemenite Jews:

> That the man does not call his wife by her name, and she, too, does not call him by his name, but with kind of syllable like *heyh* or *hayh*. [There are places where he calls her "Ya bint," that is, girl. And she calls him, "Ya walad," that is, boy. And it goes on this way among them even through old age.] And this is not related to modesty but rather a way to honor and respect, a kind of what we found owing to awe of his father and mother and his rabbi that it is forbidden to mention them by name.[244]

Similarly, R. Yiṣḥaq Raṣabi wrote about the customs of the Raṣāba community and its environs, that a couple would call each other through an allusion by the term *hyeh*. He further added about the custom in his father's house: "Yet, it is interesting that in our house that was not so. My master, my father, my teacher, my rabbi called my mother by her name, Zihrah, and she called him by his name, Nissim. My master, my father, my teacher, my rabbi told me explicitly, that in this way he deviated from custom, and he did not explain to me why. It's a pity I did not ask him."[245]

242. Interview conducted by her granddaughter Lirit Zindani of Rehovot.

243. The meeting with Mori Se'īd Ṣabari took place in Monsey, New York, in Nov 2010. On the Mori Se'īd family, see below, part 3, chap. 7, sect. 4.

244. R. Yiṣḥaq Raṣabi, *"Im mutar li-kro la-isha bi-shemah," Bet Hillel* 5 (2001): 46.

245. In a personal correspondence dated 22 Apr 2010.

ואלו הן צואות ר׳ יהודה החסיד

The ethical will of Rabbi Yehudah Heḥasid in a Yemenite manuscript. Tiklal, MS Jerusalem, Jewish National and University Library, Manuscript Department, 4⁰ 949

The ethical will of Rabbi Yehudah Heḥasid (continued)

בשם רחמן

בשם אשר לו הגדולה ומרומם על כל ברכה ותהלה בשעה מעולה

ועונה מהוללה ויד ושם ותהלה ודיצה וצהלה וחן וחסד

וחמלה ומלוי כל שאלה לחתן ולכלה ולכל

הקהלה הנקהלה זרע ישראל הסגלה ישישו וישמחו וכששון

יפריחו וכבשם יפיחו ויבנו ויצליחו כויבנו

ויצליחו מצא אשה מצא טוב ויפק רצון מה׳ בית והון נחלת אבות ומה׳ אשה משכלת

The ketubbah of Rabbi Aharon ben Sālem Hakohen – Ṣan'a 1863

CHAPTER THREE

PERSONAL NAMES AND THEIR MEANING

In 1910, Yom Tov Tzemach, visiting Yemen on behalf of Alliance Israélite Universelle, reported on naming customs in Yemen:

> Our brethren in Yemen do not have family names at all. The son is also called by his father's personal name ... and the names take many forms. Especially in the northern cities, they use Hebrew names, such as Aḥiya, Avshalom, Elisha', Ḥilkiya, Yotam, Matanya, Mevorer, Nathan, Neḥemyah, and so on. In the south, they are called by Arabic names: 'Awwad, 'Ashūra, Shūkr, Kāmil, Jāmīl, Ghīyat, Ḥassan, Hebe, Ma'ūḍa, Manṣūr, and so on. There are some, though few, women with biblical names. They are called Esther, Hannah, Leah, Miryam, Sarah, Simḥah, Yedidah, and that is all.[1] Conversely, Arabic names are numerous, while others are also heartwarming: 'Āfīyah, 'Adaniyah, Bedūr, Ghaneh, Lūlūwah, Ni'meh, Nadrah, Rūmiyah, Tūrkiyyah, Zihrah, and so on.[2]

According to Yom Tov Tzemach most Yemenite Jews did not have family names.[3] He wrote "the son is also called by his father's personal name," meaning that for the identification of the son his father's name is added to his. An example is Slaymān Ya'īsh, his personal name being Slaymān and that of his father Ya'īsh. Tzemach's comment was correct

1. Yom Tov Ṣemach was not precise. For additional names, see below in the following section.
2. Abraham Elmaleh, *Massa Yom Tov Ṣemaḥ*, pp. 313–14. See also Yehudah Ratzaby, *Be-Ma'agalot Teiman* (Tel Aviv, 1948), p. 41. On the translation and meaning of the Arabic women's names, see below in the next section.
3. On this matter, see his statements below in part 2, chap. 2, sect. 2.

that in Jewish communities in the north many of the men's names came from Jewish sources, while in the south large numbers of men bore Arabic names. Men's names in the Jewish communities in the center of Yemen reflected a middle ground.

R. Yaacov Sappir, who visited Yemen in 1859, wrote about the custom of Yemenite Jews in writing personal names in divorce documents:

> I did not see nor find that they write *ha-mekhuneh* (who is designated as) or *de-mitqare* (who is called [in addition to the given name]), only by the name they now use for him in the city, not the birth name,[4] and not the name for calling him up to the Torah. For instance, the birth name is "Avraham" while they call him Ibrāhām[5] (as in Arabic) and that is what they write. For the birth name Zekharyah, they always call "Yiḥye'," and they write Aharon as "Hārūn," Moshe as "Mūsah,"[6] Sa'adyah as "Se'īd." And as for women's names, most are in Arabic: "Naḍrah" is the moon, Nazmah[7]—star, Lūlu—pearl, Ḥusaynah—pretty, Ḥamāmah—dove (Yonah).[8]

R. Sappir was imprecise since he thought that in Yemen, too, as in Ashkenaz, the birth name was given in Hebrew and by that name a man was called to the Torah, while the byname was in the local language.[9] His error apparently derived from the fact that he saw rabbis in Yemen who were called in the marketplace and daily life, as well as to the Torah, by their Arabic name, such as Ibrāhim, while in their works, letters, and so on, these sages were noted by their Hebrew name, Avraham, the same way in which other Yemenite Jews who mentioned them in writings sometimes used their Hebrew name. The actual situation was that at the circumcision ceremony they were given their Arabic name, while in their writings they indicated, as noted, their Hebrew name. Among Yemenite Jews, the custom was that whoever was given a Hebrew

4. The name given close to the time birth.
5. It should be written as Ibrāhim.
6. It should be written as Mūsā or Mūsi'. Elsewhere in his book, R. Sappir wrote Mūsā (*Even Sappir*), p. 99a. For citation of his statements, see in the ensuing in this section.
7. Najmah, which means "star." See section 2 below, Women's Names.
8. Sappir, *Even Sappir*, p. 63a. R. Shalom 'Uzayri, who came to Israel from the Manākhe community in central Yemen, alluded also to the combination Yona-Ḥamāmah "Born was my dove, my perfect one whose Arabic name is Ḥamāmah" (R. Shalom 'Uzayri, *Sefer Iqvei Shalom*, ed. by author's family ([Tel Aviv], 2006), p. 24).
9. See also part 3, chap. 6, sect. 3.

name at circumcision also kept that name for daily use. For example, R. Moshe Yiṣḥaq Halewi, a twentieth-century Yemenite rabbi and son of the chief rabbi, R. Yiḥye' Yiṣḥaq Halewi, even though he was named Moshe after his grandfather Mūsa (Heb. Moshe) Yiṣḥaq Halewi, was given the Hebrew name at his circumcision and was always called Moshe and not Mūsa. R. Shelomo Meghori of the Ṣan'a community was called at circumcision by the name Shelomo, and that was his name in daily life, too, and not the Arabic name Sūleyman. We find this phenomenon also in the registry notebook of the emissary Shelomo Naddāf. In the Dhamār community were two brothers, Shelomo and Slayman, which were certainly the appellations given to them at circumcision. With women as well, some were called by a Hebrew name in Yemen, which was the name always used in daily life. For example, Sarah the wife of R. Avraham of the Kawkabān[10] community was never known in Yemen by the Arabic name Zihrah, the equivalent to Sarah, the name she used after her immigration to Israel.[11]

Similarly, R. Sappir was not quite correct when he wrote "For the birth name Zekharyah, they always call "Yiḥye'"; rather, as noted, the birth name was Yiḥye' and not everyone translated it to Zekharyah like the other names he mentioned, though some did translate the name Yiḥye' as Ḥayim.[12] When discussing the legend about the initial settling of the Jews in Yemen, R. Sappir wrote:

> And most of the names are for those early princes who brought them to this land (as I have said). There is no home without the name Yiḥye' (which is Zekharyah in Hebrew); Se'īd (Sa'adyah); 'Awwād (Ovadyah)[13]—for they pronounce the *ṣade* with a dot above it as a half *dal*, as in Arabic); Yosef; Harūn; Mūsa'; Dāhūd (David);[14] Sālem (Shalom); Slaymān (Shelomo). Yet, these are the majority of their names, and they refer to the tribe of Judah.[15]

Most of the men's names were from Hebrew sources, yet in daily life they were called by an Arabic name. In contrast, the overwhelming

10. R. Itamar Haim Kohen of Bnei Brak, who is their descendant.
11. In Yemen, it was unaccepted for Zihrah to be translated as Sarah.
12. For a discussion of the names Yiḥye', Zekharyah, and Ḥayim, see below chap. 4, sect. 2–3.
13. On the translation of the name 'Awad, see below, part 1, chap. 4, sect. 1.
14. Should be Da'ūd.
15. Sappir, *Even Sappir*, p. 99a. See also Erich Brauer, *Ethnologie der Jemenitischen Juden* (Heidelberg, 1934), pp. 196–99.

majority of women's names were taken from Arabic sources.[16] Yehudah Ratzaby wrote:

> The decisive majority of the men's names common among Yemenite Jews are biblical Hebrew ones, with a minority being Arabic. In contrast, the women's names, in previous generations, were almost all Arabic, and they were borrowed from the spheres of plants and animals, stars and Zodiac signs, precious gems and objects. Even the Arabic names common among them, both for men and for women, were rarely used by Arabs.[17]

R. Shalom Gamliel wrote about men's names in Yemen:

> Jews were never called by personal names such as 'Ali, Hussein, Muḥammad, or Maḥmud. There were, however, a few called by the name Ḥasan. In southern Yemen or the city Ṣa'dah, there was one fellow named Abdallah. The Muslims, in contrast, do use the names Yiḥye' [and] Ṣāliḥ, and among the Bedouins one also finds Sālem, which are among the Jewish names.[18] But they do not have the names Neḥemyah, Shemaryah, Zekharyah, Yishayah, and the like. These are names specific to Jews, like Muḥammad and 'Ali in Muslim families.[19]

R. Pinḥas Qoraḥ wrote: "They did not use Arabic names, but there were a number of names used by both the Jews and the Arabs, such as Ṣāliḥ, Yiḥye', Ḥasan, Mūsa, and the like. And in certain districts there was greater frequency of shared names, even rare ones."[20]

In his study on personal names in Yemen in the Himyarite period (third–fifth centuries), Hartwig Derenboug relied upon the archaeological findings of Joseph Halevy, who visited Yemen in the second half of the nineteenth century. He noted that the findings he examined included testimony that among the personal names of the non-Jewish population were biblical names and he presents a list. This reflects the influence of the Jews in Yemen during the Himyarite period.[21]

A similar phenomenon can be discerned in earlier times and in other places. When Abba Bendavid examined the names on the graves at

16. See above the statements by R. Yaacov Sappir and Yom Tov Tzemach.
17. Yehudah Ratzaby, *Be-Ma'agalot Teiman* (Tel Aviv, 1948), p. 41.
18. That is, names used jointly by Arabs and Jews.
19. Shalom Gamliel, *Pequdei Teiman: Mas he-Hasut be-Teiman* (Jerusalem, 1982).
20. In a personal correspondence dated April 2010.
21. H. Derenbourg, "Les noms de personnes dans l'Ancient testament et dans les inscriptions himyarites," *Revue des études juives*, 1 (1880): 57–60.

Bet Shearim, which date to the first centuries of the Christian era, he wrote: "Yet, it is amazing that almost all the men's names are Hebrew, and precisely the women's names are not Hebrew, but rather from Greek or Latin. And at this time, there is no explanation for that."[22] S. D. Goitein came to a similar conclusion when reviewing names from the Cairo Geniza. He found a large, varied range of women's names and a decided lack of biblical and Hebrew ones; he commented that he had found a similar phenomenon among Jewish women in Yemen.[23] As for women's names in the Cairo Geniza, with reference to what was customary in Yemen, Goitein wrote:

> As for women, a difference existed between Egypt and Ereṣ Israel, Tunisia, Spain, and the countries of Christian Europe. In Egypt I did not find even one biblical name among the many hundreds of women's names, while in the other countries they did appear. As we know, also among the Yemenites, "the most authentic of all Jews," it was not customary to give girls biblical names. Even the pious, educated women—and there were such in the Geniza period ... called their daughters by Arab names ...[24]

Regarding women's names, some names common among the Jewish population were identical to those used by the general population; for example, the names Jamālah, Jamīlah, Ghuṣnah, Ḥalīmah, Ni'meh, Fuḍah. Still, there were names given among the Muslims that found almost no echo in the Jewish community. Y. Ratzaby noted names common to the Muslims in Yemen that were not used by the Jews: 'Atīqah, Ṣabaḥiyah, Amnah, Fātmah.[25] The name 'Atīqah does occur in a document from 1847[26] and the name Amnah was found in the village of Zāwiyat Sha'bān in northern Yemen,[27] but it is reasonable to assume that these were the exceptions.

22. Abba Bendavid, *"Al Sifrei Atiqot, Bet Shearim," Leshonenu La'am,* 23 (1972): 14–20.
23. Shlomo Dov Goitein, *A Mediterranean Society*, vol. 3 (Berkeley, , 1978), pp. 314–15.
24. Shelomo Dov Goitein, *Sidrei Ḥinnukh bi-Ymei ha-Ge'onim u-Bet ha-Rambam: Meqorot Ḥadashim min ha-Geniza* (Jerusalem, 1962), p. 26. On biblical names for women in the other eastern countries, see Mas'ud Ben Shimon, *Shem Hadash* (Jerusalem, 1991). For a list of women's names among the Libyan Jewish community, see Mordechai Hakohen, *Higgid Mordekhai* (Jerusalem, 1979), pp. 224–31.
25. Ratzaby, *Be-Ma'agalot Teiman*, p. 41 n. 150.
26. Nissim Binyamin Gamlieli, *Teiman bi-Te'udot*, vol. 2 (Ramleh, 2009), p. 152, Doc. 102.
27. One of the daughters of Mori Se'īd Kohen. R. Aharon Ben David, *Sefer ha-Ma'asim: Ma'asim me-Hayyei Yehudei Ṣefon Teiman*, vol. 1 (Qiryat Eqron, 2010), p. 408.

Apparently, the paucity of names for women from Jewish sources derives from the fact that they were not exposed to these names. Yemenite females were not present at nor participants in synagogue rituals, whereas men were called to the Torah by the names they were given at circumcision, by Hebrew names as well as in their Arabic equivalent.[28] Biblical names were not part of the consciousness of many women in Yemen, so perhaps few women in the family preferred such a name and favored familiar, clearly understood ones. Nissim Binyamin Gamlieli of Ramleh related that his niece gave birth to a girl who was called Yael by Mori Seʻīd in line with his knowledge of numerology. The child's paternal grandmother opposed the name because it was unfamiliar and she wanted an Arabic name. The rabbi sympathized with her feelings and suggested the name Shūmays, meaning small sun. As an adult, the woman was once more called Yael.

Following are the main details of the personal names commonly used by Yemenite Jews. For some of the names, pronunciations differ slightly in various places in Yemen. For example, for certain names ending in *ṣere* (*e*), the vowel is pronounced as *pataḥ* (*a*). For the Arabic names an explanation is provided when known.[29] Not included in the list are names of new immigrants or names from Aden whose source is outside of Yemen.

1. MEN'S NAMES

Presented here are the most-common names, in descending order of frequency. The majority is from written sources and was collected from *ketubbot*, *gittin*, and R. Shelomo Naddāf's *shadarut* (rabbinic emissary) notebook. The time period for this data is the eighteenth and nineteenth centuries and the first half of the twentieth.

Following are the quantitative findings for ten men's names as found in written sources, and they constitute 77.8% of all the names:[30] Yiḥye', 15.63%; Sālem (in Hebrew: Shalem, commonly called Shalom),

28. Cf. Leah Bornstein-Makovetsky, *"Ha-Shemot ha-Peratiyyim shel Yehudei Saloniki be-Dorot ha-Aharonim al pi Reshimot Gittin, Halitsut u-Matsevot,"* in *These Are the Names: Studies in Jewish Onomastics*, vol. 4, ed. A. Demsky (Ramat Gan, 2004), p. 31.

29. The following helped in explicating the Arabic names: older immigrants from Yemen; Na'Ama Bat Ami of Petah Tikva; Mas'ud Ben Shimon, *Shem Hadash* (Jerusalem, 1991); *Al-Munjid* Arabic Dictionary (Beirut, 1984).

30. For specifications of the men's names frequency, see below chapter 6.

13.11%; Yosef, 9.42%; Se'īd, 9.29%; Slaymān (in Hebrew: Shelomo), 7.94%; Avraham (including Ibrāhim in Arabic in all its orthographic forms), 5.93%; Da'ūd (in Hebrew: David), 4.91%; Mūsa (in Hebrew: Moshe), 4.51%; Ḥayim, 3.76%; Hārūn (in Hebrew: Aharon), 3.30%.

The names from common, widespread Jewish sources are Aharon, Avraham, Binyamin, David, Levi, Me'ir, Menaḥem, Moshe, Naḥum, Pinḥas, Shelomo, Shemu'el, Shim'on, Ya'aqov, Yehudah, Yisra'el, Yiṣḥaq, Yosef.

Of note is that of the names coming from Jewish sources, some were used only in Hebrew, such as, Binyamin, Yisra'el, Levi, Me'ir, Menaḥem, Pinḥas, Shemu'el, Shim'on.

Some were generally not used in their Hebrew form but in their Arabic form. Here are the names and their orthographic manifestations or their common vocalization: Aharon – Hārūn, Harūn; Avraham – Avraham, Ibrāhim, Ibrāhīm; David – Dāwid, Dawīd; Moshe – Moshe, Mūsa', Musī; Naḥum – Naḥum, Nāḥūm; Sa'adyah – Se'īd; Shalom – Shalom, Sālem; Shelomo – Shelomo, Slaymān Ya'aqov – Ya'aqūb; Yehudah – Yehudah, Yehuda', Yuda'; Yiḥye' – Yiḥye', Ḥayim, Zekharyah; Yiṣḥaq – Yiṣḥāq; Yūda'; Yosef – Yusef.

It is important to understand that the link between the Arabic name used in daily life and its Hebrew "twin," that is the Hebrew name with a similar sound, was understood only by literate people, and they were the ones who sometimes translated Se'īd as Sa'adyah and so on. The simple folk, in contrast, when they gave their son the name Se'īd upon circumcision were not referring to the sage called Sa'adyah in the past and with the name Yiḥye' they did not mean Zekharyah; the same applied to the name Sālem.

A review of the common Hebrew names shows that all of them derive from the biblical text and almost totally absent in the corpus of names are those that became popular in the Midrash or Talmud, such as Hillel or Shamai.

Names from Arabic Sources

The common Arabic names are Yiḥye', Sālem, Se'īd, Ḥasan, Ṣāliḥ,[31] Manṣūr, 'Awād. In many instances the vocalized endings of the names differed in pronunciation in the various regions of Yemen. Below em-

31. R. Yitshaq Raṣabi wrote to me about the name Ṣāliḥ in a personal correspondence dated 22 Apr 2010:

> It is amazing that in our environment [meaning the community of Raṣāba, Yemen], the name Ṣāliḥ (the grandfather of the Mahariṣ OBM and after him all

phatics are marked with a dot below the letter (customarily in Yemen written above the Hebrew letter being used for the Arabic).

'Abdallah:	In Hebrew, Ovadyah.[32]
Abū S'ūd:	In Hebrew Avigad.[33] Father of joy or father of good luck.
Aburus:	Father of the heads [leaders]. Head in Arabic *ra's*, pl. *rus*.
Aḥsan:	Good.
'Amrān:	In Hebrew, Amram.
'Awād:	A term for recompense, substitute, compensation, usually translated as Ovadyah.
'Awjān:	Crooked or twisted.
Hibe:	Gift.
Jabīr:	Valiant, brave, from the Arabic root *j-b-r*.
Jamīl:	Handsome.
Jūm'ān:	Friday is called *jum'ah*. Perhaps the name comes from the word *jama'a*, meaning to gather, to collect.[34]
Ḥamāmī:	Dove. Rare name, found in northern Yemen.
Ḥasan:	Semantic sphere of good or beauty, usually translated as Yefet.[35]
'Īḍa':	A term for help.[36]

his family) was not considered a Jewish name at all. The proof—my father, *mmv"r*, OBM, told me that when the Jewish group first settled in the region they did not have a *shoḥet* (ritual slaughterer) among them, and they would send their chickens to be slaughtered by a *shoḥet* in the city of Ma'bar, a walking distance of a few hours. Once they sent a child with a chicken, and when he soon returned with the slaughtered chicken, his father asked him, "How did you succeed so quickly, my son?" (Gen. 27:20). He replied, "On the way I met a *shoḥet* called Mori Ṣāliḥ, and he slaughtered it for me, so I came right back." The local people came to the conclusion that this man was an Arab who wanted to play a joke, for no Jews has such a name, and they threw away the chicken. From them on, they decided to try to make sure that there was a *shoḥet* from among the community members themselves, and so it was.

32. On this name, see below chap. 5, sect. 2.
33. On this name and its translation, see below chap. 4, sect. 1.
34. In the singular *jum'ah* and with the suffix *–an* it expresses the dual, like *walad* (boy), singular, and two boys—*waldān*.
35. On this name and its translation, see below chap. 4, sect. 1.
36. Derived from the Yemenite sentence *"Alla ya'awaḍaq,"* meaning "God will help you."

Khurṣān: Jewel. In Arabic *khurṣ*, pl. *khurṣān*, meaning a ring of silver or gold.

Maḍmūn: From a term for 'guarded', usually translated as Shemaryah.[37]

Maḥfūḍ: Guarded. Usually translated as Shemaryah.

Manṣūr: Saved.

Mas'ūd: Lucky, happy.

Maṭrūd: Expelled, exiled.[38]

Ma'ūḍa: Usually translated as Me'oded.

M'īḍ: Good compensation. Apparently derived from the name Ma'ūḍa.

Minis: Usually translated as Menashe.

Musā: In Hebrew, Moshe.

Musalim: Usually translated as Meshullam.

Raḍa': In Hebrew, Raṣon.

Rashīd: Intelligent, possessor of common sense.

Sa'ad: Happiness.

Sabtān: The root *s-b-t* means to cease work, from the word *Shabbat*.

Se'īd: Helper or fortunate. Usually translated as Sa'adyah.

Ṣālih: Successful, usually translated as Ṣadōq.

Sālem: Whole, usually translated as Shalom.[39]

Salūmi: Apparently derived from the name Sālem, the term of endearment Salūmi, in translation Shelomi.[40]

37. The *nagid* of the Jews of Yemen at the beginning of the thirteenth century, Maḍmūn ben David, called himself Shemaryahu in Hebrew. Prof. Shlomo Dov Goitein wrote about this Maḍmūn: "'Maḍmūn' means only 'guarded', and perhaps for contacts with Mediterranean Jews, among whom the name Maḍmūn was not used, the *nagid* called himself 'Shemaryah'" (Shlomo Dov Goitein and Mordechai Akiva Friedman, *Maḍmun Nagid of Yemen and the India Trade – Cairo Geniza Documents, India Book II* [Jerusalem, 2010]).

38. Haim Ḥibshush, who accompanied the scholar Joseph Halevy, told of the reception given for them in Wādi Najrān in northern Yemen, and noted about the names of his hosts Mori *Maṭrūd* and Mori *Me'īd*, who is mentioned regarding "after we had conversed a bit, Mori *Maṭrūd* asked to return to his home and he took us with him. But I wished to stay with Mori *Me'īd*—since the name Me'īd (good recompense) is a sign for a blessing, while the name *Maṭrūd* (one who is bothered) is the sign for a curse." Haim Ḥibshush, *Mas'ot Ḥibshush* (Tel Aviv, 1939), p. 144.

39. On this name and its translation, see below this part, chap. 4, section 1.

40. In a personal correspondence dated 22 Apr 2010, R. Yitshaq Rasabi wrote 22 Apr

Shukr:	Translation as thanks or gratitude. It is usually translated as Yehudah, following its meaning,[41] though some translate it as Yissachar according to its letters.
Slaymān:	In Hebrew, Shelomo.
'Ūḍa':	Compensation; substitute.
Wahab:	Gift, usually translated as Nathan.
Yiḥye':	Life, usually translated as Zekharyah.[42]
Ya'īsh:	Life.
Zāhir:	Shining, beaming.

2. WOMEN'S NAMES

Listed here are female names in descending frequency. Some were taken from written sources—*ketubbot, gittin, bet din* registries in Ṣan'a, and a list of names of Jews in northern Yemen. The other names are from oral sources and were collected from questionnaires I distributed among people coming from different districts of Yemen.

Below are the quantitative findings of the ten women's name taken from written sources, and they constitute 55.28% of all the names:[43] Zihrah, 9.56%; Ḥamāmah, 7.38%; Sa'dah, 5.72%; Rūmiyah, 5.35%; Lūlūwah, 4.76%; Badrah, 4.65%; Sham'ah, 4.61%; Naḍrah, 4.5%; Se'īdah, 4.47%; Salāmeh, 4.25%.

Names from Jewish Sources

Esther, Berakhah, Ḥannah, Yedidah, Leah, Miryam, Rivqah, Raḥel, Simḥah, Sarah. Biblical names are not common. Names first mentioned in the Midrash and Talmud, such as Beruria, are almost completely absent.

Names from Arabic Sources

From an examination of the common names for women we learn that most of them were from an Arabic source. In many instances, the vocalic endings of the names differed in pronunciation in the various

2010: "Someone in our city was named Salūmi, my father's friend, and he told me his name was Sālem, and he was nicknamed Salūmi because they liked him so much."

41. See Joseph Tobi, *"Tirgumei Shemot Etsem Peratiyyim be-Tirgumei ha-Miqra ha-Arabiyyim–ha-Yehudiyyim mi-Ymei ha-Beinayim,"* in A. Demsky (ed.), *These Are the Names: : Studies in Jewish Onomastics*, vol. 3, Ramat Gan 2002, pp. 79–84

42. On this name and its translation, see below part 1, chap. 4, sect. 1.

43. For a specification of the frequencies of women's names, see below, part 1, chap. 6.

regions of Yemen. Here emphatics are marked with a dot below (customarily in Yemenite texts above the Hebrew letter being used for the Arabic).

'Adhbah: Decorative fringes descending from a hat downwards. Also sweet, pure water.

'Adīnah: Delicate.

'Āfīyah: Health.

Amīrah: Princess.

Badrah, Bedūr: The shape of the crescent of the moon, symbolizing light and beauty.

Baghlah: A female mule, symbolizing strength and health.

Banayyah: Daughter, girl.

Bint: Daughter, girl.

Bardaqūshah An aromatic plant.

Barūd: A gentle breeze, creating a pleasant atmosphere.

Faqha': A good thing that a person wants for herself as a luxury.

Farḥah: Happiness.

Fār'ah: A kind of spice, resin, i.e., incense that was burned against the evil eye.

Fāyiz: Victorious woman.

Fāyiq, Fayiqah: An animal from the ibex family. Perhaps it is an expression of strength, greatness, and beauty.

Fuḍah: Silver.

Funūn: A thing important and pleasant to a person, perhaps related to *fannan*, meaning excellent.

Ghāliyyah: Dear, precious.

Ghane', Ghaniyyah: Means singing as well as wealth; rich in spirit, generous. The name is common in women's poetry in Yemen. A Yemenite proverb states: "I lack nothing [*ghaniyyah*] from my husband and yet need a gift from my family."

Gharsah: Planting, a seedling.

Ghazāl, Ghazālah, Ghūzlān: Gazelle, a roe deer, also fresh and soft. The name appears often in Yemenite women's poetry.

Ghaziyyah: A beautiful woman taken captive; from the word Arabic *ghazu*, to raid.

Ghaydah: Beautiful.

Ghuṣn, Ghuṣūn, Ghuṣnah: A shoot sprouting from a tree trunk, symbolizing beauty, height, and strength. The name is common in Yemenite women's poetry. Compare this to Isaiah 11:1: "But a shoot shall grow out of the stump of Jesse, a twig shall sprout from his stock."

Dirhūmah: From the silver coin *dirham*.

Ḍobyah: A gazelle; expression for agility and grace.

Ḥabībah, Ḥabūbah: Beloved, pleasant.

Hādiyah: Quiet, docile.

Hadiyyah: Gift.

Ḥalawah: Sweetness.

Ḥalīmah: Wise, from the Arabic *ḥalim* "wise," "discerning."

Ḥāliyah: Pretty, sweet.

Ḥamāmah: Dove (after Song of Songs 5:2: "my faultless dove").

Ḥanūn, Ḥanūnah: Translation, merciful, from the expression *ḥanun ve-raḥum* ("gracious and merciful").

Hawīdah: Perfect, whole.

Hīnd, Hīndah: India, perhaps for the beautiful textiles imported from India.

Ḥūmḥūm: An aromatic bush with a beautiful flower. A certain genus of this bush is characterized by flowers with brown corolla and is called basil. The Yemenite Jews customarily recite over it the benediction for fragrant spices on various occasions, among them *havdala* and circumcision.

'Ibūdah: Alluding to divine service.

Jehari: Sparkling, illuminating; the word means a jewel.

Jamālah: Generous.

Jamīlah: Beautiful, charming.

Kādhiyyah: Fragrant, like the name of a fragrant bush used to give cloth a fragrance. It is mentioned in Yemenite women's poetry; it is an image for all pleasant and fragrant objects

Kāmlah: Perfect. The Arabic saying is *kamal wa-jamal,* meaning "perfect and pretty."

Kūdmah, Kūdmi: Tree trunk, or cheap, dark bread.

Khaḍra': Green tone, fresh, beauty, like a green field or green flower. Not white, not black.

Khūḍrah: Vegetables; a general name for various vegetables served at dinner.

Lawzah: Almond tree.

Layla: Night.

Lūlūwah, Lūlū: A precious stone or pearl, *lūlūwa* means one pearl; *lūlū* for a string of pearls.

Mlāḥ: Pleasant.

Malūk, Malūkah: Royal.

Mas'ūdah: Happy, lucky.

Mirjān: Good. An oyster's pearl, coral.

Mūhrah: Mare in Arabic. The name expresses nobility, agility, experience, or training.

Naḍrah: The moon; finding grace in the eyes of all her beholders.

Nafīsah: Valuable, like the expression *sekhiyyat ḥemda*, based on Isa. 2:16.

Najmah: Star.

Nakhlah: Palm or date tree.

Na'n'ah: The mint plant.

Ni'meh: In the sense of the phrase *ni'ma allah,* meaning the "goodness of God." Apparently the name expresses a good deed, such as "do anything good or bad" (Num. 24:13). Perhaps the name is meant to indicate a trait: good, demure, generous, easy-going.

Nis'ah: Braided leather straps used for various purposes. The name expresses strength, flexibility, and health.

Nūr, Nūrah: Light, radiance, from the Arabic *nur*.

Qadriyyah: A name for someone born during the night of *Shavu'ot* (Pentecost) or *Hosha'na Rabba*, nights that were called by Yemenite Jews *leilat al-Qadar,*[44] "the night of the *Qadar*," which means "the night of fate."

Qamar: The moon. Some used this name for a girl born when the moon was prominent and its light shining in the sky.

Qūmaysh: A flowery cloth.

Qumri: Animal from the ibex family. The name also means moon.

Qurṭ: A piece of jewelry worn on the forehead.

44. In the Muslim faith, *leilat al-Qadr* is the night in which the prophet Muhammad received the Quran.

Raḍa': Good will. The name was usually given to boys in Yemen; its use for a female originated in the Ḥabbān community.

Rashūshah: A vessel for spices from which one sprinkles rosewater on guests.

Rizqah: Wealth. Good livelihood.

Rūmah, Rūmiyah: Light and beautiful, and perhaps based on the noun *Rūm*, which is the term for the Turkish sultanate in the Byzantine Empire. The name expressed whiteness and beauty such as those of the Turks. Some believe the term derives from the name of a beautiful flowering aromatic plant from the basil family, called *Rūmi* in Arabic.[45]

Sa'dah, Se'īdah, Sa'diyyah: Happy, fortunate.

Ṣādqah: Real.

Saghīrah: Petite and cute.

Salamah: After the biblical name Shulamith (Song of Songs 7:1), meaning wholesomeness and well-being.

Ṣālhah: Successful, good, upright; something successfully repaired.

Sālmah: Complete. Compare to the masculine name Sālem, the translation of Shelomo.

Salwa': Salvation and joy.

Ṣan'a': The capital city Ṣan'a.

Ṣān'ah: Weaver; in Arabic *ṣāni'a,* a weaver.

Shadhrah: A grain of silver or gold;[46] also a piece of jewelry made of precious metal, such as gold or silver, shaped like a delicate flower.

Sham'ah: Candle wax. An expression for white tone and beauty, like the white color of candle wax.

Shams, Shamsiyyah, Shūmays: Sun, little sun. According to Song of Songs 6:10: "beautiful as the moon, radiant as the sun."

Shudhiyyah: A beautiful flower.

Shūmayyah: Fragrant.

45. On the name Rūmiyah, see the comment by R. Yosef Qāfiḥ, part 3, chap. 1, sect. 3.

46. In a different printing of the book *Shem Ḥadash*, in 1991, R. Yosef Qāfiḥ made a note in the margins and wrote next to this name, "It means a grain of silver or gold. It is written as follows (شذرة)." Ben Shimon, *Shem Ḥadash*, p. 256.

Ṣīniyyah: A decorated porcelain vessel used for drinking, imported from China; considered beautiful because of its luster.

Sūkarah: Sweet, from the word *sukkar*, sugar.

Sūmbūlah: Ear of sorghum, a type of grain.

Se'ūd: Happiness, in Arabic.

Sūwādah: Black. Arabic *sawd*. After Song of Songs 1:5: "I am dark, but comely."

Ṭalbah, Ṭalūb: Wish. Apparently an expression meaning that with this daughter a wish has been fulfilled.

Tamniyyah: A wish, valuable. An expression of yearning for a precious item.

Tankah: Literally, tin. Here in the sense of chest full of gold. There is an expression among Yemenite women "a chest of gold."

Ṭaybah: Good.

Thrayya': The Pleiades, after Job 9:9: "Who made the Bear, Orion, and Pleiades."

Tiranjah: Citron. Fair and fragrant like an *etrog* (citron).

Tūrkiyyah: Expressing the light coloring and beauty as those of the Turks.

Wardah, Wardiyyah: Rose, lily (based upon Song of Songs 2:2: "Like a lily among thorns, so is my darling among the maidens").

Waznah: Level-headed, wise, reasonable. From the Arabic word *wazn*, meaning a balance for weighing.

Yaman: The Arabic name for Yemen.

Zabībah: Small and sweet. From the Arabic word *zabib* meaning raisins.

Zannah: An elegant outer garment, called *'antari* in Ṣan'a.

Zar'ah: From the Hebrew word *zera'* (seed) or *zeri'a* (sowing).

Zihrah: The planet Venus.[47]

47. Mahariṣ, *Tiklal Eṣ Ḥayim,* 4 (Jerusalem, 1971), p. 223a: "And it is called Noga [Venus] for its splendor and light, as it says 'and gives off rays on every side' (Hab. 3:4) and is called in Arabic *al-zahra.* "

For the women's names Wālah,[48] 'Akah,[49] and Fiknah, I found no explanation. Concerning Fiknah, Gamliel Avivi, who emigrated from Amlaḥ in northern Yemen, told me that one of the daughters of his neighbor in Yemen, who was a sheikh, was called Fiknah, and as a sign of appreciation to his good neighbor, he, too, gave his daughter this name. After her *aliyah*, her name was changed to Penina, which sounds similar to her Arabic name.[50]

2.1 Classifying Women's Names According to Various Categories

S. D. Goitein noted that women's names in the Cairo Geniza expressed a desire for a long life of joy, happiness, and satisfaction.[51] For the Yemenite Jews, as well, names expressed the heart's desires, such as health with the name 'Āfiyah, beauty with the names Rūmiyah or Tūrkiyyah, and balance with the name Waznah. At times, a name represented multiple characteristics such as the name Tiranjah. Names are listed below according to categories and their translations or approximations are given in parentheses.

Names based on flora

Bardaqūshah (a type of plant), Fār'ah (type of perfume), Gharsah (seedling), Ghuṣn/Ghuṣūn/Ghuṣnah (a tree branch), Ḥūmḥūm (a fragrant spice), Kādhiyyah (fragrant spice), Khaḍra' (beautiful like a green field or green flower), Khūḍrah (vegetables), Kūdmah/Kūdmi (tree trunk), Lawzah (almond tree); Nakhlah (palm or date tree), Na'n'ah (mint plant), Rūmah/Rūmiyah (a fragrant herb), Shūdhiyyah (flower), Sūmbūlah (sorghum), Tiranjah (citron-like), Wardah/Wardiyyah (rose, lily), Zabībah (raisin), Zar'ah (planting).

Names of Animals

Baghlah (mule), Ḍobyah (gazelle; roe), Fāyiq/Fāyiqah (from the ibex family), Ghazāl/Ghazālah/Ghūzlān (gazelle), Hamāmah (dove), Mūhrah (mare), Qumri (from the ibex family).

48. Aharon Ben David, *Bet ha-Even, Hilkhot Yehudei Ṣefon Teiman* ([Qiryat Eqron], 5768), p. 680, nos. 311–12.

49. Ovadya ('Awad) Zandani, *Yalqut Ovadya* (Tel Aviv, 1986), pp. 172–74.

50. Gamliel Avivi lives in the town Benei Ayish. The meeting with him took place on 28 Shevat 5771 (2 Feb 2011). Similarly, there is a story about the respect Yiḥye' 'Urqabi, of the Radā' community, enjoyed by naming his daughter Ghaliyah, the same name as the wife of his Muslim friend 'Ali Shubili. See Nissim Binyamin Gamliel, *Ha-Qame'a: Sippurim me-Ḥayei ha-Yehudim be-Teiman* (Ramleh, 1980), pp. 17–18.

51. Goitein, *Mediterranean Society,* vol. 3, p. 318.

Names of Precious Commodities or Objects

Dirhūmah (silver coin), Fuḍah (silver), Ghāliyyah (dear, precious), Jehari (gem), Lūlūwah/Lūlū (pearl, string of pearls), Mirjān (coral), Qurṭ (forehead pendant jewelry), Rashūshah (perfume vessel), Shadhrah (jewelry of precious metal), Ṣīniyyah (china vessel), Tankah (chest of gold), Zannah (sumptuous outer garment).

Names of Stars

Badrah/Bedūr (lunar crescent), Najmah (star), Qamar/Qumri (moon), Shams/Shamsiyyah/Shūmays (sun), Thrayya' (The Pleiades), Zihrah (Venus).

Names after Physiological Characteristics

Badrah (beauty), Baghlah (mule; a nickname for a healthy woman), Ḍobyah (agility), Ghayda' (very beautiful), Ghaziyyah (beautiful), Ghuṣn, Ghuṣūn, Ghuṣnah (tall and strong), Ḥāliyah (beautiful), Ḥisn/Ḥusaynah/Ḥasīnah (very beautiful), Jehari (sparkle and bright), Jamīlah (graceful), Kāmlah (perfect), Nis'ah (flexibility and health), Rūmah/Rūmiyah (light), Saghīrah (petite), Sham'ah (white like candle wax), Ṣīniyyah (gleaming like china), Sūwādah (black), Tiranjah (light and aromatic), Tūrkiyyah (light), Zabība (petite).

Names after character traits

'Adīnah (delicate), Berūd (pleasant), Ḍobyah (quickness), Farḥah (joy), Ghane', Ghaniyyah (rich in spirit), Ḥabībah/ Ḥabūbah (beloved), Ḥalāwah (sweetness), Ḥalīmah (discerning), Ḥanūn/Ḥanūnah (merciful), Hawīdah (perfect), Jamālah (generous), Mlāḥ (pleasant), Mirjān (good), Mūhrah (noble and agile), Ni'meh (good), Sa'dah, Se'īdah, Sa'diyyah (happy), Ṣādqah (real), Ṣālhah (good and honest), Salwa' (joy), Sūkarah (sweetness), Ṭaybah (good), Waznah (reasonable).

Place names

Hīnd/Hīndah for the name of the country India; Ṣan'a'; Tūrkiyyah; Yaman.

Names with other meanings

'Adhbah (decoration for the head), 'Āfīyah (wish for health), Amīrah (princess), Banayyah/Bint (daughter), Faqha' (a good thing), Fāyiz (victorious), Funūn (important and likeable), Hadiyyah (gift), 'Ībūda (servant of the Lord), Layla' (night), Malūk, Malūkah (regalness), Mas'ūdah (a lucky person), Naḍrah (graceful), Nafīsah (precious), Nūr/Nūrah (light), Qadriyyah (*Leilat al-Qadar* the night of fate, is the night of *Shavu'ot* (Pentecost) or *Hosha'na Rabba*), Qūmaysh (flowery cloth), Raḍa' (good will), Rizqah (wish for happiness and good livelihood), Salāmeh (Shulamit), Sālmeh (complete), Su'ud (happiness), Ṣān'ah (weaver), Shūmayyah (fragrant), Ṭalbah/Ṭalūb (fulfillment of a wish), Tamniyyah (yearnings for a precious thing).

2.2 Women's Names Typical of Certain Regions

Some names were particular to specific communities, and one may reasonably assume that they originated through contact with the local Muslim population or from sources outside of Yemen. At times they derived from local developments.

Ṣan'a:	Rashūshah, Tiranjah.
North Yemen:	'Āfīyah, Bardaqūshah, Nakhlah, Ṣan'a', Sūkarah.
Shar'ab:	Burūd, Nūrah, Sūmbūlah.
Bayḥān:[52]	Zar'ah, Ḥalīmah, Ḥusaynah, 'Ibūdah, Funūn.
Ḥabān:[53]	Ṭaybah, Nūr.

'Aden:[54] Often, special names were given, both from Jewish and other sources. From Jewish sources there are Avigail, Ahuvah, Yedidah, Alizah, Peninah. From non-Hebrew sources we find Arnaqa, Elegra, Fortuna, Gracia, Jamilah, Kati, Katina, Linda, Luna, Marta, Rachelle, Regina, Rosa, Sarina, Sultana, and Victoria. Moreover, names of endearment were common in 'Aden, such as Esteriqa or Estrine for Esther, Mary and Marima for Miryam, Ḥanni for Ḥannah, Rachelle or Ruḥ-li for Raḥel, Sarina for Sarah. Names translated from other languages were Sultana for Malkah, Fortuna for Mazal, and Roza for Shoshanah.

The uniqueness of women's names in 'Aden, including the use of terms of endearment, which was not customary in Yemen, resides in the city's contacts with the outer world. One may assume that a few of these names belonged to members of immigrant families that settled in 'Aden.

From early tombstones from 'Aden we learn that most of the names were common to those customarily used in Yemen, such as Ghazal, Ḥali' [=Ḥāliyah], Hamāmah, Ḥanūn, Ḥasīnah, Lūlū, Qmar[55] The same was true for other matters whereby in the past 'Aden was no different

52. Southeastern Yemen. Some of the names appear in the book by S. Lahav, *Qehillat Yehudei Bayḥān* (Netanya, 1996), pp. 195–99.
53. Ḥabān is in the southeastern edge of Yemen, and in the past generation, the number of its Jews came to a few hundred.
54. Aden is a coastal city in southern Yemen.
55. See Reuven Ahroni, *Yehudei 'Aden, Qehila sha-Hayta* (Tel Aviv, 1991), p. 20.

from other districts of Yemen, especially the southern one.[56] The change occurred very slowly with the British conquest of 'Aden in 1839,[57] and became stronger in the twentieth century. The leading scholar of 'Aden Jewry, Reuben Ahroni, wrote about this:

> The Europeanization process also left its impression also on the names given to Jewish girls in Aden. Until close to the end of the thirties[58] most of the parents used to give Hebrew names, mainly biblical ones, to their daughters. So, for example, the names of the grandmothers in one family were Miryam and Ḥannah, the mother's name was Mazal, and her daughters' names were Rivqah, Esther, Rahel, Sarah, and Berakhah. From the end of the thirties, parents began to adopt foreign names for their daughters, such as Violet, Mary, Adella, Lisa, Arnaka, Betty, Sarina, and the like. The same change, of course, took place with the boys' names.[59]

Since after the British occupation, the 'Aden names no longer reflect the Yemenite custom, they are not discussed in this study and not included in the lists of men's and women's names at the beginning of this section.

56. A look into the division of a legacy between two brothers in Aden from the early nineteenth century informs us of the relations between the two centers, Aden and Ṣan'a, and of the authority the rulings of the Ṣan'a religious court had over the Aden Jews. See Aharon Gaimani, "Between the Aden and Sana Rabbinical Courts: On a Nineteenth Century Inheritance Dispute," in H. Gamoran (ed.), *Jewish Law Association Studies XIV* (Binghamton, N.Y., 2004).
57. When the British occupied Aden, it had some 600 residents of whom some 250 were Jews. The British occupation contributed to significant development of the town. In 1860 its population, including army members, came to 21,000. The Jewish community numbered about 1,500. See Ahroni, *Yehudei 'Aden*, p. 67. Ṣan'a had the largest Jewish community in Yemen. In the nineteenth century it encompassed 6,000 people. The traveler to Yemen, R. Yaacov Sappir, who visited Ṣan'a, estimated the number of Jews there in 1859 as 6,000 *batim*. "*Batim*" (literally houses) means "persons." See his book *Even Sappir*, p. 91a.
58. Referring to the 1930s. He further wrote in a note that prior to the 1930s, many of the names were Arab, such as Ḥamāmah, Salamah, and so on. See Ahroni, *Yehudei 'Aden*, p. 409 n. 47.
59. Ahroni, ibid., pp. 409–10.

3. SPECIAL NAMES

3.1 Ezra

The name Ezra alludes to Ezra the Scribe, the spiritual leader of Judea in the fifth century BCE. R. Yaacov Sappir, who visited Yemen in 1859, wrote down a tradition he heard from Yemenite Jews, namely, that they refrained from giving the name Ezra because of a dispute that had taken place between Ezra the Scribe and the Jews of Yemen. A well-known Yemenite legend ascribes the beginning of the exile of the Jews to Yemen to the time when the First Temple was still standing. This legend was cited by the sixteenth-century R. Shelomo 'Adani[60] and by R. Yiḥye' Ṣāliḥ (Mahariṣ), who lived in the eighteenth century.[61] This legend was cited by R. Yaacov Sappir with additions:

> And these are the statements I collected this time, traditions and legends, stories of Jews living in Ṣan'a, a city and mother in the land of Yemen, may the Supreme establish it. They have a tradition that there forebears came to dwell in this land 42 years before the destruction of the First Temple ... and when Ezra came up to the Land [of Israel] from Babylonia and sent letters to all Jews to go up with him, he also sent [it] to them, and they did not come. So Ezra himself came, and they did not agree to go up with him, saying from the outset that this was not total redemption, for the time for it had not come, and they will be exiled a second time from Jerusalem, so why go up before the true time of redemption has come.
>
> Even the leading Kohen, namely, Ezra, was angry at them, and he ostracized them with a severe ban. And they likewise put the "blessing" on him that he not be buried in Israel, and the curses of both came to pass. They do not have serenity and rest. It is determined that their serenity and success is not theirs forever, and a few wealthy noblemen and princes are found among them in every generation, while the rest of them do not pass it on to their children and their greatness to their sons after them, even in their lifetimes. Their honor is ephemeral and nothing remains in their possession. He, too, was not buried in the Holy Land and his place of rest was in the area of Basra. To this day they hate him and do not give his name. In the entire country, there

60. R. Shelomo 'Adani's family immigrated to Ereṣ Israel from Ṣan'a in 1571, when R. Shelomo was four years old. His statements were printed in the introduction to his commentary on the Mishnah, *Melekhet Shelomo*. This introduction was printed in the prefaces to part one of the Mishnah. See Aharon Gaimani, *Temurot*, pp. 15, 66–67.

61. See his *Megillat Teiman*, printed in Tobi's *'Iyyunim bi-Mgillat Teiman* (Jerusalem, 1986), pp. 32–33.

> is not found one man whose name is Ezra (only one child of R. Shemu'el 'Arūsi in the city of Shibām, a seven-year-old whom they called Ezra, for a miracle occurred to him prior to his birth and they called him Ezra, since God helped him, and he is the only one, none is second to him), while in Babylonia and Basra and their districts most of the names Ezra are after him.[62]

Yehudah Ratzaby extensively discussed the widespread legend about Ezra the Scribe and the Jews of Yemen, paying attention to the additions to this tale and found only in the statements of R. Sappir. He also focused on historical imprecisions in what R. Sappir wrote, such as that Ezra the Scribe came to Yemen, as well as Ezra being buried outside of Israel.[63] Ratzaby even negated the possibility that the Yemenite Jews cursed such a distinguished person as Ezra the Scribe or that Ezra ostracized the Jews of Yemen. On the claim that the Yemenite Jews hated Ezra, Ratzaby wrote that they admired Ezra the Scribe as did all Jewish communities, and he cited examples from written sources in which Yemenite men are called Ezra.[64]

On the continuation of R. Sappir, who mentioned that there was only one man in Yemen who was called Ezra, Yehudah Ratzaby wrote:

> If Yaacov Sappir found the name Ezra in only one place he visited in Yemen, this tells us nothing. Personal names are very limited in Yemen, and they are reduced to a small framework of Yiḥye', Sālem, Se'īd, Yehudah, Avraham, and so on. The name Ezra was not common in the same way that the following names are not common: Daniel, Neḥemiah, Yeḥezqel, and many other names.[65]

R. Shelomo Qoraḥ, chief rabbi of Bnei Brak, wrote in a similar vein in response to a question on this matter:

> Also our teacher R. Ḥayim Qoraḥ, his memory for the World to Come, whose generation was stirred by his wisdom and fear of God, whose grandfathers and forefathers, are my ancestors, called his youngest son the name of Ezra the Scribe, who grew and flourished and had eleven sons and daughters and became a famous *talmid ḥakham;* and lived a long life. This story, too, is proven unfounded, for we do not

62. *Even Sappir,* p. 99a. See also Erich Brauer, *Ethnologie der Jemenitischen Juden* (Heidelberg: C. Winter, 1934), p. 196.
63. According to Josephus he was buried in Jerusalem. See *Antiquities of the Jews,* 11. 5, § 5.
64. Yehudah Ratzaby, *"Ezra ha-Sofer ve-Golei Teiman,"* in *Be-Ma'agalot Teiman,* (Tel Aviv, 1948), pp. 1–5.
65. Y. Ratzaby, *"Ezra ha-Sofer ve-Golei Teiman,"* in *Be-Ma'agalot Teiman,* p. 5.

> encounter the name Neriyah or Ḥaggai, Habaquq[66] or Eldad, Medad, even not Yo'el, Elisha and Hoshe'a and others. You will not find that they gave such names in Yemen.[67]

R. Pinḥas Qoraḥ wrote:

> Many rabbis and scholars have already written to prove that the name Ezra was [found] in a number of families among Yemenite Jewry ... and in our family the name Ezra occurs, as is known, for the son of my teacher and grandfather, our honorable teacher the rabbi, R. Ḥayim Qoraḥ, blessed be the memory of the true man, and my brother, may the Lord sustain and protect him, and even I know a few who bear [the name] Ezra.[68]

Yosef Shalom Ḥubārah was a close friend of the R. Ezra noted, the son of R. Ḥayim Qoraḥ, who was among the prominent Yemenite sages of the nineteenth century. In his book, Mr. Hubarāh wrote about the question he asked R. Ḥayim concerning the name Ezra:

> I said to him: R., I heard tell that it is forbidden to the Jews of Yemen to call their offspring *Ezra*, because Ezra the Scribe called upon the Yemenite Jews to go up to Ereṣ Israel and they refused, so he cursed them and they cursed him (that he will not be buried in Ereṣ Israel), and from then on they refrained from calling their sons by this name. Now, you named your son Ezra! He answered me politely: Do not listen, do not believe! This notion has no foundation at all. Heaven forbid that Ezra the Scribe would curse Jews or that Jewish people would curse him, for it is prohibited to curse any Jew, for they are the people of the Lord. Know that there are many who call their son Ezra, and there are old and young with the name Ezra. When you have a son, name him Ezra, and he Lord will be your help [*ezrekha*].[69]

66. From among the names R. Qoraḥ mentioned, only the name *Ḥavaquq* was and it was rarely used in Yemen. See below chap. 5, sect. 2. R. Ḥavaquq Ya'beṣ immigrated to Israel with the "Wings of Eagles" *aliyah* and lived in Rosh HaAyin. He is the brother of Ovadya Ya'beṣ, chief rabbi of the city of Eqron, whose served as the last chief rabbi of the Ṣa'dah community. R. Havaquq Ya'beṣ signed as a witness to a *ketubbah* from the Ṭalḥ community in northern Yemen, on 11 Adar II 5708 (22 Mar 1948).
67. S. Qoraḥ, *'Arikhat Shulḥan,* 1–3 (Bnei Brak, 1975–1985), in the final pages of the book, section 11 (no page number). The responsum was printed again in the new edition, *Arikhat Shulḥan–Yalqut Ḥayim*, 8, sect. 706 (Bnei Brak, 2006), pp. 191–96. In this responsum, R. Shelomo Qoraḥ rejected additional details of this legend with clear proofs.
68. In a personal correspondence dated in April 2010.
69. Yosef Shalom Hubarah, *Bi-Tla'ot Teiman vi-Yrushalayim* (Jerusalem, 1970), p. 56.

The rabbi Ezra mentioned was among the teachers of the very young in Ṣan'a in the first half of the twentieth century, immigrated to Israel, and served as a rabbi in the Hatikvah neighborhood; he served as a scribe of *gittin* in the Tel Aviv *Bet Din*.[70] On this issue R. Yosef Qāfiḥ wrote:

> I must say that the widespread legend, which also R. Yaacov Sappir wrote in his book, that among the Yemenite Jews they do not call their sons by the name "Ezra" since when he called upon them to go up to Ereṣ Israel, they did not want to do so knowing that in the future the Temple would be destroyed, and owing to that he blessed them and they blessed him,[71] and the statements of both came to pass. Part of this legend was written by R. Shelomo 'Adani in his introduction to his commentary *Melekhet Shelomo*, and it was also mentioned by R. Yiḥye' Qoraḥ in the introduction to his book *Marpe Lashon*. I, however, still did not find it mentioned in the words of the ancients, and it seems to me that it was introduced to Yemen in the last three hundred years from Ereṣ Israel since Yemenite Jews have regularly given the name Ezra throughout the generations; I have seen many documents from different generations, and in many places I found the name Ezra, also in various copies of Scriptures whose scribes were called Ezra.[72]

R. Yosef Qāfiḥ commented in a similar way:

> This, too, is false, as if the Yemenite Jews do not call their sons by the name Ezra. Not only currently are many given this esteemed name, but also over the generations this name was given; we find dozens of more and less ancient manuscripts whose scribe is "Ezra." I have a manuscript that was written in 1659 SEL, which is 5108 AM [1348] and the writer's name is "Ezra b. R. Shalom b. R. Ezra."[73] This shows us that the Jews of Yemen never stopped giving their sons the name Ezra.[74]

70. Yosef Qāfiḥ, "*Ha-Rav ha-Gaon, Rabbi Ḥayim Qoraḥ, Zats"l,*" *Ketavim*, 2 (Jerusalem, 1989), p. 1004; idem, "*Kehillat Ṣan'a she-be-Teiman,*" *Ketavim*,1 (Jerusalem, 1989), p. 867; idem, "*Setimat ha-Golal al Yedidut shel 55 Shanim, Keina u-Retzufa al Yisra'el Yeshayahu, z"l,*" *Ketavim*, 2 (Jerusalem, 1989), p. 1057; Pinḥas Qoraḥ (ed.), *Anaf Etz Avot* (Bnei Brak, 1994), pp. 920–21; *Tzaddik be-Emunato Yiḥye', Pirkei Ḥayim ve-Divrei Tora le-Zikhro shel ha-Gaon ha-Tzaddik Morenu Rabbi Yiḥye' Alsheikh* (Jerusalem, 2002).
71. Euphemistic usage for the word curse.
72. *Ḥamesh Megillot*, ed. R. Y. Qāfiḥ (Jerusalem, 1962).
73. For a quote from this manuscript, see below in this section.
74. Yosef Qāfiḥ, "*Qishrei Yahadut Teiman*" p. 814. On a comment that was written that Ezra was not liked by the Yemenite Jews (see David Shelomo Shapira, "*Hash'ara al*

As to the words of R. Sappir about the name Ezra, Yisrael Yeshayahu noted, "An unfounded fact, since Ezra is one of the most pleasant names in Yemen."[75]

There are multiple occurrences of the name Ezra. In the listing of a birth, written at the beginning of the book *Lekaḥ Ṭov* by R. Sa'adyah Buṭa:

> The good flower has been born, likened to a moist tree, may the Lord give him good, and fashion him well, Ezra ben Shemu'el Buṭa', *yṣ"v*, 6 Elul 2229 SEL [5678 AM/1918], may he be a good sign for his father and mother and see long-lived descendants, Amen.[76]

R. Azaryah Basis, from the Rad'a community, wrote:

> They would give the name Ezra. From what I remember now, there was one very old man, a *talmid ḥakham*, whose name was Ezra al-Farḥi from Jerusalem. And one named Ezra Mhaṣri. And my friend, the rav, the gaon, Ezra Qoraḥ—his brother is the rav, the gaon, Pinḥas Qoraḥ, *shlita*. In Rosh HaAyin is R. Ezra Qāfiḥ, a native of Yemen "al-'Arūs." There is another one as well, born in Yemen, with the name Ezra Qāfiḥ, the son of the *shoḥet* and *mohel* from the city of Dhamār. Ezra 'Eden, previously "'Adani." In Rad'a—Ezra 'Ūrqubi, Ezra Ma'ūḏah.[77]

R. Almog Akhlufi wrote:

> The name Ezra was common, such as my great-uncle, the rav, R. Shemu'el called his son Ezra, that's one. And second, in Sūq al-Ithnayn, and the third, in Shaḥdiye. And fourth, Ezra b. Mūsa (a cousin of my grand-uncle Yehudah Mnos) of Mhāṣir. And fifth was Ezra in Baraṭ in northern Yemen.[78]

In the list of Jews who lived in northern Yemen in the first half of the twentieth century, and which is found in the book by R. Dr. Aharon Ben David, are five men who were named Ezra.[79] While examining the

---

Devar Alila Muslamit," Sinai 71 (1972): 149), R. Qāfiḥ noted "And these statements are simply nonsense, because Ezra was liked and esteemed the Jews of Yemen, no less than any other central figure in the Bible (Qāfiḥ, ibid.).

75. Yisrael Yeshayahu, *"Shevilei ha-Aliya mi-Teiman le-Tziyyon," Shevut Teiman*, ed. Y. Yeshayau and A. Tzadok (Tel Aviv, 1945), p. 40.
76. *Lekaḥ Tov*, introduction to the book.
77. In a personal correspondence dated 8 Mar 2010.
78. In a personal correspondence dated 16 Feb 2011.
79. See Aharon Ben David, *"Shemot Yehudim bi-Ṣefon Teiman al pi ha-Sefer 'Beit ha-Even'," Mesora le-Yosef* 6 (2009): 444, 456–457; idem, *Bet ha-Even*, p. 711, nos. 1476–1480.

name Ezra in a number of Yemenite communities, thirty men's names were Ezra.[80] In the list of the remnants of Jews in Yemen written by Mori Ṣemaḥ Yiṣḥaq Halewi (Qādi), who visited Yemen in the 1980s and helped the Jews of northern Yemen, were four men named Ezra.

In Yemenite *ketubbot* the name Ezra occurred six times. In a *ketubbah* dated 17 Sivan 5670 (24 June 1910), from the 'Arūs community, the name of one of the witnesses at the bottom of the document is Yiḥye' ben Ezra. In a *ketubbah* from 17 Elul 5693 (8 Sep 1933), from the Shibām community, the groom's name is give as Yiḥye' ben Ezra ben Yiṣḥāq called al-Maqlūb. In a *ketubbah* dated 17 Elul 5696 (4 Sep 1936), from the 'Arūs community, the name of one of the witnesses who signed it is Ezra ben Yiṣḥāq. In a *ketubbah* dated 11 Av 5699 (27. July 1939), from the Khamer community, the name of one of the witnesses appears on it appears as Ezra Ibrāhim Jerashi. In a *ketubbah* from 28 Iyyar 5702 (15 May 1942), from the 'Arūs community, the name of one of the signing witnesses is Yiḥye' ben Ezra. The groom's name in a *ketubbah* from 21 Elul 5702 (3 Sep 1942), from the Ḥuṣn bin Sa'd community, was given as Ezra ben Yiḥye' Sharārah who is called al-'Uzayri.

In five colophons of Yemenite manuscripts, the name Ezra is mentioned in the lineage lists of the copyist or of the commissioner of the work. In a manuscript of Ecclesiastes from 24 Nisan 5108 (24 Mar 1348), from the Ṭawīlah community, the copyist listed the name of the owner "May it be for a good omen for Mori Ezra ben R. Shalom from the tribe of Judah."[81] The son of the Ezra mentioned, who was from the family of copyists from Ṭawīlah, noted his family lineage in a copy of Rambam's *Moreh Nevukhim* from 5140 (1380): "Shalom b. R. Ezra ben Shalom b. Ezra b. Shalom ben Abu al-Sa'd ben Shalom ben Oded ben Zekharyah ben Ya'akov ben Yosef ben David ben Shemaryah known as al-'Ansi ben Yosef ha-Qenazi."[82] In a manuscript of Rambam's *Mishneh Torah* from Tishri 5114 (1353), which was also copied in Ṭawīlah, the copyist gave the name of its owner, "May it be a good omen for Mori Amram b. R. Maimon b. R. Ezra b. R. Sa'adyah."[83] In a manuscript of the *Mishneh*

80. See Yehuda Levi Naḥum, *Hasifat Genuzim mi-Teiman* (Holon 1971), p. 375.

81. MS R. Yosef Qāfiḥ, *Oṣar Kitve Yad Ivriyim mi-Ymei ha-Beinayim*, 2, no. 32, and see also no. 33. See also *Ḥamesh Megillot* (Qāfiḥ), p. 8.

82. MS London, British Library Arabic MSI. O. 3679 (IMHM 49322). For a description of the manuscript, see Aharon Gaimani, *"Ha'ataqah Qedumah mi-Teiman le-*Moreh Nevukhim *le-ha-Rambam," Tehuda* 14 (1994): 15–20. See also above, chap. 2, sect. 1.

83. G. Margoliouth, *Catalogue of the Hebrew and Samaritan Manuscripts in the British*

Torah (1409), the copyist gave the name of the commissioner of the work: "Ezra, may the spirit of the Lord guide him, ben Rav, the most holy, reverent Shalom, *ng'*, bar the most holy, reverent Zekharyah, may he repose in good, the most holy, reverent ben Rav Gad ben Rav ben the most holy, reverent Meshullam, his memory should live in eternity ben the most holy, reverent Ḥoter al-Ḥabayshi."[84] In a manuscript of Rambam's *Mishneh Torah* from 10 Adar II 5193 (2 Mar 1433), copied in Qaryat Thele, the copyist listed his name "Yehudah b. R. Dawid b. R. Ezra."[85]

In Yemen, the sanctified, wonder-working Torah scrolls [a Yemenite tradition], and sometime even regular Torah scrolls, were given names.[86] R. Gilad Ṣadoq compiled a list of names of 150 holy Torah scrolls in Yemen, and many of them had identical names.[87] Six of them were called by the name Ezra, and they were located in different Yemenite communities.[88] The highly important civic leader R. Shalom 'Irāqi donated three Torah scrolls to the Ṣan'a synagogue in which he prayed, and one of them was called Ezra.[89]

Some of the Yemenite children who immigrated to Israel changed their name to Ezra from a name with a similar sound that they had been given in Yemen. For example, Ezra 'Arūsi of Ramat Gan was born in Ṣan'a and his name was 'Azri and after immigration to Israel changed his name to Ezra. Ezra Qaro [=Qara] of Petah Tikva was born in Ṣan'a, and his name was 'Azar; after moving to Israel, he changed his name to Ezra.

From all the foregoing, we understand the imprecision in the statements by R. Sappir about Ezra the Scribe and the Jews of Yemen. His

Museum, 2 (1965), serial no. 497, p. 108. For a photograph of the colophon, see Yehuda Levi Naḥum, "Revelation of Yemen's Treasures," p. 373.

84. Margoliouth, *Catalogue*, 1, serial no. 88, pp. 61–63/
85. MS Jerusalem, JNUL, Yah. MS Heb. 2; *Oṣar Kitve Yad Ivriyim mi-Ymei ha-Beinayim*, 1, no. 91.
86. See Yiṣḥaq Raṣabi, *Shulḥan Arukh ha-Mequṣar*, vol. 5 (Bnei Brak, 1989), Section 165, pp. 180–81 n. 131. See extensively on that below, part 3, chap. 6, sect. 2.
87. For a list of ninety-five of them, see G. Tsadok, *Livneikhem Sappeiru—Ma'aseihem shel Tzaddiqim Nissim ve-Nifla'ot* (Bnei Brak, 2000), pp. 279–81. For a fuller list, see G. Ṣadoq, *Zikhron Teiman—Sippurei Nifla'ot, Demuyot Hod u-Minhagim mi-Yahadut Teiman* (Bnei Brak, 2006), pp. 160–64.
88. G. Ṣadoq, *Livneikhem Sappeiru*, p. 281; idem, *Zikhron Teiman*, p. 163.
89. Aharon Gaimani, *"Mekorot Ḥadashim le-Po'alo shel R. Shalom 'Irāqi bi-Kehillot Teiman ba-Me'ah ha-18,"* *Pe'amim* 55 (1993): 141.

statement that "to this day they hate him and do not give his name" is in serious error, since the Jews of Yemen observe Ezra's regulations and study and copy his book.[90] Of further note, among the Yemenite Jews there are few Hebrew names deriving from the holy tongue.[91] The fact that among this paucity of names one finds the name Ezra, and not other names from the late biblical books, attests to their admiration for him.

3.2 Tūrkiyyah and Tūrki

Tūrkiyyah as a personal name for women was widespread in Yemen, while the name Tūrki as a personal name for men or as a family name was rare. These names had originated when the Turks were ruling in Yemen, 1546–1629 and 1872–1918. The Jews preferred Turkish rule, even though it was Muslim, since it was less strict toward the minority than the local regime, which was composed of Muslims known for their zealousness.[92] An interesting phenomenon is the frequency of the name Tūrkiyyah in the Ṣan'a community in the first half of the twentieth century. In a roster of 179 girls who in 1943 attended the girls school in Ṣan'a,[93] there are twenty-two named Turkiyyah,[94] about 12% of all pupils. This fact can be explained by the moderate regime the Jews of Ṣan'a experienced during the Turkish administration, which was centered in Ṣan'a, and ruled, as noted, from 1872 to 1918.

90. For instance, R. Yiḥye' Sāliḥ wrote in his commentary on *Siddur Eṣ Ḥayim*: "And Ezra made a rule for them, the Jews, that they should read 10 verses for the 10 *batlanim*, who are proper people idle from their trade to deal with public affairs and to come to the synagogue so that ten people will be there at prayer time ... and Ezra also set the rule that they should read at Minḥah on the Sabbath ..." (Mahariṣ, *Tiklal Eṣ Ḥayim*, 1, p. 86a).

91. See above, sect. 2.

92. Robert W. Stookey, *Yemen: The Politics of the Yemen Arab Republic* (Boulder, CO, 1978), pp. 142–49. See also Yehudah Ratzaby, *"Mered al-Qasim: Parsha be-Qorot Yehudei Teiman ba-Me'ah ha-17,"* *Zion* 20 (1956): 32; idem, *"Be-Matsor u-be-Matsoq (Le-Parshat ha-Ra'av ha-Aharon be-Shanim 5663–5665),"* in *Bo'i Teiman: Mehkarim u-Te'udot be-Tarbut Yehudei Teiman*, ed. Yehudah Ratzaby (Tel Aviv, 1967), pp. 67–102; Yehudah Nini, *Teiman ve-Ṣiyyon: Ha-Reqa ha-Medini ha-Hevrati ve-ha-Ruhani la-'Aliyyot ha-Rishonot mi-Teiman* (Jerusalem, 1982), pp. 97–99.

93. Tsuri'eli, *Temurot be-Ḥinukh*, doc. no. 16, photo of the doc. on p. 66, and transcription of the doc. on p. 67.

94. Ibid., p. 67 nos. 2, 24, 37, 41, 49, 50, 58, 71, 90, 96, 106, 112, 114, 120, 121, 125, 141, 158, 161, 170, 177, 179.

The name expresses lightness and beauty, traits associated with the Turks, who were known for their light skin color. It also means health and courage, possessed by the Turkish soldiers. A common proverb among the Jews of northern Yemen gives voice to this idea, namely, that about children who were born healthy and of full weight they used to say "Qad hu'a mithl al-Turki" (He is healthy and strong like the Turk).[95] The names Tūrkiyyah and Tūrki were also given to newborns even when Yemen was not under Ottoman rule. Apparently, some people had experienced Turkish rule or had heard about it, and so gave these names to their children.

R. Shelomo Qoraḥ and R. Pinḥas Qoraḥ wrote me about what was customary in the Ṣan'a community, where the name Tūrkiyyah was given to a girl who was quite beautiful when born, in line with the image of the Turks and their women as perceived by the Yemenite Jews.[96] R. Ovadyah Ya'beṣ, who served as the chief rabbi of the Jews of Ṣa'dah in northern Yemen, wrote to me about his local custom: "The names Tūrkiyyah or Tūrki were very rare, and I heard that they were given to fat children."[97] Yehudah Ratzaby reports that he heard from S. D. Goitein that lighter-skinned daughters born in Yemen were called by one of the three names: Tūrkiyyah—as a symbol of the Turks, who came from light-toned stock; Ṣīniyyah—as a symbol for porcelain (originating in China), which is lighter than pottery vessels; or Sham'ah—as a symbol for white as the color of candle wax.

In the list of Jews from the first half of the twentieth century in northern Yemen, there is one man whose personal name was Tūrki, Tūrki al-Sha'bali, and five women called Tūrkiyyah.[98] Mentioned in the *pinkas Bet ha-Din* (religious court registry) of Ṣan'a are five unrelated men from the eighteenth century whose byname was Tūrki: David Tūrki,[99] Yiḥye' Tūrki,[100] Yiṣḥaq Tūrki,[101] Yosef Tūrki,[102] and Harūn

95. Aharon Ben David, *"Shemot Yehudim,"* p. 461.

96. In a personal correspondence from R. Shelomo Qoraḥ received in May 2010 and in a personal correspondence received from R. Pinḥas Qoraḥ in April 2010.

97. In personal correspondence dated 4 Mar 2010.

98. Ben David, *"Shemot Yehudim,"* pp. 445, 462; idem, *Bet ha-Even,* p. 717, nos. 1695–1699.

99. See *Misawwadeh,* 1, par. 139, pp. 52–53.

100. Ibid., par. 232, p. 94; par. 207, p. 80; par. 1255, p. 433; par. 1355, p. 464. See also Gamliel, *Pequdei Teiman,* p. 200.

101. Ibid., par. 287, p. 113; par. 752, p. 272; par. 1303, p. 448.

102. Ibid., par. 485, pp. 180–81.

Tūrki.[103] In one of the rulings given in Ṣan'a in 1787, one of the four signatories was Shalom ben Yosef Tūrki.[104] Found in a Yemenite manuscript is one copyist whose byname was Tūrki. In a manuscript of *Meqor Ḥayim* by R. Yiḥye' ben Ya'aqov Ṣāliḥ, the copyist wrote in the colophon: "*Sefer Meqor Ḥayim* on 20 Iyyar 5685 (14 May 1925), with the help of the sustainer of life, by the humble Moshe ben Shemuel al-Tūrki, *yṣ"v* ....[105]

In the 1,506 Yemenite *ketubbot* I have examined, the name Tūrkiyyah (תורכיה) occurs thirteen times. Here I present the names while noting the place and dates of the *ketubbot* in chronological order. In a *ketubbah* from the 1770s, from the 'Aqba Ḥusn Wad community, the bride's name was written as Turkiyyah bint Yiḥye' al-Ḥamdi al-Lewi. A *ketubbah* dated 24 Tevet 5612 (17 Jan 1852), from the Ṣabar community, presents the bride's name as Turkiyyah bint Yosef al-Shāḥidi. In a *ketubbah* from 15 Shevat 5631 (6 Feb 1871), from the Ṣan'a community, the bride's name is written as Turkiyyah bint Slaymān ben Avraham. A *ketubbah* dated 4 Tevet 5650 (27 Dec 1889), from the 'Imrān community, the bride's name appears as Turkiyyah bint Sālem ben Yiḥye' al-Manṣūrah. In a *ketubbah* from 20 Elul 5650 (6 Sep 1890), from the Ṣan'a community, the bride's name is Turkiyyah bint Sālem b. Slaymān b. Sālem al-Mishriqi. A *ketubbah* dated 15 Av 5653 (28 July 1893), from the Ṣan'a community, presents the bride's name as Turkiyyah bint Harūn b. Yiḥye' 'Amr al-Lewi. In a *ketubbah* from 15 Shevat 5670 (25 Jan 1910), from the Ṣa'dah community, the bride's name is written as Tūrkiyyah bint Yiḥye' Hashāsh. A *ketubbah* from 2 Shevat 5677 (25 Jan 1917), from the Maḥwīt community, the bride's name appears as Tūrkiyyah bint Se'īd al-Būsāni.[106] In a *ketubbah* from 17 Adar 5691 (6 Mar 1931), from the Yafīd community, the bride's name is Tūrkiyyah bint Ya'īsh b. Sālem al-Khalūfi. In a *ketubbah* from 18 Adar I 5692 (25 Feb 1932), from 'Imrān, the bride's name is written as Turkiyyah bint Yiḥye' b. Yūda' Sham'ah. A *ketubbah* dated 27 Shevat 5693 (23 Feb 1933), from the Ṣan'a community, gives the bride's name as Turkiyyah bint Shemu'el b. Sālem al-Akhlūfi called Shalīṭ. In a *ketubbah* from 24 Elul 5709 (18 Sep 1949), from

103. Ibid., par. 1329, p. 456.

104. Yehudah Ratzaby, "*Golat Teiman*," in *Bo'i Teiman: Meḥqarim u-Te'udot be-Tarbut Yehudei Teiman*, ed. Yehudah Ratzaby (Tel Aviv, 1967), pp. 187–90.

105. MS Chicago, Spertus College B 5 (IMHM 40230).

106. In a document written on the back of the *ketubbah* the name is written as *Trkiyya*, without the *waw*.

the Ṣan'a community, the bride's name is written as Tūrkiyyah bint Yosef al-Mazūlah. A *ketubbah* from 21 Adar 5710 (10 Mar 1950), from the Ḥajjar Sūq al-Ithnayn community, the bride's name is given as Turkiyyah bin Avraham Ḥibshūsh.

In the 174 Yemenite divorce documents I examined, there are three instances of Tūrkiyyah. In a nineteenth-century *get*, from the village of Qaṣr Mlāha', the name of the divorcee is Tūrkiyyah bint Yosef; in a *get* dated 3 Adar 5673 (21 Feb 1912), from the village of Darb al-Mahras, the name of the divorcee is written as Turkiyyah bat Slaymān; and in a *get* from 9 Shevat 5701 (5 Mar 1941), from the village of Khamer, the name of the divorcee is written as Turkiyyah bat Yiṣḥāq.

In the Ṣan'a *Bet Din* registry there were thirty women named Tūrkiyyah.[107]

R. Azaryah Basis, formerly of the Radā' community, wrote that "in Rosh HaAyin there is an extended family with the name of Tūrkiyyah from the 'Afār district."[108]

Yemenite rabbis discussed how to spell the name Tūrkiyyah when writing a *get*.[109] R. Shalom Yiṣḥaq Halevi noted: "Similarly with the name Turkiyyah (except that after the *tav* there is no *waw*, as the author wrote above [meaning the Maharis, *Shut Pe'ulat Ṣaddiq*, 3, par. 95] as for all names when they are *mil'el* or *milra'*), some read it with two vowels Turki[y]yah, while some read it with one vowel and with one *yod* Turkiya."[110] From the statements by the Yemenite rabbis, we see that in Yemen they usually wrote the name Turkiyya without the letter *waw*, but with two *yods*, the reason for the doubling stemming from the *dagesh* in the reading of the letter *yod*.[111] From the name lists, we learn that the

107. See *Misawwadeh*, 1, par. 65, p. 25; par. 66, p. 25; par. 80, p. 30; par. 216, p. 86; par. 217, p. 87; par. 274, p. 110; par. 298, p. 119; par. 309, p. 125; par. 355, p. 141; par. 378, p. 148; par. 432, p. 164; par. 479, p. 179; par. 481, p. 179; par. 496, p. 183; par. 528, p. 193; par. 542, p. 197; par. 601, p. 219; par. 620, p. 226; par. 625, p. 228; par. 630, p. 231; par. 639, p. 233; par. 678, p. 249; par. 796, p. 281; par. 889, p. 284; par. 1048, p. 362; par. 1192, p. 411; 1266, p. 436.

108. In a personal correspondence dated 8 Mar 2010. The village of 'Afar is in central Yemen. Moshe Gavra, *Enṣiqlipedya le-Qehilot ha-Yehudiyyot be-Teiman*, 2 (Bnei Brak, 2005), p. 443, entry 'Afar.

109. See below, part 3, chap. 1.

110. See the comment by R. Shalom Yiṣḥaq Halewi in Maharis, *Shut Pe'ulat Ṣaddiq* 3 (Jerusalem, 2003), sect. 98.

111. Maharis, *Shut Pe'ulat Tsaddik*, 3, sect. 98; R. Yiḥye' ben Yosef 'Amud, *Petah ha-Ohel* (Jerusalem, 1980), sect. 1, 30; R. Avraham Alnaddaf, *'Anaf Ḥayim—Shut Zikhronei Iy"sh* (Jerusalem, 1981), *Even ha-Ezer*, sect. 59, p. 224.

name Tūrkiyyah was not written uniformly among the Yemenite communities, appearing with four different spellings: תורכייה, תרכיה, תורכיה, תרכייה (Tūrkiyyah, Tūrkiyah, Turkiyyah, Turkiyah).

The count to the destruction of the First Temple and the Second Temple. Tiklal, 1889, MS Asaf Haetzni, Elad

CHAPTER FOUR

NAMES AND THEIR FORMS

1. ARABIC NAMES

Some personal names are Arabic and are pronounced as the Arabic name in daily life. However, for a few of these names, people sought a Hebrew translation, an issue with which some Yemenite sages dealt.

R. Ḥoṭer ben Shelomo (in Arabic: Manṣūr ibn Sulēmān) wrote at the beginning of his philosophical work on Maimonides' Thirteen Principles, *Sharḥ al-Qawā'id* ("Explanation of the Principles"): "[I] Ḥoṭer ben Abba Mori Shelomo, he should find peace in Eden, ibn al-Mu'allem." In the introduction to responsa that he wrote, we find: "Said the author Manṣūr ibn Slaymān al-Dhamāri."[1] R. Sa'adyah ben Dawid al-'Adani in his introduction to a commentary on Maimonides' *Mishneh Torah* wrote: "I Sa'adyah ben R. David, may he find peace in Eden, his great loving-kindness upon me." In the continuation, however, he wrote: "The dependent upon the help of the Lord, who awaits the mercy of God, Se'īd ibn Da'ūd, may he find peace in Eden, al-'Adani."[2]

The Arabic name of R. David ben Yesha' Halevi is noted in the title of his commentary on the laws of ritual slaughter, *Sharḥ Ghiyat*. The Arabic name Ghiyat is Yesha' in Hebrew.[3]

The name Banayah appears in many colophons of sixteenth- and seventeenth-century manuscripts that were copied by R. Banayah b. R. Sa'adyah or members of his family. We learn about the source of the

1. Yehudah Ratzaby, *Toratan she-li-Bnei Teiman* (Qiryat Ono, 1994), pp. 28–31.
2. Ibid., pp. 32–33.
3. Ibid., p. 35.

name Banayah through another source. In one of the manuscripts, the copyist renders his lineage as "David *beirav* Banayah *beirav* Sa'adyah." In a bill of sale, this name appears as "Da'ūd ben 'Amr ben Se'īd." R. Amram Qoraḥ noted that the name 'Ammar [builder] appearing in the bill of sale is the writer Banayah, who is often cited by his Arabic name 'Amar, which in Hebrew means *binyan* (building).[4] This means that 'Amr was his real name and Banayah was his pen name.

R. Yosef Qāfiḥ noted the name of R. Netanel ben Yesh'ayah, a fourteenth-century Yemenite sage, who in his introduction to his midrashic work *Nur al-Dalām*, whose Hebrew translation is *Me'or ha-Afela* [The Light in the Darkness], wrote: "Said the poor collector Netanel b. R. Yesh'ayah, *tanṣeba"h*."[5] On the author's Hebrew name, R. Yosef Qāfiḥ commented, "It is highly probable that this was the author's name, but since the names Netanel and Yesh'ayah do not occur frequently and are unusual in Yemen, one may assume that the name of our author is Wahab ben Ghiyat."[6] A review of fourteenth- to sixteenth-century manuscripts shows that these names were rare, as R. Qāfiḥ stated. The name Netanel occurs four times and the names Yesh'ayah and Ghiyat one time each. In a manuscript copied in 1351, the copyist's name appears: Ye[fet b. R. [Neta]nel b. R. Yesh'ayah."[7] A manuscript copied in 1454 contains the name of the copyist "Netanel be[n] ha-Zaqen Ḥisdai, may the Lord protect him [*sha"ṣ*], son of R. Netanel *tanṣeba"h* son of ha-Zaqen Dav[id], may the spirit of the Lord let him rest, son of Yesh'ua, OBM, bar Ḥisdai, *zekhurim li-vrakha*."[8] In a manuscript of the Torah copied in 1496, the name of the copyist is "Me'oded ben Yosef ben Sa'adyah ben Yosef ben Shelomo ben Netanel Yadi'a Ibn Ḥasān al-Qaysi."[9] In a Torah manuscript copied between 1478 and 1483, the name of the person who ordered it appears as "Avraham [*sha"ts*] known as Alṣārim [*sha"ts*] ben Yosef, may the spirit of the Lord make him rest, ben Ghiyat, *ng'*."[10]

4. Amram Qoraḥ, *Sa'arat Teiman* (Jerusalem, 1954), p. 137 n. 1. In contemporary times, too, some Hebraicized their family name 'Ammar into Banayahu. See below, part 3, chap. 7, sect. 3.
5. *Me'or ha-Afelah le-R' Netanel ben Yeshaya*, ed. Y. Qafiḥ (Jerusalem, 1957), Introduction, p. 1.
6. Ibid., Introduction, p. 10 n. 1.
7. *Halakhah u-Midrash*, MS JTS NY 693 (IMHM 41433).
8. *Halakah u-Midrash*, MS San Francisco Sutro 75.
9. MS San Francisco Sutro 74.
10. Manuscript Cambridge 1728 (IMHM 17483)

R. Yosef Qāfiḥ made similar comments about Hebrew names in the lineage of R. Shalom Shabazi. In the introduction to his book *Ḥemdat Yamim*, R. Shabazi mentioned his father and his grandfather: "I of weak knowledge and reason, Shalem son of my master and teacher, Yosef, master and teacher, Avigad, son of my master Ḥalfon, OBM."[11] As for the Hebrew names Avigad and Ḥalfon, R. Qāfiḥ noted:

> In my opinion, the name Avigad is not the personal name of his grandfather ... but a byname, as this name is not common in Yemen, but rather is the translation of the name Abu Sa'ūd by which it is customary in Yemen to call a happy person. For Abu S'ūd is the literal translation of "Father of happiness" or "Father of good fortune" so Rabbenu Abu S'ūd was translated as Avi Gad because Gad is good fortune as our Sages OBM explicitly wrote that Leah said about Gad (Gen. 30:11), *Ata gada de-beita.*[12] Or he had another son named Sa'ūd and because of his name, his father was called Abu Sa'ūd, as is common in Yemen. The name Ḥalfon is also not usually used, while it is merely a translation of the Arabic name Khalaf, which some of the ancient in Yemen used to call an important person, a personage who takes the place of his ancestors, by the name Khalaf, in the name of "all the time of my service I wait until my replacement (*ḥalifati*) comes" (Job 14:14). They interpret this as until I will have a son to replace me (and not according to the interpretation of R. Sa'adyah Gaon, who explained *ḥalifati* as I will pass from the world), and our rabbis translated the name Khalaf in Yemen as Ḥalfon.[13]

We learn from the following example that the name Avigad is the Hebrew translation of the name Abu Sa'ūd. In the introduction to one of the poems written by the father or R. Shabazi we find "a beautiful poem about the astrological signs from a work of our master and teacher [Yosef] son of his father Avigad on what they asked the Sheikh Kamil." At the end of the poem the poet gave his name as "My name remains *yod waw* and *sin* and *pe* [= Yosef] and Avigad, he is the father."[14]

Regarding the Arabic name Sālem, the Yemenite rabbis discussed whether it should be translated Shalom or Shalem in regard to the name of R. Shalom Shabazi. R. Avraham Naddāf wrote:

11. Shabazi, *Ḥemdat Yamim* (Jerusalem, 1977), Introduction by R. Yosef Qāfiḥ.
12. Gen. Rabba 71:9.
13. Shabazi, *Ḥemdat Yamim*.
14. Joseph Tobi, *"Yedi'ot Hadashot le-Toledot R. Shalom Shabazi,"* in *Shalom ben Yosef Shabazi, Qovets bi-Mlot 350 Shana le-Holadeto*, ed. Joseph Tobi (Nisan 1972), p. 35.

> And it is known that it is not because of pronunciation[15] that one reads his name Shalem without a *waw* between the *lamed* and the *mem*, but because of the difference between the word Shalem and Shalom according to the grammar of the underst[anding] of the word, since *Shalem* comes from the idea of "Jacob arrived safe [*shalem*] in the city of Shechem" [Gen. 33:18], and R. Sa'adyah Gaon interpreted this as the Arabic Sālem. But Shalom means *selām* and the Must'arabs say to each other "Selām 'aleikum," and in Hebrew, *Shalom 'aleikhem*, and they do not say *"Sālem aleikum," Shalem 'aleikhem*. And everyone is used to calling people Sālem in Arabic, which is Shalem in Hebrew, and they call a woman Salāmah instead of Shulamit in Hebrew. And only those who do not know the grammar of the language call Sālem Shalom, and not because of the accent.[16]

R. Qāfiḥ wrote: "Our rabbi in his book and his poetry translates his name as Shalem and not Shalom as customary among Yemenite Jews, and that is really the precise translation of the Arabic name *Sālem*, Shalem. R. Sa'adyah Gaon translated "Jacob arrived safe [*salma*], but Shalom is the translation of the word *Selām*."[17] Y. Ratzaby wrote: "Shalem is also the precise translation of the Arabic form of the name Sālem that the poet frequently uses."[18] In any event, one can understand the name Sālem to mean "whole," so that it corresponds to the Hebrew name Shalom. The meaning of the name Shalom is *shalem* [whole], in line with Psalms 38:4: "There is no soundness in my flesh because of Your rage, no wholeness [*shalom*] in my bones because of my sin."[19]

Meir Benayahu and Joseph Tobi remarked on the writing of this name with the defective spelling שלם (Shalem). According to Benayahu, "The Jews of Morocco as well usually signed their name with defective spelling as in the Bible, Shalem and not Shalom, since it is one of the names of God, and there is no proof that the name of the Yemenite poet was not the traditional Shalom."[20] Tobi noted, however, "that in Yemen

15. That is the accent of the Jews in southern Yemen who pronounce the *ḥolam* as a *ṣere*.
16. Avraham Naddaf, *"Le-Toledot ha-Meshorer ha-Teimani R. Shalem beirav Yosef Shabazi ve-Shirato ha-Ivrit," Mizraḥ u-Ma'arav*, 1 (Sivan-Elul 5680 [1920]): 329.
17. Shabazi, *Ḥemdat Yamim*, See also Y. Qāfiḥ, *"Rabbi Shalom Shabazi,"* in *Ketavim*, 2 (Jerusalem, 1989), p. 991.
18. Yehudah Ratzaby, *"Rabbi Shalem Shabazi ve-Shirato," Sefunot*, 9 (1965): 136 n. 10.
19. See Academy of the Hebrew Language, letter 9, *"Shalom, shalom le-raḥoq u-le-qarov,"* 7 Nov 2010.
20. His comments appears in Ratzaby's article, *"Rabbi Shalem Shabazi ve-Shirato,"* p. 136 n. 10.

the name Shalem was never heard,"[21] citing responsa by rabbis outside of Yemen from the sixteenth and seventeenth centuries, from which one may learn that some used to write this name with defective spelling. He further commented, "We thus see that there was a tradition for hundreds of years among Jewish communities in eastern and northern Yemen to write the personal name 'Shalom' in defective writing [שׁלֹם], and one may assume that this tradition is what guided R. Shalom Shabazi, too."[22]

R. Yiḥye' Ṣāliḥ (Mahariṣ) commented in his responsa work *Pe'ulat Ṣedek* about translated names, regarding issues of *gittin*:

> I further considered to be meticulous about another change, namely, with the signing of names by witnesses who wrote Yefet ibn Yeshu'a, while everyone knows his usual, well-known name and the one by which he is also called to the Torah is Ḥasan.[23] For this name is not a byname for Yefet, since the name Yefet does not have an Arabic correspondent. And this is a sign that Rabbenu Sa'adyah aligned the name Moshe in Arabic with Mūsa; Aharon, Harūn; Ya'aqov, Ya'aqūb; while the name Yefet was given no alternate name at all but just as it is written in the Bible. If so, he should not have signed his name as Yefet, as if someone had told him this was a byname for Ḥasan. We have also seen errors made by someone called Ma'ūḍah signing Me'oded, and someone whose name is Yiḥye', and they call him Zekharyah as a byname. This is nonsense and false for which there is neither rhyme nor reason.[24]

In another responsum on this issue, Mahariṣ commented in a similar manner:

> As for the facet you mentioned regarding the names Yefet, Ḥoṭer, and similarly Me'oded, Zekharyah. The issue is simple since the names

21. Joseph Tobi, "*Yehudei Teiman be-Shut Ḥakhmei Mitsrayim ve-Erets Israel ba-me'ot ha-Shesh Esreh ve-ha-Sheva Esreh,*" in *Benei Teiman, Meḥqarim be-Yahdut Teiman u-Morashtah*, ed. A. Gaimani, R. Arusi, S. Regev (Ramat Gan, 2011), p. 90.
22. Ibid., p. 91.
23. It is a custom among Yemenite Jews that when one is called to the Torah, he is called by the name he was given upon circumcision even if it was in Arabic, and not as in the Ashkenazi custom whereby they call him by the Hebrew name he was give at circumcision and not the vernacular name used in daily life. See further statements of the Mahariṣ in another responsum as well as those of R. Amram Qoraḥ, and see below part 3, chap. 6, sect. 3.
24. R. Yiḥye' Ṣāliḥ, *Shut Pe'ulat Ṣaddiq*, 1–3, ed. M. Ratsabi (Jerusalem, 2003), section 105.

> Yefet, Ḥoṭer, and such as these are not bynames because Arabic does not correspond to the Holy Tongue. Here, since it has already been done, over what has been done, one should not consider it for a number of reasons we find written among us. Of course, from now on, one must take care to sign his Arabic name with which he goes up to the Torah, which is familiar and known to everyone. And this should tell you that Yefet is not a byname for Ḥasan nor Ḥoṭer for Manṣur and so on, since R. Sa'adyah aligned the name Moshe, in Arabic with Mūsa; Aharon, Harūn; Ya'aqov, Ya'aqūb; and so on, and for the name Yefet he gave no byname at all. Also Ḥoṭer, he translated as Qaḍib. Verily, R. Sa'adya wrote Yefet as in the Bible, and said that Ḥasan is a byname for Yefet and Ḥoṭer a byname for Manṣūr. And whoever is named Ma'ūḍa, how could he sign 'Oded, as well as some named Yiḥye' who is called Zekharyah? This is nonsense and false for which there is neither rhyme nor reason.[25]

In the first part, the Mahariṣ wrote the translation for the name Aharon as Harūn and in the second part as Ha'rūn (with the addition of an *alef* after the *he*). R. Shalom Yiṣḥaq Halevi noted that the custom among Yemenite Jews is to write this name in two ways, plene and defective.[26] A review of 165 *gittin* from Yemen, a few from the sixteenth and seventeenth centuries and most of them from the eighteenth, nineteenth, and (the first half of the) twentieth century, shows that the name Aharon appears 37 times: 31 times in plene spelling Hārūn, five times with defective spelling Harun, and once as the Hebrew name Aharon.

Looking into the *Tafsir* of R. Sa'adyah Gaon on the Torah[27] informs us that this agrees with what the Mahariṣ wrote. For example, Ex. 5:1, "And afterwards Moses and Aaron went," is translated by Sa'adyah as "And after that entered Mūsa and Harūn"; Gen. 25:26, "He named him Jacob," Sa'adyah translates "And he named him Ya'aqūb"; Gen. 10:27, "May God enlarge Yafet" he translates "God will do well for Yefet." As for the translation of 'Awāḍ, R. Shelomo Badīḥi wrote in his commentary on the Torah: "I understood the reason for this in the writing of my brother 'Awāḍ, who is called in the Holy Tongue 'Iddo."[28]

R. Amram Qoraḥ agreed with the statements by Mahariṣ that for a number of name pairs, the Arabic name and the Hebrew name osten-

25. Ibid., section 106.
26. Ibid., section 106, Neve Tsedeq, n. 4.
27. The translations in Sa'adya's are on the basis of the *Keter Torah, Taj*, ed. Hasid.
28. Shelomo Badiḥi, *Olat Shelomo, Al ha-Torah ve-ha-Megillot*, ed. R. Itamar Hayim Cohen, (Jerusalem, 1994), Gen. 31:34–35, p. 108.

sibly translating it, there is no correlation between the two names. On a very old document from Ṣan'a, dealing with a regulation on limiting the meals at celebrations, one of the sages signed his name as Ḥoṭer ben Yosef. Regarding the name Ḥoṭer, R. Qoraḥ commented:

> This is the name Manṣur in Arabic. Thus wrote Mahariṣ in his responsa, sec. 106, that a few had the custom of giving Hebrew bynames for Arabic names. [For] the name Ḥasan—Yefet. Ma'ūḍa—Me'oded. The name 'Awāḍ—'Oded. And the name Manṣur— Ḥoṭer. And the name Yiḥye'—Zekharyah. And all this is nonsense and false. And he is right, for in none of these Arabic names is there any affinity to the translation into Hebrew. Should one say they did not intend translating but rather sought similarity, look at the name Manṣūr and the name Yiḥye'. One is hard-pressed to find any similarity between them. If so, the rabbi was correct when he asserted that there was neither rhyme nor reason for these bynames.[29]

As for the analogy between the names Manṣūr and Ḥoṭer, Amnon Shlomi wrote: "We may presume that this analogy derives from the verse: 'But a shoot shall grow out of Jesse, a twig shall sprout from his stock' (Isa. 11:1), in which there is parallelism between the words *ḥoter* and *neṣer* (*n-ṣ-r* being reminiscent of Manṣūr)."[30]

As for the names Ma'ūḍa and Me'oded, note the family lineage of Shalem Bashāri, who lived in the nineteenth century. In the introduction to riddle poems that he wrote, he listed his family's lineage: "The humble Shalem son of my master, my father Ma'ūḍa, may he find rest in Eden son of my honorable master and grandfather Yiḥye', may he see long-lived descendants, Amen, son of our honorable teacher, the rabbi Ma'ūḍa Bashari, May the memory of the righteous and holy (be) for a blessing, may his merit protect us, Amen, may it be His will. Moreover, in the colophon to a prayer book that he copied in 1820 in al-Ma'īda, Yemen, he wrote: "Shalem son of *abba mori* Me'oded son of *mori* my grandfather Yiḥye' son of the great, honorable, holy, may the memory of the righteous be for a blessing, Me'oded al-Bashari." Thus in Arabic he wrote Ma'ūḍa and in Hebrew Me'oded.[31]

29. Qoraḥ, *Sa'arat Teiman*, p. 130 n. 14.
30. Amnon Shlomi, "'*Sharḥ Shalom–Ha-Ḥibbur, Ofyo, ve-Zehut Meḥaber*," *Tehuda* 20–21 (2000–2001): 99–101.
31. Yehudah Ratzaby, "*Shirei Ḥida Halakhiyim le-R. Shalem Me'oded*," *Sefunot*, NS 1 (1980): 274–77. In "*Shirei Ḥida*" he noted the name *Ma'ūḍah* in Hebrew as Me'oded or 'Oded. Ibid, pp. 274, 282–83. See also the *Ohel David Catalogue*, 1 (Paris 1972), p. 334.

R. Amram Qoraḥ commented on the name Zekharyah occurring in a 300-year-old *sheṭar* signed by R. Yiḥye' ben Avraham Halewi from Yemen, in which he gave his personal name as Zekharyah:

> He is the one who built the first synagogue,[32] and in this signature he gave his name as Zekharyah, and a few rabbis and scribes did the same, with no connection between them. Perhaps they took this from Arab books that call Zekharyah "Yiḥye'."[33] Even so, anyone named Yiḥye' is not called Zekharyah by his family and the residents of his city, and also when he is called to the Torah, he is called only Yiḥye'. So, when the name Yiḥye' is written in a *get* or the witness signs a *get*, they write the name Yiḥye' without any byname, since they do not usually call Yiḥye' by the name Zekharyah, except for a few people, and just when signing *sheṭarot* or in works. The Mahariṣ, as well, did not find this byname pleasing and referred to himself as Ḥayim.[34] In truth, this word is both Hebrew and Arabic, but in Hebrew it is written with a final *heh* and in Arabic a final *alef*.[35]

We do find, however, rabbis in Yemen who were called Yiḥye' and indicated their name in writing as Zekharyah or Ḥayim. Combinations of Yiḥye', Zekharyah, and Ḥayim are found in the Muslim world and in Spanish Jewry.[36]

2. INTERCHANGE OF THE NAMES ZEKHARYAH, YIḤYE', AND ḤAYIM

R. Zekharyah Harofe (Harazah) is the fifteenth-century R. Yiḥye' al-Ṭabīb [the physician]. He apparently lived in the town of Maṣna'at Bane Qīs in central Yemen,[37] where he produced midrashic and halakhic lit-

---

32. The reference is to R. Yiḥye' who built the Alsheikh synagogue, in Qaa Bir al-Azab, their new location in Ṣan'a, after the return of the exiles from the expulsion to Moze that took place in 1680.

33. Prof. Shlomo Dov Goitein wrote the same, and he cited proof from the prophet Zekharyah who is called Yiḥye' in the Quran. See the note in the book by Haim Ḥibshush, *Mas'ot Ḥibshush* (Tel Aviv, 1939), p. 7 n. 19. Perhaps the source of the name Yiḥye' comes from the Jews from whom Muhammad heard about the prophet Zekharyah.

34. On the Mahariṣ, see below in the next section.

35. Qoraḥ, *Sa'arat Teiman*, p. 150 n. 7.

36. See the comprehensive discussion by Prof. Yehudah Ratzaby, "*Gilgulei ha-Shemot Yiḥye', Zekharyah, and Ḥayim,*" in his *Be-Ma'agalot Teiman* (Tel Aviv, 1948), pp. 6–9.

37. At the end of his work *Midrash ha-Ḥefeṣ*, he wrote "וכאן תמאמה פי אכ'ר שנת הק"ץ ליצירה, תהא סוף וקץ לכל גלויותינו, וכאן תאליפה במצנעה' בני קיס ,תחרוב ותצדי

erature, the most famous being *Midrash Ḥefeṣ*.[38] Since he wrote in Arabic (in Hebrew script), he gave his name in Arabic, "al-Ḥakim Yiḥye' ibn Slayman al-Mu'allam," that is, the physician Yiḥye' ben Shelomo the teacher.[39]

In his *Midrash Ḥefeṣ*, he signed his name at the end of each *ḥumash*: in the first four books with the name Zekharyah, apparently because he interpolated his name into a rhyme he wrote in Hebrew, and at the end of the work with the name Yiḥye'. At the end of the books he wrote: in Genesis, "I, Zekharyah Harofe, the least worthy and most minor of all existence ...";[40] in Exodus, "I, Zekharyah Harofe, I will declare to His name power ...";[41] in Leviticus, "I, Zekharyah Harofe, will glorify and up lift to my master";[42] in Numbers, "I, Zekharyah Harofe, will ask of Him that He make me worthy of the special sages;"[43] and written in the colophon of Deuteronomy, "the physician Yiḥye' ben Slaymān al-Mu'allem said."[44]

The sixteenth-century rabbi R. Zekharyah Alḏāhari was one of the most important rabbis of Yemen and one of the greatest poets of Yemenite Jewry. He lived in Kawkabān in central Yemen. His most notable writings include an ethical work in which he presents, in rhymed prose, his impressions of his journey to various countries, including Ereṣ Israel,[45] and *Ṣedah la-Derekh*, which is a commentary on the Torah.[46]

וירושלם תתבני ותשתכלל, אכי"ר," which means, "And may its completion at the end of the year 5190 AM (1430), may it be the end of all our exiles. And it was written in Maṣna'at Bane Qis, may it be destroyed and desolate, and Jerusalem will be built and be perfect, Amen, may it be His will (*Midrash ha-Ḥefeṣ le-R' Zekharyah ha-Rofe*, ed. Meir Havatzelet (Jerusalem, 1991), Deut., p. 483; Ratzaby, *Toratan she-li-Bnei Teiman*, pp. 23–24; Yehudah Levi Naḥum, *Ḥasifat Genuzim mi-Teiman* (Holon, 1971), p. 184).

38. *Midrash ha-Ḥefeṣ*, Introduction, pp. 11–12.
39. See Ratzaby, *Toratan she-li-Bnei Teiman*, pp. 23–28; Naḥum, *Ḥasifat Genuzim*, pp. 180–91.
40. *Midrash ha-Ḥefeṣ Bereishit*, p. 261 n. 11; Naḥum, *Ḥasifat Genuzim*, p. 183.
41. *Midrash ha-Ḥefeṣ*, Shemot, p. 450; Naḥum, *Ḥasifat Genuzim*, p. 183
42. *Midrash ha-Ḥefeṣ*, Vayikra, p. 190, n. 63.
43. *Midrash ha-Ḥefeṣ*, Bemidbar, p. 323; Naḥum, *Ḥasifat Genuzim*, pp. 183–84.
44. *Midrash ha-Ḥefeṣ*, Devarim, p. 483; Ratzaby, *Toratan she-li-Bnei Teiman*, pp. 23–24; Naḥum, *Ḥasifat Genuzim*, p. 184.
45. Alḏāhari, *Sefer ha-Musar* (Ratzaby; Jeusalem, 1965); Alḏāhari, *Sefer ha-Musar* (Yiṣhari; Rosh haAyin, 2008).
46. *Perush Ṣedah la-Derekh le-R' Zekharyah Alḏahari*, in *Ḥamisha Ḥumshe Torah, Bet David u-Shelomo* (Jerusalem, 1964)

We also have 270 *piyyutim* integrated into *Sefer ha-Musar*, as well as recently discovered poems of his.[47]

In two places in *Sefer ha-Musar* he lists his name as Zekharyah. He began the book with the words "The humble Zekharyah ben Sa'adya ben Ya'aqov Alḍahari"[48] and in a notebook that concludes his work he wrote "And now the young servant/Zekharyah ben Sa'adyah ben Ya'aqov notes."[49] In four *piyyutim* he noted his name as Zekharyah in an acrostic and in two as Yiḥye'. In a *piyyut* beginning "God is hiding" (*El mistater*), he created an acrostic with the letters of the *alef-bet*, from *alef* to *tav*, and he ended with "I am Zekharyah ben Qa'adyah."[50] In a *piyyut* opening with the words *matoq le-maṣof u-fanag* he wrote a double-letter acrostic "from Zekharyah ben Sa'adya."[51] In a *piyyut* beginning with *libbi alai ṣal'ai* and in the *piyyut* opening with the phrase *li-krat pene Shabbat,* he created an acrostic with *le-Zekharyah.*[52] In a *piyyut* starting with *yaḥid meromem,* as well as in one opening with the words *mar li mi-yaqshan,* he arranged an acrostic of Yiḥye'.[53]

R. Yiḥye' Bashīri, a famous seventeenth-century rabbi active in the al-Raḥabe district of Yemen,[54] is known also by his pen name, Avner ben Ner Hasharoni.[55] When copying books, R. Bashīri used to write his personal name in the colophon as Ḥayim or Zekharyah. The name Ḥayim occurs in four manuscripts and Zekharyah in one.

In his copy of *Sefer Or Yaqar* by Moshe Cordovero, he wrote in the colophon: "And it was written by the scribe Ḥayim son of our honorable teacher, R. Avraham *beirav* Sa'adyah *beirav* Avraham *beirav* Sa'adyah ibn Shemaryah al-Bashīri."[56] In copying *Sefer Seder ha-Yom* by

47. Yehudah 'Amir, "*R. Zekharyah Alḍāhari be-Shevah R. Yosef ben Yisra'el: Le-Qesher bein Shene Gedole ha-Shirah ha-Ivrit be-Teiman ba-Me'ot ha-16–17,*" *Pe'amim,* 59 (1994), p. 77 n. 3.
48. Alḍahari, *Sefer ha-Musar* (Ratzaby), author's introduction, line 3.
49. Ibid., notebook 45, lines 45–46.
50. Ibid., notebook 14, lines 22–58.
51. Ibid., notebook 23, lines 65–90.
52. Ibid., notebook 15, lines 54–85; 23, lines 25–56.
53. Ibid., notebook 22, lines 22–35; Alḍahari, *Sefer ha-Musar* (Yiṣhari), pp. 387–88.
54. The al-Raḥabe district is some twenty km north of the capital Ṣan'a.
55. *Encyclopaedia Judaica,* 4:296, s.v. "Bashīri, Yahya"; Aharon Gaimani, *Ḥavaṣelet ha-Sharon by Rabbi Yiḥye' Bashiri* (Jerusalem, 2008), pp. 16–18.
56. *Qovets be-Qabbalah,* JTS, New York 1767/8 (IMHM 10865). See Aharon Gaimani, *Temurot be-Moreshet Yahadut Teiman: be-Hashpa'at ha-Shulḥan 'Arukh ve-Qabalat ha-Ari* (Ramat Gan, 2005), p. 282.

R. Moshe ben Makhir, he wrote in the colophon: "I, the humble copyist Ḥayim, son of my honorable teacher and rabbi Avraham, may he rest in Eden, *beirav* Sa'adyah *beir*[*av*] Avraham, *ng'*, *beir*[*av*] Sa'adyah, *yenon shemo la'ad*, Shemaryah, *tanṣeba"h*, al-Bashīri."[57] In *Taj* he wrote in the colophon: "I, the lowly, humble Ḥayim son of the honorable R. Avraham, his memory should live in eternity, *beirav* Sa'adyah, his soul in Eden, *beirav* Avraham, *tanṣeba"h*, *beirav* Sa'adyah, "he shall live a happy life and his descendants inherit the earth" (Ps. 28:13) *beirav* Avraham, the spirit of the Lord gave him rest, son of Shemaryah, may his name be eternal, known as al-Bashīri. I wrote this precious, pleasant, esteemed book for my own use, to study it, I and my children and my children's children from now and forever..."[58] In the colophon to the Ari's *Sefer ha-Kavvanot*, he wrote: "And may the completion of the second copy from the print to the manuscript, I Ḥayim son of *kmhr"r* Avraham al-Bashīri ..."[59]

When copying selections from *Sefer Ḥaredim* by R. Ela'zar Azkari along with other pieces from Kabbalah in an anthology, he wrote in the colophon: "The copyist Zekharyah ben Avraham al-Bashīri, *yṣ"v*, [the book is] completed but mercy of the Heavens is not ended, or the copy is ended but not complete, for God is complete.[60] In R. Yiḥye' Bashīri's *takkanah* on the change in the value of money that occurred in Yemen in 1646, he signed his name as "the humble Ḥayim, the son of *kmhr"r*, Avraham al-Bashīri."[61]

R. Yiḥye' Sāliḥ (Mahariṣ), according to his system, was careful to note his Hebrew name Ḥayim. His commentary to the *Tiklal*, the Yemenite rite prayer book, is called *Eṣ Ḥayim*, according to the verse Proverbs 11:30: "The fruit of the righteous is a tree of life." He called his

57. *Seder ha-Yom* by Moshe ben Makhir, MS Rabbi Shimon Ṣāliḥ, Bnei Brak. See Gaimani, *Temurot be-Moreshet*, pp. 282–83; idem, *Ḥavatselet ha-Sharon*, p. 12 n. 19.

58. *Taj*, Manuscript Zekharyah Samina, Elyakhin. See Aharon Gaimani, *Ḥavaṣelet ha-Sharon*, p. 14.

59. *Sefer ha-Kavvanot le-ha-Ari*, MS R. Yosef Qāfiḥ. See Gaimani, *Temurot be-Moreshet*.

60. MS Jerusalem, JNUL, Manuscript Department 8^0 2428; see Gaimani, *Temurot be-Moreshet*, pp. 280–81.

61. See *Tiklal Kadmonim*, the prayer book of R. Yiḥye' Bashīri, which was copied in the twentieth century by R. Shalom Qoraḥ, p. 215a. R. Bashīri's *takkanah* is cited in the prayer book of Mahariṣ, *Eṣ Ḥayim*, pt. 1, p. 299b. The text and the translation of the *takkanah* were included in the book by R. Yiṣḥaq Raṣabi, *Tofes Ketubbot* (Bnei Brak, 1995), p. 127; see also the photograph on p. 223. See also S. Qoraḥ, *Arikhat Shulḥan*, 3 (Bnei Brak, 1985), pp. 405–6.

responsa books *Pe'ulat Ṣaddik*, based on the verse Proverbs 10:16: "The labor of the righteous man makes for life." His work *Ḥeleq ha-Dikduk* is called *Toṣa'ot Ḥayim*, based on the verse Proverbs 4:23: "For it is the source of life."[62] Mahariṣ noted other rabbis in Yemen known by the two names Yiḥye' and Ḥayim. For instance, in one of his responsa, he cited one of his teachers, R. Yiḥye' 'Irāqi, writing, "Our distinguished rav, R. Ḥayim ben R. Shalom ben Aharon Kohen Tzedek called 'Irāqi";[63] in his commentary on the prayer book support for Yemenite Jewry's custom from R. Yiḥye' Bashīri, he wrote "and also our teacher, the rav, R. Ḥayim Bashīri vocalized it thusly."[64] Apparently, rabbis who noted their name in writings as Zekharyah, such as R. Zekharyah Harofe, were usually referenced by Mahariṣ with the name Zekharyah—even though this ran counter to his system—because that was how they were actually called.[65]

R. Yiḥye' Qoraḥ, a famous nineteenth-century Yemenite rabbi, noted his name using three alternatives: Yiḥye', Zekharyah, and Ḥayim. He began the introduction to his work *Marpe Lashon*, in which he explicated Yemenite Jewry's version of Targum Onkelos, with: "Let the servant say to the servant of the Lord, the lowliest of the scribes, Zekharyah son of my master, my father Shalom of the Qorḥi"m family." He ended the introduction with:

> Furthermore, as it is said "a healing tongue is a tree of life" (Prov. 15:4), Yiḥye', which is Ḥayim, as well like my name Eṣ Ḥayim *ge[matria]* Zakhar with the *kolel*, which is the main part of my name Zekharyah, and my prayer is pure before the Lord who helps the oppressed, will help me in honoring His name, that I not be abashed or ashamed, not in this world or in the World to Come, and He will fulfill through this book of mine what is written, "Let not the foot of the arrogant tread on me, or the hand of the wicked drive me away" (Ps. 36:12), as well as what is written, "She is a tree of life, and whoever holds on to her is happy" (Prov. 3:18), and this shall be by the end of my words.[66]

62. Some think that R. Yehuda Gispan, a nineteenth-century Ṣan'a rabbi, is the one was called the work *Ḥelek ha-Dikduk* for the title *Totza'ot Ḥayim*. See R. Yiḥye' Ṣāliḥ, *Shut Pe'ulat Ṣaddiq*, part 1 introduction, chap. 6, p. 68, comment by Qāfiḥ.
63. Ibid., Par. 65, p. 75.
64. Mahariṣ, *Eṣ Ḥayim*, pt. 1, p. 168a.
65. See, for example, ibid., pt. 1, pp. 8b, 10b, 55b, 60b, 63a; Mahariṣ, *Shut Pe'ulat Ṣaddiq*, pt. 2, par. 42; pt. 3, par. 252.
66. Y. Qoraḥ, *Marpe Lashon*, in *Keter ha-Torah—Ha-Taj ha-Gadol*, (Jerusalem, 1970),

He selected these particular verses since they contain an allusion to his name. The calculation according to *gematria* is as follows: Eṣ Ḥayim = 228. Zakhar = 227 + 1 = 228. For the name Zekharyah, he considered only the root *z-kh-r* and added another one that is called *"kolel"* as it gives the word an extra number.

In *Berit ha-Lashon*, in which R. Qoraḥ discusses the importance of Aramaic, as well as a collection of rules, he opens with the words "Said Zekharyah the Scribe."[67] In his introduction to his work on the Torah, *Maskil Doresh*, he writes:

> Said *Ḥayim* asking from the merciful God, through my simple-mindedness and my great energy, I thought to write this booklet on what I have found new in the *parashiyot* of our holy Torah. Perhaps, it will be of use to others beyond me and my sons, the Lord should protect and sustain them. And I named this booklet *Maskil Doresh* (*gema*[*tria*] of *Ḥayim sha'al* ["Ḥayim asked"]), as is its name, so it is, for when I was discerning and looked closely at a statement in our holy Torah, as it sa[ys] in it, "The promise he gave for a thousand generations" (Ps. 108:8), I wrote.[68]

He began another introduction with the words "Ḥayim said asking."[69] Likewise, in his work *Maskil Doresh,* when he finds a challenge in a verse, he starts with the words "Ḥayim asked," meaning I, Ḥayim, am asking about the verse.[70] The calculation of the names *Maskil Doresh* and *Ḥayim sha'al* is as follows: *maskil* = 400; *Ḥayim sha'al* = 399, and with the addition of 1 = 400. In the title of the work, he calculated only the first word, *maskil,* while in the expression *Ḥayim sha'al* he added one, which is called *kolel.* Elsewhere R. Qoraḥ links the three names Zekharyah, Ḥayim, and Yiḥye'. In his commentary on Genesis 8:1, "And God remembered Noah," he writes that God remembered Noah to give him life:

> And to explain all this, we will introduce what seems to be the reason for saying in the High Holydays prayer, "Remember [*zokhreinu*] us for life," using the term for remembrance and not another notion, since

Introduction, p. 4; *Keter ha-Torah– Ḥazon Shimon – Ha-Taj ha-Shalem ke-Minhag Teiman,* ed. R. Shimon Ṣaliḥ (Bnei Brak, 1996–2002), p. 17b.

67. In *Keter ha-Torah—Ha-Taj ha-Gadol*, p. 8; *Keter Torah–Ḥazon Shimon*, pp. 18a, 21a.
68. R. Yiḥye' Qoraḥ, *Maskil Doresh al ha-Torah* (Tel Aviv, 1964), Introduction, p. 23.
69. Ibid., *Maskil Doresh* [appendices], p. 201.
70. See, for example, ibid., Gen. 48:19 (p. 77); Ex. 13:14 (p. 97); 18:1 (p. 101).

> the term *zekhira* [remembrance] belongs to life. And one must give a reason why. To be sure, through *sod* [the mystical meaning] the reason is simple, since remembrance is through the powers of the Moḥin Qadishin (the first three Sfirot), which are the life of the King, as we know from the *sod* of the *tefillin* and a number of places. Therefore, remembrance means life.[71]

He wrote further:

> And from this we certainly understand our tradition that the name Yiḥye' is the name Zekharyah. Just as this is an ancient custom, just as we see from 600 years ago, great rabbis whose name was Yiḥye' in Arabic, which is shared with the Holy Tongue, and they sign their name in the Holy Tongue as Zekharyah, as we found with Rabbenu Zekharyah Harofe author of *Midrash ha-Ḥefeṣ* and Rabbenu Zekharyah Alḍāhari, OBM, author of a collection of poems,[72] and thus a number of scribes and *dayyanim* sign their name. And this is how we received it, since when we were exiled from our land, the Holy Land, to this country, the land of the Arabs, those whose name was Zekharyah were called by the byname Yiḥye', since there were sages well-versed in the holy tongue who knew the meaning of the name Zekharyah, which means Yiḥye', so they called them Yiḥye' since that was its explanation.[73]

From his statements we see that R. Qoraḥ used Yiḥye', Zekharyah, and *Ḥayim* to denote his name.

From R. Zekharyah Ṭabīb (15th c.), R. Zekharyah al-Ḍāhari (16th c.), R. Yiḥye' Bashīri (17th c.), R. Yiḥye' Sālih (18th c.), and R. Yiḥye' Qoraḥ (19th c.), we learn of parallel usage of the names Yiḥye', Zekharyah, and Ḥayim. In addition to the name Yiḥye', which was the most widespread name in all generations, the name Zekharyah was widely used until the sixteenth century, and beginning in the seventeenth century the name Ḥayim was common.

R. Yiḥye' Bashīri did not present his name in writings as Yiḥye', perhaps owing to the Arabic source of this name or simply for a literary reason. R. Yiḥye' Bashīr wrote Ḥayim instead of the Arabic name

71. Ibid., *parashat* Noah, p. 38.

72. He is referring to Alḍāhari's book *Sefer ha-Musar*. The book was published in two editions: *Sefer ha-Musar* (Ratzaby); *Sefer ha-Musar ha-Shirah ve-ha-Piyyut le-R. Yiḥye' (Zekharyah) Alḍahari*, edited by Mordechai Yitshari (Rosh HaAyin, 2008).

73. Y. Qoraḥ, *Maskil Doresh.*

Yiḥye', as other rabbis wrote Shalom in place of Sālem, Shelomo in place of Slaymān, Moshe in place of Mūsa, and so on.[74]

The most common name among Yemenite Jews is the name Yiḥye', meaning "life." The Arabs pronounce this name as Yaḥya, while the Jews pronounce it as Yiḥye'.

2.1 The Names Zekharyah, Yiḥye', and Ḥayim in Yemenite Manuscripts

In fourteenth- to nineteenth–century colophons from Yemen, we can discern that until the sixteenth century the names Yiḥye' and Zekharyah were used, whereas the name Ḥayim was not. Copyists or those who ordered the copy who are named in colophons are cited here according to their earliest appearance. Owing to the large number of occurrences, I cite only representative examples.

In a fourteenth-century colophon, even earlier than the sages discussed above, the name Zekharyah was noted in three copies and the name Yiḥye', in two: The person who ordered the manuscript copied in Ṭawīlah in 1357 is "Mas'ūd Halevi ben Zekharyah Halevi ben Yefet Halevi."[75] A copyist from the town of Thila in 1359 wrote his name as "and the writer Yiḥye' ben Ḥasan."[76] A copyist in 1384 wrote his name as "Yosef b. R. Abba Mori Zekharyah."[77]

In fifteenth-century colophons, the name Zekharyah is mentioned in nine copies, and the name Yiḥye' in two copies.[78] The person who ordered a manuscript of the Torah in 1409 wrote the name Zekharyah in his family lineage: "Ezra, the spirit of the Lord gives him rest, b. R. the great and holy Shalom, the spirit of the Lord gives him rest, son of the great and holy Zekharyah, his soul will rest in Eden, ben R. the great and holy Gad b. R. the great and holy Meshullam OBM for eternity b.

74. R. David Jamal wrote down hearsay from Zekharyah Say'ani in the name of R. Zekharyah Badihi. The two rabbis mentioned are known by their personal name Yiḥye'; the latter is R. Yiḥye' Badihi, author of *Ḥen Tov*. R. Jamal preferred to call them by the name Zekharyah, apparently because it seemed more Hebrew to him. See R. Yiḥye' Badiḥi, *'Im Ḥen Ṭov, Ḥenah shel Torah*, with annotations, notes, and commentaries by R. Itamar Ḥayim Kohen (Bnei Brak, 2008), p. 368.

75. *Halakhah u-Midrash*, MS New York, JTS 328.

76. Manuscript Yehudah Levi Naḥum, *Mif'al Ḥasifat Ginze Teiman*, Holon, single page.

77. *Halakhah u-Midrash*, MS London 10738 (Gaster 1382); *Halakhah u-Midrash*, MS New York, JTS 290.

78. The mention of Zekharyah Harofe was discussed above and is not taken into consideration in this section.

R. the great and holy Ḥoter al-Ḥabīshi."[79] The buyer of the manuscript in 1419 was "Ḥoter Halevi ben Zekharyah."[80] A copyist of a manuscript of Former Prophets in 1471 wrote the name Zekharyah in his family's lineage: "Avraham ben R. Shalom Halevi ben Me'oded Halevi ben Zekharyah Halevi."[81] In a manuscript on the sciences and medicine, copied in 1499, the name of the commissioner is "Mūsa, may the Lord protect him, b. Amran b. Yiḥye', the spirit of the Lord gives him rest b. Yosef, *tanṣeba"h.*"[82]

In sixteenth-century colophons the name Zekharyah is noted in five copies, and the name Yiḥye' in one.[83] In a manuscript of the Hagiographa copied in 1505, in Khamer, the name of the copyist is "Shelomo ben Zekharyah Halevi."[84] In a manuscript of *Midrash ha-Ḥefeṣ* by R. Zekharyah Harofe, copied in 1532, in 'Imrān, the name of the commissioner appears: "Slaymān ibn Yiḥye' Al Ḥarīzi."[85] In a manuscript of *Sefer Tola'at Ya'aqov* by R. Meir Gabbai that was copied in 1593, in al-Ṣulbi, the name of the copyist is "Zekharyah ben Yosef Ḥoṭer."[86]

In a seventeenth-century colophon, the name Zekharyah occurs ten times, the name Ḥayim three times, and the name Yiḥye' once.[87] In a manuscript of *Midrash ha-Gadol* by R. David 'Adani, which was copied in 1616, in Qaryat Dhanaḥ, the name of the commissioner of the work is "Shelomo *beirav* David *beirav* Zekharya' al-Khalafi."[88] In a Zohar manuscript copied in 1645, in the Radā' community, the name of the copyist was "Zekharyah ben Yosef, the spirit of the Lord gave him rest, ben Sa'adyah, his memory should live in eternity, ben Shelomo, his memory should live in eternity, his soul in Eden."[89] In a *Tiklal* manu-

79. MS London
80. *Halakhah u-Midrash*, MS San Francisco Sutro 104 (Brinner 115)
81. Former Prophets, MS Rabbi Yosef Qāfiḥ; *Oṣar Kitve Yad Ivriyim* (Paris, 1972).
82. MS London 14059 (IMHM 7928).
83. The mention of Zekharyah Harofe was discussed above and is not taken into consideration in this section.
84. Maimonides' *Sefer ha-Mitsvot*, MS Moscow Ginzburg 1014 (IMHM 48303).
85. MS London 2381; Margaliot Catalogue, 2, no. 366, pp. 26–27.
86. MS Sassoon 568 (IMHM 9789); *Ohel David* Catalogue, 1, p. 435.
87. Mentions of R. Yiḥye' Bashīri were mentioned above and not included in this count.
88. MS Tel Aviv, Y. Ratzaby [5] (IMHM 39664).
89. MS Menahem Feldman, Jerusalem, no. 52 (IMHM 42662).

script copied in 1647, in Majadla Ḥaql, the name of the copyist is "Ḥayim son of *mv* Shalom ben David ben Yiṣḥaq ben Shelomo ben Ya'aqov known as al-Ḥajāji."[90] In a manuscript of a prayer book copied in 1674, in the Dhamār community, the commissioner of the work was "Se'īd ben Yiḥye', *yṣ"v*."[91]

In eighteenth-century colophons the name Yiḥye' was indicated five times, the name Zekharyah' four times, and the name Ḥayim once.[92] In a manuscript of *Sefer Pardes Rimmonim* by R. Moshe Cordovero, which was copied in 1707, the name of the one who commissioned the copy is "Ṣāliḥ Yiḥye' ibn Yosef ibn Ṣāliḥ, *nefesh, ru'aḥ, u-neshamah*."[93] In a manuscript of the *Shulḥan Arukh* copied in 1720, in Qaryat al-Ṣayīḥ, the name of the copyist is "the humble Ḥayim son of my master, *mori* Sa'adya, His Rock and Redeemer should guard him."[94] A manuscript of the *Shulḥan Arukh* that was copied in 1720 in the village of Qaṣba fī Balīd Ḍalīma, the name of the copyist is "Yosef ibn Zekharyah ibn Ḥisdai al-Marḥabi."[95] In a manuscript of the *Shulḥan Arukh* copied in 1740, in Bane Manṣūr, the name of the person who commissioned the work is "Sa'adyah ben Zekharyah Ḥusāni."[96] In a manuscript of the *Shulḥan Arukh* copied in 1741, the name of the copyist is "Yiḥye' ben my master, my father, Moshe ben Shalom known as al-Qāraṭeh, His Rock and Redeemer should guard him."[97]

In nineteenth-century colophons the name Yiḥye' appears in 36 copies, the name Zekharyah in 9, and the name Ḥayim in 7.[98] In a manuscript of *Sefer Qeri'e Mo'ed*, copied in 1801 in Ṣan'a, the client was "Zekharyah ben Master Sa'ad al-Sirri."[99] In a manuscript of Rashi's commentary on

90. MS Ramat Gan, Bar-Ilan University 398 (IMHM 36881).
91. MS England, Leeds Roth 76 (IMHM 15307); Aharon Gaimani, *"Ha-Sofer R. Pinhas ben Gad ha-Kohen," Tema* 7 (2001): 123.
92. Mentions of R. Yiḥye' Ṣāliḥ were mentioned above and not included in this count.
93. MS Munich, Bavarian State Library HEBR 924. According to the lineage of the copyist, he is the grandfather of Mahariṣ. See below, part 3, chapter 5, section 3.
94. MS Chicago, Spertus College (IMHM 40226); Gaimani, *Temurot*, pp. 299–300.
95. MS New York, Public Library 112 (IMHM 31114); Gaimani, *Temurot be-Moreshet*, pp. 300–301, no. 36.
96. MS New York, Public Library Heb MS 111 (IMHM 31113); Gaimani, *Temurot be-Moreshet*, pp. 304–5, no. 47.
97. MS New York, Public Library Heb MS 109 (IMHM 31111); Gaimani, *Temurot be-Moreshet*, p. 305.
98. Mentions of R. Yiḥye' Qoraḥ were discussed above and were not in this account.
99. MS Jerusalem, Hubara [5] (IMHM 40441).

the Torah, which was copied in 1804, the name of the copyist is "the humble Yiḥye' ibn Sa'adya' ibn Ḥayim ibn Sālem al-Sirri al-Maz'aqi, *yṣ"v*."[100] In a manuscript of Rashi's commentary on the Torah, 1805, in the village of al-Ḥays in the district of Thila, the name of the person commissioning the work is "Yosef son of *mmv"r* Yiḥye' 'Afjīn Jamal al-Ṣan'āni."[101] In a manuscript of the *siddur* of R. Y. Wanneh, copied in 1819, the name of the copyist is "Shalem son *abba mori* Me'oded ben *mori zekeni* Yiḥye' ben of the great, honorable holy, OBM, Me'oded al-Bashāri, may he live a long life."[102] In a manuscript of the book *Tola'at Ya'akov*, copied in 1827, the name of the commissioner is "Zekharyah' ben Yosef al-Khalfi."[103] In a manuscript of *Pirqei Rabbi Eliezer*, copied in 1841, the copyist's names is "Avraham Yiḥye' *ysh"l* ben Aharon, may the spirit of the Lord give him rest, ben Shalem, *tanṣeba"h*."[104] In a manuscript of *Sefer Ḥen Ṭov* by R. Yiḥye' Badīḥi, copied in 1889 in Ṣan'a, the name of the copyist is "Avraham ben Ḥayim Shalem al-Naddāf, *yṣ"v*, his end be for the good, and the person who commissioned the copy was "Yosef ben Yiḥye' al-Tām, may his memory be long lasting."[105]

A review of colophons shows that use of the name Ḥayim began in the seventeenth century, during the time of R. Yiḥye' Bashīri, as one sees from those in which he wrote his name; in other colophons from this period and onward the name Ḥayim was written. We are also informed by scrutinizing colophons that in the fifteenth and sixteenth centuries the name Zekharyah was also common. The shift from preferring Zekharyah to favoring Yiḥye' began in the eighteenth century. The name Yiḥye' was very widespread in the nineteenth and twentieth centuries.

One can learn of the increasing use of the name Yiḥye' from the eighteenth century on by reviewing Yemenite *ketubbot* and *gittin* from the eighteenth century to the mid-twentieth century. The name Yiḥye' appears 2,057 times, the name Ḥayim 496 times, and the name Zekharyah 13 times—8 times with the *heh* and five times with an *alef.*

100. MS Jerusalem, Mosad Harav Kook 731 (IMHM 10233).

101. MS Yehudah Levi Naḥum, *Mif'al Ḥasifat Genuzim mi-Teiman* 64; Naḥum, *Mi-Ṣefunot Teiman* (Tel Aviv 1987), p. 35, serial no. 102.

102. MS Sassoon 339–340; *Ohel David Catalogue,* 1, pp. 329–34.

103. MS Sassoon 568 (IMHM 9789); *Ohel David Catalogue*, 2, p. 1018.

104. MS Ramat Gan, Bar-Ilan University 496 (IMHM 37015).

105. MS Jerusalem, Mosad Harav Kook 943 (IMHM 26427).

These findings show us that in recent generations use of the name Zekharyah as a parallel to Yiḥye' has declined. Here are two examples of the parallel use of Yiḥye' and Zekharyah during the first half of the twentieth century: Yiḥye' Ma'ūḍa of the Ḥārf Bane Maṭar community wrote in the registration of the birth of his oldest son in 1936 "Shalom ben Zekharyah," in the registration of his other sons on 22 Dec 1939 "Slayman ben Yiḥye'," and in 1945 "Ma'ūḍa ben Yiḥye'."[106] Yet, R. Shalom 'Uzayri, one of the rabbis of the Manākhe community, noted in a birth listing he wrote for one of his children in 1945, "And I gave him the name of my grandfather Yiḥye' in [Arab]ic, in our language Zekharyah."[107]

The name Zekharyah was written also as Zekharya' (זכריא) to avoid writing God's name. Conversely, some wrote Yiḥye'h instead of Yiḥye'. There were places in Yemen where they wrote Iḥye', and it seems that this referred to the name Yiḥye', and it was written the way it was heard in the spoken language in their region. Below are written testimonies, in chronological order. In a colophon written by R. Shalom Shabazi in 1665, he gave the name of the commissioner of the work as ונסכת לאלתלמיד אלעזיז, meaning, it was copied for the dear student Iḥya' ibn Haba.[108] In a bill of sale of a *Tiklal Mashta–Shabazi,* the name of the seller appears as "Se'īd ibn Iḥye'."[109] In a *ketubbah* from the village of Maqruḍ, from 1924, the name of the groom is listed as Reuven ben Iḥye'. A *ketubbah* from the village of Maḍrāb, from 1937, the name of the groom was written as Sālem ben Iḥye'. In a *ketubbah* from the village Dayrā' Ashū'bi, from 1946, a witness signed his name as Iḥya' ibn Isra'īl.[110] In a *ketubbah* from the village of Ashīqa, from 1949, the witnesses signed as Wahab ibn Iḥye' Hakohen, Ḥasan ibn Iḥye'. In another *ketubbah* from Ashīqa, from 1949, the name of the witness was written as Iḥya' ibn Wahab.

106. The registration within a printed book, *Nahal Qedumim.* In the possession of Shalom Ben Porath of Netanya.

107. R. Shalom 'Uzayri, *Sefer Iqvei Shalom,* ed. by author's family (Tel Aviv, 2006), p. 24.

108. Ratzaby, *Toratan she-li-Bnei Teiman,* p. 55.

109. *Tiklal Mashta–Shabazi,* 2, photo edition, published by Binyamin Odded-Yefet (Jerusalem, 1986), p. 714.

110. Isra'il is the biblical name Israel. On this name see this part, chap. 5, sect. 2.

3. SUMMARY

From the foregoing discussion, we see that part of the names from Jewish sources were pronounced and written in Hebrew orthography as pronounced in Arabic, such as Harūn for Aharon and Mūsa for Moses. As for the name Sālem, the Jews of Yemen usually translated it as Shalom even though the correct translation is Shalem. Until the seventeenth century, the common name Yiḥye' appeared in writing as Zekharyah, and from the eighteenth century onward the use of Yiḥye' became the more prevalent.

R. Avraham 'Arusi related that in the eighteenth century there was a Muslim judge by the name of Yiḥye' Ṣālih al-Khubasi, who asked R. Yiḥye' Ṣāliḥ (Mahariṣ) to change his name, since the Muslims mocked him saying that among the Jews there was a famous sage whose name was also Yiḥye' Ṣāliḥ.[111]

Y. Ratzaby told me that in a dispute that broke out in Ṣan'a in 1914 about the Kabbalah and its customs. The disputants, Chief Rabbi Yiḥye' Yiṣḥaq Halevi and R. Yiḥye' Qāfiḥ came before the *imam* Yiḥye', who remarked to the chief rabbi, "You are Yiḥye' and he is Yiḥye' and I am Yiḥye'; together we must end this controversy."

An interesting thing occurred with R. Yiḥye' Yiṣḥaq Halevi, who served as chief rabbi of Yemen in the first third of the twentieth century. In his correspondence with personages in Ereṣ Israel, he gave his name as Yiḥye' Mūsa, the way it is commonly written in Israel: Yiḥye' ben Moshe.

111. See his work *Qore ha-Dorot*, in Sa'adya Ḥozeh, *Toledot ha-Rav Shalom Shabazi u-Minhagei Yahadut Shar'ab be-Teiman*, 1 (Jerusalem, 1973), pp. 78–79.

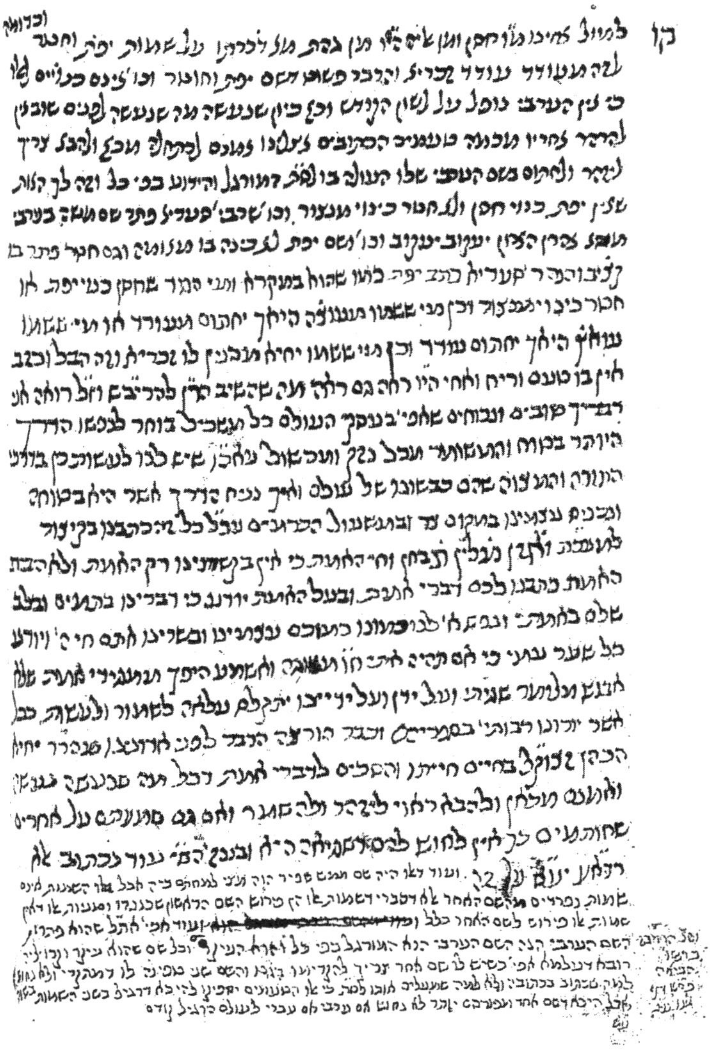

Arabic names and the way they appear in a *get* in *Shut Pe'ulat Ṣaddiq* by Rabbi Yiḥye Ṣāliḥ (Mahariṣ), in author's handwritten manuscript. Manuscript in possession of RM"Ḥ, Bnei Brak

CHAPTER FIVE

RARE NAMES

The rare names to be discussed come from written as well as oral sources, some from the early period but mainly from more recent times. In the works of the Yemenite rabbis and in the questionnaires completed, there are names rare in one district but not in another, and so they have not been included in the list. Nor did I include rare names found among the remnant of Yemenite Jewry who left the country in the last two decades. The names presented in this chapter are only some of those that occur infrequently in the inventory from the various sources cited.

1. MEDIEVAL NAMES

In the period of the economic flourishing of Yemenite Jewry and the India trade in the twelfth and thirteenth centuries, we find rare personal names, such as Maḍmūn ben Yefet, *nagid* of the Jews of Yemen, who was also called by the Hebrew name Shemaryah; his brother, Bundār, which indicates his family's origin in Persia; and Maḥrūz, translated as *Shamur*, meaning one guarded by the Lord.[1]

At the beginning of *Iggeret Teiman,* Maimonides wrote in reply to R. Ya'aqov Fayyūmi, *negid* of the Jews of Yemen: "To our great, holy teacher and rabbi Ya'aqov the wise and discerning, the charming, precious, honorable, son of our great, holy teach[er] and rab[bi] Fayyūmi."[2]

1. Shlomo Dov Goitein, *"Negidei Erets Teiman,"* in *Ha-Teimanim—Mivḥar Meḥqarim,* (Jerusalem, 1983), pp. 75–83; idem, *"Me-Ḥalifat ha-Mikhtavim shel Yeqirei Teiman be-Et Periḥat Saḥar Hodu,"* in *Ha-Teimanim—Mivḥar Meḥqarim* (Jerusalem, 1983), p. 100; Shlomo Dov Goitein and Mordechai A. Friedman, *Maḍmun Nagid of Yemen and the India Trade* (Jerusalem, 2010), pp. 12–18.
2. R. Yosef Qāfiḥ, *Iggeret Teiman* (Jerusalem, 1987), p. 15.

On the name Fayyūmi mentioned in *Iggeret Teiman*, R. Amram Qoraḥ wrote: "If we focus on this appellation and try to make assumptions, we will achieve nothing, and until now, I have not seen this appellation for any rabbi except him."[3] Some scholars believe that the name Fayyūmi attests to the family's origin from the Fayyūm in Egypt,[4] but in R. Yosef Qāfiḥ's opinion the name Fayyūmi is a private one. R. Qāfiḥ expanded on this, writing:

> The name Fayyūmi is not a family name as many thought, leading them to the supposition that a family that came from the city of Fayyūm, Egypt, which is the biblical Pithom, was the leading one among the rabbis of Yemen. This is definitely not so. We have a tradition from our forefathers that the name Fayyūmi is not a family name but a personal one. And this tradition of ours has support since if it were a family name it would be written as "al-Fayyūmi," as it is customary to add the article, the prefix "al" to the family name, such as al-Ladāni and al-Ḥamāmi.[5]

R. Qāfiḥ cited proofs from a number of manuscripts in which were written "*beirav* Fayyūmi" or "Ben Fayyūmi," which shows that Fayyūmi is a personal name. On the use of this name in Yemen, R. Qāfiḥ wrote:

> And we have a tradition from our forefathers that with the spreading of knowledge of the teachings and books of R. Sa'adyah Gaon, he was admired by a huge number of people who revered his teachings, in those same generations in Yemen, with evidence from that the fact that many of his books were found only in Yemen and nowhere else, so out of admiration for R. Sa'adyah Gaon, the father of R. Fayyūmi called his son by the name Fayyūmi.[6]

R. Sa'adyah Gaon was called Rav Sa'adyah Gaon al-Fayyūmi because of his place of origin in the Fayyūm district of Egypt, and he was a revered figure among Yemenite Jews throughout the generations.

3. R. 'Amram Qoraḥ, *Sa'arat Teiman* (Jerusalem, 1954), p. 95 n. 5.
4. Simcha Assaf, "*Al ha-Qesherim shel Yehudei Teiman im ha-Merkazim be-Bavel u-be-Erets Yisra'el*," in *The First World Congress of Jewish Studies* (1952), p. 393; Avraham Alnaddaf, *Shut Zikhronei Ish*, in his *Anaf Ḥayim* (Jerusalem, 1981), sect. 71, p. 249. On the name Fayyumi as a family name, see part 2, chap. 3, section 8.
5. See R. Qāfiḥ's edition of *Gan ha-Sekhalim* (Jerusalem, 1984), introduction, p. 13; see also R. Yosef Qāfiḥ, *Iggeret Teiman*, in his edition of *Iggerot ha-Rambam* (Jerusalem, 1987), p. 15 n. 3.
6. *Gan ha-Sekhalim*, introduction, p. 13.

In a work of responsa on philosophy composed no later than 1357, the author wrote his name as "I the most humble of the students Peraḥyah ben Meshullam OBM."[7] Concerning the author's name, R. Qāfiḥ wrote: "The name 'Peraḥyah' is rare in Yemen, and I know of no other sage or person with this name."[8] In a collection in the handwriting of R. Shalom Shabazi, the author wrote his name in the title of a new poem—beginning with the words "שמץ שמעתי באזני"—with the words *"Siman shalem beirav Yosef Mashta al-Shabazi mi-Bnei Peraḥyah."*[9] In the colophon of a manuscript written by R. Yisra'el, the son of the seventeenth-century poet R. Yosef ben Yisra'el, he wrote the family lineage, enumerating twelve generations back to Peraḥyah.[10] Perhaps all the names mentioned alluded to that rabbi.

The name Banayah is the translation of the Arabic name 'Amr, "builder."[11] The fifteenth-century scribe Banayah copied many manuscripts that are known for their precision and beautiful calligraphy.[12] In a manuscript of the Torah that he copied in 1461, he indicated his name in the colophon: "The weak, miserable scribe, the least esteemed, Banayah ben Sa'adyah ben Zekharyah ben Marjaz."[13] In a manuscript of Maimonides' *Sefer Zemanim* of the Mishneh Torah, which he copied in 1464, he noted his name in the colophon: "The humble writer Banayah ben Zekharyah al-Marjazi."[14] His sons Yehosef and David as well as other copyists from his family mentioned him by this name. For example, in a manuscript of the Torah, copied by his son Yehosef in 1508, he indicated his name in the colophon: "I have written it, the humble Yehosef ben Banayah, born to Ḥazmaq [in *atbash*, Se'īd]."[15]

In a 1509 manuscript of the Pentateuch copied by his son David, the copyist wrote his name in the colophon as "The humble scribe David, His name shall endure forever, *beirav* Banayah, OBM, son of the scribe

7. R. Yosef Qāfiḥ, *"Arba'im She'elot u-Teshuvot be-Filosofya le-Rav Peraḥyah b"R. Meshullam," Ketavim*, 1 (Jerusalem, 1989), p. 133.
8. Ibid., p. 131.
9. Manuscript in the possession of R. Assaf Haetzni and R. Ḥaim Genasia, Elad, Israel.
10. See below, part 3, chapter 5, sect. 3.
11. See the comment by R. Amram Qoraḥ on this name, above chap. 4, sect. 1.
12. See Michael Riegler, *Colophons of Medieval Hebrew Manuscripts as Historical Sources* (Jerusalem, 1995), pp. 163–66.
13. MS London 2370 (IMHM 6036); Margoliouth Catalogue, 1, ser. no. 127, p. 94.
14. MS Sassoon 1012 (IMHM 4743); Ohel David Catalogue, 2, no. 1012, p. 700.
15. MS Jerusalem, JNUL Heb 4^0 1133; *Oṣar Kitve Yad Ivriyim* (Jerusalem-Paris, 1972) 1, no. 171.

Sa'adyah, the spirit of the Lord rests upon him, son of Zekharyah, resting in Eden, son of Banayah, *tanṣeba"h.*"[16] In a manuscript of the *Tiklal*, copied by the grandson Avigad in 1540, he wrote his name in the colophon: "Avigad ben David ben Banayah ben Sa'adyah ben Zekharyah ben 'Oded ben Margaz."[17]

R. Zekharyah ha-Ḥalfoni, a Yemenite rabbi from the early seventeenth century, is known by his byname R. Yoḥanan Mizraḥi.[18] About the name of this sage, R. Yitsḥak Ratsabi wrote:

> This rabbi is not known to us from any other source, and even the name "Yoḥanan" does not occur at all among the Yemenites throughout the generations. Perhaps he thought that this is a translation into the holy tongue in place of the Arabic name "Yiḥye'" (the same way that the byname "Mizraḥi" is in exchange for "Mishriqi" that is used in the holy tongue for people originating in east Yemen. Or, perhaps, he is one of the forefathers of the Maharad ([Morenu ha-Rav David] Mishriqi family who have olive saplings)...and now we have learned a new thing, that the translation of Yiḥye' – Yoḥanan, matches the beginning of the word.[19]

The name Ḥisdai is rare in Yemen though known from several sources. From the poet Ḥisdai, we have a poem beginning: "חוס אלהי ממעונך על חבצלת שרונך" (Have mercy, my God, from your dwelling over your rose of Sharon).[20] Similarly, there are two Yemenite manuscripts by two scribes named *Ḥisdai*, one from the fifteenth century and one from the nineteenth. In copies from 1467 and 1473 of the Pentateuch, in the village of 'Aram in central Yemen, the copyist wrote his name in the colophon: "Ḥisdai ben Ḥoṭer ben Shalom ben Yosef known as Ibn Mahdi;"[21] "Ḥisdai ben Ḥoṭer ben Shalom ben Yosef ben Mahdi."[22] While in 1899, copying the dedication page to R. Yiḥye' Sāliḥ with

16. MS Philadelphia 304.
17. MS London 2227; Margoliouth Catalogue, 2, serial no. 711, pp. 396–402.
18. He wrote a commentary on tractates of the Mishnah and Talmud and on the Rif and was called "Ha-Mizraḥi." On him, see M. Gavra (ed.), *Mishna ve-Talmud im Peirush Ha-Mizraḥi, Berakhot u-Pesaḥim*, 1 (Bnei Brak, 1997), Introduction, pp. 71–73.
19. R. Y. Raṣabi, *"Ofan ha-Merkavah,"* in his edition of *Sefer Wanneh, Rekhev Elohim* (Bnei Brak, 1992), p. 42 n. 1.
20. Avraham Zevi Idelsohn, N. H. Torczyner, *Shirei Teiman* (Cincinnati, 1931), pp. 33–34.
21. MS NY, JTS 136.
22. *Mahberet ha-Tijan be-Aravit*, MS Jerusalem, JNUL Yah. MS Heb 5; *Oṣar Kitve Yad Ivriyim*, 1, no. 124.

the commentary *Leḥem Toda* by R. Yiḥye' Badīḥi, the copyist wrote his name in the colophon: "The lowly, miserable Ḥisdai son of my master, my father Yiḥye' who is called al-Dawwar?"[23] The name Ḥisdai appears in the lineage of another scribe who copied *Midrash ha-Ḥefeṣ* in 1500. He listed his family's lineage in the colophon: "I, Shelomo ben R. Sa'adyah b. R. Dawid b. R. Shelomo b. R. Sa'adyah b. R. Avraham b. R. Ḥisdai b. R. Sa'adyah b. R. Gad."[24]

2. NAMES IN RECENT GENERATIONS

Men's Names

'Abdallah: Abdallah is the brother of R. Ya'beṣ, who was the chief rabbi of the Ṣa'dah community in the first half of the twentieth century.[25] R. Ya'beṣ' grandson as well, R. Ovadyah Ya'beṣ, who served as the last chief rabbi of the Ṣa'dah community and today is the chief rabbi of Qiryat Eqron, is called 'Abdallah.[26]

'Ābiṣ: Ni'mah bat 'Ābiṣ[27] and Yosef ben 'Ābiṣ from the village of Ṣāghir[28] in northern Yemen.

Adam: The name was found in the Ṣan'a community in the Hakohen family.[29]

Adīb: The name was found in the Ṣan'a community in the Dar family[30] and in the Shar'abi family.[31]

'Amiel: The son of Shukr of the Qāfiḥ family.[32]

23. MS Bill Gross, Tel Aviv, no. 3, (IMHM 37726).
24. MS Sassoon 262 (IMHM 9753); *Ohel David Catalogue* (Oxford, 1932), 1, pp. 50–57.
25. Ibid., p. 673, no. 56. He signed his name as Abdallah on a *ketubbah* from Sa'adah, dated 16 Heshvan 5641 (21 Oct 1880).
26. Using the name Abdallah, he signed a *ketubbah* from the village of Sharamāt when copying it, on 6 Tammuz 5707 (24 June 1947).
27. Ibid., p. 676, no. 140; p. 684, no. 464.
28. Ibid., p. 703, no. 1174.
29. Oral testimony of R. Hayim Ṣadoq, Gederah.
30. Oral testimony of R. Gilad Ṣadoq of Bnei Brak.
31. Tsefanya Shar'abi, *Bet al-Shar'abi, Quntres odot "Yeshivat Bet al-Shar'abi," Rabbaneha, Ḥakhameha, u-Mishpaḥtah bi-Mdinat Ṣan'a be-Erets Teiman* (Qiryat, Sefer 2002), p. 20; R. Shalom Gamliel, *Pequdei Teiman: Mas he-Ḥasut be-Teiman* (Jerusalem, 1982), p. 204.
32. Yaron Harel, "'*Hu Domeh le-Ishah Ra'ah u-ketubbahtah Merubbah'—Le-Berur Yaḥasehah shel Qehilat Ṣan'a im he-Ḥakham Bashi ha-Sefardi Yitsḥaq Shaul,*" *Mi-Mizraḥ u-mi-Ma'arav*, 7 (2004): 69.

'Amram: The name was found in the Ṣan'a community. In the Qoraḥ family, R. 'Amram was the last chief rabbi of Yemenite Jewry in their Diaspora.[33]

Avshalom: The name was found in the Ṣan'a community in the 'Uzayri family,[34] the Būsāni family,[35] and the Naddāf family.[36]

'Azar: The name was found in the Ṣan'a community[37] and in the Ṣarūm family.[38]

'Azarya: The name was found in the Ṣan'a community. In the Ḥibshūsh family[39] and in the Ṭayri family.[40]

Banīn: From the Jāhli family of the Mādān (pronounced Modan) village in northern Yemen.[41]

Barhein: R. Shelomo ben Barhein was a resident of Sīnwān in southern Yemen. Some believe that Barhein is a compromise byname for the name Avraham, since the Muslims in the area forbade the Jews from giving the name Avraham.[42]

Barukh: From the village of Māfiush, in the 'Ūdayn District in southern Yemen.[43]

Bureh: From the village Raf', in the Shamūr district in southern Yemen.[44]

Daniel: From the Ṭobi family of the Ṣan'a community.[45]

33. R. 'Amram wrote the book *Sa'arat Teiman* (Jerusalem, 1954).
34. Gamliel, *Pequdei Teiman*, p. 195; Yosef Tsuri'eli, *Temurot be-Ḥinukh be-Teiman (5663–5708; 1903–1948)* (Jerusalem, 1990), doc. no. 16, p. 67; doc. 118.
35. Ibid., p. 201.
36. Ibid., p. 204.
37. Gamliel, *Pequdei Teiman*, p. 198.
38. Ibid., p. 199.
39. Ibid., p. 199.
40. Ibid., p. 197.
41. Ben David, *Bet ha-Even*, p. 697, nos. 941–42.
42. Efraim Ya'akov (ed.), *Timna—Mavo le-Ereṣ al-Ḥūgariya le-Mori Yosef Raḍa'* (Jerusalem, 2005), p. 41.
43. Oral testimony of R. Gilad Ṣadoq of Bnei Brak.
44. Oral testimony of R. Gilad Ṣadoq of Bnei Brak.
45. Gamliel, *Pequdei Teiman*, p. 195.

Elishah:	In the Ramaḍan family from the village of Aḥwād in central Yemen.[46] From the village Ḥaymeh in central Yemen.[47] In the notebook of the emissary R. Shelomo Naddāf, he mentions his family name without explanation: "my teacher and master, Elisha."
Firnīṣ:	From the village of Ṭalḥ in northern Yemen.[48]
Ghubeyr:	In the Ḥarīzi family in northern Yemen.[49]
Ḥakham:	From the Ṣāliḥ family of the Ṣan'a community.[50]
Ḥamāmi:	Ḥamāmi in Hebrew is Yona (dove). The name was found in Jewish communities in northern Yemen. For example, Ḥamāmi Jāhli of the village Miḥtawiya;[51] Ḥamāmi Maḥdūn and Ḥamāmi Shūtbān of the Hajar village.[52]
Ḥanash:	Ḥanash Maḥdūn from the village of Majz in northern Yemen.[53]
Ḥanīnah:	Ḥanīna Dhamāri from the village of Majz in northern Yemen.[54]
Ḥarīf:	The name was found in the Manākhe community, the son of Ṭov and Rūmiyah Ṣāliḥ.[55]
Ḥavaquq:	The brother of R. Ovadyah who served as the last chief rabbi of the Ṣa'dah community.[56]
Ḥilqiyah:	From the Ṣarūm family of the Ṣan'a community[57] and

46. Oral testimony of R. Gilad Ṣadoq, Bnei Brak.
47. In a personal correspondence dated 16 Feb 2011 from R. Almog Shelomo Akhlufi of Jerusalem.
48. Ben David, *Bet ha-Even*, p. 676, no. 140; p. 684, no. 464.
49. Ben David, *Bet ha-Even*, p. 675, no. 106.
50. As related by R. David Ḥakham, Qiryat Ono. Ḥakham was the grandfather of the informant, and among his descendants this family name was exchanged for the previous family name, Sāliḥ.
51. Ben David, *Bet ha-Even*, p. 682, no. 370.
52. Ibid., nos. 372, 374.
53. Ibid., no. 378.
54. Ibid., no. 377.
55. As related by Tov Tsadoq, Qiryat Ono. Tov is Ḥarīf's brother. The origin of the name is in Nehemiah 7:24: "The sons of Hariph—112." After immigration to Israel, Ḥarīf took the additional name of Ḥayim.
56. Ibid., p. 681, no. 335. See also above, chap. 3, sect. 3.
57. Yosef Tsuri'eli, *Devarim be-'Iqvot ha-Sefer Kalkalah ve-Ḥinukh Moderni be-Teiman ba-*

the Ḥaddād family, also of Ṣan'a.[58] In a manuscript of *Zera ha-Shalom* by R. Yiḥye' Ṣarūm, in one of the birth lists we find: "The firstborn was born *Natan ben Ḥilqiyah*, on Thursday, 23 Elul 5628 AM [10 September 1868]. May Ha-Makom, blessed be He, open his heart to Torah study, and raise him to His service, and protect and sustain him, *'ky"r*."[59]

Ḥūti: From Arabic "fish." The name was found among communities in northern Yemen. Ḥūti from the Ṣabari family from the village of Amlaḥ told me that he was born smaller than usual so he was called by this name because he was small like a fish.[60] Other instances include Ḥūti Maḥdūn from Majz,[61] Ḥūti Madār from Sāqein,[62] Ḥūti Maḥdūn of Ḥilf.[63] This appellation was given as a byname to one of the Muslim judges who ruled in a dispute over synagogues in Ṣan'a in the 1930s. The judge was Yiḥye' ben Muhammad ben Abbas called al-Ḥūthi, and R. Gamliel noted his byname as coming from Ḥūth, a city in northern Yemen, which is one of the fortress cities of the forefathers of the *imam*.[64]

Isra'īl: In a *ketubbah* from 19 Av 5675 (30 July 1915), from the Kharfa community, the name of the groom was written as Yosef ibn Isra'īl Ma'ūḍa. In a *ketubbah* from the village Dayrā' Ashū'bi from 19 Adar II 5706 (22 Mar 1946), the witness signed his name as Aḥiya ibn Isra'īl. *Isra'īl* is the biblical name *Yisra'el* (Israel).[65]

'Et ha-Ḥadasah (Jerusalem, 2005), pp. 23, 84; Yosef Hubarah, *Bi-Tl'aot Teiman u-Yerushalayim* (Jerusalem, 1970), p. 42.

58. Gamliel, *Pequdei Teiman*, p. 194.
59. *Zera ha-Shalom*, MS Yehudah Levi Naḥum, Mif'al le-Ḥasifat Genuzim mi-Teiman, p. 102b, MS Yehuda Levi Naḥum, *Ṣohar le-Ḥasifat Ginzei Teiman* (Tel Aviv, 1986).
60. He immigrated to Israel in 1962 and lives in Bnei Ayish. The meeting with him took place on 28 Shevat 5771 (2 Feb 2011).
61. Ben David, *Bet ha-Even*, p. 681, no. 337.
62. Ibid., p. 680, no. 297; p. 681, nos. 346, 350.
63. Ibid., p. 681, no. 347. For additional instances, see ibid., nos. 338–45; p. 688, no. 617.
64. Shalom Gamliel, *Batei Kneset be-Ṣan'a Birat Teiman*, 1–3 (Jerusalem, 1987–1988), p. 308 n. 3.
65. One must take note that the name Yisra'el is one of the names not pronounced by

Jabīr:	The name was found in the Ṣan'a community in the families Sirri,[66] 'Uzayri,[67] and Shar'abi.[68]
Janāḥ:	In the Lewi family, the 'Irji family, and the Ḥubḥubi family from the villages 'Amīda, Ḥurum, and al-Hajar.[69]
Jarādi:	From the 'Iraqi Kohen family of Bir 'Ali in north Yemen.[70]
Jim'ān:	In the Ṭeiri family and the Qeha' family from al-Tiḥsein and al-Qābīl in northern Yemen.[71]
Khūrsān:	The name was found in Jewish communities in northern Yemen: in the Kūbāni family from al-Hajar,[72] and in the Ridi family of Sharamāt.[73]
Maḥbūb:	In the Ṣa'di family of the Ṣa'dah community.[74]
Maḥli:	The name was found in Jewish communities in northern Yemen. For example, Maḥli ben Sālem from Majz;[75] Maḥli from the Jābr family of Ṭalḥ;[76] Maḥli ben Ṣīniya from 'Amīda.[77]
Malki'el:	From the Badīhi family of the Ṣan'a community.[78]
Mathanyah:	In the Badīhi family of the Ṣan'a community; this name was given since he was born eight years after his mother last delivery; previously only daughters had been born.[79]

Jews in Yemen in Arabic, and only Arabs called Jews named Yisra'el, in their spoken and written language, Isra'īl, and here the name was written as pronounced in Arabic, Isra'īl.

66. Gamliel, *Pequdei Teiman*, p. 199.
67. Ibid., p. 201.
68. Ibid., p. 204.
69. Ibid., p. 676, nos. 148–50.
70. Ibid., p. 676, no. 150.
71. Ibid., p. 676, nos. 141–44; p. 678, no. 214.
72. Ibid., p. 693, no. 799. See also p. 690, no. 686.
73. Ibid., p. 703, no. 1175.
74. Ben David, *Bet ha-Even*, p. 694, no. 829.
75. Ibid., p. 676, nos. 174–75; p. 690, no. 670; p. 694, no. 830.
76. Ibid., p. 694, no. 831.
77. Ibid., p. 684, no. 459.
78. Yosef Tsuri'eli, *Kalkalah ve-Ḥinukh Moderni be-Teiman ba-'Et ha-Ḥadasha* (Jerusalem, 2005), p. 29.
79. As related by Michal Badihi, Givatayim. Matanyah was Michal's great-grandfather. See also Gamliel, *Pequdei Teiman*, pp. 73, 196.

Maṭrūd:	Maṭrūd ben Yosef from Waṭan al-Maqāsh in northern Yemen.[80]
Mattat:[81]	In the Ṣāliḥ family of the Ṣan'a community.[82]
Me'īḍ:	From the 'Alāfi family of 'Amīda in northern Yemen.[83]
Meivīn:	The son of Slayman and Naḍrah Ḥibshush of the Ṣan'a community.[84]
Meshullam:	In the Kohen family of the Ṣan'a community.[85]
Mevorakh:	In the Qāra family of the Ṣan'a community.[86]
Neḥemyah:	From the Ṣarūm family of the Ṣan'a community,[87] and from in northern Yemen.[88]
Naḥman:	From the Danūkh family of the Ṣan'a community.[89]
Qūlāṣah:	In the Ḥarīzi family of the Jūrba village in northern Yemen.[90]
Rashīd:	In the Ḥarīzi family of Waṭan al-Maqāsh in northern Yemen.[91]
Sabtān:	The name occurs in Jewish communities in northern Yemen, e.g., Sabtān in the Madūn family from Majz;[92] Sabtān from the Manṣūr family from Damāj;[93] Sabtān from the 'Aṣār family from Jūrba.[94]

80. Ibid., p. 694, no. 843.
81. Mattat from the term *matanah* (gift).
82. Gamliel, *Pequdei Teiman*, p. 193.
83. Ibid., p. 681, no. 342.
84. See *Keter Torah shel Mishpaḥat Ḥabshush* (Tel Aviv, 1985), title pages.
85. Gamliel, *Pequdei Teiman*, p. 197.
86. Yehudah Tovi, *Aharit le-Ish Shalom* (Bnei Brak, n.d.), p. 36; Gamliel, *Pequdei Teiman*, pp. 193, 202; Tsuri'eli, *Kalkalah ve-Ḥinukh*, p. 25. See also Mevorakh Efrayim; Tsuri'eli, *Temurot be-Ḥinukh be-Teiman*, doc. no. 16, p. 67, no. 131.
87. Ibid., p. 199.
88. Ben David, *Bet ha-Even*, p. 686, no. 530.
89. Tsuri'eli, *Kalkalah ve-Ḥinukh*, p. 24.
90. Ibid., p. 714, no. 1600.
91. Ibid., p. 715, no. 1615.
92. Ben David, *Bet ha-Even*, p. 686, no. 547; p. 690, p. 672; p. 703, no. 1155.
93. Ibid., p. 703, no. 1153.
94. Ibid., p. 704, no. 1154.

Sa'd:	From Gharīr in northern Yemen.[95]
Ṣadoq:	From the Saddi family of the Ṣan'a community.[96]
Sason:	From the Maḥdūn family of Majz in northern Yemen.[97]
Ṣemaḥ:	The name occurs in the Ṣan'a community in the families Yiṣḥak Halevi (Qāḍi),[98] Naddāf,[99] Kisār,[100] Maḍmūn,[101] and Ṭaybi.[102] It was also used by the Madhala family of Ḥidān in northern Yemen.[103]
Ṣevi:	From the Ṭayri family of the Ṣan'a community.[104]
Shemayah:	R. Yiḥye' Ḥayim Mu'allam of the Dhamar community had four girls, though he had prayed each time for a son. When his fifth child was a boy, he called him Shemayah, meaning God had listened to his prayer.[105]
Shem Ṭov:	The name of a nineteenth-century copyist. In a copy of a translation of the *haftarot*, he indicated his name as Shem Ṭov ben Ḥasan ben Shaul.[106]
Siman:	The name was found in the Ṣan'a community. In the Ṣadoq family[107] and the Mishriqi family.[108]
Siman Ṭov:	In a manuscript of *Zera ha-Shalom* by R. Yiḥye' Ṣārūm, written in one of the lists of births is "The good flower was born, whose name was called Siman Ṭov, on Tuesday on which good was doubled twice, Rosh Hodesh Adar II [in the year] 2189 SEL [5638 AM/5 Mar 1878].

95. Ben David, *Bet ha-Even*, pp. 704–5, nos. 1226–27.
96. Ibid., p. 203.
97. Ben David, *Bet ha-Even*, p. 717, no. 1692.
98. Living today in New York, the father of R. Eliyahu Yitsḥak Halevi (Qaḍi).
99. Gamaliel, *Pequdei Teiman*, p. 196.
100. Tsuri'eli, *Kalkalah ve-Ḥinukh*, p. 24.
101. Ibid., p. 25.
102. See Tsuri'eli, *Temurot be-Ḥinukh be-Teiman*, doc. no. 25, p. 77.
103. Ben David, *Bet ha-Even*, p. 714, no. 1598.
104. Gamliel, *Pequdei Teiman*, p. 203.
105. As related by Simha Melammed Marx, Tel Aviv. Simha is the eldest daughter, and the son Shemayah lives in Jerusalem.
106. See Introduction by R. Yoav Pinhas Halevi, *Torah Qedumah* (Beit Dagan, 2001), p. 7 n. 23.
107. As related by his son Gilad Ṣadoq of Bnei Brak.
108. Gamliel, *Pequdei Teiman*, p. 202.

May God, blessed be he, protect him and sustain him, and open in heart for Torah study, *'ky"r.*"[109]

Ṭov:[110] The name occurs in the communities of Ṣan'a and Manākhe. In Ṣan'a the son of Slaymān and Naḍrah Ḥibshūsh;[111] in the Ṣārūm family.[112] In Manākhe, as well, the son of Ṭov Ṣāliḥ[113] who called his son by the same name, Ṭov.[114]

Ṭovim: From the village of Ḥada, in the Shar'ab district in southern Yemen,[115] in one of the birth registrations.[116]

Ṭovyah: The son of Shalom Ṣarūm of the Ṣan'a community.[117]

Yadīd: Yadīd Yosef from the Ṣan'a community.[118]

Ya'īr: In the Ṭabīb family from Ḍūbr Maḥwīt.[119]

Yamani: From the Yeshu'ah family of the Ṣan'a community.[120]

Yamīn: From the Qoraḥ family of the Ṣan'a community.[121]

Yeḥezqel: From the Meghori family of the Ṣan'a community.[122] From the Shar'abi family of the Manākhe community.[123]

109. *Zera ha-Shalom*, p. 109a, MS Yehuda Levi Naḥum, Mif'al le-Ḥasifat Genuzim mi-Teiman.

110. Some understand the verse in Ruth 3:13, "If he will act as a redeemer, good [*tov*]," such that the name of the redeemer was "Tov." They read this as "If the one who redeems you is the person named 'Tov', this will be a good thing." See, for example, Midrash Tanhuma (*parashat* Behar, par. *ḥet*): "That he will have an older brother whose name is Tov."

111. See *Keter Torah shel Mishpaḥat Ḥabshush* (Tel Aviv, 1985), title page. See also Gamliel, *Pequdei Teiman*, p. 199.

112. Ibid., p. 199.

113. Oral testimony of R. Gilad Tsadoq of Bnei Brak.

114. As related by Tov Ṣadoq, Qiryat Ono. See below, part 3, chap. 4, sect. 1.

115. Oral testimony of Rabbi Gilad Ṣadoq of Bnei Brak.

116. The list is written in a printed book owned by Nira Yahav, Holon.

117. See Tsuri'eli, *Temurot be-Ḥinukh be-Teiman*, doc. no. 25, p. 77.

118. Gamliel, *Pequdei Teiman*, p. 204.

119. In a personal correspondence dated 23 Iyyar 5770 (7 May 2010).

120. Ibid., p. 197.

121. Gamliel, *Pequdei Teiman*, p. 195.

122. Tsuri'eli, *Kalkalah ve-Ḥinukh*, pp. 62, 118.

123. Immigrated to Israel and lives in Bnei Berak.

Yesha'yah:	The son of Yosef Drāmi of the Radā' community,[124] and the son of Khūrṣān from al-Qal'ah in northern Yemen.[125]
Yishai:	From the Būsāni family of the Ṣan'a community;[126] and in the Zindāni family from Rajūza in northern Yemen.[127]
Yom Ṭov:	From the Ghiyat family of the Ṣan'a community.[128]
Zāhir:	The name was used in Jewish communities in northern Yemen. For example, Zāhir from the Qafri family from Qafra; Zāhir from the Damarmari family of Alwa; Zāhir from the Madār family and Zāhir from the Rashīd family of Hajar.[129]
Zevulun:	From the Ḥibshūsh family of the Ṣan'a community.[130]

Women's Names

'Akah:	From the Dūkhmah family from Rajūzah in northern Yemen.[131]
Avigail:	From the Kisār family of Ṣan'a.[132]
Bekhorah:	From the Ṣāliḥ family of Manākhe.[133]
Fār'ah:	The name was found in Jewish communities in northern Yemen: in the Manṣūrah family from Waṭan al-Maqāsh, the daughter of Yosef ben Aharon from Ḥaḍan, and in the Marḥabi family from the Blād al-Baḥri.[134]

124. Dromi family, pp. 20, 23.
125. Ben David, *Bet ha-Even*, p. 690, no. 686.
126. Ibid., p. 199.
127. Ben David, *Bet ha-Even*, p. 690, no. 685.
128. Ibid., p. 199. For a photo of the Ghiyat family with their son Yom Tov, see Yeḥi'el Haybi, *Ṣan'a u-Sevivatah be-Ṣilumei Yeḥiel Ḥaybi*, ed. Yosef Sha'ar, published by Ruma Haybi (Tel Aviv, 1985). p. 11, photo no. 8.
129. Ben David, *Bet ha-Even*, p. 680, nos. 322–25.
130. Tsuri'eli, *Kalkalah ve-Ḥinukh*, pp. 21, 24, 28.
131. Ben David, *Bet ha-Even*, p. 696, no. 897; p. 700, no. 1066. See also Ovadya ('Awad) Zindani, *Yalqut Ovadya* (Tel Aviv, 1986), pp. 172–73.
132. Tsuri'eli, *Temurot be-Ḥinukh*, doc. no. 16, no. 30.
133. Oral testimony of Tov Tsadoq, Qiryat Ono. Tov is Bekhorah's brother. After immigration to Ereṣ Israel, Bekhorah changed her name to Farḥa. On the name Bekhorah, see above chap. 1, sect. 1.
134. Ben David, *Bet ha-Even*, p. 712, nos. 1503–5.

Farāshah:	In the Zindāni family from Rajūzah in northern Yemen.[135]
Funūn:	Daughter of Sālem of the Bayḥān community.[136]
Ḥasina:	Daughter of Sālem of the Bayḥān community.[137]
Hinda:	Of the Zindani family in Rajūzah in northern Yemen.[138]
'Ibūda:	Daughter of Mūsa, of the Bayḥān community.[139]
Jamālah:	The name was found in Jewish communities in northern Yemen: Jamālah bat Yosef and Jamālah bat Yiḥye' of Ḥaḍan,[140] Jamālah bat Yiḥye' of Fala,[141] Jamālah bat Firniṣ from Ṭalḥ.[142]
Khūḍra:	Of the Matana family of the Bayḥān community.[143]
Laya:	The name occurred in Jewish communities in northern Yemen: in the Najjār family, the Marḥabi family, and the Manṣūr family, from the villages of Saqin, Sharamāt, and Damāj.[144]
Layla:	From the Ma'ūḍa family of the Bayḥān community.[145]
Miṣva:	From the 'Azāni family of the Radā' community,[146] and the Levi family in one of the communities near Radā'.[147]
Nakhlah:	From the Qeha family in the villages of al-Taḥsein and al-Qābil in northern Yemen.[148]

135. Ben David, *Bet ha-Even*, p. 704, no. 1214.
136. Shalom Lahav, *Kehillat Yehudei Bayḥān* (Netanyah, 1996), p. 195.
137. Ibid., p. 198.
138. Ibid., p. 693, no. 783.
139. Lahav, *Kehillat Yehudei Bayḥān*, p. 198.
140. Ben David, *Bet ha-Even*, p. 675, nos. 111–12.
141. Ibid., p. 675, no. 114.
142. Ibid., p. 675, no. 115.
143. Ibid., p. 196.
144. Ben David, *Bet ha-Even*, p. 692, nos. 759–62.
145. Lahav, *Kehillat Yehudei Bayḥān*, p. 195.
146. Dromi family, p. 215.
147. Lives today in Rosh HaAyin; she does not know why she was given this name. Related by Yehonatan Halevi, Rosh HaAyin.
148. Ben David, *Bet ha-Even*, p. 698, no. 979–80.

Qafla:	The name was found among Jewish communities in northern Yemen: in the Zindāni family from Rajūzah,[149] and in the Ṣa'di family from Rāziḥ.[150]
Rizqah:	From the Jamal family from Majz in northern Yemen.[151]
Savtah:	In the Yiqneh family from the Ṣa'dah community in northern Yemen.[152]
Sūkara:	In the Jāhli family from Baraṭ in northern Yemen.[153]
Sūrya:	In the Marḥabi family of the Blād al-Baḥri in northern Yemen.[154]
Wāla:	Of the Ṣa'di family from al-Naḍīr in northern Yemen.[155]
Zar'ah:	From the Ma'ūḍah family of the Bayḥān community.[156]

149. Ibid., p. 714, no. 1602.
150. Ibid., p. 715, no. 1603.
151. Ibid., p. 715, nos. 1614–15.
152. Ibid., p. 1156, no. 1156–57.
153. Ibid., p. 695, no. 866.
154. Ibid., p. 1156, nos. 1156–57.
155. Ibid., p. 680, nos. 311–12.
156. Lahav, *Kehillat Yehudei Bayḥān*, p. 189.

CHAPTER SIX

FREQUENCY OF NAMES

The study contains data from the following sources: 1,506 *ketubbot*, 175 *gittin*, and the emissary's notebook of the *shadar* (fund-raising emissary) R. Shelomo Naddāf. An examination of the data in each group shows that the common names are identical in each source group. For a name written in a number of ways, the most frequent form is given first and then the others. Names with identical frequency are listed in alphabetical order. In a few isolated cases, names were counted more than once, such as when witnesses signed a number of *ketubbot*. Similarly, there are some individuals who had two *ketubbot*, as in instances of second marriages, or the father's name at the marriages of his sons and daughters. In those occurrences they were counted according to what was written in the *ketubbot*, but these cases do not change the general findings.

1. THE CORPUS OF NAMES

Some names were written a number of ways, and they are cited according to their frequency of occurrence, with a dash between them. Below is the corpus of names in Hebrew alphabetical order.

Men's names

א. Aburus. Abūsa'ūd. Aḥsan. Avigad. Avraham – Ibrāhim – Ibrāhīm – Ibrahīm – Brāhīm – Bīrhīm – Barhūn – Ībrahim – Brahīm – Brāhim. Efrayim. El'azar. Elisha'. Eliyah. Eliyahu.

ב. Binyamin. Binyan. Barukh.

ג. Gershom. Jabīr. Jamīl. Jūm'ān.

ד. Dan. Dā'ūd – Dawid – Dawīd – Dāwīd.

ה. Hārūn – Harūn – Aharon – Aharōn. Hibah – Hībah.

ו. Wahab. Walad.

ז. Zekharya' – Zekharyah.

ח. Ḥamāmi. Ḥanan'el. Ḥasan. Ḥabaqūq. Ḥayim. Ḥilqiyah. Ḥizqiyah. Ḥoter. Ḥūti.

ט. Ṭov.

י. Ya'aqūb – Ya'aqov. Ya'īsh. Ya'beṣ. Yefet. Yeḥezqel. Yeḥī'el. Yehonatan. Yesha'. Yeshū'ah. Ye'ūda' – Yūda' – Yehūdah – Yehūda' – Yūda; – Yedūda' –Ye'ūda' – Yedūda'. Yiḥye' – 'Iḥye – Yiḥyah – Yāḥya'. Yish'ayah. Yisra'el – Īsra'īl. Yissakhar. Yiṣḥāq – Yiṣḥaq. Yosef.

כ. Khurṣān.

ל. Lewi.

מ. Maḍmūn. Maḥfuḍ. Ma'īḍ. Manṣūr. Masallam – Mūsallam. Mas'ūd. Mthana'. Maṭrūd. Ma'ūḍah – Ma'ūḍa'. Maymūn. Me'ir. Me'awdad. Menaḥem – Manāḥim. Menasheh. Meshullam. MeshumMar Minis. Mordekhai. Mūsa' – Mūsya' – Mosheh – Mūsī – Mūsah.

נ. Naḥūm – Nāḥūm. Nathan. Neḥemyah. Nethan'el. Nissim – Nīssim.

ס. Sabtān. Se'id – Sa'adya' – Sa'adyah. Sālem – Shalom – Sālīm – Shalem – Salem – Salīm. Selūmi – Qalūmi. Shiloh. Si'd. Slaymān – Shelomo – Sulē[mān] –Sūlēmān – Sulēman.

ע. 'Abdāllah. 'Amar 'Amrān – 'Amram. 'Awāḍ – 'Awaḍ –'Awūḍ. 'Awḍa'. 'Awdad. 'Awjān. 'Iḍa'. 'Azar. 'Azarya' – 'Azaryah. 'Azri. 'Ezra. 'Imanū'el. 'Ovadyah.

פ. Pinḥas – Pīnḥas

צ. Ṣāliḥ – Ṣadoq. Ṣemaḥ. Ṣevi. Ṣiyyon.

ר. Raḍa' – Raḍah. Raḥamīm. Refa'el. Re'uven.

ש. Sha'ul. Shelumi'el. Shemaryah'. Shemu'el. Shim'on. Shiloh. Shukr –Shukūr.

Women's names

א. Amān. Amīrah. Esther.

ב. Badūr. Badrah. Banayyah. Bint. Bardaqūshah. Barūd. Berakhah.

ג. Ghaliyah. Ghane. Ghaniyyah. Gharsah. Ghayda'. Ghazal. Ghaziyyah. Ghuṣnah, Ghūṣnah, Ghūṣna'. Ghuṣūn. Ghūzlān. Jamālah. Jamīlah.

ד. Darah.

ה. Hadiyah. Hawidah. Hind. Hūdiyyah.

ו. Wardah. Wardiyyah. Waznah.

ז. Zihrah.

ח. Ḥabībah. Ḥalīmah. Ḥāliyah. Ḥamāmah. Ḥannah. Ḥaṣībah. Ḥisn.

ט. Ṭaybah.

י. Yamān. Yedīdah.

כ. Kādhiyyah. Kāmlah. Khūḍra.

ל. Leah. Lūlah. Lūlūwah.

מ. Māri. Mlāḥ. Mlūk. Malūkah. Mas'ūdah. Mazal. Miryam. Mūhrah – Muhrah.

נ. Naḍrah. Nafīsah. Naḥūmah. Najmah, Najrah. Ni'meh. Nīni.

ס. Sābarah. Sa'dah. Se'īdah. Sa'īdiyyah. Sakhītlah. Salāmeh. Salwah. Subūlah. Sūkarah. Swādah.

ע. 'Afiīyah. 'Atīqah.

פ. Fākhah. Fakhnah. Falfalah. Farāsah. Fāyīq. Fāyīza. Fuḍah – Fūḍah.

צ. Ḍobyah. Ṣādqah. Ṣālḥah. Ṣīniyyah.

ק. Qadriyyah. Qmar. Qifriyah. Qamāsh. Qurṭ.

ר. Raḍa'. Raḥel. Rā'iyah. Rashusha. Rivqah. Rizqah. Rūmah. Rumīyah. Rūza'.

ש. Sarah. Shadhrah. Sham'ah. Shams. Shamsiyyah. Shikhah. Shi'tālah. Shoshanah. Shudhiyyah. Simḥah – Samḥa'.

ת. Tamniyyah – Tamniyah. Tankah. Thrayya'. Tiranjah. Turkiyyah – Turkiyah.

2. FREQUENCY OF NAMES

Men's names

The total number of names is 114, which appear 17,509 times in the corpus. The ten most frequent names appear 13,622 times, constituting 77.8% of all occurrences of names. The other 104 names appear 3,887 times, constituting 22.2%. Presented below are the names in descending order of frequency. Alternate spellings of a name are given in square brackets with the number of occurrences.

Yiḥye' – 2,737 [including 'Iḥye – 7; Yiḥyah – 6; Yāḥya' – 2]. Sālem – 2,296 [including Shalom – 59; Sālem – 16; Shalem – 9; Sālīm – 4; Salīm – 2].[1] Yosef – 1,649. Se'īd – 1,627 [including Sa'adya' – 38; Sa'adyah – 13].

1. *Sālem* in Hebrew is Shalem. Shalom was translated into Arabic as Salām. For a discussion of this name, see above chap. 4, sect. 1.

Slaymān – 1,391 [including Shelomo – 145; Sulē[mān] – 54; Sūlēmān – 18; Sulayman – 9]. Avraham – 1,038 [including Ibrāhim – 251; Ibrahīm – 53; Ibrāhīm – 47; Brāhīm – 10; Bīrhīm – 3; Barhūn – 2; Ībrahim – 1; Brahīm – 1; Brāhim – 1]. Dā'ūd – 859 [including Dawid – 57; Dawīd – 4; Dāwīd – 2]. Mūsa' – 789 [including Mūsya' – 281; Mosheh – 105; Mūsī – 60; Mūsah –3]. Ḥayim – 658. Hārūn – 578 [including Harūn – 52; Aharon – 10; Aharōn– 5]. Ye'ūda' – 381 [including Yūda' – 134; Yehūdah – 53; Yehūda' – 47; Yūdah – 9; Ye'ūda' – 1; Yedūda' – 1]. Ya'aqūb – 332 [including Ya'aqov – 37]. 'Awāḍ – 296 [including 'Awaḍ – 64; 'Awūd – 9]. Ḥasan – 266. Yiṣḥāq – 246 [including Yiṣḥaq – 57]; Ṣāliḥ – 192 [including Ṣadoq – 4]. Ya'īsh – 189. Shukr – 163 [including Shūkr – 6]. 'Amrān – 142 ['Amram – 15]; Shim'on – 135; Mas'ūd – 106; Nissim – 97 [including Nīssim – 6]. Ma'ūḍah – 95 [including Ma'ūḍa' – 1]. Menaḥem – 89 [Manāḥim – 2]. Maḥfuḍ – 87. Yisra'el – 80 [including Īsra'īl – 6]. Yeshū'ah – 79. Pinḥas – 74 [including Pīnḥas – 2]. Shemu'el – 72. Manṣūr – 63. Wahab – 59. Jamīl – 39. Naḥūm – 38 [including Nāḥūm – 4]. Binyamin – 32. Zekharya' – 29 [including Zekharyah – 13]. Raḍa' – 28 [including Raḍah – 2]. Si'd – 21. Hibah – 20 [including Hībah – 1]; Masallam – 19 [including Mūsallam – 2]. 'Īḍa' – 18. Efrayim – 17. Re'uven – 17. Mthana' – 15. 'Awḍa' – 15. Sha'ul – 14. Selūmi – 13 [including Salūmi – 2]. 'Awdad – 13. 'Azri – 12.

10 times	Aḥsan, 'Amar, Banyan, 'Ezra, Maḍmūn, Refa'el
9 times	Menashe, Walad
6 times	Ṭov, Ya'beṣ
5 times	Abūs'ūd, Barukh, Ḥizqiyah, Nethan'el, Ṣiyyon
4 times	Abūrūs, Neḥemyah, Shiloh
3 times	'Awjān, Dan, Ḥabaqūq, Ḥilqiyah, Jabīr, Me'awdad, Ṣevi, Yeḥi'el
2 times	Avigad, 'Azarya' [including 'Azaryah – 1], El'azar, Elisha', Eliyah, 'Imanū'el, Ma'īḍ, Maṭrūd, Meshūmar, Nathan, Raḥamīm, Rāshid, Ṣemaḥ, Yefet, Yeḥezqel
1 time	'Abdallah, 'Azar, Eliyahu, Gershom, Ḥamāmi, Ḥanan'el, Ḥoṭer, Ḥūti, Jūm'ān, Khurṣān, Maymūn, Meshūlam, Ovadyah, Sabtān, Shelumi'el, Shemaryah', Yehonatan, Yesha', Yesha'yah, Yissakhar

Women's names

The total number of names comes to 116 and appear 2,708 times in the corpus. The ten most common names appear 1,497 times, constituting 55.28% of all the occurrences of the names. The other 106 names appear 1,211 times, constituting 44.72%. Presented below are the names in descending order of frequency. Alternate spellings of a name are given in square brackets with their number of occurrences.

Zihrah – 259. Ḥamāmah – 200. Sa'dah – 155. Rumīyah – 145. Lūlūwah – 129. Badrah – 126. Sham'ah – 125. Naḍrah – 122. Se'īdah – 121. Salāmeh – 115. Ghane – 109. Ni'meh – 109. Ghazāl – 108. Miryam – 97. Śimḥah – 93 [including Simḥa' – 7]. Ḥannah – 63. Turkiyyah – 57 [including Turkiyah – 4]. Banayyah – 41. Ḥabībah – 40. Kādhiyyah – 29. Berakhah – 22. Yedidah – 19. Tiranjah – 19. Ghāliyyah –18. Ḍobyah – 18. Shūdhiyyah – 18. Leah – 15. Raḥel – 14. Ṣīniyyah – 13. Mlāḥ – 12. Fuḍah – 12 [including Fūḍah – 1]. Jamīlah – 11. Mazal – 11. Barūd – 10. Ghuṣne [including Ghūṣne– 2, Ghūṣna' – 1]. Hawidah – 9. Shams – 9. Qamr – 8.

7 times	Amān, Ḥisn, Lūlah, Malkah, Mas'ūdah, Shamsiyyah, Tamniyyah [including Tamniyah – 2], Wardah
6 times	'Afīyah, Mlūk, Mlūkah, Qurṭ
5 times	Hadiyah, Salwah, Sarah
4 times	Bedūr, Bint, Esther, Ghūzlān, Fakhnah, Fāyīq, Nafīsah, Qadriyyah, Rivqah, Shadhrah, Thraya'
3 times	Darah, Ghaniyyah [including Ghanyah –1], Ghuṣūn, Khūḍrah, Se'īdiyyah, Ṣādqah
2 times	'Atīqah, Bardaqūshah, Ḥāliyah, Jamālah, Kāmlah, Mūhrah [including Muhrah – 1], Qmāsh, Rashūsh, Sūkarah, Swādah
1 time	Amīrah, Fākhah, Falfalah, Farāsah, Fayīzah, Gharsah, Ghaydah, Ghaziyyah, Hind, Hūdiyyah, Ḥaṣībah, Māri, Naḥūmah, Najmah, Najrah, Nīni, Qifriyah, Raḍa', Rizqah, Rūmah, Rūza', Sābarah, Sakhītlah, Sbūla, Shi'tālah, Shikhah, Shoshanah, Ṣālḥah, Tankah, Taybah, Tiranjah, Wardiyyah, Waznah

The results show a similarity in the range of names between the two genders, 114 for men, 116 for women. Yet, the ten most common names among the men constitute the overwhelming majority with 78%, whereas among the women they come to little more than 55%. Apparently, there were not many more names for women than for men, since they found it sufficient to call a woman by her personal name and her family name, such as my mother's name, Ghaṣūn bint [= daughter] al-Raḥbi, or by ascribing her to her husband, *marat* [= wife of] al-Gaymāni. As for the men, a man was usually called according to his father's name, such as Hārūn Slaymān or Yosef Ya'īsh.

From this overview we see that most of the men's names come from Jewish sources, though a few stem from Arabic. Among the women, the situation is reversed: most of the names are Arabic and a few from Jewish sources. Some names with a similar sound were used for men and women: Ḥamāmi – Ḥamāmah; Ṣāliḥ – Ṣālḥah; Mas'ūd – Mas'ūdah; Se'īd – Se'īdah. There was also the name Raḍa', used jointly by men and women.

Some of the names that were customary among the Jews in Yemen were used also by the non-Jewish population.[2] Generally, among Yemenite Jews newborns were not given two names.[3] When they did call a person by two personal names, the first one was his personal name and the additional one referred to his father's name.[4] Moreover, almost totally lacking were names used for both men and women. Also the use of names of angels, such as Michael, Gabriel, Raphael, a phenomenon that spread after the time of the Ari,[5] as well as names of animals, such as Eyal, Arye, Ṣevi, gained no foothold in Yemen.[6]

2. See above chap. 3, sect. 2.

3. In the Jewish communities in eastern countries as well, it was not customary to give a child two names, while in Ashkenazi countries, only in recent centuries did the phenomenon of giving two names begin to spread. See Yosef Rivlin, *"Mattan shnei shemot la-noladim,"* in *These Are the Names: Studies in Jewish Onomastics*, vol. 5, ed. A. Demsky (Ramat Gan, 2011) [in Hebrew], pp. 135–47.

4. See, for example, in the Libyan Jewish community in the book by Mordechai Hakohen, *Higgid Mordekhai* (Jerusalem, 1979), p. 223. The German anthropologist Erich Brauer was impressed by the custom among Yemenites to note the name of the father along with the family name. For additional customs regarding this issue, see his *Ethnologie der Jemenitischen Juden* (Heidelberg, 1934), pp. 196–99. In the replies written by R. Avraham Ṣan'ani of the 'Ayāshiya community in southern Yemen to questions from R. Avraham Yitshaq Hakohen Kook, he notes that the name of the addressee in his introductory remarks as "Avraham ben Yitshaq Hakohen Kook" (Shmuel Yavne'eli, *Ha-Massa le-Teiman* (Tel Aviv 1952),p. 199). The term of address "Avraham ben Yitshaq" instead of "Avraham Yitshaq" occurred because the rabbi thought that R. Kook's father was named Yitshaq, and the Yemenite custom was to say Avraham Yitshaq in place of Avraham ben Yitshaq, so he added "ben"; he also did this because in Yemen they did not usually call someone by two names.

5. Y. G. Gumpertz, *"Qeri'at Shemot be-Yisra'el," Tarbiẓ*, 25 (1957): 454–55. R. Shemu'el ben Yosef Yeshu'a 'Adani, one of the most prominent sages of Aden in the early twentieth century, wrote in his book *Naḥalat Yosef* (Jerusalem, 1988): "It is known that all of creation arises to the sound of man's call. For that reason, the kabbalists agreed not to orally mention the names of angels, but only in thought from the mouth inwardly, except for those alluded to in "Argaman," namely, the initials of Uriel, Refa'el, Gavri'el, Micha'el, Nuri'el, that can be stated aloud, because many have delved into them and also written about them. For that reason, it is permitted

DISTRIBUTION OF MEN'S NAMES[7]

The Group	Quantity	Relative Percentage
10 most common names	13,622	77.80%
All other names	3,887	22.20%
Total in corpus: 114 names	17,509	100.00%

Names	Quantity
Yiḥye'	2737
Sālem	2296
Yosef	1649
Se'īd	1627
Slaymān	1391
Ibrāhim	1038
Da'ūd	859
Mūsa'	789
Ḥayim	658
Hārūn	578
Total:	13622

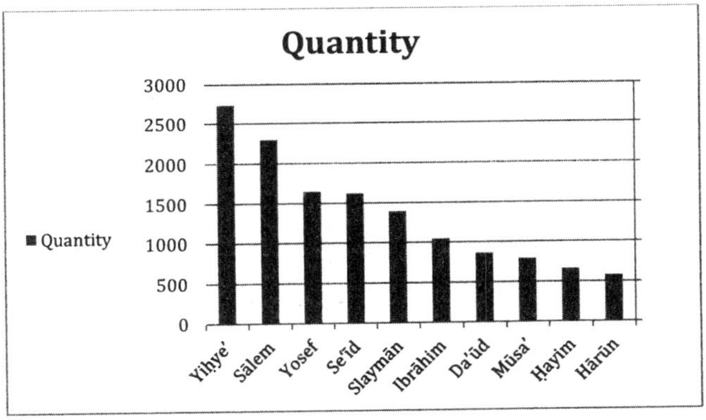

to give people those names. Some say that it is also allowed to mention the angel Raziel orally, but not to call people by his name." 'Adani, *Naḥalat Yosef*, pt. 1, chap. 9, p. 48b. See also Yiṣḥaq Raṣabi, *Shulḥan Arukh ha-Mequṣar*, vol. 1 (Bnei Brak, 1989), sect. 6, par. 29, p. 27.

6. R. Raṣabi wrote about this: "And they did not usually give the names of angels, such as Micha'el, Gavri'el and so on; nor names of animals, such as Arye, Ze'ev and so on. Although there are few names, such as Refa'el, Ṣevi, it seems this is only a recent usage, so they are not frequent" (Raṣabi, *Shulḥan Arukh ha-Mequṣar*, 5, sect. 159, 10, par. 43, p. 14).
7. In the table, similar names were consolidated.

DISTRIBUTION OF WOMEN'S NAMES[8]

The Group	Quantity	Relative Percentage
10 most common names	1497	55.28%
All other names	1211	44.72%
Total in corpus: 116 names	2708	100%

Names	Quantity
Zihrah	259
Ḥamāmah	200
Sa'dah	155
Rumīyah	145
Lūlūwah	129
Badrah	126
Sham'ah	125
Naḍrah	122
Se'īdah	121
Salāmah	115
Total:	1497

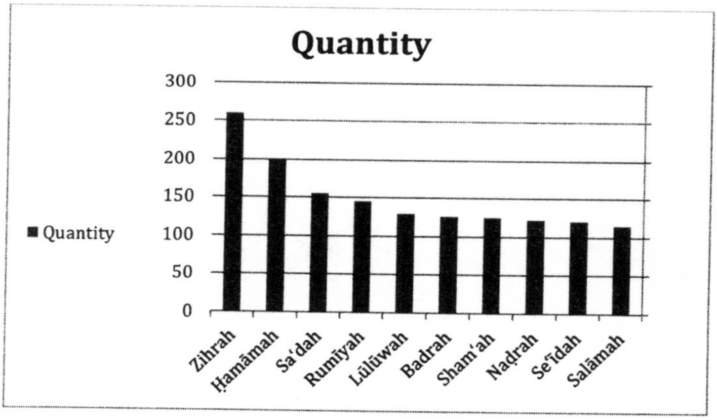

8. In the table, similar names were consolidated.

PART II
FAMILY NAMES AND BYNAMES

CHAPTER ONE

GENERAL INTRODUCTION

The standard practice in Yemen was to call a person by his personal name in combination with his father's, and for a woman by her personal name with the addition of "daughter of X" or "wife of X." At times, a byname was added. Family names, that is, a name that identified one as a member of a particular family, were common in the larger communities and less frequent in smaller ones.

1. FAMILY NAMES AMONG JEWISH COMMUNITIES

For many generations, Jews were identified by their personal name, but there were some who added an auxiliary appellation so as to express membership in a particular familial line, a status, or a link to a function or event. This name became a symbol and became attached to the family. On ascribing a familial line, Nachmanides wrote in his Torah commentary:

> For this was the custom among the Jews to make for themselves heads of families; all of his descendants eternally referred to this man, and called themselves by his name to honor him, as is done even today by all the Muslims and all Jews who live in their lands to be called all of them as the Ibn Ezra [or] Ibn Shushan family, and that is what is meant by "the following are the heads of their respective clans" (Ex. 6:14).[1]

The combining of a family name with the personal name began to spread during the Golden Age in Spain. Among the famous family names from that period are Benveniste (welcome); Astruc (star; *mazal*); Albo (white); Abulafia (father of health); Gerondi (of the city Gerona in

1. Nachmanides commentary on Num. 26:13.

Castille). After the expulsion from Spain, the Jews took with them family names based on their cities of origin in Spain, such as Cordovero (from Cordoba), Toledano (from Toledo), and Saragosti (from Saragossa). At the same time, Italian Jews were adopting family names taken from their city of origin.[2] Throughout Europe, the phenomenon began to take root in the eleventh century and expanded during the Renaissance, at first among the nobility and then through imitation by other sectors of the population. In the modern era the use of family names became widespread among the general European population and moved beyond Europe to places controlled by the Europeans.[3]

Among the Jews of Western Europe, in a few cities in Germany and Austria it was customary to indicate family names as early as the fourteenth century, but the phenomenon became widespread only in the modern era, from the end of the eighteenth century on. When emancipation was granted to the Jews, legislation was enacted in a number of countries so as to have Jewish names be in harmony with those of the general population, making contact with the authorities easier. For example, an edict promulgated on 27 July 1787 by Joseph II of Austro-Hungary required the Jews of his empire to append permanent family names to their personal names. The order stemmed from the need to prevent confusion in political and legal listings. In 1804, the Russian Jews were obligated to add family names to the official documents they carried. On 20 July 1808 Napoleon published an edict requiring French Jews to have family names. This decree also included countries under French occupation. In 1812, in a decree published by Friedrich Wilhem, the Jews of Prussia were ordered to have family names. Sometimes they were forced to select a family name from a pool of names presented by the authorities. As a result of these laws, the phenomenon of noting a family name spread among all the European Jews, even in places where the Jews were not required to do so.[4]

2. See *Hebrew Encyclopedia*, vol. 31, entry "*Shem, Shemot*," col. 1012; Yohanan Arnon, "*Ivrut Shemot ha-Mishpaḥah eṣel Yehudei Teiman ba-Shanim 1947–1957*," *Yeda Am* 26 (1995): 188.

3. *Hebrew Encyclopedia*, ibid., cols. 1009–1010.

4. *Encyclopaedia Judaica*, (Jerusalem 1972), "Names," 809–12; Adolf Kober, "Jewish Names in the Era of Enlightenment," *Historia Judaica* 5 (1943): 165–82; Abraham Stahl, *Shemot Mishpaḥah Yehudiyim* (Jerusalem, 1987), pp. 12–14; *Hebrew Encyclopaedia*, "*Shem, Shemot*," cols. 1012–13; Arnon, "*Ivrut Shemot*, ibid.

2. KEYWORDS AS AN EXPRESSION OF FAMILY ATTRIBUTION

It was a common tradition in Yemen to identify oneself solely by the personal name. Most Yemenite Jews did not have a family name and even those who had one did not usually use it in daily life. Y. Ratzaby in his article on R. Shalom Shabazi, who was known by his byname of Mashta, wrote, "One may assume that 'Shabazi' and 'Mashta' were simply bynames. Proof is that people of the south do not have family names but are called by their given name and their father's personal name, 'ploni ben ploni'."[5] Ratzaby's statement applies as well to the other Jews of Yemen who lived in small communities in which it was sufficient to add the father's name to a person's designation and sometimes also the grandfather's for the purpose of identification. The same was true for a woman; added to her personal name was "bat ploni" (her father's name) or "wife of ploni" (her husband's name).

In recent centuries, in the large Yemenite communities, such as Ṣan'a, Radā', Dhamār, and Ṣa'dah, there were permanent, i.e., inherited, family names that were part of the family lineage. R. Azaryah Basis wrote about this: "It was very common in all of Yemen that a person or his family was named after his location or profession, such as Ṣan'ani, Radā'i, Bayḍāni and so on, or Najjar or Naqqāsh. Najjar indicating the profession of a carpenter, and Naqqāsh for the one who decorates a vessel with dots or the henna coloring on the hands."[6] In Ṣan'a, home to the largest Jewish community in Yemen and one in which its members had family names, the custom was to add a byname to the family name, since many people had identical personal and family names.

Tractate Megillah (28a) of the Babylonian Talmud states, "The disciples of R. Zera asked, "By what merit have you lived long?' He replied '... I did not call my fellow by his *ḥakhina* (nickname)—and another version says, by his *'ḥanika'* (personal name)" In the rabbinic period, we find the addition of bynames to common combinations. The Mishnah tractate of Baba Bathra (10:7) states:

5. Yehudah Ratzaby, *"Rabbi Shalem Shabazi ve-Shirato," Sefunot* 9 (1965): 136–37 n. 13. In the phrase "ploni ben ploni" the word *ben* (son of) was written as an explanation, but in practice a person was called by his personal name and his father's without the intervening *ben*. See above, part 1, chap. 6, end of sect. 2. On the bynames Shabazi and Mashta, see below part 3, chap. 3, sect. 1. On the meaning of the name Mashta, see below chap. 3, sect. 3.

6. In a personal correspondence dated 8 Mar 2010.

> If there were two in the same town, and the name of the one was Yosef ben Shim'on and the other was Yosef ben Shim'on—neither can bring forth a bill of indebtedness against the other, and another person cannot bring forth a bill of indebtedness against them ... What should they do? They should write their names to the third generation, and if the names of the three generations are alike, they should give themselves a descriptive name, and if their descriptive names are alike they should write "Cohen." [Herbert Danby, *The Mishnah* (London, 1933), p. 381]

"They should write their names to the third generation," that is, they should add the grandfather's name. And if the names of grandfather's are identical, the solution is to write a "description," that is, a distinguishing byname making each person unique; for example, they should write "the tall Yosef ben Shim'on" or "the dark Yosef ben Shim'on."

This type of byname is found among people in the Second Temple period, in the Mishnah, and in the Talmud. Some of them describe a situation while others indicate some disgrace owing to a deed of one of the family's forefathers.[7] For instance, R. Yoḥanan ben Arza is mentioned in 'Avodah Zara (58a). Arza may, perhaps, be his father's name, but another source mentions that the name Arza without the accompanying Ben informs us that the name is a nickname alluding to height.[8] In contrast, Ben Nanas, who is mentioned in Mishna Baba Bathra (7:3) and in Mishna Shevu'ot (7:5), was given this sobriquet because he was of short stature.[9] R. Yoḥanan ben Durmaskit, who is mentioned in Megilla (7a), was so called because his mother was a convert from Damascus.[10] R. Yoḥanan ben Torta is mentioned in the Jerusalem Talmud (4, 5). Ben Torta means son of a cow, and he was given this nickname because he approached Judaism because of the act of a cow.[11] Nedarim (22a) states, "The grandson of R. Yannai the Elder came before R. Yannai the Elder." In Megillah (32a) we read, "R. Yannai the son of the old R. Yannai said in the name of the great R. Yannai." The addition of the

7. S. Klein, *"Le-Ḥeqer ha-Shemot ve-ha-Kinnuyim," Leshonenu* 1 (1929): 330–45; Rachel Hakhlili, *"Shemot ve-Kinnuyim eṣel Yehudim bi-Tkufat ha-Bayit ha-Sheni," Ereṣ Israel* 17 (1984): 195–204.
8. Klein, *"Le-Ḥeqer ha-Shemot,"* p. 330; Hakhlili, *"Shemot ve-Kinnuyim,"* p. 195.
9. Klein, ibid., p. 341.
10. Ibid., p. 334.
11. On this act, see Pesiqta Rabbati, 56b–57a. See also Klein, ibid., p. 344.

"old" apparently is aimed at emphasizing his very advanced age or perhaps the word "old" is intended to differentiate him from the great R. Yannai, who was apparently greater than he in Torah learning.

We find bynames not only for individuals but also for families. Mentioned in Mishna 'Arakhin (2:4) are "the families of Bet ha-Pegarim, and Bet Ṣipporya, and they were from Emmaus." These were distinguished families from Emmaus.[12] The family name Bet ha-Pegarim is a contemptuous byname, while Bet Ṣipporya seemingly alludes to a bird (*ṣippor*).[13] We see the same phenomenon in Bereishit Rabbah (98:8):

> A genealogical scroll was found in Jerusalem in which it was written that Hillel was descended from David, R. Ḥiyya the Elder from Shefatya the son of Avital, the house of Kalba Savu'a from Caleb, the house of Ṣiṣit ha-Keset from Avner, the house of Kovshin from Aḥav, the house of Yaṣah from Asaf, the house of Yehu from Ṣipporin, the house of Yannai from 'Eli, R. Yose b. R. Ḥalafta from Yonadav the son of Rekhav, and R. Neḥemyah from Neḥemyah the Tirshata.

Mentioned in this section are bynames of great families, which ascribe them to a specific branch.[14] For example, one sees R. Ḥiyya the Elder, whose branch descends from David, not from the offspring of Shelomo his son but from the descendants of Shefatya ben Avital. The word *bet* indicates a family appellation: Bet Kalba Savu'a, stems from Kalev ben Yefune; Bet Kovshin, from Aḥav, king of Israel; Bet Yannai, from 'Eli Hakohen, who officiated in the Tabernacle in Shiloh.[15]

R. Shalom Gamli'el distinguished between the large and small communities in which most Yemenite Jews lived, writing: "These bynames and family bynames were, as noted, [found] almost solely in Ṣan'a and part of the cities. The situation was different in most of the towns and villages. They preserved the ancient tradition of Ploni ben Ploni without any byname or family nickname."[16] He noted further:

> "In Yemen, Jews did not have family names like the Arab or Muslim names, except for two or three families.... In most sites in Yemen in

---

12. An ancient settlement on the way between Jerusalem and the Lowland. Cf. also Jerusalem Talmud, Shevi'it 9, 2, "R. Yoḥanan said, 'Still there is Mountain, Lowland, and Valley from Bet Horon to Emmaus.'"
13. Klein, "*Le-Ḥeqer ha-Shemot*, p. 348.
14. Ibid., pp. 345–346.
15. See the commentary of M. A. Mirkin on the Midrash cited.
16. Shalom Gamliel, *Pe'amei ha-Aliyyah mi-Teiman* (Jerusalem, 1988), p. 181.

the villages and towns, they used to call a person only according to his father's name: Re'uven ben Ya'aqov, Shim'on ben Ya'aqov, Sālem ben Yiḥye', Slayman ben Ḥayim, Yiḥye' ben Sālem, Ya'aqov ben Re'uven, Ḥayim ben Slayman, in line with the rabbis' statement, a person should not call his fellow by a *ḥanikha* nor a *ḥakhina*, and here we have neither a *ḥanikha* nor a *ḥakhina*. In Ṣan'a and central Yemen families were called with a *ḥanikha* but not a *ḥakhina*."[17]

R. Yosef Shalom Ḥubāra wrote in a similar vein that in Ṣan'a there are family names and bynames, while in Shar'ab in southern Yemen and in other districts family names are not used, but rather they call one by the personal name and that of his father, such as Sālem ben Yiḥye' or Ḥayim ben Yosef.[18] R. Gamliel presented examples of the custom among Yemenite Jews in the large communities, who added a *ḥanikha* expressing place, occupation, or bodily characteristic,[19] such as 'Imrāni for the location 'Imrān; Ḥaṭṭābi for wood-cutter; Qāfiḥ for a lean body. He also notes that there were those who bore a *ḥakhina* as an addition to an existing *ḥanikha*, for example, Badīḥi al-Fitlah—Badīḥi was the *ḥanikha* while al-Fitlah, "string," was the *ḥakhina*, used as an addition indicating his being a seller of string; 'Amr al-'Aṭṭār—al-'Aṭṭār, "perfume," was an added *ḥakhina* to note a seller of perfumes; al-Ḥaybi al-Ṣalāṭ—al-Ṣalaṭ, "oil," to indicate a purveyor of oils;[20] Ghiyāt al-Sha'not—Sha'na lulav (palm branch) and the supplement is to inform us that he was a seller of *lulavim* before Sukkot.[21] Ḥubārah al-Meshulash—people were given this byname because they used to bring *hadas meshulash* (a myrtle branch that has at least three leaves on each row) to Ṣan'a for Sukkot.[22]

There were families whose profession was passed down from father to son and so was used to identify the family. For example, a branch of the 'Uzayri family, which engaged in the tobacco business (in Arabic, *burdeqān*), was called Bayt al-'Ūzayri al-Mabradaq; the part of the Sham'ah family that dealt with the production of shoes was called Bayt al-Sham'ah al-Mubshamāq; members of the Sirri family who engaged

17. Shalom Gamliel, *Pequdei Teiman: Mas he-Ḥasut be-Teiman* (Jerusalem, 1982), p. 56.
18. Yosef Shalom Ḥubarah, *Bi-Tla'ot Teiman vi-Yrushalayim* (Jerusalem, 1970), p. 38.
19. See also below, part 2, chap. 3, sect. 5.
20. Gamliel, *Pe'amei ha-Aliyyah*, pp. 180–81.
21. Gamliel, *Pequdei Teiman*, p. 56.
22. As related by Yehiel Hubarah, Qiryat Ono. See also Gamliel, *Pequdei Teiman*, p. 328.

in soldering metals were named Bayt Sirri al-Mulḥim;[23] the part of the Pinḥas family that engaged in casting silver and gold for jewelry was called Pīnḥas al-Khallāṣ, "caster."[24]

In addition to the foregoing, Ṣan'a families split up according to bynames. The Ladāni family[25] broke into four divisions according to traits of the children. To distinguish among them, each was given an apt nickname, which turned into the family name. R. Shalom Gamliel, a scion of this family, wrote:

> I heard from my paternal grandfather, our honored teacher and master, R. Ḥayim ben Slayman al-Jamal, may the memory of the righteous be a blessing, that a Jew by the name of Shemu'el ben Menaḥem al-Ladāni (after his place "Ladān"), had four sons. The first was merry and lived simply, and his contemporaries called him Shiryān. The second was handsome and generous and was called Jamāl. The third was uncompromising and would always say "let the law pierce the mountain," so he was called Qoraḥ. And the fourth had a lean and weak body; he was called Qāfiḥ. Over the years these four sons' units became four large, diverse families that spread over central, southern, northern, and western Yemen.[26]

In older documents, these family members were still mentioned with the addition of Ladāni. For example, in the bill of sale for a house that was written in Ṣan'a in 1669, the name of the buyer is given as "Yiḥye' ben Se'īd ben Slayman al-Ladāni, who is called al-Qāfiḥ."[27] In a 1699 manuscript of a collection of writings on Kabbalah, the copyist gave his name: "And the most humble, insignificant writer, servant of the Hebrews, Yosef ben David ben Shelomo son of our distinguished teacher and rabbi, Rav Zekharyah al-Ladāni called al-Qāfiḥ."[28] In a

23. Y. Ḥibshush, *Mishpahat Ḥibshush* (Tel Aviv, 1986), p. 404 (Hebrew).
24. Ibid., p. 409.
25. Named after the village of Ladān in central Yemen. In 5252 (1492), Shalom ben Zekharyah Ladāni copied Maimonides' *Sefer ha-Miṣvot* and in (5253) 1493 his *Sefer Hafla'ah* of the *Mishneh Torah*. See *Sefer ha-Miṣvot*, ed. Y. Qāfiḥ (Jerusalem, 1971), introduction, p. 11; Maimonides, *Mishneh Torah*, ed. Y. (Jerusalem, 1967), *Hafla'ah*, in the introduction, pp. 8–9; Yosef Qāfiḥ, *"Divre Ṣaddiqim ve-Zikhronam be-Teiman," Reshimat Ḥibburei Ḥokhmei Teiman le-Rav Yiḥye' Qāfiḥ, zaṣal," Tema* 1 (1990): 14–15 n. 18.
26. Shalom Gamliel, *Pe'amei ha-Aliyyah* (Aliyah to Israel), (Jerusalem, n.d.), p. 179.
27. See Amram Qoraḥ, *Sa'arat Teiman* (Jerusalem, 1954), p. 143.
28. Qiryat Ono ms, Shim'on Kisar.

ketubbah written in Ṣan'a in 1767, the groom's name is "Sālem ben Yuda' al-Jamal who is called al-Ladāni."[29] Such cases show that over time the original family name occasionally was forgotten and replaced by a byname.

As for the name of the Qoraḥ family, S. D. Goitein told of a conversation he had with R. Amram Qoraḥ in Jerusalem:

> I recall that I once asked him about the origin of this large family's name, the Qoraḥ family. Even though I knew he was not a Levite, I put forward, being polite, the notion that his forefathers were great singers, as had been the Levite sons of Qoraḥ in Psalms, and therefore had been given this appellation. The elderly rabbi laughed, "That is not how family names were created in Yemen. Rather, most certainly one of my ancestors was a great pest and was called "Qoraḥ" as a pejorative term, and the name stuck to the whole family."[30]

After the Jews returned from the expulsion in the Tihāma plain in southwest Yemen, in 1681, a new location was assigned to them for building their neighborhood at a distance of 3 km from their former neighborhood.[31] Jews from other districts gathered there, too; in other cities as well, such as Radā' and Dhamār, Jews who had not lived there before also took up residence. The way they indicated family names after their return from the Mawza' exile was attested to by R. Ḥayim Ḥibshūsh: "And the Jews gave names to all the families who had come from the villages, each for the name of the city of his birthplace from which he had been exiled."[32] R. Qāfiḥ wrote:

---

29. Yehudah Levi Naḥum, *Ḥasifat Genuzim mi-Teiman* (Holon, 1971), file 61, no. 77.
30. See the introduction of S. D. Goitein to R. Qoraḥ's book, *Sa'arat Teiman*, p. 11; see also Yiṣḥaq Raṣabi, *"Ofan ha-Merkavah,"* in his edition of *Sefer Rekhev Elohim* (Bnei Brak, 1972), p. 37 n. 1.
31. After the expulsion order was rescinded, part of the exiles returned to Ṣan'a. They were not permitted to return to the neighborhood they had lived in before the expulsion, and they built a new neighborhood for themselves outside the city wall, about 3 km for their first residential area, and the neighborhood was ringed by a separate wall. On the Mawza' exile and its aftermath, see Ratzaby, *"Galut Mawza',"* *Sefunot* 5 (1961): 337–95; idem, *"Geirush Mawza' le-Or Meqorot Ḥadashim,"* *Zion* 37 (1972): 197–215; Aharon Gaimani, *Temurot be-Moreshet Yahadut Teiman: be-Hashpa'at ha-Sulhan 'Arukh ve-Qabalat ha-Ari* (Ramat Gan, 2005), pp. 145–58; Reuben Ahroni, *Yemenite Jewry* (Bloomington, 1986), pp. 121–35.
32. Yosef Qāfiḥ, *"Qorot Yisra'el be-Teiman le-R. Ḥayim Ḥabshuh,"* ed. Rabb Yosef Qāfiḥ, *Ketavim*, 2 (Jerusalem, 1989), p. 706.

> Also within Yemen itself there was migration to Ṣan'a. As early as the settlement of the Jews in their new neighborhood after the "Mawza'" exile, we find among the names of the community leaders and *Bet Din* presidents, family names based on villages outside of Ṣan'a, such as Manzali, Ṣabaṭāni, Ḥamdi, Bashāri, Ṣa'di, Qarawāni, Mishriqi, and so on. Some believe that these families originated in Ṣan'a. But they lived during varying times of decrees and emergencies in those cities and villages, and when the tempest was over, they returned to Ṣan'a; attributed to them as a distinctive sign was the name of the place from which they returned, in addition to their original family name. In time, the original family name disappeared, leaving only their differentiating indication. To this day, many families living in Ṣan'a bear names of well-known cities and villages.[33]

When he says, "some believe that these families originated from Ṣan'a," perhaps R. Qāfiḥ meant to note that his family, the Qāfiḥ family, stems from Ṣan'a; it is also called by the name Ladāni, because they were expelled from Ṣan'a to the town of Ladān, though they did not originate there. There is some basis for R. Qāfiḥ's supposition, since sometimes names were given to Ṣan'a families for places in Yemen. This was due to certain events among those families that are linked to one or another settlement in Yemen, even though the family did not come from there originally. R. Yiṣḥaq Raṣabi wrote about this:

> For it is well known about distinguished families in 'Ūzal[34] (meaning Ṣan'a), which are mainly from the villages such as Qoraḥ, Qāfiḥ, who came from the village of Ladān … while on the other hand, there are families in the villages known for coming from 'Ūzal. It is also reasonable to distinguish these things by the family bynames ending in the letter *yod*, which relate to place names, such as Manzili, from the village called Manzal. Also the family of the rabbi, president of the Bet Din, *morenu* R. Shlomo Qāreh, ment[ioned] above, probably were

33. Yosef Qāfiḥ, "*Kehillat Ṣan'a she-be-Teiman*," *Ketavim*, 1 (Jerusalem, 1989): 864.
34. A tradition of Yemenite Jews considers 'Ūzal as the ancient name of Ṣan'a, which also befits the traditions of Jewish and Muslim residents of Yemen, similar to the ancient Arabic by name (Azāl; Yazāl). See entry אוזל in *Encyclopedia Biblica*. See also Malachi Bet Aryeh, "*Emunah Yoṣerah eṣlo Amanah*," in Shai Lehman, *Meḥqarim ba-Sifrut ha-Ivrit Mugashim le-A. M. Haberman* (Jerusalem, 1977), pp. 44–46. In their poetry the Yemenite poets also use the name Yazāl as an alternate name for Ṣan'a. See *Ḥafeṣ Ḥayim—Shirei Rabbeinu Shalom Shabazi* (Jerusalem, 1966), pp. 539–544. See also Se'īd Ibn al-Asbaṭ's poem, Yehudah Ratzaby, "*Galut Mawza'*," *Sefunot* 5 (1961): 368.

> named for their origin from the known village of al-Qāra in western Yemen...and we see that people from all kinds of places have already been mixed together, especially from the period of the Mawza' expulsion and afterward.[35]

This means that family names for the Mawza' exiles who settled in new locations were determined according to their previous place of residence.[36] Indeed, there are numerous families named for locations in Yemen, and it is clear that there are names such as those that preceded the Mawza' exile and were determined because of changing one's place of residence. However, the Mawza' expulsion intensified the phenomenon. For example, a member of the Manzili family mentioned by R. Yosef Qāfiḥ and R. Yiṣḥaq Raṣabi was one of the sons of R. Shelomo ben Sa'adyah Manzili, a *dayyan* in Ṣan'a before the expulsion to Mawza', who later served as president of the rabbinic court in Ṣan'a.[37]

On family names in Ṣan'a, R. Pinḥas Qoraḥ wrote:

> A portion of the family names was taken from their location, such as "al-'Arūsi" after the name of the village 'Arūs, "al-Ḥamdi" after the name "Ḥamdeh," "al-Kūḥlāni" after "Kūḥlān," and in this manner tracing migration from district to district owing to tribulations and famine and the like. Also of note is that part of the family names mentioned in the *Misawwadeh*[38] did not exist in recent generations in Ṣan'a, and perhaps famine caused reverse migration, or "*Ḥawzat al-Nafar*," which caused the loss of most of [the residents of] Ṣan'a.[39]

35. Yiṣḥaq Raṣabi, *Shulḥan Arukh ha-Mequṣar*, vol. 6 (Bnei Brak, 1989), par. 205, 5, p. 343.
36. From this we also learn about Jewish settlements prior to the expulsion, and even about places that ceased to exist as time went by. Yehudah Ratzaby, *"Galut Mawza',"* p. 339 n. 1.
37. Qoraḥ, *Sa'arat Teiman*, pp. 14, 143–50. R. Yiḥye' Ṣāliḥ (Mahariṣ) in his commentary of the *siddur* wrote about this:
38. *Misawwadeh* is the notebook registry of the *Bet Din* of the Ṣan'a community, in which the courts renderings were registered in brief. Vol. 1 covers the years 1765–1776, while vol. 2 encompasses 1786 to 1867.
39. In a personal correspondence received in April 2010. *Ḥawzat al-Nafar* is the siege imposed by the Imam Yiḥye' on Ṣan'a at the end of 1904, with the aim of ousting the Turks from Yemen, and because of it many Muslims died as did most of the Jewish population of the Ṣan'a community. This event is among the most difficult that ever befell the Yemenite Jews in their exile and the most severe visited upon them in the twentieth century. See Yehudah Ratzaby, *"Be-Maṣor u-be-Maṣoq,"* in *Bo'i Teiman: Mehkarim u-Te'udot be-Tarbut Yehudei Teiman*, ed. Yehudah Ratzaby (Tel Aviv, 1967), pp. 67–70.

Below are a few examples from the seventeenth and eighteenth centuries of people whose family names indicate their previous place of residence. In an inheritance document for a home in Ṣan'a signed in 1670, the disputants were Avraham, Yiḥye', and Se'īd, the sons of Yosef ben Se'īd ben Ṣāliḥ al-Ḥaydāni.[40] The family was called Ḥaydāni apparently as coming from the Jewish community of Ḥaydān in northern Yemen. In a *ketubbah* from the village of 'Imrān, on 5 Shevat 5426 (11 Jan 1666), the name of the groom is written as Mūsa' ben Se'īd Tan'ami. The family name Tan'ami alludes to the family's origin from the town of Tan'em. Similarly in a *ketubbah* from Ṣan'a, dated 11 Nisan 5535 (11 Apr 1775), the name of the groom was registered as Ḥanna bint Se'īd al-Tan'ami. In a *ketubbah* from the village of Ṭawīlah, dated 5458 (2 Aug 1698), the bride's name was written as Ḥamāmah bint Yosef ben Slaymān al-'Adani. The family name 'Adani alludes to the family's origin in the city of 'Aden. A Ṣan'a *ketubbah* from 28 Av 5530 (19 Aug 1770) lists the bride's name as Ḥamāmah bint Avraham al-Ladāni. The family name Ladāni refers to the family's source in the village of Ladān. In a *ketubbah* from Ṣan'a, dated 17 Tevet 5534 (31 Dec 1773), the groom's name appears as Yiḥye' ... al-Sayyāni. The family name Sayyāni alludes to the family's origin in the village of Sayyān. In a *ketubbah* from Marwāje, dated 12 Tishri 5536 (6 Oct 1775), the bride's name was written as Se'īdah bint Se'īd Hārūn al-Kawkabāni. The family name Kawkabāni refers to the family as coming from the town of Kawkabān. In a Ṣan'a *ketubbah*, dated 15 Av 5549 (7 Aug 1789), the bride's name is given as Yedīdah bint Yūda' ben Moshe al-Raṣābi. The family name Raṣābi alludes to the family as coming from Raṣāba.

Some families have a tradition that they arrived in the place where they settled only after their return from the Mawza' exile. For example, the Badīḥi family from Ṣan'a has a tradition that they came from the Radā' community;[41] and the Ḍāhari family from Radā' has a tradition that it came from Kawkabān and from Ṣan'a, where in the sixteenth century the poet R. Yiḥye' al-Ḍāhari lived and worked.[42] Conversely, the Shar'abi family of Ṣan'a has a tradition that they settled in Ṣan'a even

40. Qoraḥ, *Sa'arat Teiman*, pp. 146–48.

41. Support for this tradition can be found in the fact that prior to expulsion to Mawza' manuscripts are found by the scribe Me'oded ben Sa'adya Badīḥi from the Radā' community. Moshe Gavra, *Enṣiqlopedya le-Qehilot be-Teiman*, 1 (Bnei Brak, 2005), pp. 34–35, entry Badiḥi, Me'oded ben Sa'adya.

42. Joseph Tobi, *Kehillat Yehudei Radā' ba-Me'ah ha-18* (Jerusalem, 1991), p. 19.

before the expulsion. R. 'Azri ben R. Sulēmān Shar'abi told of their initial arrival in Ṣan'a from Shar'ab:

> Elders tell that the original source of the Shar'abi family of Ṣan'a was from the Shar'ab district in Yemen, and they arrived in the city of Ṣan'a a few generations before the Mawza' expulsion. The family forefathers made their living from retrieving pearls from designated areas of the Red Sea. They knew the time of the year when pearls were found by the edges of the sea; they would go down to the seashore once a year at a specific time, and whatever they could fish out they would take to Ṣan'a to sell to the al-Abyad [Abyaḍ] family that for generations dealt with jewelry making in gold and silver. Among others, the al-Abyad family would sell their hand-made products to the royal family and its ministers. Once, when the day came and the Shar'abi family went to retrieve pearls from the edges of the sea, the Lord came to their aid and in their haul they found twelve magnificent, large pearls. When they went to sell them to the al-Abyad family, the latter was stunned by their size and beauty, but did not know their value. They tried to find out, but could not since there was nothing comparable. Finally, they had to offer them to the *imam*'s family, and so became exceedingly wealthy from this transaction, moving their place of residence to the city of Ṣan'a.[43]

In Yemen, someone called Shar'abi is not from Shar'ab, but rather his ancestors originated there. The reason for this is clear. There was no benefit for anyone living in Shar'ab to identify himself by the byname Shar'abi, since everyone who lived there was Shar'abi. The same holds true for anyone whose name is Ṣan'āni, meaning he does not come from Ṣan'a; anyone with the family name Ṣa'di is not from Ṣa'dah, and anyone with the family name 'Adani is not from Aden.

R. Se'īd Ṣa'di, who wrote *"Dofi ha-Zeman,"* and his brother, R. Yehudah, who wrote the introduction to the Yemenite version of the prayer book, both of whom belong to eighteenth-century Yemenite sages, lived in Ṣan'a.[44] R. Avraham Ṣan'āni, a descendant of the al-Sheikh family in Ṣan'a, lived in the nineteenth century in the 'Ayāshiya community near Radā'.[45] In the introduction to his commentary on the Mishnah, *Melekhet Shelomo*, R. Shelomo 'Adani wrote about his family, which emigrated from Ṣan'a to Israel in the sixteenth century, that his

43. Tsefanya Shar'abi, *Bet al-Shar'abi* (Qiryat Sefer, 2002), p. 6
44. Gaimani, *Temurot be-Moreshet*, pp. 160–61, 182–83.
45. Yehudah Ratzaby, *Toratan she-li-Vnei Teiman* (Qiryat Ono, 1994), p. 86. See also Gaimani, *Temurot be-Moreshet*, p. 238. On him, see below chap. 3, sect. 2.

father, R. Yeshu'a had been the rabbi of Ṣan'a and that his grandfather, R. David, had been a teacher of younger children in Ṣan'a.[46] The Zindani family, which for a few generations had lived in the town of Rajūza in northern Yemen, had originated, according to their tradition, in the village of Zindān in central Yemen and their family name before they moved to their new place had been Ṣabari.[47] The Jerāfi family, which had resided in the village of al-Maḥtawiya in northern Yemen, originated, as their tradition tells it, in the village of Jerāf in central Yemen, where their family name had been Lewi.[48]

One must note that the ancient sages who were called 'Adani did indeed live in 'Aden, but they were called so because their works were disseminated outside of their place of residence, and others called them 'Adani; certainly their fellow town residents did not call them 'Adani. There are similar instances. For example, R. Sa'adya b. David 'Adani, who lived in the fifteenth century, immigrated to Israel and settled in Safed. He used three appellations for himself in his works: Ha-Yisra'eli, Ha-'Adani, Ha-Teimani. In his introduction to his commentary on Maimonides' *Sefer Tohorah*, he wrote, "the one in need of God, who looks forward to His mercies, Se'īd ben Da'ūd, *n'* (*nuḥo 'eden*), the Yemenite." In the introduction to his midrash, "Rescue of the Drowning," which is a commentary on the Torah and the *haftarot*, he began with "Said Se'īd ibn Da'ūd, *n'*, al-'Adani." In the introduction to his work, "The Stirring Introduction to the Distracted," he wrote, "I hope for mercy of the heavens, Sa'adya b. David, OBM, Ha-Yisra'eli ha-Teimani."[49] The byname 'Adani is used to indicate the name of his community in Yemen; the byname Teimani is to mark his land of origin after he left Yemen; and the term Yisra'eli is to identify himself as a Jew.

The end of the Yemenite diaspora came with the operation "On the Wings of Eagles" in 1949–1950. Jewish immigrants came from all over Yemen to Aden, where they stayed until their flight to Israel. The campaign to fly in the immigrants to Israel began in June 1949 and ended in September 1950. Airlifted from Aden to Israel during that period

46. See the introduction to his commentary on the Mishnah, *Melekhet Shelomo*. See also below, chap. 2, sect 1; Gaimani, *Temurot be-Moreshet*, p. 15 n. 1, 66–67.

47. Ovadya ('Awad) Zindani, *Yalqut Ovadya* (Tel Aviv, 1986), p. 44.

48. In a personal correspondence received in September 2010 from Shelomo Jarafi. Shelomo Jarafi is a member of this family and he lives in Gederah.

49. Yehudah Ratzaby, *Toratan she-li-Bnei Teiman*, pp. 32–33. See also Gaimani, *Temurot be-Moreshet*, pp. 270–71.

were some 44,000 immigrants on 430 flights.[50] Some people tried to arrange the list of those waiting for flights according to family names. In many instances, in lieu of a family name, the organizers added a family name according to place of origin of those waiting or according to their trade or profession or by a nickname they bore. In creating these administrative lists stress was put on family names. When many of those waiting were called up by the family names, which sometimes were new to them, chaos ensued.[51] Order was restored after identification was made according to personal name, then by the father's name, and last according to the newly proposed family name. The Joint emissary, Yosef Zadok, wrote:

> But this time, we did not read the names in the order of the lists (family name first, then personal name, and finally, the father's name), but in the way they were used to: first, the personal name, then the father's name, and after that the family name. It was just "wondrous"! Everyone was located immediately. Let it be said, that the names we "stuck" them with, even though they sounded nice, were not accepted by them.[52]

So, for example, most people coming from the Shar'ab community in southern Yemen did not have family names since they lived in tiny villages, and there was no need for family names for identification. After they immigrated to Israel, many of them were called by the name Shar'ab.[53]

3. FAMILY NAMES ASCRIBED TO TRADITION

Among Yemenite Jews there are families whose names, according to their traditions, go back to a very early period and are connected to the people from ancient times and to tribes. R. Yaacov Sappir, who visited Yemen in 1859, cited the traditions of the priestly families Pinḥas and Meghori, as well as of the Dan family. On the priestly families in Ṣan'a he writes: "And among the priests there are those who trace their lin-

50. See Yosef Zadok, *Be-Se'arot Teiman*, p. 232; N. A. Stillman, *The Jews of Arab Lands in Modern Times* (Philadelphia, 1991), p. 157; Aharon Gaimani, *"Ha-Hanhagah ha-Yehudit be-Ṣan'a 'im Ḥissul Golat Teiman," Miqqedem Umiyyam*, 7 (2000): 185–216.
51. Zadok, *Be-Se'arot Teiman*, pp. 39–41.
52. Ibid., p. 42.
53. A similar phenomenon occurred with immigrants from various communities in the east who did not have family names, and after they came to Israel were called by the name Mizraḥi.

eage to Pinḥas, son of El'azar Ha-Kohen, and are called Beit Pinḥas, and also to Yehoyariv, head of the *mishmarot* (priestly courses of Temple service), and named Bet al-Meghori."[54] About the family of *kohanim* in the village of Hajareh, he wrote, "Here there is a family of *kohanim*, and they too are refugees from Ṣan'a; they are called Bet al-Pinḥas,"[55] and consider themselves to be descendants from the line of Pinḥas ben El'azar ben Aharon Hakohen."[56] Perhaps, it is more reasonable to accept the tradition that the members of the priestly Bet Pinḥas family were named after the famous Mori Pinḥas, to whose grave the Jews of Ṣan'a used to make pilgrimages.[57]

Sappir wrote about the Meghori family in the town of Shibām:

> Here among the city dignitaries is a dear, wise, god-fearing man, R. Ya'īsh, may his light shine, a good person acting beneficially, a respected god-fearer ... the *kohen* of the Bet al-Meghori, and this family traces its lineage to the chief priests of the division of Yehoyariv (I Chron. 24:7; TB Ta'anit 27b), and they are also of the pedigreed people of Ṣan'a and they fled here because of the disturbing violence.[58]

R. Pinḥas Meghori Hakohen, who lived in Ṣan'a in the nineteenth century, cites at the end of work on the Torah, *Or Torah*, the family tradition, that it is aligned with the Yehoyariv division of priests, "May the Lord bring our redemption soon, we will go up to our land with singing, and merit serving in the Holy Temple, in the reserved division of Yehoyariv."[59] The Dan family believed that they went back to the tribe of Dan:

> There is a family in Ṣan'a that is called the "Hadani family." I spoke with distinguished members of it and they told me that the family's progenitor was from the tribe of Dan that lives in an unknown country. He and another person with him from the tribe of Asher,[60] who live among them, lost their way in the desolation and did not find the path

54. See Sappir, *Massa Teiman*, ed. A. Yaari (Jerusalem, 1945), p. 166.
55. Should have been written as "Bet Pinhas."
56. Ibid., p. 96.
57. As related by R. Itamar Ḥayim Kohen, Bnei Brak. The Mori Pinḥas mentioned is R. Sālem Pinḥas, who died in the seventeenth century on the way to Mawza'. Many people did not know his private name, and they called the site the grave of R. Pinḥas. See Joseph Tobi, *'Iyyunim bi-Megillat Teiman* (Jerusalem, 1986), p. 158 n. 22.
58. Sappir, *Massa Teiman*, p. 136.
59. *Rekhev Elohim le-R. Yiṣhaq Wanne*, ed. Yehudah Ratzaby (Bnei Brak, 1992), p. 37 n. 1.
60. אָשֵׁר [my vocalization—A.G.].

> to return to the place of their dwelling and their tribe, and so they continued on their way, wherever it may have been, until they arrived here in Ṣan'a. And the Asherite died here just after coming, and the Danite married a women and had sons and daughters, and they are their descendants and called by the name "Hadani" to this day.[61]

Among the Halewi-Alsheikh[62] family there is a tradition relating them to the earliest Jewish settlement in Yemen. In the nineteenth century, three brothers from this family engaged in striking coins on behalf of the *imam*, and were suspected of counterfeiting by the new regime in Ṣan'a. On their way to execution, the three brothers conversed among themselves, saying:

> "This is the day to admire and sanctify the Holy One of Israel! Let us remember our patriarch, the saintly Mori Yiḥye', prince of the Levites,[63] who is descended from the progeny of the Jerusalem exile at the beginning, and we shall not let our honor be disgraced by our adversaries and shamed by those who hate us!"[64]

Another well-known family in Yemen is the Qoraḥ family. This lineage produced many famous rabbis, including the last chief rabbi of the Yemenite exile, R. 'Amram Qoraḥ. According to the family's tradition the name refers to the sons of Qoraḥ from Ḥevron of the tribe of Judah, who are mentioned in I Chron. 2:43.[65]

---

61. Yaacov Sappir, *Massa Teiman*, pp. 164–65.
62. The addition Alsheikh to the family name will be discussed below in this part, chap. 3, sect. 2.
63. The reference is to R. Yiḥye' Halewi, who returned in 1681 from the Mawza' expulsion and built the first synagogue in Ṣan'a. R. Yaacov Sappir wrote about him: "I have already told of the distinguished Levite family al-Sheikh which is in the holy community of Ṣan'a, the capital of Yemen, and two hundred years ago there lived there Mori Yiḥye' Halewi al-Sheikh, head of this family, the leader and head of the Golah, a man steeped in Torah learning, in God-fearing, in wisdom, and in wealth, and he brought the exile of Ṣan'a back for Tihama to where they had been expelled" (Sappir, *Massa Teiman*, p. 218). See there also pp. 169, 171. Aharon Gaimani, *"Sheṭar ha-Tseva'a u-Sheṭar Ḥaluqat ha-Yerusha shel ha-Nasi ha-Rav Avraham al-Sheikh,"* in *Bnei Teiman, Meḥqarim be-Yahadut Teiman u-Morashta*, eds. Aharon Gaiman, Ratson 'Arusi, and Shaul Regev (Ramat Gan: Bar-Ilan University, 2011), p. 49
64. Sappir, *Massa Teiman*, p. 220.
65. See Shimon Jaraydi, *Mi-Ginzei ha-Yehudim be-Teiman* (Tel Aviv, 1948), p. 15. See also Yiḥye' Qoraḥ, *Maskil Doresh 'al ha-Torah* (Tel Aviv, 1964), Introduction, p. 7;

The Zabīb (lit. raisins) family, whose members lived in various communities in Yemen, has a tradition that they are descended from the Salmon lineage mentioned in Ruth. In the family book they wrote:

> For many years, in oral discussions and in stories passed down from father to son, it was always told that the original name of the tribe of the Zabīb family was Salmon. This name occurs in the Bible: "Salmon begot Boaz, Boaz begot Oved, and Oved begot Yishai and Yisha begot David" (Ruth 4:21). That means that even in the time of the kings of Judah, before the destruction of the First Temple, our families were a strong, stable branch related to the kingdom of the House of David.[66]

One may reasonably assume that other families have traditions such as these, apparently created by an ancestor through metaphor or allusion, and so should be understood as legend.[67]

Shelomo Qoraḥ, *Masekhet Avot im Peirush Ḥokhmat Ḥayim* (Bnei Berak, 2011), at the end of the Introduction. For a different opinion concerning the tradition of the Qoraḥ family, see above, sect. 2.

66. Yisrael Soreq, *Album Mishpaḥat Zabib le-Doroteha* (Tel Aviv, 2004), p. 7. See also below, part 3, chap. 7, sect. 3.

67. For example, the *'Amr* family which is Levitic—some wish to see an allusion in biblical texts, that the source of their name is in the Amrami family (Num. 3:27; 1 Chron. 26:23) of the descendants of Kohath the Levite. That is, if one deletes the suffix of the name Amrami, the Amrami, what remains is the name 'Amr (in a personal correspondence from Prof. Zohar 'Amr of Neve Tzuf, whose family immigrated from Ṣan'a). The Manṣura family has a tradition that it left for Yemen from Manṣura in Ereṣ Israel even prior to the destruction of the First Temple (as related by Yiḥye' Manṣura who immigrated to Israel from 'Amran in the "Wings of Eagles" operation and lived in Givat Shemuel [d. 2010]). On the settlement of Manṣura in Ereṣ Israel, see Zev Vilnay, *Ha-Yishuvim be-Yisra'el* (Tel Aviv, 1951), pp. 188–89.

CHAPTER TWO

HISTORICAL REVIEW

Beginning in the twelfth century, there is written evidence, enabling us to follow family names. Sources include Geniza fragments, tombstones (only in Aden), inscriptions and colophons in Yemenite manuscripts, travelogues, and the registration of those who stopped in Aden during the mass immigration to Israel.

1. THE EARLIER PERIODS

Tombstones were discovered in Aden that dated to the Middle Ages. The names inscribed on them were Avraham ben Yeshu'ah ben Ya'aqov, Aharon ben Yeshu'ah, Ya'aqov bar Yiṣḥaq, Yiṣḥaq ben Ḥalfon, Maḍmūn ben Ḥalfon, Moshe ben Yiṣḥaq, Pinḥas ben Moshe, Shalom ben Ḥoṭer, Bayti bat Yiṣḥaq, Ḥāmāmah bat Yosef, Ḥoglah bat Moshe Tūbo, Ḥalāti bat Avraham, Ḥasīnah bat Ṭov ben Shiloh, Lūlū bat Avraham, Mlāḥ bat Yisra'el, Miryam bat Avraham, Mashta'[1] bat David, and Sarah bat Shiloh ben Ya'aqov.[2]

In letters from the eleventh and twelfth centuries found in the Cairo Geniza occur Maḍmūn bar Ḥasan,[3] Maḥrūz[4] ben Yehudah Hakohen

1. Mashta is both the name of a woman and a family name, see also below chap. 3, sect. 3.
2. Yaacov Sappir, *Even Sappir*, 2 (Mainz, 1874), p. 10; Reuven Aharoni, *Yehudei 'Aden: Qehila she-Hayeta* (Tel Aviv, 1991), pp. 19–21; Yitzhak Ben-Zvi, *"Sefunei Temunei Ḥol* (Ṣiyyunei Qevarim mi-Paras ve-'Aden)," *Tarbiẓ* 22 (1951): 198–201; M. A. Levy, "Jüdische Grabsteine aus Aden," *Zeitschrift der Deutschen morgenlandischen Gesellschaft* 21 (1867): 156–60.
3. Shlomo Dov Goitein, *"Me-Ḥalifat ha-Mikhtavim shel Yeqirei Teiman be-'Et Periḥat Saḥar Hodu,"* in *Ha-Teimanim—Mivḥar Meḥqarim* (Jerusalem, 1983), p. 94.
4. Translation: guarded.

ben Ya'aqov ben Yosef Hakohen,[5] Maḍmūn ben David, Ḥalfon ben Maḍmūn,[6] David ben Amram, Yosef bar Avraham ben Bundār bar Ḥasan,[7] 'Amram b. R. Yehonatan,[8] Ya'aqov ben Sālem.[9]

From listings on the tombstones and Geniza documents, we learn that the names indicated are personal names without family names, except for Hakohen and Tūbo, which is apparently a byname. We cannot conclude from this that they did not have family names, for to this day there are situations, such as being called to the Torah, in which a person is designated by his personal name and that of his father, even in times and places when or where most people or everyone had a family name.

Another source for names and bynames of the Yemenite sages comes from Yemenite rabbinic literature and from colophons in Yemenite manuscripts, in which we can already discern names with the nature of family names. The names indicate ascription to places, occupations, character traits, and so on. These markings show that they usually note, in addition to the individual's personal name, that of the father. However, there are a few who were using a family name. The following are family names based on place of origin, and then names with other ramifications.

Ladāni—After the city Ladān. In a copy made in Tan'em in 1492, the copyist cites his name in the following: "And may the writer, the most simple of the simpletons and the humblest of the scribes, Shalom *beirav* Abba Mori Zekharyah al-Ladāni."[10]

'Adani—After the coastal city in southern Yemen. R. Yeshu'ah 'Adani was a rabbi in Ṣan'a and immigrated to Palestine in the sixteenth century, settling in Safed. His son, R. Shelomo, notes in the introduction to his commentary on the Mishna, *Melekhet Shelomo*:

5. Goitein, *Yeqirei Teiman,* p. 101.
6. Shlomo Dov Goitein, *"Negidei Erets Teiman,"* in *Ha-Teimanim—Mivḥar Meḥqarim,* (Jerusalem, 1983), p. 83.
7. Shlomo Dov Goitein, *"'Ashirei Teiman,"* in *Ha-Teimanim—Mivḥar Meḥqarim* (Jerusalem, 1983), pp. 107, 118.
8. Shlomo Dov Goitein, *"Temikhatam shel Yehudei Teiman bi-Yshivot Bavel ve-Ereṣ Yisra'el u-bi-Yshivat ha-Rambam,"* in *Ha-Teimanim—Mivḥar Meḥqarim* (Jerusalem, 1983), pp. 19–32.
9. Jacob Mann, *The Jews in Egypt and in Palestine under the Fatimid Caliphs,* vol. 2 (London, 1920–1922), pp. 366–67; reprint: 1970, p. 367.
10. *Oṣar Kitve Yad Ivriyim mi-Ymei ha-Beinayim,* vol. 3, Descriptions (Jerusalem–Paris, 1980), no. 122.

"Thus says the youngest servant among all those in the city, Shelomo son of my master and father Ha-Rav R. Yeshu'ah ben Ha-Rav R. Dawid ben Ha-Rav R. Ḥalfon ha-'Adani, may the spirit of G-d give them rest...and especially my young family, all of whom were, according to what I have gleaned and found to be true according to the distinguished speakers of truth, fearers of heaven, and Torah scholars, students of my master and father, OBM, for he was the rabbi of the city 'Ūzal, which is called Ṣan'a, and also the grandfather of my father had previously been a teacher of small children there."[11]

Ṣa'di—After the name of the city Ṣa'dah in northern Yemen. At the end of the fifteenth century the name R. Dawid Sa'di is mentioned in a dispute between the sages of Ṣan'a and the rabbis of Ṣa'dah over *Sefer Ha-Amitot* [*Book of Truths*] written by a scholar from Ṣa'dah.[12] In a manuscript of a *siddur* copied by Pinḥas ben Gad Hakohen of the Dhamār community, in 1680, the name of the commissioner of the work was given: "Written at the request of the distinguished gentleman, for a good name and praise, who is known in public by the name Yehudah ben Shelomo, may he have descendants, live a long life, Amen, who is known as al-Ṣa'di, *yṣ"v*.[13] Other scholars from the Ṣa'di family were also known in Ṣan'a. In the seventeenth century, there was a *dayyan* in Ṣan'a with the name of R. Shalom ben Sa'adyah Ṣa'di.[14] Among the Ṣan'a

11. Introduction to his commentary to the Mishnah, *Melekhet Shelomo,* commentary to the Mishnah by R. Shelomo 'Adani, printed in *Mishnayot 'im Peirushim* (Jerusalem, 1960).

12. R. Qāfiḥ wrote on this issue: "The foremost rabbi in Ṣa'dah at the time was 'Harav Yehudah Birbi Shelomo' and he had no family name, as was usual in the Ṣa'dah district and lower Yemen. And the leading Ṣan'a rabbi was 'Harav Da'ūd ben Sa'ad ben Suleman al-Ṣa'di. (R. Yosef Qafiḥ, *"Ketav Haganah mi-Teiman 'al ha-Shitah ha-Alegorit be-Peirush ha-Miqra," Ketavim* 1 (Jerusalem, 1989): p. 342). R. Qāfiḥ wrote this because he believed that the selection in which the names of these scholars were mentioned is a reply to a letter of protection. According to another finding in the manuscript, it turned out that it concerns a totally different issue, so we do not know the names of the sages involved with that debate. Thus, for the names given, we do not know where these people lived. See idem, "*Ha-Pulmus 'al Shitat ha-Parshanut ha-Aligoristit be-Teiman,*" in Le-Rosh Yosef, ed. Joseph Tobi (Jerusalem, 1995), p. 11. See also Qāfiḥ, *Kitāb al-Ḥaqā'īq*.

13. Aharon Gaimani, *"Ha-Sofer R. Pinhas ben Gad ha-Kohen," Tema* 7 (2001): 125.

14. Moshe Gavra, *Enṣiqlopedya le-Qehilot ha-Yehudiyyot be-Teiman*, vol. 1 (Bnei Brak, 2005), 533, entry "Sa'di, Shalom ben Sa'adyah.

scholars at the end of the seventeenth century and in the first half of the eighteenth were R. Se'īd Ṣa'di, who wrote *"Dofi ha-Zeman,"*[15] and R. Yehudah Ṣa'di, who wrote the introduction to a *siddur* with the traditional rites of Yemenite Jewry.[16]

An examination of Yemenite manuscript colophons informs us that some scribes indicated their family names. For instance, the 'Ansi family is noted in copies from the fourteenth century among copyists and commissioners of books. In a colophon from 1342, the scribe indicated the name of the client: "May it be for a good sign for Mori Shelomo b. R. Yosef b. R. Se'īd b. Manṣūr b. Se'īd b. Yiḥye' b. Dawid b. Kathīr b. Dawid b. R. Yosef ben Maḥfūḍ al-'Ansi b. R. Yosef ha-Qenīzi."[17] The 'Ansi family is cited also in the name of the person who ordered a manuscript in 1351[18] and in the name of the copyist of a manuscript from 1357.[19] In a manuscript from 1380, the family is cited in the lineage of the commissioner and in that of the copyist as well.[20] The Khalīfi family is cited in a copy from 1328, in which the copyist cites his name: "I, Yiṣḥaq ben Dukhn al-Khalīfi."[21] In a copy from 1412, the scribe notes: "May the writer have merit, Yosef Halewi ben Se'īd al-Farḥi of the al-Farīghiyin family."[22] In a copy from 1460, the copyist cites his name: "The weak and poor scribe, Shelomo ben Yehudah *beirav* Marduk *beirav* 'Oded known as al-'Uzayri al-Ḥashfi."[23]

In seventeenth-century Yemenite *ketubbot*, family names appear that are names used in later generations. In a *ketubbah* from the village of Ḥatab, dated 23 Adar 5371 (9 Mar 1611), listed are the names of the groom, Slayman ben Sālem ben Maḥfuḍ ben al-Musa'yiy, and the bride, Ghaziyyah bat Shim'on ben Binyamin al-Qabāli are listed. Listed in a

15. Aharon Gaimani, *Temurot be-Moreshet Yahadut Teiman: be-Hashpa'at ha- Shulḥan 'Arukh ve-Qabalat ha-Ari* (Ramat Gan: Bar-Ilan University, 2005), pp. 160–61.
16. Ibid., pp. 160, 182–83.
17. *Oṣar Kitve Yad Ivriyim mi-Ymei ha-Beinayim*, vol. 2, Descriptions, no. 28 (Jerusalem-Paris, 1980). See also Yehudah Levi Naḥum, *Mi-Ṣefunot Teiman* (Tel Aviv, 1987), pp. 252, 257.
18. MS JTS NY 2770.
19. MS JTS NY 328.
20. Aharon Gaimani, *"Ha'ataqah Qedumah mi-Teiman le-*Moreh Nevukhim *le-ha-Rambam," Tehuda* 14 (1994): 17–18.
21. MS Berlin 2415.
22. *Oṣar Kitve Yad Ivriyim mi-Ymei ha-Beinayim*, 1, Descriptions, no. 81 (Jerusalem-Paris, 1972).
23. Ibid., no. 116.

ketubbah from the village Maghrabo, from 14 Ḥeshvan 5416 (4 Nov 1655), are the names of the groom, Yiṣḥaq ben ʿAmr al-Hawās, and the bride, Ṣīniyyah bat Masʿūd Ashwal.[24] A *ketubbah* from Ḍūwāleʿ, dated 2 Ḥeshvan 5419 (19 Oct 1658), listed the names of the groom and bride as Seʿīd ben Yūdaʾ Shiʿtāl and Ghane bat Yiḥyeʾ Ghiyat, respectively. In a *ketubbah* from ʿImrān, dated 5 Shevat 5426 (11 Jan 1666), the names of the groom and bride were listed as Mūsa ben Seʿīd Tanʿami and Niʿmah bat Sālem Khalaf. A *ketubbah* from Hizm, dated 7 Tishri 4930 (4 Oct 1669), lists the names of the groom and bride as Sālem ben Mori Yiḥyeʾ Qarawāni and Hawīdah bat Shimʿon al-Nehāri, respectively. Listed in a *ketubbah* from Faṣīrah, from 11 Ṭevet 5439 (16 Dec 1678) were the names of the groom and bride as Yiḥyeʾ son of *mori rabi* Slay[man] Najjār, Ghazāl bat Yiḥyeʾ Naḥūm Manṣūr, respectively. In a *ketubbah* from Ṣanʿa, from 5 Tammuz 5439 (16.6.1679), the names of the groom and bride were listed as Maʿūḍah ben Yosef ben Moshe al-Sayyāni and Mlāḥ bat Sālem al-Sayyāni.

2. THE MODERN ERA

R. Shalom Gamliel, a native of Ṣanʿa who immigrated to the Land of Israel in 1944, wrote that many of the Yemenite Jews, including city inhabitants, did not have family names; he even presents a relevant short list.[25] From the lists of travelers in the nineteenth and twentieth centuries, as well as from the *ketubbot* documents from Yemen, one may learn of the custom of the Yemenite Jews in modern times regarding family names and bynames, as well as the scope of the phenomenon in the various districts of Yemen. These lists also underscore the differences between large and small settlements.

Yom Tov Tzemach, the AIU emissary to Yemen in 1910, wrote:

> Our Jewish brethren in Yemen have no family names at all. The son is also called by his father's proper name....In the well-known cities, there are some families called by the name of their place of origin, ʿIrāqi, ʿArusi, Tanʿami, Khulāni; others by their trade: Ḥaddād,

24. For a photo of the *ketubbah*, see Shalom Sabar, *Ketuba: Jewish Marriage Contracts of the Hebrew Union College Skirball Museum and Klau Library* (Philadelphia, 1990), p. 364, no. 245.
25. Shalom Gamliel, *Pequdei Teiman: Mas he-Ḥasut be-Teiman* (Jerusalem, 1982), pp. 180–83. See also Yosef Shalom Ḥubarah, *Bi-Tlaʾot Teiman vi-Yrushalayim* (Jerusalem, 1970), p. 38; Nissim Binyamin Gamliel, *Ḥadrei Teiman—Sippurim va-Aggadot* (Tel Aviv, 1978), pp. 184–85.

> Naqqāsh, Najjār, Sayyāgh, Maddār; and some are called with nouns, Abyaḍ, Ūsṭa, Mu'allam, Naddāf,[26] Ḥibshūsh, Kisār.[27]

One may reasonably assume that his statement "Our Jewish brethren in Yemen have no family names at all" is a general impression from visiting the smaller communities, in which most people did not have family names. In contrast, when he stayed in Ṣan'a, he registered the names of the quarters of the Jewish community that had been built at the end of the seventeenth century and he noted: "A few of them are called after the names of the first families who had settled in them: Būsāni, Sayyāni, Ḥūbarah, Ūsṭa."[28]

R. Ḥayim Ḥibshūsh, who, in 1870, traveled throughout Yemen with Yosef Halevi, who had been sent by the French Academy to copy ancient inscriptions, cited the names of people who had family names, as well as those identified by their name plus their father's name. During his visit to the Jawf community, he noted the names of eight families he felt originated outside the local community. Four of them were called by their communities of origin: Bet Ṣa'ūd from the city of Ṣa'dah, al-Arḥabi from the land of Arḥab, Ḥijāzi from the land of al-Ḥijāz, and Jawfi apparently for the village of Jawf. As for the four other families, Sharārah and Asad stemmed from the village of Nihm, al-Bāsel from Ṣan'a, and Jalākh from Kūlān.[29] In the village of Milḥ he met Yiḥye' ben Se'īd[30] and Shukr al-Maswari, who originated from Ṣan'a.[31]

An important source on the customs of Yemenite Jews in modern times is the book by the traveler R. Ya'aqov Sappir, who visited Yemen in 1859. In his travels throughout Yemen, he wrote down the names of people from the important communities with whom he had contact. His

26. He was not precise in this categorization, and he should have assigned him to artisans, for it means upholsterer.
27. Abraham Elmaleh (trans.), *"Massa Yom Tov Ṣemah le-Teiman," Shevut Teiman*, ed. by Y. Yeshayahu and A. Tzadok (Tel Aviv, 1945), p. 313. See also above, part 1, chap. 3, sect. 1.
28. Elmaleh, *"Massa Yom Tov Ṣemah le-Teiman,"* p. 279.
29. Ḥaim Ḥibshush, *Mas'ot Hibshush* (Tel Aviv, 1939), pp. 122–23. S. D. Goitein believed that the family name Ḥijāz apparently came from the occupation of one of the family members in commerce in the land of Ḥijāz. See ibid., p. 122 n. 71; S. D. Goitein, *"Ḥayim Ḥibshush ve-Sifro* Ḥizzayon Teiman," in *Sefer Magnes:Koveṣ Meḥqarim*, eds. J. N. Epstein et al. (Jerusalem, 1983), p. 91 n. 10.
30. Ibid., p. 69.
31. Ibid., p. 80.

jottings inform us about the Jewish leadership in the middle-sized and large communities in Yemen, which, like other Jewish groupings, relied on two mainstays. At the head of the spiritual leadership stood the *Mori* and at the head of the political leadership stood the *Nasi*.[32] His sketches reveal the internal migration within Yemen for reasons such as famine or threats against the main ruling authority in Ṣan'a, which occurred in the second third of the nineteenth century, a situation that resulted in exacerbating the authorities' attitude toward the Jews in Ṣan'a to the point that part of them were forced to leave their homes and settle in other communities.[33] The ones who took root elsewhere were called by R. Sappir "Ṣan'a refugees." In the Jirwāḥ community he mentioned R. Yosef ben Se'īd, the community rabbi, as well as R. Yiḥye' 'Ūmaysi, Mori Slaymān Ta'īzi, and Avraham 'Adani.[34] The chief rabbi's family name is not mentioned, while the others are given: 'Ūmaysi, Ta'īzi, and 'Adani, all of which refer to places in Yemen. In Muḍmār, the community rabbi was Mori Yosef Yehoshua, and the *nasi* was Lewi Ḥamdi.[35] The community *nasi* is mentioned with a family name; the *nasi*'s family originated from the city of Ḥamdeh in northern Yemen. In Yafīd, the community rabbi was Mori Slaymān al-'Imrāni. Another *ḥakham* was Avraham al-Ḥarāzi.[36] The family names inform us of the origins in 'Imrān and Ḥarāz, as well.

The Shibām community was composed of local residents and Ṣan'a refugees. The leaders of the local inhabitants were R. Aharon and his father, R. Yiḥye'. The heads of those coming from Ṣan'a were R. Yosef Shi'tāl and R. al-'Arūsi.[37] The native residents were not mentioned by family name, whereas others were: the Shi'tāl and 'Arūsi families. R. Sappir further relates that Mori Se'īd 'Amār, a Ṣan'a refugee, married his son to the daughter of the religious court president, Kawkabān Mori Yiḥye' al-Badīḥi, who had also fled Ṣan'a.[38] In the Thila community he met Yosef al-Thayri (=Ṭayri) from the Ṣan'a community.[39] In the 'Imrān community was a community leader named Mori Slaymān al-Tanī'mi

32. See Gaimani, *Temurot be-Moreshet*, pp. 171–72.
33. Yehudah Nini, *Teiman ve-Ṣiyyon* (Jerusalem, 1982), pp. 11–14, 43–62.
34. See the Ya'ari edition of Sappir's book, pp. 55–58.
35. Ibid., p. 96.
36. Ibid., pp. 106–7.
37. Ibid., p. 121.
38. Ibid., p. 132.
39. Ibid., p. 123.

(should be Tan'ami);[40] the family originated from Tan'em. In the market in the vicinity of Ḥajjah, he came to the store of the merchant Avraham al-Kūḥlāni, a resident of Ḥajjah,[41] whose family originated in Kūḥlān. In the Ḥajjah community, he met the community leader Mori Sālem ben Yiḥye' and his son-in-law, Mori Yosef Sirri Halewi.[42] In the Rawḍah community, he met Mori Sālem al-Qāfiḥ, a Ṣan'a refugee.[43] In Dhamār, the community heads were Mori Avraham al-Qāfiḥ[44] and Mori Avraham al-Naddāf. In Damt, the community leader was Mori Salīm al-Ḥarāzi; and in the Radā' community, the community heads were Mori Sālem Ma'na [i.e., Menayah] and Mori 'Awaḍ Sulaymān.[45]

From these lists, we see that some of the locals bore family names whereas others did not. Some derived from internal circumstances, for purposes of identification among the community members, and the authorities in Yemen did not interfere in this issue. There were family names citing locations, informing us as to the family's origin in preceding generations.

3. THE MASS IMMIGRATION TO ISRAEL

The main source for a large pool of family names is made from R. Shalom Gamliel's registration of immigrants who came from all over Yemen and stayed in Aden.[46] R. Gamliel immigrated to Israel in 1944. In 1949, at the time of the mass immigration to the State of Israel, he went to the Geulah camp in Aden on behalf of the Ministry of Religion and the Aliyah Department of the Jewish Agency, in order to help organize the new *olim*.[47] His list contains 330 place names and under each appears the main family names,[48] which, it is estimated, encompass about one-third of the Yemenite *olim*.

40. Ibid., p. 145,
41. Ibid., p. 183.
42. Ibid., p. 184.
43. Ibid., p. 187.
44. It seems that he originated from Ṣan'a. His grandson is R. Yiḥye' Qāfiḥ of the Raṣāba community. R. Yiḥye' is the grandfather on the mother's side of R. Yiṣḥaq Raṣabi as well as a relative of R. Yiḥye' Qāfiḥ of Ṣan'a, the grandfather of R. Yosef Qāfiḥ.
45. Sappir, ibid., p. 194.
46. Cited in his book *Ha-Naḥshonim 'al Kanfei Nesharim mi-Teiman* (Jerusalem, 1996).
47. Ibid., Introduction, pp. 4–5.
48. The list of place names appears in the index located at the beginning of the book. The Jews of Yemen lived in over one thousand locations. Many were small settlements, and their Jewish population sometimes numbers only a few families.

Below are various categories of family names as collected from the lists. The listing below contains minor updates, and a few family names were deleted on the assumption that they were erroneous. Owing to the differences in pronunciation among the regions in Yemen, in a few instances the name endings are not vocalized.

Family names derived from personal names

Avraham, Binyamin, Dawid, Efrayim, Ḥasan, Ḥayim, Menashe, Meshūlam, Meshūmar, Moshe, Mūsa, Naḥūm, Nissim, 'Ovadyah, Pinḥas, Sālem, Se'īd, Shelomo, Shemaryah, Shemū'el, Shim'ōn, Slaymān, Ṣadōq, Ṣevi, Ya'aqov, Ya'īsh, Yehudah, Yeshū'ah, Yiḥye', Yisra'el, Yiṣḥaq, Yosef, Zekharyah.

Family names from places and districts

Appearing in parentheses are place or district names.

Abyani (Abyān), Akhwa' (Khaw'i), 'Ammār ('Ammār), 'Arāmi ('Arām), Arḥabi (Arḥab), 'Arūsi ('Arūs), 'Āshri (al-'Ashūr), 'Athāri ('Athār), 'Awāmi ('Awām), 'Awdi ('Awd), 'Azzāni ('Azzān), Baraṭi (Baraṭ), Bawsi (Bayt Baws), Bayḍa'/Bayḍāni (Bayḍa'), Beshāri (Beshār), Busāni (Busān), Damti (Damt), Dehāri (Dehār), Dhahbāni (Dhahbān), Dhamāri (Dhamār), Dharāḥi (Dharāḥ), Ḍāhri (Ḍāhareh), Ḍāl'i (Ḍāl'e), Ḍulā'i (Ḍuwāle'), Ḍūr'āni (Ḍūr'ān), Farawi (Farwah), Ghirasi (Ghiras), Hizmi (Hizm), Ḥabbāni (Ḥabbān), Ḥāfdi (Ḥāfid), Ḥajbi (Ḥajbeh), Ḥamdi (Ḥamdeh), Ḥāshdi (Ḥāshid), Ḥāzi (Ḥāz), Ḥubāshi (Ḥubaysh), Ḥūbayshi (Ḥūbayshiyyah), Ḥūdhayfi (Aḥdhūf), Ḥūgari (Hūgariyyah), Ḥūgeyrah (Ḥūgeyrah), Ibbi (Ib), Jadasi (Jadīs), Ja'di (Ja'ūd), Jāhli (Jāhaliyah), Jerāfi (Jerāf), Jerāsi (Jerās), Jerūfi (Jerūf), Jawbi (Jawb), Jeḥāfi (Jeḥāf), Jibli (Jiblah), Jūbāani (Jūbān), Kawkabāni (Kawkabāni), Khūbāni (Khūbān), Kūḥlāni (Kūḥlān), Kūmaymi (Kūmaym), Ma'bari (Ma'bar), Mraysi (Mrays), Maswari (Maswarah), Maṭari (Bane Maṭār), Maz'aqi (Mazā'qah), Nihmi (Nihm), Qahlāni (Qahlān), Qa'ṭabi (Qa'ṭabah), Raḍmi (Raḍma), Saddi (Saddeh), Sahwān (Sahwān), Sanḥāni (Sanḥān), Sa'wāni (Sa'wān), Saybhi (Saybhi), Sayyāni (Sayyān), Shabazi (Shabaz), Shaddādi (Shaddād), Shaghadari (Shaghādarah), Sinwāni (Sinwān), Sirri (Sirr), Ṣa'di (Ṣa'dah), Ṣabari (Ṣabar), Ṣan'āni (Ṣan'a'), Ṣubāri (Ṣubārah), Ta'izzi (Ta'īzz), Tan'ami (Tan'em), Thālabi (Thālabi), Ṭawīli (Ṭawīlah), 'Ūdayni ('Ūdayneh—synonym for Ta'īz), Wāwah (Wāwah), Wi'lāni (Wi'lān), Yanā'i (Yanā'), Yarīmi (Yarīm)

Family names after animals

Dajāj = chickens, Ḥamāmi = male dove, Jaḥsh = young ass; Khayl = horse, Qu'ūd = young camel, 'Ūqāb, 'Ūqabi = kinds of birds, Waḥsh = wild animal from the leopard family (usually translated as lion).

Family names after plants and fruits

'Aravah = willow tree, Balas = figs, Jawzi = nut-like, Dukhan = species of legume, millet, Ḥilbeh = fenugreek, Wabal = species of grass (symbol from steadfastness and survival), Wajīmah = stalk of sorghum, Zabīb = raisins.

Family names derived from professions and occupations

Ḍrāb = striker of coins; Ḥaddād = smith; Khayyāṭ, Mebawrit = gunpowder maker; Maddār = potter; Mallāj = plasterer; Maṣrafi = money changer; Mejahez = maker of sword sheath;[49] Mkhayyīt = tailor; Mu'allem/Muqari/Mori = teacher, rabbi; Mughāni/Shā'ir = poet-singer; Naddāf = upholsterer or carder; Najjār = carpenter; Nanajjim = fortuneteller; Saqqāl = burnisher of copper; Sayīgh/Sayyāgh = goldsmith, jeweller; Ṣāni' = weaver; Shammā' = wax chandler; Ṭabīb = physician.

Family names taken from tools and other objects

Būta = a bowl used when heating silver and gold; Ḥallah = laundry basin; Ku'aydah = small pitcher for washing hands; Madhalah = precious container for storing oil and honey; Maṭraqah = hammer; Mezuzah; Mid'i = nargila; Nūṣayf = vessel for dry measure; Qindīl = oil lamp; Ṭāṣah = bowl, basin.

Family names based on physical characteristics

Afhal = unkempt; Aḥwal = cross-eyed; Aḥmar = red, ruddy; Aḥraq = burned; 'Amya' = blind; A'raj = lame; Aqḍa' = bald (in front); Ashwal = left-handed; Ashram = rough; Ashtar = missing an ear; Azraq = blue, apparently referring to eye color; Qa'ashe = unkempt forelock; Qaṭī'i = whose member is cut off; Sheḥib = hoarse; Zindāni = wrist, biceps, perhaps referring to strong-armed; Zūghayir = rather small.

49. Cf. Avraham Ṣan'ani, *Qodesh Hillulim* (Jerusalem, 1971), p. 145.

4. FAMILY NAMES IN THE LISTINGS OF RABBI SHALOM GAMLIEL

In his 1996 book *Ha-Naḥshonim al Kanfei Nesharim me-Teiman*, R. Shalom Gamliel assembled a list of family names among the immigrants, which he wrote at the time of his mission to Aden. There are family names in his book that do not appear here since they seem to not have been properly written. For a few family names we have no explanation, apparently because they were given in earlier times owing to an event that has since been forgotten. Some names are listed with a Hebrew translation, and it is reasonable to assume the translation was made when the list was compiled in Aden. The names cited are the following:

Abbi, Abdar, 'Abiṣ, Abyani, 'Adani, Ahfa'l, Ahfal, Aḥmar, Aḥraq, Aḥwal, Akhwa', Alzaq, 'Āmel, 'Āmi, 'Ammār, 'Amr, 'Amya, 'Anjil, Aqḍa', A'raj, 'Arāmi, 'Aravah, Arḥabi, 'Arji, 'Arūsi, 'Aṣab, Ashram, 'Āshri, Ashtar, Ashwal, 'Athāri, Avraham, 'Awāḍ, 'Awāmi, 'Awdi, 'Awwāwi, 'Aydah, 'Ayna', Ayṭamus, Azraq, 'Azzani, Badīḥi, Badūḥ, Balas, Bandalah, Bane, Baraṭi, Bashāri, Basīs, Baṭīḥah, Batiyyah, Bayḍa, Bayḍāni, Ba'zah, Bilḥaj, Binyamin, Būni, Burah, Burhan, Būsāni, Būsi, Būṭa, Būtayl, Dahāri, Dajāj, Damarmari, Damti, Danūkh, Dār, Dawid, Dawṭāthi, Dawwaḥ, Dha'rūr, Dhahbāni, Dhamāri, Dhanīn, Dharāḥi, Dhiyāb, Diḥbāsh, Di'ri, Dughmah, Duḥūḥ, Dūkhān, Dūkhn, Dūrayb, Du'ūs, Ḍāhari, Ḍāl'i, Ḍarāb, Ḍārḥi, Ḍūlā'i, Ḍūr'āni, Efrayim, Faḍl, Faq'ah, Farāj, Farawi, Fayyūmi, Ga'di, Gershom, Ghadqah, Gharābi, Gharāmah, Ghayār, Ghayda, Ghazāl, Ghirāsi, Ghiyāt, Ghūmdāni, Ghuni, Habari, Halewi, Harari, Hārūn, Hashash, Hibih, Hikri, Hilal, Ḥaddād, Ḥaddi, Ḥādri, Ḥāfdi, Ḥajbi, Ḥalhalu, Ḥallah, Ḥamāmi, Hiṭali, Hizmi, Hudi, Ḥamdi, Ḥāmi, Ḥarāzi, Ḥarīzi, Ḥasan, Ḥāser, Ḥāshdi, Ḥathūkah, Ḥatrūsh, Ḥawa'īya', Ḥaybi, Ḥayim, Ḥaza, Ḥāzi, Ḥibshūsh, Ḥijāshi, Ḥabāni, Ḥilbah, Ḥirfūf, Ḥisha'i, Ḥomri, Ḥūbārah, Ḥubāshi, Ḥubayshi, Ḥūdhayfi, Ḥūgari, Ḥūgariyyah, Ḥumādi, Ḥūnen, Ḥusāni, 'Idwi, 'Ijash, 'Immanu'el, 'Imrān, 'Imrāni, 'Irāqi, 'Iṭwār, Ja'rabi, Jābar, Jabāsah, Jadasi, Jaḥāfi, Jāhli, Jaḥsh, Jamāl, Jamali, Jamīl, Janāh, Jarashi, Jarūfi, Jawzi, Jeredi, Jerufi, Jibli, Jidār, Jishjūsh, Jizfān, Ju'ayd, Jūbani, Jūbayr, Jūbbi, Jūḥf, Jum'i, Jumāzah, Ka'tarah, Kawkabāni, Khabrah, Khabti, Khalaf, Kharbi, Khaw'I, Khayl, Khayyāṭ, Khubāji, Khubāni, Khurṣān, Kisār, Kisrah, Kīzah, Kohen, Ku'aydah, Kūḥlāni, Kūmaymi, Kūtah, Lewi, Libi, Lūlūwi, Ma'aṭi, Ma'bari, Ma'dāni, Ma'saji, Ma'ūḍah, Mabawrit, Madāni, Madawwil, Maddār, Madhalah, Madīnah, Madrafi, Maḍmun, Maghīlah, Maghrabi, Mahalla, Mahāṣri, Maḥbūb, Maḥdūn,

Maḥfūḍ, Maḥzari, Maj'ar, Makhāḥil, Makhayyiṭ, Makhorish, Malāj, Malayḥi, Manajjim, Manqadhah, Manqadhi, Manṣūr, Manṣūrah, Maqayṭin, Marabiḥ, Maraysi, Marḥabi, Mas'ūd, Masallam, Maṣayni', Maṣrafi, Maswari, Mathanah, Maṭari, Maṭraqah, Maṭrūd, Māwari, Mawashir, Mawbadi, Mawqa'ah, Māwri, Maydāni, Maz'aqi, Mazāḥni, Mazūzah, Meghori, Menaḥem, Menashe, Meshūlam, Meshūmar, Mi'wil, Mid'i, Minis, Mishriqi, Mori, Moshe, Mu'allam, Mughānni, Muqari, Mūqi, Naddāf, Nafarayn, Naḥshon, Naḥum, Najjār, Nehāri, Nihmi, Nīssim, Nūni, Nūṣayf, 'Ovadyah, Pinḥas, Qā'ah, Qa'ashe, Qa'ṭabi, Qadri, Qāhiri, Qahlāni, Qaḥm, Qamās, Qanimmiḥ, Qapari, Qāra, Qārah, Qarawāni, Qarītti, Qarna, Qarni, Qārni, Qarṭah, Qashame, Qaṣir, Qathar, Qathū', Qaṭī'i, Qehah, Qindīl, Qirnān, Qoraḥ, Qūbaysi, Qūḍā'i, Qūlaṣah, Qūmali, Quraysh, Qū'ud, Qūzi, Raḍa', Raḍmi, Raḥabi, Rakhīṣ, Ramādi, Raṣābi, Rashīd, Ray'āni, Raydi, Rizqān, Ṣa'di, Ṣabbari, Ṣadoq, Ṣafādi, Ṣafar, Ṣāliḥ, Ṣan'āni, Ṣāni', Ṣārūm, Ṣevi, Ṣubāri, Ṣubayri, Sa'ādi, Sa'īgh, Saddi, Sahwān, Sālem, Salūs, Sandaḥ, Sanhāni, Saqqāl, Satāḥi, Sa'wāni, Say'ad, Saybhi, Sayyāgh, Sayyāni, Se'īd, Sha'bali, Shā'ir, Sha'ul, Shabazi, Shaddādi, Shaghadari, Shaghn, Sham'ah, Shammā', Shar'abi, Sharafi, Sharāmah, Sharkhasi, Shawāqi, Shawḥam, Shawkiya, Shawniya, Shawwabal, Shayyāḥi, Sheḥib, Shelomo, Shemaryah, Shemū'el, Shim'on, Shir'ah, Shiryān, Shi'tal, Shū'ah, Shū'aybi, Shukr, Shūzayf, Shūzayfi, Si'd, Simḥi, Sinwāni, Sirri, Slaymān, Subā'i, Suḥāni, Ṣūtaḥi, Ṭabīb, Ṭahbāsh, Ṭāṣah, Ṭawīli, Ṭaybi, Ṭayri, Ṭov, Ṭovim, Ta'izzi, Ta'sah, Tālabi, Tām, Tan'ami, Tarāban, Tayram, 'Ūdayni, 'Ūdayri, 'Ūmari, 'Ūmaysi, 'Ūqāb, 'Ūqabi, 'Ūrāshi, 'Ūrqubi, 'Ūzayri, Wabal, Wahb, Waḥsh, Wajīmah, Wanneh, Washdi, Wāwah, Wi'lāni, Ya'aqov, Ya'īsh, Yadūmi, Yahūd, Yamani, Yanā'i, Yaqna', Yarimi, Yehudah, Yeshu'ah, Yiḥye', Yiṣḥaq, Yisra'el, Yosef, Za'īri, Zabaṭāni, Zabīb, Zāhir, Zakharyah, Zamīmi, Zārib, Zāyid, Zindāni, Zūghayir, Zukhmi, Zūqā'

5. BYNAMES IN YEMENITE MARRIAGE DOCUMENTS

In Yemenite *ketubbot* the byname, when there is one, is listed as an appendage to the names of the bride and groom and sometimes as an addition to the family name. For example, in a *ketubbah* 12 Shevat 5691 (30 Jan 1931) from Ghaymān, the name of the groom is listed as Yosef ben Ya'ish ben Se'īd called al-Malāḥi. After immigration into Israel, the byname was dropped and the name of the town or village noted; the groom was my uncle R. Yose Ghaymani, who led the synagogue in moshav Zavdiel. In a *ketubbah* from 11 Sivan 5708 (18 June 1948), from the Tan'em community, the name of the groom was written as Salīm ben Salīm who is called al-Abhar. After immigration into Israel, this byname became the family name, and the groom is R. Shalom Abhar, who in Israel served as the rabbi of the Yemenite community in Ashkelon. In a *ketubbah* dated 9 Shevat 5507 (9 Jan 1747), from the Ṣan'a community, the bride's name appears as Ghazāl bint Yosef ibn Salīm Ṣāliḥ who is called al-Ḥaydāni. The byname Ḥaydāni is used to indicate that the family originated in Ḥaydān in northern Yemen. In a *ketubbah* from 19 Elul 5684 (18 Sep 1924), from the Radā' community, the name of the groom was listed as Yehuda' ben Salīm ben Ṣāliḥ Ma'ūḍah al-Ḥathūkah called Waqiyah. R. Azaryah Basis, from among those who came from Radā', wrote to me about the appellation Waqiyya: "The family was called Waqiyah because someone in it could estimate weight precisely without weighing an object, because the *waqiyya* is a small weight, and he would take, for example, some spices in his hand and say this is a *waqiyya*, and after him, people would weight it and see that he was precise."[50] From R. Basis's statement, we learn that over time the byname Waqiyya replaced the family name for that part of the Ḥathūkah family that came from Radā'.

Below is the corpus of bynames that appear in Yemenite *ketubbot* from the seventeenth to the twentieth centuries. The categorization of the bynames or family names follows what is noted in each *ketubbah*. A name that was added to the personal name and the father's name and is preceded by the word *ha-mekhuneh* ("called") is considered a byname; a name added to a personal name and a father's name without the term *ha-mekhuneh* is considered to be a family name. Yet, it may still be that this classification, faithfully reflecting what is listed in the *ketubbot*, does not coincide with the academic categorization that we apply to these names. Listed alongside the byname is a family name, if noted, and the place and date. For bynames that appear a number of times in the same place, only the first instance is listed here. Some names were written in various ways, such as Adukam and Adūkam or 'Uzayri, 'Uzayyri, and each is cited just as it was listed.

50. In a personal correspondence dated 8 Mar 2010.

Byname	*Family*	*Location*	*Date*
Abhar	—	Tan'em	19 Aug 1927
Abu Sāra	—	Sha'ab al-Aswad	19 Mar 1919
Abu Sit	Sirri	Ṣan'a	29 Oct 1897
Abusara	Azīn	Sha'ab	9 Apr 1946
'Adani		Maru'āgah	30 Jul 1879
'Adani		Garyat Yehude al-Sūd	29 Mar 1940
Aḥmar	—	Ḍūwāle'	20 Jun 1929
Aḥmar	Minnis	Ḥallah	23 Jun 1940
Aḥmari	—	Bagkal	6 May 1841
Aḥsan	—	Adhre'a	11 Mar 1867
A'me'	—	Ṣan'a	14 Aug 1870
A'me'	—	Qārah	23 Jan 1873
'Arūsi		Ḍubr	6 Dec 1901
'Āshri		Ṣan'a	18 Feb 1949
'Āshri	Zayīd	'Arūs	4 Jun 1936
Ba'zah	—	Ja'are'	30 Jan 1940
Ba'zah	—	Maṣ'ab	19 Feb 1907
Būsāni	—	Maḥwīt	23 Feb 1897
Damti	—	Ṣan'a	4 Apr 1944
Dan	'Awāmi	Maḥwīt	29 Aug 1856
Deqel	Najjār	Dāyān	29 Jan 1931
Dukhān	—	Tan'em	17 Mar 1933
Ḍāhiri		Ḍubr	19 Oct 1884
Ḍāhiri		Rawd	20 Dec 1888
Ḍāhiri	Abūrūs	Maru'āgah	21 Jan 1859
Ḍrāb		Gaṣr Mlāḥa'	12 Aug 1938
Faḍal		Ḥajbeh	9 Mar 1939
Ftayḥi		Sūq Ḍrāb	23 Nov 1939
Ftayt	Hashāsh	Ṣan'a	9 Jan 1947
Gadqah	—	Nuwayid	
Gafri		Lakamat Rubī'i	17 Apr 1905

Gafri		Naghd	3 Sep 1942
Gafri		Nawīd	6 May 1937
Gafri		Ḍalīm	26 Jan 1940
Gaharāni	—	Qāreh	17 Feb 1933
Gaḥm		Maḥwīt	7 Jul 1944
Gaḥm	Ḍurāni	Bīr al-Darb	7 Mar 1947
Gaḥm	Ḍurāni	Maḥwīt	29 Aug 1856
Garawāni		Ḥafeh	10 Dec 1918
Garawāni		Ladān	1 Feb 1934
Garawāni		Mawrah	19 Aug 1910
Gārni		Shibām	2 Aug 1949
Gārṭah		Sayyān	11 Sep 1862
Gasgas	Hashāsh	'Imrān	20 Jul 1933
Gaṭr		'Iddid	13 Jun 1919
Gaysi		Sūq Ḍrāb	19 Feb 1943
Gharameh	—	Adhre'a	11 Mar 1867
Ghayār	—	Ja're'	30 Jan 1940
Ghayār	—	Dajih	3 Jun 1935
Ghīyat	—	Shibām	26 Apr 1949
Ghīyat	Danūkh	Shibām	24 May 1940
Gūfārah	—	Madīd	4 Aug 1898
Gulūb		Ṣan'a	4 Apr 1946
Gu'ūd		Ḥajareh	12 Oct 1730
Gūzi	Ṣabaṭāni	Ṣan'a	4 Sep 1846
Hadiyyah		'Imrān	22 Aug 1949
Hikri		Ṭawīla	1 Jun 1934
Hindi		Qaṣr Mlāḥa'	12 Apr 1946
Ḥāḍari		Masiyab	9 Sep 1949
Ḥaddi	She'ūbi	Bayt Baws	31 Aug 1877
Ḥāḍri		Kawkabān	9 Jul 1943
Ḥajbi		'Ūgla	12 Mar 1937
Ḥamāmi		Ḥagal	9 Jun 1933
Ḥamdi	Dhumrāni	Ṣan'a	25 Mar 1768

Ḥaydāni		Ṣan'a	9 Jan 1747
Ḥāzi		Ṣan'a	18 Sep 1949
'Idwi		Maghrabat Bane Ḥijāj	25 Jun 1948
'Idwi	Ḥarāzi	Ḥajar Sūq Ithnayin	30 Jan 1946
'Imrāni		Shāhir	20 Feb 1942
Jarādi	—	Bane Zayid	26 Jan 1932
Jihsi	—	Tan'em	2 Mar 1945
Jūbani	—	Ṣan'a	23 Sep 1948
Jūbani	—	Naghd	25 Jan 1940
Kalib		Madīd	4 Aug 1898
Khabra		Ḥāfa	10 Dec 1918
Khabra		Gāreh	23 Jan 1873
Khabra		Qaṣr Mlāḥa	19 Apr 1929
Khabra	Sughayir	Adukam	14 Dec 1922
Khadhāb		Qaryat Ṣafa	26 Feb 1909
Khameri	Mardam	Ṣan'a	2 Nov 1891
Khāwli		Maru'āgha	25 Aug 1803
Khlūfi		Bayt Sālem	13 Mar 1936
Kohen		Bayt al-Shār'ah	26 Aug 1949
Lewi		Dār 'Amr	6 Mar 1925
Lewi		Ma'urah	31 Jul 1942
Lewi		Shibām	26 Apr 1949
Lewi		Tan'em	17 Mar 1933
Lewi	Nehari	Jir'ān	25 Dec 1931
Lewi	Sawīlam	Maru'āgah	22 Mar 1944
Lewi	'Amr	Sayyān	15 Oct 1909
Lidāni	Jamal	Ṣan'a	1767
Maddār		Bayt al-Shāri'eh	4 Apr 1944
Maḍmūn	Sawīlam	Rau'ūd	20 Dec 1888
Maḍmūni		Naghd	25 Jan 1940
Maḍmūni		Sayān	4 Sep 1942
Maḍmūni		Ḍaba'āt	21 Feb 1913
Maḍmūni		Ṣan'a	1808

Maḍmūni		Gāreh	17 Feb 1933
Maḍmūni		Gaṣr Mlāḥa	12 Nov 1873
Maḍmūni		Sha'b al-Sūd	19 Mar 1919
Maḍmūni		Sha'b	25 Jun 1940
Maḍmūni	Abghāni	Sha'b	25 Jun 1940
Maḍmūni	Ṭabīb	Ḥāfed	13 Feb 1873
Maglūb		Shibām	8 Sep 1933
Maḥfūḍ	Ṭawīli	Kawkabān	9 Jul 1943
Maliḥ		Maḥwīt	23 Feb 1897
Manṣūr		'Alāniyyah	15 Jul 1949
Marḥab		Sūq Ḍrāb	12 Aug 1949
Marḥab	Mūwashir	Sūq Ḍrāb	11 Aug 1927
Maswari	Ghīyāt	Ṣan'a	24 Jan 1746
Mid'i		Mlḥah	3 Nov 1948
Mid'i		Ḥāz	25 Aug 1949
Mid'i		Kawkabān	7 Jun 1901
Mid'i		Masyab	28 Feb 1923
Mid'i		'Alāniyyah	26 Jun 1942
Mid'i		'Arūs	15 May 1942
Mid'i		Ṣan'a	9 Jan 1945
Mid'i		Qaryat Ḥāz	27 Feb 1947
Mid'i	Wahb	'Arūs	4 Sep 1936
Mid'i	Ḥāzi	Ḥāz	23 Dec 1881
Mid'i	Najjār	Ibn Ḥājeb	25 Mar 1930
Mid'i	Najjār	Ḥaz	19 Feb 1926
Mid'i	Ga'eh	Shibām	2 Apr 1929
Mid'i	Qarawānni	Ṭawīla	22 Mar 1912
Mlāḥi		Ghaymān	30 Jan 1931
Moshe		Naghd	3 Sep 1942
Najjar		Ṭawīla	14 Mar 1924
Najjār	Ṭawīli	Ṣan'a	14 Dec 1943
Naqqāsh		Tan'em	24 Nov 1925
Nehāri		Bane Zayid	26 Jan 1932

Nehāri		Jabal	31 Aug 1923
Nehāri		'Arūs	31 May 1912
Nehāri		Ḍubr	6 Dec 1901
Nehāri	Halevi	'Arūs	15 May 1942
Raḥabi		Danah	7 Jun 1928
Raḥabi		Sa'diyeh	12 Mar 1703
Raḥabi		Ṣarfah	6 Sep 1938
Raḥabi	'Ināgi	Khaḍara'	29 Feb 1932
Ramaḍān		Kharbat Sa'wān	15 Feb 1935
Raṣabi		Khamer	12 Sep 1930
Raybi		Dā'iyān	11 Mar 1943
Raybi		Khamer	12 Sep 1930
Raybi	Manṣūr	Khamer	28 Feb 1901
Raybi	Na'ūs	Khamer	1 Apr 1946
Rūbayḥ		Bayḥān	16 Mar 1950
Sa'ad		Bayt al-Shāri'eh	9 Jul 1948
Sabaṭāni		Maḥwīt	22 Jun 1861
Sāhi		Mawra	17th century
Sai'd		Garn	29 Jan 1942
Sai'd	Hibeh	Hijreh	16 Jul 1943
Sai'd	Hibeh	Garn	29 Jan 1942
Shaddādi		Gaṣr Mlāḥa	12 Apr 1946
Shāhili		Mezā'gah	19 Feb 1948
Shalit	Khlūfi	Ṣan'a	23 Feb 1933
Shanīf		Sa'diyah	12 Mar 1703
Sharāreh	'Izayri	Ghayl	21 Jun 1883
Shawnim		Tan'em	26 Sep 1928
Shayleh		Sayyān	13 Sep 1949
Shḥib		Sūq Ḍrāb	11 Aug 1927
Sībahi		Khamer	1 Apr 1946
Sībahi	Jawbi	Ṣan'a	26 Aug 1920
Sībahi	Malgab Asiri	Khamer	1 Apr 1946

Ṣabari		Jabal	31 Aug 1923
Ṣabari		Dā'i'ān	27 Sep 1901
Ṣabari		Majrabat Bane Ḥajāj	25 Jun 1948
Ṣabari		Mobad	7 Nov 1944
Ṣabari		Maṣwi	25 Jan 1924
Ṣabari		'Alāyina	17 Jun 1932
Ṣabari		Rubu'	27 Jul 1923
Ṣabaṭāni		Maḥwīt	5 Jun 1868
Ṣabaṭāni		Maru'āgah	9 Jun 1864
Ṣabaṭāni	Dukhān	Maru'āgah	10 Feb 1882
Ṣabaṭāni	Gūzi	Bagkhal	6 May 1841
Ṣā'igh	'Imrāni	Maḥwīt	1 Mar 1883
Ṣfīrah		Mḥālīn	15 Sep 1944
Ṣfīrah		Tan'em	24 Nov 1925
Ṣubarah		Maru'āgah	5 Jul 1909
Ṣubarah		Maru'āgah	26 May 1944
Ta'izzi		Mirwāgah	30 Jan 1798
Ta'izzi	Yamani	Ṣan'a	14 Mar 1746
Ta'uzzi		Ṭawīla	20 Aug 1937
Tāba'i		Ḍalīm	26 Jan 1940
Tan'ami		Tan'em	19 Aug 1927
Ṭabīb		Shiraghe	13 Oct 1949
'Urqabi		Gaṣr Mlāḥa	30 Dec 1937
'Uzayri	Ḥāser	Shibām	8 Sep 1933
'Uzayri		Maru'āgah	14 Jun 1717
'Uzayri	Zaqīn	Ghayl	9 Oct 1889
'Uzayri		Mawrah	19 Aug 1910
'Uzayri		Maḥālīn	15 Sep 1944
'Uzayri		Maṣala'	2 Mar 1948
'Uzayri		Muḍmār	11 Aug 1916
'Uzayri		Ḍubr	8 Oct 1805
'Uzayri		Ṣan'a	14 Mar 1913
'Uzayri	Bāsil	Ghayl	21 Jun 1883

‘Ūzayri	Bāsl	Ghayl	9 Oct 1889
‘Ūzayri	Sfarjal	Maru’āgah	28 Aug 1730
Wa‘lāni		Sayyah	2 May 1927
Waqiyya	Ḥatūkah	Radā‘	18 Sep 1924
Yadā‘i		Adūkam	5 Apr 1949
Yadā‘i		Ḥamāmi	15 Mar 1932
Yadā‘i		Marbakh	22 Apr 1949
Yadā‘i		Shiraghe	13 Oct 1949
Yadā‘i	Ḍanīn	Adūkam	16 Aug 1929
Yadā‘i	Ḍanīn	Khamer	27 Nov 1905
Yanā‘i		Mazā‘iqah	19 Feb 1948
Yanā‘i		Shibām	25 Feb 1950
Yarīmi	Ḍāhiri	Ṣan‘a	7 Mar 1871
Zaqen		Ṭawīla	1 Jun 1934

CHAPTER THREE

BYNAMES AND SPECIFIC FAMILY NAMES

It was common among the Yemenite communities to assign a byname for the purpose of identification. Sometimes the byname was insulting or embarrassing, perhaps referring to an unattractive physical feature or alluding to an unpleasant event. So as not to humiliate people, community rabbis often refrained from using them. Nonetheless, even when there was a family name, the nickname often replaced it, and eventually, in later generations, any negative connotation disappeared.

1. BYNAMES ADDED FOR EASE OF IDENTIFICATION

Occasionally, another name was added to the family name, which was a common one, to make it distinctive. The examples below were selected because each has a tale to tell, and most of them are from the Ṣan'a community, where, owing to the community's large size, they customarily used bynames so as "to provide indications,"[1] to differentiate among households with the same name.[2]

Mori Shim'on Dhahbāni of the Ṣan'a community tells that when a person was called by his own name and that of his father and there were similar names in the family, to make identification easier they would append a nickname, that is, an "indication" according to some prominent feature of that person. As a result, there often are humorous bynames.[3] But, as discussed above, these names could also be embarrassing.

1. Cf. M Bava Batra 10:7.
2. If a source is not specifically noted, the information was taken from R. Ezra Qoraḥ of Bnei Brak, from R. Itamar Ḥayim Cohen of Bnei Brak, or from Eleazar Gamliel of Tel Aviv.
3. Interview conducted by R. Raṣon Arusi of Qiryat Ono.

Priestly Families

The names Efrayim, Pinḥas, Meghori, or 'Irāqi were added to priestly families. Efrayim and Pinḥas are relatively rare in Yemen, so they were often chosen as names identifying families of *kohanim* in Yemen. R. Itamar Ḥayim Kohen wrote about his great-grandfather, R. Aharon [b. R.] Efrayim Hakohen:

> Everyone called him Harūn [=Aharon] Efrayim, on the name of his father, since the name Efrayim was not found in the city of Ṣan'a, and from then the family was called by the name Efrayim. In *shetarot* and *ketubbot* and the like, they wrote Hakohen or al-Kohen.[4]

Priestly families that did not include a rare name simply retained the usual bynames: Kohen, Hakohen, al-Kohen.[5]

Levitic Families

For Levitic families the names appended were Alsheikh, Yiṣḥaq, Sirri. The family names Ḥamdi, 'Amr, 'Arūsi, and Naḥūm were used by Levites and Israelites. The 'Arūsi clans originally came from the city of 'Arūs. The Levites from these families moved to Kawkabān and from there to Ṣan'a and elsewhere, such as R. Avraham 'Arūsi who moved to the Maḥwīt community; and the Israelites arrived in Ṣan'a from 'Arūs. All the Naḥūm families were Levites, except for those who reached Ṣan'a from the Dhahr 'Amr community.

Bynames for the Sirri Family

The name *Sirr* refers to the location Sirr in Yemen.

Sirri Minḥah—one of the members of the Sirri family had a store in the Arab market in Muslim Ṣan'a. Owing to the distance to the synagogue in the Jewish neighborhood, the owner of the store tried to see that all the Jewish merchants in the market would gather in his store for the Minḥah (afternoon) service. That was how he and his descendants earned this nickname.

Sirri Rosh Ḥodesh—In this family it was customary that every Rosh Ḥodesh (new moon), they would refrain from working and celebrate with fine clothing and a meal. This event was so impor-

4. Itamar Ḥayim Kohen, *Sar ha-Shalom, Toldotav shel ha-Rav Shalom Efrayim Hakohen,* printed together with *Shevet Kehunah* (Bnei Brak, 2012), 59 n. 4. In a document dated 23 Av 5699 (8 Aug 1939), his name is written as Harūn Efrayim Hakohen.
5. On the Meghori family, see above, this part, chap. 1, sect. 3. On the 'Irāqi family, see below part 3, chap. 5.

tant that if one member of the family had to leave Ṣan'a on business, he would be sure to come home in time to celebrate Rosh Ḥodesh. This custom was unique in Yemen to this family.

Sirri Yatom—One of the family members whose father died young used to say, "I am Ben Sirri, whose father has died, and I am not used to being an orphan." This is the response of a simple man, and because of this statement his family was called "Sirri Yatom."

Sirri Kū'dah—One of the family members was a seller of *Kū'ad*, which are dessert saucers, and so the family name.

Bynames for the 'Ūzayri family

The name 'Ūzayri is one of the most common among Yemenite Jews.[6]

'Ūzayri Shuqri—*Shuqri* is a small chicken, a chick. According to one account, one of the family members once raised chickens and when he fed them he would call out *"shuqri"* several times so they would gather around him to feed. The family has another origin of this byname. A family member, Yisra'el, the brother of R. Sālem 'Ūzayri, used to go for his mother to the *shoḥet* (ritual slaughterer) with chicken in hand. When he would be asked where he was going, he would joke, "I am going to slaughter the chick," and because of this reply the byname stuck to the family.[7] Yet another story tells that when young R. Sālem 'Ūzayri attended the class of the chief rabbi, R. Yiḥye' Yiṣḥaq Halevi, and in a debate with the chief rabbi the latter quipped endearingly, "You are still a chick [i.e., young]."[8]

'Ūzayri Sawwagh—*Sawwagh* means "man of the market," and this referred to a family member who delivered goods to the market, and so received the name.

'Ūzayri Dubba—*Dubba* means squash. One of the family members was a squash seller and so was dubbed with this name.[9]

6. Prof. Joseph Tobi thinks that this is the most common family name among Yemenite Jews. See Joseph Tobi, *"Yosef Halevi ve-Ḥeqer Yehudei Teiman," Pe'amim* 100 (2004): 40 n. 41.
7. Shalom 'Uzayri, *Sefer 'Iqvei Shalom*, ed. by author's family ([Tel Aviv], 2006), p. 5.
8. Ibid., p. 8.
9. Shalom Gamliel, *Pequdei Teiman: Mas he-Ḥasut be-Teiman* (Jerusalem, 1982), 56–57.

'Ūzayri Aḥmar—*Aḥmar* means "red." Owing to their ruddy complexion, the term was appended to the name of family members.[10]

'Ūzayri Mashḥūn—*Mashḥūn* means "overflowing," and "full." The *imam* besieged Ṣan'a during his 1905 war against the Turks, who ruled the area. Owing to the great famine raging during the siege, many Ṣan'a Jews left for other Jewish communities. A member of the 'Ūzayri family who remained in Ṣan'a had a wealthy neighbor with whom he shared a common wall. That neighbor eventually left Ṣan'a. When he realized that his neighbor was not returning, he tore down the joint wall and used his neighbor's apartment. Lodged within that shared wall, he found a trove of money. So from that time on, he was "full," that is, fixed for life and so his family was nicknamed 'Ūzayri Mashḥūn.

'Ūzayri Zaṭāṭ—*Zaṭūṭ* means "being emotional." There was a family member who tended to overreact in certain situations, while in other situations he behaved like a person thrilled to receive a gift. Because of this behavior the nickname Zaṭāṭ was appended to him and his descendants.

Bynames of the Jamāl family[11]

Jamāl Meshari—*Meshari* means "singer," and this byname derived from one of the family members named Se'īd, who had a good voice.

Jamāl Qala'—*Qalai* means "roaster," because a family member's occupation was as a roaster of legumes.

Jamāl ha-Zahav— *Zahav* means "gold," reflecting a family member being a goldsmith and silversmith, a maker of jewelry.

Jamāl 'Aṭṭār—*'Aṭṭār* means "perfumer," and this byname indicates that a family member was a seller of perfumes.

Bynames for the Mishriqi family

Mishriqi Dabāb—*Dabāb* denotes "a narrow place." The nickname derives from the narrow street on which the family lived.

10. Ibid., p. 57.
11. All the bynames of the Jamāl family come from the book by R. Shalom Gamliel, *Pequdei Teiman*, p. 56.

Mishriqi 'Aravah—One of the Mishriqi families was tall in stature, thus *Aravah* (tall like) "a willow tree" was added to his personal name.[12]

Bynames for the Ṣāliḥ family

Ṣāliḥ ha-Zahav—*Zahav* means "gold," reflecting a family member being a goldsmith and silversmith, a maker of jewelry.[13]

Ṣāliḥ al-Jazzār—*Jazzār* is Arabic for "butcher." Avraham ben Yiḥye' Ṣāliḥ al-Jazzār was called thus by his contemporaries because of his occupation.[14] Yiḥye' Ṣāliḥ, too, was given this byname because of his trade, and apparently to distinguish him from other community members named Yiḥye' Ṣāliḥ.[15]

Ṣāliḥ Ḥarṭūh—One family member spent a long time in Ḥartum (Khartoum), presumably on business, and owing to this event, the family was called Ṣāliḥ Ḥarṭūh, which seems to be a corruption of the place name Ḥartum. R. Shalom Gamliel wrote about one member of this family, "Avraham Ṣadōq called Ḥarṭūh."[16]

Ṣāliḥ al-Mittarib—*Trab* is Arabic for "soil." One of the family members used to dig up the soil outside of Ṣan'a and bring it to his city by donkey. From the soil, his wife would make large pots, pitchers, and kitchen implements, and this was the source of their livelihood.[17]

2. FAMILY NAMES BASED ON EVENTS IN COMMUNITY LIFE

The Qaṭī'i and Kisār families

Both names indicate "cutting" or "breaking." Multiple explanations for the adoption of these names as family names have been pre-

12. On the Mishriqi 'Aravah family, see Shimon Jaraydi, *Yamim Yedabberu* (Tel Aviv, 1995). One of the female members of this family was known as Ghane bat Suleman Mushriqui 'Aravah; see Ḥayim Gamliel, *Pirqei Ḥayim* (Ramat Gan, 1998), p. 40.
13. 'Uzayri, *'Iqvei Shalom*, p. 5.
14. Shalom Gamliel, *Batei Kneset be-Ṣan'a Birat Teiman*, 1 (Jerusalem, 1987–1988), pp. 129, 133 n. 1.
15. Ibid., 3: 341 n. 2.
16. Gamliel, *Batei Kneset*, 2: 123 n. 14. In Israel many members of the Ṣāliḥ family were called Ṣadōq. R. Sa'adyah Gaon, in his Arabic commentary on the Torah, explained *ṣadīq* as *ṣāliḥ* (see, for example, *Keter ha-Torah – Ha-'Taj' ha-Gadōl*, Gen. 18:23). Apparently, Ṣadōq according to the sound derived from the word *ṣadīq*.
17. Nissim Binyamin Gamlieli, *Ḥivayon Teiman: Zikhronot, Sippurim, Aggadot Ḥayim me-'Olam Aḥer* (Ramla, 1983), p. 95.

served. The two simplest for the Qaṭī'i family are by Joseph Tobi, who suggested that the family name Qaṭī'i derives from the al-Qaṭī'a quarter, located in the eastern part of Ṣan'a,[18] and by Y. Ratzaby who posited that the name was given because a family member had been an amputee. There are, however, more fanciful explanations.

R. Yiḥye' Ṣāliḥ (Mahariṣ), who lived in the eighteenth century, wrote in *Megillat Teiman* about the miracle that happened to R. Yosef Qaṭī'i, who lived in Ṣan'a hundreds of years earlier and for whom the family was called Qaṭī'i. There was a spring with foul-smelling water where non-Jews were living that was causing plague. The non-Jews asked the Jews of Ṣan'a to exchange locations so they could move to the safety of where the Jews were. The Jews, having no choice, settled around the spring, but prayed incessantly that no harm should befall them as had happened to their Gentile neighbors. Mahariṣ writes:

> In those days, there was a great person in his generation, his name was Mori Yosef Qaṭī'i, may his rest be glorious. And he stood in prayer with the congregation, and God heard their prayer and he ceased the functioning of the spring and there is no sign of it to this day. So owing to this miracle, they gave the nickname of Qaṭī'i to this Mo[ri] Yosef because he eliminated and cut off and stopped this spring.[19]

Another explanation concerns one of the most important rabbis of seventeenth-century Ṣan'a, R. Slaymān Jamāl, who was seized by the great messianic fervor surrounding Shabbetai Zevi. As a result of the ensuing messianic turmoil within his community, he was summoned before the *imam* and beheaded.[20] R. Avraham Naddāf wrote "and in everlasting memory the Jews called this R. Slaymān's family by the name al-Qatā'i instead of 'Jamīl,'[21] because his head had been cut off."[22]

R. Shalom Gamliel cites a tradition he heard from his grandfather, R. Avraham Badīḥi, about one of the families in Ṣan'a called *Qatī'i* that had recently changed its name to Kisār. Among the descendants of the

18. Ibid., p. 38 n. 34.

19. Joseph Tobi, *'Iyyunim bi-Megillat Teiman* (Jerusalem, 1986), pp. 37–38.

20. See Yehudah Ratzaby, *"He'arot li-Nequdot Yehudiyyot bi-Khroniqa shel Ibn Nāṣr," Peamim* 43 (1990), pp. 136–41. Tobi doubts that the family name Qati'i was given as a result of this event; see his *'Iyyunim bi-Megillat Teiman*, p. 108 n. 97.

21. Jamīl should have been written Jamāl.

22. Avraham Alnaddaf, *Shut Zikhronei Ish*, in his *Anaf Ḥayim* (Jerusalem, 1981), sect 71, p. 258. See also Yosef Qāfiḥ, *"Qorot Yisra'el be-Teiman le-R. Ḥayim Ḥibshush,"* ed. R. Yosef Qāfiḥ, *Ketavim* 2 (Jerusalem, 1981): 711–12.

Qatī'i family in the nineteenth century was R. Yisra'el ben Yiḥye' Qatī'i, who dealt in commerce. Owing to his campaign against those who raised market prices unfairly, he would lower his prices, thus "breaking" the stranglehold on prices imposed by the other merchants. For this, the family name was changed from Qatī'i to Kisār, which means to "break." R. Gamliel further said of him: An incident in Ṣan'a in 1874 posed a danger to the Jewish community, whose members were suspected of having taken part in the killing of one of the sheikhs in the vicinity. The community gathered in the city square opposite the cemetery to pray. (The aforementioned) R. Yisra'el Qatī'i, who was the prayer leader, read the verse from Psalms (10:15), "Break the power of the evil man," and to symbolize the act of breaking he would raise his right hand against the left. As R. Gamliel wrote: "From that day on the members of that generation called Yisra'el Qatī'i, Yisra'el Kisār for his having prayed 'Break the power of the evil man,' and it was broken. Also, because he had previously 'broken' the market, as noted. So his family has been called Kisār to this very day."[23]

However, the family name Kisār occurs in documents prior to the events noted by R. Gamliel. One of the synagogues in Ṣan'a is called the "Kisār Synagogue." A document dated 1793 states that the synagogue called *"Kanīs bet al-Kisār"* had been destroyed upon the command of the *imam* along with other synagogues in Ṣan'a in 1762, and that some thirty years later Slaymān ben Shukr al-Kisār interceded with the authorities of Ṣan'a and received permission to rebuild it.[24] In a *ketubbah* from Ṣan'a, dated 5 Adar 5574 (25 Feb 1814), the bride's name is listed as Rūmiyah bat Yosef ben Slaymān al-Kisār. According to a manuscript copied in 1845, the person commissioning the copy was Shim'on ben Sālem al-Kisār.[25]

Halewi Alsheikh

R. Yaacov Sappir wrote about the Levitic Halewi-Alsheikh family of Ṣan'a, which had a distinguished lineage.[26] The *nasi* R. Avraham ben Shalom Halewi, who died in 1829, had been one of the distinguished Jews of the city and was responsible for striking coins on behalf of the

23. R. Shalom Gamliel, *Pa'amei ha-Aliyyah mi-Teiman* (Jerusalem, 1988), pp. 174–76.

24. Yehiel Nahshon, *Batei Keneset be-Ṣan'a (Me'ot 18 u-19)* (Netanya, 2000), pp. 105 160–62.

25. Manuscript in the possession of Ratson Halevi, Tel Aviv.

26. Yaacov Sappir, *Massa Teiman*, ed. A. Yaari (Jerusalem, 1945), pp. 171, 218–20.

imam. Owing to his leading position within the community, R. Avraham was called Alsheikh, "leader."[27] R. Amram Qoraḥ writes that "from then on his family as well as the synagogue and ritual bath, were named for him, 'Alsheikh' instead of 'al-Lewi'."[28] Thus Alsheikh was appended to the name Lewi. Sometimes, however, only the appended name was used. In a *ketubbah* from Ṣan'a dated 17 Tevet 5497 (10 Dec 1736) the bride is registered as "Yedidah bint Sālem ben Yosef [ben] *mv* Yiḥye' Alsheikh al-Lewi." The bride is the great-granddaughter of R. Yiḥye' Halewi, who served as a *dayyan* after the return of the Mawza' exiles in 1681.[29] The appellation Alsheikh for R. Yiḥye' shows that the assumption that the brother of the bride, R. Avraham, who served as the *nasi* of Yemenite Jewry, was the first to be called Alsheikh is unfounded. Yet, even if R. Yiḥye' Halewi had been called Alsheikh, the term was only ascribed to the family from the time of the *nasi* Avraham onward owing to his activity on behalf of the community.[30]

R. Avraham Alsheikh's descendants continued to engage in striking coins on behalf of the royal house. However, some were suspected

27. Amram Qoraḥ, *Sa'arat Teiman* (Jerusalem, 1954), p. 24. The article *"Zekhor le-Avraham"* by Yehudah Ratzaby was printed in the anthology Avraham Naddaf, *Zekhor le-Avraham* (Jerusalem, 1976), p. 5. Yehudah Nini, *Teiman ve-Ṣiyyon: Ha-Reqa ha-Medini ha-Ḥevrati ve-ha-Ruḥani la-'Aliyyot ha-Rishonot mi-Teiman* (Jerusalem, 1982), p. 105; Yehiel Nahshon, *Dyuqanot be-Hanhagah ha-Yehudit be-Teiman ba-Me'ah ha-18–19* (Netanya, 1994), p. 170; idem, *Batei Keneset be-Ṣan'a*, p. 124; Moshe Gavra, *Enṣiqlopedya le-Qehilot ha-Yehudiyyot be-Teiman*, 1–2 (Bnei Brak, 2005), p. 22; *Ṣaddik be-Emunato Yiḥye, Pirkei Ḥayim ve-Divrei Tora le-Zikhro shel ha-Gaon ha-Tzaddik Morenu Rabbi Yiḥye Alsheikh* (Jerusalem, 2002), p. 3.

28. Qoraḥ, *Sa'arat Teiman*, p. 24 n. 26.

29. The family patriarch, R. Yiḥye' Halewi was one of the leaders of the exiles who left Ṣan'a for Mawza' and the Jewish community leaders in Ṣan'a after their return from the exile in 1681. On him, see Yehudah Ratzaby, *"Mi-Shivḥei R. Yiḥye' ben Avraham Halevi,"* *Yeda Am* 8 (1963): 56–58. See also Erich Brauer, *Ethnologie der Jemenitischen Juden* (Heidelberg, 1934), pp. 38, 306. The traveler to Yemen in 1859, R. Yaacov Sappir wrote about him that "I have already told of the distinguished family Bet Halewi al-Sheikh, which is in the Holy Community of Ṣan'a, the capital of Yemen, and two hundred years ago living there was Mori Yiḥye' Halewi al-Sheikh, the head of this family, *nasi* and *rosh golah*, a man steeped in Torah learning, reverence to the Lord, wisdom, and wealth, and he led the return of the Ṣan'a exile from Tihāma to where they were expelled" (Sappir, *Massa Teiman*, p. 218; see also ibid., pp. 169, 171). On the Mawza' exile, see above chap. 1 n. 31.

30. On his activity, see Aharon Gaimani, *"Sheṭar ha-Ṣeva'a u-Sheṭar Ḥaluqat ha-Yerusha shel ha-Nasi ha-Rav Avraham al-Sheikh,"* in *Bnei Teiman, Meḥqarim be-Yahadut Teiman u-Morashta*, ed. Aharon Gaimani, Ratson 'Arusi, and Shaul Regev (Ramat Gan: Bar-Ilan University, 2011), pp. 49–58.

of counterfeiting and were tortured, causing one of them to flee to the community of 'Ayāshiya, located south of Ṣan'a and east of Radā', where he was dubbed Ṣan'āni. This appellation was also applied to his descendants in his new community, one of them being R. Avraham Ṣan'āni.[31] A Yemenite manuscript writes about R. Avraham Ṣan'āni's being a member of the Alsheikh family: "A request of the great R. Avraham Ṣāliḥ[32] ... Halewi called Asheikh from the glorious city of Ṣan'a, who lived for a number years in eastern cities, the city of 'Amad and its satellites, and taught Torah in this region, a number of students learning from his teachings, may his merit defend us, *'ky"r.*"[33]

Qāḍi

Arabic for "judge" (Hebrew *dayyan*). R. Yosef Yiṣḥaq Halevi Qāḍi was a Yemenite rabbi in the early twentieth century and his brother was chief rabbi Yiḥye' Yiṣḥaq Halevi. R. Yosef's son, R. Ṣemaḥ, wrote about the name Qāḍi being given to his father:

> In his spare time, many Muslim dignitaries began to visit him in Ṣan'a—especially on Fridays, which is the Muslims' day of rest—so as to ask his advice, as well as to have him judge between them concerning various conflicts and legal suits. This was astonishing, since the Muslims did not usually do such a thing at all—to turn to a Jew for the purposes of judgment. It turns out that they trusted his integrity and wisdom more than that of the Muslim judges. From then on, the nickname *al-qāḍi*—"the *dayyan*"—was applied to him.[34]

31. See R. Avraham Ṣan'ani, *Qodesh Hillulim* (Jerusalem, 1971), introduction by Joseph Tobi, pp. 25–26; introduction by the author's grandson, Yehiel Ṣan'ani Halevi, pp. 3–4. On the story of their departure from Ṣan'a because of the machinations of the king, see Sappir, *Massa Teiman*, p. 221. Shemuel Yavnieli was sent to Yemen by the Zion Organization in 1911–1912 to bring them information about Ereṣ Israel and to prepare organized *aliyah* to it. He wrote about his impression of R. Avraham Ṣan'ani: "Mori Avraham Ṣan'ani, whom I met there, in the area of 'Amid, east of Rada [meaning the city of Radā', was one of the most revered figure in Yemen of his day. He was a *talmid ḥakham*, completely devoted to Torah learning but it was not the source of his livelihood, a person with a poetic soul, full of yearning for the Redemption and for Ereṣ Israel (Shmuel Yavnieli, *Ha-Massa le-Teiman* [Tel Aviv, 1952], pp. 199–200).

32. R. Avraham Ṣan'āni's father was called Ṣadōq, which in Arabic is Ṣāliḥ.

33. Yosef Tobi, *Kitvei Yad Teimaniyyim be-Makhon Ben-Zvi* (Jerusalem, 1982), Manuscript no. 228, par. B, p. 143.

34. Yosef Yiṣḥaq Halevi Qāḍi, *Sefer Edut bi-Yehosef al Miqra ha-Qodesh im ha-Quntres Qorot ha-Zeman be-Teiman* (Jerusalem, 2004), on the figure of the author, p. 14. After R. Yosef immigrated to Ereṣ Israel, he served as the rabbi of the Nordiya neighborhood in Tel Aviv. His grandson is R. Eliyahu Yiṣḥaq Halevi Qāḍi of New York.

Dafni

Dafn in Arabic means "burial." A priest (*kohen*) from the Shar'ab region in southern Yemen married a woman who was divorced from her first husband and widowed from her second. The regional rabbinical court tried to persuade him to divorce her because it is forbidden for a priest to marry a divorcee. Out of his love for her, however, he refused to divorce her notwithstanding the warning that he would have to waive his priestly privileges. To make sure that his offspring would not be considered *kohanim*, a burial rite for an earthenware jug was performed in the cemetery, symbolizing the burial of his priesthood. The descendants of this priest were therefore given the family name Dafni, "burial."[35]

Ramaḍān

Ramaḍān is the Muslim month of fasting. This appellation or family name is found in various seventeenth-century Yemenite sources.[36] In three colophons to Yemenite manuscripts from the sixteenth and seventeenth centuries we find that the copyist belonged to this family. In a 1575 manuscript of the Taj, from the village of Ma'bar, the copyist wrote his name as Zekharyah ben Sa'adyah ben Ḥoṭer ben of the Me'oded known as ben Ramaḍān.[37] In a 1683 manuscript of the Zohar and in a 1687 manuscript of *Sefer Sha'arei Orah* from the village of Dlāj, the copyist signed his name as Zekharya' b. David. b. Sa'adya' ben Zekharya' known as Ramaḍān.[38] This name is also found in *ketubbot* from various settlements in Yemen. In a *ketubbah* from the city of Tanem, dated 17 Tevet 5673 (27 Dec 1912), the name of the groom was written as Yūda' b. *mori ve-rabbi* Slaymān Ramaḍān. A *ketubbah* from Kharbat Sa'wān, prepared on 12 Adar 1 5695 (15 Feb 1935), the name

35. Sa'adya Ḥozeh, *Toledot ha-Rav Shalom Shabazi u-Minhagei Yahadut Shar'ab be-Teiman*, 2 (Jerusalem, 1982), pp. 64–66.

36. Nissim Binyamin Gamliel, *Ḥadrei Teiman—Sippurim va-Aggadot* (Tel Aviv, 1978), pp. 183–84. See Joseph Tobi, *'Iyyunim bi-Mgillat Teiman*, p. 176; Ratson Halevi, *Shirat Yisra'el be-Teiman* (Qiryat Ono, 1998), 1: 533–39.

37. Yehudah Levi Naḥum, *Mi-Ṣefunot Teiman* (Tel Aviv, 1987), p. 252; photo of the colophon, p. 261. See also Yitshak Raṣabi, *Ofan ha-Merkavah*, in his edition of *Rekhev Elohim le-R. Y. Wanneh* (Bnei Brak, 1992), p. 39 n. 3.

38. Yehudah Levi Naḥum, *Ṣohar le-Ḥasifat Ginzei Teiman* (Tel Aviv, 1986), p. 167; manuscript in possession of Amalya Dahan, Ashdod, and see also Aharon Gaimani, *Temurot be-Moreshet Yahadut Teiman: be-Hashpa'at ha-Shulḥan 'Arukh ve-Qabalat ha-Ari* (Ramat Gan, 2005), p. 99 n. 186.

of the groom appears as Sulēmān ibn Yūda' who is called Ramaḍān. In a *ketubbah* from the village of Majma'a, from 18 Adar 1 5703 (23 Feb 1943), the groom's name appears as Ya'ish b. Elisha Ramaḍān, and on the back of the *ketubbah* his name is written as Elisha al-Khawlāni known as Ramaḍān.

According to the Ramaḍān family tradition, this appellation was given to a family member who, because of his piety, would not eat food prepared by non-Jews.[39] So as not to offend his host's feelings, he would thank him for the hospitality and say, "It is Ramaḍān for me," meaning "I am fasting." He hosts respected his wishes because of his religiosity but his Jewish comrades would make fun of him, calling him *Ramaḍān*. The name stuck with his descendants until they immigrated to Israel.[40]

Ṣayḥi

Ṣayḥi in Arabic means "to shout." Avshalom Raṣabi, whose parents emigrated from the Sa'wān community in central Yemen, wrote that Ṣayḥi was the name of his mother's family and related that there were two explanations for it. One is that family members tended to speak in a whisper, so listeners would say *"Ṣiḥ,"* that is, "shout, so we can hear you." Another explanation is that family members were the town-criers and since they had to yell out their announcements, they were given the nickname Ṣayḥi.[41]

Qar'ah

Bayt Qar'ah is an Arab village in Yemen. Shelomo Raṣhabi, from the Raḍa'i community in the Amlukh district of southern Yemen, told of an orphan who was forced to wander among the local villages in order to earn a living. One time, upon his return to his village, he was asked where he had been. He replied "to Bayt Qar'ah," and so from then on

39. Yemenite Jews did not implement a prohibition against bread of non-Jews. R. Amram Qoraḥ wrote about this, "In the days of the Sages of the Mishnah, they levied a decree against non-Jewish bread, but in all the districts of Yemen they did not hear of its being prohibited, and even after the Mishnah came to the regions of Yemen. To this day, they have permission to use the bread of the homeowner, as was their previous custom, even when not an urgent need" (Qoraḥ, *Sa'arat Teiman*, p. 94). See also extensively Raṣabi, *Ofan ha-Merkavah,* in his edition of *Rekhev Elohim*, pp. 37–39 n. 2.

40. Part of the family changed their last name after immigration to Ramati or Haramati. I heard the story of the name from a number of family members. See also Raṣabi, *Ofan ha-Merkavah,* in his edition of *Rekhev Elohim*, p. 39 n. 3.

41. In a personal correspondence dated 11 Apr 2010.

his family called him by that nickname. After the family immigrated to Israel, they changed the family name to Malkho, for the district from which they had come.[42]

Ḥanash

Ḥanash in Arabic means "snake." In the city of Raṣāba, there was a man who always gave evasive answers with twisting body movements. One community member remarked to him about his behavior, "Look, I see you are writhing like a snake," and from then on the family nicknamed him ḥanash. In Israel, they changed the family name to Naḥshon, which sounds similar to the old name.[43]

Qehe

A cow had run away from one of the butchers in Ṣan'a and someone who witnessed this ran after the cow yelling out 'Ilqihe' meaning "Find it" or "Grab it." Because of his repeated cry *'Ilqihe'*, he was nicknamed Ilqihe. The nickname turned into a family name and was listed in family documents. In recent generations the family is Alqehe' or, in short, Qehe. In Israel some members changed it to Qehati.[44]

Dhanīn

Dhanīni means "my love" as said by a mother to her small son in one of the villages in central Yemen, and became an identification for her family.[45]

Ḥāser

Means "lacking." It is told that one person from the village of Jiḥzān complained that he needed money. And so his relatives nicknamed him Ḥāser, and the name stuck to the family. In Israel the family sought to avoid the negative nuance accompanying the name and replaced it with the name Ḥasid.[46]

---

42. Interview conducted by R. Gilad Zadok of Bnei Brak.
43. In a personal correspondence dated 22 Apr 2010 from R. Yiṣḥaq Raṣābi. A member of this family is Dr. Yehiel Nahshon of Hod Hasharon.
44. See Ezra Kehati, *Yeqirai be-Teiman u-be-Ṣiyyon* (Jerusalem, 1989), pp. 213–15. For documents mentioning the family, see ibid., pp. 16–18.
45. I heard this from my parents Slaymān [= Shelomo] and Ghusūn [= Mazal] Gaimani. See also Nehama Danin, *"Peraṭim Odot Rishonei Mishpaḥat Danin ba-Areṣ," Afikim* 136–37 (2011): 33.
46. As related by Ilanit Ḥasid, Moshav Sha'ar Efraim.

Yiqne

Means "He will buy." In Ṣa'dah in north Yemen lived a family by the name 'Iḍa'. A nearby parcel of land with an airport was offered for sale and for some time people said that a wealthy member of the 'Iḍa' family would purchase it. After he did, everyone nicknamed him 'Iḍa' Yiqne. So part of the family bears the appellation Yiqne.[47]

Bāsha

Pāsha was a noble, high title in the Ottoman Empire, which controlled Yemen from 1870 to WWI. A wealthy Jew of the family Ḥamdi-Halewi from Ghūrbān in central Yemen became accepted in Arab society. Many of the Arabs, and later the Jews, of that place prefixed his name with the honored title *ya-bāsha*. In a book in the possession of the family, the owner's name appears as "Yiḥye' ben Aharon [written in *atbash* order] al-Ḥamdi Halewi who is called Bāsha." Over time the nickname stuck to the family and the former name Ḥamdi-Halewi was dropped and the nickname Bāsha became the family name.[48]

Ṭayri

Ṭayr in Arabic means "bird." Nissim Ṭayri from Radā' relates that in an earlier generation one of the family members had taken care to feed the birds and so the family was called Bet al-Ṭayri.

Samīnah

The former name of the Samīna family was Mlīḥ. Zekharyah Samīnah of Elyakhin, from the town Bīr al-Darb in the Reḥabe district of Yemen, explained the name change. His grandfather, Moshe, as a leader in his community, would purchase cows when needed by his constituency. Once, he bought a cow that was too fat, and after the people had divided up the meat and eaten it, they came to Moshe and complained that he had brought them a cow full of fat, in Arabic, *samn*. One of those who had eaten the meat stuck him with the name Samīnah. Among his descendants this nickname was taken as the family name to this day, replacing the previous family name Mlīḥ. In a Yemenite *ketubbah* from 15 Adar 5707 (7 Mar 1947) from the village of Bīr al-Darb, the groom's name was written as Yosef ben Sālem al-Mlīḥ, and on the back of the document his name was given as Yosef ben Sālem a-Samīnah.

47. As heard from Avivit of the Yiqne family, Qiryat Eqron. The name *'Iḍa' Yiqne* appears in the membership list of the Ṣa'da community. See Aharon Ben David, *Bet ha-Even, Hilkhot Yehudei Ṣefon Teiman* ([Qiryat Eqron], 5768), p. 703, no. 1156.

48. As related by Einat Basha, Yavneh.

Ta'sah

This family name became well known in 1981 with the election of Mrs. Miriam Ta'sah Glazer to the Knesset and her appointment as deputy minister of education. A family member, David Ta'sah, tells of the origin of the name. The Ta'sah family lived in towns and villages in Shar'ab in southern Yemen. A few generations ago, one of the heads of the family was a bit inarticulate, and whenever he had to count something, he would say the number nine in Arabic as *ti'sah* instead of *tis'ah*. Many people pointed this out to him, but he could not correct himself, so they attached the name Ti'sah to him, and so this nickname became the family name for all his descendants.[49]

Ḥandali

Ḥanẓal is a bitter fruit, a kind of small watermelon.[50] In Yemen, the ḥanẓal was used as a decoration at festive events, and among the non-Jews, on their holiday, some would decorate their cattle with this fruit. R. David Kimchi (Radak) explains it as "wild vine" (2 Kings 4:39): "And we have found in the commentary of the Geonim, OBM, field orbs like a kind of small melon and they are bitter and oil is made from their seeds; this is what our rabbis, OBM, said of the oil of the orbs and it is called in the language of Ishmael *ḥandal*." Eitan Ḥandali from south Yemen tells of a game the young men play in which they throw the fruit called ḥanẓal. Once, a family member had thrown the fruit too hard at his friend and from then on family members were called Ḥandali.[51] The name Ḥanḍal as a family name occurs in a 1469 bill of sale for a manuscript of the Torah and Former Prophets for the synagogue of Avraham ben Yosef ben Se'īd Ḥanḍal.[52] Also, in a *siddur* copied in Dhamār in 1674, the name of the person who ordered it is given in the colophon:

49. The informant, David Ta'sah from Tel Aviv, told me that he had heard this explanation from his father and other family sources.

50. The Yemenite rabbis identify the *ḥanẓal* with the biblical wormwood. See the annotations of R. David Ṣāliḥ to the *Siddur "Eṣ Ḥayim"* of R. Yiḥye' Ṣāliḥ, 4, p. 174a. See also the commentary of R. 'A. Qoraḥ, *"Neve Shalom"* on the Torah, printed in *Sefer Keter ha-Torah—Ha-Taj ha-Gadol*, Deut. 29:17. See also Yehudah Feliks, *Olam ha-Ṣome'aḥ ha-Miqra'i* (Ramat Gan, 1968), pp. 200–3.

51. As related by Eitan Ḥandali, Manhattan, New York. I wrote elsewhere that perhaps the source of the family name stems from dealing with medicines, since this fruit is also used in remedies. See Aharon Gaimani, *"Ha-Sofer R. Pinhas ben Gad ha-Kohen," Tema* 7 (2001): 123 n. 31.

52. Yehudah Levi Naḥum, *Mi-Yeṣirot Sifrutiyyot mi-Teiman* (Holon, 1981), pp. 196–97. On two other bills of sale for books for the "Bane Ḥanḍal" synagogue, see ibid., p. 198.

"And it was written in the name of the good friend, who is like a moist tree, may the Lord also give him good, and form him well, the wise and esteemed, for a good name and praise, Yiṣḥaq ben Binyamin who is called Ḥanẓal, *yṣ"v*, who lives where the governors of the city of Dhamār are."[53]

Hazaqen

Means "The Old One." R. Sa'adya Sharāra Hazaqen lived in Barāqīsh. His descendants tell that toward the end of his life his wife died and his sons made sure that he had a younger woman to help him run the house. Shortly thereafter he married the woman, by whom he had several more children, and the family name by which these children were called was Bet Sharārah hazaqen, "House [dynasty] of Old Shararah."[54]

Qo'dah

A man from Gharāne' in southern Yemen used to travel to a nearby village to sell spices and notions to the Arabs. He would carry a vessel called *qo'dah,* made from a dried squash, in which he would keep butter. Once, returning from work, he came upon a band of idlers from his community. They asked him what he was carrying and he told them a *qo'dah* containing butter. From then on, they nicknamed him Qo'dah, after the vessel. When his son immigrated to Israel in 1949, the family was registered in the Ministry of the Interior with the name Qa'īda, and years later some members of the family changed their name to Qedar.[55]

Da'rūr

In the eighteenth century one of the Mishriqi family members in Ṣan'a used to sell spices for use in preparing incense mixtures. The per-

53. Gaimani, *"Ha-Sofer R. Pinhas ben Gad,"* p. 123.

54. In a personal correspondence dated 16 Feb 2011 from R. Almog Shelomo Akhlufi.

55. As related by Yaniv Qedar, Tel Aviv. The incident related happened to his great-grandfather.

56. The information was received from R. Gilad Zadok of Bnei Brak by Yehudah Ra'anan from Rekhasim, who immigrated from al-Ḥajareh and is related to the Da'rūr family. On the Da'rūr family in the Radā' district see M. Yiṣhari, *Shim'on Drumi u-Mishpaḥto* (n.p. [Israel], 2004), p. 215.

57. As related by Ya'aqov Tobi, from the Aden community emigrés, London.

58. As related by Ya'aqov Tobi, from the Aden community emigrés, London. In Ṣan'a, *'aṣīt* was made from flour and not from grains, as in Aden. See above, part 1, chap. 1, sect. 2.

son who actually prepared the mixture was called in Arabic *Yeda'rir*. This family was dubbed Da'rūr because of its business and so the family name was changed from Mishriqi to Da'rūr. This family lived in Ṣan'a until the mid-twentieth century, when it moved to al-Hajareh in the Ḥarāz district of central Yemen. In Israel some changed the name to Deror, which sounds similar to the former name.[56]

Sha'ban

Ya'aqov Tobi from 'Aden was a famous singer who performed at weddings and other festive events. One day there were two weddings at the same time, one for a wealthy family and one for a poor one. Ya'aqov chose to participate in that of the poor family, and so was given the nickname Sha'ban, from Arabic *sha'abi*, "common," "popular." Today his son Ya'aqov Tobi is called Ya'aqov Tobi Sha'ban.[57]

'Aṣīṭah

The maternal great-grandmother of Ya'aqov Tobi mentioned above awoke one morning and asked to eat *'aṣīt*, which is cooked oats with butter, because she was cold and this dish would warm her up. Because of this, she was called 'Aṣiṭah. To this day one family of her descendants is called 'Aṣidah, which sounds similar to the name of the cooked cereal.[58] This story is unusual in that the nickname was given to a woman, not a man, and still passed on to her descendants.

3. FAMILY NAMES MARKING MIRACLES AND COURAGEOUS ACTS

Mashta, the seventeenth-century R. Shalom Shabazi, greatest of Yemenite poets, said of his name: "I, humblest of authors, Shalem *beirav* Yosef *beirav* Yisra'el, who is called after the name of my family of the sons of Mashta' and after my city al-Shabazi."[59] As to the origin of the name, there is a famous tale about a miracle that happened to one of the ancestors of R. Shalom Shabazi in which he was saved from death by a utensil called *mashta*, which was used for mixing flour and water. Therefore, the family was called Bene Mashta' and an indication of his city was appended to R. Shalom Shabazi's name. Some believe the

59. See Avraham Alnaddaf, *"Toledot ha-Rashb"i al-Shabazi, z"l,"* in his *Oṣar Seridei Teiman* (Jerusalem, 1992), p. 3; Sa'adya Ḥozeh, *Toledot ha-Rav Shalom Shabazi u-Minhagei Yahadut Shar'ab be-Teiman*, 1 (Jerusalem, 1973), p. 1. If this place was named thus only because of Sham'a's grave, then perhaps a place called Mashta was destroyed and forgotten.

name Mashta signifies a place,[60] while other think that it derives from the personal name of the family progenitor.[61]

Keter

Means "crown." R. Aharon Cohen of an 'Irāqi family was given the nickname Keter. R. Shalom Harari notes in his account of his visit to Ṣan'a that "rumors running among the public say that R. Aharon, son of R. Shalom Cohen al-'Irāqi-al-Awsṭa, was named R. Aharon Keter, because on a Sabbath afternoon the likeness of a crown of fire was seen on his head and only the select few had the privilege to see it."[62]

Hibeh

In the Ībrahīm family from Ḥarāz there were several children who died a few days after birth. The family, in the hope of averting such danger for the next baby, turned to a sage adept at consulting a special book for the purpose of finding a "safe" name. The sage proposed calling a son Hibeh, "gift" and holding the circumcision ceremony in the *dayma*, which is the term for a kitchen in Yemen. From then on, the infants stopped dying. The name has been retained to this day.[63] In the first half of the twentieth century, there was a family in Ṣan'a called "Hibeh al-Shar'abi."[64]

'Awād

The name of the 'Awad family in Ṣan'a had been Damti. One of my students told me that a few generations ago all but one of the infants in his family died soon after birth. The name of the child who survived was 'Awād, which means "exchange" or "compensation." This "lucky" personal name became the family name. In Israel, a number of family members changed their name to 'Oved, which has a similar sound.

60. See Avraham Zevi Idelsohn, *"Ha-Meshorer ha-Teimani R. Shalom ben Yosef Shabazi ve-Shirato ha-Ivrit," Mizraḥ u-Ma'arav* 1 (1919): 11. The gravesite of Sham'a, R. Shalom Shabazi's daughter, was called Mashti'iya; see Ḥozeh, *Toledot ha-Rav Shalom Shabazi*, 1, p. 6.

61. Shalom Medina, *"Le-Maqor Moṣa'an shel Mishpaḥot Teimaniyot," Afiqim* 29 (1969): 8. The name *Mashta* is also a women's name, see above part 2, chap. 2, sect. 1.

62. R. Shalom Harari, *"Ṣaddiq be-Emunato Yiḥye'," Nefesh*, a memorial pamphlet for R. Sa'adya b"R Yosef 'Uzayri, OBM (Tel Aviv, 1954), p. 9.

63. As related by Orit Marmorstein, Petaḥ Tiqva.

64. As related by R. Itamar Ḥayim Kohen, Bnei Brak.

Qaḥm

In Israel this family is known by the Hebrew equivalent, Aryeh "lion." The family name stems from an act of bravery by one of its members when confronted by a lion in the vicinity of Ṣan'a.[65] In a *ketubbah* dated 28 Av 5616 (1856) in the Maḥwīt community, the groom's name was written as Yiḥye' ben Sulēmān ad-Ḍūr'āni who is called al-Qaḥm.[66] The synagogue in Maḥwīt where the family prayed is called *Kanis Bayt al-Qaḥm.*[67]

Da'ōs

The source of the name is Arabic *da's*, which means "stepping" or "trampling." A number of generations ago in the town of Bayḍa' in southeastern Yemen, people were having difficulty bringing an ox down so they could slaughter him. One of the participants managed to get him down by stepping hard on him. From then on his descendants were nicknamed Da'ōs, which became the family name.[68] In the eighteenth century, one of the Bayḍa' rabbis, who taught ritual slaughtering in the Ḥabbān community, was called R. Moshe ben Shalom Da'ōs.[69]

4. FAMILY NAMES ACCORDING TO OCCUPATION

Madhala

Madhala is a vessel used for storing oil or honey. The family stems from northern Yemen, branching out from the Ṣāliḥ family of Ṣan'a. One tradition states that a family member, Avraham, owned many *madhala* vessels full of oil and honey. When times were difficult, other businessmen used to purchase *madhala*s of oil and honey from him. To find his location, they would ask "Where is Avraham Madhala?" rather than refer to him by his name, Avraham Ṣāliḥ. From then on his descendants bore the appellation Madhala.[70] Another tradition is that a

65. Family tradition has two versions regarding the act of bravery. See Avraham Arye, *Ohel Yosef* (Be'er Ya'aqov, 1973), pp. 15–18 n. 10.
66. For a photo of the *ketubbah*, see ibid., p. 19.
67. Ibid., p. 14.
68. As related by Yonatan Du'us, Azor.
69. Sa'adya Ma'ṭūf, *Yahadut Ḥabbān (Ḥadramawt) be-Dorot ha-Aharonim* (Tel Aviv, 1987), p. 78. On the Du'us family among the immigrants from the Bayḍa' community to Ereṣ Israel, see Menashe Zekharyah, *Aliyat Qehilat Yehudei Beyḍa' mi-Teiman u-Hishtalvutam ba-Areṣ* (Herzliyah, 2003), pp. 110, 220; Shalom Gamliel, *Ha-Naḥshonim 'al Kanfei Nesharim mi-Teiman* (Jerusalem, 1996), p. 39.
70. K. Madhala, *Toledot Mishpaḥat Madhala* ([Rehovot], 1973), p. 44.

family Madhala lived in al-Hajar, and was named for the *madhala* vessels that the head of the family would produce and sell.[71]

Qalazān

The Qalazān family has a tradition that the family name originated with an ancestor who traded in small glass bottles. Arabic *Qalazān* sounds similar to the English word "glass."[72]

Aldār

R. Yiḥye' Badīḥi of the Ṣan'a community, who was involved with gold- and silver-smithing, was given the byname Aldār, which, in Arabic, means "palace." He was a partner of ha-Rav ha-Gaon Yiḥye' Abyaḍ and his sons in contracting for the striking of silver coins for the king's mint, which was situated in the king's palace called *Dar al-Sa'ādah.* From then on this byname became a sign of recognition because there are many named Yiḥye' Badīḥi.[73]

Zabīb

Zabīb means "raisin." According to family tradition, beginning at least three hundred years ago, the family's trade had been the production, transport, and sale of raisins. They built in their places of residence warehouses for storing the raisins, and so were called Bayt al-Zabīb ("House of the Raisin").[74]

Megari

Means "teacher." The Megari family lived in southern Yemen, where, as their livelihood, they taught children. In a *ketubbah* belonging to this family from the village of Najīd, dated 28 Dec 1920, the name of the groom was Yiḥye' ben Ya'īsh al-Megari. In Israel they changed the family name to Melamed, which is the Hebrew equivalent.[75]

---

71. In a personal correspondence dated 13 Jan 2010 from R. Dr. Aharon Ben David of Qiryat Eqron. On the *madhala,* see the note by Prof. S. D. Goitein, in Ḥibshush's book, *Massa'ot Ḥibshush* (Tel Aviv, 1939), p. 144 n. 22.
72. As related by R. Moshe Qalazān.
73. Shalom Gamli'el, *Ḥakhmei ha-Yehudim be-Teiman be-Doreinu ve-'ad Samukh li-Tqufat ha-Tana'im* (Jerusalem, 1992), p. 58. One must note that the family name *Dār* had already existed in Yemen. For example, in a *ketubbah* from Ṣan'a, dated 5454 (1694), the groom's name appears as 'Awāḍ ben Yiṣḥaq Aldār. In another Ṣan'a *ketubbah,* from 17 Shevat 5606 (13 Feb 1846), the groom's name was written as Sālem ben Sālem Aldār.
74. Yisrael Soreq, *Album Mishpaḥat Zabib le-Doroteha* (Tel Aviv, 2004), p. 7.
75. In a personal correspondence dated 4 Apr 2011 from Mazal Bushari of Petaḥ Tiqvah.

5. FAMILY NAMES REFLECTING PHYSICAL CHARACTERISTICS

The Ma'ṭūf and Shamukh families

The chief of a clan in Ḥaban southeastern Yemen, though old and bent over, married a younger woman and so he and his clan were called Ma'ṭūf, "bent over." Another clan in Ḥaban was named Shamūkh, which means "very tall."[76] In Israel, some members of the Ma'ṭūf family changed their name to Mah Tov or Ki Tov, and the Shamūkh family to Same'aḥ, names with a similar ring to their previous ones.

Samīn

The family name in the Khamer community was Sūdami, meaning from the Sdum community. They were given the appellation Samīn ("fat") because the grandfather was old and fat, and so the nickname became the family name.[77]

Zayyid

In Arabic means "addition." Yiḥye' 'Adan, who lived in Ḥūtayib in the district of Bane Bahlūl in central Yemen, was given the nickname Zayyid because he had six fingers on each hand.[78]

Bīsbās

A very sharp pepper. Naḥum 'Aravah related that one of his relatives, Shalom Ṣan'āni, from Naḍrah in south Yemen, loved to eat *bīsbās*, so he was dubbed with the nickname Bīsbās. This nickname became into the family name and upon immigration into Israel, his name was registered as Shalom Bīsbās.[79]

6. BYNAMES AND FAMILY NAMES FROM WELL-KNOWN PERSONAGES

a. Family names from names of personalities

Ṣāliḥ

Means "righteous" or "successful."[80] There are a few families in the

76. Yosef Sha'er, *"Yehudei Haḍramawt (ha-Ḥabānim),"* in *Harel—Koveṣ Zikkaron le-ha-Rav Refa'el Alsheikh*, ed. Y. Ratzaby and Y. Shabti'el (Tel Aviv, 1963), p. 234. See also Sa'adya Ma'ṭūf, *Yahadut Ḥabān (Ḥadramawt) be-Dorot ha-Aharonim* (Tel Aviv, 1987), p. 26.
77. As related by family members. Yosef Samin lives in Petaḥ Tiqva.
78. Oral communication from Raḥamim Aden, Kfar Sava.
79. In the questionnaire I received from Naḥum Arava, Qiryat Eqron.
80. On the family names *Ṣāliḥ* and *Ṣadoq*, see Mahariṣ, *Shut Pe'ulat Ṣaddiq*, 1–3, ed. M. Raṣabi (Jerusalem, 2003).

Ṣan'a community by this name, though unrelated to each other. One of them is of the lineage of the greatest *poseq* of Yemen, who lived in the eighteenth century, R. Yiḥye' Ṣāliḥ (Mahariṣ); the name apparently originated with his grandfather, Ṣāliḥ ben Yiḥye', who was steeped in Torah learning. Another family is Ṣāliḥ al-Baraṭi, which seems to descend from the *parnas* (community dignitary) R. Yiḥye' ben Yehudah Ṣāliḥ who lived in the first third of the nineteenth century, and whose forefathers came from the village of Baraṭ in northern Yemen.[81] The third is the Ṣāliḥ al-Ḥaydāni family that apparently originated in Ḥaydān in northern Yemen.[82]

Pinḥas

Men and women went to pray and make requests at the grave-site of R. Sālem Pinḥas. Healing powers were attributed to the spring water near the grave, and the mud at its base was thought to cure skin diseases. During drought, the Jews of the Ṣan'a community used to gather at this site to pray for rain. Many people did not know the personal name of R. Sālem Pinḥas.[83] R. Yosef Qāfiḥ wrote about him that "the public and all the unfortunates used to go every Monday and Thursday to pray at his grave-site known by the name 'the grave of Mori Pinḥas,' and to this day his descendants are called the 'Pinḥas' family."[84]

Ya'beṣ

The most outstanding personage in the leadership of the Jewish community in recent generations and the authority figure in northern Yemen was R. Yiḥye' ben Ya'aqov, known by his byname, R. Ya'beṣ. He was active in the first half of the twentieth century and was located in Ṣa'dah. Owing to his greatness in Torah learning, his descendants adopted the name Ya'beṣ as their family name.[85]

81. See Qoraḥ, *Sa'arat Teiman*, p. 25.

82. Moshe Zadok, "*Mi-Mivḥar ha-Sifrut ha-Toranit shel Yehudei Teiman*," in *Se'i Yonah: Yehudei Teiman be-Yisra'el*, ed. Shalom Sirri (Tel Aviv, 1983), p. 347.

83. See Joseph Tobi, *'Iyyunim bi-Mgillat Teiman*, p. 158 n. 22. See also Yosef Shalom Hubarah, *Bi-Tla'ot Teiman vi-Yrushalayim* (Jerusalem, 1970), pp. 266–67; R. Pinḥas Qoraḥ, *Bet Mo'ed* (Bnei Brak, 2000), pp. 381–82.

84. R. Yosef Qāfiḥ, "*Sefer Dofi ha-Zeman le-R. Se'īd Sa'd*," *Ketavim*, vol. 2 (Jerusalem, 1989), p. 784 n. 287.

85. His grandson is R. Ovadya Ya'beṣ, who was the chief rabbi of Qiryat Eqron. R. Ovadya wrote about Aharon, the brother of his grandfather R. Ya'beṣ, who left Ṣa'dah and settled in "Jabal Bara'"; upon immigration to Ereṣ Israel, he met his sons who were called the Sa'di family because of their origin in Ṣa'dah. See R. Ovadya Ya'beṣ, *Yehudei Ṣa'dah u-Sevivoteha* (Qiryat Eqron, 2012), pp. 28–29.

Maimūn

The Qahalani family, which originated in the Ḥaydān community in northern Yemen, was called Maimūn after one of the progenitors of the family whose personal name was Maimūn.[86]

Bane Yehudah and Bane Moshe

R. Yiṣḥaq Raṣabi, whose family originates from this lineage, wrote: "Our family was called Yehudah for the name of the head of the family nine generations ago. The second branch of the family was named for his brother Moshe, and these are Bane Yehudah and Bane Moshe."[87] In a similar vein, R. Raṣabi wrote in commemoration of his father, noting nine generations beginning with the head of the family, R. Yehudah: "In whose name our family is called 'Bane Yehudah'. Now, R. Yehudah had a brother named R. Moshe, *n'"g*, and his descendants are called 'Bane Moshe'."[88] And for his signature in one of his books, he wrote: "Yiṣḥaq son *'mv"r*, the Rav ha-Gaon, Nissim, blessed be the memory of the true man, from the Yehudah family, who are called Raṣabi."[89]

b. Bynames for identical or similar names

Ha-Rav Yiḥye' ben ha-Rav Yosef Ṣāliḥ, known by the acronym Mahariṣ (*morenu ha-rabbi Yiḥye' Ṣāliḥ*, "our teacher, the rabbi Yiḥye' Ṣāliḥ"), who lived in eighteenth-century Ṣan'a, is considered the greatest of the *poseqim* (religious decisors) of Yemen. Active a generation after him was Ha-Rav Yiḥye' ben ha-Rav Ya'aqov Ṣāliḥ, one of the important leaders of Ṣan'a; he served in the capacity of head of the Alsheikh synagogue. The latter Rav Yiḥye' Ṣāliḥ did not belong to the family of the former: *Meqor Ḥayim* on the laws of ritual slaughter and 70 *terefot* is a condensed version of *Zevaḥ Todah*, and *Torah Ḥakham* is a shortened version of the responsa *Pe'ulat Ṣaddiq*. In order to distinguish between the two rabbis mentioned, Moshe Ṣadoq wrote: "But the following generations used to differentiate between these two men: the first, Mahariṣ, was called Mori Yiḥye' Ṣāliḥ al-Kabīr (the big), and the second, Mori Yiḥye' Ṣāliḥ ben Ya'aqūb."[90] Also R. Shim'on Ṣāliḥ, who printed Ma-

86. As related by Avshalom Maimun, Rishon Lezion.
87. In a personal correspondence dated 22 Apr 2010.
88. Yiṣḥaq Raṣabi, *Shulḥan Arukh ha-Mequṣar*, vol. 3 (Bnei Brak, 1989), p. 4; ibid., 8, end of the book, p. 236. See also below, part 3, chap. 5.
89. Raṣabi, *Shulḥan 'Arukh Mequṣṣar*, 1, introduction to the book—*Nokhaḥ ha-Shulḥan*, p. 47.
90. Moshe Zadok, *"Mi-Mivḥar ha-Sifrut ha-Toranit,"* p. 347.

hariṣ's prayer book, *Eṣ Ḥayim,* and listed at its end his lineage that is linked to the Mahariṣ, wrote about him, "son of the rabbi, the author, Yiḥye', who is called *al-kabir* [the bigger]."[91] Others added a byname for the second R. Yiḥye' and called him Mahariṣ *ha-qatan* (the smaller),[92] while R. Yiḥye' Qāfiḥ called him the last Mahariṣ.[93]

R. Yiḥye' Ṣāliḥ (Mahariṣ) cites in his commentary to the prayer book *Eṣ Ḥayim* statements by R. Yiḥye' al-'Akhbari.[94] Apparently, the source of the latter's name comes from the village 'Akhbara in Israel, and a name akin to this is that of R. Ḥananyah bar 'Akhbari, who is mentioned in the Jerusalem Talmud (Shabbat 2, 1).[95] Out of respect, there were some who changed his name and called him al-'Akbari, "The Great One."[96]

7. PERSONAL BYNAMES FROM PERSONAL EVENTS

These bynames became attached to a specific person owing to an event that occurred to him or an act he performed, but the term was not passed on to his descendants and did not become a family name. Here are a few examples.

Hayashish

R. Yiḥye' Qāfiḥ, one of the outstanding sages of Yemenite Jewry in the twentieth century, was called Hayashish [the old one] by his students. He was awarded this appellation as he was the oldest among the great rabbis of Ṣan'a in his generation.

Ḥāfi

R. Yiḥye' 'Arūsi was one of the sages of Ṣan'a in the second half of the twentieth century. The nickname Ḥāfi, "barefoot," was given to him because, being very pious, he went about barefoot to atone for his sins.

91. See Mahariṣ, *Tiklal Eṣ Ḥayim* (Jerusalem, 1971), 4, p. 352a. See also above, chap. 1, sect. 2.

92. Yehudah Ratzaby, *Toratan she-li-Vnei Teiman* (Qiryat Ono, 1994), p. 70.

93. See the responsum by R. Yiḥye' Qāfiḥ in the *Responsa Ḥen Ṭov—Ḥenah shel Torah,* end of section 34.

94. In the Sabbath morning service, the *seder ha-qorbanot* section (see Mahariṣ, *Tiklal Eṣ Ḥayim,* 1, p. 112b); Yom Kippur service, *seder seliḥot* (ibid., 2, p. 137b); and in the Ne'ilah service (ibid., p. 121a).

95. On this name, see Yosef Ṣubayri, *Siddur Keneset ha-Gedolah,* vol. 2, Introduction (Tel Aviv–Jerusalem, 1986), p. 14.

96. Yiṣḥaq Raṣabi, *Megillat Ester be-Nusaḥ Teiman* (Jerusalem, 1988), author's introduction *Binah ba-Miqra.*

About this habit we read, "And we found no one barefoot except for the rabbi, R. Yiḥye' ben Shalom al-'Arūsi, and when we asked him why he goes barefoot, he replied that he decided to do so to atone for his iniquities, since there is no one on earth who does only good and does not sin. He brought support for his custom from what was written by R. Be'er Heitiv (end of section 2) in the name of Eliyahu Rabba and in [the name of the] Shelah, that if one does so to atone for his iniquities, it is permitted, and King David also went barefoot, as it is written (2 Sam. 15:30), 'His head was covered and he walked barefoot'."[97]

Eliyahu

There was a Jew who traveled from Shar'ab to Ṣan'a and was dubbed Eliyahu, since he went to every circumcision he heard about, and he used to say that one should go to a *berit mila* even three-days distant.[98]

Sha'tan

There was a man who would read according to the printed edition of Mishna tractate Niddah 1: 1, "For all women their time [*sha'tan*; שַׁעְתָּן] is enough," rather than according to the Yemenite version *sha'ton* [שָׁעָתָן]. Owing to his variant pronunciation, he was given the nickname for the way he read, *sha'tan*.[99]

Hayle

Hayle derives from the spice *hal*, "cardamom." In the Khamīr community there was a man called Se'īd al-Hayle since he often would ask jokingly for only one grain of *hal*.[100]

Bayt al-Ṣudq

Ṣudq in Arabic means "truth." The Shalom family from Sada in southern Yemen was nicknamed Bayt al-Ṣudq because they were known for their integrity and truthfulness.[101]

97. *Emunat Hashem* (Jerusalem, 1938), p. 49. R. Shelomo Qoraḥ writes that R. 'Arusi used to go barefoot in memory of the destruction of the Temple; see Shelomo Qoraḥ, *'Arikhat Shulḥan*, 2 (Bnei Berak, 2012), *Hashkavah ve-Qaddish*, Sect. 71, p. 261.

98. In a personal correspondence dated 22 Apr 2010 from R. Yiṣḥaq Raṣābi. The story's source is R. Nissim, the father of R. Raṣābi.

99. In personal correspondence dated 22 Apr 2010 from R. Yiṣḥaq Raṣabi.

100. In a personal correspondence dated 8 Mar 2010 from R. Azaryah Basis.

101. One of the family members is R. Shalom Shalom, OBM, founder and head of the kollel Sha'arei Yosef in Bnei Brak. Oral communication from R. Itamar Ḥayim Kohen, Bnei Brak.

Maḥlīq

Means "one who differs." R. Se'īd al-Qāfiḥ was one of the sages of Ṣan'a. He was given the appellation al-Maḥlīq because in halakhic disputes he would cling to his understanding of the *halakhah* even when he was in the minority.[102]

Muhandis

'Amr 'Amr was called Muhandis ("the engineer") because of his skill with mechanical devices.[103] Some emigrés from Ṣan'a tell that he had made a motor so a rooster could fly.

Ḥami

Ḥāmi in Arabic and *ḥam* in Hebrew mean "hot." An elderly man in the Radā' community who was holding a hot pita yelled out "ḥami ḥami," and from then on the nickname ḥami stuck to him.[104]

Būrmah

A man from northern Yemen received this nickname because of his love for Sabbath *ḥamīn* that was prepared in the vessel called *būrmah*.[105]

Wanne

The Yada'i family lived in Dār Ḥayd in central Yemen. It is told about one of the family members that when he was ill he would give out, as an expression of his pain, exaggerated groans. A person groaning from pain in Yemen was called *biwīn*, and the word *wīn* describes the groan. From then on, his family name was changed from Yada'i to Wanne.[106]

Yarmukh

Aharon Yarimi told me about his nickname Yarmukh: At a wedding in Ṣan'a a worker slaughtered and prepared an ox as was the cus-

102. R. Yosef Qafīḥ, *"Rabbanim Yoṣe'ei Teiman bi-Yrushalayim,"* in *Se'i Yona* (Tel Aviv, 1984), pp. 83–84.

103. Yosef Zadok, *Ma'avaqim u-Temurot* (Tel Aviv, 1989), p. 64.

104. In a personal correspondence from Avraham Levi of Jerusalem in received in 2006.

105. In a personal correspondence dated 13 Jan 2010 from R. Dr. Aharon Ben David of Qiryat Eqron. In the language of the Ṣan'a Jews this vessel is called *bīrmah*. This nickname appears in a list of Jewish names from northern Yemen in the village of Daḥḍah. See Ben David, *Bet ha-Even*, p. 706, 1271; p. 715, nos. 1616–1617.

106. As related by his sister, Rinat Yid'i. His son, Ḥayim Wanneh of Bnei Brak, is my sister Rina's brother-in-law. Cf. Raṣabi, *Ofan ha-Merkavah*, in his edition of *Rekhev Elohim*, pp. 36–39.

tom. When the task was finished, the worker was given drink in appreciation. After he had drunk three glasses of ʻaraq, the groom's father called him Yarmukh, like the Yarmuk River, which flows unceasingly, and from then on this nickname was used by his acquaintances.

8. FAMILY NAMES ORIGINATING OUTSIDE YEMEN

S.D. Goitein noted that during the time of trade with India, mainly in the twelfth century, when Jews of South Arabia, that is Yemen including Aden, were a dominant factor, immigrants arrived from different places. Goitein remarks:

> As I made my statement, I had the opportunity to indicate the various foundations of which Yemenite Jewry is composed: immigrants from the Land of Israel, Iraq, and Iran, and a few even from the west. We ultimately found that the Yemenites themselves contributed something to the composition of other Jewish communities. The centuries in which commerce with India flourished were the times in which these foundations merged into a unit that developed in the following generations into a tribe with a unique nature—the Yemenites.[107]

In a *maqama* dating, apparently, to the twelfth or thirteenth century, Shelomoh tells of his origin: "First came my father from Spain / and to settle in Ṣoʻan[108] he went down / ... and behold a voice from before the loyal Lord / it said to him, arise, go to the land of Yemen / ... and he took himself from the land of Yemen a praiseworthy wife / perfect in her beauty / and she had boys and girls for him / in a nation of people with great faith."[109]

Y. Ratzaby has discussed information from a Yemenite manuscript about the emigration of Jews from Egypt to Yemen in the mid-fourteenth century. Written in the preface to a question asked of Maimonides about a Torah scroll was "I have found in papers that came from Egypt in 1677 SEL [5126 AM/ 1366] in the handwriting of Jews who moved their dwelling place from Egypt to Ṣanʻa. They mentioned them in the following terms: Found in the cupboard in the *bet midrash* of Rabbenu Moshe ben Maimon, may the memory of the righteous, holy one be for a blessing, and this is its text."[110]

107. Ibid., p. 43.
108. The reference is to Egypt or to one of its cities. Ṣoʻan is a city in ancient Egypt, Tanis in Greek; cf. Ṣoʻan Miṣrayim (Num. 13:22).
109. Simcha Assaf, *"Meqorot le-Qorot ha-Yehudim bi-Sefarad," Zion* 6 (1941): 44–45.
110. Yehudah Ratzaby, *"Teʻudot le-Toledot Yehudei Teiman," Sefunot* 2 (1958): 288.

S. D. Goitein commented on the Jews coming from Iran to Yemen: "In the tenth century, part of Yemen came under the rule of the Zaydi *imams*. They [the Jews] originated in north Iran, from around the Caspian Sea, and in Yemen they made the city of Sa'dah their center. The way of the Jews is to accompany the rulers and to settle in the capital."[111]

About the families that arrived in Yemen, R. 'Amram Qoraḥ noted: "Undoubtedly during the times, people moved from Egypt and India and the district of Iraq and they took hold in Yemen, and there were families called by the name of their location."[112] R. Yosef Qāfiḥ observes: "There are also family names whose Spanish names have remained to this day, such as the 'Ḥarizi' family with the same family name as R. Yehudah Ḥarizi, the author of *Taḥkemoni*.[113]

Y. Ratzaby writes:

> Active among Yemenite Jews were personages whose non-Yemenite origin is proven by their names and their forefathers' names, whether it be R. Ya'aqov Netan'el Fayumi, *"Negid Ereṣ Teiman,"* to whom Rambam sent the famous *"Iggeret Teiman,"* or the 'Irāqi family, from whom came *nesi'im* and leaders of Yemenite Jews in the seventeenth and eighteenth centuries, and the like: emissaries, merchants and simply travelers, who wanted Yemen as their place of residence and settled in it."[114]

Joseph Tobi, in his discussion about the 'Irāqi family, which originated outside Yemen, wrote:

> The 'Irāqi family is the only one that existed in Yemen until our times for which there was maintained a clear tradition, since its origin is outside of Yemen. Undoubtedly, and there is firm proof from various sources, that at least over the past thousand years, Yemenite Jewry was nurtured by immigrants who came from elsewhere. Many among them were merchants who happened to come to the country for business, whether in the Middle Ages or in modern times, and found it good for them as a place to live. There is not always documented proof of this, but one may assume that families such as Ḥarāzi, Ṭobi, and

111. Shlomo Dov Goitein, *"Yahadut Teiman ve-Saḥar Hodu ha-Yehudi,"* in *Ha-Teimanim —Mivḥar Meḥqarim* (Jerusalem, 1983), p. 38.

112. Amram Qoraḥ, *Sa'arat Teiman* (Jerusalem, 1954), p. 95 n. 5.

113. Yosef Qāfiḥ, *"Kehillat Ṣan'a she-be-Teiman," Ketavim* 1 (1989): 863. There were a number of rabbis in Yemen with the family name *Ḥarizi*. See *Enṣiqlopedyah le-Ḥokhmei Teiman,* 1, pp. 177–78, entries: Ḥarizi David; Ḥarizi David ben Yosef; Ḥarizi Nissim.

114. Yehudah Ratzaby, *"Te'udot le-Toledot Yehudei Teiman,"* p. 288.

Maymūni, are not from among the ancient residents of the exile in Yemen.[115]

It would be accurate to say that in the last few hundred years there has been practically no immigration into Yemen. Perhaps the *Maymūni* family originated in the town of Bane Maymūn, which is located north of Ṣan'a.[116] Possibly the name Ṭobi derives from the Yemenite family name Ṭaybi. Regarding other names, such as Ḥarīzi, Basīs, Naqqāsh, Maddār, and 'Iṭwār, it is difficult to determine whether these families originated outside of Yemen, even though we have found family names such as these in communities outside of Yemen.[117]

There are a few families that, based on written sources and oral traditions, apparently did originate outside Yemen:

Bundār

S. D. Goitein wrote that this extended family, which led Yemenite Jewry from the end of the eleventh century until the first half of the thirteenth, was apparently of Persian origin, since its founder was called Bundār, which is a Persian word. This family had close ties to the heads of the Babylonian *yeshivot* and with the Rosh ha-Golah, in Baghdad.[118]

In Aden, Yefet ben Bundār was "Peqid ha-Soḥarim," the legal representative of the foreign merchants who came there. His son Maḍmūn attained a respected position of authority,[119] being responsible for the port of Aden, as well as being a business partner of the ruler of Aden. Maḍmūn had connections with the *yeshivot* in Babylonia and with the Jewish community in Fustat, Egypt. One of the letters sent from Babylonia tells that Maḍmūn "has been appointed by the *rashei galuyot* (exilarchs) and by the *rashei yeshivot* to be over all the Jews, and a trustee of the rulers wherever they may be in foreign countries or in the desert." Maḍmūn's high standing is further seen in that the Palestinian *yeshiva*

115. Tobi, *'Iyyunim bi-Mgillat Teiman*, pp. 151–52.
116. Gavra, *Enṣiqlopedya le-Qehilot ha-Yehudiyyot be-Teiman*, vol. 1, p. 63, entry בני מימון.
117. One of my students, Naomi Cohen of Rehovot, whose maiden name was Ḥarīzi and who stems from northern Yemen, wrote to me that her older brother, when visiting Bet Hatefutsoth in Tel Aviv—where family names from the different Jewish communities are concentrated—asked about the family name Ḥarīzi. He was told that it comes from Spain. That reply, obviously, was given because of the documentation of the Ḥarīzi family in Spain.
118. Goitein, *Saḥar Hodu*, p. 38.
119. Maḍmun had a brother named Bundār. See Goitein, *"Negidei Erets Teiman,"* in Ha-Teimanim—*Miḥar Meḥqarim* (Jerusalem, 1983),p. 81; Shlomo Dov Goitein and Mordechai Akiva Friedman, *Maḍmun Nagid of Yemen and the India Trade - Cairo Geniza Documents, India Book II* (Jerusalem, 2010), p. 16 [in Hebrew].

in Egypt granted him honorifics, among them Nagid Ereṣ Teiman, Yedid ha-Yeshivah, and Segulat ha-Yeshivah. Maḍmūn died in 1151, and his son Ḥalfon replaced him, holding the office of Nagid Ereṣ Teiman.[120]

Nīhāwandi

In the twelfth century, there lived in Aden a Jew by the name of Khalaf al-Nīhāwandi who set customs' rates for the city. His family name indicates his origin from the city of Nīhāwand in Iran.[121]

Hīndi

Apparently this is the family name of Jews who came from India, which is known by the name Hindiyya. It may be that, upon their return to Yemen, this name was affixed to those Jews from Yemen who had traveled to India to serve as cantors, ritual slaughterers, teachers, printers of books, and merchants.[122] In a *ketubbah* from 13 Ḥeshvan 5673 (24 Oct 1912), from 'Ūqlah, the name of the groom is written as Sālem b. al-Hindi. A *ketubbah* from 22 Sivan 5687 (22 June 1927), also from 'Ūqlah, we find the name of the groom registered as Se'īd ibn Sālem Yiḥye' al-Hindi, and the name of one of the witnesses was Yosef al-Hindi. In a *ketubbah* from 13 Tammuz 5706 (12 July 1946), from Qaṣr Mlāḥa', the name of the groom is given as Ḥayim ben Yosef called al-Hindi.

Kūtah

According to the family tradition, one of the family members arrived in Yemen from Calcutta, India, in the nineteenth century. The family lived in the village of Aqmah in central Yemen.[123] Perhaps, this name became attached to families of emigrants who returned to Yemen, or of merchants who would travel from Yemen to Calcutta.

120. Goitein, *Saḥar Hodu*, pp. 38–42; idem, *"Negidei Ereṣ Teiman,"* in *Ha-Teimanim—Mivḥar Meḥqarim* (Jerusalem, 1983), pp. 78–80; Shlomo Dov Goitein and Mordechai Akiva Friedman, *Maḍmun Nagid of Yemen and the India Trade – Cairo Geniza Documents, India Book II* (Jerusalem, 2010), pp. 7–16 [in Hebrew]. See also Reuven Ahroni, *Yehudei Aden, Qehila sha-Hayta* (Tel Aviv, 1991), pp. 24–28.

121. Goitein, *Saḥar Hodu*, p. 38; idem, *"Negidei Ereṣ Teiman,"* p. 78; Goitein and Friedman, *Maḍmun Nagid of Yemen*, p. 5.

122. On the links between Yemenite Jewry and India, see Shlomo Dov Goitein, *"Yahadut Teiman ve-Saḥar Hodu,"* p. 42; Yehudah Ratzaby, *"Yehudei Qochin vi-Yhudei Teiman ba-Me'ah ha-18," Sinai* 89 (1981): 69–86; idem, *Be-Ma'agalot Teiman* (Tel Aviv, 1948), p. 121; R. Yosef Qāfiḥ, *"Zeror Mikhtavim bein Manhigei Yehudei Kochin le-vein Yehudei Teiman," Ketavim* 2 (1989): 831–60.

123. As related by Iris Eshel, Petah Tikva. Some family members wrote their last name as Qūṭah.

'Aṣab

'Aṣab is a city in Eritrea opposite the coast of Yemen. Many Yemenite laborers worked there, and they apparently received the name of the city as their family name. This family lived in the Ḥadād community in southern Yemen.[124]

'Irāqi

There are various traditions about the origin of this family and about the time it arrived in Yemen. Joseph Tobi believes that the family came from Iraq to Yemen in the sixteenth century.[125] R. Ḥayim Ḥibshush feels that the source of the name is in Egypt.[126] In Yosef Qāfiḥ's opinion the family stemmed from Iraq, "but it may be that they were first exiled to Egypt and thence to Yemen."[127] We have seventeenth-century manuscript copies made by R. Aharon ben Shelomo ben Yosef 'Irāqi, which were copied in the Ma'bar, Radā', and Dhamār communities.[128] From the seventeenth century until the end of the Yemenite Golah, 'Irāqi families lived in Ṣan'a,[129] and in the eighteenth century, R. Aharon and his son, R. Shalom, served as *nesi'ei ha-qehilah*.[130] 'Irāqi families lived in northern Yemen as well, in the al-Hajjar community.[131]

124. For support for this family name, see Shalom Gamliel, *Ha-Naḥshonim 'al Kanfei Nesharim*, p. 155; Gavra, *Enṣiqlopedya le-Qehilot be-Teiman*, 1, entry "*Ḥadād.*"

125. Joseph Tobi, *"Peniyyat Peqidei Qushta el R. Shalom 'Irāqi Nesi Yehudei Teiman be-Shnat TQ"B (1742),"* *Shalem* 1 (1974): 262.

126. Qāfiḥ, "*Qorot Yisra'el be-Teiman*, p. 718.

127. Ibid., p. 718 n. 156.

128. Gavra, *Enṣiqlopedya le-Qehilot ha-Yehudiyyot be-Teiman*, vol. 1, p. 466, entry ,עראקי אהרן בן שלמה בן יוסף.

129. Tobi, *'Iyyunim bi-Mgillat Teiman*, p. 154.

130. Gaimani, *Temurot be-Moreshet Yahadut Teiman*, pp. 175–78.

131. See Tobi, *'Iyyunim bi-Mgillat Teiman*, p. 155. Prof. Bat-Zion Eraqi-Klorman's family originated in the al-Hajar community in northern Yemen. R. Yosef 'Irāqi Ha-Kohen wrote to me on 30 Apr 2010 about the origins of the 'Irāqi family: "Or, lest it be, about the origin of the family that is perhaps in Babylonia as heard from the family name that refer to your statement, conversely, this is its greatest *yiḥus* [lineage]. Apparently you did not miss seeing the statements of our teacher, the R. Yiḥye'] Qoraḥ in his commentary *Maskil Shir Yedidot*, for the song לבבי יחשקה עפרה, on what the divine R. Shalom [meaning, R. Shalom Shabazi] 'and all members of the group and *ofer bavali*,' stating that both he and we are called *Bavliyyim*, after where we were initially, and from there our forefathers came to live in this land ... and even though we have a tradition that our exile began at the time of the first destruction [of the Temple], do not believe that we are still only from them, but

Fayyūmi

We already find the family name Fayyūmi in Yemen in an early period.[132] In a copy from Yemen of *Moreh Nevukhim* made in 1380, a note was written in the margins that begins "Rabb[enu] Sa'adyah ha-Kohen al-Fayyūmi." Y. Ratzaby concluded that this does not refer to Sa'adyah Gaon, since he was not a *kohen*, but to a sage from Fayyum in Egypt who had come to Yemen. In his hometown, he was known as Sa'adyah ha-Kohen and, owing to the plethora of "ha-Kohen" names, people added the byname al-Fayyūmi to make identification of him easier.[133] A bill of sale from 1652 for a Mishna that was bought from the Jiblah community in southern Yemen was signed by Avraham ben Shalom Fayyūmi.[134] The name Fayyūmi occurs also in nineteenth- and twentieth-century documents from the region of the Damt community. In a document from 1847 concerning a dispute between neighbors, one of the litigants was Ma'ūdah al-Fayyūmi.[135] In a 1912 document concerning the sale of a home, one of the witnesses signed the *sheṭar* as Sālem Fayyūmi.[136]

Madīnah

According to the tradition of the Madīnah family that lived in Ṣan'a, the family's origin is Medina del Capo in northern Castile, Spain.[137] This tradition, however, is probably incorrect, since there is no link between the name of this family and families outside Yemen. Perhaps there was some incident that had occurred in Ṣan'a, that is in the *"madina"* [the city], and so this byname was given to the family.[138]

also from Halah, and Habor that remain from the ten tribes, and from Babylon and from Egypt who come for their livelihood we ... and, to be sure, the *galuyot* of Babylonia are superior to the *galuyot* in the other lands ... Rav Huna said in the name of Rav saying [Menaḥot 110a], 'Bring My sons from far—These are the exiles in Babylon, who are at ease like sons' ... and see there all his statements extensively."

132. On the name Fayyūmi as a personal name, see above part 1, chap. 5, sect. 1.

133. See Aharon Gaimani, *"Ha'ataqah Qedumah mi-Teiman le-*Moreh Nevukhim *le-ha-Rambam," Tehuda* 14 (1994): 17.

134. In the possession of Yehudah Levi Nahum, *Ḥasifat Genuzim mi-Teiman* (Holon 1971), file 63. See also Nahum, *Ṣohar le-Ḥasifat Ginzei Teiman*, p. 187, no. 145.

135. Nissim Binyamin Gamlieli, *Teiman bi-Te'udot*, vol. 2 (Ramleh, 2009), p. 152, doc. 102.

136. Ibid., vol. 1, pp. 308–10, doc. 73, photo of the document on p. 311.

137. See the list of Talya Argaman-Medina, *"Le-Nishmat R. Ḥayim Medina," Afikim* 117–18 (Adar II 2000): 80.

138. Cf. Raṣabi, *Ofan ha-Merkavah*, in his edition of *Rekhev Elohim le-R. Y. Wanneh*, p. 37 n. 1.

Shalīṭ

The family has a tradition that it originated in France. *Shalīṭ* as a family name is found in France to this day.[139] Some three hundred years ago, three wealthy brothers fled from France to Aden in southern Yemen in fear for their lives, where they then went their separate ways. One immigrated to Syria; the second remained in Aden and, having only daughters, the family name ceased; the third brother settled in Ḥima in central Yemen, where it lived for generations.[140] In three *ketubbot* from Ṣan'a the Shalīṭ family is mentioned with the term serving as a family name, as well as a byname. In a *ketubbah* dated 14 Tishri 5625 (14 Oct 1864), the groom's name is registered as Yiḥye' be Sālem al-Shalīṭ. In a *ketubbah* from 22 Sivan 5672 (7 June 1912), the groom's name is listed as Shemu'el ben Sulēmān al-Shalīṭ. In a *ketubbah* dated 27 Shevat 5793 (23 Feb 1933), the bride's name is Turkiyya bint Shemu'el ben Sālem al-Akhlūfi who is called Shalīṭ.[141]

139. The family of Gilad Shalit, the soldier kidnapped by Hamas, stems from France.
140. According to the testimony of Ḥayim Shalit, who immigrated to Israel from the Ḥima community in Yemen and lives in Ramat Gan.
141. For a photo of one of the Shalīṭ families in Ṣan'a, see *Ṣan'a u-Sevivatah be-Ṣilumei Yeḥiel Ḥaybi*, ed. Yosef Sha'ar, published by Ruma Haybi (Tel Aviv, 1985), p. 61, photo no. 112.

PART III
Additional Aspects

CHAPTER ONE
ORTHOGRAPHY OF NAMES

Differences exist concerning the way names are written in different Jewish communities. For example, there is the orthography of biblical names as pronounced in Arabic, names written in plene or defective spelling, the denoting of emphatics in Arabic names, and so on.

1. MATRES LECTIONIS

Yemenite Jews did not pronounce biblical names according to the vocalization. For example, the name Avraham, which was vocalized in the Tiberian tradition as אַבְרָהָם (Avraham), was read with the vowel *ḥiriq* under the *alef* and the *heh* (Ibrahim). This pronunciation is found in a number of written forms: אבראהם, איבראהים, איברהים, איבראהם (Ibrāhim, Ībrāhīm, Ībrahim, Ībrāhīm). יצחק (Yiṣḥaq), whose pronunciation did not differ from that of other Jews was written as יצחאק (Yiṣḥāq). יעקב, which was pronounced with a *shuruq* (Ya'aqub), written as יעקוב. There were also biblical names that were transformed into names with a similar Arabic sound: שלמה (Shelomo) was pronounced as Suliman and written as סלימאן (Slaymān) (and sometimes as סולימאן, Sūlēmān); שלום (Shalōm) was pronounced Sālem and written as סאלם (Sālem).

Writing Hebrew biblical names following the Arabic sometimes caused an uneasy feeling. R. Yiḥye' 'Amud, an Aden resident, turned to the Rishon Lezion, R. Ya'aqov Elyashar, and asked him to write a *haskamah* (approbation) for his book *Petaḥ ha-Ohel*. In his reply, R. Elyashar referred to the custom of Yemenite Jews, who added *otiyot hemshekh* (the matres lectionis) to biblical names:

> And I myself was thoroughly shaken, for names written in the Torah, such as Avraham, Yiṣḥaq, Ya'aqov, Sarah, Rivqah and the like of this type of name, Heaven forfend, for one should not add them nor detract

> from them [God forbid] but only as one writes them in the Bible ... only for names not written in the Torah is it necessary to provide them with matres lectionis so no error will be made in reading them.[1]

R. 'Amud sought the opinion of the Ṣan'a rabbis and, after considering the attitude of the Rishon Lezion, R. Elyashar, they defended the Yemenite orthographical customs:

> Indeed, in the regions of Yemen and the like, where they read Avraham with a *pataḥ* under the *resh*, and Yiṣḥaq with a *pataḥ* under the *ḥet*, and Da'ūd with a *pataḥ* under *dalet alef*, and Ya'aqūb with a *shuruq*, at all times and when reading in a Torah scroll as well as when signing, then one must write an *alef* after the *resh* in Ibrāhim (אבראהם), as well as for all the noted, and as noted by Me'or ha-Golah, Morenu ha-Rav Yiḥye' Ṣāliḥ in his responsa, and as explained as such by all the *poseqim*, *Rishonim* and *Aḥaronim*.[2]

As a result of the reply of the Ṣan'a rabbis, R. 'Amud wrote that a person appending a signature and spelling his name as Ibrāhim (אבראהם), though when he is called to the Torah it is by the name Avraham (אברהם), should he be mentioned in a *get* both names should be written, that is, "Avraham who is called Ibrāhim."[3]

Moreover, R. Elyashar thought that the Yemenite Jews added matres lectionis for those called by their Hebrew name. However, the Ṣan'a sages responded that this was not so and that matres lectionis were inserted only for people called by the Arabic name. For example, for someone named Avraham upon his circumcision, and who was called thereby to the Torah, and who so signed his name, in such a case in a *get* the name Avraham was written. But for someone who was called Ibrāhim at the *brit*, and was called thereby to the Torah and who so signed his name, in such a case in a *get* it was written as Ibrāhim as well. Thus, in reality, there was no controversy between R. Elyashar and the Yemenite rabbis; R. Elyashar simply was not familiar with the situation in Yemen.

R. Amram Qoraḥ wrote, "The Religious Courts did indeed insert matres lectionis also in Arabic names, such as Ibrāhim, Yiṣḥāq, Harūn, Da'ūd, Slaymān and the like. Only if the word or the name was Hebrew

1. Yiḥye' ben Yosef 'Amud, *Petaḥ ha-Ohel*, printed at the end of *Sefer Meqor Ḥayim*, published by Yosef Hasid (Jerusalem, 1980), approbation, p. 3.
2. Ibid., p. 86.
3. Ibid., p. 87.

would they write it in *gittin* according to the grammar of biblical language."[4] And R. Yosef Qoraḥ reinforces the Yemenite Jews' custom, "Since the earliest Religious Courts wrote that way ... we follow their custom."[5]

2. THE WRITING OF ARABIC NAMES

The tradition of the Yemenite Jews when writing Arabic names differs in a few cases from that of their brethren in other Islamic countries, which at times resulted in disputes with members of other communities. This stems from the difference in pronunciation of the names as enunciated by the Jews of Yemen.

R. Shalom Yiṣḥaq Halevi, who served as a member of the Tel Aviv Bet Din, was asked in 1934 by immigrants from Yemen about writing the name 'Awaḍ in a *get*. The possibilities were עוואד ('Awwād), עואד ('Awād), עוואץ̇ ('Awwāḍ), עואץ̇ ('Awāḍ). In his letter to R. Reuven Katz, then the chief rabbi of Petaḥ Tiqvah, he notes that the tradition among Yemenite Jews for this name is to write it as 'Awāḍ with one *vav* and an emphatic *ṣade*, that is, to place a dot over the letter *ṣade* as in Arabic transcription. He appended to his letter the testimony of the president of the Tel Aviv Beit Din, R. Yosef Halevi, that this is also what he customarily does in a case when the litigants belong to the Yemenite community.

In another letter to R. Reuven Katz, who believed that it was necessary to write the name with two *vavs*, he notes that the orthography of the names derives from the pronunciation of the Yemenites:

> First of all, I wish to draw the attention of your revered self to two things that are different between the pronunciation of the Yemenite community and all others, from which one can gain a notion relevant to our issue, namely, your revered self should know that language purists such as ourselves do not pronounce the *vav* as a (fricative) *vet*; because among us, according to grammar, there is a special point of origin for the *vav* and the pronunciation of the *vav* is not the same as the *vet*, and we always sense the difference between *vav* and *vet*, not the usual pronunciations as produced in other communities ... and since the name 'Awāḍ is written with one *vav* in Arabic, and it is our tradition to write one *vav* as usual in Arabic script and as we read it, since among us we do not read the *vav* as a fricative *bet*, as I mentioned

4. Amram Qoraḥ, *Sa'arat Teiman* (Jerusalem, 1954), p. 149 n. 5.
5. Pinḥas Qoraḥ (ed.), *Anaf Eṣ Avot* (Bnei Brak, 1994), p. 591.

above, and especially since there is no fricative *bet* in Arabic at all, it is incumbent upon us to write it with only one *vav*.[6]

In a 1936 letter to the Egyptian Beit Din that dealt with the divorce of a couple who came from Yemen, he notes the Yemenite Jews' tradition for writing the names Yiḥye' and Mūsa':

> Now for these names Yiḥye'' and Mūsa' and the like, the tradition the Yemenites have for generations is to write them with an *alef* at the end. The reason is that any name written in Arabic with a *heh* at the end is with a *mappiq*, such as Sa'dah, Sham'ah, Ni'meh, Badrah, Ḥabībah (that is its pronunciation in Yemenite Arabic) ..., which is not so for Yiḥye' and Mūsa' as well as for Raḍa' and Ghane' and the like that are written with an *alef* at the end, they are read with a furtive *alef*.[7]

In his conclusion, he makes use of R. Sa'adyah Gaon's translation of the names mentioned. In a discussion of the orthography of the name Yiḥye', whether to use one *yod* or two, a footnote in the work *Shem Ḥadash* states, "My humble opinion tends toward writing Yiḥye' with one *yod* between the *ḥet* and the *heh*. And in the North Africa and Yemenite cities proficient in Arabic, they write [it] with one *yod*. And should they write with an *alef* at the end, this causes no harm, since they also do so in Arabic."[8]

R. Aviran Yiṣḥaq Halevi, who, like his grandfather mentioned above, serves as a *dayyan* in the Tel Aviv Beit Din, wrote to me about similar cases that occurred in the Tel Aviv Rabbinic Court. In regards to spelling of the name Ma'ūḍah or Ma'ūdah he wrote:

> There was a case of a person whose name was Ma'ūḍah, and the *av bet din* (president of the Court) and his colleague were divided over whether to write Ma'ūḍah or Ma'udah. And they called me to the hall of their Court and asked me for my opinion. I told them that the custom in Yemen was to write and pronounce it as Ma'ūḍah, and the *av bet din* immediately ordered to write it that way. And come morning, the Lord will make known, and the following day I brought them responsa of the rabbis and the serious dispute of my paternal grandfather over the issue of the name 'Awaḍ.[9]

6. Shalom Yiṣḥaq Halevi, *Shut Divrei Ḥakhamim* (Jerusalem, 1972), *Even ha-Ezer*, par. 7, p. 143.
7. Ibid., p. 144.
8. Mas'ud Ben Shim'on, *Shem Ḥadash* (Jerusalem, 1991), p. 88.
9. In a personal correspondence dated 12 Oct 2010.

And R. Aviran Yiṣḥaq Halevi had another case about the writing of the name והב (Wahb) with one *vav* or two:

> And I had a case where a Yemenite couple came for a divorce and the husband's name was Wahb, and the honorable president of the Bet Din ordered the scribe to write ווהב (Wwahb) with two *vavs*. And when I remarked to him that the custom in Yemen was to write it with one *vav,* he replied that the custom in Tel Aviv is to write it with two. The scribe went and wrote the *get.* In any case, we used to trade back and forth about this, and he showed me the statement of the rabbi *Shem Ḥadash*, and I showed him what my paternal grandfather said.[10] The scribe returned with the *get* in hand and the *get* in which [the name] was written with two *vavs* was given. But upon handing over the *get*, the heart of the revered president of the Court was uneasy, and again he asked me what is wrong with writing it with two *vavs*, for this is simply for greater clarification of its reading. And I answered him that that is not so, that a Yemenite accustomed to Yemenite writing would read and pronounce the two *vavs*. The *av bet din* was shocked and said, if so we must consider this explanation, and he erased one of the *vavs*, and they once again gave the *get* to the woman as it should be.[11]

R. Avraham Naddāf, one of the leaders of the Yemenite community in Jerusalem at the beginning of the twentieth century, commented to R. Refa'el Aharon Ben Shim'on, the rabbi of the Egyptian community, about the writing of the woman's name Lūlūwa. In his letter to the Bet Din of the Yemenite community in Jerusalem, dated 9 Tevet 5679 (12 Dec 1918), R. Ben Shim'on described the situation:

> This is to inform you that this woman was divorced the first time in the cities of Yemen, and afterwards became a widow, as written in the evidentiary document about her divorce that was granted by the sages and rabbis of Yemen. And when she was on route by ship, she married a Yemenite man on board, but they did not get along, and she was divorced from the *erusin*. To be sure, this woman was divorced twice with the name Lūlūwwah (לולווה), since we came to understand that the name Lūlūwwah is to be written according to the writ of the Rabbinic Court of the rabbis of Yemen who wrote to the current court

10. He is referring to his grandfather Shalom Yiṣḥaq Halevi mentioned in this section, who wrote annotations to the book *Shem Ḥadash* about writing names in divorce documents. These annotations, which deal with issues of names in the tradition of the Jews of Yemen, were written apparently at the behest of his fellow *dayyanim* and were used by the members of the Bet Din.
11. In a personal correspondence dated 12 Oct 2010.

> as expressed in a notification of the old Rabbinic Court, and by this name she was also divorced in our Rabbinic Court on 4 Shevat 5668,[12] Lūlūwwah, who is called Lūli, since in Egypt it was difficult for them to pronounce the name Lūluwwah so they used the diminutive Lūli, and in any event there the name Lūlūwwah did not become her usual one as the Yemenites call her, and it is her birth name as well as what is written in her *ketubbah*. Later she was divorced by the name Lūlūwwah both in Yemen and in Egypt, but in Egypt they added "who is called Lūli." And it is impossible to change her name in the third *get* and to only write Lūlū, since in Yemen and in Egypt this did not take root, and it is the place of her marriage with the gentleman Menaḥem ben Avraham Halewi, so that the eyes of *ṣaddiqim* should behold what is right, wisdom and knowledge is with them.[13]

We learn from the statements of R. Ben Shim'on that the actual name of the woman was Lūluwah, but when she came to Egypt people began to call her Lūli, which is a nickname or in the language of the *poseqim* a diminutive used in one's youth.[14] R. Ben Shim'on wrote in the *get* "Lūlūwah who is called Lūli," and the reasons for writing Lūlūwah were (1) the name did not fall into oblivion, that is, it was not forgotten, and the Yemenites called her by this name; (2) this is the name given to her upon her birth;[15] and (3) this name was written in her *ketubbah*. For these reasons, one must write Lūlūwah, but also write the name Lūli, as she was called in Egypt. R. Ben Shim'on did one more thing: he wrote the name with three *vavs*. Beside the first *vav*, he wrote two consecutive *vavs*, לולווה (Lūlūwwah); he gave no reason for this since he just thought that was how it should be written.

12. 7 Jan 1908.
13. Avraham Alnaddaf, *'Anaf Ḥayim—Shut Zikhronei Iy"sh* (Jerusalem, 1981), *Even ha-Ezer*, par. 59, pp. 222–23.
14. Erroneously in the printed texts of the Shulḥan Arukh, *Even ha-Ezer*, par. 129, 15, the phrase was set as *"shem ha-neharot"* instead of *"shem ha-na'arut"*, since the printers did not understand that the term *"shem ha-na'arut"*, stemming from *na'ar* [lad], should be written.
15. R. Ya'aqov Emden wrote about how meticulous people must be when giving a birth name: "One must take care when giving a name to a daughter, to give clearly a Torah name, and not a childish name, such as Rekhela, Raikhela, but Raḥel, in any event the principal name so there should be no doubt in the writing of *ketubbot* and *gittin*. Also for males, one should be aware of this. But this [diminutives, nicknames] is not as frequent as among females" (R. Ya'aqov Emden, *Sefer Birat Migdal Oz, Shoqet* 2, 18 [Warsaw 1882], p. 22.)

R. Naddāf disagreed with him and wrote to him on 31 Mar 1919:

> Indeed, one is astonished by what is written in the *ketubbah*; moreover in the letter by your good self the name Lūlūwah appears with 3 *vavs*, which is the opposite of our pronunciation in our reading of it, for we in Yemen and here in the Holy Land, never read it as if it were Lūlūwa with a *ḥaṭaf*, that is with a *schwa* under the second *lamed* and without placing a *dagesh* in the *vav* that follows it. Also when writing it, we have never seen anyone write it with three *vavs*, whether in *ketubbot* or in other writings. We do have in our possession *ketubbot* from Ṣan'a, capital of Yemen, in which the Bet Din signed upon it in a very early period, with one "*vav*" after the second *lamed*, which means that they wrote it the way they pronounced as it is read by people in Yemen.[16]

R. Naddāf noted that the custom in Yemen, as well as among the Yemenite immigrants in Jerusalem, is to read and write this name with two *vavs*: לולוה. He commented on R. Ben Shim'on, who wrote that he had asked a bet din in Yemen, inquiring whether R. Ben Shim'on had clarified just the pronunciation of the name or its orthography as well. For if it were on the writing of the name, there would be a different question before the Bet ha-Din of Yemen, because this would be contrary to the widely known accent. But the Bet Din in Yemen replied that it was according to the pronunciation of his location at the time he was asked. And in relation to the accent of our times, this name should be written with one *vav* after the second *lamed*. Another issue on which R. Naddāf disagreed with R. Ben Shim'on concerned two names noted in the *get*, "Lūlūwwah who is called Lūli," and he commented:

> And, behold, according to the statements by your good self, who believes that both in Yemen and Jerusalem, may it be built and established, we call her by the two names mentioned. The truth is that this is not so, for she is called only Lūluwah, which is her birth name, and we have never heard, neither in Yemen nor in Jerusalem, may it be built and established, that she is also called Lūli at all. And for what is under discussion, also when she came to Jerusalem, may it be built and established, they called her only by the name they knew for her in Yemen, Lūlūwah. If so, regarding her there is no need to write "who is called" since she was not so called in her place of birth and not in the place of the writing and handing [it over]. Even though for a bit in Egypt, they added the name Lūli to her, we, on this issue, have no reason to guess why they called her that there. In addition, they did

16. Naddaf, *'Anaf Ḥayim, Even ha-Ezer*, par. 59, p. 223.

not change her name at all owing to illness, for then there might be place to assume.[17]

R. Naddāf cited support for his statements from R. Yosef Qaro in the *Shulḥan Arukh* and from the book *Get Pashut* that if some of the people call her by her main name and others by a diminutive and term of endearment, that is, by a nickname, then in the *get* only the main name should be written. For instance, Sarah, Sarūlah—then in the *get* they only write *Sarah.* R. Naddāf concluded his reply: "What difference does it make for me Sarah, Sarūla? What difference does it make to me Lūluwah, Lūlū, or Līli?"[18] So according to Yemenite custom, one does not add childhood names to a *get*, as R. Refa'el Aharon Ben Shim'on wrote.

R. Mas'ūd Ben Shim'on wrote this name in his book *Shem Ḥadash* with three *vavs*. R. Shalom Yiṣḥaq Halevi noted that "according to the Yemenite tradition Lūluwah is written with one *vav* after the second *lamed*."[19] In a 1991 reprint of the book *Shem Ḥadash*, R. Yosef Qāfiḥ made notations in the margins, "This name is to be written as Lūluwah, and it is an error to write it with two *vavs* between the *lamed* and the *he* لولوة ."[20]

In 1,506 *ketubbot* the name Lūluwah appears 47 times. Of these, 45 are written as Lūluwah (לולוה), with two *vavs*, and only twice was it written as Lūlūwwa (לולווה) with three *vavs*. In 152 *gittin*, the name Lūluwah appears eight times. Of these, seven are written as Lūluwah, with two *vavs*, and only once as Lūluwwah with three *vavs*.

3. OTHER GRAMMATICAL ISSUES

The ending heh in biblical names

In his discussion of the writing of the name Yehūdah (יהודה)—whether it should be Yehūdah (יהודה) or Yehūda' (יהודא)—R. Yiḥye' Ṣāliḥ (Mahariṣ) determined that it should be written with a final *heh*, as it is written in the Torah. Non-biblical names, however, should be written with a final *alef*, such as Yiḥye' (יחיא) rather than Yiḥye'h (יחיה),[21] and names that have a *mappiq* should be written with a *heh.*[22] An exam-

17. Ibid., p. 224.
18. Ibid., p. 225.
19. I received a photocopy of his annotations to the book *Shem Ḥadash* from his grandson, the *dayyan* R. Aviran Yiṣḥaq Halevi.
20. Ben Shim'on, *Shem Ḥadash*, p. 208.
21. See Mahariṣ, *Shut Pe'ulat Ṣaddiq*, 3 (Jerusalem, 2003), par. 95. See also Shulḥan Arukh, *Even ha-Ezer*, par. 129, 34.
22. Cf. the statement by R. Shalom Yiṣḥaq Halevi, above sect. 2.

ination of the names in *gittin* shows that the name Yehudah was written in Ṣan'a twice with the ending *heh* and twice with the ending *alef* in the locations of Maru'āgha and Khamer. In a *get* from Ṣan'a, dated 10 Sivan 5641 (8 Jun 1881), the name of the divorcing husband was written as Yehudah ben Slayman and in another Ṣan'a *get*, dated 13 Elul 5769 (30 Aug 1909), the divorcing husband's name appears as Yehūdah ben Yehūdah. In a *get* from Maru'āgha, dated 22 Adar 5527 (22 Feb 1767), the divorcing husband's name is Yūda' Ibn Da'ūd; and in a *get* from Khamer, dated 11 Iyyar 5706 (12 May 1946), the name of the divorcing husband is written as Yehūda' ben 'Imrān.

Women's names written with two yods

There is a disagreement over whether to write the names בנייה (Banayyah), קדרייה (Qadriyyah), and תורכייה (Tūrkiyyah) with one *yod* or two. In Yemen they were customarily written with two *yods*, owing to the *dagesh* (dot) in the *yod*.[23] R. Shalom Yiṣḥaq Halevi told of the debate between his father, the Yemenite chief rabbi, R. Yiḥye', and the Ḥakham Bashi of Egypt, over a *get* that was sent from Ṣan'a to Egypt and in which the name Rūmiyah (רומיה) was written with one *yod*. The Egyptian Bet Din wanted to annul the *get*, while he argued that after the fact the *get* was properly acceptable. In his conclusion R. Shalom Yiṣḥaq Halevi wrote:

> It turned out, therefore, that every name follows the way it is pronounced in a given place. And one cannot rely on what is written in book X for location Y, since that author did not know however it was pronounced elsewhere. For example, the name Mūsa is written in Yemen with an *alef* at its end; the way R. Sa'adyah Gaon represented the name Moshe). And why not with *heh* as it is written in books (of names on how to write names in a divorce document)? Because in Yemen the pronunciation of *heh* in pure Arabic is always a *mappiq* (diacritic dot in a *heh*) with a *dagesh*, but there is no voiceless glottal *heh* except in our holy Torah.[24]

In the 1991 reprint of *Shem Ḥadash*, R. Yosef Qāfiḥ commented in the margins of the book, and wrote next to this name: "This name is destined to be with one *yod* not two, and it does not mean European woman,[25] but

23. See Mahariṣ, *Shut Pe'ulat Ṣaddiq*, 3, par. 98; 'Amud, *Petaḥ ha-Ohel*, section 1, 30; Naddaf, *'Anaf Ḥayim, Even ha-Ezer*, par. 59, p. 224.
24. See his comment in Mahariṣ, *Shut Pe'ulat Ṣaddiq*, ibid.
25. This is expressing the idea that the name *Rūmiyah* does not allude to Rome, the capital of Italy. On the meaning of *Rūmiyah*, see above part 1, chap. 3, sect. 2.

rather it is the name of an aromatic plant and its correct spelling is Rūmiyah."[26] The name Rūmiyyah is found in *gittin* five times, four times with two *yod*s and once with one *yod.*

In an examination of the women's names in *gittin,* the following names were written with two *yod*s: Hadiyyah (הדייה), Ḥāliyyah (חאלייה), Ṣīniyyah (ציניייה), Tūrkiyyah (תורכייה), Turkiyyah (תרכייה). The name Rūmiyyah (רומייה) appears four times with two *yod*s and once with one *yod*. The name Ghāliyah (גאלייה) is found twice in *gittin*: once with two *yod*s, and once with one. Of note is that in *gittin* written in Ṣan'a, these names appear with two *yod*s, and it is reasonable to assume that the orthography with one *yod* elsewhere reflects a different pronunciation.

Differentiation between similar letters

For some Arabic names written with Hebrew letters one must add letters as guides to their proper reading, since there are not enough letters in Hebrew to represent all the Arabic consonants. The Yemenite Jews were meticulous about this. R. Yiḥye' Ṣāliḥ (Mahariṣ) wrote:

> If so, in this instance too, one must add a diacritic in 'Awāḍ, for if not so its meaning will be understood differently even to someone well versed in the Arabic language. This is similar to the case of the name *Naḍrah,* if one does not vocalize the *ṣade* the meaning will also be turned into something else. This is the reason for the custom of the Rishonim who add a diacritic to the emphatic letters in a *get,* so that this name should not look like another.[27]

R. Yiḥye' 'Amud wrote in a similar vein:

> The Arab names with emphatics such as the name 'Awāḍ or Naḍrah and the like must have a dot above those emphatic letters so that they will not take on a different meaning. And this was the custom of the Rishonim.[28]

Also when writing names in a *ketubbah,* the Jews of Yemen marked the emphatics or velar fricatives, such as נצרה (Naḍrah) or גזאל (Ghazāl) and גנא (Ghane').

26. Ben Shim'on, *Shem Ḥadash*, p. 251.
27. Mahariṣ, *Shut Pe'ulat Ṣaddiq*, 1, par. 105. The statement of Mahariṣ was quoted in Naddaf, *'Anaf Ḥayim, Even ha-Ezer*, par. 61, p. 229.
28. 'Amud, *Petaḥ ha-Ohel*, sect. 1, par. 29.

4. THE WRITING OF NAMES IN DIVORCE DECREES

Divorce decrees well serve as a source for the study of names, since, more than in any other type of document, meticulous care must be taken in the spelling of every name to ensure the validity of the *get*. A *get* generally provides a range of men's names: the name of the divorcing husband, the father of the woman being divorced, names of two witness, and the names of their fathers; a feminine name occurs in the *get* only as the name of the woman being divorced. Our analysis here will be based solely on the names of the parties being divorced.

This is the corpus of names of divorcing men:

> 'Amr; 'Awāḍ/'Awaḍ; Binyamin; Da'ūd; Hārūn/Harūn; Ḥasan; Ḥayim; Ibrāhīm/Ibrāhim/Ibrahīm; Imrān; Jamīl; Lewi; Manṣūr; Mas'ūd; Minis; Mūsa'; Nissim; Se'īd; Sabtān; Ṣāliḥ; Sālem; Shim'on; Shukr; Si'd; Sūlēmān/Slaymān; Ya'aqūb; Ya'īsh; Yehuda'/Yehudah/Yūda'; Yiḥye'; Yiṣḥāq, Yosef.

The corpus of the names of the divorcing men in order of declining frequency:

> Yiḥye'—29; Sālem—24; Se'īd—20; Yosef—13; Slaymān (including 1 Sūlēmān); Ibrāhim (including Ibrahīm–2, Ibrāhīm—1); Hārūn—8 (including 1 Harūn); Mas'ūd—5; Ṣāliḥ—5; Da'ūd—4; Ḥayim—4; Yehudah—4 (including 1 Yehuda', 1 Yūda'); Ya'aqūb—4; Mūsa'—3; Si'd—3; Shim'on—3; 2 times—'Awāḍ (including 1 'Awaḍ); Binyamin; Ḥasan; Manṣūr, Shukr; once—'Amr; 'Imrān; Jamīl; Lewi; Minis; Nissim; Sabtān; Yiṣḥāq; Ya'īsh.

The corpus of women's names among the divorcees:

> Amnah; 'Āfiyah; Badrah; Barūd; Berakhah; Bedūr; Fuḍah; Ghazāl; Ghaliyah/Ghaliyyah; Ghane; Ḥabībah; Hadiyyah; Ḥāliyah; Ḥamāmah; Ḥannah; Kādhiyyah; Lūlūwwah /Lūlūwah; Malkah; Miryam; Naḍrah; Narmah; Ni'meh; Qmāsh; Qurṭ; Rivqah; Rūmiyah /Rūmiyyah; Sa'dah; Ṣādqah; Se'īdah; Skaytaleh; Salāmeh; Sham'ah; Shams; Śimḥah/Simḥah; Ṣīniyyah; Tiranjah; Tūrkiyyah/Turkiyyah; Wardah; Zihrah.

Names of divorcees in descending order of frequency:

> Ḥamāmah—17; Zihrah—14; Ni'mah—13; Sa'dah—12; Se'īdah—11; Sham'ah—11; Miryam—10; Lūlūwah—8 (including 1 Lūlūwwah); Ghane—7; Ghazāl—5; Salāmeh—5; Rūmiyyah—5 (including 1 Rūmiyah); Badrah—4; 3 times—Berakhah, Ḥannah, Malkah, Śimḥah (including 1 Simḥah); Tiranjah; 2 times—Ghaliyyah (including 1 Ghaliyah); Hadiyyah; Wardah; Naḍrah;

Ṣīniyyah; Shams; Tūrkiyyah (including 1 Turkiyyah); once—Amnah; Bedūr; Barūd; Ḥāliyah; Ḥabībah; Kādhiyyah; Najrah; Skaytaleh; ʻĀfiyah; Fuḍah; Ṣadaqah; Qmāsh; Qurṭ; Rivqah.

CHAPTER TWO

SIGNATURES ON DOCUMENTS

Widespread among the eastern rabbis was the practice of ornate signatures on the documents they wrote. In documents from Yemen we find two types of signatures—regular and ornate.

1. THE FORM OF THE SIGNATURE

The Talmud tells of Amoraim who used a well-known form of signature on the *sheṭarot* they signed, even though halakhically one should sign a *get* with a clearly legible signature:

> Rabban Gamaliel said: [The rabbis] set a most important regulation, namely, that the witnesses should write their names in full in a *get*, to prevent abuses. But is not a mark enough? Did not Rav sign by drawing a fish, and R. Ḥanina by drawing a palm-branch, R. Ḥisda with a *Samek*, R. Hosha'ya with an *'Ayin*, and Rabbah son of R. Huna by drawing a sail? Regarding the rabbis, things are different, because everyone knows their marks. How did they make these signs known to begin with? In letters.[1]

These rabbis signed solely with symbols even in *sheṭarot*, since these symbols were understood by all. Rav's signature was *kavara*, which is a drawing of a fish.[2] R. Ḥanina's signature was *ḥaruta*, which is the drawing of a palm branch[3] or palm tree.[4] R. Ḥisda drew the letter

1. Gittin 36a; see also Gittin 87b and Bava Batra 161b. See also Jerusalem Talmud, Gittin 9, 8.
2. Bava Batra, ibid., Rashbam, incipit *kavvara*.
3. Gittin 36a, Rashi, incipit *ḥaruta*.
4. See Bava Batra, 161b, commentary of Rabbenu Gershom.

samekh. R. Hosha'ya drew the letter *'ayin*. And as his signature, Rabba bar R. Huna drew *makuta*, which is a ship's sail,[5] a ship's mast,[6] or a ship.[7] Some people offered reasons for the shape of these signatures. Rav used to eat fish and R. Ḥanina used to eat dates[8] or because Rav usually bought a large fish for Sabbath eve and R. Ḥanina used to buy fine dates.[9] R. Ḥisda signed with the letter *samekh* because it was the prominent letter in his name; the same was done by R. Hosha'ya when signing with an *'ayin*. Rabbah bar R. Huna often sailed the seas, so he signed with a symbol reflecting it.[10]

2. ORNATE SIGNATURES

Common among the eastern rabbis were ornate signatures. But unlike the Amoraim mentioned above, whose name did not appear in their signature, in the ornate signature of the eastern sages—through careful scrutiny—one can read their name, their father's name, and the family name.[11] R. Ḥayim Yosef David Azulai (the Ḥida) tells that the signature of his grandfather, R. Ḥayim Azulai, was in the shape of a ship, in commemoration of a miracle that had happened to him: "He is the rabbi, the ḥasid, our master elder, in memory of a true man, who arrived by boat in Kapotakia; they all debarked to dry land, leaving all their belongings on the boat. Immediately, a storm rose up, the boat broke apart, and everything went to the bottom of the sea, and they lost everything but their lives. In commemoration of this miracle of his being saved, he formed his signature in the shape of a boat, and I have seen his signature, OBM."[12] Other rabbis in the lineage of the Ḥida family signed ornately.[13]

5. Gittin 36a, Rashi, incipit *makuta.*
6. See Bava Batra 161b, Rashbam, incipit *makuta,* and the commentary of Rabbenu Gershom, ibid.
7. *Sefer ha-'Arukh* by R. Natan ben R. Yeḥi'el mi-Romi (Lublin, 1874), entry *makuta.*
8. See BB 161b, Rashbam, incipit with *Rav ṣiyyer kura.*
9. See Mahrashal, *Hokhmat Shelomo, Bava Batra* 161b.
10. See *Tosefot Ḥakhmei Angliya, Gittin,* ed. E. D. Pines (Jerusalem, 1968), p. 43.
11. For ornate signatures of rabbis on *ketubbot* in the eastern lands, see, for example, Eliyahu Bar Shalom, *Mishpat ha- ketubbah,* vol. 2 (Jerusalem, 1995), pp. 878–83; David Davidowitz, *Ha- ketubbah be-'Itturim* (New York, 1968), pp. 32, 36, 79, 81, 83. For the ornate signatures of the eastern sages on various letters, see documents in the collection of Eliyahu Elyachar, ed. by E. Ḥayim (Tel Aviv, 1971), pp. 37–38, 55–58. Islamic scholars also customarily signed with ornate signatures. I have a collection of documents of Islamic scholars in Yemen who signed in this manner.

On *sheṭarot*, in responsa, and *pisqei ha-din* (rabbinical rulings) from Yemen, some witnesses signed with a regular signature, while others added flourishes to theirs. Like their colleagues, the rabbis of the east, the sages of Yemen added flourishes to their name, their father's name, and the family name. However, on *gittin* they signed only with their regular signature, and usually listed their name and that of their father but not a family name.

Until the end of the seventeenth century, the sages of Yemen generally signed a *ketubbah* in the ordinary way. The ornate signature appeared toward the end of the first half of the eighteenth century[14] and became common in the second half.[15] The first to sign with embellished signatures were the rabbis of Ṣan'a: R. Shalom ben Yosef Bashāri, R. Yiḥye' ben Yosef Ṣāliḥ (Mahariṣ), and R. Yiḥye' ben David Mishriqi. The first signatures of R. Shalom ben Yosef Bashāri were on a *sheṭar* written on the back of a *ketubbah* dated 11 Tishri 5508 (4 Sep 1747); on the value of the dowry on 27 Nisan 5526 (6 Apr 1766); and a signature in the body of the *ketubbah*, on 7 Nisan 5528 (25 Mar 1768). The first signatures by R. Yiḥye' ben Yosef Ṣāliḥ (Mahariṣ) were on the *ketubbot* from 28 Av 5530 (19 Aug 1770); 17 Tevet 5534 (31 Dec 1773); 11 Nisan 5535 (11 Apr 1775). The first signatures of R. Yiḥye' ben David Mishriqi were on a *ketubbah* from 23 Iyyar 5548 (30 May 1788); on the value of the dowry on 7 Adar II 5551 (13 Mar 1791); and in a *ketubbah* dated 15 Av 5549 (7 Aug 1789). This practice occurred mainly among the Ṣan'a rabbis, but spread to other communities. For example, the signature of R. Yosef ben Ya'aqōv Ḥamdi, from Dār 'Amr, on a *ketubbah* from 23 Shevat 5649 (18

12. *Shem ha-Gedolim le-ha-Ḥida* (Jerusalem, 1992), *Ma'arekhet Gedolim*, entry מה' אברהם אזולאי, p. 9.

13. For the ornate signature of the Ḥida, see M. Benayahu, *Ha-Ḥida*—synagogue lecture in Jerusalem (Jerusalem, 1957), cover of the book and p. 16; idem, *Ha-Ḥida*, Part One, *Toledot Ḥayav* (Jerusalem, 1959), cover; Part Two, *Meḥqarim u-Meqorot*, cover. On additional rabbis in the Ḥida family, see ibid., pp. 307, 494, 503.

14. Yehudah Levi Naḥum noted that in the seventeenth century the Jews of Yemen began to use an embellished signature, and he called it "spider form". See Yehudah Levi Naḥum, *Ḥasifat Genuzim mi-Teiman* (Holon, 1971), p. 166; and see also Yiṣḥaq Raṣabi, *Tofes Ketubbot* (Bnei Brak, 1995), pp. 247–48. As for the explanation and decoding of the Mahariṣ's ornate signature, see ibid., pp. 148–49.

15. Some people wrote the sum of the dowry on the back of the *ketubbah* or in its lower margin, a week or a month or the like after the wedding, accompanied by the witnesses' signatures. In the ensuing, information will be provided also about the signatures on the value of the dowry.

Feb 1819); the signatures of R. Se'īd Waḥsh and R. Naḥum Ya'beṣ from 'Azīrat on a *ketubbah* dated 14 Sivan 5591 (26 May 1831); the signature of R. Yosef Ben Shalem from Bayt Salm on a *ketubbah* dated 29 Adar II 5600 (3 Apr 1840); and the signature of R. Yiḥye' ben Yosef from Dūmrān on a *ketubbah* from 14 Adar 5607 (2 Mar 1847).

In the eighteenth century, ornate signatures comprised some 35 percent of all the signatures on *ketubbot* and in the nineteenth century they made up about 65 percent. In the first half of the twentieth century there was a noticeable decline in embellished signatures to about 30 percent. Some of the outstanding Yemenite rabbis of the twentieth century did not customarily sign with ornate signatures, among them the members of the Ṣan'a Bet Din, R. Yiḥye' Qāfiḥ and R. Aharon Ha-Kohen, as for example on *ketubbot* from 15 Elul 5661 (30 Aug 1901); 21 Kislev 5666 (19 Dec 1905); 25 Adar 5666 (22 Mar 1906); and 8 Adar 5667 (22 Feb 1907). Even the president of the Bet Din and the chief rabbi in the first third of the twentieth century, R. Yiḥye' Yiṣḥaq Halevi, who still signed with an embellished signature, changed his style. Most of the Ṣan'a Bet Din members in the eighteenth and nineteenth centuries who signed wills, responsa, and *pisqei din* did so with ornate signatures. For example, a court rendering given in Ṣa'dah in northern Yemen in 1777, about *mezonot* for a widow and the inheritance of a firstborn, was signed by R. Yiḥye' ben Yosef Ṣāliḥ (Mahariṣ) with an embellished signature, whereas the *dayyanim* R. Shelomo ben Yeshu'ah and R. Shalom ibn Sa'adyah Ha-Kohen signed in ordinary style.[16] In a judgment rendered in the Ṣa'dah community in 1806, in the matter of construction in a joint courtyard, the *dayyan* R. Yiḥye' ben Yehudah Sa'di signed in the regular way, and the *dayyanim* R. Yiḥye' ben Dawid Mishriqi and R. Avraham ben Yiḥye' Ṣāliḥ with ornate signatures.[17] On the copy of the will of R. Yiḥye' Ṣāliḥ (Mahariṣ) in 5571 (21 Nov 1810), the *dayyan* Yosef ben Sālem Naqqāsh wrote an ordinary signature, while the *dayyanim* R. Yosef ben Shalom al-Qāreh and R. Avraham ben Aharon Manzali used embellished signatures;[18] on a judgment rendered in the Ṣa'dah community in the first half of the nineteenth century, in the matter of the marriage of a nursing woman, all the *dayyanim* signed with

16. See Aharon Gaimani, *"Bein Beit Din Ṣa'ada le-Beit Din Ṣan'a," Dinei Israel*, 20–21 (2000–2001): 316–17.

17. Gaimani, ibid., p. 322. On another *pesaq din* with their signatures, see ibid., p. 319.

18. For a photo of the signatures, see Aharon Gaimani, *"Sheṭar ha-Ṣeva'ah ha-Shalem shel Rabbi Yiḥye' Ṣāliḥ (Mahariṣ)," Pe'amim* 103 (5765): 138–39.

ornate signatures: R. Yosef ben Shalom Qāreh, R. Avraham ben Aharon Manzali, and R. Yiḥye' ben Slaymān Abyaḍ.[19] On the 1888 copy of the will of R. Slaymān Qārah all the *dayyanim* signed ornately: R. Yosef ben Dawid Manzali, R. Slay[mān] ben Sālem Ṣāliḥ, and R. Sālem Ḥibshūsh;[20] on a responsum by the Ṣan'a rabbis to the Ghayl community in 1895, on the matter of *aliyah* to Ereṣ Israel, the *dayyanim* signed with ornate signatures: R. Avraham ben Ṣāliḥ, R. Sulēmān ibn Sālem Ṣāliḥ, and R. [Yosef ben ...] Ṣāliḥ;[21] in a judgment given in the Ṣa'dah community in 1900, in the matter of a pregnant widow according to the renderings of Islam, R. Sālem ben Sālem Shemen signed with his regular signature, while the other rabbis' signatures were embellished: the *dayyan* R. Yiḥye' be Slay[mān] Qāfiḥ, R. Sulēmān ben Sālem Ṣāliḥ, R. Ḥayim ben Yosef Qoraḥ, and the *dayyan* Av[raham] ben Ṣāliḥ. The *dayyan* R. Yiḥye' Qāfiḥ also added a stamp next to his signature.[22]

3. SIGNATURE EMBELLISHMENTS

From the sixteenth to the eighteenth centuries, we find on documents from Yemen witnesses who embellished their signatures by adding small letters above and below the name. Such decorations are found also in documents from the Cairo Geniza. On these signature adornments, Mordecai Akiva Friedman wrote:

> These "embellishments" were written for various motives. Some were aimed at adding to one's pedigree and noted the names of ancestors or honorifics. Some people added a blessing or a verse or another noted phrase. Some repeated the same "embellishment" on all their signatures, while some noted a special event by a special "embellishment". Despite the differences between one signature and the next, obviously whoever signed with an "embellishment" considered it an addition of beauty and elegance. Generally, the tiny letters were written alternately above and below, that is, the first letter above, the second below, third above and so on, and they graced the signature with a pleasing appearance.[23]

19. See Gaimani, *Ṣa'dah–Ṣan'a*, pp. 315–16.
20. For a photograph of the signatures, see Gaimani, *Ṣa'dah–Ṣan'a*, p. 92.
21. For a photograph of the signatures, see Aharon Gaimani, *"Qehilat Gheil u-Qeshareha 'im Ṣan'a," Mi-Mizraḥ u-mi-Ma'arav* 8 (5768): 256.
22. See Gaimani, *Ṣa'dah–Ṣan'a*, pp. 320–21.
23. Mordecai Akiva Friedman, *"'Itturei Ḥotemim ve-Shittah Meyuḥeddet le-Ṣiyyun Ta'arikh," Tarbiẓ* 48 (1979): 160. On embellishments in *ketubbot* from the Cairo Geniza, see Mordecai Akiva Friedman, *Jewish Marriage in Palestine, A Cairo Geniza Study*, 2 (Tel Aviv and New York, 1980–1981), p. 185 [16]; 310 [32].

The embellishers of signatures in documents found in the Geniza used to write above and below the name initials abbreviating a verse, or the indication of a year, or names noted in *atbash* order.[24]

The practice of adding letters above the names of those signing documents as well as below them was customary in Yemen until the beginning of the eighteenth century. In the body of a *ketubbah* from Ṣan'a dated 16 Shevat 5296 (9 Jan 1536), the witnesses who signed were R. Avraham ben David and R. Avigad ben David; and on a *sheṭar* written on the back of the *ketubbah* are the signatures of the witnesses, R. Avigad ben David and R. Sa'adyah ben Avraham. Letters were written above and below the names of the witnesses. In the text of the *ketubbah* the letter ח (*ḥet*) appears above the first witness's name, and beneath it—the letters ט (*ṭet*) and ק (*qof*). Above and below the name of the second witness, the letter ש (*shin*) was written twice. On the back of the *ketubbah* appears the letter ש twice above and twice below the witnesses' name.[25]

On a *taqqanah* (regulation) that was written in 5367 (1607), in the town Ghunub in Qaryat Ḥame in the Raḥabe district, north of Ṣan'a, concerning settlement of a dispute within the community, there were thirteen signatories, whom we may assume were among the communal leaders, the rabbis, and the community activists. Most of the signatures are faded, but one can still see that the signers embellished their signatures with letters above and below. In five of the six signatures that can be made out, the letter ש (*shin*) appears four times: once above and below the name, once above and below the father's name. The sixth signature is adorned with the letters נבת (*nbt*) above the signature and the letters ויא (*wy'*) below it as well as with the initials of a verse from Psalms (25:13), נפשו בטוב תלין וזרעו יירש ארץ ("His soul shall abide in prosperity; and his seed shall inherit the land").[26]

In a *taqqanah* from 5459 (1699), dealing with matters of women's modesty in Ṣan'a, six of the sixteen rabbis from among the community leaders who signed it embellished their signatures with letters above and below their signing. In five cases the letter ש (*shin*) appears four times: once above and once below the name, and once above and once below the father's name. The signatories who acted in this manner are

24. Friedman, "'Itturei Ḥotemim," pp. 161–63.
25. Yehudah Levi Naḥum, *Ḥasifat Genuzim mi-Teiman*, File 61, *ketubbah* no. 1.
26. With permission of Sagiv Maḥfud, Rosh HaAyin. See Aharon Gaimani, "*Taqqanah Qedumah mi-Teiman mi-Shenat 5367 (1607)*," *Tema* 11 (5771): 95.

Shalom ben 'Amram Halevi, Moshe ben Sa'adyah, Yehudah ben Yeshū'ah, Shelomo ben Abba Shalom, Se'īd ben Yosef Ghiyāt. In the signature of Sa'adya' ben Yosef the letter *shin* appears above and below his name; above his father's name is the letter נ (*nun*) and below the name the letter ע (*'ayin*). Perhaps, the resolution of נ"ע, the initials for *nuḥo 'eden* (He should find peace in Eden).[27]

In a seventeenth-century document registering a debt between two men, three witnesses signed: R. Shelomo ben *'"m* [for *adoni mori*, my master, my teacher] Sa'adyah *ysh"l*, R. Shelmo ben Sa'adya' al-Manzali *ysh"l*, R. Zekharya' ben Yosef Ha-Kohen *ysh"l*. The first and the second witnesses embellished their signatures with the letters ש. Above the name of each witness and above the father's name and beneath it the letter ש was written four times, twice above the name and twice below it.[28]

In a seventeenth-century *ketubbah*, from Bīr al-Darb, the first witness signed his name as Zekharya' ben *kmh"r* Sa'adya' ben *'"m* Zekharya'. Written above and below the witness's name is the letter ש four times, twice above the name and twice beneath it; above the father's name נתב (*ntb*) appears and ויא (*wy'*) below it, as noted above they are an acronym of the verse "His soul shall abide in prosperity; and his seed shall inherit the land." Written above the grandfather's name is תנצ (*tnṣ*) and beneath it is בה (*bh*), which make up the initials תנצב"ה (*tanṣeba"h*).[29]

On a *ketubbah* from 6 Nisan 5463 (12 Mar 1703), from the town Sa'adiyah Khārij Dhamār, the witnesses signed: R. Sa'adya' ben Me'oded *ysh"l*, R. Yūda' ibn Zekharya' Ha-Kohen *ysh"l*. Above the name of the first witness and above the father's name, and below them, the letter ש is written four times, twice above the name and twice below it. Also written above the name of the father, Me'oded, was נע"ג (*n'"g*), the initials of *"nuḥo 'eden gan,"* and its purpose is to indicate the father's death.[30]

On a *ketubbah*, dated 16 Tammuz 5477 (14 June 1717), from Mirwāgah, the witnesses who signed were R. Avraha ben Sa'adya' *ysh"l* and R. Sa'adya' ben Yehshu'a *ysh"l*. Written above the name of the sec-

27. Aharon Gaimani, *"Taqqanah Qedumah li-Ṣeni'ut Nashim be-Ṣan'a," Tarbiẓ* 74 (5765): 445–46, especially p. 447.

28. Naḥum, *Ḥasifat Genuzim mi-Teiman*, File 63, no. 4.

29. By permission of Sagiv Maḥfud, Rosh HaAyin.

30. Naḥum, *Mif'al Ḥasifat Ginzei Teiman*, File 61, *ketubbah* no. 3.

ond witness and above his father's name, as well as beneath them, is the letter ש, twice above the name and twice below it.[31]

4. ADDITIONS TO A SIGNATURE

Accompanying the signatures were various additions. Before the name, they usually added the word הצעיר (*ha-ṣaʿīr;* lit., the young) or abbreviated as 'הצ (*ha-ṣ'*), which is a byname of modesty, while some used the Aramaic זעיר (*zaʿīr,* the small), for the same purpose. Other prefixes are *hṣby*, for *ha-ṣaʿīr be-alfei Yehudah* (least among the clans of Judah) or *ha-ṣaʿīr be-alfei Yisra'el* (the least of the clans of Israel), קה"ק *(qhq)* for *qal ha-qalim* (the most insignificant), ער"ה (*ʿrḥ)* for *ʿafar raglei ḥakhamim* (dust at the feet of the Sages, i.e., of no value). Following the writing of the name, they added: יש"ל *(ysh"l)* for *yinon shemo le-ʿolam yehi/yeḥi shemo le-ʿolam* (May his name last forever);[32] יצ"ו (*yṣ"v*) for *yishmero ṣuro ve-yoṣero;*[33] ס"ט (*sin ve-ṭin*), which is an expression of humility, meaning "mire and mud," on the basis of the Aramaic *targum* of Isaiah 57:20, "whose waters toss up mire and mud," Aramaic *"ve-okhrin mohi sin ve-ṭin."*[34]

As for the additions after the name, the Yemenite rabbis usually wrote two acronyms. The common ones are יצ"ו, ס"ט, and יש"ל. In isolated instances they used the following: נו"א (נבזה וחדל אישים, "the most despised and worthless of persons"); יזיי"א (יראה זרע יאריך ימים אמן, "May he see offspring and have long life"); נר"ו (נטריה רחמנא ופרקיה, "The Merciful one will protect him and save him" or an acronym for נצרו רם ונישא, "his offspring is elevated and lofty");[35] שצ"ו (שומרו צורו ויוצרו, *shṣw;* "His Protector, his Rock, and his Creator"); ליי"ש (לעד יינון שמו, *lysh;* "forever Yinon is his name"); שי"ל (שמו יהי לעולם, *shyl;* "May his name be forever");[36] הי"ו (*hy"v*, ה' ישמרהו ויחייהו, "May the Lord pro-

31. Sasoon Collection, no. 1069.

32. See Yehudah Ratzaby, *Oṣar Leshon ha-Qodesh she-li-Bnei Teiman* (Tel Aviv, 1978), p. 123, entry יש"ל. Found in the Geniza is יהי שמו לעולם (*yehi shemo le-ʿolam*). See Mordechi Akiva Friedman, *Ribbui Nashim be-Yisra'el: Meqorot Ḥadashim mi-Genizat Qahīr* (Tel Aviv, 1986), p. 180.

33. Some read this as *yishmereihu ṣuro ve-go'alo.* See Raṣabi, *Tofes Ketubbot*, p. 26.

34. Y. Ratzaby, *"S"Ṭ," Haaretz, Tarbut ve-Sifrut,* 9 Oct 1963. Some Yemenite rabbis wrote the full expression *"sin ve-ṭin"*; see Yehudah Levi Naḥum, *Mi-Ṣefunot Teiman* (Tel Aviv, 1987), p. 247. I have a photograph of a Yemenite manuscript whose copyist had the same custom.

35. Ratzaby, *Oṣar Leshon ha-Qodesh*, p. 187, entry נר"ו.

36. Ibid., p. 274, entry שי"ל.

tect him and sustain him"). Also used were acronyms alluding to the death of the witness's father: נע"ג (נוחו גן עדן, *n'"g*; "May he find rest in Eden"); רי"ת (רוח ה' תניחנו, *ry"t*; "May the spirit of the Lord guide him"); זלה"ה (זיכרונו זכרו לחיי העולם הבא, *zlh"h*; "May his memory be for the World to Come").

With regard to the expression R. 'Amram Qoraḥ, the last chief rabbi of the Yemenite Diaspora, wrote to his acquaintance in Israel Yehudah Levi Naḥum: "Concerning your query as to the way in which a few of the early rabbis used to write at the end of their signatures *s"ṭ*, I heard from some of them that these are initials for *sin ṭin*, the transla[tion] for *refesh ve-ṭiṭ* [mud and mire]."[37]

Even in a very early period, the Jews of Yemen used to add the expression *s"ṭ* to their name. Some twelfth-century documents from the Cairo Geniza were written by Yemenite personages who added the acronym *s"ṭ*[38] to their signature.[39]

There were some Yemenite rabbis who, by adding the acronym *s"ṭ* to their signature, understood the meaning as "mud [and] mire" [=the lowly]. In a *ketubbah* from 'Ãthayin, dated 24 Adar II 5692 (1 Apr 1932), the witness signed *Ha-Ṣ[a'ir]* Se'īd Ma'ūḍah סי"ט (*sy"ṭ*), which proves that he understood it as "mud [and] mire." Some witnesses wrote this acronym with the addition of a ו (*w*), so that it meant "mud and mire." For example, in a *ketubbah* from the 'Imrān community from 8 Adar 5687 (10 Feb 1927), the witness signed his name ornately, *Ha-Ṣa'ir* Pinḥas [ib]n Hārūn Ha-Kohen *ys"l sw"ṭ*; on a *ketubbah* from the village of Wādi Sharamāt in northern Yemen, dated 16 Sivan 5691 (1 June 1931), the chief rabbi of Sa'adah, R. Ya'beṣ signed his name as יעב"ץ בכמ"ו יעקוב סי"ט ; on a *ketubbah* from the village of Shaṭ, from 8 Nisan 5709 (7 Apr 1949), a witness signed his name as Ṣāliḥ ibn Ibrāhīm *sw"ṭ*. There is also a signature that includes the addition of a *yod,* סי"ט (*syw"ṭ*). On a *ketubbah* dated 24 Adar II 5684 (30 Mar 1924), a witness signed his name with embellishment, *Ha-Ṣa'ir* Avraham [ib]n Shelomo al-Ṣabari *yṣ"w syw"ṭ*.

R. Yiṣḥaq Raṣabi wrote that the custom of adding *s"ṭ* is not old in Yemen, and the Yemenites followed the Sephardim in this matter.[40]

37. Naḥum, *Mif'al Ḥasifat Ginzei Teiman*, File 71, 99a.

38. E. Strauss, *"Massa le-Hodu (Mikhtav me-'Aden le-Miṣrayim bi-Shenat 1153) la-Sefirah ha-Noṣrit), Zion* 4 (1939): 222.

39. See E. Strauss, *Toledot ha-Yehudim bi-Miṣrayim u-ve-Surya*, 3 (Jerusalem, 1970), pp. 32, 62, 67, 77.

40. See Raṣabi, *Tofes Ketubbot*, p. 248.

Perhaps he means that at some unspecified time, the Yemenite rabbis ceased writing *s"ṭ*, and the custom was revived in the last third of the eighteenth century; this same conclusion can be drawn from the Yemenite *ketubbot* as shown by the illustrations mentioned here.

Presented here in chronological order are examples from *ketubbot* that include all the phrases mentioned above. In a *ketubbah*, dated 2 Ḥeshvan 5419 (19 Oct 1658), from the town of Ḍūwāle', one of the witnesses signed in an ordinary way: *Ha-Ṣa'ir* Yūda' ibn Yiṣḥāq Sha'tāl *nw"'*; on a *ketubbah* from the village of Delāj, dated 6 Tammuz 5493 (8 June 1733), one of the witnesses signed as regular: Shukr ibn Se'īd Ashar'abi *shy"l*; on a *ketubbah* from the Radā' community, from 13 Tishri 5514 (11 Oct 1753), the witnesses signed in the ordinary way: *Ha-Ṣa'ir* Sa'adya' ben Ḥoṭer *Ry"t*, *Ha-Ṣa'ir* 'Oded *k'"m* Shelomo *zlh"h n'"g*; on a *ketubbah* from the village of Qaṣbat Ḍalayme; dated 19 Av 5517 (5 Aug 1757), one of the witnesses signed in the ordinary way: Sa'adya' ben R. Ḥayim 'Abāhil *n'"g*; a *ketubbah* from the Ṣan'a community, from 28 Av 5530 (19 Aug 1770), bears the ornate signature of R. Yiḥye' Ṣāliḥ: *Ha-Ṣa'ir* Yiḥye' ben Yosef Ṣāliḥ *yṣ"w s"ṭ*; on a *ketubbah* from the village of Ma'zub, dated 27 Elul 5576 (20 Sep 1816), one of the witnesses signed in the regular way: Sulēmān ibn Sālem *ly"sh*; a Ṣan'a *ketubbah*, from 16 Adar I 5616 (21 Feb 1856) was signed by R. Ḥayim Qoraḥ with an ornate signature: *Ha-Ṣa'ir* Ḥayim ibn Yosef Qoraḥ *yzyy"' s"ṭ*; on a *ketubbah* from Ṣan'a, dated 11 Ḥeshvan 5645 (1 Nov 1884), R. Yiḥye' Qāfiḥ signed in the usual manner: *Ha-Ṣa'ir* Yiḥye' ben Sulē[mān] al-Qāfiḥ *yṣ"w*; a *ketubbah* from Ṣan'a from 5 Adar 5666 (2 Mar 1906), was signed by Chief R. Yiḥye' Yiṣḥaq Halewi with an embellished signature: *Ha-Ṣa'ir* Yiḥye' ben Musa' Yiṣḥāq *yṣ"w s"ṭ;* on a *ketubbah* from the Kawkabān community, dated 13 Tammuz 5666 (6 July 1906), one of the witnesses signed an ordinary signature: *Ha-Ṣa'ir* Avraham *shṣ"w* ibn Yiḥye' al-Jarashi *s"ṭ*; on a *ketubbah* from 18 Iyyar 5671 (16 May 1911), from the Maḥwīt community, one of the witnesses signed by proxy: *Ha-Ṣ[a'ir]* Yeshu'a ibn Sālem al-Ḥarāzi *nr"w*; on a *ketubbah* from the Ḥāfid community, from 19 Av 5672 (2 Aug 1912), one of the witnesses signed with the common style signature: *Ze'ir* Sālem ibn *m"w* Ya'aqūb *s"ṭ*. On a *ketubbah* from the Manākhe community, dated 15 Sivan 5676 (16 June 1916), the *shadar* R. Shelomo Naddāf signed as *Ha-Ṣa'ir* Shelomo ben Avraham al-Naddāf *hy"w s"ṭ*. In a *ketubbah* from the village Qafle, from 2 Adar I 5681 (10 Feb 1921), one of the witnesses signed in the ordinary manner: *hṣb"y* Yiḥye' ibn '"' [א"א, *adoni avi* (my master, my father)] *mw"r* Yiḥye' 'Umaysi *yṣ"w s"ṭ*; in a *ketubbah* from the Radā' community, dated 9 Shevat 5706 (11.1946), one of the witnesses signed an ordinary signature:

'r"ḥ Yehudah ibn *l'"'* Da'ād 'Ūrqubi; on a *ketubbah* from Madīd, from 13 Elul 5707 (28 Aug 1947), one of the witnesses signed the usual way: *qh"q, 'r"ḥ* Yosef ibn Yiḥye' Ḥadād *ysh"l.*

Ketubbot from Yemen inform us that until the end of the eighteenth century, they appended mainly *ysh"l*. In that century there were also a few with *yṣ"w*. From the nineteenth century on the most common combinations were *yṣ"w* and *s"ṭ*, which almost totally replaced the other acronyms. This conclusion is in keeping with a 1699 *taqqanah* from Ṣan'a, signed by sixteen rabbis of the community. The acronyms used by these rabbis, in descending order of frequency, were *ysh"l, yṣ"w, n'"g.*[41]

Of interest is the signature of R. Sālem ben Yiḥye' Ḥibshūsh, head of the Yeshiva ha-Gedolah in Ṣan'a, who signed in an ornate manner. He usually appended to his signature יצ"ו ס"ט,[42] and in two *ketubbot* in place of ס"ט he wrote סי"ח, the initials of his name.[43]

Some believe that the witness signing the *ketubbah* must append to his signature the word עד (*'ed*; witness), even though this is not imperative for the validity of the *ketubbah.*[44] The Yemenite Jews did not usually add it. Those *ketubbot* in which we do find that the witnesses added the word *'ed* after their signature do not come from the big cities.[45]

In summation, embellishment of letters in Yemenite rabbis' signatures occurred mainly up to the beginning of the eighteenth century. Then followed the phenomenon of ornate signatures, which became increasingly common in the nineteenth century. As for combinations of words added as acronyms with the signature, until the end of the eighteenth century the term added was principally *ysh"l*, and from the nineteenth century on the dominant acronym was *yṣ"v s"ṭ*.

41. Gaimani, *"Taqqanah li-Ṣeni'ut Nashim,"* p. 446, and photo of the *taqqanah*, p. 447. On the matter of the *taqqanah*, see the previous section.
42. See, for example, *ketubbot* from 7 Adar 5622 (7 Feb 1862); 15 Av 5630 (14 Aug 1870); 24 Tevet 5635 (1 Jan 1875).
43. *Ketubbot* from 26 Iyyar 5760 (25 May 1900); 9 Shevat 5663 (6 Feb 1903).
44. Shmuel Eliezer Stern, *Ketubbah ke-Hilkhatah*, chap. 8, sections 21–22 (Bene Brak, 1996), p. 39.
45. See, for example, a *ketubbah* from Mirwāgah, dated 5 Kislev 5631 (29 Nov 1870); a *ketubbah* from Ṣaf'a, dated 3 Nisan 5633 (2 Apr 1873); a *ketubbah* from Muḍmār, from 16 Adar 5634 (5 Mar 1874).

EMBELLISHED SIGNATURES

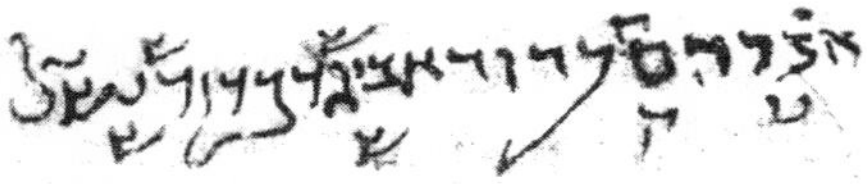

16 Shevat 5296 (9 Jan 1536)
Avraham ben David, Avigad ben David, *ysh"l*
Location of signing: Ṣan'a

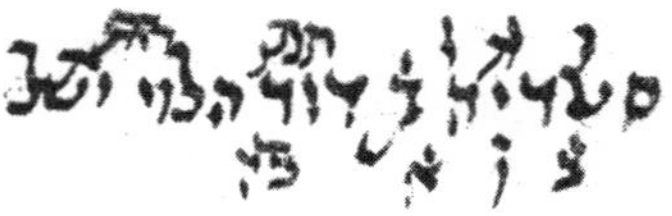

9 Nisan 5453 (15 Apr 1693)
Sa'adyah ben David Halevi *ysh"l*
Location of signing: Ṣan'a

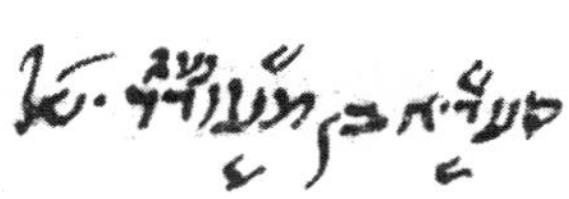

6 Nisan 5463 (12 Mar 1703)
Sa'adyah ben Me'oded *ysh"l*
Location of signing: Sa'adiyah Khārij Dhamār

ORNATE SIGNATURES

28 Av 5530 (19 Aug 1770)
Ha-Ṣa'ir Yiḥye' ben Yosef Ṣāliḥ *yṣ"t s"ṭ*
Location of signing: Ṣan'a

12 Shevat 5589 (17 Jan 1829)
Ha-Ṣa'ir Yosef ibn Shalom al-Qāreh *yṣ"v s"ṭ*
Location of signing: Ṣan'a

10 Tishri 5625 (13 Oct 1864)
Ha-Ṣa'ir Yiḥye' ibn Shukr al-Badīḥi *yṣ"v s"ṭ*
Location of signing: Kawkabān

CHAPTER THREE

ENCODING NAMES

The encoding of names by Yemenite poets and writers was designed to stimulate thought and intellectual effort in the reader.

1. ENCODING IN THE POETRY OF RABBI SHALOM SHABAZI

R. Shalom Shabazi, the greatest of the Yemenite poets, lived and worked in southern Yemen in the seventeenth century. He is buried in the city of Ta'īz in south Yemen,[1] and his grave-site used to be visited by many Jews in Yemen. He is one of the most outstanding Yemenite rabbis in the fields of Torah, philosophy, and Kabbalah, and he wrote a number of works, the salient being *Ḥemdat Yamim* on the weekly Torah readings and the *haftarah*. He is, however, best known for his poetry, and in that genre there is no one greater than he among Yemenite Jewry. Thus far, we know of 800 poems, which comprise about one quarter of all Jewish poetic works in Yemen. He composed his poems in three languages: Hebrew, Aramaic, and Arabic. His corpus consists mainly of religious poetry, and his poems are among the most famous of the works of Yemenite poets.[2]

R. Shalom Shabazi, like many other Jewish poets, alluded to his name in an acrostic in his poems. This system, used extensively by R. Shabazi, assisted in identifying him as the author of the poem and even helped in arranging the stanzas within the poems, for at times they were

1. Some 250 km south of the capital, Ṣan'a. See Maqḥafi, p. 69.
2. Yehudah Ratzaby, *Toratan she-li-Bnei Teiman* (Qiryat Ono, 1994), pp. 51–55.

shifted by mistake.[3] On Shabazi's habit of indicating his name in his poems, Y. Ratzaby wrote:

> From all the acrostics, he liked most his family name "al-Shabazi", and it was used most frequently. Next comes *"Mashta',"* which R. Shalom Shabazi frequently attached to the word *mekhuneh* (called). We understand that *mashta* is a byname ... In his poems, the poet often refers to his father Yosef, but not to his grandfather or earlier ancestors. In one of the heretofore unpublished poems, he does refer to his grandfather, Avigad, as well.[4] R. Shalom Shabazi customarily notes his sons, Shim'on and Yehudah, but not his daughters—although in one acrostic he does cite the name of his daughter Miriam.[5]

R. Shalom Shabazi was the only poet who used the name *al-Shabazi* in his acrostics. In contrast, the byname Mashta' was used by several poets.

Here are a few examples from his poems in which he presented an acrostic of his name in different forms.[6] The acrostic שלם בן יוסף אלשבזי משתא appears in a *piyyuṭ* beginning with שבח נזכיר לצורנו, וננעים שיר שפתינו,[7] and in a *piyyut* opening with שמחו ביום שבת ילדי גבירה.[8] The acrostic שלם בירב יוסף אלשבזי משתא occurs in a *piyyuṭ* that starts with שחתי לעפר מיגוני, ושינה נדדה מעיני.[9] The acrostic שלם בירב יוסף משתא is found in a *piyyuṭ* that begins שובו שובבים וחכו לצור ישעכם.[10] The acrostic שלם בירב יוסף אלשבזי appears in the *piyyuṭ* that begins with שחר אהלל צור ואעיר כל נרדם.[11] The acrostic שבזי משתא occurs in a poem opening with שישי גברת, שמחי ללבי.[12]

---

3. Yehudah Ratzaby, *Shirei R. Shalom Shabazi—Bibliografia* (Tel Aviv, 2003), introduction, p. 9. This applies to other poets among the Yemenites. See David Yellin, *"Ginzei Teiman," Hashiloach* 2 (1897): 148.
4. Joseph Tobi, *"Yedi'ot Hadashot le-Toledot R. Shalom Shabazi,"* in *Shalom ben Yosef Shabazi, Qoveṣ bi-Mlot 350 Shana le-Holadeto*, ed. Joseph Tobi (n.p., Nisan 1972), p. 35; cf. above, part 1, chap. 4, sect. 1.
5. Ratzaby, *Shirei R. Shalom Shabazi—Bibliografia*, introduction, pp. 14–15.
6. The identification numbers of the poems are according to the bibliography prepared by Prof. Yehudah Ratzaby for the poems of R. Shalom Shabazi, which contains 744 items.
7. Ratzaby, *Shirei R. Shalom Shabazi—Bibliografia*, p. 54, no. 645.
8. Ibid., p. 58, no. 703.
9. Ibid., p. 56, no. 674.
10. Ibid., p. 55, no. 654.
11. Ibid., p. 58, no. 673.
12. Ibid., p. 56, no. 679.

There are also instances in which R. Shalom Shabazi interpolates in an acrostic his name and that of his father by writing שׂ instead of ס, writing שׂאלם in place of סאלם, יושׂף instead of יוסף.[13] As an illustration, the acrostic שאלם appears in a poem beginning שג'אני עוהג'י אלגזלאן.[14] The acrostic שלם יושף occurs in the poem opening with שובי בתום ידידה,[15] the poem beginning שועת גברת יה שמע כי חרדה,[16] and in the poem starting שושבינים בואו נחזה הוד רעיה.[17] The acrostic שלם בן יושף is found in a poem opening with שוכן שחקים חון עלי עם נבחרו.[18] In the introduction to his work *Ḥemdat Yamim* he created an acrostic with the opening lines, שלם בן יושף הקטן.[19]

Sometimes, he wrote the acrostic with the addition of descriptors in the family lineage. For example, we find the addition of י"צ (*y"ṣ)* which means ישמרו צורו ("His Rock shall protect him"), in the acrostic שלם י"צ, and it appears in the poem beginning with the words שלום לך רבי ממלאכי מעלה.[20] The addition ש"צ [*sh"ṣ*], meaning שמרו צורו ("His Rock protected him"), appears in the acrostic שלם בן יוסף ש"צ as well as in the *piyyuṭ* starting with שבח אל חי, אשר ברא לכל חי[21] and in the poem beginning with the words שושן עמקים, חלי לשוכן שחקים.[22] The addition שה"צ (*shh"ṣ*), meaning שמרו הצור ("The Rock has protected him"), occurs in the acrostic שלם שה"צ and is found in the poem opening with שלום רב לכל החבורה.[23] The initials רי"ת (*ry"t*) seen in the acrostic

13. Other poets did the same. For example, R. Se'īd ben Merḥav, who was a *dayyan* in Aden, sent a letter in 1153 to his acquaintance in Fustat, Egypt. In the poetic beginning of the letter, he indicated his name at the start of the verses שעיד בן מרחב חזק יצו (Joseph Tobi, *Shirei Avraham ben Ḥalfon* [Tel Aviv, 1991], p. 17; Yehudah Ratzaby, *Shirat Teiman ha-Ivrit* [Tel Aviv, 1989], p. 105). R. Se'īd Manṣūra, one of the nineteenth-century Yemenite rabbis, indicated his name in an acrostic, in a poem beginning with the words שמעתי שיר מכנף ארץ, as S'id Manṣūra (*Shirei Shabazi* [Maqaytin], pp. 521–22).
14. Ratzaby, *Shirei Shabazi—Bibliografia*, p. 55. n. 650.
15. Ibid., p. 55, no. 655.
16. Ibid., p. 55, no. 663.
17. Ibid., p. 56, no. 669.
18. Ibid., p. 55, no. 659.
19. *Ḥemdat Yamim* of R. Shalom Shabazi (Jerusalem, 1977), Introduction.
20. Ratzaby, *Shirei Shabazi—Bibliografia*, p. 56, no. 682.
21. Ibid., p. 54, no. 640.
22. Ibid., p. 56, no. 670.
23. Ibid., p. 56, no. 683.

שלם יוסף רי"ת stand for רוח ה' תניחנו ("May the spirit of God guide us") and allude to his father's having passed away; they occur in the *piyyuṭ* beginning שבח אל חי, מרומם על כל שבחים.[24] The addition הקטן (*ha-qaṭan*, the small) to the acrostic שלם משתא הקטן is an expression of humility and is found in the *piyyuṭ* starting שומרי מחיצות, עורו עד חצות.[25] The insertion נע"א (*n''g*) in the acrostic שלם יושף נע"א stands for "נוחו עדן אמן ("He should find peace in Eden"), and appears in the poem opening with שמעתי קול תוף וגם [נ"א וקול] מחול.[26] R. Shalom Shabazi used additional bynames in acrostics, such as for his sons Shim'on and Yehudah and for his daughter Miriam.[27] For example, the opening words and the acrostic אבו שמעון (father of Shim'on) occur in the poem beginning אבו שמעון יקול יא מזור אלעין.[28] The acrostic אבו שמעון אלשבזי. appears in the poem beginning with the words אבטית יא גריב, מא דֹא גרא לך.[29] The acrostic אבו יהודה שבזי (father of Yehudah Shabazi) is found in the poem opening with המעולה על כרובים איומה.[30] The acrostic אבו יהודה שבזי משתא occurs in the poem beginning אלא תקארן זחל ומשתרי ומריך.[31] The acrostic אבו שמעון ויהודה שבזי is found in the poem opening with אלבס אלנור אמיר אלכואכב ואלזהרה.[32] The acrostic אבו מרים ויהודה שבזי is seen in the poem starting with the words אבתדא אלקול ברבן לא סואהו.[33]

Sometimes he alluded to his name at the end of a poem. For example, in the poem beginning אני הדל, ועזי עיר ומגדל, based upon the acrostic אלשבזי משתא, he hinted at his personal name in the final stanza with the words ושי"ן למ"ד ומי"ם בשמי ילמד / זכות עלי / ועל חברת זקיני[34] In the poem beginning אסבח כאלקי, based on the *alef-bet* acrostic אלשבזי משתא, he wrote his name and that of his father in the last stanza with the words ואם תדע בשם זה המחבר / שמו שלום ויוסף יולדהו.[35] In a poem

24. Ibid., p. 54, no. 641.
25. Ibid., p. 55, no. 661.
26. Ibid., p. 59, no. 721.
27. Yehudah Ratzaby, *"Rabbi Shalem Shabazi ve-Shirato," Sefunot*, 9 (1965): 135–37.
28. Ratzaby, *Shirei R. Shalom Shabazi—Bibliografia*, p. 16, no. 13.
29. Ibid., p. 17, no. 17.
30. Ibid., p. 22, no. 104.
31. Ibid., p. 25, no. 162.
32. Ibid., p. 25, no. 169.
33. Ibid., p. 17, no. 23.
34. *Shirei Shabazi* [Maqaytin], p. 25.
35. *Shirei Shabazi* [Maqaytin], p. 31.

opening with the words אקוה ישעך אל ממעונים, he alluded to his name, while he wrote his father's and his grandfather's name at the end of the poem, as follows:

ושם הקל אשר דבר בשיר זה / הלא יוזכר באותיות ספורים.
שלש מאות ספור הוסף שלשים / וקח עתה לארבעים גמורים.[36]
ושם אבי יהוסף בן אביגד/ יחיהו אשר יצר יצורים.[37]

Additional allusions to his name are found in the byname Ibn al-Mu'llem, which perhaps hints to his father having been a teacher and in אלמשתאי חבר אליהוד, which means "Mashtai a *ḥakham* of the Jews," which he used in acrostics in his poems.[38]

The bynames famous in his poems are אלשבזי and משתא. אלשבזי alludes to his place of residence, שבז (Shabaz), while משתא (Mashta') is an allusion to his family name, which is linked to a miraculous deed that occurred to one of the family forefathers. This is what R. Shabazi wrote in the colophon to a commentary on the *haftarot*:

שַמָש סופרים, הצעיר שלם בא"מ [=בן אבא מורי]
יוסף בא"מ [=בן אדוני מורי] אביגד ב"א [=בן אדוני] חלפון,
מכונה על שם עירינו אלשבזי ,ועל שם משפחתי מן בני משתא

"Servant of scribes, the humble Shalem ben Abba Mori Yosef ben Adoni Mori Avigad ben Adoni Ḥalfon, called by the name of our city al-Shabazi, and for my family name from the Mashta' clan".[39]

In one of his poems, he indicated his name with the words מכונה לבן משתא ("called a member of the Mashta' clan"),[40] and in the poem

36. An allusion to his name Shalem.

37. Ratson Halevi, *Shirat Yisra'el be-Teiman*, vol. 1 (Qiryat Ono, 1998–2003), p. 43.

38. Ratzaby, *"Shabazi ve-Shirato,"* pp. 137–38; idem, *Shirei R. Shalom Shabazi—Bibliografia*, p. 61.

39. S. Shabazi, *Peirush ha-Haftarot le-R. Shalom Shabazi*, in *Torah Qeduma*, ed. R. Yoav Pinhas Halevi, vol. 2 (Bet Dagan, 2001), p. 130. On the bynames Shabazi and Mashta that were used by R. Shalom Shabazi, see the statement by Prof. Yehudah Ratzaby, above part 2, chap. 1, sect. 2. For an explanation of the byname Mashta, see above part 2, chap. 3, sect. 3.

40. Other sages in his family used the byname Mashta. For example, the poet R. Yosef ben Yisrael (about him, see below sect. 4), apparently from the Shabazi family, in poems usually used an acrostic of his and his father's name, while he used the byname Mashta a few times, from example in the *piyyut* beginning אם אשמרה שבת נפשי שמורה and in the poem starting with יקול אלשאער אלנאטים. See *Shirei Shabazi* [Maqaytin], pp. 410–12, 593–94. R. Yisra'el ben Yosef Mashta copied the

beginning with שמעו קול שופר, R. Shalom wrote פתור שין בית זאן יוד ידידי כינויי.[41]

2. THE ATBASH CIPHER

Atbash is a cipher in which one substitutes the first letter of the Hebrew alphabet, *alef*, with the last letter, *tav*, the second letter, *bet*, with the next to last letter *shin*, *gimel* with *resh*, and so on with other letters in order.[42] In the Bible we find use of the *atbash* letters, *alef–tav*, *bet–shin*, and so on. For example, Jeremiah's prophecy referring to Babylon (51:41) is an *atbash* cipher: "How has Sheshakh been captured, the praise of the entire world has been taken." The word ששך (Sheshakh) in *atbash* cipher is בבל (Bavel; Babylon).[43] In Jeremiah's prophecy (51:1), we read, "Behold, I will raise up against Babylon and against them that dwell in Lev-Qamai (לב קמי)." Lev-Qamai in the *atbash* cipher is *Kasdim* (כסדים).[44]

David Yellin remarks on the custom of Yemenite poets to use *atbash*:

> The openings of stanzas are generally with letters spelling their author's names, but these names are written explicitly by some, though others substitute *atbash* or the like for them, such as *ḥazmaq* (חזמק) in place of Se'īd (סעיד), *bakhyaṣ* instead of Shelomoh (שלמה), and *qfmaq* (קפמק) instead of Dawid (דויד). On the whole, we have seen that [the authors] wanted the readers to know by whom these words were written, for beside the combinations of the letters at the beginning of stanzas, there are those who remind the reader, at the end of their poem, to pay attention to these combinations ... yet these mach-

Tikhlāl in 1642; see *Tiklal Mashta–Shabazi*, photo edition, published by Binyamin Odded-Yefet (Jerusalem, 1986), v. 1, p. 1. Another rabbi belonging to the family, who copied the Midrash *"Ḥemdat Yamim"* in 1983 SEL [5432 AM/1672], noted his name in the colophon משה בן אברהם הידוע מן בני משתא (Moshe ben Avraham known as from the sons of Mashta). In the nineteenth century, R. Yiḥye' ben Sālem Mashta copied a collection of the laws of ritual slaughter; about him see below in the next section.

41. *Shirei Shabazi* [Maqaytin], p. 729.
42. See, for example, Shabbat 104a.
43. See also Jeremiah 25:26, "The king of Sheshakh shall drink, after them."
44. The rabbis and biblical exegetes decoded this system. See, for example, *Oṣar Midrashim*, collected and edited by Julius D. Eisenstein (1915), entry *"Lamed-bet Middot ba-Aggadah,"* p. 269. See also Rashi, Radak, and Meṣudat David on the verses noted. On the use of *atbash* in Jeremiah and Lamentations, see the comprehensive study by Aharon Demsky, *Yedi'at Sefer be-Yisra'el ba-Et ha-Atiqah* (Jerusalem, 2012).

inations have helped us know their names in detail today without having recourse to a great deal of investigation.[45]

The poets of Yemen used to apply *atbash* letters not only at the opening of verses but also within the body of the poem. Below are a few examples of the use of *atbash* by Yemenite rabbis. R. Shelomoh b. R. Se'īd wrote a poem beginning with the words *Shema ha-El 'inyani bi-tefillah.*[46] The poem is constructed as an acrostic of the writer's name, *Shelomoh.* This poem, replete with emotion of the outpouring of the soul before its creator, is famous at parties of the Yemenite Jews. Written in the last stanza is the following: "Is not *bakhyaṣ* whose poem it completes, offspring of *ḥazmaq*, I am worth less than an ant (*mi-nemalah*, מנמלה)." The words *bakhyaṣ* and *ḥazmaq* allude to the author having encoded with *atbash* letters his name and that of his father, Shelomoh ben Se'īd. It seems that the writer's family name is al-Naddāf, and he concealed this with the word *mi-nemalah,* which in *gematria* with the *kolel* (that is, with the addition of 1) adds up to 166 as does the family name al-Naddāf.[47]

In a poem beginning with *Libbi le-'almah hadurah,* R. Yosef ben Yisra'el Mashta, one of the famous poets of the seventeenth century, made a dedication for his friend who lived far away: *Ḥazmaq geviri ve-uzi, yoshev ba-'ir ha-perzai, al na tegaleh le-razi* ("*Ḥazmaq* my master and strength, living in a distant city, do not reveal my secret"). He concealed his friend's name, Se'īd, with the letters *ḥazmaq*. His own name he encoded in the words, "And my name is explicit in the intelligence of a Jewish child."[48] In this sentence, he apparently is referring to his personal name, Yosef, which is found in the opening phrase of the second stanza: *Yosef be-ḥayyekha 'aneni, mori ve-ribboni* (Joseph, I beseech answer me, mori and ribboni).

45. David Yellin, *"Ginzei Teiman,"* p. 148.

46. *Ḥafeṣ Ḥayim—Shirei Rabbeinu Shalem Shabazi* (Jerusalem; ed. Maqaytin, 1966), p. 609.

47. Sa'adya b. R. Ḥayim al-Naddaf, *Sefer Eṣ ha-Ḥayim*, Introduction (Jerusalem, 1995), p. 10. There were a number of rabbis names Shelomoh ben Sa'adya who lived in the seventeenth century, and this poem was apparently erroneously attributed to Shelomoh ben Sa'adya Ḥarāzi, a sage from south Yemen. See *Beit Tefillah le-R. Shelomoh Ḥarāzi,* ed. Z. Bar Maoz (Ramat Gan, 1992), pp. 13–14, 17–18.

48. Avraham Zevi Idelsohn and N. H. Torczyner, *Shirei Teiman* (Cincinnati, 1931), p. 50–51, no. 38.

R. Dawid ben Se'īd Ramaḍan, who lived in the seventeenth century, encrypted his name in one of the verses of the poem beginning with

שלום לבן דוד אשר נקרא מני אני דוד ילוד חזמ"ק /מולך אני אקרא שׂלומותי.
אבי סעדיא הוא ילוד מסמ"ת / בן גיהתט.[49]

In the acronym חזמ"ק he encoded his father's name, Se'īd; with the initials מסמ"ת he encrypted his grandfather's name, Yiḥye'; and with the word גיהתט, he hid his family name, Ramaḍan.

In a poem beginning אני אשיר לאל חי ואזמר, the author revealed his name in the words שמי דוי" ילוד בכי"ץ מכונה בד"ל מי"ם רי"ש ומי"ם יו"ד רי"ש כפולים. Here, the writer is alluding to his father's name in the *atbash* system, Shelomo, and to his full name, David Shelomo Damarmari.[50]

In a poem opening with יקול אלשזער אלנאצׂם, with the words שמי חזמ"ק ולד מצפ"ק, the writer was alluding to his name in the *atbash* system, Se'īd ben Yehudah.[51]

Poets in Yemen for whom we do not have biographies used to employ *atbash* to allude to their name. A poet named Se'īd would list as an acrostic in his poems חזמ"ק (*ḥazmaq*). In poems beginning with the words חכמים פרשו דברי שמועה חשקי בבת מלכים תמה the opening words of the stanzas make up *ḥazmaq*,[52] and in the poem beginning חמדת הימים השביעי נקרא, he wrote חזמ"ק יצ"ו (*ḥazmaq yṣ"w*).[53] R. Dawid ben Se'īd indicated his name in the poem beginning יצו האל לחסדו ממרומים as follows: הלא זה אשר הוא עלה בשכלי ,שמי דֹוֹד חדל אישים צעירים, ילוד הרב שמו חֹזֹמֹק גבירי, יקימהו אשר יצר מאורים.[54] In the poem beginning ילוד חזמ"ק שהוא כהן לאל חי, שמו: אשורר שיר לאל נורא תהלה he wrote דוד צערי כל הקהילה.[55]

In 1674, the scribe R. Pihḥas ben Gad Ha-Kohen copied the *siddur* of R. Yiṣḥaq Wanne in the city of Dhamār. On the title page of the *siddur*,

49. Ratzaby, *Shirat Teiman ha-'Ivrit*, p. 159
50. *Ḥafeṣ Ḥayim—Shirei Rabbeinu Shalem Shabazi* ([Maqaytin]), p. 24.
51. Apparently this is referring to R. Se'īd Manṣūra, a nineteenth-century Yemenite rabbi. See Itamar Ḥayim Kohen, *"Perushei Shirim ve-Ḥidushim Rabbi David al-Jammal (Harda"g)"* in Y. L. Naḥum, *Ha-Te'udah mi-Ḥasifat Ginzei Teiman* (Holon, 1996), 226–311.
52. Idelsohn and Torczyner, *Shirei Teiman*, p. 75, no. 64; p. 76, no. 66.
53. Ibid., pp. 75–76, no. 65.
54. Ibid., p. 72, no. 60.
55. Ibid., p. 73, no. 61.

he noted his name as: אלה דברי זעירא דמן חבריא, צעיר ספריא וחכימיא העציר פינחס הכהן בן ר"ק הכהן ילוד בכי"ץ הכהן יצ"ו [=ישמרו צורו ויוצרו]. With the term ר"ק, he indicated in the *atbash* cipher, the name of his father, Gad, and with the term בכי"ץ he indicated the name of his grandfather, Shelomo.[56]

In 1720, Yosef Marḥabi, in the town of Ḍlayme, copied R. Karo's Shulḥan 'Arukh. In the colophon of the division *Ḥoshen Mishpat*, he indicated his name, ספרא קלא ומסכינא, זעירא דמן חברייא, יוסף ן' זכריה ן' חסדאי אלמרחבי and in the colophon to the *Even ha-'Ezer* division, he noted his name as ספרא קלא ומסכינא מפחו שט מסמת שט סחקתם שט חזמק אלמרחבי. With the words מפחו שט מסמת שט סחקתם שט חזמק he is alluding to his family lineage in the *atbash* cipher יוסף בן יחיא בן חסדאי בן סעיד (Yosef ben Yiḥye' ben Ḥisdai ben Se'īd).[57]

In the nineteenth century, Sālem ben Yiḥye' Mashta' copied a collection of the laws of ritual slaughter.[58] In the colophon (p. 69b), on which the copyist listed a lineage of 16 generations, he noted his name in the *atbash* cipher: "The least skilled, lowliest of the scribes, most lightly esteemed, humble, least of the clans, youngest in my father's house" with the sentence שמי בכפ"י ובלשון ערב שמי חתכ"י so as to allude to his name in the *atbash* code in Hebrew and Arabic: בכפ"י = Shalom; חתכ"י = Sālem.

In 1825, Se'īd ben Yiḥye' al-'Uzayri copied a *diwan* in Sūq Ḍrāb in central Yemen.[59] In the colophon he gave his name as follows: והכותב קל הקלים חזמ"ק בא"מ [=בן אבא מורי] מסמ"ת בא"מ [=בן אדוני מורי] מפח"ו בא"מ יב"ץ הידוע אלעזירי יש"ל. The terms חזמ"ק, מסמ"ת, מפח"ו, and יב"ץ allude to the family lineage in *atbash* cipher: Se'īd ben Yiḥye' ben Yosef ben Moshe 'Uzayri.

Of special note among the messianic movements that arose among the Yemenite Jews in their exile is that of Shukr Kuhayl II, who was ac-

56. *Siddur*, Manuscript England, Leeds Roth 76 (IMHM 15307); Aharon Gaimani, "*Ha-Sofer R. Pinhas ben Gad ha-Kohen*," *Tema* 7 (2001): 123.

57. Shulḥan 'Arukh, MS New York, Public Library 112 (IMHM 31114); Aharon Gaimani, *Temurot be-Moreshet Yahadut Teiman: be-Hashpa'at ha- Shulḥan 'Arukh ve-Qabalat ha-Ari* (Ramat Gan, 2005), p. 301. On the interchange of the names Yiḥye' / Zekharyah, see above part 1, chap. 4, sect. 2.

58. MS Jerusalem, Menahem Feldman 113 (IMHM 42715). See also below, chap. 5, sect. 3.

59. MS Tel Aviv, Bill Gross 160 (IMHM 46202).

tive from 1868 to 1875. A letter of reply sent by Jews of Ghūle of northern Yemen after receiving a letter from Shukr Kuhayl was signed by four people, two of them sons of Manas and two, sons of Ya'aqov, formulated as follows: הצעיר שלום ן' יט"ח, הצעיר חזמ"ק ן' יט"ח, אהרן בן יעקב, חזמ"ק בן יעקב. Three of the signers used the *atbash* cipher to encode their names. The first signer encrypted the name of his father, *Manas*, and wrote in *atbash* style יט"ח. The second encoded his name and his father's name, Se'īd ben Manas, with the letters חזמ"ק ב יט"ח. The fourth signer encrypted his personal name, Se'īd, with the letters חזמ"ק.[60]

3. GEMATRIA AND ACRONYMS

The rabbis of Yemen used various methods of *gematria* and notarikon/ acronyms to encrypt their names. Some were simple, others sophisticated.

R. Avraham Ṣan'āni, who lived in 'Ayāshiya in the nineteenth century, called one of his compositions קֹדֶשׁ הִלֻּלִים (without a *waw*).[61] The work's name in *gematria* adds up to 519, identical to the value of the author's name, Avraham Ṣan'āni.

R. Ḥasan ben Sālem Se'īd, who was active in the nineteenth century and lived in Ḍal'i in southern Yemen, called his innovations on the Torah *Ḥoq Ne'eman* (חק נאמן).[62] In *gematria*, the title חק נאמן comes to 249, the same value as the author's name חסן סאלם (Ḥasan Sālem).

R. Yosef Badiḥi, a nineteenth-century Ṣan'a rabbi, wrote an introduction to *Sefer ha-Dīwān* in which were collected many of the poems of Yemenite Jewry. In the introduction he speaks with admiration of R. Shalom Shabazi. In his words, appearing below, he encrypted the name of R. Sh. Shabazi, writing: שפתותיו שושנים, בש"ע אורות שונים, שכן עולה כאשר רשם בפזמונים ["his lips are roses, in 370 different lights, for his name comes [to the sum] as written in verses"].[63] With the initials ש"ע, he is alluding to the name of R. Shalom Shabazi, since ש"ע = 370, and in his poems R. Shabazi indicated his name by ש"ע = 370. At the end of

60. Aharon Gaimani, "The Messianism of Shukr Kuhayl II: Two New Letters," *Jewish Quarterly Review* 92 (2002): 354.

61. The work was published in Jerusalem in 1971. See also part 2, chap. 1, sect. 2. On the author and his works, see Ratzaby, *Toratan she-li-Bnei Teiman* p. 86.

62. Ibid., p. 138.

63. *Dīwān Efteḥah Shir* ('Irāqi), Introduction by R. Yosef Badiḥi (Bnei Brak, 1999), pp. 15–16.

the introduction, R. Yosef ben Shalom Badiḥi (הרב יוסף בן שלום בדיחי) encoded his name, writing:

> Until here the words of the little in quantity and few in quality, considered as nothing, a worm and not a man. If you wish to know my name, my name is חציו, חצי חציו, ועוד נוסף, חצי נוסף ("half of it, half of half of it, and more, and half more"). Or this way, the end of my name is the beginning of my name and ואמצע הסוף [אמצע] שמי ("the middle of the end [is the middle] of my name"), and וסוף הסוף סוף שמי ("the end of the end is the end of my name"). Ben le-Shalom Hd"L [Badiḥi in gematria D"L [34]).[64]

His personal name, *Yosef*, he encrypted in two ways. The first is "half of it, half of half of it, and more, and half more." That is, the name is encoded with the system of half, meaning half the word alluded to. "Half of half" refers to the letters יו, which comprise the last part of the word חציו, and the first part of his name יוסף; "half more" alludes to the letters סף, which make up the last part of the term נוסף and the last part of his name יוסף. The other method, "the end of my name is the beginning of my name" alludes to the letter י (*yod*) at the end of his name, which is the end of the word שמי. ואצמע הסוף [אצמע] שמי refers to the letters וס, which are the middle of the word הסוף. וסוף הסוף סוף שמי alludes to the letter ף, which is the final letter of the word סוף. The family name בדיחי he encoded in the *gematria* of the term ד"ל = 34, which is the sum of בדיחי, also 34.

R. Yiḥye' Badiḥi, the head of the most important yeshiva in Ṣan'a in the second half of the nineteenth century, wrote innovations on the Torah and responsa entitled *Ḥen Ṭov*. At the end of the introduction to his book he encrypted his name and that of his work using *gematria*:

> And may the blessed Lord assist me in doing his will, and let me merit preparing this book in an upright manner and with good grace. And my humble name is alluded to with the byname of *hd"l* (עם כינויי הד"ל) with the letters, as the number of the name of the book *Ḥen Ṭov* with the *kolel* (an addition of 1).[65]

By the words "with the byname *hd"l*" he is alluding to his family name Badiḥi, which in *gematria* adds up to 34, the same as ד"ל = 34. As for decoding the name of the author and the title of the book, there are two

64. Ibid., p. 41.
65. *Ḥen Ṭov* by R. Yiḥye' Badiḥi, MS Jerusalem, Mosad Harav Kook 943 (IMHM 26427), Introduction, p. 17.

systems. One is that of R. Yiḥye' Alsheikh, who preferred to indicate the name of the author Yiḥye' (יחיא) with the *alef*, and the other, that of R. Itamar Ḥayim Kohen, who preferred to indicate the author's name with the letter *heh*. Thus, R. Yiḥye' Alsheikh's solution is that *Ḥen Ṭov* using *gematria* adds up to 75. Yiḥye' Badiḥi using *gematria* comes to 63 + number of letters composing the name (9) + the number of words comprising the name (2), with the *kolel* (that is, an addition of 1), for a total of 75.[66] The solution of R. Itamar Ḥayim Kohen is as follows: Yihyeh Badiḥi using *gematria* adds up to 67, and with the nine letters of the name, to 76. Moreover, the title of the book *Ḥen Ṭov* comes in *gematria* to 75, and with the *kolel* (the addition of 1), equals 76.[67]

R. Shelomo 'Amr, a nineteenth-century Ṣan'a rabbi, wrote a commentary on R. Yosef Qaro's *Shulḥan 'Arukh* entitled *Shetilei Zeitim*, for the *Even ha-Ezer* division. He had been preceded by R. Dawid Mishriqi, one of the eighteenth-century Yemenite rabbis, who wrote a commentary *Shetilei Zeitim* to the *Shulḥan 'Arukh*, on the divisions *Oraḥ Ḥayim* and *Yoreh De'ah* up to *siman* 110.[68] R. 'Amr's commentary matches that of R. D. Mishriqi in structure and content. In his introduction to this work, R. Shelomo 'Amr encoded his name and wrote:

> I the most meager in my father's house and the most humble in my family and the least among the people of my city, while passing through the courts of five synagogues, to learn a bit from the great amount in this book,[69] with a few rabbis and colleagues, and to debate with them as far as my poor [אבי"ן] hand can reach … and after I informed you that I have followed in the way of the author of *Shetilei Zeitim* [שתלי זתים]. I also took its name to call it *Shetilei Zeitim*, and this is one of the reasons. And another reason is that the number of these words in *mispar qatan* [calculating the value of each letter, while truncating all the zeros], they are the number of my name and my nickname in *mispar qatan* with two words. For this book of mine versus *Sefer Shetilei Zeitim*, has fewer pages and less quality, like the sum of the *mispar qatan* regarding *mispar gadol* to those who know the mystical teachings … May Hamaqom, blessed be He, say enough to my trou-

66. Ibid., Introduction by the Mahar"i Alsheikh, p. 9.
67. Ibid., Introduction, Badihi, *Ḥen Ṭov*, see there annotations *Ḥenah shel Torah* (Bnei Brak, 2008), p. 17 nn. 37–38.
68. On the *Shetilei Zeitim* commentary by R. D. Mishriqi, see Gaimani, *Temurot*, pp. 106–7, 178–82.
69. The reference is to the Shulḥan 'Arukh, *Even ha-'Ezer*.

bles and my sadness, and let me merit being one of those who serve his always in love, and show me my descendants engaged in Torah and mitzvot. And fulfill the desire of my heart and objective to complete the part on *Yoreh De'ah,*[70] as I intend to do. And let me see the consolation of Zion and the building of Jerusalem. And complete my portion and my cup סוכתי לפנינת יקרת מסיבת אהובים נדיבים ענוים מחיצתם רמה בעדן גן אלהים. So be it before the Lord my King, my Helper, my Redeemer, Amen. Such is the appeal of the humble and despised, who prays with an aggravated heart, and he read this, and said, סלימאן בלא"א סלימאן עמר יצ"ו (Slaymān son of my master my father Slaymān 'Amr, may his Rock protect and redeem him.[71]

In three places in the introduction to this book, R. Shelomo 'Amr encrypted his name. The word אביו"ן in *mispar qatan* comes to 15, calculated as follows: *alef* – 1, *bet* – 2, *yod* – 1, *waw* – 6, *nun* – 5 = 15. This word contains an allusion to his name, Shelomo, which comes to the same sum in *misapar qatan* reckoning, as follows: *shin* – 3, *lamed* – 3, *mem* – 4, *heh* – 5 = 15. The words שתלי זתים (*Shetilei Zeitim*) have eight letters which, in *mispar qatan* calculations, come to the sum of 35, as follows: *shin* –3, *tav* – 4, *lamed* – 3, *yod* – 1, *zayin* – 7, *taav* – 4, *yod* – 1, *mem* – 4 = 27 + 8 = 35. His name, Slaymān 'Amr, two words – 2, totals, in *mispar qatan* calculations, the same sum: *samekh* – 6, *lamed* – 3, *yod* – 1, *mem* – 4, *alef* – 1, *nun* – 5, *'ayin* – 7, *mem* – 4, *resh* 2 = 33 + 2 = 35. At the end of the introduction, with the words סוכתי לפנינת יקרת מסיבת אהובים נדיבים ענוים מחיצתם רמה, he indicated his personal name in Arabic, סלימאן (Slaymān), and his family name, עמר ('Amr).

In the closing poem to his work *Shem Ṭov* on Maimonides' Mishneh Torah, R. Ḥayim ben Shemu'el Kisār, one of the outstanding Yemenite rabbis in the twentieth century, encoded his name in the initials of the words of one of the stanzas: חלקי ה', פעת יקרת מנתי / שמו מכתירת וצניף אור לראשי / כונני סומכי אוהדי רונני.[72]

70. Since R. Dawid Mishriqi did not complete his commentary on *Yoreh De'ah.*

71. Yiṣḥaq Raṣabi, *Shulḥan Arukh ha-Mequṣar*, vol. 7 (Bnei Brak, 1989), Introduction, p. 13, 16–17.

72. Maimonides, *Mishneh Torah le-ha-Rambam im Peirush "Shem Ṭov" le-R. Ḥayyim Kesar* (Jerusalem, 1982), on the final page of the last volume.

4. ENCODING NAMES IN RIDDLE POEMS

In riddle poems, the sages of Yemen used to encode topics, mainly from the sphere of halakhah and midrash as well as their names. Riddle poems from Yemen are not numerous, there being only a few dozen extant. The most outstanding of the Yemenite sages who wrote them are R. Zekharyah al-Ḍāhari in the sixteenth century, R. Yosef ben Yisra'el at the end of the sixteenth century, and R. Shalem ben Me'oded Bashāri in the nineteenth century.[73]

R. Shalem ben Me'oded Bashāri encoded his name in three of the eight halakhic riddle poems he wrote. In one of the poems, we find: "And if you know the name of the writer / is it not after the name [ע"ש] of the youngest of the children of the comrades."[74] In another poem, he wrote in a similar manner: "And if you know the name of the writer / is it not after the name dust at the feet of the upright."[75] He describes himself in humble terms, and alludes to his name using *gematria* with the term ע"ש = 370, which is equal to his personal name, Shalem = 370. In another poem he encrypted his name in the last part of the poem in a very vague way.[76]

Here are six lines from the poem:

225=	ואם תשכיל בשם זה המחבר /
	קחה מנין לאלף בית[77] כפולים[78] גם ישרים.[79]
64=	וקח מנין לאותיות אנשים / עלי תומים מפותחים ואורים.[80]

73. 'Amir, *"Shirei ha-Ḥida shel Yosef ben Yisra'el," Bikkoret u-Parshanut* 32 (1998): 137–39.
74. Yehudah Ratzaby, *"Shirei Ḥidah Halakhiyim le-R. Shalem Me'oded," Sefunot,* n.s. 1 (1980): 281, poem 3, line 9.
75. Ibid., p. 283, poem 5, line 14.
76. The solution as cited in Prof. Ratzaby's article, ibid., does not come to 370, and seemingly it should understood as in the solution given below.
77. According to the enumeration of the letters of the *alef-bet* and the final letters in the tradition of the Yemenite Jews, their sum is 75: *alf, be, jimel, dal, ha, waw, zān, ḥet, ṭet, yud, kāf, lamed, mayim, nun, ṣād, fa, khaf.*
78. *Kefulim* (doubles) as an allusion to double the number 75 + 75 + 150.
79. Alludes another time to the letters of the *alef-bet* (including the final letters) = 75, for a total of 150 + 75 = 225.
80. Letters for the 12 tribes (see Maimonides, *Klei ha-Miqdash* 9, 9): ראובן, שמעון, לוי, יהודה, יששכר, זבולן, נפתלי, דן, גד, אשר, יהוסף, בנימן, = 50 + 14 letters of אברהם יצחק ויעקב (including the conjunctive *waw*), which are also written in the Urim and Thummim (ibid., Halakhah 7) = 64.

12= וקח מנין נשיאי השבטים / אשר המה כמו נרות מאירים.[81]
9= וקח מנין שנים הנביאים / מפורשים והמה בכתובים.[82]
60= וקח מנין לארבע הברכות / סמוכים הם לקרבן הנשיאים.[83]
ושם אבי מפורש בכתובים בשיר דוד וסמוך לענוים

The sum reached in the five first lines is 370, equal in value to the name שלם (Shalem). The sixth line alludes to his father's name, Me'oded, according to the verse in Psalms (147:6): מעודד ענוים ה'.

The poet R. Yosef ben Yisra'el wrote three riddle poems whose entire content is the encoding of his name. About these riddle poems, Yehudah 'Amir wrote:

> These poems are rather simple, are not characterized by sophisticated means of encoding or a challenge in solving them, and in fact, are no more than one riddle in different variations. Yet, they do have a distinctive facet: unlike the Spanish poets, this poet does not deal with meaningless combinations of numbers or with allusions through words, them or parts of them or combinations of their parts, but bases his riddle on familiarity with the Bible, imbuing them with the breath of life and adding a didactic nuance. Another unique aspect is the very three-time repetition of the name riddle in a different version. To be sure, the Spanish poets have already provided us with various riddle poems on the same topic or the same name, but three poems almost identical in their formulation, solely with changes in the allusions, and moreover, concerning the poet's name, constitute an exceptional phenomenon that must be investigated. It seems that in this case, too, as with most Yemenite riddles, the educational-practical consideration was operative; the riddles were intended for reviewing biblical passages in a way amusing to students, for the poet was involved in studies, and repetition is, apparently, a result of the teaching routine.[84]

81. Cf. Num. 1:44: "the princes of Israel, being twelve men." See also Num. 1:5–16.
82. Num. 11:26: "But there remained two men in the camp, the name of the one was Eldad, and the name of the other Medad; and the spirit rested upon them; and they were of them that were recorded, but had not gone out to the tent; and they prophesied in the camp." This allludes to the number of letters in Eldad and Medad (including the conjuctive *waw*).
83. In the priestly blessing are 60 letters. Num. 6:24–26: יברכך י-ה-ו-ה וישמרך. יאר י-ה-ו-ה פניו אליך ויחנך. ישא י-ה-ו-ה פניו אליך וישם לך שלום. The last verse is considered two blessings.
84. 'Amir, "*Shirei Ḥida,*" pp. 140–41.

R. Yosef ben Yisra'el lived in the Shar'ab region in southern Yemen, and his family name was Mashta, like that of R. Shalom Shabazi, so we may reasonably assume that they belonged to the same family.[85]

Riddle No. 1[86]

קח נא סכום הדברות שנתנו / מתוך ערפל על ידי איש עניו.[87]	= י
וסכום סדרים מזקנים שננו / לידע מגמת אל וכל עניניו.[88]	= ו
וסכום למסכתות אשר בם כוננו / גלו למסתריו וכל מצפוניו.[89]	= ס
וסכום אנשים חוצבי אגור ביום / בנה לבית עמלו בו בוניו.[90]	= ף
וסכום בני רחל, שהיא אם צפנת / מלך עלי פרעה בתוך ארמוניו.[91]	= ב
וסכום שני יובל , אשר בם תגאלה / תשיב לרעיך כמנין שניו.[92]	= ן
וסכום לימים מתקיעה עד עבור / כפור עון עם, מעלו וזדוניו.[93]	= י
וסכום לתיבה נמלטו בה נושעים / נח ונשיו[94] עם שלשת בניו.[95]	= ש
וסכום למוהר הבתולה תידעה[96] / וסכום בני דן גור ארי במעוניו.[97]	= ר,א

85. Yehudah 'Amir, "The Poetry of Yosef ben Yisra'el (Yemen—end of the sixteenth and beginning of the seventeenth centuries)" (doctoral dissertation, Bar-Ilan University 2001), p. 80. Also Prof. Yehudah Ratzaby believed that R. Shalom Shabazi and R. Yosef ben Yisra'el, an older member of his generation, were related and that R. Shalom Shabazi was influenced by him with regard to literature and music. Ratzaby, *Shirei R. Shalom Shabazi—Bibliografia*, introduction (Tel Aviv, 2003), p. 12.
86. Published by Idelsohn and Yellin. See Idelsohn and Torczyner, *Shirei Teiman*, pp. 58–59, 404; David Yellin, *"Ginzei Teiman,"* pp. 147–61.
87. The Ten Commandments, which were given to Moshe. Ex. 20:17.
88. The Six Orders of the Mishnah.
89. Sixty Mishnah Tractates.
90. "[A]nd 80,000 quarriers in the hills" (I Kings 5:29). Alluding to the letter *peh*.
91. The two sons of Raḥel. The word צפנת infers Yosef, who was called צפנת פענח (Gen. 41:45).
92. The intention is to the years of one Jubilee period, 50 years.
93. The Ten Days of Repentance, from Rosh Hashanah to Yom Kippur.
94. Another version: ואשתו.
95. Gen. 6:15: "The length of the ark shall be three hundred cubits." In his comments Torczyner solved this verse: 8 people entered the ark alludes to the letter ש, from the word שמונה. His solution is not precise, and the reference is rather to the length of the ark, the value of the letter ש. See Yehudah 'Amir, *"Shirei ha-Ḥida shel Yosef ben Yisra'el,"* p. 159 n. 69.
96. Deut. 22:28–29. "If a man find a damsel that is a virgin, that is not betrothed, and

וסכום לארך היריעה תקחה / תשלים בארכה מעשה משכניו.[98] = ל
מי הוא חכם לבב ונבון עד מאד / ימצא שמי כתוב לנגד עיניו.[99]
יקבץ סכומותיו[100] ולהם ידרשה / ושמי ושם אבי בראש סימניו.[101]

Riddle No. 2[102]

קח נא סכום בנים לבנימין, אשר נקרא: צעיר הצאן לנין איתנים.[103] = י
וסכום בני שמעון, אשר נאסר ביד יוסף, אשר כלכל לאב עם בנים.[104] = ו
וסכום לערי עוג אשר כבש יקותיאל[105] וארבעת דגלים[106] חונים.[107] = ס
וסכום שני משה ביום עמד למול פרעה,[108] אשר נקרא "גדול תנינים."[109] = ף
וסכום בני משה אשר נתברכו בהון ובעשר עשרת מונים.[110] = ב

---

lay hold on her, and lie with her, and they be found; then the man that lay with her shall give to the damsel's father fifty shekels of silver." According to a rabbinic regulation, 50 shekels of silver are worth 200 zuz (Ketubbot 38a).

97. Gen. 46:23: And the son's of Dan, Ḥushim = 1. Dan is called גור אריה (lion's whelp) in Moshe's blessing, Deut. 33:22: דן גור אריה יזנק מן הבשן.
98. Ex: 26:8, 36:15: ארך היריעה האחת שלשים באמה.
99. Alludes to the topic of the riddle being the author's name.
100. Another version: סתומותיו.
101. Alludes that the solution of the riddle is his name and his father's name.
102. Published by Idelsohn. See Idelsohn, *Shirei Teiman*, pp. 59–60, 404–5.
103. The ten sons of Binyamin. Gen. 46:21: ובני בנימן בלע ובכר ואשבל גרא ונעמן אחי וראש מפים וחפים וארד (And the sons of Benjamin: Bela, and Bekher, and Ashbel, Gera, and Na'aman, Eḥi, and Rosh, Muppim, and Ḥuppim, and Ard).
104. The six sons of Shim'on. Gen. 46:10: "And the sons of Simeon: Yemuel, and Yamin, and Ohad, and Yakhin, and Zohar, and Sha'ul the son of a Canaanite woman."
105. A byname for Moshe Rabbenu; see TB Megillah 13a.
106. The people of Israel who camped in the desert with four flags, and the reference is to Moshe and the people of Israel.
107. Deut. 3:4: "Sixty cities, all the region of Argov, the kingdom of Og in Bashan."
108. Ex. 7:7: "And Moses was 80 years old, and Aaron 80 and 3 years old, when they spoke to Pharaoh."
109. Ez. 29:3: "I am against you, Pharaoh King of Egypt, the great monster that lies in his rivers."
110. Ex. 2–4: "And Jethro, Moses' father-in-law, took Zipporah, Moses' wife, after he had sent her away, and her two sons; of whom the name of the one was Gershom; for he said: 'I have been a stranger in a strange land'; and the name of the other was Eliezer: 'for the God of my father was my help, and delivered me from the sword of Pharaoh.'"

וסכום קרסים שלזהב תקחה / זכים ומזהירים כמו שושנים.[111] = ן
וסכום לדורות מבריאה עד ימי מבול אשר בו נשטפו זידונים.[112] = י
וסכום לתיבה נמלטו בה נושעים / כלה שמונה עם שאר המינים.[113] = ש
וסכום לכלאים וערלה תקחה / תדע בסודם עם שאר ענינים.[114] = ר
וסכום בני דן בעת שנספרו / עת ירדו למצרים, באב עם בנים.[115] = א
וסכום לארך היריעה תקחה / תשכיל במספר עם שאר ענינים.[116] = ל

Riddle No. 3[117]

קח נא סכום פסקי תשובות חוטאים / נאה הגות בהם ביום כפרה.[118] = י
וסכום לפרקי התמידין תקחה / כלם מקשרים בשם אל נורא.[119] = ו
וסכום לאותיות בברכת כהנים / תדע ותבינה וגם תחקרה.[120] = ס
וסכום שני יצחק אשר נתוספו / יותר עלי מאה כמנין תורה.[121] = ף

---

111. Ex. 26:11: "And you shall make fifty clasps of brass."
112. Ten generations from Adam to Noaḥ.
113. Three hundred amah, and see the note to line 8 of the previous riddle.
114. Mishna Kilaim 5, 6: "[The vegetable] is forbidden even if it has grown by a two-hundredth."
115. Equals one, and see the note to line 10 in the preceding riddle.
116. Thirty amah. See also the note to line ten in the previous riddle. In another manuscript, the riddle concludes, from the second half of line 9 as follows:

    תבין בשיעור סופרים וגאונים. וסכום בני יאיר אשר נתגברו על כל בני קדם ומעונים.
    מי הוא חכם לבב ונבון עד מאד / ימצא שמי פנים כנגד פנים

    (Idelsohn, *Shirei Teiman*, p. 405).
117. Published twice by Ratzaby. See Yehudah Ratzaby, "*Mi-Shirat Teiman* (*13 Shirim Ḥadashim*)," *Biqqoret u-Parshanut* 20 (1985): 139; idem, *Shirat Teiman ha-'Ivrit*, pp. 163–64. In the version Ratzaby published, stanza 7 and half of stanzas 8 and 9 were omitted, and they were completed by the research of Yehudah Amir. See Amir, *Shirei ha-Ḥida*, p. 146.
118. *Hilkhot Teshuva* in Maimonides' *Mishneh Torah* contains 10 chapters.
119. *Hilkhot Temidin* in Maimonides' *Mishneh Torah* contains six chapters.
120. In the priestly blessing are 60 letters. Num. 6:24–26: יברכך י-ה-ו-ה וישמרך יאר י-ה-ו-ה פניו אליך ויחנך ישא י-ה-ו-ה פניו אליך וישם לך שלום.
121. Gen. 35:28 "And the days of Isaac were a hundred and fourscore years." The amount above one hundred is 80.

וסכום בני יוסף אשר נתברכו / מפי גביר תמים בנפש ברה.[122]   = ב
וסכום לגבורי אדניה קחה / רצים לפניו לאחז בשררה.[123]   = ו
וסכום אחי יוסף אשר באו לנוף / לשבר למחיתם בנפש מרה.[124]   = י
וסכום לכסף מיהוסף שקלו / לתת לאחיו עם לבוש תפארה.[125]   = ש
וסכום רחלי יעקב יום הלכו / לתת לאיש שעיר לחן ותשורה.[126]   =ר
וסכום בני דן האהוב הנאמן / נמשל כאריה או כגור במערה.[127]   = א
וסכום ברואים מערבות עד יסוד / מהם דמות גלם ומהם צורה.[128]   = ל
מי הוא חכם לבב ונבון עד מאד / ימצא שמי כתוב בראש השירה.
יקבץ סכומותיו ולהם ידרשה / הוא אנוש משכיל ובעל תורה.

5. ENCODING AND ALLUSIONS TO FAMILY NAMES

In various family names, allusions were found to have hidden meanings through initials, or *gematria*, or metathesis. These occurrences happened after the fact, as it were, and there was no reason to choose this name.[129] Here are a few examples:

---

122. Gen. 46:27: "And the sons of Joseph, who were born to him in Egypt, were two souls." He further noted the blessing of Jacob to the sons of Joseph in Gen. 48:9–20.
123. I Kings 1:5: "Now Adonijah the son of Haggit exalted himself, saying: 'I will be king'; and he prepared himself with chariots and horsemen, and fifty men to run before him."
124. Gen. 42: 3: And Joseph's ten brethren went down to buy grain from Egypt."
125. Gen. 45: 22: "To all of them he gave each man changes of raiment; but to Benjamin he gave three hundred shekels of silver, and five changes of raiment."
126. Gen. 32:15: "Two hundred ewes."
127. Equals one. See the note on line 9 in the first riddle.
128. Cf. Rambam, *Hilkhot Yesodei Torah* 2, 3: "Everything created by the Holy One blessed be He in this world is divided into three categories. Creations which are a combination of matter (גולם) and form (צורה) …" The word גולם alludes to the *galgalim* (wheels), while the word צורה refers to *mal'akhim* (angels). Apparently, the number 30 is reached as follows: The number 10 is related to the *mal'akhim* about whom it states "there are 10 levels of angels" (ibid., 2, 7), and another 20 come from the *galgalim*, which number 9 (ibid., 3, 1), and the ninth one is divided into two parts (ibid., 3, 6). Eight *galgalim* and the 12 parts of the ninth *galgal* come to 20. Or, perhaps, the number 30 alludes to what is written TB Berakhot 32b: "The Holy One, blessed be He, said to her, 'My daughter, I have created twelve constellations in the firmament, and for each constellation I have created thirty hosts, and for each host I have created thirty legions, and for each legion I have created thirty cohorts, and for each cohort I have created thirty maniples, and for each maniple I have created thirty camps, and to each camp …'"

Menajjim (מ'נג'ים) – *Menajjim* means fortune-teller. The Menajjim family originated in Shar'ab. In Israel they changed the family name to Ḥozeh or Kokhavi. R. Sa'adyah Ḥozeh wrote about the roots of the family: "Manajjim was a *talmid ḥakham*, and he had no way to chastise the people who were sinning secretly. He fled from Ṣan'a and declared about himself, *shem"i Menajjim*, with an allusion to Ps. 19:13–14: ש'גיאות מ'י י'בין מ'נסתרות נ'קיני ג'ם מ'זדים ("Who can discern his errors? Clear me from hidden faults.... also from presumptuous sins"), which forms the acronym *shem"i Menajjim*.[130] In a manuscript from 2119 SEL (5568 AM; 1808), the copyist wrote his name in the colophon: "Natan ben Ya'īsh ben *km"w* Ḥasan ben Se'īd ben Ma'uḍa ben Amram who is called al-Menajjim, initials of ...מִנסתרות נִקני גם מִזדי."[131]

Morḥi (מוֹרְחִי) – In one of the settlements near Dhamār, R. Ḥayim Yosef Morḥi served as the local rabbi. His descendants have explained the name מורחי as the initial letters of מורנו ורבנו חיים יוסף ("Our teacher and rabbi Ḥayim Yosef").[132]

Wahab (וַהַב) – The name means "giving." Some of the family members have indicated the initial letters of the verse (Deut. 4:4 ואתם הדבקים בה') as the basis of the name. After immigrating to Israel they were called Yahav, and this new name as well has been marked as the initial letters of יהבך השלך בה' on the basis of the verse (Psalms 55:23) השלך על ה' יהבך והוא יכלכלך.[133]

Kashāt (כַּשַּׂאת) – This family emigrated from the Dhamār community, and in Yemen the name was written כשאת. The family's pedigree is derived from the tribe of Lewi and its descendants have explained the name as the initial letters of a verse in Deut. (11:22) כי אם שמור תשמרון. After immigrating, the name was registered in a corrupted form as קשת (Qeshet). For this new

129. See also Avshalom Raṣabi, *"Ha-Humor shel Yehudei Teiman,"* in *Meḥqarim be-Yahadut Teiman*, ed. J. Tobi and E. Isaac (Princeton-Haifa, 1999), pp. 66–67. In the list I did not include allusions with negative overtones.

130. Sa'adya Ḥozeh, *Toledot ha-Rav Shalom Shabazi u-Minhagei Yahadut Shar'ab be-Teiman*, 1 (Jerusalem, 1973), p. 71.

131. *Sefer ha-Hafṭariyyot*, Nissim Binyamin Gamli'eli manuscript, Ramle.

132. As related by Orit Marmorstein, Petaḥ Tiqva.

133. As related by family members. In a personal correspondence dated 11 Apr 2010 from Avshalom Raṣabi of Tel Aviv, he noted other initials for this name: וזאת הברכה.

name, too, an allusion was found in the verse in Deut. (7:12) עקב תשמעון את in the second letters, which was even considered an improvement (*'aliya*) over the first letters alluding to the original name.[134]

Sha'tāl (שַׁעְתַּאל) – A tradition of the family, which lived in the village of Ibn Ḥājeb located in central Yemen north of Ṣan'a, ascribes them to the tribe of Levi. The family members interpreted the family name (without the *alef*) as the initials of the verses in Deut. 19:2, 7: שלוש ערים תבדיל לך.[135]

Jeraydi (גְרֵדִי) – R. Yisra'el, brother of R. Sulēmān Ma'ūḍah, political leader of the Dhamār community, tells of the tradition of the Dhamār Jereydi family that they are descendants of King David, as supported in the *gematria* of the family name: גרדי = 217, חטר = 217, based on the verse (Isa. 11:1) ויצא חטר מגזע ישי ("and a shoot shall go forth from the trunk of Jesse").[136]

Daḥbāsh (דַחְבַּאש) – R. Ḥizqiya Daḥbāsh explained the family name (without the *alef*) as an acronym for D*ivrei* Ḥ*akhamim be*-N*aḥat* Sh*om'im* (!) (Eccl. 9:17: "The words of the wise spoken in quiet are heeded" [*Nishma'im*]). In a *ketubbah* from the Radā' community, dated 11 Nisan 5517 (1 Apr 1757), the bride's name is written as "[...] Bint Yiḥye' Daḥbāsh." In a *ketubbah* from the Ṣan'a community, from 30 Adar I 5643 (9 Mar 1883), the bride's name is "Sa'dah bint Yosef ben Shukr Daḥbāsh." In these citations the family name is written with the addition of the *alef*, and apparently, people did not include it in the initials because it was not pronounced. Or, perhaps, the acronym came about after *aliyah* to Israel, since many have the custom of writing the family name without the *alef*.

'Ukkaysh (עֻכַּיְש) – The family name was explained as the initials of the verse in Genesis (49:10): עד כי יבא שילה.[137]

134. As related by R. Levi Qeshet, Benei Brak.

135. As related by Shalom She'alti'el, Netanya. Many members of the family changed their name in Israel from Sha'tāl to She'alti'el, while some took the name Levi. In Yemen the family name was pronounced Shi'tāl.

136. As related by family members. One can reasonably assume that this allusion was ascribed in Israel, when the family name is pronounced Geredi. In Yemen, the pronunciation of the family name was Jeraydi.

137. In a personal correspondence dated 8 Mar 3010 from R. Azaryah Basis.

Qa'ashe (קַעְשֶׁה)– This family name was understood as an acronym for Qahal 'Adat Shevet Halewi (the assembly of the congregation of the tribe of Levi).[138]

Haparṣi (הפרצי) – a rearrangement of the letters in צפירה (Ṣefirah). Ṣefirah is the name of a family of scholars from the Tan'im community. In the second half of the nineteenth century Mori Slaymān Ṣefirah led the community.[139] In a colophon dated 1882, the copyist Yosef Ṣefirah of Tan'em cites his name as "I, the young writer, simplest of simpletons, Yosef son of my master and father Se'īd ben Yosef Haparṣi."[140]

Ner Miṣvah – a rearrangement of the letters of the name Manṣūrah. R. Sa'adyah Manṣūrah wrote *Sefer ha-Maḥshavah*, which is written in rhymed prose. The book was published as *Sefer ha-Galut ve-ha-Ge'ulah*.[141] R. David Jamal calls him Sa'adyah Ner Miṣvah.[142] His brother, R. Shalom Manṣūrah, also called his work on the Torah *Ner Miṣvah*, alluding to the family name Manṣūrah.[143]

138. In the correspondence cited in the previous note. Cf. Num. 14:5: קהל עדת בני ישראל (the assembled congregation of the Israelites).

139. Sappir, *Massa' Teiman*, ed. A. Yaari (Jerusalem, 1945), p. 191.

140. *Sefer Oṣerot Zahav*, MS Tel Aviv – Bill Gross 141 (IMHM 49219).

141. Yehudah Ratzaby, *Toratan she-li-Vnei Teiman*, p. 230.

142. Itamar Ḥayim Kohen, "*Perushei Shirim ve-Ḥidushim le-Rabbi David al-Jammal (Harda"g)*" in Y. L. Naḥum, *Ha-Te'udah mi-Ḥasifat Ginzei Teiman* (Holon, 1996), p. 232.

143. Ratzaby, *Toratan she-li-Vnei Teiman*, p. 74.

CHAPTER FOUR

THE EFFICACY OF NAMES

Yemenite Jewry, like other Jewish communities, applied different systems as charms to improve one's luck. For example, if children had died in childhood, other newborns were given temporary names or specific names to ensure life. Similarly, it was customary to add a new name at the time of a serious illness in order to change the heavenly decree. Sometimes they gave a new name as a charm for good luck in a new stage of life or to have children as well as for health and a good life.

1. TEMPORARY NAMES

If a man's children had died when quite young, some people had the custom of calling a newborn by one of the charms for life as a temporary name.[1] In *Yalqut Shim'oni*, the issue of a temporary name is discussed concerning Noah's name.

> *He begot a son*. Why did it not state his name, as it did for Kenan, Mahalel, Jared, and Enoch. This teaches us that Methuselah was a great wise man, and he warned Noah' father not to call him by his name, since the members of the generation of the flood were sorcerers, lest they kill him with sorcery. And since he had been born, he called him Noah, and to his father he said, "Call him Menaḥem, for he will comfort his generation." As it says, "This one will provide us with relief" (Gen. 5:29). He said to them, if you repent, he will comfort you.[2]

1. For a discussion of this topic, see Avishai Teherani, *Keter Shem Ṭov,* 2 (Jerusalem, 2000), siman 6, pp. 62–76.
2. *Yalqut Shim'oni*, Genesis, siman 42.

When Lamech had a son, Genesis states (5:28), "When Lamech had lived 182 years, *he begot a son*," and only in the ensuing was his name mentioned: "And he named him Noah" (29). While in noting the other births in that lineage, the name of the newborn is given immediately. For example, "When Enosh had lived 90 years, *he begot Kenan*."[3] The midrash relies upon this difference and on the reason provided for giving the name Noah, "This one will provide us relief ...," so as to understand that the name Noah is temporary, while Menaḥem in intended to be his permanent name; and this was meant to protect him so that the people of the generation would not harm him through sorcery.[4]

In Ashkenaz, some people called a son Alter, "old man," and a daughter, Alte, "old woman." After the infant had grown into childhood, he was given the name originally chosen for him, while other times he retained the temporary name. R. Abraham Isaac Sperling of Lvov wrote in his book *Ta'amei ha-Minhagim* (Reasons for Jewish Customs and Traditions):

> The reason we call a boy or girl by the name Alter or Alte for a person whose children do not live, heaven forbid, is to conceal his name so that Satan will not have the power to harm him. And they call him "old," that is, that he should merit old age, and this is used by all as a blessing.[5]

A Meritorious Name for One Born after the Death of Previous Children

[1] Wald, bint [boy; girl].

R. Yosef Qāfiḥ observes:

> There were only two cradle names whereby they call a son Wald and a girl Bint, and this was in the case when their other children had died, they thought or felt that this was a charm for life. But at their wedding, they would change the name Wald to Yiḥye', and the name Bint to Banayyah. And in the case of divorce, they would write Yiḥye' who is called Wald. For everyone knows that Wald is a temporary name. Also, Banayyah who is called Bint, since everyone knows that Bint is a temporary name.[6]

---

3. Gen. 5:9. See also Gen. 5:12, 15, 18.
4. See also the interpretation by R. Avraham "Abeleh," *Zeit Ra'anan* on *Yalkut Shim'oni;* ibid., par. 51.
5. Shmu'el Pinḥas Gelbard, *Oṣar Ṭa'amei ha-Minhagim* (Petaḥ Tiqvah, 1996), Circumcision, par. 929, p. 396.
6. In a personal correspondence dated 20 Tammuz 5753 (9 July 1993). See also his

R. Pinḥas Qoraḥ wrote on this matter:

> There were names like "Wald" or "Bint" or "Banayyah," and I heard that this was determined when other children died, so they called the next children "Wald" or "Bint." And I heard that one was called "Wald" and at his wedding they changed his name to "'Azaryah." Even when they came to the Land of Israel they changed names, such as "Bint" being replaced with the name "Batyah."[7]

Furthermore, R. Shelomo Qoraḥ writes that the names Wald and Bint were permanent names for a *segula* (beneficial charm) that they should live.[8] Mori Shim'on Dhahbāni of the Ṣan'a community says that they usually gave the temporary names noted when previous infants had died, and they did so as a *segula* for life. When they grew to be healthy, some called them by other names.[9]

R. Adam Bin Nun writes:

> I spoke with two Ṣan'a-born, elderly people: one, R. 'Azri Ṣāliḥ of Herzliya, and the other, R. Ḥayim Ṣāliḥ from Gedera (they are not related). Both of them (each separately) spoke to me about "name change," mainly in cases when a boy or girl had not been given a name soon after birth (because previous siblings had died), and they were called simply "Wald" [boy] or "Bint" [girl], and when they were somewhat older they were given a new name. Yet, also in rarer instances, when someone decided to change his name—in both these cases, they would arrange a festive meal, whose main feature was that they would prepare *lasis* and distribute it to neighbors and relatives.[10]

R. Almog Shelomo Akhlufi wrote:

> As for the names Wald or Bint, it is known that these names were given for fear of the evil eye, as I heard that the rabbi, the gaon, the mequbbal, R. Shalom Manṣūr, *zlhh*, one of the rabbis of Shibām community, many of whose male children had died, until he called his son Wald, and he is still alive and well over the age of ninety, may he merit a good long life, *'ky"r*. My grandmother (my father's mother) was also called Bint

edition of Maimonides' *Mishneh Torah*, 6, *Sefer Nashim*, 2 (Jerusalem, 5748), *Hilkhot Gerushin*, ch. 3 n. 10, p. 89. On a similar custom among Bukharan Jews, see Abraham Zevi Idelsohn, *"Yehudei Bukhara," Mizraḥ u-Ma'arav* 1 (1920): 323.

7. In a personal correspondence dated Iyyar 5770 (Apr 2010).
8. In a personal correspondence dated May 2010.
9. Interview conducted by R. Zion Arusi of Qiryat Ono.
10. R. Adam Bin Nun lives in Bnei Brak.

for this reason. As far as I know, this name was never changed and accompanies them their whole life through.[11]

R. Shalom Manṣūr listed the dates of birth of his four children at the end of a manuscript of the three *megillot*. He registered the birth of his son Wald as follows:

> Praise and gratitude to the blessed Lord, the good child, who resembles a moist tree, has been born, my child Wald, on the 26th of Adar, in the year 2231 SEL [5680 AM/16 Mar 1920]. May he merit Torah, the marriage canopy and good deeds, sons and daughters, and a great deal of assets.[12]

Naomi Badiḥi from the Ṣan'a community said that in her family there was a woman called Bint since her parents' other children had died when young and when she married she called her daughter Bint as well, as a charm for a long life.[13] Aviva Himoff, whose parents emigrated from Ṣan'a, told me that her grandmother Rūmiyah Shameh had 13 deliveries and 9 of the newborns died soon after birth or when very young. One of the boys who survived was called Wald, and he died when about five.[14] R. Yiṣḥaq Raṣabi wrote about the customs of the Raṣabah community and its surroundings: "In our environs I never heard of this at all, but I did hear of this from people from elsewhere."[15]

In 1943 a boys school and a girls school were opened in Ṣan'a.[16] Registration of the girls studying in the school was made according to the girl's name, her father's name, and the family name.[17] On the list, which contains 179 pupil's names, are four girls called Bint: Bint Yiḥye' Ḥaybi,[18] Bint Slayman 'Adani,[19] Bint Ḥayim Ḥubārah,[20] Bint 'Azar

11. In a personal correspondence dated 16 Feb 2011.
12. The manuscript was copied in the city of Shibām, on 10 Nissan 5626 (26 Mar 1866), by the scribe Sulēmān ben Yūda' Jizfān. In the possession of R. Almog Shelomo Akhlufi, Jerusalem.
13. Interview conducted by her granddaughter Michal Badiḥi of Givatayim.
14. Aviva Himoff, Manhattan, New York.
15. In a personal correspondence dated 22 Mar 2010.
16. Yosef Tsuri'eli, *Temurot ba-Ḥinukh be-Teiman (5663–5708; 1903–1948)* (Jerusalem, 1990), pp. 20–24.
17. For the list of girls, see ibid., document no. 16, photo of the document on p. 66, and a transcription of it on p. 67.
18. Ibid., p. 67, no. 64. *Bint* here and in the other examples means "the name *Bint*" and not "the daughter of."

Shar'abi.[21] On the boys' list, which contains 66 names of pupils, the name Wald appears once: Wald ben Ḥayim 'Irāqi.[22]

In a 1947 document from the Ḥajāji Synagogue in Ṣan'a, the name of one of the congregation's worshippers who signed the synagogue's bylaws was "al-Wald ben Yiḥye' Māsa'."[23] In the list of contributors assisting the publication of one of the books of the legacy of Yemenite Jews a name listed is "Ha-Rav Wald ben Yosef."[24]

Avshalom Raṣābi, whose parents emigrated from the Si'wān community in central Yemen, wrote me that there were two families related to his mother. One was called al-Wald, since only boys had been born to it and all of them had died, and the other was called al-Bint, since only girls had been born to it and all of them had died.[25]

[2] The segula name Wald/Bint as a substitute name

Aharon Yehudah, from the Ra'ūḍah community, related that his older brother, Wald, was the first boy after nine girls, and at the circumcision he was given the name *Yehudah*. He was a sickly child, so he name was changed to Wald, as a *segula* for strength and health.[26]

In the body of a *ketubbah* dated 17 Sivan 5670 (26 June 1910), from the 'Arūs community, we find written after the signatures of the witnesses: "Previously her name had been Rūmiyah, now her name is Bint." In the text of the *ketubbah*, one can see signs of the erasure of the bride's name *Rūmiyah*, which was replaced by the writing of Bint.

[3] Personal name identical to that of the parents

Sarah Kohen, who was born into the Shibām community, told that someone whose children died in childhood would name another child as a *segula* for a son with his father's name and for a daughter by the

19. Ibid., no. 77.
20. Ibid., no. 119.
21. Ibid., no. 164.
22. Ibid., document no. 25, photo of the document on p. 76, transcription of the document on p. 77. See the transcription of the document, on the second list, no. 12.
23. Aharon Gaimani, "*Bet Keneset Ḥajāji she-be-Ṣan'a ve-Hanhagato shel ha-Rav Me'ir Subīri*," doc. 1, *Kenishta* 4 (2010): 124–25.
24. *Shisha Sidrei Mishna Menuqqadot al yedei ha-Mahariṣ, Zera'im*, introductory pages.
25. In a personal correspondence dated 11 Apr 2010.
26. Interview conducted by Idan Yehudah of Petaḥ Tiqva. Wald is Idan's grandfather.

mother's name.[27] Naomi Badiḥi of the Ṣan'a community told of a woman named Sham'ah who gave her daughter the name Sham'ah, with the name being a *segula* for a long life, since her other children had died in childhood. Ṭov Ṣadoq, who immigrated to Israel from the Manākhe community in 1949, said that his father, Ṭov, named him by the same name, Ṭov, as a *segula* for a long life, since before he was born two of his brothers had died in childhood.[28] Aviva Himoff tells that her grandmother, Rūmiyah, called her mother Rūmiyah, the same as her name, as a *segula* for life, since a few of her children had died in childhood.[29] R. Ya'aqov Shar'abi wrote that he heard from his grandmother about his uncle (his mother's brother), who at age two became ill with smallpox, and his grandfather (that is, the father of the ill child) Yisra'el changed the child's name to Yisra'el, the same as his, as a *segula* for life.[30] Mori Faiz Jarādi, who left the village of Raidah in northern Yemen, tells of a woman named Lawzah, the wife of the late R. Moshe Nehari,[31] who changed her daughter's name a few times as a *segula* to cure an illness and when she gave her daughter the name Lawzah, identical to her own, the daughter became healthy and so the name remained her permanent one.[32]

[4] Ṣedaqah as a personal name

A daughter was born to the Jerāfi family of the Ṣan'a community after other children had died while small, and they called her Ṣedaqah ("Righteousness"). Her father, R. Maḥfuḍ, wrote about the giving of this name: "Afterwards Ṣedaqah was born after prayer, and we said, it shall be righteousness [*ṣedaqa*] to us (Deut. 6:25)."[33] The Maz'aqi family of the Shibām community in Yemen named one of their daughters

27. Interview conducted by her son, R. Itamar Ḥayim Kohen of Bnei Brak. For examples of calling a son by his father's name, see above, part 1, chap. 2, sect. 2.
28. Ṭov Ṣadoq lives in Qiryat Ono. After *aliyah* to Ereṣ Israel, his father, Ṭov, added for himself the name 'Azri as a *segula* for health and a full cure for an illness.
29. Aviva Himoff, Manhattan, New York. Her grandmother, *Rumiya* Sham'a had 13 deliveries but only three daughters survived: Ni'mah, Rumiyyah, and Turkiyyah.
30. In a personal correspondence dated 2 Dec 2010.
31. R. Moshe Nahari was murdered in Yemen in 2008.
32. The meeting with Mori Faiz Jeraydi took place in Monsey, New York, in December 2007.
33. Aharon Gaimani, *"Treisar Nisyonot she-Nitnasa bahem Ben Teiman ve-Qibbel Yesurav be-Ahava,"* in *Mikhtam le-Yona*, ed. Yosef Dahu'ah Halevi (Tel Aviv, 2004), p. 455.

Ṣedaqah, since other children had died when small;[34] apparently they were referring to the verse "righteousness delivers from death" (Prov. 10:2; 11:4).

[5] Personal name identical to the Family Name

Some gave the family name as a personal name to the new born as a charm for life, while others at the time of serious illness changed the given name and replaced it with the name identical to the family name. R. Ya'aqov Shar'ab tells of a few examples of this custom in the Ṣan'a community. 'Amr ben Ḥayim 'Amr was named Shim'on, and since he was ill for a long time as a child they changed his name and called him by the family name. On this practice, people used to say that his name shall be called *"min rāsahu,"* which means "from his head." Similarly, there was the case of Drayan ben Yiḥye' Drayan. R. Shar'abi heard this story from Yiḥye' the son of Drayan. The initial name given to his father was Ḥayim, and he suffered from a lengthy illness as a child and was unable to walk under his own power until the age of three. The family decided to change his personal name to that of the family and he was called Drayan (*min rāsahu*); his former name, Ḥayim, was forgotten.[35] Yiḥye' added that in issues of name change it was mostly women who were involved. Similar to the cases mentioned, is that of Meghori ben Yiḥye' Meghori (the brother of R. Shar'abi's grandfather), who in the event of *Ḥawzat al-Nafar* in 1905,[36] fled to Australia and never returned from there; other examples are Mori Tan'ami Tan'ami; 'Adani 'Adani;[37] Ṣāliḥ Ṣāliḥ; 'Amr 'Amr (al-Dawmeh); Yamani ben Yeshu'a Yamani.[38] R. Yiṣḥaq Raṣabi also wrote about this and cited examples from Ṣan'a community members.

34. As related by Sarah (Zihrah) Kohen Efrayim, Bnei Brak.

35. One of his sons wrote his name and that of his father in the following text: "A gift from Aharon Drayn for *ilui nishmat* of his dear parents Drayn Drayn ..."

36. In this event, Imam Yiḥye' besieged the Turks in Ṣan'a. About the event, see Yehudah Ratzaby, *"Be-Maṣor u-be-Maṣoq (Le-Parshat ha-Ra'av ha-Aharon be-Shanim 5663–5665),"* in *Bo'i Teiman: Mehkarim u-Te'udot be-Tarbut Yehudei Teiman*, ed. Yehudah Ratzaby (Tel Aviv, 1967), pp. 67–102; Yehudah Nini, *Teiman ve-Ṣiyyon: Ha-Reqa ha-Medini ha-Ḥevrati ve-ha-Ruḥani la-'Aliyyot ha-Rishonot mi-Teiman* (Jerusalem, 1982), 97–99.

37. For a photograph of a person named 'Adani 'Adani, see *Ṣan'a u-Sevivatah be-Ṣilumei Yeḥiel Ḥaybi*, ed. Yosef Sha'ar, published by Ruma Haybi (Tel Aviv, 1985), p. 44, photograph no. 76.

38. In a personal correspondence dated 2 Dec 2010.

> For someone whose children do not live long, Heaven forbid, does not give a child a name when he is born but rather the family name. For example: well known is the instance of an elderly man here in Bnei Brak in Shikkun Vav, the father of R. Aharon Drayan, who was called by the name of Drayan Drayan, for this reason.[39] That is, his family name as well as his personal name, they came from the great city of Ṣan'a. Or Wald, that is son. If the child is a female, they call her Bint or Banayyah, that is, daughter. These names were never replaced but were retained their whole life through. In my childhood, I knew in our area one old woman with the name Banayyah,[40] but I did not know nor ever heard the reason for the name, and in any event, she came from Ṣan'a.[41]

In a 1910 document bearing the stamp of the Ṣan'a Bet Din, that grants a rabbi authority in religious matters as the rabbi in one of the communities in central Yemen, his name is given as follows: "Therefore, we have sent to our friend, the worthy sage, pious and humble, R. Tan'ami, may God protect and sustain him, son of the distinguished, deceased Sālem al-Tan'ami...." Later, in 1933, he again received authorization in a document from the Ṣan'a rabbis, and his name appears as in the foregoing: Ha-Rav, R. Tan'ami son of the deceased Sālem Al-tan'ami. Tan'ami is a family name, not a private one. A few of his descendants gave the reason for this name, saying that his personal name was Sālem and the family name Tan'ami. His grandson Efrayim further noted that when his father, Yosef, was called to the Torah or when they were saying a *Mi she-berakh* prayer they would use Yosef ben ha-Rav Sālem Tan'ami. Efrayim says that Ṭov Ṣadoq, an acquaintance of his grandfather R. Tan'ami, related to him that children had been born to Sālem Tan'ami, the father of R. Tan'ami, but had died soon after birth. For advice, he turned to the Ṣan'a sages, who suggested that he call a newborn son by the family name. And so when his grandfather was born, his father gave him the family name Tan'ami as his personal name, and that was how he survived. The personal name of Rabbi Tan'ami Tan'ami was changed to Sālem, the same as his father's.[42]

39. His name appears on the tax rolls in Ṣan'a; see Shalom Gamliel, *Pequdei Teiman: Mas he-Ḥasut be-Teiman* (Jerusalem, 1982), p. 196,
40. My maternal grandmother was called Banayyah, and she was born in the village of Ṣarfah in central Yemen.
41. In a personal correspondence dated 22 Apr 2010.
42. R. Tan'ami died in Aden in 1949 on his way to immigrate to Ereṣ Israel. I wish to

Change of the Temporary Name to a Permanent Name

R. Itamar Ḥayim Kohen,[43] whose parents immigrated to Israel from Ṣan'a, relates that his grandfather, R. Shelomo Efrayim Ha-Kohen, was given the name Wald, since his brothers had died very young. When he began to study with the Mori, he came home one day and complained that the children were making fun of him. His parents told him to pick a name, and he chose Slaymān [Heb., Shelomo], and that became his permanent name. R. Sālem Jamal of the Ṣan'a community, who served as the Ḥakham Bashi,[44] called his oldest son, Wald. This remained his set name even after he married in Yemen. After he immigrated to Israel, he changed his name from Wald to Yeḥi'el.[45]

Sālem and Ni'meh al-Jamal al-Qaleh (someone who roasts legumes) had a boy whom they called Wald. In the caption beneath a picture of him as a young man, his name appears as Wald Jamal.[46] At his wedding, they changed his name to 'Azaryah.[47]

R. Shalom Abhar, from the Tan'em community in central Yemen, listed the birth of one of his sons at the end of a printed prayer book: "The good flower was born, Wald ben Shalom Abhar, on Wednesday, 17 Av 2257 SEL [5706 AM/14 Aug 1946]. *Ha-maqom barukh hu,* will give him a good, long life, and pleasant years, *'ky"r.*"[48] Written above the name *Wald* in parentheses is the name Barukh, which was given to him later, about five years after his *aliyah* to Israel.[49] Shalom Ashwal was born in 1936 in the Ḥūfāsh community in central Yemen, and when young his parents called him Wald. The children of his parents, Yiḥye' and Badrah, had died soon after birth, so they decided that if they

thank Shalti'el Tan'ami for giving me his grandfather's document and his brother, Efrayim, of Qiryat Ata, who told me the story of the name.

43. Lives in Bnei Brak.

44. He was born circa 1859 and died in 1934. The Turks captured Ṣan'a in 1872 and ruled there until 1918. Rabbis who served in the Turkish period were granted the title "Ḥakham Bashi." R. Sālem Jamal served from some two years as the Ḥakham Bashi (1897–1899). On him see, Amram Qoraḥ, *Sa'arat Teiman* (Jerusalem, 1954), pp. 59–60.

45. As related by his daughter, Ziona Gamliel, Bat Yam.

46. See *Ṣan'a u-Sevivatah be-Ṣilumei Yeḥiel Ḥaybi*, p. 21, no. 23.

47. As related by his brother, El'azar Gamli'el, Tel Aviv. For the family picture in Ṣan'a, see *Ṣan'a u-Sevivatah be-Ṣilumei Yeḥiel Ḥaybi*, p. 21, no. 24.

48. I wish to thank his son Eliyahu of Ashkelon, who gave me his father's writings.

49. As related by Barukh Abhar of Ashkelon.

would have a son they would call him Wald, and turn him over for three months to the mother's sister, Zihrah. When he was six years old, he chose the name Sālem for himself, and after immigrating to Israel in 1949, he changed his name to Shalom, as others had done, replacing Sālem with Shalom.[50] On the name Wald as a permanent name, R. 'Azaryah Basis wrote: "As for the name Wald, someone in Rosh HaAyin had the name Wald and so he was called until the day he died, and there is also a Wald family."[51] R. Avraham Arye wrote that he knew someone in the Maḥaneh Yehudah neighborhood in Petaḥ Tiqvah who was called Wald Zā'īd. As for the name Bint, he mentioned R. Avraham Manṣūr, of the Maḥwīt community, who had from his two wives daughters with the name Bint:

> Many people called their daughters Bint, and that was the name of my grandmother (my mother's mother), Bint (Manṣūr), and her sister had the same name. The reason for calling them this comes for our notion that this is a charm so that the children will not die. But when these girls were married, they were given another name by which they were called in the *ketubbah*. So, for example, my grandmother, mentioned above, was called Bint, and when she married they gave her the name Esther. Likewise with her sister, when she married she was called by the name Ḥamāmah (Yona).[52]

Naomi bat Yiḥye' 'Irāqi of Ṣan'a, the wife of R. Ḥayim Pinḥas Kohen of Bnei Brak, was called Bint until her wedding. Then it was changed to Ni'meh, and after her *aliyah* to Israel the name was changed to Naomi, which sounds similar to her previous name.[53] Michal Badiḥi[54] said that her great-grandmother, from the Ṣan'a community, had the name *Bint*, but when she married it was replaced by Rūmiyah. Re'uma Ṣadoq, from the Manākhe community, related that her sister was called *Bint*, and as a child, at her own initiative, she changed it to Rina.[55] The older daughter of Ḥamāmah and Ḥayim 'Uzayri was called Bint, but later this name was replaced by Batyah.[56] Binat 'Efroni, who was born

50. Shalom Ashu'el lives in Qiryat Ono.
51. In a personal correspondence dated 8 Mar 2010.
52. In a personal correspondence dated 7 May 2010.
53. As related by R. Adam Bin Nun of Bnei Brak.
54. Lives in Givatayim.
55. Interview conducted by her granddaughter Vardit Yonati of Qiryat Ono.
56. For a picture of the mother and daughter, see *Ṣan'a u-Sevivatah be-Ṣilumei Yeḥiel Ḥaybi*, p. 45, no. 78.

in the Shibām community in Yemen, was given the name Bint as a temporary name by her parents. After her *aliyah*, her name was registered as *Binat*, which sounds similar to the temporary name.[57]

Permanency of the Temporary Name or Its Replacement

R. Ya'aqov Shar'abi wrote about the custom in Ṣan'a and central Yemen in which the temporary names Wald for a boy and Bint for a girl were given as a charm for life and that it was believed that if a child did not have a personal name, the demons could never harm him. People bearing these temporary names had their appellations changed at the time of their marriage. Wald Abu-Sit had his name changed to Ḥayim; the name of Wald of the Jamāl family became Yiḥye'. Bint the daughter of Yosef Meghori was changed to Tūrkiyya. Bint of the Mishriqi family became Banayyah. R. Shar'abi further noted that even though the temporary name had been replaced, there were still some people whose acquaintances continued to use it because they were accustomed to doing so.[58]

As noted, sometimes a temporary name remained, even though there was a permanent one, and was even listed before the latter.

In a *ketubbah* dated 21 Av 5704 (10 Aug 1944), from the Mazā'qah community, the name of the groom is al-Wald ibn Yiṣḥāq Yehudah al-Shāli. In a *ketubbah* from 13 Av 5670 (18 Aug 1910), from the Ṣan'a community, the name of the bride is registered as "Bint who is now called Naḍrah bint Yosef be Ibrāhim al-'Imrāni." In a *ketubbah* from 9 Adar 5678 (21 Feb 1918), from the Dhamār community, the name of the bride is written in the formulation "the daughter of Abraham Kohen who is called Bint." As the bride's name is Bint, they did not use the usual text, "He said to her the *bint* [daughter], bint Avraham," since using the term *bint* twice would have looked odd; so they changed the usual wordage to the foregoing, "who is called Bint." In contrast, in a *ketubbah* from 10 Elul 5686 (20 Aug 1926), from the Ṣan'a community, they did not refrain from this doubling when writing the bride's name: Al-Bint bint Yiḥye' ibn Yosef Pinḥas Ha-Kohen. In a *ketubbah* from 6 Tamuz 5703 (9 July 1943), from the Kawkabān community, the bride's personal name was changed from the temporary name Bint to the permanent name Sham'ah. The body of the *ketubbah* contains the bride's new name, "Sham'ah bint

57. Binat 'Efroni lives in Rehovot.

58. In a personal correspondence dated 2 Dec 2010.

m"w Sālem ben *m"w* Shukr who is called al-Ḥāḍri," but on the verso of the document, on which the sum of the dowry is written, we find the temporary name "al-Bint bint Sālem Shukr." In a registration of births and deaths in the family of R. Ḥayim Ṣāliḥ of Ṣan'a, the name of one of the daughters is listed as "Born was the daughter al-Bint, Shavu'ot night, 6 Sivan 5600 AM [12 June 1940]";[59] and when she married she was given the name Batyah.

Sometimes the temporary name became permanent. Yiḥye' Manṣūra, who came from the 'Imrān community, relates that his sister was called Bint, and this name became permanent.[60] Yisra'el 'Uzayri, of the Ṣan'a community, who is known by his byname of Asawwagh (the transporter) after his occupation of transporting passengers and merchandise on donkeys he owned, called his eldest daughter Bint. She married into the Wād'i family and her name was never changed.[61]

Selling an Infant to Another Family as a Segula.

Some people would make a virtual sale of an infant to another family as a *segula* that it should remain alive. The children of Naḍrah of the Ṣabari family, who married R. Yehudah Tobi of Ṣan'a, died when small. During one of her pregnancies, she went to the grave of R. Shalom Shabazi to pray that the child she was carrying would live. The son was named Shalom, after R. Shalom Shabazi; she later sold her son to a woman belonging to the Sa'adi family. This woman would come to their home to tend to the child, and with her money she would feed and clothe him, and the infant would call her "Mama."[62]

Tamniyyah Avraham, who emigrated from 'Ūdayn in southern Yemen, reported that the children of two of her sisters died when young, so upon the advice of rabbis of the community they changed the names of her two sisters. Her sister Rūmiyyah changed her name to Ḥannah and when she had a boy, she put an earring into a hole she had made in his ear and sold him to another woman. A number of months later she took the child back and eventually gave birth to four boys and three

59. The list was written on a page before the title page of the *siddur Tikhlāl*, part one (Jerusalem, 5654). In the possession of 'Azri ben R. Ḥayim Ṣāliḥ, Herzliya. I received a photocopy of the list from R. Adam Bin Nun, Bne Brak.

60. Yiḥye' Manṣūra, OBM, lived in Givat Shemuel.

61. As related by Ya'aqov Adani, Ramat Gan.

62. Yehudah Tobi, *Aḥarit le-Ish Shalom: Masekhet Ḥayyav shel R. Shalom Ṭobi* (Bnei Brak, 1990), p. 21.

girls, all of whom survived. Nine daughters born to her sister Miriyam all died, but after they changed her name to Naḍrah, she gave birth to two daughters and a son, all of whom lived.[63]

On this issue, R. Itamar Ḥayim Kohen tells that his grandfather, R. Yisra'el Mishriqi from the Shibām community, whose brothers died when small, was sold to the family of R. Yiḥye' Ghiyat of Ṣan'a. Their son, R. Moshe Ghiyat, used to jokingly call R. Yisra'el "my brother."

2. CHANGE OF NAMES

There was a widespread custom among Jewish communities to change the name of a critically ill person as a *segula* for complete recovery. We find support for this custom in the Talmud, in works by *poseqim*, and in *midrashim*. In the Babylonian Talmud, a name change is listed as one of the factors that can change one's fate for the better:

> R. Yiṣḥaq said: four things cancel the judgment against a man, namely: charity, beseeching, change of name, and change of behavior...change of name, as it is written, "As for Sarai your wife, you shall not call her name Sarai but Sarah shall be her name," and it is written, "And I will bless her, and moreover give you a son from her" (Gen. 17:15–16).[64]

Genesis Rabbah discusses the efficacy of name change as seen in Genesis 15:3, "And Abram said, 'Behold, to me You have given no seed'":

> R. Samuel bar R. Yiṣḥaq commented: My planetary fate oppresses me and declares, "Abram, you cannot beget a child!" Said the Holy One, blessed be He, to him: "Let it be even as your words: Abram will not beget, Abraham will beget." "As for Sarai your wife, you shall not call her name Sarai" (Gen. 17:16)—Sarai cannot beget but Sarah can beget.[65]

Maimonides discussed this issue in his *Mishneh Torah*:

> In the course of repentance the penitent cries out constantly before God with tears and supplications; gives as much to charity as he can; distances himself quite far from the thing brought him to sin; and

63. In an interview conducted by Meir Ben Ḥayim of Nahariya in April 2010.
64. TB Rosh Hashana 16b.
65. Genesis Rabbah 44:10. As for the name changes of Avraham and Sarah, see the commentary of R. Yehudah Jazfan, a nineteenth-century Yemenite rabbi, who commented on the matter in a mystical manner. Jazfan, *Minḥat Yehudah*, Gen. 17:16, p. 69ab.

> changes his name, as if to say I am now different person and not the person who did those sins but someone else; and changes all his actions for the better and on the straight path. He should also remove himself from his place, for exile atones for sin, as it causes him to be submissive as well as humble and meek.[66]

Rabbenu Menaḥem Hameiri and R. Yosef Qāfiḥ point out the benefit of a name change by a repentant. Hameiri stresses the psychological aspect expressed by name change. It is as if one were opening a new page in his life, an act that makes one forget all the past, since remaining steeped in the past is liable to bring a person to think that perhaps there is no way for him to atone for his deeds.[67] On Maimonides' statements cited above, R. Yosef Qāfiḥ noted: "Our rabbi added about changing a name, that is, 'I am now different person…,' to rebuff the opinion that the numeric total of a man's name and his mother's name influence the events of his life; but the name change is to remind him every moment that he is a repentant and that his should not stumble again."[68] R. Qāfiḥ's words bear a critical note, with perhaps a hint of derision for those people who change their name according to numerical calculations; in his opinion, positive deeds change the negative image of the past.

On the custom of changing the name of a seriously ill person, R. Moshe Isserles (the Rama, Poland, 16th c.) wrote: "This is what they did, to bless an ill person in the synagogue by calling them a new name, since a name change will rend his fate asunder."[69]

Among the Jewish communities different customs became associated with name changes. Some added the new name to the previous one, while others substituted one name for the other. Until sometime in the Middle Ages, the usage was for the new name to replace the old one, but in later periods the new name became an addition to the previous one. R. Yeḥi'el Epstein (Minsk, 19th c.) wrote in *Arukh ha-Shulḥan*:

66. *Hilkhot Teshuva* 2:4.

67. R. Menaḥem ben R. Shlomo *le-bet Me'ir ha-Mekhuneh Hameiri, Bet ha-Beḥira 'al Masekhet Rosh ha-Shana*, ed. Avraham Sofer (Jerusalem, 1969), 16b; see also Sarah Munitz, *"Shemot Benei Adam—Minhag ve-Halakhah"* (MA diss., Bar-Ilan University, 1989), p. 87 [Hebrew].

68. See his commentary on the *Mishneh Torah, Hilkhot Teshuvah* 2, ṣiyyun 7, pp. 590–91.

69. His commentary on the *Shulḥan Arukh, Yoreh De'ah*, siman 335, 10.

> As is known, in the days of the sages and the Rishonim, a person was not called by two names at all, as we see in the Babylonian and Jerusalem Talmuds and Midrashim, that you do not have a *tana* or an *amora* who had two names. But that we do find Abba Sha'ul, this is nothing but one name, Sha'ul, with a modifier, like rav, rabbi. Among the Rishonim, too we do not find (except in Tosafot Ketubbot 98: beginning with "He said: They also did not have nicknames in their day").[70] Moreover, a change of name because of illness was an actual name change where they substituted a new name for the old, and not as we do it by adding a name. We also saw in the Torah name changes and not the addition of a name, such as Sarai to Sarah, Avram to Avraham, Hoshe'a to Yehoshu'a. And the Patriarch Ya'aqov, when the Holy One, blessed be He, said to him: "No longer Ya'aqov ... but Yisra'el,"[71] we did not find in the entire Bible that they called two names, but either Ya'aqov or Yisra'el. This shows that the name Ya'aqov was not completely uprooted, because that is what God wanted as the rabbis explained (at the end of the first chapter of Berakhot[72]).[73]

R. Mordechai Brisk (Hungary, 19th–20th c.) wrote in a similar vein. When referring to the statements in the Talmud, *Rosh Hashanah* (16b), cited above, he noted that in the rabbinic period it was customary that when they changed a person's name, they would use only the new name and not follow the custom of also appending the previous name: "And even now, when people change the name of an ill person, Heaven forbid, they call him by his former name and do not forgo the previous name, but from the Gemara mention, this should not be." R. Brisk gave further reasons for joining the two names, as in the Midrash Rabbah cited above, so as not to uproot the earlier name that had been given for his relatives:

> Thus, in our days when a son is named for his grandparents or for great *ẓaddiqim* (the righteous) and no one wants the name of the grandparents and *ẓaddiqim* to be forgotten and disappear, so they change the name also leaving the previous name, so their will be a memorial of the soul of the grandparents and the *ẓaddiqim*...and since it is possible to maintain both; both so the name of the grandparents will not be forgotten, and since the name was actually changed, the two names

70. This is not precise, and he apparently means that this was rare. On nicknames in the rabbinic period, see above part 2, chap. 1, sect. 2.

71. Gen. 32:29.

72. Berakhot 13a.

73. Yeḥi'el Mikhal Epstein, *Arukh ha-Shulḥan*, *Even ha-Ezer*, siman 129, 12.

> are now one, so they made it customary to leave the former name as well.[74]

R. Ovadia Yosef (Israel, 20th c.) wrote that the first given name should not be taken away:

> Know that according Lurianic Kabbalah, a person's name should not be completely changed, even for an ill one, as it is written: "whatsoever the man would call every living creature, that was to be the name thereof."[75] We learn that every person receives his vitality from the root letters of his name, and if the name he was given at birth is taken away, it may be that the replacement name does not belong to his vitality, and his vitality will cease, Heaven forbid, so that is what they do at the *meṣal'im 'anaḥna* prayer.[76] When they bless the name of the ill person, they do not remove the first given name but rather they add to it.[77]

R. Ḥayim Yosef David Azulai (the Ḥida) wrote: "The name change [is made] by a pious Ḥakham with great devotion to imbue him with a new holy soul."[78] Similarly, we find that R. Mordechai Eliyahu (Israel, 20th c.) wrote, "This is a warning not to be hasty to make a name change for a person except with a halakhic ruling from an ordained rabbi."[79]

Under the influence of the disciples of the Ari, the Ḥida recommended particular names: "When making a name change for a women,

74. Mordechai of Brisk, *Shut Mahram mi-Brisk ha-Ḥadashot* (1990), 2, Section 7.
75. Gen. 2:19.
76. According to the beginning of the מצלאין אנחנא [we are praying] prayer, in which the name of an ill person is changed. For the text of this prayer as well as others recited upon the occasion of a name change, see, for example, Shelomo Qoraḥ, *'Arikhat Shulḥan – Yalquṭ Ḥayim, Yoreh De'ah*, 1 (Bnei Berak, 2003), pp. 6–8; Mishael Rubin, *Qorei Shemot, Halakhot u-Minhagim be-'Inyenei Shemot u-Qeri'atam* (Qiryat Arba, 2002), pp. 349–53; Avraham Levi, *Va-Yiqare Shemo be-Yisra'el* (Jerusalem, 2008), pp. 631–38; Avishai Teherani, *Keter Shem Ṭov*, 2, pp. 409–14.
77. Ovadia Yosef, *Halikhot 'Olam*, pt. 7 (Jerusalem, 2002), p. 232. This change is similar to the solution proposed in the ethical will of R. Yehudah Heḥasid that the name of a groom should not be the same as his father-in-law's and so on, for if they are adding another name it is not at all the same at the first one, for it is a completely different name. See above, part 1, chap. 2, sect. 4.
78. Ḥida, *Sansan le-Ya'ir*, in *Oṣerot ha-Ḥida, Musar ve-Hanhagot* (Jerusalem, 1976), Siman 11, Ot 7; the Ḥida was given the birth name of Yosef, while the names Ḥayim and David were added later. See Meir Benayahu, *Rabbi Ḥayim Yosef David Azulai*, Jerusalem, 1959 [Hebrew], p. 10.
79. In the approbation he gave for Mishael Rubin, *Qorei Shemot*, p. 5; see also p. 303.

do not call her Raḥel, Bat Sheva, Tamar, [or] Leah, but Ḥannah, Sarah, Yokheved."[80]

Names were sometimes chosen that expressed long life and good health (such as Ḥayim, Ḥai, Ḥayyah) or that contained the theophoric element. Others picked a name at random or chose according to a *petiḥa* (opened passage) in the Torah. Still others chose through the manipulations of letters such that the new name would not have any letters included in the previous name, or numerical calculations, so that the new name, for example, would have a larger sum in *gematria* than the previous name.

In a few locations, they would publicly proclaim the new name and even hold a special ceremony with the congregation in attendance in the synagogue, along with the recitation of prayers and blessings.[81] In Ṣan'a and the nearby communities the custom of name-changing was not common. R. Shelomo Qoraḥ wrote, "Few were those who used to make name changes"[82] and R. Pinḥas Qoraḥ wrote, "And in the Holy Community of the Jews of Yemen, the custom of changing names did not spread,"[83] stating further:

> On the whole, they did not customarily change names, except on very rare occasions, and especially when a person bore the name of a relative the name was not changed. Only in cases of illness did they used to change a name, and this was so as to change a decree about the person and as a charm for a long life, but there was no special prayer for this, and among the prayers and *baqqashot*, no prayer was included for adding or changing a name. Even though Rambam did write in *Hilkhot Teshuva* that one of the signs of a repentant is that "he changes his name," in any event, no name change took place in Yemen. Some people do say a *Mi she-Berakh* and give the person a new name.[84]

In the other Yemenite communities, however, the custom of changing a name was accepted, and it was applied in various situations, as a charm for healing as well as for ensuring good luck. R. Avraham Arye

80. Ḥida, *Sefer Devash le-Pi*, which is part 2 of the kunteres of מדב"ר קדומו"ת (Tarna 1929).
81. Munitz, *"Shemot Benei Adam,"* pp. 100–5; Teherani, *Keter Shem Ṭov*, 1, fifth branch, siman 1, 4–13, pp. 300–15; Yishayahu Zussya Wilhelm, *Ziv ha-Shemot* (New York, 1987), chap. 28, pp. 98–101.
82. Sh. Qoraḥ, *'Arikhat Shulḥan, Yalqut Ḥayim, Yore De'ah*, 1, *siman* 335, 22, 6.
83. Pinḥas Qoraḥ, *Bet Mo'ed*, 1 (Bnei Brak, 2000), chap. 1, p. 9.

cited two examples, one from his family, which emigrated from the Maḥwīt community in central Yemen, and the other from his wife's family, which immigrated to Israel from the 'Ūdayn community in southern Yemen.

> My revered father, my teacher my elder, OBM, on the day of his *brit*, was given the name Aharon, and he cried all the time, so his uncle R. Avraham (who had only one daughter) suggested calling the infant by his name, Avraham; that is what they did and he stopped crying, and from then on he was called by that name (an issue of a charm).
>
> In southern Yemen, in many instances they used to give a new name to a women getting married. My mother-in-law, OBM, was called soon after her birth by the name Ghazāl, and on her wedding day she was given the name Yaman, and in Israel she was called Yemima.[85]

Shelomo Raṣhabi, from the Raḍa'i community in southern Yemen, told of a name change made for a ten-year-old child. This child, whose name was Sālem, was very short and looked like a four-year-old. His parents decided to change his name, so they turned to the *bet din* in their town, which decided to change his name to Manṣūr. The name change took place in the *bet midrash* accompanied by light refreshments, in the presence of the Mori and the pupils in the *bet midrash* in which the boy studied. The Mori declared that from now on they would call the boy *Manṣūr*. After the name change, Manṣūr developed rapidly, being even taller than usual for his age.[86]

Shelomo 'Adani, from the Ḍāli' community in southern Yemen, related that if a person was ill or had no children, the rabbi would advise his father to change his name. After the name was replaced, the new name would become known by word of mouth, without any special ceremony.[87] Shalom Sa'ad, whose parents came from the village Nābāt in central Yemen, related that the reasons for name change were illness, problems of livelihood, and barrenness. Before the changing of the name, people would consult the rabbi or a person who would open a book used for the purpose of suggesting the giving of a name. The new name would be declared in the synagogue or at an event with the par-

84. In a personal correspondence of April 2010.
85. In a personal correspondence dated 7 May 2010.
86. Interview conducted by R. Gilad Ṣadoq of Bnei Brak.
87. Interview conducted by R. Gilad Ṣadoq of Bnei Brak.

ticipation of congregation members, though there were instances when the name change was not announced publicly because of shame.[88]

Na'ama Qa'ṭabi, whose parents emigrated from the Baraṭ community in northern Yemen, wrote that her father Se'īd ben Se'īd Ṣabari was first called Yiḥye' but when he became ill, his name was changed to that of his father.[89]

Amos Raṣon, who was born in the Geula transit camp in Aden in 1947, tells that a few months after his birth a furuncle was discovered under his chin that made breathing very difficult and threatened his life. His parents treated him as was customary in Yemen through *makwa*, that is, burning his body with a hot iron, and the wound healed. At the same time, his parents changed his name to Shim'on, like the name of R. Shalom Shabazi's son, and his mother took an oath that R. Shabazi should consider him as his son and protect him from diseases and all harm. When he was twenty, he returned to using the name Amos, which had been his birth name, and now he uses both names, with the name Amos primary.[90]

Announcement of the new name was sometimes accompanied by a ceremony. In the Ṣan'a community, some people used to hand out roasted food items and sweets to the young children, while the new name was declared aloud. Sarah Alsheikh, from the Ṣan'a community, told that if a child was ill or cried for no reason, they would go to the rabbi, who would open a book and decide whether to give him/her a new name as a sign for a good life. She gave the example of her daughter, whose name had been changed from Tūrkiyah to Ḍobyah, "Good." Announcement of the new name was made and they would invite children from the Mori and feed them *lasis*, made from cooked wheat, lentils, and sorghum.[91] Yeḥi'el Ṣan'āni,[92] an emigré of the 'Ayāshiya com-munity in southern Yemen, tells that in his community they would give each child a full handful of sweets after he repeated the new name. Moshe Ben David, coming from the Bayḥān community, informed us that in his community they mainly changed names for children in the case of illness or misfortune, and the substitution was made at a special celebration of

88. Interview conducted by Yehonatan Levi of Rosh HaAyin.
89. In a personal correspondence dated April 2009.
90. In a personal correspondence dated 3 Mar 2010.
91. Interview conducted by David Ben Shalom Qāfiḥ of Jerusalem.
92. Lives in Rosh HaAyin.

sweet things so that the children should remember from that day on that his name had been changed.[93] R. Almog Shelomo Akhlufi reported that in the Ḥaymeh and Mhāṣr communities changes were done only in the case of illness or danger, and this happened rarely.[94]

In the villages and in southern Yemen, people usually consulted a *menajjim* (a fortune-teller) who could see according to the *tanjīm* (examination of the names of the ill person and his mother through *gematria* calculations) what the proper name should be. With the help of the rabbi arranging the *ketubbah* and the *kiddushin*, the woman was offered the name in line with her mother's name and according to the *gematria* calculations. R. Sa'adyah Ḥozeh, a native of Shar'ab, tells of the customs there:

> Just as they take care that the *mazal* (astrological sign) match that of the man. This means they make a calculation with the woman and her mother and reduce by 12 the number that results and from what remains they know which *mazal* it belongs to: that is, Aries 1, Taurus 2, Gemini 3, Cancer 4, Leo 5, Virgo 6, Libra 7, Scorpio 8, Sagittarius 9, Capricorn 10, Aquarius 11, Pisces 12. The same way they calculate the name of the groom and his mother's name, and take away 12, 12. And whatever remains is his zodiac sign as above. And then before the groom meets the bride to become matched to her, or if he already was matched with her, they change her name, so that the *mazal* will befit the both of them the best way.[95]

R. Yiṣḥaq Raṣabi writes:

> Usually before marriage the name of the groom or the name of the bride was changed by those familiar with dealing with names, a person who has a book of names and who understands calculations of the *mazalot*, so that the couple will merit domestic tranquility and have children; and I went into this at length in *Shulḥan Arukh ha-Mequṣar*, the *Yoreh De'ah* section, the laws of diviners and soothsayers, and in *Even ha-'Ezer*, laws of *kiddushin* and marriage, and from there you will learn it.[96]

93. Interview conducted by 'Omri Portugez of Nes Ziona.
94. In a personal correspondence dated 16 Feb 2011.
95. Sa'adya Ḥozeh, *Toledot ha-Rav Shalom Shabazi u-Minhagei Yahadut Shar'ab be-Teiman,* 1 (Jerusalem, 1973), p. 89; see also p. 86. The arithmetic procedure described here may be the division by 12 and categorization of the remainder according to the zodiac signs.
96. In a personal correspondence dated 22 Apr 2010. See also Yiṣḥaq Raṣabi, *Shulḥan Arukh ha-Mequṣar*, vol. 4 (Bnei Brak, 1989), sect. 108, par. 15, p. 414; ibid., 7, section 69, pp. 44–46.

As for name change, R. Raṣabi wrote of three instances in his family:

> *Adoni, avi, mori, ve-rabbi* [My father] was called by the name Nissim when he was born. Before his wedding, one of his friends, who understands the *mazzalot*, changed his name to Naḥum. About a year later, *"mv"r* took back the name Nissim. Apparently, he had found an error in the calculation. For some reason it was just the name *Naḥum* that became known. If you would say Mori Nissim, they thought you meant his father. But even decades after his father's death, they knew him only by the name Mori Naḥum. I remember that he signed his name then in at least two places as Naḥum ben Mori ve-R. Nissim. But, as noted, afterwards he himself did not agree to that though the name Nissim remained known only among the family members, and thus he always signed with the name Nissim. His mother's name is Salāmeh, though previously her name was Ni'meh, and that is what is written in her *ketubbah*. The name change came about after several years had passed and she had not given birth or only to daughters. My aunt, my mother's sister is called Ḥannah; she was whiny and fragile; her husband, my uncle, ha-Rav R. Yisra'el used to say that she was "finicky," meaning too fastidious and refined. Her father-in-law, my grandfather ha-Rav R. Nissim, OBM, always told her, when she cried, using the cantillation and stress of the verse " Ḥannah, why are you weeping? and why don't you eat? and why is your heart grieved?" (I Sam. 1:8). Finally she was fed up with the name Ḥannah, and so it was changed to Lulūwa. Apparently, since then in our family the name Ḥannah is derogatory. When my father, the distinguished, honorable rabbi, wanted to scold one of his daughters, he would address her by the name Ḥannah.[97]

R. Raṣabi wrote that the new name was made known from one man to another and from a woman to another woman, and they made no *Mi-she-berakh* in honor of the new name.

In Yemen, name changes were more common among the women. My father's sister was named Zihrah, and the father of her future husband, who was expert in the practice of changing names, proposed to switch it to Ni'meh; and the new name was written in the *ketubbah*. Shalom Maḥfūd, from Bane Ṭayba in the Dhamār district, who dealt with amulets and astrological signs, changed the name of his intended wife, Simḥah, to Miriyam, which matches her *mazal*; his wife's new name was identical to her sister's name.[98] Se'īdah Aharon, who immigrated to Is-

97. In a personal correspondence dated 22 Apr 2010.

98. *Be-Derekh Lo Selula, Ovadya Ben Shalom: Mish'ol Ḥayim u-Mif'al Ḥayim*, ed. Avshalom Mizrahi ([Netanya], 2000), pp. 13–14, 17–18.

rael from the village Adūfa in the Shar'ab district, related that her name had been Ghaniya, and when she married it was changed to Se'īdah.[99]

In some instances they changed a woman's name at the beginning of her pregnancy to "ensure" the desired sex of the newborn. Nissim Binyamin Gamlieli told of such a case involving the wife of his brother Shalom. The couple had three sons and during the fourth pregnancy, the grandfather was afraid that his daughter-in-law would give birth to a son and to increase the love between the couple it was preferable that she give birth to a daughter. The grandfather, who dealt with this issue of matching names, changed his daughter-in-law's name from Shadhrah to Miryam. After the name change, she had six girls in a row and after them two boys.[100] I think that the grandfather's aim was the fulfillment of the commandment to be fruitful and multiply, which the rabbis state is completed with the birth of one boy and one girl. R. Itamar Cohen of Bnei Brak told me that he was present on an occasion when someone asked for a blessing from R. Ḥayim Kisār that he should have sons, and the rabbi blessed him to have *zekharim u-neqevot* (males and females), with the rabbi stressing the word *u-neqevot*.

In Yemenite *ketubbot* and in the Ṣan'a Bet Din registry, we find support for the custom of name changing, with the new name registered next to the previous one. In Yemenite *ketubbot* there are several indications of former names both within the *ketubbah*, as well as on the verso of the document.[101] In a 1536 *ketubbah* from the Ṣan'a community, the name of the bride is given as "Salāmeh whose former name was Shamsiyyah." In a *ketubbah* dated 13 Tishri 5617 (25 Sep 1855), from the Sadam community, the name of the bride is written as "Rūmiyyah whose former name was Zihrah." In a *ketubbah* from 28 Shevat 5630 (30 Jan 1870) from the Sayyān community, the woman's name change is written in the last part of the *ketubbah*, "and we acquired from Slaymān the groom herein for the bride Qurṭ who was formerly called Rūmiyyah."

We also find a name change on the verso of the *ketubbah*, since it took place after the wedding. On the back of a *ketubbah* from Ṣan'a from

99. Interview conducted by Ya'ir Shunem of Rosh HaAyin.

100. Nissim Binyamin Gamlieli lives in Ramleh. He immigrated to Israel in 1949 with "On the Wings of Eagles" operation.

101. Some people customarily listed the name change on the verso of the *ketubbah*. See Yiḥye' Ṣāliḥ [Mahariṣ], *Shut Pe'ulat Ṣaddiq*, ed. M. Raṣabi, part 1 (Jerusalem, 2003), par. 68.

1774/5, the passage on the obligation of the dowry opens with the words "May it be for a good sign, the name Zihrah has become the name Rūmiyyah." On the verso of a *ketubbah*, from the Ṣan'a community, whose date has become blurred but which was earlier than 1684, the husband wrote a *sheṭar* in which he noted the change of his wife's name from Simḥah to Salāmeh, and noted her rights to everything written in the *ketubbah*.

Sometimes we find a fuller text about the name change on the back of a *ketubbah*, perhaps years after the marriage. For example, in a *ketubbah* from Ṣan'a, dated 5 Adar 5574 (25 Feb 1814), beneath the sum of the dowry on the back of the document an indication of the name change appears:

> [Changed was] the name Rūmiyyah to the name Ghazāl. May it be His will that the change of her name is for a good sign and [good] luck and for sons involved in Torah and observing the commandments of Israel, and may they merit...in their Torah, their wedding canopy, and their g[oo]d deeds, *'ky"r*. Thursday, of the weekly reading[102] "that you may live, you and your offspring" (Deut. 30:19). *'ky"r*, 2130 SEL [5579 AM/1819].[103]

In this case the motive for the name change was the desire for children, with five years having passed since the wedding. In such instances, it was the woman's name that was changed. Many *ketubbot* provide us examples of changes of the woman's name, but not even one case of a name change for a man. This can, perhaps, be explained in that they thought that usually it was the woman who was barren and not the man, or by the man's being able to marry another woman and have children with her, or it may be that this is an expression of the status of the woman, being subordinate to her husband.

Written on the back of a *ketubbah* from the Ṣan'a community, dated 13 Shevat 5683 (24 Jan 1823), under the sum of the dowry, after twenty years from the marriage day, we find:

> For a good sign and success with children, who live, the name of Ghazāl was changed to Ghane. May it be His will [that] this name change will be for the good and for blessing and for success. And Ghane has already acquiesced to her husband, this aforementioned

102. Alluding to the weekly Torah reading, *parshat Pequdei,* in which the verse cited occurs.

103. This text was signed by the *dayyan,* Ha-Rav Avraham ben ha-Rav Aharon Manzali.

> Yosef *qirsh ḥajar*, who paid her to buy the children[104] that she would give birth to from now and forever, by the virtue of the Mighāleḥi,[105] may its merit protect us. And she vowed, this is the *qirsh* in the name of her children that they should live for a long time by the merit of this Torah scroll. Wednesday, 23 Sivan 2153 SEL [5602 AM/1 June 1842].[106]

From the expressions "living descendant" as well as "so that her children should live," we see that this was not a barren woman and that the reason for the name change was that her children had died. In a *ketubbah* from the Ṣan'a community, dated 15 Adar 5617 (11 Mar 1857), written on the verso of the *ketubbah*, beneath the sum of the dowry, about twelve years later, we read:

> The name of this Rūmiyyah has been changed to Salāmeh, may it be His will that it will be for success and for raising children and for life and for good and for blessing, *Hamaqom barukh hu*, and the Lord will bless with the blessing "higher than the frontlet,"[107] *'ky"r*. Monday, 14 Sivan 2180 SEL [5629 AM/24 May 1869].[108]

Here, too, from the blessing cited, one may understand that the reason for the name change is that her children had died. Written on the back of a *ketubbah* from the Maṣwi community, dated 15 Tevet 5632 (28 Dec 1871), about ten years after the wedding day:

> On this date the name of Salāmeh, Se'īdah. For a good sign and blessing and success. And this was on Monday, 8 Tishri 2192 SEL (5641 AM/13 Sep 1880), and all is confirmed.[109]

The reason for the name change was apparently for a blessing and success in daily life. Written about a year later, on the back of a *ketubbah*

104. The buying of children was done as a *segula* that the children she would give birth to would stay alive, since they were somebody else's children. See examples above at the end of sect. 1.

105. *Mighāleḥi* is a sanctified Torah scroll. On sanctified Torah scrolls, see below chap. 6, sect. 2.

106. This text was signed by the Av Bet Din, the *dayyan* ha-Rav Yosef ben Shalom Qāra.

107. An allusion to the priestly blessing in the Temple in which the priests would raise their hands above their heads, except for the High Priest about whom it is written "except for the High Priest who lifts his hands only as high as the frontlet" (M Sotah 6:6).

108. This text was signed by R. Ḥayim ben R. Yosef Qoraḥ.

109. This text was signed by R. Se'īd ben Yiḥye' Sāmari.

from the Ṣan'a community, dated 30 Adar I 5643 (9 Mar 1883), beneath the sum of the dowry, we find:

> On this date the name of Sa'dah was changed to Ghazāl, may it be His will, before the God in the heavens that this change of name will be for a good *mazal* and to her husband for *mazal*, sons and long life and plentiful sustenance, so may the Merciful one say, Amen, so may it be. Sunday, 5 Adar 2195 SEL [5644 AM/ 2 Mar 1884].[110]

Apparently this is for domestic tranquility, health, good livelihood, and children. On a *ketubbah* from the Ṣan'a community, dated 17 Av 5644 (8 Aug 1884), written about eight months later on its verso, beneath the sum of the dowry, we find

> On this day the name Berakhah was changed to another name, Salāmeh, may it be pleasing to the Lord of the heavens that she be called by the name Salāmeh for a blessing and success and long life and sons who deal with Torah and *miṣvot* and have long lives and plentiful sustenance, so shall say the Merciful one, *'ky"r*. The *s[eder]* [weekly portion] "And Moses blessed them" (Ex. 39:43), Adar 2196 SEL [5645 AM/ 1885].[111]

This name change was apparently made to gain a blessing and the birth of children.

As to the writing of the names in *gittin* in the case of a name change, some of the *poseqim* believe that one must also write the former name. First they write the new name and after it the previous one, inserting the word *ha-mekhuneh* or *demitqare* (for a man)/*demitaqarya* (for a woman), meaning "who is called."[112]

A review of the names of the divorcing couple in 175 *gittin* from Yemen informs us that in contrast to *ketubbot*, in which former names are noted, in *gittin* name changes are barely noted, except in one case. In a *get* written on 22 Sivan 5690 (18 June 1930), in the Qahrah community, the name of the wife was registered as "Ghaliyyah who is called Zihrah bat Hārūn." R. Yaacov Sappir wrote in his remark about the Yemenite custom of writing personal names in *gittin*: "I did not see or find that they would write *ha-mekhuneh* or *demitqare*, only according to the name

110. This text was signed by R. Avraham Ṣāliḥ.

111. This signatory to this text is the *dayyan*, R. Avraham Ṣāliḥ.

112. For sources on the rabbis who deal with the issue of writing names in *gittin*, see Avishai Teherani, *Keter Shem Ṭov*, Section 1, pp. 299, 311.

that they call him now in the city, not the birth name or when called up to the Torah."[113]

In contrast to *gittin*, in the Bet Din registry in Ṣan'a, in which divorces were briefly noted, the former names of the divorcing couple are listed. In 30 of the 500 divorces listed from 1765 to 1780,[114] the previous name is also noted. Sometimes this listing is extremely brief, such as, "Slaymān ben Yiḥye' Sa'ādi divorced his wife Lūlūwah who is called Ghazāl bat Yosef Alḥajāji. Wednesday, 11 Elul 2086 SEL [5435 AM/6 Sep 1775";[115] "Ya'ish ben Se'īd Duḥān divorced his wife Badrah who had been called Ghazāl bat Yiḥye' al-Ḥadād. And she relinquished her *ketubbah* and other obligations. Sunday, 27 Tammuz 2090 SEL [5439 AM/11 July 1779]. And this remission was made in order to obtain the *get*, since she requested the separation... And *shalom*."[116]

Listed below is the corpus of names written in *ketubbot* from Yemen and the Ṣan'a *Pinkas Bet Din* (Religious Court Registry). The entries first present the former name, then the new name, and in parentheses the source is noted. For the Ṣan'a *Pinkas Bet Din*, the serial number given to the listing and the page numbers are cited; for the *ketubbot*, the name of the community and the date are given.

Badrah ➛	Ghane (Pinkas, 497, p. 184)
Badrah ➛	Ghazāl (Pinkas, 785, p. 279)
Badrah ➛	Ḥamāmah (Ketubbot, Ṣan'a, 17 Jan 1907)
Badrah ➛	Simḥah (Pinkas, 399, p. 155)
Banayyah ➛	Malūk (Pinkas, 407, p. 157)
Bint ➛	Naḍrah (Ketubbot, Ṣan'a, 18 Aug 1910)
Ghazāl ➛	Badrah (Pinkas, 379, pp. 148–49)
Ghazāl ➛	Badrah (Pinkas, 633, 232 = 679, 249)
Ghazāl ➛	Salāmeh (Pinkas, 374, p. 147)

113. Yaacov Sappir, *Even Sappir*, 1 (Lyck, 1866), p. 63a. For a discussion of Sappir's statements, see above part one, chap. 3, sect. 1.

114. *Misawwadeh*, 1, par. 319–828, pp. 129–289.

115. In the source, the listings were written in the *Misawwadeh* in Arabic (in Hebrew letters), and was translated into Hebrew by N. B. Gamlieli. *Misawwadeh*, 1, par. 495, p. 183.

116. *Misawwadeh*, 1, par. 677, p. 248. In another ruling concerning this couple made half a year later, it was written: "Ya'īsh ben Se'īd Dukhan divorced his wife Badrah Dahut who is called Ghazāl bet Yiḥye' Alḥadād. And she has given him all her rights, as decided between them, in writing, Alqāḍi. Sunday, 23 Shevat 2091 SEL, 5440 [30 Jan 1780]" (*Misawwadeh*, 1, par. 633, p. 232).

Ghazāl ➛	Salāmeh (Pinkas, 451, p. 170)
Ghazāl ➛	Simḥah (Pinkas, 460, p. 173)
Ghane ➛	Lūluwah (Pinkas, 404, p. 156)
Ghane ➛	Simḥah (Pinkas, 561, p. 204)
Zihrah ➛	Rūmiyyah (Ketubbot, Sudum, 25 Sep 1855)
Zihrah ➛	Rūmiyyah (Ketubbot, Ṣan'a, 1774–5)
Zihrah ➛	Simḥah (Pinkas, 750, p. 240)
Ḥabībah ➛	Zihrah (Pinkas, 343, p. 137)
Hannah ➛	Badrah (Pinkas, 727, p. 265)
Kādhiyyah ➛	Ghazāl (Pinkas, 430, p. 164)
Lūluwah ➛	Ghazāl (Pinkas, 495, p. 183)
Lūluwah ➛	Ghazāl (Pinkas, 519, p. 189)
Lūluwwah ➛	Ghazāl (Pinkas, 341, p. 137)
Miryam ➛	Zihrah (Ketubbot, Sāma, 10 Oct 1924)
Nakhlah ➛	Ghuṣna (Ketubbot, Zāwyat Shi'bān, 10 Apr 1946.)
Naḍrah ➛	Rūmiyyah (Pinkas, 357, p. 141)
Salāmeh ➛	Simḥah (Pinkas, 701, p. 257)
Se'īdah ➛	Lūluwah (Pinkas, 392, pp. 152–53)
Se'īdah ➛	Rūmiyah (Pinkas, 402, p. 156)
Ṣan'a ➛	Miryam (Ketubbot, Ṣa'dah, 1 Jan 1907)
Rūmiyah ➛	Banayyah (Pinkas, 408, p. 186)
Rūmiyah ➛	Salāmeh (Ketubbot, Dhamār, 30 Aug 1877)
Rūmiyah ➛	Salāmeh (Pinkas, 509, p. 187)
Rūmiyah ➛	Qurṭ (Ketubbot, Sayyān, 30 Jan 1870)
Simḥah ➛	Salāmeh (Ketubbot, Ṣan'a, before 1684)
Simḥah ➛	Salāmeh (Pinkas, 525, p. 192)
Simḥah ➛	Rūmiyah (Pinkas, 381, p. 149)
Shamsiyyah ➛	Salāmeh (Ketubbot, Ṣan'a, 9.1.1536)
Tamniyyah ➛	Wardah (Ketubbot, Ṣa'dah, 17.4.1916)
Yedidah ➛	Ghane (Pinkas, 474, p. 177)

All these name changes inform us that they did not customarily add a name to an existing one, but exchanged it for a new one, as was the custom in earlier times. Similarly, carefully maintained customs that prevailed elsewhere on the matter of name changes, such as using the letters of the former name, did not gain a foothold in Yemen.

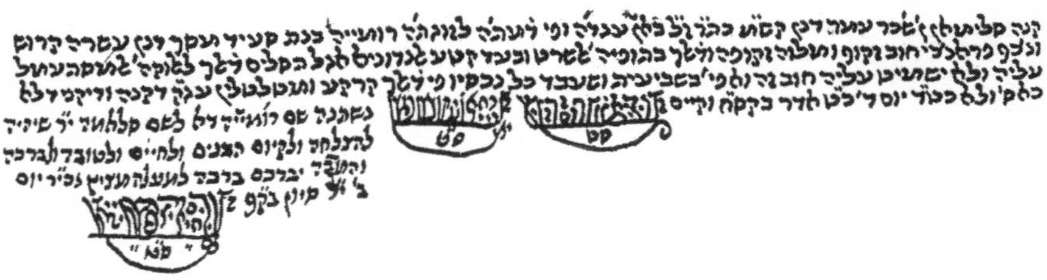

A bride's name change in 5629 (1869),
on the back of a ketubbah from the Ṣan'a community
In the possession of Rabbi Eliyahu Yiṣḥaq Halevi (Qādi), New York

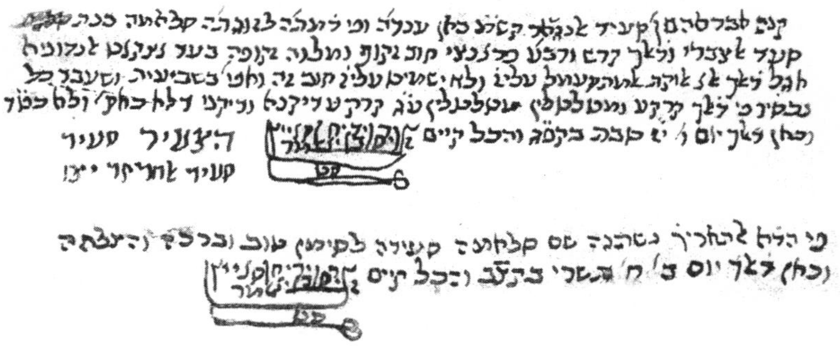

Change of a bride's name in 5629 (1869),
on the back of a ketubbah from the Maṣui community
In the possession of Natan Qa'ṭabi, Gederah

CHAPTER FIVE

LINEAGE

1. LINEAGES AMONG THE JEWS

Some Yemenite family trees can be traced back hundreds of years. In fact, some claim to trace their lineage to the period of the founding fathers of the nation. The lineage lists that were maintained by many Yemenite families served as a way to express one's admiration for the history of the family, as well as to preserve the heritage for the next generation. Yet, in many of these lineages there are errors deriving from incorrect copying and so in some lineages the people listed do not match historical reality.[1]

Prevalent among the Yemenite Jews is a tradition that their family trees go back to the patriarchs. Some families in Yemen had a tradition that their lineage went back many centuries, but they did not have a document to prove it. For example, R. Yaacov Sappir cites the tradition of the Hadani family in Ṣan'a, which attributes itself to the tribe of Dan that reached Yemen; a tradition of the Priestly family Meghori, that ascribes this family to the division of Yehoyariv; the Pinḥas family that traces its lineage to Pinḥas ben El'azar ben Aharon Ha-Kohen.[2] The poet Raṣon Halevi, who originated from Shar'ab in southern Yemen, wrote about the traditions of a number families from Shar'ab. For example, one of the them has a tradition of a lineage that stretches back to the tribe of Zebulun; the Shumali and Yemini families ascribe themselves to the tribe of Benjamin; and the Yehud family traces its lineage to King

1. Shlomo Englard, *"Le-Ḥeqer ha-Yoḥasin be-Yisra'el,"* *Sefunot* 10, no. 2 (1991): 101–8.
2. Sappir, *Even Sappir* (Lyck, 1866), pp. 68a, 87a, 96a, 99b. See also above part 2, chap. 1, sect. 3.

David.[3] One of the interviewees from the Moshe family of the village Jiḥzān in southern Yemen explained the source of the family pedigree to the prophet Moses (Moshe ben 'Amram).[4]

According to rumor, these lineage documents were burned in the eighteenth century. R. Amran Qoraḥ wrote alluding to their disappearance in Yemen:

> The powerful hand of a foe acted swiftly to remove them from the places where they lived, to the point that they were forced to leave all precious items from their memoirs of events, which had been written down by sages of the generations from the beginning of the Yemenite exile, and their lineage registrations that had been a tradition from one generation to the next, and they were unable to save these precious works by their ancestors, which became spoils for their enemies.[5]

R. Qoraḥ linked the disappearance of the lineage documents to the Mawza' exile, which occurred in 1679–1680.[6] In this exile, the *pinkasim* (registry books) of the Bet Din were lost. R. 'Amram Qoraḥ, was unable to reconstruct these documents from the Ṣan'a Bet Din.[7] When trying to trace the lineages of the famous families in Yemen, it is difficult to uncover their roots prior to the Mawza' exile.[8] There are bits of information about the burning of the lineage documents of the Yemenite Jews dating from the nineteenth and twentieth centuries.

In his book, the missionary Joseph Wolff wrote about the rumor on this matter even before he reached Ṣan'a in 1836. He heard it in the Mokha port, during his meeting with Jews originating from Ṣan'a.

> Eighty years ago, the Jews of Sanaa pretended that they could ascertain their genealogy, and were in possession of ancient documents; but a dispute having arisen among them as to whom the superiority ought to belong, the respectable princes of that nation came forward, and said, "Children of Israel, hear the words of your elders, and listen to the advice of your old men. Through the jealousy, hatred, and enmity among ourselves, and on account of our impiety, our ancestors lost all their privileges, and were driven away from the Land of Israel, and

3. Ratson Halevi, *Shirat Yisra'el be-Teiman*, vol. 1 (Qiryat Ono, 1998), p. 16.
4. As related by Yefet Moshe, Rehovot.
5. Amram Qoraḥ, *Sa'arat Teiman* (Jerusalem, 1954), p. 9.
6. On the Mawza' expulsion, see above part 2, chap. 1, sect. 2.
7. Qoraḥ, *Sa'arat Teiman*, pp. 173–74.
8. See, for example, Joseph Tobi, *'Iyyunim bi-Megillat Teiman* (Jerusalem, 1986), p. 151.

> we, their children, are sighing in captivity; but why should be now quarrel among ourselves? Have we not trouble and tribulation enough? We live in the midst of Ishmaelites; of what use then is it, that one should pretend to be of the tribe of Judah, and the other of the tribe of Reuben? This only excites hatred; let us cast into the fire our doubtful documents; for, when the Lord shall be pleased to gather the scattered sheep of Israel, then every one of use will know what tribe he is; He himself will reveal it to us; and Messiah, the son of David, will reign among us, even at Jerusalem, and upon His holy hill of Zion. No disputes will then take place among us; but there will be peace and quiet and harmony."[9]

According to this rumor, the burning of lineages was done in light of a joint decision by the Ṣan'a rabbis in the eighteenth century.

R. Yaacov Sappir visited Ṣan'a in 1859, twenty-three years after the visit by Joseph Wolff, and reported on what he heard in Ṣan'a:

> And they say that until two hundred years ago all their families, every single one, had family tree documents. Until a wise, rich man came to them from Egypt, Mori Aharon Irāqi Ha-Kohen, *zaṣa"l*, and he was the banker of the king, very dear to and honored by him, and he did many good things for the Jews, and he lived there, and wanted to take from them a woman for his son, Mori Shalom, and they did not give him [one], since he did not have a written lineage. So he said to them, "Bring me your lineage books"; and they brought them to him. And he said, "All Jews are pedigreed," and he burned all their lineage books. Only one family retained [it], "Bet Mori Ṣālīḥ," and I tried very hard to see it but could not. One especially from among them, Mori Avraham ha-Sofer,[10] may his light shine, and the head of this community (whose home I lived in for a few weeks), promised to show me it, and it is hidden with his valuable things in the treasure he has in the

9. *Travels and Adventures of the Rev. Joseph Wolff, D.D., LL.D.*, vol. 2, 2nd ed. (London, 1861).

10. The reference is apparently to R. Avraham Ṣāliḥ, who served as a *dayyan* in Ṣan'a. Elsewhere he wrote, "And located there is a god-fearing man, Mori Avraham, may his light shine, one of the grandsons of the great rabbi Mori Yiḥye' Ṣāliḥ, may the memory of the righteous be for a blessing [the reference is to Mahariṣ, the greatest *poseq* of Yemen, who lived in the eighteenth century], and he is skilled *sofer*, ritual slaughterer and examiner, and the *ḥazzan* of the synagogue of his grandfather mentioned, whose house has always been a gathering-place for scholars, and through his loving-kindness took pity on me and brought me to his house, and I stayed with him until I saw which way I should return safely" (Yaacov Sappir, *Even Sappir*, 1 (Lyck, 1866), p. 106b.

> fortress (for the important heads of household have treasure lockers or guarded, rented storehouses in the fortress) and when he has an opportunity he will bring it to me. Until I went and pressed him, and he did not bring it.[11]

Abraham Zevi Idelsohn (1882–1938), the musicologist and historian of Yemenite Jewish song, wrote in a similar vein in the first half of the twentieth century what he heard in Israel, apparently from immigrants from Ṣan'a:

> Ṣan'a Jews consider themselves pedigreed, and by tradition they had a family tree that reached as far back as the exiles from the First Temple, and they did not assimilate to their Arab neighbors. This lineage document was burned owing to a particularly singular incident, about which the Jews tell the following: At the beginning of the fourth century,[12] a wealthy, distinguished Egyptian Jew came to Yemen, and his name was Shalom 'Irāqi, and with him came his brother Aharon. At first they settled in Ḥudaydah[13] and from there they moved to Ṣan'a. Through his wealth and wisdom he established connections with the court of the *Imam* (he was the high priest and ruled the land), and all the Jews respected him greatly. Then, his son reached maturity and he sought to take a wife from the local Jewish girls. But they did not give him any of their daughters, saying that they were careful to not become mixed with Jews without pedigreed stock. So Shalom 'Irāqi became furious and demanded that the Ṣan'a Jews show him their family tree documents. And when they brought him the book, and he took it from them and he burned it in the fire, and he said: All the children of Israel are sons of royalty. And nothing remained of that pedigree document, and only the Alsheikh family still has a family tree document, and it is stored in their synagogue in Ṣan'a, called the synagogue of Mori Alsheikh.[14]

11. See Sappir, *Even Sappir*, p. 100b. See also Yehudah Levi Naḥum, *Mi-Yeṣirot Sifrutiyyot mi-Teiman* (Holon, 1981), pp. 192, 311.
12. Indicating time as "the beginning of the fourth century" probably means the years after the year 'ה'ש (1540) to the creation, that is, the mid-sixteenth century. Yet, comparing this version of the event with that of R. Yaacov Sappir, cited above, and with the chronological information about Shalom or Aharon 'Irāqi, one tends to think that this is referring to the mid-seventeenth century. Perhaps, therefore, Idelsohn erred in stating the time he gave, and it should be the beginning of the fifth century.
13. A coastal city on the Red Sea.
14. Abraham Zevi Idelsohn, *"Yehudei Teiman, Shiratam u-Neginatam," Reshamot*, 1 (1925): 5.

R. Sappir and A. Z. Idelsohn ascribe the disappearance of the lineage registers of the Yemenite Jews to either Aharon 'Irāqi or his son Shalom in the eighteenth century.[15] The traditions mentioned differ on some points. Aharon is Shalom's father, as noted in Sappir's tradition, and not his brother, as indicated in Idelsohn's tradition. In R. Sappir's tradition Aharon was involved in the *imam*'s court in Ṣan'a, whereas in Idelsohn's it was Shalom who was in contact with the *imam*'s court.[16] In both traditions, the motive for their deeds is that the people did not want to have them join their families in marriage since they did not have a pedigree. In R. Sappir's tradition, Aharon wanted to marry off his son Shalom to one of the local girls, whereas in Idelsohn's tradition, it was Shalom who wanted to have his son marry. According to R. Sappir's version the remaining lineage registry is of the Ṣāliḥ family, in the other tradition the surviving family tree is from the Alsheikh family. In the three traditions—that of R. Qoraḥ, R. Sappir, and Wolff—each family had a personal lineage document, while Idelsohn thought there was one document for all that included the lineages of each of the families.[17]

Aviva Ṣabari analyzed the explanations of Joseph Wolff and R. Sappir and concluded that the family genealogies were burned in the 1820s by Aharon 'Irāqi, since he wanted to have his grandson Yiḥye' marry one of the girls of Ṣan'a.[18] R. Yosef 'Irāqi Ha-Kohen, from the line of Ha-Sar Shalom 'Irāqi, wrote:

> If you directed your question to the legend regarding the "burning of the lineage documents by Ha-Sar Shalom 'Irāqi, who is called 'Ūsṭa' (the artisan), when he wanted to marry off his son and encountered refusal," you might think this is no legend, but rather it is empty palaver and baseless suppositions that have left no trace in the words of those who wrote the events at the time of Ha-Sar Shalom, this despite the highly doubtful fact if at all written (as opposed to oral) documents of lineage were kept by any of the families in that period. Even an igno-

15. Tobi, *'Iyyunim bi-Mgillat Teiman*, pp. 151–54.
16. Aharon Gaimani, *Temurot be-Moreshet Yahadut Teiman: be-Hashpa'at ha-Shulḥan 'Arukh ve-Qabalat ha-Ari* (Ramat Gan, 2005), p. 175.
17. Cf. in the continuation of this section, the statement of R. Sa'adya Ḥozeh, in which he comments about the lineage document of the Shar'ab families in southern Yemen.
18. See Aviva Klein-Franke, *"Ha-Mishlaḥat ha-Mada'it ha-Rishonah li-Derom 'Arav ke-Maqor le-Toledot Yehudei Teiman,"* *Pe'amim* (1984): 86.

> ramus knows and a fool understands this, since in the five generations preceding Sar Shalom (as learned from the documents that were preserved and now available) and operating in Yemen also on the spiritual plane as well as on the profane, the family's lineage in the time of Ha-Sar Shalom was not an unknown, and its standing was firm, and this is attested to by many *ketubbot* of the family that were kept by us and elsewhere, in which one can see with which families our family joined in marriage.[19]

These traditions on the burning of lineage scrolls are probably not historically accurate, but rather legendary.[20] In light of this, we better understand the statement of R. Sappir about his attempts to obtain the lineage document of the Ṣāliḥ family: "And this pedigree book, I tried very hard to see it and couldn't … and until I left I pleaded with him but he did not bring it." Likewise, R. Yiḥye' Badiḥi wrote in his letter from Ṣan'a to a friend in Israel:

> Be aware, my friend, that according to what is accepted among us, the Yemenite exiles, that our ancestors go back to ancient times, that when they heard the prophecies of our prophets, Jeremiah and Ezekiel and others during the time of the First Temple prophesying about the destruction of the Temple, they went in exile to Yemen before its destruction. Moreover, this seems so from the statements by the Mahariṣ in his commentary on the elegies of the night of the Ninth of Av![21] And according to the words of one of the greats of our ancient ones, namely, R. Netanel ben Yesha' in his book *Nur al-Ḍalām* (The Light in the Darkness),[22] all the Jews of Yemen are the remnants of the Ten Tribes that Sennacherib exiled to Halah and Habor,[23] and there came against them from the kings of the Muhammadeans,[24] and they fought against them, killing them in great numbers, and these exiles in Yemen are the surviving remnant of them![25] And owing to the length of the exile of 2,300 and more years and owing to the subjugation of our ancient ones by nations of the world, they no longer turned to their lineages and the source of their roots, for it was enough for

19. In a personal correspondence dated 30 Apr 2010.
20. Part 1, chap. 3, sect. 3.
21. For a discussion of the statements of the Mahariṣ, see above part 1, chap. 2, sect. 3.
22. The Hebrew title is *Ma'or ha-Afelah* (A Light in the Darkness).
23. 2 Kings 17:1–6.
24. The reference is to a ruler descending from Muhammad, the Prophet of Islam.
25. *Ma'or ha-Afelah*, p. 475.

> them that they remained with their Jewish religion, however that may be! Therefore, it is impossible to obtain any lineage for any family, whether a family of Kohanim or Levites or Israelites, for all of them are only by presumption![26]

The noted Sar Shalom 'Irāqi was known by his byname of *al-'Ūsṭa'*, and he was the most famous political leader of the Yemenite Jews. From his own money he built a large synagogue in Ṣan'a; he helped other communities in Yemen and was instrumental in spreading *nuṣaḥ Sefarad* (the Sephardi prayer rite) and the rulings of the *Shulḥan 'Arukh* in Yemen.[27] In nineteenth-century *ketubbot* his descendants listed a lineage that goes back to Sar Shalom, and they mentioned him in admiration. For example, in a *ketubbah* from Ṣan'a, dated 16 June 1831, at a marriage of relatives of the 'Irāqi family the name of the groom was written as "Mūsa' ben *m"v* Harūn ben *k-h-r* Yosef ben *kmh"r* Yiḥye' son of our master, the prince Sālem al-Kohen al-'Irāqi," and the name of the bride was listed as "Ghane bint Yiḥye' ben Yosef ben Harūn al-Kohen al-'Irāqi, may the memory of the righteous and holy be for a blessing." In another *ketubbah* from Ṣan'a, from 24 Nov 1836, the groom's name was written as "Mūsa' ben Hārūn ben *kevod ha-rav* by *kmhr"r* Yiḥye' son of our master al-sheikh Sālem al-Kohen al-'Irāqi." In a Ṣan'a *ketubbah*, dated 29 Jan 1858, the groom's name was registered as "Hārūn ben Da'ūd son of al-sheikh Harūn ben *kh"r* Yiḥye' son of our master al-sheikh *al-'Ūsṭa'* Sālem al-Kohen al-'Irāqi."

On a similar tradition of the burning of lineage documents in Shar'ab in southern Yemen, Rabba Sa'adyah Ḥozeh wrote:

> There are families who to this day know from which tribe they come, according to a lineage document that is hidden in the Shar'ab district, and there are also some who burned them themselves. For example, there was the incident of Yosef al-Jamal, who was the treasurer of Shabazi[28] and the leader of the Jews. One time at night, in the Shar'ab district, people were gathered feasting and they were joyous and in

26. *Qeta'im me-Iggerot R. Yiḥye' Qāfih z"l, Shevut Teiman,* ed. Y. Yeshayahu and A. Zadok (Tel Aviv, 1945), p. 227. In a similar vein, the rabbis of Yemen replied to R. Avraham Yitzhak Hakohen Kook that the families in Yemen are proper only by presumption. See Aharon Gaimani, *"Teshuvot Ḥakhmei Teiman li-She'elot ha-Rav Kook,"* in *Halikhot Kedem be-Mishkenot Teiman*, ed. S. Sirri and Y. Kesar (Tel Aviv, 2006), pp. 40–41.
27. Aharon Gaimani, *Temurot,* pp. 175–78.
28. That is of the grave of R. Shalom Shabazi.

> their cups, and they began to talk about matters of lineage. One of them asked the distinguished guest, Yosef al-Jamal, the treasurer of Shabazi, *zṣ"l*, to let them look at his parchment lineage document, and written in it were the Shar'ab families and their lineages to the tribes of Jacob. He saw it and thought himself very clever, and advised them to burn the document so that the non-Jews would not be jealous of them, especially the Arab who have no pedigree; they burned it at night while drunk, but in the morning all of them rued their action, including the distinguished guest, and also the residents of the area, and they mourned for the error they had made.[29]

He wrote also about another lineage document that was in a ruined synagogue in Shar'ab. Before the mass *aliyah* of 1948, people wanted to retrieve it from the synagogue, but fear of demons and evil spirits kept them for entering the synagogue.

2. EXAGGERATED LINEAGES IN MANUSCRIPTS

In a manuscript of the Taj, which was copied in Ṣan'a in 1498, commissioned by Aharon ben 'Amram ben Yosef, four birth dates were registered: of the three sons of the client, Yeshu'a in 5263 (1503), Moshe in Marheshvan 5268 (1508), 'Amram in 5270 (1510), and a grandson, Aharon ben Moshe in 5305 (1545). In the list of the first son, Yeshu'a, after giving the date of birth, the client Aharon ben 'Amram added the family tree. The lineage of the other sons and the grandson can be completed according to the registration under the first son. Below is the list, which contains 91 generations:

> The good flower has been born, one who resembles a moist tree, Yeshu'ah ben Aharon, Sunday, 5 Elul 1814 SEL [= 5263 AM/1503]. May God make him a good sign for his father and his mother, and fulfill with him the Holy Writ stating, "May the Lord bless and protect you, may the Lord shine his countenance upon you and be gracious to you, may the Lord lift up his face to you and grant you peace."[30] And fulfill with him the Holy Writ stating, "For a child is born to us, a son is given to us, and the government is upon his shoulder, and his names is called Pele Yo'eṣ Elgibbor Abi ad-Sar Shalom.[31]

29. R. Sa'adya Ḥozeh, *Toledot ha-Rav Shalom Shabazi u-Minhagei Yahadut Shar'ab be-Teiman*, 1 (Jerusalem, 1973), p. 84.
30. Num. 6:24–26.
31. Isa. 9:5.

> And this is his lineage: Yeshu'ah ben Aharon ben 'Amram ben Yosef ben 'Oded ben 'Amram ben Sa'adyah ben Avigad ben Shalom ben 'Oded ben Zekharyah ben Ya'aqov ben Shemaryah al-'Ansi ben Yosef ha-Qenazi ben Ya'aqov ben Maḍmūn ben Yefet ben Yesha'ya ben Yefet ben Moshe ben Avigad ben Ya'aqov ben 'Eli ben Fayis ben Ya'ir ben Yeḥezqe'el ben Aharon ben Ezra ben Daniel ben Yehonatan ben Elīshūv ben Qadmi'el ben Mikha ben Yirmiya ben 'Aminadav ben Zeraḥ ben Eytan ben Heman ben 'Azarya ben Yeraḥme'el ben Kesalon ben 'Aminadav ben Naḥshon ben Shelomo ben Bo'az ben 'Oved ben Eli'av ben Avinadav ben Yoav ben Tash'al ben Yeter ben Shuv ben Arnon ben Efrat ben Ḥur ben Uri ben Beṣalel ben Seguv ben Ya'ir ben Makhir ben Ram ben Yamin ben Sason ben Shammai ben Amnon ben Dani'el ben Shefaṭya ben Shama''el ben Natan ben 'Ami'el ben Reḥav'am ben Yehoyaqim ben Yokhonya ben She'alti'el ben Shafat ben Qenaz ben Otni'el ben Ṣadoq ben Pinḥas ben Oshri'el ben 'Amihud ben 'Aminadav ben Omri ben Boni min Benei Pereṣ ben Yehudah ben Ya'aqov whose name is called Yisra'el. The Merciful one will hasten the end and bring the Redemption nigh in our lives and days, Amen.[32]

An additional lineage is found in the colophon page of a manuscript of the Torah, from the beginning of the sixteenth century, by the copyist Yeter ben Shelomo,[33] who listed a lineage of 88 generations:

> I have gone over this complete Torah, which is for the eyes of those seeking its enlightenment, and I have vocalized and been meticulous as the Lord has graced me, I, Yeter *beirav* Shelomo *beirav* David *beirav* Maymum *beirav* 'Oded 'Amram *beirav* Sa'adyah *beirav* Avigad *beirav* Shalom *beirav* 'Oded *beirav* Zekharyah *beirav* Ya'aqov *beirav* Yosef *beirav* Shemaryah known as al-'Ansi *beirav* Yosef ha-Qenazi *beiravbei-rav* Ya'aqov *beirav* Maḍmūn *beirav* Yefet *beirav* Yesha'ya *beirav* Yefet *beirav* Moshe *beirav* Avigad *beirav* Ya'aqov *beirav* 'Eli *beirav* Fayis *beirav* Ya'ir *beirav* Yeḥezqe'el *beirav* Aharon *beirav* 'Ezra *beirav* Dani'el *beirav* Yehonatan *beirav* Elyashuv *beirav* Qadmi'el *beirav* Mikah *beirav* Yirmiya *beirav* 'Aminadav *beirav* Zeraḥ *beirav* Eytan *beirav*[34] Heman *beirav* 'Azaryah *beirav* Yearḥmi'el *beirav* Kesalon *beirav* 'Aminadav *beirav* Naḥshon ber[av] Shelomo ber[av] Bo'az ber[av] 'Oved *beirav*

32. For a photo and copy of the colophon of the *Taj*, see Naḥum, *Mi-Yeṣirot Sifrutiyyot mi-Teiman*, pp. 191–92.
33. For a photo and copy of the colophon of the *Taj* whose copying he completed in 5278 (1518), see Naḥum, ibid., p. 311, 316.
34. In the source this word was erroneously written twice.

> Eli'av ber[av] Avinadav ber[av] Yo'av b[erav] Yiratshe'el *beirav* Yeter ber[av] Shuv ben Arnon ben Efrat ben Ḥur ben Uri ben Beṣalel ben Seguv ben Ya'ir ben Makhir ben Ḥeṣron ben Ram ben Yamin ben Sason ben Shammai ben Amnon ben Dani'el ben Shefaṭya ben Shama''el ben [Shafa]ṭ ben Qenaz ben Otni'el ben Ṣadoq ben Pi[n]ḥa[s] ben ['Utay] ben 'Amihud ben 'Aminadav ben Omri ben Boni min Benei Pereṣ ben Yehudah ben Ya'aqov whose name is called Yisra'el. May the [Mer]ciful one hasten the end and bring the Redemption nigh in our lives and days, Amen, Neṣaḥ, Selah, La'ad.[35]

At the closing of these two lists, there is no continuum of generations and we find written "from the sons of Peretz," i.e., "from the descendants of Peretz." Moreover, the two lists were written in the same period, and except for the beginning of the list, both of them are parallel for the 88 generations. Doubt should be cast on their trustworthiness. Beyond that, the list contains a group of copied biblical lineages, which was apparently a literary convention.

Another dynasty is listed on one of the colophons of a manuscript of *Sefer Qinyan* of Maimonides' *Mishneh Torah.* According to it, the year of the copying was 1491. On a second manuscript colophon, the copyist, Shelomo ben David Tawīli, listed a dynasty of 23 generations of the commissioner of the manuscript:

> A weak, meager scribe, Shelom[o] ben R. Dawīd ben Maimun [al]-Ṭawīli ... This text was completed on Thursday, which is the twenty-seventh day of the month of Elul in 1802 SEL (1491 AM), in Qaryat al-Sūd that should be built until the city of Jerus[alem] will be built. May this be for a good sign for Mori Yeter Halevi ben Kokhav Halevi ben 'Amram Halevi ben Mas'ūd Halevi ben Kokhav Halevi *beirav* Mas'ūd Halevi *beirav* Khalīfa Halevi *beirav* Mas'ūd Halevi ben Peraḥ Halevi ben Ḥassan Halevi ben Shelomo Halevi ben Zekharyah ben Merari Halevi ben Ḥayim Halevi ben 'Oded Halevi ben Mas'ūd Halevi ben Menaḥem Halevi ben Shelomo Halevi ben Merari Halevi ben 'Oded Halevi ben Peraḥ Halevi of the Tribe of Merari ben Levi ben Ya'aqov, may he rest in peace. May the Lord make him worthy of understanding his laws and being meticulous in his matters, *'ky"r*. And make his sons who follow after him be worthy of all the commandments in it, and may nothing be hidden from them, may this be the will of the Heavens, and now say, [Amen].[36]

35. For a photograph of the lineage from the manuscript and a copy of it, see Naḥum, *Mi-Yeṣirot Sifrutiyyot mi-Teiman*, pp. 313–14.

36. Manuscript of R. Yosf Qāfiḥ, Jerusalem; *Oṣar Kitve Yad Ivriyyim mi-Ymei ha-Beinayim*, 1, Descriptions (Jerusalem–Paris, 1980), no. 163.

In total, exaggerated lineages lists appear in three of 684 colophons of manuscripts from Yemen that are in my possession, and all three are from the same period; this casts doubts on the reliability of these lineages.

3. RELIABLE LINEAGES IN MANUSCRIPTS

Below are the lineages of families of scribes and sages in Yemen, noted in the colophons of manuscripts from Yemen and in introductions and conclusions of books, which are undoubtedly reliable.

In the colophon of a manuscript completed in 1342, the copyist Benayah ben Sa'adya noted the lineage of the person who commissioned the work, which contains twelve generations:

> This book was completed on Tuesday, the tenth day of the month of Iyyar 1653 SEL (5103 AM/1342). May it be a good sign for the owner of the manuscript Shelomo *bera*[*v*] Yosef, *beirav* Se'īd, ben Manṣūr, ben Se'īd, ben Yiḥye'['], ben Dawid, ben Kathīr, ben R. Yosef, ben Maḥfuḍ al-'Ansi, b. R. Yosef ha-Qenazi. May he merit to study it, he and his offspring and his offspring's offspring, and may it be fulfilled through him the verse as it is written: May the Lord bless you and keep you, shine, lift up, *Amen, Neṣaḥ, Sela.* Blessed is [the Lord] that bestows good on to those who are guilty. May God forgive me for where I erred and made a mistake, as it is written, "Who can discern his errors? Clear me from hidden faults." The writer is the humble Benayah ben R. Sa'adyah ben R. Kalev ben Maḥfūḍ al-Khawli, *tanṣeba"h.* Blessed [is He] who has granted us life and sustained us in life and has brought us to this day.[37]

In another manuscript, copied in 1497, connected to the family lineage of the commissioner of the previous manuscript; the copyist noted in the manuscript colophon thirteen generations in the lineage of this family:

> This book was finished, on Wednesday, which was the twenty-seventh day of the month of Adar, in the year 1808 SEL [1497/5257 AM], in the place Ṣu[bar]ah. May it be for a good sign for its owner and his sons and his sons' sons forever, Zekharyah Ha-Kohen ben R. Ḥoṭer Ha-Kohen. May the Lord give him merit to learn, he and his children and his children's children, Amen, Neṣaḥ, Sela. And may the writer Ḥalfon b. R. Dawid, b. R. Avraham, b. R. Yesha', b. R. Shalom, b. R. 'Ezra, b. R. Shalom, ben Manṣūr, ben Yiḥye', ben Yosef, ben

37. Yehudah Levi Naḥum, *Mi-Ṣefunot Teiman*, 2 (Tel Aviv, 1987), no. 28.

> Maḥfūḍ al-'Ansi, b. R. Yosef ha-Qenazi. May the Lord forgive me for all my errors and mistakes, and inscribe me for life.[38]

R. Yosef ben Yisra'el (Yemen; sixteenth-seventeenth centuries) was a poet who lived in the district of Shar'ab in southern Yemen,[39] in a copy of *Sefer ha-Haftarot*, which was written by his son, R. Yisra'el, in 1605, he wrote the family genealogy in the colophon, which lists twelve generations:

> This haftarah was completed on the fifth day of the month of Elul in the year 1916 SEL, which is the year 5365 AM. May the Merciful one hasten the end and bring the Redemption nigh, in our lifetime and in our days and in the lives of all his people, all the House of Israel, *'ky"r*. The least among the scribes of Israel, *beirav* Abba Yosef, may his Rock protect him, *beirav* Abba Mori Yisra'el, ben Abba Mori Yosef, ben Abba Mori Moshe, ben Abba Mori Sa'adyah, ben Abba Mori Dawīd, ben Abba Mori Avram, ben Abba Mori Me'oded, ben Abba Mori Shemu'el, ben Abba Mori Daniel, ben Abba Mori Perḥya.[40]

In a 1740 copy of the *Shulḥan 'Arukh* by R. Yosef Qaro, the copyist noted in the colophon eight generations:

> This book that has been completed herewith is the *Shulḥan 'Arukh*, blessed be God, 8 Elul in the year 2051 SEL [5500 AM = 1740], the writer is the slightest, the least of the scribes, who is covered with dust at the feet of the rabbis and disciples, the most humble Yosef ben A' [ben] Avraham son of my master and teacher [*m"w*] Sa'adyah son of *m"w*

38. Maimonides' Commentary on the Mishnah, MS Berlin, State Library OR. QU 574 (IMHM 1793).

39. Yehudah 'Amir, *"Shirato shel Yosef ben Yisra'el (Teiman—sof ha-Me'ah ha-16 ve-reishit ha-17)."* (Ph.D. diss., Bar-Ilan University, 2001), pp. 80–82; on this poet, see above part 3, chap. 3, sect. 2.

40. *Sefer Hafṭariyyot*, Ratzon Halevi Manuscript, Tel Aviv. For a photograph of the colophon, see the introduction by Rav Yosef Subayri to *Tiklal Mashta-Shabazi*. See also Amir, "Poetry of Yosef ben Yisra'el," p. 80. Of note here is that we see the custom of giving names while skipping the grandfather's name. See above part 1, chap. 2. In another manuscript, copied in 1622, nine generations are listed. Written in the colophon, we find: "This *siddur* was completed, with the help of heaven, on Monday, the tenth of Nisan in the year 1622 SEL, in the village of al-A'dān, of the approaching salvation ... the least of the scribes, the youngest of the observers, Yisra'el, may his Rock protect him, Berav Abba Mori Yosef, Berav Abba Mori Yisra'el, ben Abba Mori Yosef, ben Abba Mori Moshe, ben Abba Mori Sa'adyah, ben Abba Mori David, ben Abba Mori Avraim, ben Abba Mori Me'oded OBM" (Jerusalem Manuscript, Jewish National and University Library, 1140; Amir, "Poetry of Yosef ben Yisra'el," pp. 80–81).

> Yosef ben *m"w* Shelomo son of ma"t Ḥisdai son of *m"w* Sa'adyah ben *m"w* Avraham Halevi known as al-'Arūsi. Hashem, thankfully, will forgive me for all that I have erred and mistaken and have overlooked, as stated Messiah of the God of Ya'aqov and the sweet singer Israel: Who can discern his errors? You shall clear me from hidden faults. Keep back your servant also from presumptuous sins. And written in the name of the commissioner, similar to a moist tree, the Lord, too, will give him good, and settle him in a good oasis, and bequeath him a goodly portion, Amen, so the good, Amen, the good God will also bless him, Sa'adya ben Zekharyah Ḥusāni, Hashem, thankfully, will make him worthy to meditate on it and he and his descendants and his descendants' descendants until the end of all generations.[41]

In a copy of a collection of the laws of ritual slaughter, from the nineteenth century, the copyist listed in the colophon a lineage of sixteen generations of his family:

> The most meager, unfortunate scribe, the most humble, dust at the feet of the sages, the most unimportant of the clans and the youngest in my father's house, my name is *Bkf"y* (in *atbash*, Shalom), and in Arabic my name is *Ḥtk"y* [in *atbash*, Sālem] ben of my honorable father, *mmv"r*, Yiḥye' son of his honorable father, his teacher and rabbi, Ya'aqov son of his master and teacher, 'Amram son of his master and teacher Yisra'el the scribe who is called Mashta, son of his master and teacher, Yosef son of his master and teacher, Yisra'el, son of his master and teacher Yosef son of his master and teacher, Moshe, son of his honorable master and teacher, Sa'adya, son of his honorable master and teacher, Dawīd, son of his honorable master and teacher, Avram, son of his honorable master and teacher, Me'oded, son of his honorable master and teacher, Shalom, son of his honorable master and teacher, Daniel, son of his master and teacher Faraḥya, who is called Mashta.[42]

In a copy of the book *Sefer Menorat ha-Ma'or* from the mid-nineteenth century copied by R. Levi of the al-Sheikh family dynasty in Qāryat al-Qabel in central Yemen, his son Sālem added in the colophon the family lineage that encompassed eleven generations:

> This *Menorat ha-Ma'or,* written by hand by Abba Mori in Qarya al-Qābel, may Hashem make it for a good commemoration and for merit

41. Manuscript New York, Public Library Heb MS 111 (id. no. in IMHM 31113); see Gaimani, *Temurot,* pp. 304–5.
42. Menaḥem Feldman Manuscript, Jerusalem, no. 113 (IMHM 42715). See also above, chap. 3, sect. 2.

> for him and his descendants, it shall not be sold or redeemed ever, as it is written, "and your righteousness shall go before you" (Isa. 58:8). The humble Sālem ibn Līvi [should be Levi], *ng'*, ibn Yiḥye', ibn Shalom, ibn Avraham, ibn Shalom, ibn Yosef, ibn Yiḥye', ibn Yeshu'a, ibn Maḥfuḍ Shalom of the House of a-Levi, *yṣ"v*.[43]

The Alsheikh family was among the families with distinguished lineage in Ṣan'a, and it had property in Qaryat al-Qābel.[44] In the continuation of the page, beneath the colophon, R. Netan'el, son of R. Shalom who copied the colophon, wrote the date of his father's passing: "Abba Mori, may his merit be for us, is no more, Wednesday, of the weekly portion Va-Yera, 17 Ḥeshavan 2210 SEL, 5659 AM (2 Nov 1898), [ornate signature]: Netan'el [ib]n Shalom Alsheikh."[45]

R. Shalom Yiṣḥaq Halevi, at the end of the introduction to his work *Divrei Shalom*, which he completed in Jerusalem in 1968, listed seven generations of his family lineage:

> This is the statement by *Ha-Ṣa'ir* of the clans of Israel (Jud 6:15), dust at feet of the sages, Shalom ben ha-rav ha-gaon, moreinu ha-rav, R. Yiḥye', [ib]n Mūsa', [ib]n Yiḥye', [[ib]n Sāliḥ][46] [ib]n Harūn, [ib]n Sālem, ben Yiṣḥaq of the Sason Halewi family.[47]

R. Yosef Qāfiḥ, after completing his translation of Maimonides' commentary on the Mishna, and under the influence of Maimonides adding his own genealogy, listed thirteen generations of his family tree:

> And now completed was its preparation for printing, its proofreading, and its printing, in Jerusalem city of the great king, in the year 5728 AM, by me, I am Yosef, ben R. David the rabbi, b. R. Yiḥye' the *dayyan*, b. R. Slaymān, b. R. Sālem, b. R. Slaymān, b. R. Yiḥye' the rabbi, b. R.

43. David ben Shalom Qāfiḥ, Jerusalem. The wife of the manuscript owner is Ilana Alsheikh. Her father was Levi, the brother of R. Yiḥye' Alsheikh, who is mentioned in the continuation of the passage. For an additional list of the Alsheikh family lineage, see Shalom Harari, *"Ṣadiq be-Emunato Yiḥye',"* *Nefesh*, a memorial pamphlet for R. Sa'adya b"R Yosef 'Uzayri, OBM (Tel Aviv, 1954), pp. 2–3.

44. Aharon Gaimani, *"Shetar ha-Ṣeva'a … al-Sheikh,"* in *Bnei Teiman, Meḥqarim be-Yahadut Teiman u-Morashta*, ed. Aharon Gaimani, Ratson 'Arusi, and Shaul Regev (Ramat Gan, 2011), pp. 49–77.

45. For a photograph of this passage noting the *haftarah*, see Tzipporah Ben Aharon (Alsheikh), *Bet Alsheikh le-Dorotav* (Tel Aviv, 1987), p. 26.

46. This addition follows a comment by R. Shalom's grandson, R. Aviran Yiṣḥaq Halevi.

47. Yiṣḥaq Halewi, *Divrei Shalom*, p. 4.

> Slaymān, b. R. Yiḥye', b. R. Slaymān the rabbi, b. R. Yiḥye', b. R. Yosef the *dayyan*, b. R. Se'īd al-Qāfiḥ.[48]

In 1971, R. Shimon Ṣāliḥ, after he had completed the preparatory work towards publishing the prayer book with the *Eṣ Ḥayim* commentary by R. Yiḥye' Ṣāliḥ (Mahariṣ),[49] with his own annotations, listed in his concluding statement ten generations of his family lineage:

> I *Ha-Ṣa'ir*, dust at the feet of the sages, Shim'on ben Yiḥye', ben Yiḥye', ben Sālem, ben R. Yosef, son of the author R. Yiḥye' known as al-kabīr [the Great],[50] ben R. Yosef, ben R. Ṣāliḥ,[51] ben R. Yiḥye', ben R. Yosef Ṣāliḥ, the memory of all of them for life in the World to Come.[52]

After completing the preparation for printing of his book *Arikhat Shulḥan—Yalqut Ḥayim* (2003), part one, R. Shelomo Qoraḥ presented in his closing statement seven generations of his family tree:

> Shelomo son of my honorable father, my teacher and my rabbi Yiḥye' son of *mv"z* R. 'Amram son of the holy Mahariq (= Morenu ha-Rav Yiḥye' Qoraḥ) son of the holy Maharashal (= Morenu ha-Rav Shalom) son of the holy Maharasa' (= Morenu ha-Rav Sa'adyah son of the distinguished (Morenu ha-Rav Yosef) of the House of Qorḥi, the memory of all of them for life in the World to Come.[53]

R. Yiṣḥaq Raṣabi, whose parents emigrated from the Raṣāba community, noted in memorial remarks about his father, R. Nissim (Naḥum), nine generations of his family's lineage.

> The righteous shall be had in everlasting remembrance, I am setting a memorial in the memory and for the transcendence of the soul in honor of the teaching of my father, my teacher and master, the Rav the Gaon the Ḥasid and the Modest, who dwells in humbleness ..., *adoni*, my father, my teacher and master, Nissim (Naḥum) Raṣābi, OBM, who

48. Maimonides, *Peirush ha-Mishna* [Qāfiḥ], *Tohorot*, closing statement, n. 79; on the lineage of Maimonides, see above section 1. In R. Qāfiḥ's listing we see the naming custom of skipping the grandfather's name. See above, part 1, chap. 2.
49. On R. Yiḥye' Ṣāliḥ (Mahariṣ) and his commentary *Eṣ Ḥayim*, see Gaimani, *Temurot*, pp. 182–96.
50. The reference is to R. Yiḥye' Ṣāliḥ (Mahariṣ).
51. The reference is to Maharaṣ, author of *Peri Ṣadīq*.
52. See Mahariṣ, *Tiklal Eṣ Ḥayim*, 4 (Jerusalem, 1971), 354a. See also *Keter Torah—Ḥazon Shim'on, Bereishit* (Bnei Brak, 1986), introduction, p. 15b.
53. Shelomoh Qoraḥ, *'Arikhat Shulḥan–Yalqut Ḥayim, Oraḥ Ḥayim*, 1 (Bnei Brak, 1975), author's introduction, p. 22.

> was the head of the Bet Din and rabbi of the community of Raṣabā and its environs, Yemen. The descendant of saints, stock of rabbis, ben *morenu ha-rav* (our teacher, rabbi) Nissim ben *mh"r* Shalom ben *mh"r* Sa'adyah son of the great rabbi, the divine kabbalist, Shelomo *beirav* Ya'aqov ben *mh"r* Shelomo *beirav* Yosef *beirav* Yehudah, *ng'*, on whose name our family is called as "Benei Yehudah."[54]

As for the lineage of the 'Irāqi family, S. D. Goitein put together from family documents a family tree of ten generations before the eighteenth century;[55] and R. Yosef 'Irāqi Ha-Kohen, who also uses family documents, continued the 'Irāqi family lineage down to our own times. Presented here are seventeen generations of the 'Irāqi family lineage as given to me by R. Yosef 'Irāqi Ha-Kohen of Bnei Brak and it begins with his eldest son: "Shemu'el ben Yosef ben *adoni avi* Shim'on ben Yosef ben Yehudah ben *mori va-adoni* Ḥayim ben Yiḥye' ben *mori va-adoni* Sālem ben *mori va-adoni*, Yosef ben *mori va-adoni* Aharon ben *mori va-adoni* Yiḥye' ben *ha-sar* Shalom ben *ha-nagid* Aharon ben Sālem ben *mori va-adoni* ben Yosef ben Avraham ben David 'Irāqi Kaṣ."[56]

54. Yiṣḥaq Raṣabi, *Shulḥan Arukh ha-Mequṣar*, vol. 8 (Bnei Brak, 1989), end of the book, p. 236.

55. See Shlomo Dov Goitein, *"Batei ha-Yehudim u-Shekhunoteihem ba-'Ir Ṣan'a le-Or Shetarot Ketuvim lifnei Galut Mawza" (li-Shtarot 1678–1680),"* in *Ha-Teimanim—Mivḥar Meḥqarim* (Jerusalem, 1983), p. 146.

56. Personal correspondence of 30 Apr 2010.

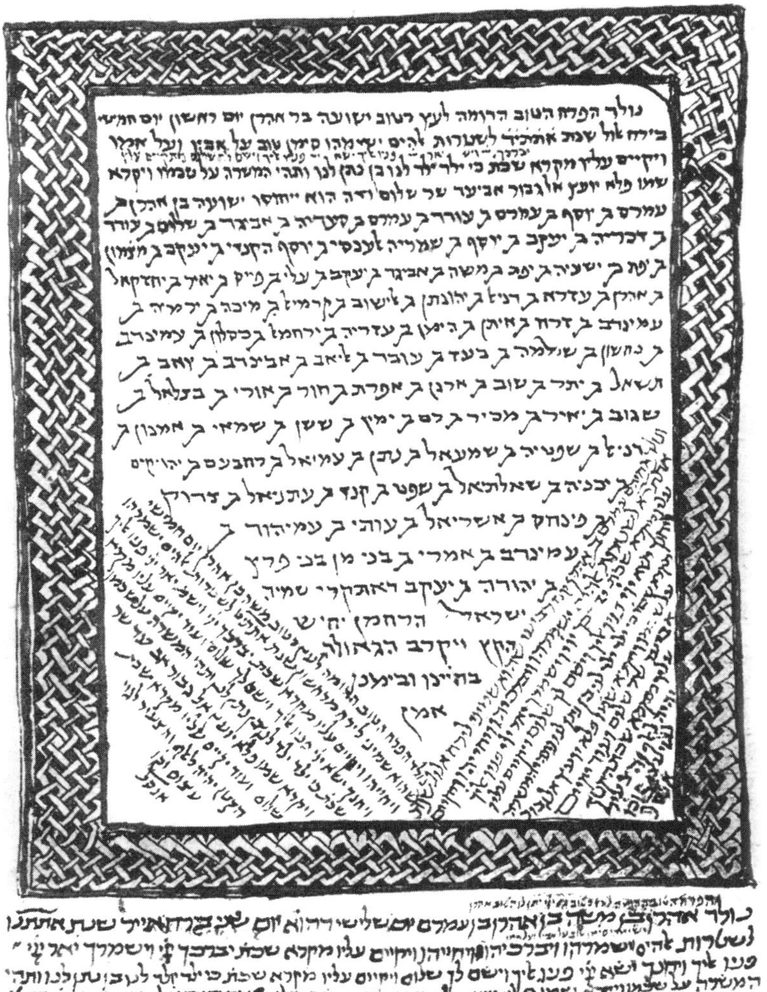

Lineage to Ya'aqov Avinu in a Yemenite manuscript.
Y. L. Nahum, Mi-Yeṣirot Sifrutiyyot mi-Teiman*, p. 191.*

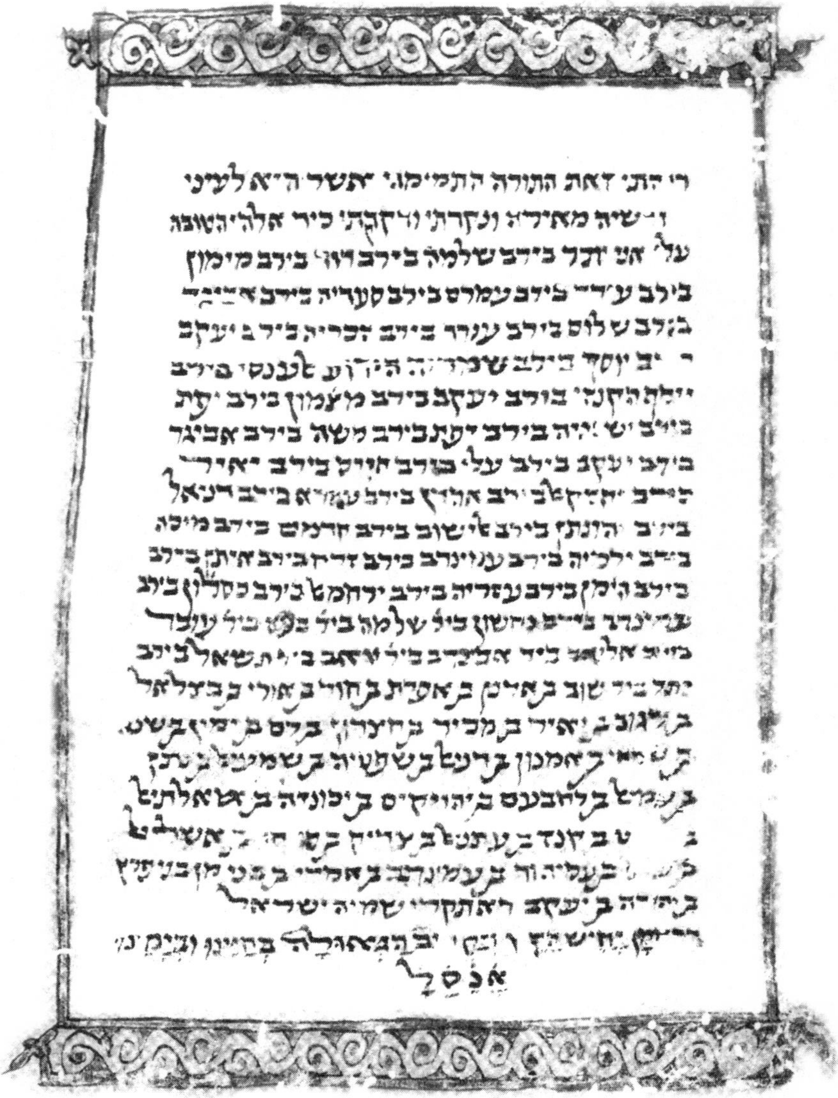

Lineage to Ya'aqov Avinu in a Yemenite manuscript.
Y. L. Nahum, Mi-Yeṣirot Sifrutiyyot mi-Teiman, *p. 313.*

CHAPTER SIX

USE OF PERSONAL NAMES IN THE SYNAGOGUE

1. PERSONAL NAMES TO IDENTIFY SYNAGOGUES

Ṣan'a Community

The synagogues that served the Ṣan'a Jews in recent centuries were built after the Yemenite Jews return from the Mawza' exile in 1681.[1] The synagogues in Qa' al-Yahūd (the Jewish Quarter) were destroyed in 1762 at the order of the Imam al-Mahdi 'Abbās ibn al-Manṣūr Ḥasīn. They were desolate for about 30 years, and the Jews had to pray in private homes.[2] Other synagogues were erected after the Turks captured the city in 1872.[3]

Concerning the names of the Ṣan'a synagogues, R. Yosef Qāfiḥ wrote: "No plaque was affixed to a synagogue announcing its name, and no name was initially given to the synagogue; but the public, as if by itself, called the synagogue by the name of the person who persevered in its construction or by the name of the first rabbi who served in it if he was distinguished."[4]

1. On the Mawza' exile, see above Part two, chap. 1 n. 29.
2. See Yehiel Naḥshon, *Batei Keneset be-Ṣan'a (Me'ot 18 u-19)* (Netanya, 2000), pp. 52–59. See also Amram Qoraḥ, *Sa'arat Teiman* (Jerusalem, 1954), pp. 18–19, 22–23; Qāfiḥ, *"Batei Keneset be-Teiman," Ketavim* 2 (Jerusalem, 1989), p. 953. According to the traveler Carsten Niebuhr, 12 of the 14 Ṣan'a synagogues were destroyed. See Aviva Klein-Franke, *"Ha-Mishlaḥat ha-Mada'it ha-Rishonah li-Derom 'Arav ke-Maqor le-Toledot Yehudei Teiman," Pe'amim* 18 (1984): 88.
3. On the building of synagogues after the Turkish conquest, see Qoraḥ, *Sa'arat Teiman*, p. 43.
4. Yosef Qāfiḥ, *Halikhot Teiman* (Jerusalem, 1961), p. 65.

Synagogues Founded after the Mawza' Exile

1. The 'Ūsṭa' synagogue was built by the dignitary Sar Shalom Kohen 'Irāqi, and it is called *Kanīs al-'Ūsṭa'*. *'Ūsṭa'* (the Artisan) was the appellation of the benefactor.[5]
2. The Alsheikh synagogue was built by R. Yiḥye' ben Avraham ha-Lewi; it was first called Bet Kneset Mahar"i ha-Lewi,[6] and later was named for the family known as the Alsheikh family.[7]
3. The Jizfān synagogue was named after its founder and first owner, Avraham Jizfān.[8]
4. The Dhamāri synagogue, was named after its first owners, who built it, and whose name has been forgotten.[9]
5. The Ḥubārah synagogue, named after its first owners, who built it, the Ḥubārah family.[10]
6. The Ḥajāji synagogue named after its first owners, who built it, and whose names have been forgotten.[11]
7. The Ṭayri synagogue was named for its founder and its first owner, Avraham Ṭayri.[12]

---

5. Qoraḥ, *Sa'arat Teiman,* p. 107; Aharon Gaimani, *Temurot be-Moreshet Yahadut Teiman: be-Hashpa'at ha-Shulḥan 'Arukh ve-Qabalat ha-Ari* (Ramat Gan: Bar-Ilan University, 2005), pp. 176–77.
6. See, for example, Qoraḥ, *Sa'arat Teiman,* p. 152, in an elegy the Mahariṣ wrote starting with the words *"Qehillat Ṣan'a"*; Yehudah Ratzaby, "Batei Kenesiyyot be-Ṣan'a," in *Bo'ii Teiman* (Tel Aviv, 1967), pp. 239–42.
7. See, for example, Qoraḥ, *Sa'arat Teiman,* p. 107; Naḥshon, *Batei Keneset be-Ṣan'a,* pp. 122–25.
8. Qoraḥ, *Sa'arat Teiman,* p. 107; Shalom Gamliel, *Pequdei Teiman: Mas he-Ḥasut be-Teiman* (Jerusalem, 1982), p. 71.
9. Qoraḥ, *Sa'arat Teiman,* p. 107; Shalom Gamliel, *Pequdei Teiman,* p. 72.
10. Qoraḥ, *Sa'arat Teiman,* p. 107; R. Shalom Gamliel this synagogue is not included among the first synagogue built after the return of the exiles from the Mawza' expulsion. See Gamliel, *Pequdei Teiman,* p. 73.
11. Qoraḥ, *Sa'arat Teiman,* p. 107; the family name *Ḥajāji* is not known in Ṣan'a in recent generations. In the seventeenth century, there was a prolific scribe named Ḥayim ben Shalom Ḥajāji, who lived in the town Migdala' Ḥaqal, southwest of Ṣan'a, and one may reasonably assume that after the return of the exiles from Mawza' the Ḥajāji family moved to Ṣan'a and built the synagogue under discussion. See Aharon Gaimani, *"Bet Keneset Ḥajāji she-be-Ṣan'a ve-Hanhagato shel ha-Rav Me'ir Subīri,"* *Kenishta* 4 (2010): 113 n. 3.
12. Qoraḥ, *Sa'arat Teiman,* p. 107.

8. The Kuḥlāni synagogue was named for its first owners who built it, and whose name was forgotten.[13] The will of Se'īd ben Moshe Kuḥlāni of 1787 states that he owns the synagogue, so it is safe to assume that he built it or inherited it.[14]
9. The Kisār synagogue was handed over to the public realm by Mrs. Malāḥ bat Avraham 'Amr, who was its owner.[15] At the end of the eighteenth century, after the decree calling for the destruction of the synagogues, the synagogue was rebuilt by Slaymān Kisār, and he served at its leader.[16]
10. The Maswari synagogue was named for its first owners who built it, whose names have been forgotten.[17]
11. The Sayyāni synagogue.[18] At present, we have no details about the founders of the synagogue, but a Ṣan'a Bet Din document from Kislev 5550 (1789) mentions Se'īd ben Sayyani who took upon himself the responsibility for guarding the Torah scroll in the synagogue safe from theft or loss.[19]
12. The Sa'ādi synagogue.[20] Currently, we do not have details about the founders of the synagogue, but a Ṣan'a Bet Din document from 5571 (1810), mentions Se'īd be Musa Sa'ādi, who dedicated the synagogue for the public.[21]
13. The 'Awāḍ synagogue was named for its first owners who built it and whose names have been forgotten.[22]
14. The 'Izayri synagogue named for its first owners, who built it and whose names have been forgotten.[23] In a Ṣan'a Bet Din document from 5557 (1797), the synagogue is mentioned in a dis-

13. Qoraḥ, *Sa'arat Teiman*, p. 107.
14. Naḥshon, *Batei Keneset be-Ṣan'a*, p. 103.
15. Qoraḥ, *Sa'arat Teiman*, p. 107.
16. Ratzaby, "*Batei Kenesiyyot be-Ṣan'a*," pp. 232–33; Naḥshon, *Batei Keneset be-Ṣan'a*, p. 105.
17. Qoraḥ, *Sa'arat Teiman*, p. 107; Gamliel, *Pequdei Teiman*, p. 72.
18. Qoraḥ, *Sa'arat Teiman*, p. 107; Gamliel, *Pequdei Teiman*, p. 73.
19. Naḥshon, *Batei Keneset be-Ṣan'a*, p. 109.
20. Qoraḥ, *Sa'arat Teiman*, p. 107; Gamliel, *Pequdei Teiman*, p. 73.
21. Naḥshon, *Batei Keneset be-Ṣan'a*, p. 109.
22. Qoraḥ, *Sa'arat Teiman*, p. 107.
23. Ibid., p. 107; Gamliel, *Pequdei Teiman*, p. 71.

cussion about the division of the estate of Slaymān ben Yosef 'Izayri, and in another document from that court in 5572 (1812) Harūn ben Yosef 'Izayri dedicated three Torah scrolls to the synagogue.[24]

15. The 'Irq synagogue was named for its first owners, who built it and whose names have been forgotten.[25] Mentioned in a Ṣan'a Bet Din document from 1798 is the matter the sale of part of the synagogue by Yehudah 'Irq.[26]
16. The Ṣāliḥ synagogue named after its first owners, who built it—the Ṣāliḥ family.[27]
17. The Ray'āni synagogue was named for its first owners, who built it, and whose names have been forgotten.[28]
18. The Shar'abi synagogue.[29] When first founded it was called *Kanis Ḥoṭer*, after the first owners who built it, the Ḥoṭer family. In the first half of the eighteenth century, it was led by the president of the Rabbinic Court, R. Dawid ben Yiḥye' Ḥoṭer, who perhaps was its builder.[30] At the end of the eighteenth century, the synagogue was acquired by Sālem Shar'abi, and from then it was called for the purchaser, *Kanis Shar'abi*.[31]
19. The Tan'ami synagogue was built by Manṣūr ben Se'īd Ma'bari and was named for Sālem ben Se'īd Tan'ami, who bought it in the first half of the eighteenth century.[32]

24. Naḥshon, *Batei Keneset be-Ṣan'a*, p. 112.
25. Qoraḥ, *Sa'arat Teiman*, p. 107; Gamliel, *Pequdei Teiman*, p. 71.
26. Naḥshon, *Batei Keneset be-Ṣan'a*, p. 113.
27. Qoraḥ, *Sa'arat Teiman*, p. 107.
28. Ibid., p. 107; Gamliel, *Pequdei Teiman*, p. 74.
29. Qoraḥ, *Sa'arat Teiman*, p. 107. R. Shalom Gamliel thinks that the Shar'ab synagogue is not one of the very old ones. See Gamliel, *Pequdei Teiman*, p. 74.
30. Qoraḥ, *Sa'arat Teiman*, p. 15.
31. Ṣefanya Shar'abi, *Bet al-Shar'abi, Quntres odot "Yeshivat Bet al-Shar'abi"* (Qiryat Sefer 2002), p. 7; Naḥshon, *Batei Keneset be-Ṣan'a*, p. 125; Yosef Ṣubayri, *Siddur Keneset ha-Gedolah*, vol. 1, introduction (Tel Aviv–Jerusalem, 1976), p. 125; Shalom Gamliel, *Batei Keneset be-Ṣan'a Birat Teiman*, 1 (Jerusalem, 1987), pp. 66–70, doc. 6.
32. Naḥshon, *Batei Keneset be-Ṣan'a*, pp. 126–27; Gamliel, *Batei Keneset be-Ṣan'a*, 1: 110–14, doc. 303.

Synagogues Established during the Turkish Occupation

20. The Badīḥi synagogue was built by Sālem Badīḥi in 1873–1874.[33]
21. The Jamal synagogue was built by Ya'īsh al-Jamal in 1876.[34]
22. The Jarashi synagogue was built by Yiḥye' Jarashi in 1878.[35]
23. The Qarya al-Jadīd synagogue was constructed from the donations by residents of the neighborhood in the last third of the nineteenth century.[36]
24. The Yiṣḥāq synagogue was built by the Yiṣḥaq Halewi family in 1888.[37]
25. The Pinḥas synagogue: in the final quarter of the nineteenth century, the Pinḥas family, a wealthy family of Kohanim, devoted one of its houses as a place of prayer, and it served as a synagogue.[38]

A Synagogue Erected in the Time of the *Imam* Yiḥye'

26. The Shim'on synagogue was built in the first half of the twentieth century, with the permission of *Imam* Yiḥye', by builders, brothers, from the Shim'on family, who were the builders of one of the *imam*'s palaces.[39]

Synagogues Whose Founding Date is Unknown

27. The Misk synagogue: From a Ṣan'a Beit Din document, we see that the synagogue was located in the home of R. Se'īd Misk and was owned by him.[40]
28. The Sa'di synagogue: at present, we do not know when this synagogue was founded. It was situated in the home of R. Yehudah Sa'di, one of the famous Ṣan'a rabbis in the first half of the eighteenth century.[41]

---

33. Qoraḥ, *Sa'arat Teiman*, p. 43.
34. Qoraḥ, *Sa'arat Teiman*, p. 43; Gamliel, *Pequdei Teiman*, p. 72.
35. Qoraḥ, *Sa'arat Teiman*, p. 43.
36. Qoraḥ, *Sa'arat Teiman*, p. 43.
37. Qoraḥ, *Sa'arat Teiman*, p. 43; Gamliel, *Pequdei Teiman*, p. 73.
38. Gamliel, ibid., p. 75.
39. Ibid., p. 75.
40. Naḥshon, *Batei Keneset be-Ṣan'a*, p. 105.
41. Naḥshon, *Batei Keneset be-Ṣan'a*, p. 119.

29. The Qāfiḥ synagogue was located in the home of R. Yiḥye' Qāfiḥ (d. 1932), one of the outstanding rabbis and the founder of the Dor De'ah movement.[42]

The large synagogues were 'Ūsṭa', Alsheikh, Ṣāliḥ, Sa'ādi, Sayyāni, Kisār, and Jarashi,[43] with the important ones being 'Ūsṭa', Alsheikh, and Ṣāliḥ.[44] Of the twenty-nine synagogues noted, twenty-four functioned until the mid-twentieth century, and they were, in alphabetical order: (1) Alsheikh; (2) 'Awāḍ; (3) Badīḥi; (4) Dhamāri; (5) Ḥajāji; (6) Ḥubārah; (7) 'Irq; (8) Jadīd; (9) Jamal; (10) Jarashi; (11) Kisār; (12) Kuḥlāni; (13) Maswari; (14) Pinḥas; (15) Qāfiḥ; (16) Ray'āni; (17) Sa'ādi; (18) Ṣāliḥ; (19) Shar'abi; (20) Shim'on; (21) Ṭayri; (22) 'Ūzayri; (23)'Ūsṭa'; (24) Yiṣḥaq.[45]

From the synagogues listed above, we learn that they were named either for the person who was instrumental in the construction of the synagogue or for an important rabbi who served as its leader, though there were some synagogues named for a person who bought an already existing one, such as the Shar'abi synagogue, whose previous name had been Ḥoṭer.

Names of Synagogues in the Radā', Dhamār, and Ṣa'dah Communities

The Radā' community had nine synagogues: the names of the three ancient ones were Kanīs Wahb, which later was called Kanīs al-Ḍāhiri; Kanīs al-Badīḥi; Kanīs Ṣāliḥ. The other synagogues were called Ma'uḍah, Ṭayri, Ḥatuka, Basīs, 'Umaysi, and al-'Ammaysah—another sector of the 'Umaysi family that built the synagogue.[46]

42. Ibid., p. 120.

43. R. Amram Qoraḥ listed the six large synagogues built in the eighteenth century; see Qoraḥ, *Sa'arat Teiman*, p. 107. The Jarashi synagogue, too, which was built later, was a large synagogue and had a very sizable courtyard, so large community prayer services were held there. See Naḥshon, *Batei Keneset be-Ṣan'a*, p. 99.

44. Ratzaby, "Batei Kenesiyyot be-Ṣan'a," p. 239.

45. R. Maḥfuḍ Jarūfi visited the synagogues operating in Ṣan'a in the past generation and wrote a short description of each. See Aharon Gaimani, "*'Maggid Ṣedeq'—al Batei Keneset she-be-Ṣan'a,*" *Kenishta* 3 (2007): 83–94. On the Ṣan'a synagogues in the twentieth century, see Ṣubayri, *Siddur Keneset ha-Gedolah*, vol. 1, pp. 12–17; Shalom Yiṣḥaq Halevi, *Ḥeleq ha-Diqduq la-Mahariṣ al ha-Torah im Be'ur Divrei Shalom* (Jerusalem, 1970), Introduction, p. 15. For a comprehensive book on the Ṣan'a synagogues, see Naḥshon, *Batei Keneset be-Ṣan'a*. See also Qāfiḥ, *Halikhot Teiman*, p. 65; Gamliel, *Pequdei Teiman*, pp. 71–75; idem, *Batei Keneset-be-Ṣan'a*, 1–3.

46. See the Introduction by M. Yiṣhari to his *Shim'on Drumi u-Mishpaḥto* (Israel 2004), p. 13. For additional details on the Radā' community, see below chap. 7, sects. 1, 3

In the Dhamār community there were seven synagogues: Bendawid, Jaraydi, Mqālḥi, Ma'ūḏah Jaraydi, Yosef Ma'bari, Sālem (al-'Ūsṭa), and Qahlāni.[47] The Sālem (al-Ūsṭa) synagogue was named for its founder, the leader Shalom (Arabic: Sālem) ha-Kohen Irāqi and was called by his appellation, al-'Ūsṭa.[48]

The Ṣa'dah community had four houses of worship: 'Afjin, Maz'al, Jamīl, Ha-Qodesh.[49]

Even though we do not have at hand details about the founders of most of the synagogues, one may reasonably assume that as in Ṣan'a in the Radā', Dhamār, and Ṣa'dah communities as well, the names of the synagogues were for the person who had them built or for a great rabbi who had led the synagogue.[50]

2. PERSONAL NAMES FOR TORAH SCROLLS

Yemenite Jews gave names to some of the Torah scrolls in their possession. For example, in the public document of the will of the *nasi* R. Shalom 'Irāqi, written in 1780, he donated three Torah scrolls to the Great Synagogue he had built, and their names were Ha-Zaqen, Nihmi, and Ezra.[51] In a clarification of ownership among partners in Torah scrolls carried out in 1927, their names of the scrolls were noted as Moshe and Aharon.[52] In a 1936 document concerning verification of the acquisition of Torah scrolls, we learn that R. Shalom Ḏarāb of the Raḏma community had donated to the synagogue he owned four Torah scrolls that he had purchased, and their names were Zikhron, Shem Ṭov, Eliyahu, and Refa'el.[53] About the custom of Yemenite Jews to give names to Torah scrolls, R. Yiṣḥaq Raṣābi wrote:

47. For additional details on the Dhamār community, see below chap. 7, sect. 3.
48. See Aharon Gaimani, *"Mekorot Ḥadashim le-Po'alo shel R. Shalom 'Irāqi bi-Kehillot Teiman ba-Me'ah ha-18," Pe'amim* 55 (1993): 138, 140. On the Great Synagogue he built in Ṣan'a, see the beginning of the section.
49. Ovadya Ya'veṣ, *Yehudei Ṣa'dah u-Sevivoteha* (Qiryat Eqron, 2012), p. 11.
50. Shelomo Amihud wrote that in Radā', the Badīḥi, Ṭayri, and Ṣāliḥ synagogues had been named for their founders. See Shelomo Amihud, *Qoveṣ:* chapter *"Iggerot Ḥokhma u-Musar"* (Bat Yam, 2003), p. 53.
51. See Gaimani, *Shalom 'Irāqi*, pp. 137, 141.
52. Yehudah Ratzaby, *"Halikhot ha-Ḥayim be-Golat Teiman le-Or Te'udot Ḥadashot," Asufot* 4 (1990): 375.
53. See Nissim Binyamin Gamlieli, *Teiman bi-Te'udot*, vol. 2 (Ramleh, 2009), p. 200, document 143.

> There are places in which it is customary that the owner of the scroll gives it a certain name for identification, such as Yosef, Binyamin, Beṣal'el, Shemu'el, Eliyahu, just as they give a name to a newborn baby. And some people who have no children, call the scroll after their own name, and they write their name on it.[54]

R. Avraham Arye, who parents emigrated from the Maḥwīt community, says that in his family's synagogue in Yemen three Torah scrolls had names: Shemu'el, Yequti'el, Tam.

A number of Torah scrolls were considered to be holy and were given fitting names. These Torahs were recognized for their special sanctity and were known among the public as miracle workers; Jews would visit these Torah scrolls to pray and beseech, the same way they would visit the graves of *ṣaddiqim*.[55]

There were synagogues in Yemen in which, on special occasions, they would take out the holy Torah scrolls and lay them on the podium, such as before the Kol Nidrei prayer on Yom Kippur night, or read from them on Yom Kippur.[56] R. Gilad Ṣadoq compiled a list of 150 sanctified Torah scrolls that were found among the various communities throughout Yemen; many of them had identical names.[57] Some of them were called by personal names, or for some external trait of the Torah scroll, while still others had place names or the family names of the scribes who wrote them:

54. R. Yiṣḥaq Raṣabi, *Shulḥan Arukh ha-Mequṣar*, vol. 8, *Torah u-Miṣvot* (Bnei Brak, 1989), *Siman* 165, p. 180 n. 131.
55. R. David Mishriqi, one of the outstanding eighteenth-century Yemenite rabbis, did not refer respectfully in his statements to the issue of the holy scrolls, but as is known the other sages of Yemen did not share his opinion. See *Sefer Ravid ha-Zahav le-Rabbeinu David Mishriqi u-Beno Rabbi Yiḥye' Mishriqi*, ed. Y. L. Nahum (Tel Aviv, 1956); ed. S. Ghiyat (Betar Ilit, 2002), *siman* 1. For stories about the holy Torah scrolls in Yemen, see Erich Brauer, *"Qivre ha-Qedoshim ve-Sifre Torah 'Ose Nifla'ot,"* in *Qoveṣ mi-Teiman le-Ṣiyyon*, ed. by S. Jaraydi and Y. Yeshayahu (Tel Aviv, 1938), pp. 169–71; Gaimani, *"Bet Keneset Ḥajāji she-be-Ṣan'a,"* pp. 122–24, 134–36; Sappir, *Even Sappir* (Lyck, 1866), p. 104a. R. Gilad Ṣadoq wrote stories about some of the holy scrolls. See his books *Livneikhem Sapperu—Ma'aseihem shel Tzaddiqim Nissim ve-Nifla'ot* (Bnei Brak, 2000), pp. 229–78 and *Zikhron Teiman—Sippurei Nifla'ot, Demuyot Hod u-Minhagim mi-Yahadut Teiman* (Bnei Brak, 2006), pp. 139–59.
56. Ṣubayri, *Siddur Keneset ha-Gedolah*, 4, pp. 79–80.
57. Ṣadoq, *Zikhron Teiman*, pp. 160–64.

Personal names: Eliyahu—21; Shem Ṭov—9; Shemu'el—8; Ezra—6; Zakkai—4; Ṣemaḥ—4; Moshe—2; once—Aharon; Beṣalel; David; Yehonatan; Yosef; Yiṣḥaq; Me'ir; Mikha'el; Menaḥem; Mordekhai; Siman Ṭov; 'Azri; Pinḥas; Raḥamim; Shem ve-'Ever.

Family names: Farḥi—2; Ḥamāmi—1.

Place names: 'Adani—23; Marghazi —7; Bayḍani—4; Ḍāhiri—2; Maqāleḥi—2; once—Manzali; Mishriqi; 'Azāni; Shabazi; Sharafah.

Other names: Tam—15; Māqḍa'—3; Gadol—2; Jaloḥ—2; Zaqen—2; Kekhov—2; once—Aḥmar; al-Bom; Ba'al ha-Nes; Dal'ah; Ha-Bahir; Maghoz; Mezarar; Qu'ud; unknown.

About half the noted Torahs have personal names, most of which were used in Yemen. Many of the names derived from place names were common family names in Yemen, such as 'Adani, Ḍāhiri, Manzili, Mishriqi, Shabazi, Azāni; Marjazi. In general, most Torah names were private or family names.

Presented here are the names of a few of the sanctified Torah scrolls. The scrolls called Bayḍani are named for the scribe who wrote them, R. Sālem Bayḍani.[58] The scrolls called Farḥi are named for the scribe from the Farḥi family who wrote them.[59] The Torah scroll called Sharafah is for the village Sharafah where the Torah was located.[60] The Maqāleḥi Torah scrolls, one of which was located in the Dhamār community, were named for their place of origin, the village Maqāleḥ.[61] Some of the Torah scrolls called 'Adani are named for the scribe who wrote them, R. Yehudah 'Adani, while others are called by the city, 'Aden, in which they were copied.[62] The Torah scroll called Aḥmar, which means the red one, was apparently named for its scribe, who came from the Aḥmar family, or because the parchment had a reddish tone.[63] Concerning this R. Yiṣḥaq Raṣābi wrote, "There are some old, holy scrolls

58. G. Ṣadoq, *Livneikhem Sapperu*, p. 269.
59. G. Ṣadoq, *Zikhron Teiman*, p. 155.
60. G. Ṣadoq, *Livneikhem Sapperu*, p. 238.
61. Ibid., p. 255. This scroll was brought to Ereṣ Israel and is located in the Maqāleḥi synagogue in the Hatiqvah neighborhood in Tel Aviv. See Uzziyahu Meshullam, "*Qehilat Yehudei Dhamār: Zikhronot me-Ari Shim'on,*" *Tema* 11 (2011): 248 n. 3.
62. Ibid., p. 260.
63. G. Ṣadoq, *Zikhron Teiman*, p. 147.

called by the names of their righteous scribes or their place, such as 'al-'Adani' from the city of 'Aden, 'al-Maqālḥi' from the city of Maqālaḥ."[64]

The al-Bom scroll is located today in Rosh HaAyin; as for the name there several suppositions. Perhaps it alludes to the verse אדני בם סיני בקדש [*Adonai bam, Sinai ba-qodesh*] (Ps. 68, 18), or the verse ודברת בם [*Ve-dibbarta bam*] (Deut. 6:7). Maybe al-Bom is in the sense of to halt, to be silent, reflecting the scribe's asking his family to be quiet while he wrote the scroll or the scribe declaring himself a *ta'anit dibbur* (taking upon oneself not to speak words unrelated to Torah). Another possibility is that it referred to the system of substituting letters by the system אלב"ם גנד"ם and so on, based on dividing the letters into two equal groups and switching to the appropriate letters in each group.[65]

3. NAME USED TO CALL A MAN TO THE TORAH

The custom among the Jews of Yemen is to call a person to the Torah by his personal name and his father's personal name. R. Amram Qoraḥ, the last chief rabbi of the Yemenite Jews in their exile, wrote, "Anyone whose turn it is to read in the Torah scroll, the hazzan calls him by name, and he goes up and recites the blessing and reads by himself."[66] With the words "Anyone whose turn it is" he is referring to the custom of Yemenite Jewry according to which they go up to the Torah according to the order of their seating in the synagogue.[67] About the statements made, his grandson R. Shelomo Qoraḥ noted, "Even though my grandfather, in *Sa'arat Teiman* on page 108, did not mention his father's name, in actuality care is taken to say Ploni son of Ploni.[68] In a similar vein, R. Yosef Ṣubayri, who served as the chief rabbi of the Yemenite Jews in Tel Aviv, wrote "And the custom is to call each *oleh* by his name and

64. Y. Raṣabi, *Shulḥan Arukh ha-Mequṣar*, part 5, *Torah u-Miṣvot, siman* 165, p. 180 n. 131.

65. Ibid., pp. 180–81. See also G. Ṣadoq, *Livneikhem Sapperu*, p. 231.

66. Qoraḥ, *Sa'arat Teiman*, p. 108.

67. Cf. the statement by R. David Mishriqi about the *din* that whoever is called up to read in the Torah not in accordance with the seating arrangement in the synagogue: "And it seems to me that this is the rule if he is out of order but that the hazzan erred and he called him, but he does not to go up" (Mishriqi, *Shulḥan 'Arukh, "Oraḥ Ḥayim" 'im Peirush "Shetilei Zeitim," siman* 139, *siman qatan* 2. See also ibid., *siman qatan* 6).

68. Shelomoh Qoraḥ, *'Arikhat Shulḥan—Yalqut Ḥayim, Oraḥ Ḥayim*, 2, calling up to the Torah by name, *siman* 139, *ṣiyun* 3, (Bnei Brak, 2012), p. 50

his father's name, and respectfully, such as Adoni Yosef ben Ya'aqov, *barekh* [bless]."[69]

R. David Mishriqi (Yemen, 18th c.), who copied the *Shulḥan Arukh* and wrote a commentary on it entitled *Shetilei Zeitim,* did not omit the annotation of the Rama on this issue. The latter wrote "They call them by their name, Ploni ben Ploni," since this coincided with R. Mishriqi's approach, to cite the customs of the Rama that matched Yemenite ones.[70]

R. Yiṣḥaq Raṣābi expanding on the customs of Yemenite Jewry:

> Our custom is to call a person to the Torah by his name and his father's name as follows, Sayyidi (Arabic: "sir", "mister") Ploni ben Ploni, bless ... and not as those who initially state "The first should rise [*ya'amod*] in honor, the second should rise in honor, and so on. Also the custom of the Ashkenazim on this is like our custom, to call by his name and his father's name, but they do follow the pattern mentioned, *Ya'amod R. Ploni ben R. Ploni.*[71]

Elsewhere he wrote:

> Our custom is that the ḥazzan calls [people up] in the order in which they sit in the synagogue, one after the other. And he mentions each one by his name and his father's name, Ploni ben Ploni, *barekh.* And that is the proper custom, the reason being that there should be no argument. Furthermore, by doing so the entire public will come to know his precise name and will not encounter any stumbling block over the matter of a *get* and the like. In addition, the name and soul of every Jewish person is alluded to in the Torah and he has a part in it.[72]

If the person being called to the Torah is a *talmid ḥakham,* the ḥazzan precedes his name with *Mori,* and for the others Sayyidi. But if the ḥazzan is calling up his father or his brother, he does not call his father by name but says, "The honorable father *mori, barekh,*" while for his brother, he says his personal name and adds "son of the honorable father *mori, barekh.*"[73]

69. Yosef Ṣubayri, *Siddur Keneset ha-Gedolah,* 1 (Tel Aviv, 1976), p. 211.

70. Mishriqi, *Shetilei Zeitim, siman* 139, 3. On R. David Mishriqi's system, see Gaimani, *Temurot be-Moreshet Yahadut Teiman,* pp. 212–15.

71. Yiṣḥaq Raṣabi, *Piskei Mahariṣ,* 2, *Hilkhot Qeri'at Torah* (Bnei Barak 1993), commentary *Be'erot Yiṣḥaq, siman qatan* 10, p. 427.

72. Raṣabi, *Shulḥan Arukh ha-Mequṣar,* 1, *siman* 22, 13, pp. 183–84.

73. Ibid., *ṣiyyun* 34, p. 184.

Even though the custom of the Ashkenazi and the Yemenite Jews is to call to the Torah by the personal name, there is a difference between them. The Ashkenazi Jews use the Hebrew name that had been given at the time of circumcision and not by the vernacular name that was used in daily life. However, among the Yemenite Jews the name given at circumcision is the name used in daily life, so they would call one up to the Torah with his personal name, even if it was in Arabic.[74]

In Israel today, some Yemenite Jews have adopted the Sephardi custom of not calling a person to the Torah by his personal name. On this phenomenon R. Shim'on Ṣāliḥ [Yemen–Israel, 20th] wrote:

> Our custom, from time immemorial until today, is to call and invite the person going up to the *sefer Torah* as ploni ben ploni, and for which see Shulkhan 'Arukh, par. 139, sect. 3. Now, to our sorrow, some *sheliḥei ṣibbur* [prayer leaders] have arisen who did not know the *halakhah* and the custom which is also law, and do as they please, namely, the first will please arise, the second will please arise, and this is not as it is written, and they should be made aware of their error and cease it, and the good Lord shall atone for them.[75]

When people recite in the synagogue or at other gatherings the *Mi she-Berakh* for the benefactors or the ill, as well as at the burial ceremony for the deceased, there are some Jewish communities that usually mention the mother's name.[76] Some offer an explanation that the biological link of a son to his mother is greater than that to his father and that a woman has fewer complaints about her, since she is released from the time-bound commandments and from the iniquity of *bittul Torah* (wasting time not studying Torah learning).[77] In contrast, the Yemenite Jews' custom is to mention only the father's name, and as R. Shelomo Qoraḥ has commented, "Mentioned are the name of the deceased and his father's name. It has never been heard that they cite the mother's name,

74. See also above, part 1, beginning of chap. 3.
75. Mahariṣ, *Tiklal Eṣ Ḥayim*, 1 (Jerusalem, 1971), notes, p. 87a.
76. Support for this custom is found in the statement in the Zohar, Lekh Lekha (part 1, p. 84a), for Ps. 86:16: "Save the son of your handmaid, that David mentioned his mother and not his father." See also the *Ta'amei ha-Minhagim*, Shabbat matters, par. 353, p. 164.
77. Yosef Ḥayim ben Eliyahu, *Shut Torah li-Shmah* (Jerusalem, 1976), *siman* 399; see also R. Ovadia Yosef, *Shut Yabi'a Omer*, part 2 (Jerusalem, 1956), *Oraḥ Ḥayim*, *siman* 11.

for this is associated with magic and the way of demons."[78] He wrote further to underpin the custom of the Jews of Yemen on this matter:

> One must say about the custom of our forefathers that they were not sensitive to all this, since one must mention only merit and satisfaction and not offensive thoughts to detract from him lest (one might think) he not be this father's son ... and I am not coming, Heaven forbid, to find fault in the customs of the other holy communities, may the Lord protect them and sustain them, far be this from me, but I am interested in placing our children on the knees of our forefathers, resting in Eden, that they should not falter, Heaven forbid ... so our custom is good and not to be changed, and the same as in his lifetime it is customary to mention the name of the father when called up to the Torah and in all kinds of documents, so it is after death.[79]

Further, R. Qoraḥ cites statements from the Zohar about the ways of witches and demons to mention only the mother's name, and he concludes with "from all this, we see that our ancestors had a custom to distance themselves from the ways of witches and demons, and to note only the father's name. And even if our ancestors are not prophets, they are the sons of prophets."[80] R. Pinḥas Qoraḥ says that the Yemenite Jews' custom is based on Num. 1:2, "by their families, by their father's houses," and adds that perhaps the mother's name is not added out of modesty:

> This is the simple custom that has wended its way down through the generations in our communities [i.e., the Yemenite communities] that they always mention a person along with his father's name, and from the day he leaves his mother's womb until he dies, he is called by his father's name. On the day of the *brit*, mercy is sought for the infant and they say, "May health be sent for the life and mercy ... that he name be called Ploni ben Ploni; and when he is called to the Torah he is called by his father's name, in *ketubbot* and *gittin* and when acting as a witness, he is called Ploni ben Ploni, and even at the burial rite they mention his name and his father's name, and the proof is that it states by their families, by their father's houses, and they

78. S. Qoraḥ, *Arikhat Shulḥan—Yalqut Ḥayim*, Yod, 1, Burial and Qaddish, *siman* 376, section 27, p. 162.
79. Ibid., pp. 162–63.
80. Ibid., p. 164.

> never mention a person by his mother's name. Perhaps, the reason is also out of modesty that the mother's name is not invoked.[81]

R. Yiṣḥaq Raṣabi wrote about this issue:

> As for what I wrote about his name and his father's name, this is always our custom, as in the formula of *Mi-she Berakh*, both for a regular person as well as for an ill one, to cite the name of the father and not the mother, and even for a woman, they mention then her name and her father's name, and so it is at the burial ceremony ... only for matters of *mazalot* and healing incantations they deal with them with his name and that of his mother, this is also so for incantations against the Evil Eye and in amulets.[82]

On the issue of mentioning the name of the deceased, R. Raṣabi wrote, "And they always mention his name and his father's name but not his mother, and for a woman, her name and her father's name, such as Yokheved bat Levi."[83]

81. P. Qoraḥ, *Bet Mo'ed*, 1 (Bnei Brak, 2000), chap. 1, section 20, p. 42.
82. Raṣabi, *Shulḥan Arukh ha-Mequṣar*, 5, *siman* 175, *ṣiyun* 10, p. 364. Support for mentioning the mother's name in incantations is found in tractate Shabbat 66b: Abbaye said, "My mother told me: Many things in the name of the mother." And on this text, Rashi explained, "Many things—all the incantations. And since they are doubled, there are also three times and more, they are called in the incantations"; "in the name of the mother—Ploni ben Plonit."
83. Raṣabi, ibid., *siman* 187, 14, p. 443. In Ereṣ Israel, there are some Yemenite rabbis who when saying *"Mi she-Berakh"* add after the father's name the family name as well. See *Ha-Tiklal ha-Mevu'ar*, ed. and proofread under the direction of R. Pinas Qoraḥ (Bnei Brak, 5766).

CHAPTER SEVEN

CHANGES AS A RESULT OF IMMIGRATION TO ISRAEL

Immigration of Jews from Yemen to the Land of Israel began in 1881 and culminated in the major immigration operation *'Al Kanfei Nesharim*, 1949–1950. New names appeared in Yemen in the twentieth century as a result of the awakening for *aliyah*, along with the transformations of private, as well as family names, after arriving in Israel.

1. NEW NAMES IN YEMEN IN THE TWENTIETH CENTURY

An expression of *aliyah* is the name Ṣiyyon, Zion, which was reintroduced into Yemen in the first half of the twentieth century. On the name Ṣiyyon from that period in Ṣan'a and Manākhe, R. Ya'aqov ben Avraham Shar'abi writes:

> But in the last generation, they gave the name Ṣiyyon (and perhaps under the influence of the awakening of interest in Ṣiyyon that pulsed in them), and from what I remember just now, I will list a few of them: Ṣiyyon b. Shalom Ghiyat (Manākhe); and may he have a long life, Ṣiyyon b. Sālem Yisra'el Shar'abi; Ṣiyyon b. Yiḥye' Shelomo Kisar; Ṣiyyon b. R. Sālem Raḥabi; R. Ṣiyyon b. Yiḥye' Ḥubarah; all of them from Ṣan'a.[1]

In the list of pupils who studied in 1943 in the Ṣan'a schools, are four boys named Ṣiyyon,[2] and among the girls Bat Ṣiyyon Jamal.[3] In the first

1. In a personal correspondence dated 16 Marḥeshvan 5758 (16 Nov 1997). For a photo of Ṣiyyon Sha'ir with his parents in Ṣan'a, see *Ṣan'a u-Sevivatah be-Ṣilumei Yeḥiel Ḥaybi*, ed. Yosef Sha'ar (published by Ruma Haybi; Tel Aviv, 1985), p. 57, photo no. 105.
2. See Yosef Tsuri'eli, *Kalkalah ve-Ḥinukh Moderni be-Teiman be-Et ha-Ḥadashah* (Jerusalem, 2005), doc. 25, p. 77.

half of the twentieth century, the name Ṣiyyon is also found in the Jewish communities in northern Yemen: Ṣiyyon b. Yosef from Sha'bān,[4] Ṣiyyon b. Sālem from Majz,[5] Ṣiyyon Ḥarizi from Qarḥaw.[6] In the extended Drumi family in the Radā' community, they named children Ṣiyyon, Ṣiyyonah, and *Ge'ulah* (Redemption).[7]

In the 1940s, immigrants waiting for *aliyah* to Israel were assembled in the Ge'ulah Camp (Aden). At that time, newborns in the camp were given names expressing the spirit of redemption, such as Go'el, Yinon, Ṣiyyon, Ben Ṣiyyon, and Ge'ulah in the extended Avraham family.[8] A few days before immigration to Israel, R. Shalom and Niḍra Tobi had a son and called him Ṣiyyon.[9] R. Maḥfuḍ had a daughter in 1949 on the way from Ṣan'a to Aden and wrote, "She was called Ṣiyyonah, meaning 'To Zion we shall ascend'."[10]

Ziona Aharoni told me of the stages in the development of her name. Her family emigrated from the Radā' in the *'Al Kanfei Nesharim* operation. On the way to Aden, her four-year-old sister Ḥamāmah (Dove) died. Her father, who had deeply loved Ḥamāmah, called the daughter born after the girl's passing Yonah. He subsequently decided that since the family had obtained its heart's desire to live in Zion, he would add the letter *ṣade* to his daughter's name, thus Ṣiyona.[11] Naomi Badiḥi related that her father was called Yiga'el (meaning, "he will be redeemed") because he had been born about a week after they arrived in Israel.[12] One of the Yemenite immigrants to Israel wrote in the 1940s about his son's birth:

3. Ibid., doc. 16, p. 67, no. 4. Bat Ṣiyyon is the daughter of R. Shalom Gamliel, who immigrated to the Land of Israel in 1944 and lived in Jerusalem.
4. Aharon Ben David, *Bet ha-Even, Hilkhot Yehudei Ṣefon Teiman* ([Qiryat Eqron], 5768), no. 1576, p. 714.
5. Ibid., no. 1577–1578.
6. Ibid., no. 1579, p. 714.
7. M. Yiṣhari, *Shim'on Drumi u-Mishpaḥto* (n.p., 2004), pp. 214–15.
8. R. Shalom Gamliel, *Pe'amei ha-Aliyyah mi-Teiman* (Jerusalem, 1988), pp. 184–85.
9. Yehudah Tobi, *Aḥarit le-Ish Shalom: Masekhet Ḥayyav shel Rabbi Shalom Tobi* (Bnei Brak, 1990), p. 43.
10. Aharon Gaimani, *"Treisar Nisyonot she-Ninasa bahem Ben Teiman ve-Qibbel Yesurav be-Ahava,"* in *Mikhtam le-Yona—Meḥqarim be-Tarbut Yehudei Teiman u-be-Sugyot Ḥevrati'ot ve-Ḥinukhiyyot*, ed. Yosef Dahu'ah Halevi (Tel Aviv, 2004), p. 456.
11. Ziona Aharoni lives in Gedera. In a personal correspondence dated 19 Oct 2010.
12. Interview conducted by her granddaughter Michal Badiḥi from Givatayim.

> The good flower was born, may the Lord give him all good, *Ṣiyyon* ben Shalom Naḥum, *yṣ"v*, make him worthy of a good year and of great Torah learning, born on 1 Iyyar 5706 (1946), may God educate my son, and save you from all trouble and distress.[13]

This phenomenon of giving names related to the redemption is found also among the last Yemenite immigrants, from the end of the twentieth century through the beginning of the twenty-first: A boy was born in 1993 to the 'Aṣar family, which immigrated to Israel in this period, and he was given the name Go'el (redeemer);[14] R. Binyamin Kubāni called his daughter, born in 1995, Besorah (tidings), because of the message about leaving Yemen;[15] in the Jarādi family, which came to New York in 2005 from the village of Raidah, one of the children born after they had left Yemen was named Yenon, a name expressing tidings of the redemption.[16]

2. CHARACTERISTICS OF CHANGING PERSONAL NAMES

After immigration to Israel many names were translated or shifted from Arabic to Hebrew: both women's names, the majority of which in Yemen were in Arabic, and those of men. For some of them the translation was precise, while for others a Hebrew name sounding similar to the Arabic one was chosen, even if there was no relation to the Arabic meaning; in some cases a new name was selected. R. Yosef Qāfiḥ wrote, "Indeed, with our *aliyah* there are many name changes ... with no relation to their main name, such as Turkiyyah who is called Yehudit, or Sham'ah who is called Shoshanah, without any link to their previous name."[17] R. Pinḥas Qoraḥ wrote in a similar vein about given as well as family names:

> Hebraization of names is not always parallel to the original name. For example, the name Sham'ah was Hebraized as Shoshana, Turkiyya was turned into Yehudit, Bint became Batya, the family name Dha'rur

13. Written on the back of the title page of a *Kol Peh* prayer book for the High Holidays in the Yemenite rite; in the possession of R. Shelomo Almog, Jerusalem. For a piece on the birth of another son of Shalom Naḥum, see above part 1, chap. 2, sect. 2.
14. From the registration of the Absorption Ministry.
15. As related by R. Yisachar Kubāni, London.
16. As related by Mori Shim'on Jaraydi, New York. Yenon is one of the names of the Messiah; cf. Pesaḥim 54a; Sanhedrin 98b.
17. In a personal correspondence dated 9 July 1993.

> became Deror, Manṣūra turned into Ben Ṣur, Jarūfi was turned into Yig'ali ... this is so for many of the Hebraized or distorted names ...[18]

R. Yiṣḥaq Raṣabi wrote, "Know that when they immigrated to Israel, they changed many of the Arabic names into Hebrew ones similar in sound rather than by their meaning, such as Ya'ish (meaning life) [into] Yeshayah. Shukr (thanks, that is, Yehudah) [to] Yissakhar; Zihrah (Venus) to Sarah. All kinds of transformations like this."[19] R. Aviran Yiṣḥaq Halevi wrote concerning the Hebraization of the name Tūrkiyya that "there were some who used to call by the name Yehudit, while others chose Rivqah. And my paternal grandfather, Rabbenu Shalom Yiṣḥaq Halevi, gave his daughter the name Tūrkiyya, but in Israel the name was changed to Yehudit. My maternal grandfather, R. Yehudah Kisar, called his daughter Tūrkiya, and in Israel they changed her name to Rivqah because of the similar sounds *resh kaf/qof*, and in time she became the wife of Yehudah Ratzaby, OBM."[20] On the making the name Yiḥye' equivalent to Zekharyah, Y. Ratzaby noted:

> It is accepted among Yemenite Jews, from the distant past, that the Arabic name Yiḥye' is none other than the Hebrew Zekharyah. This is so in Yemenite literature, and immigrants from Yemen, when they come to Ereṣ Israel, usually change their name from Yiḥye' to Zekharyah. Researchers studying Yemen have not found any reasonable explanation linking these two names.[21]

Many names that had been common in Yemen were not given to children born in Israel. This is so for Yiḥye', Sālem, and Ya'ish for men, and the names Rūmiyyah, Ḥamāmah, Banayyah, and Sham'ah for women. There were those who wanted to name their child for a parent or relative, but after *aliyah*, in the spirit of the times, instituted a name change.

Shalom Katriel, whose parents had lived in the Ḍāhare community in southern Yemen, wrote, "My father, my master, OBM, was called Sālem Yiḥye' Qatar. Apparently, this name was his and his father's,[22]

18. In a personal correspondence dated April 2010.
19. Yiṣḥaq Raṣabi, *Shut Olat Yiṣḥaq,* 2, par. 251, section *gimel*, pp. 427–28 (Bnei Brak, 1992).
20. In a personal correspondence dated 12 Oct 2010.
21. Yehudah Ratzaby, *Be-Ma'agalot Teiman* (Tel Aviv, 1948), p. 7. For a discussion concerning the names Yiḥye', Ḥayim, and Zekharyah, see above, part 1, chap. 4, sects. 1–2.
22. Originally written erroneously: that is the name of his father and the name of his grandfather.

exactly the same as he called his sons. The older one was called Yiḥye', while the younger Sālem, who is the writer of these lines."[23] The writer changed his personal name from Sālem to Shalom, and his family name, based on the sound, from Qathar to Katri'el; he called his son Avishai "since this name corresponds to the name of our parents: Avi-Shai, that is, Avinu Shalom Yiḥye'."[24] Aviva Himoff, whose parents emigrated from Ṣan'a, said that her brother Ḥayim Meghori Kohen named his son Yosef after his father and his daughter Re'umah after his mother, Rūmiyyeh.[25] A member of my family, Pinḥas, named his son Yeḥi'el after his father's name Yiḥye'. After the death of my grandfather Ya'ish, my father called my brother Yeshayah, which is quite similar in sound to his father's name, and later changed my brother's name to Shai. After the passing of my uncle, my teacher R. Yosef ben Ya'ish Gaimani, OBM, my brother Barukh named his son Yosef, while I named my son Amiḥai, because we used to call my uncle 'Ami (the customary way in central Yemen to call the brother of one's father); this was combined in 'Amiḥai since the righteous after their death are called living (*ḥayim*).[26]

After the passing of my maternal grandmother Banayyah, my brother called his son Benayah, and another relative called his daughter Nivah, which is composed of a rearrangement of the letters of the name Benayah. Sāli Ḥarīr told me that her paternal grandfather emigrated from the Ḥaja community in central Yemen. She was born about a year and a half after his death and they called her Sāli after her grandfather's name, Sālem.[27]

The following are some of the Arabic names that, on the basis of meaning or homophony, were transformed into Hebrew ones.

23. Shalom Katriel, *Ha-Mal'akh ha-Go'el Oti* (The Story of the Tribulations, the Exile, and the Redemption) (Modi'in Ilit, 2006), p. 9. On the custom of Yemenite Jews to name their children for themselves or for their parents, see above part 1, chap. 2, sects. 1–2.
24. Ibid., in place of an introduction, p. 6.
25. Aviva Himoff lives in Manhattan, New York.
26. Cf. TB Berakhot 18a: "These are the righteous who in their death are called living."
27. In personal correspondence dated 10 Nov 2011. Shira Talmud from the settlement Revava wrote me on 13 Nov 2011 that during her National Service in Netivot in 2009–2010, she met young men and women named *Sāli*, and they explained to her that this name was for the Baba Sāli, the Kabbalist, and R. Yisra'el Abuḥaṣera, who is buried in Netivot.

Men's names based on meaning:

Abu S'ūd – Avigad
'Amran – 'Amram
Harūn – Aharon
Ḥasan – Yefet
Mūsa' – Moshe
Raḍa – Raṣon
Sālem – Shalom
Se'īd – Sa'adya
Shukr – Yehudah
Slaymān – Shelomo
Ṣāliḥ – Ṣadoq
Wahab – Nathan
Ya'ish – Ḥayim

Men's names based on homophony:

'Awaḍ – 'Ovadyah
Banīn – Binyamin
'Īḍah – 'Ovadyah, 'Oded
Jamīl – Gamliel
Methane– Menashe
Shukr – Yissakhar
Ya'ish – Yeshayah
Yiḥye' – Yeḥi'el

Women's names based on meaning:

Banayyah – Batyah
Bint – Batyah
Ḍobyah – Ṣviyah
Fuḍah – Kaspit
Ghaliyah – Yeqarah
Ghane – Rinah
Ghazāl – Ayyalah
Ḥabībah – Ahuvah
Ḥāliyah – Yafah
Ḥamāmah – Yonah
Ḥīsin– Yafah
Jamilah – Yafah
Lūluwah – Margalit
Maḥbubah – Ḥavivah

Naḍrah – Orah
Najmah – Kokhavah
Qamar – Levanah
Sa'dah – Mazal, Oshrah
Salāmeh – Shulamit
Se'īdah – Mazal
Sham'ah – Nurit
Shams – Shemesh
Tiranjah – Etrogah
Tūrkiyyah – Yehudit

Women's names based on homophony:

Badrah – Devorah
Barūd – Berakhah, Vardah, Beruryah
Ghazāl – Galyah
Ghusnah – Osnat
Hawidah – Yehudit
Kamlah – Karmelah
Lūluwah – Le'ah
Niḍrah – Orah
Ni'meh – Na'omi
Nurah – Nurit
Qamar – Margalit, Tamar
Rashūshah – Shoshanah
Rūmiyyah – Re'umah, Miryam, Rinah
Se'īdah – Sarah
Shadhrah – Shoshanah
Sham'ah – Shoshanah, Bat Sheva'
Ṣīniyyah – Ṣiyyonah
Tūrkiyyah – Rivqah
Yaman – Yemimah
Zihrah – Sarah

3. CHARACTERISTICS OF CHANGES IN FAMILY NAMES

Upon immigration to Israel during operation "On the Wings of Eagles," those Yemenite Jews who did not have family names were requested to add one to make identification easier.

The Ṣa'īri family emigrated in the first decade of the twentieth century from southern Yemen. The poet Ḥayim Nachman Bialik met with R. David ben Yisra'el Ṣa'īri, one of the outstanding figures among the

Yemenite settlers at Kinneret, and was quite impressed with him. As a result of that meeting, most of the Ṣa'īri family changed their name to

> Margalit. As it is told, when he was strolling with the children of Degania on Sabbath eve Hayim Nachman Bialik came to their neighborhood at Lake Kinneret. After a discussion with R. David ben Yisra'el Ṣa'īri Shar'abi (this was his full name), Bialik was interested in the explanation for the name Ṣa'īri ("elevated", "sublime"), however, he rejected it, claiming it was a "*Galut* name." Bialik proposed the name be changed to Margalit ("pearl") instead, since this "name befits someone from whose mouth comes forth pearls, like the mouth of the sage rabbi." Indeed, all the Yemenites of Kinneret accepted Bialik's suggestion (almost all of them were related), except for the rabbi himself, who retained the name Ṣa'īri.[28]

The Zabīb ("raisins") family wrote: "The source of the name Zabīb, as handed down by the parents, is the ancient trade of the family—dealing with the production, transportation, and selling of raisins … therefore, they were called Bet al-Zabīb."[29] We learn of the changes to the family name once in Israel:

> Today, part of the family has adopted the custom that spread in our society—Hebraization of a family name. In a discussion held about this … the idea was raised to base themselves on the Bible and to use the family name "*Soreq*" in the sense of a noble grape, as it is written, "I planted you with noble vines, all with choicest seed" (Jer. 2:21), as well as other names: Gefen, Sarig, Aviv, Raviv, Karmon.[30]

An examination of the family album shows that the family names mentioned were actually used: Shmuel and Miriam Soreq,[31] Pinḥas and Ṣiona Sarig,[32] No'aḥ and 'Atara Karmon,[33] 'Azriel and Sarah Gafni,[34] and Raḥamim and Miriam Gefen.[35]

28. Dina Greitzer, "*Marmorek—Moshav ha-'Ovdim ha-Rishonim shel Yehudei Teiman ba-Areṣ,*" in *Se'i Yona: Yehudei Teiman be-Yisra'el*, ed. Shalom Sirri (Tel Aviv, 1983), p. 161 n. 13.
29. Yisrael Soreq, *Album Mishpaḥat Zabib le-Doroteha* (Tel Aviv, 2004), p. 7. See also above part 2, chap. 1, sect. 3.
30. Ibid.
31. Ibid., p. 32.
32. Ibid., p. 35.
33. Ibid., p. 59.
34. Ibid., p. 80.
35. Ibid., p. 82.

On the giving of different family names to members of the same family, Dr. Ni'mah ben 'Ami wrote concerning her family:

> In some cases, brothers, children of the same parents, received different family names in Israel, as for example, my father and his two brothers; something I could not understand when I was young: the family name of my uncle Slaymān is Ben Shelomo, after his father's name, Slaymān; while my father's family name is Ḥezi (Ḥāzi). Only when I grew up did I realize that when they immigrated to Israel each one of them gave a different name to the Inhabitants Register: the first, his father's name (Slaymān); the second, the family name as it was in Yemen ('Imrān), while my father, gave the name of the village in which he lived (Ḥāz).[36]

Shiran Yosef of Kiryat Ono writes that her family name had been chosen by her grandfather and his brothers:

> My grandfather, Ḥayim Raṣon Yosef, OBM, immigrated to Israel from the 'Ūzla community in southern Yemen. In Yemen, my grandfather's father was called Raḍa' (in Hebrew, Raṣon) Yosef, and my grandfather's grandfather was called Yosef Se'īd (following the custom of Yemenite Jews that a person was called by his name and his father's name). Upon the immigration of my grandfather and his brothers to Israel, they were asked to choose a family name for their Identification Card. My grandfather selected the name of his grandfather Yosef as a family name, and he was called Ḥayim Yosef. His brother Yosef chose the name of his grandfather's father as a family name, and he was called Yosef Se'īd. His brother Yefet followed suit and was called Yefet Se'īd, though later he changed the family name to Sa'ar. The other brothers, David and Avraham, picked their father's name, Raḍa', as their family name, and they were called in Hebrew the Raṣon family.[37]

An error of registration of the family name for one of the Yemenite immigrants is related by Shemu'el Ḥofi:

> When my father came to Israel on *aliyah*, his turn with the Jewish Agency clerk came, and he asked him, "Who are you?" My father replied, "I am Ḥudhayfi," since he came from the Aḥdhuf district in southern Yemen. The clerk, who did not understand Arabic well, heard Ḥofi instead of Ḥudhayfi and that is what remained the family name to this day. There was actually an IDF general by the name of

36. Na'ama Ben Ami, *"Ha-Maqor ha-'Aravi shel Shemot ha-Yehudim she-'Alu mi-Teiman," Tema* 10 (2007): 207 n. 31.

37. In a personal correspondence dated 21 Apr 2011.

> Yiṣḥaq Ḥofi, who was of Ashkenazi origin, and during my childhood I was asked a number of times if I was related to him, sometimes jokingly and sometimes seriously.[38]

Lirit Zinadani wrote about another case of erroneous registration:

> My grandfather immigrated to Israel from the village of Bane-Ḥajāj in the Ḥaymeh district of Yemen. He told me that in Yemen, even when they had family names, they would still be identified by the father's and grandfather's names. My grandfather, for example, was called Yiḥye', his father was called Sūlēman (= Shelomo), and his grandfather was named Nissim, and when he was asked what his name was, he would reply: Yiḥye' ben Sūlēman Nissim, meaning, they would add the father's name to that of the grandfather and that was how they identified them, even though he did have a family name: Ṣūbara. But when he arrived in Israel, he was asked, "What is your family name? He gave them the name of his grandfather, Nissim, and that is what they listed for him in his certificate.[39]

As a result of the incident noted, the family's name to this day is Nissim. Lirit Zindani further told about the name change in the Nissim family:

> My mother's uncle (my grandfather's brother) is named Ḥayim Yanai, even though the family name of the other brothers is Nissim. My grandmother told me that Uncle Ḥayim was an academic in the 1970s and 1980s and changed his family name to Yanai (no one knows the reason for picking "Yanai"). He earned a master's and a doctorate, was principal of a school, and now that he has retired he has added to his name "Ḥayim Yanai" the original family name Ṣūbara, before it was changed to Nissim upon arriving in Israel.[40]

Mazal Būshari, whose parents emigrated from southern Yemen, wrote about the family name Naddūf. Her great-grandfather's name was Sayyagh [jeweler]. Because of economic hardship, he went to Aden, where he worked with a cotton gin, where the cotton fibers were separated from the seeds and underwent their first cleaning. From then on he was called al-Naddūf, the carder or cotton cleaner. As to the name upon immigration to Israel, she writes:

38. In response to a questionnaire that Shemu'el Ḥofi gave me in Dec 2010.
39. In a work Lirit Zindani turned in 2009.
40. In response to a questionnaire given to me by Lirit Zindani in July 2010.

> The immigration clerk had never heard of the family name Naddūf, but had heard of other immigrants who had come from Ṣan'a and its surroundings with the family name Naddāf. So he wrote on my parents' Immigrant Certificate Naddāf. In time, my two brothers decided to change their family name to Yehonadav, because they did want that they or their children should be labeled as belonging to a specific ethnic group as a result of the family name.[41]

Ilanit David, whose family emigrated from the village of Qūbāt in southern Yemen, relates that her great-grandfather's name had been Da'ūd, and so upon coming to Israel they adopted his name as the family name and thus were the David family.[42]

The Qo'dah (cauldron) family lived in the town Gharāne' in southern Yemen. Upon *aliyah* to Israel the family was registered with the name Qa'īda; in later years some members of this family changed the name to the Hebrew Qedar.[43]

The Si'dīd family lived in the village of Sharafe in central Yemen. They immigrated to Israel in 1949 and lived in moshav Ge'ulim in the Sharon. A few of them had the same name, which caused the moshav secretary Immanu'el to confuse various bills and payments, and sometimes he would "clear a debt and oblige someone not required to pay." So he took the initiative and changed the family name of some of them, such as 'Ami'el, Re'uveni, Gamli'el, No'aḥ, Arzi, and they have kept this name to this day.[44] One family member, Yiḥye' Yosef Si'dīd, said that his cousin had the exact same name, and this resulted in confusion in letters as well as payment of salaries and other bills. To solve the problem, he went to the Interior Ministry in Netanya, where the clerk suggested that he change his family name to Semadar, which he did. Eventually, the cousin mentioned changed his family name to Shrafi after their home in Yemen.[45]

The Raḥabi family emigrated from central Yemen and settled in moshav Zavdi'el. Two of them had the identical name, Yiḥye' Menaḥem Raḥabi. It happened that one of them, who worked in agriculture, would

41. In a personal correspondence dated 4 Apr 2011.
42. In a questionnaire I received from Ilanit David of Rishon Lezion.
43. In a questionnaire turned in by Yaniv Qedar, Tel Aviv. For the family story, see above, part 2, chap. 3, sect. 2.
44. As related by Zion Petaḥya, who lives in moshav Ge'ulim.
45. As related by Yosef Semadar, who lives in moshav Ge'ulim.

market his merchandise, but when the payment would arrive at the post office, which was in a private home in the moshav, the mailman would notify the other Yiḥye' Menaḥem Raḥabi. As a result, one of the sons of Yiḥye' Menaḥem Raḥabi changed his family name to Raḥamim so that the payment would reach its proper destination. The sons of Yiḥye' Menaḥem Raḥabi bore the new family name, Raḥamim, except for the eldest, Shalom, who took the family name Menaḥem. Yiḥye''s brother Shalom did not change his family name, but kept Raḥabi.[46]

The Qa'ṭabi family, which had lived in Miḏraḥ in southern Yemen, immigrated to Israel in 1935. They went to Rehovot and were asked by the local council if they would mind changing their family names to Katabi, which is shorter and easier to pronounce, and so they did.[47]

At times, the changes occurred at the request of the family. For example, the family Sībahi, which means "apathetic," emigrated from Bilad Ans. In Israel, they replaced it with the similar-sounding name Zehavi.[48] In a similar instance, the Ḥāser family, which had resided in Ghiḥzān, and after their immigration to Israel changed its name to the similar-sounding name Ḥasid.[49]

Some in the Māwreḥi family (called Morḥi in Israel), who emigrated from the city of Dhamār, changed their name to Ma'or or Ma'or-Ḥai.[50] The origin of the Yaf'i family is the Yafa' district in Yemen. After making *aliyah* to Israel, some of them changed their name to the homophonous Yafe.[51]

We see this type of name change in the names of well-known personalities. The family name of Yisra'el Qesar, who was deputy prime minister and minister of transport under Rabin had been Kisār;[52] that of the singer Yigal Bashan had been Bashāri; that of the singer Uri She-

46. In a personal correspondence dated 15 Dec 2011 from the granddaughter Niva Raḥamim of Ra'anana, on 15 Dec 2011. Yiḥye' Menaḥem Raḥabi and his brother Shalom Raḥabi are my uncles, brothers of my mother. Menaḥem is the name of my maternal grandfather and he died in Yemen.
47. In a questionnaire I received from Yonit Katabi of Rehovot.
48. In a questionnaire I received from Idit Zehavi of Rehovot.
49. In a questionnaire I received from Ilanit Ḥasid from moshav Sha'ar Efrayim. For the family's story, see above, part 2, chap. 3, sect. 2.
50. In a questionnaire returned to me by Orit Marmorstein of Petaḥ Tiqvah.
51. In a questionnaire I received from Shlomi Yafeh, Ramat Gan.
52. On the development of the family name Kisār, see above part 2, chap. 3, sect. 2.

vaḥ had been Shḥib; that of Nehemiah Lahav, mayor of Hedera, had been Aḥraq; and that of Gen. Yishai Eduard was Adū'ar. The previous personal name of the Afula Town Council member Yosef Goshen was Jishjush and that of the singer Zion Golan was Bagdalān.

In some instances, the placement of a letter in the family name was changed, creating a Hebrew name for the family. The 'Amran family had lived in one of the villages near the city of Ibb. After *aliyah* to Israel, some of the family members felt they had to make identification easier and to differentiate themselves from other families with the name 'Amran, who had come from the same district where they had resided in Yemen. To do so, they added a *yod* and changed their name to 'Amiran. They added a homiletic interpretation to the name change: 'Ami Ran, "the Jewish people are happy."[53]

The family name Shar'abi was given to many who emigrated from Shar'ab in southern Yemen, and is the most common family name today in Israel among those originating in Yemen.[54] Regarding the name change in the Shar'abi family, R. Adam Bin Nun writes:

> As for my family name Bin Nun: my father's family was Shar'abi; and my mother's family was Shar'abi (even though they were not related). For a short time after they married the kept the name Shar'abi, but afterwards they thought about changing their name to something more Israeli, specifically biblical. That's how they came to Yehoshu'a Bin Nun, the leader of the Jewish people when they began to enter Israel. This is not translating into Hebrew, nor preserving the sounds of the former name, but choosing an entirely new name.[55]

Of the families who bear the name of locations in Yemen, some have a family name reflecting the name of their former place of residence, such as the 'Adani and Sa'di families who lived in Ṣan'a,[56] while others because they actually came from that place, such as the name Ghaymāni, since they came from the town of Ghaymān, which lies

53. As related by Shmuel Amiran, Jerusalem.

54. From among the unique family names among Yemenite emigrants, the family name *Shar'abi* is the most common and is thirty-seventh among the two hundred most common in Israel. See Avraham Ariel, *Sefer ha-Shemot: 200 ha-Mishpaḥot ha-Nefoṣot be-Yisra'el* (Tel Aviv, 1997), p. 42. Among the Yemenite names, the family name Ṣabari comes next, and it holds place 176. See ibid., pp. 140–41.

55. R. Adam Bin Nun lives in Benei Brak.

56. See above part 2, chap. 2, sect. 1.

some 15 km southeast of Ṣan'a, the capital. See also Dhamāri (from the place name Dhamār), Yarīmi (from Yarīm), 'Adani (from Aden), Ṣan'āni (from Ṣan'a), Ṣa'di (from Ṣa'dah), Radā'i (from Radā'), Raṣābi (from Raṣabah), Tan'ami (from Tan'em), Ta'īzzi (from Ta'īzz). Amiel Raṣabi told of what transpired with the Raṣabi families as they moved from Yemen to Israel as he heard from a family member, Y. Ratzaby:

> Yehudah once told me, I do not remember exactly when, that there are three Raṣabis in Israel: one is R. Yiṣḥaq Raṣabi of Bnei Brak; the second is Shalom Raṣabi, who is also a poet and also a professor of Jewish history at Tel Aviv University; and the third Raṣhabi—that's me. There is no family link among us, other than the family name, and each contributed or contributes to Israeli culture. I am adding to Yehudah's statements. The two dignified gentlemen, Rabbi Yiṣḥaq Raṣabi and the poet and historian Shalom Raṣabi, were born after 1950, and the difference in age between them and Yehudah is some thirty years, so that the name Raṣabi (with or without an *alef*) was known among the Israeli public because of him. He turned this name into a label and made a small change it in: in place of the *alef* in the middle of the word he put in *heh*—and created a nice Hebrew name. That is how the name is marked today. In the past, I enrolled in a number of classes at the Hebrew University and was asked on several occasions by the lecturer or teaching assistant whether I was connected to Yehudah, and I answered yes with undisguised pride. Also Mori Yosef Qāfiḥ, when I once turned to him with a question, and introduced myself, immediately asked me if I am the Raṣabi of Yehudah.[57]

One must note that Yehudah Ratzaby emigrated with his family from the Sa'awān community in central Yemen in 1924; the family of Shalom Ratsaby emigrated from Ṣan'a in the early twentieth century; and the family of R. Yiṣḥaq Ratsabi came from Raṣāba in 1949.

Yohanan Arnon remarked that family names adopted by Yemenite Jews based on place names in Yemen, such as Dhamāri, 'Adani, Shar'abi, meshed well with the Hebrew language, much better than the family names based on toponyms that the European Jews brought with them, such as Braslavsky, Litvack, and Prager.[58]

57. Statements by Amiel Raṣabi at a memorial service marking two years to the passing of Prof. Yehudah Ratzaby, on 29 Shevat 5771 (3 Feb 2011). The service was held in the Shevet Aḥim Synagogue on 5 Klisher Street in Tel Aviv, the one which Prof. Ratzaby regularly attended.

58. Yohanan Arnon, "*Ivrut Shemot ha-Mishpaḥah etzel Yehudei Teiman ba-Shanim 1947–1957,*" *Yeda Am* 26 (1995): 199–200.

There are some who translated or transformed their family name. For example, the Waḥsh (wild beast) family changed their name in Israel to Aryeh (lion). Some made only minor changes, as for example the Hārūni family, which emigrated from the city of Ta'īz, made their name Aharoni.[59] Others sufficed with changing the spelling of the previous name without changing its meaning or sound; examples are Ḍurāni – Durani (צוראני – דורני), Ḍāhari – Dahari (צאהרי – דהרי).

We further note that in most cases the new names are Hebrew ones; but in a few instances the new name is neither Hebrew nor originally Yemenite. However some are derived from the original with a slight orthographic change. For example, Adū'ar was changed to Eduard; Qārah became Qaro.

Sometimes an addition or change to a family name resulted in difficulties in identification: Dr. Yosef Tzuri'eli looked for one of the Yemenite leaders who had emigrated from Aden in southern Yemen and settled in Naḥli'el. This leader used to sign his letters in Yemen with the name Re'uven Ka"ṣ, and when Dr. Tzuri'el visited Naḥli'el no one he asked claimed to know him. After the evening prayers there, he approached the synagogue's rabbi to seek his help in locating the resident Re'uven Ka"ṣ. The rabbi told him that it was he and that he had changed the family name to Kohen. In explaining the reason for the change, the rabbi said:

> After I came on *aliyah* to Ereṣ Israel, I approach the *aliyah* official to obtain an immigrant's certificate and when I identified myself by the name Re'uven Kaṣ, the *aliyah* clerk told me that in Israel the name means "cat". On the spot I decided to erase the term *kaṣṣ* and asked that they list my name as Re'uven Kohen.[60]

The poet Raṣon Halevi relates that he had known a girl from south Yemen named Sham'ah bat Ya'aqov, who was called Sham'at Ya'qub (which in general Hebrew usage is Shoshanat Ya'aqov). When she died in Israel in 1993, death announcements listed her name as Shoshana Shar'abi, which meant nothing to him until people drew his attention to the fact that the deceased was, in fact, Sham'at Ya'qub.[61]

59. In a questionnaire given to me by Ḥanan'el Aharoni from the settlement of Nofim-Yaqir.
60. Yosef Tsuri'eli, *Devarim be-'Iqvot ha-Sefer Kalkalah ve-Ḥinukh Moderni be-Teiman ba-'Et ha-Ḥadasah* (Jerusalem, 2005), p. 33.
61. See Raṣon Halevi, *Shirat Yisra'el be-Teiman*, vol. 1 (Qiryat Ono, 1998), p. 14.

There were women among the emigrés from Yemen who, after their marriage, adopted the name of their father's family. Below are a few of the from the academic world: Bat Tsion Eraqi, who parents emigrated from the Hajjar community in northern Yemen, whose name after marriage is Eraqi Klorman; after her marriage, Dr. Aviva Ṣabbari, whose parents emigrated from the Ṣan'a and Tan'em communities in central Yemen, had the family name Klein-Franke Ṣabbari; the family name of Ṣila Sinwāni, whose parents emigrated from the Shar'ab district in southern Yemen, was Sinwāni Stern; the married family name of Mithqa Ratzaby, whose parents came from the Ṣan'a and Sa'wan communities in central Yemen, was Ratzaby Golub.[62]

There are cases of deriving family names from personal names, places, occupation, or special cases.[63]

Translation of the Name

Abu S'ud – Avigad
Abyaḍ – Livni, Halivni, Levanon
Aḥmar – Admoni, Shani
Alsheikh – Nasi
'Amr – Banai, Benayahu
'Amrān – Amram
Asad – Lavi
Ben Da'ūd – Ben David
Da'ūdi – Davidi
Dhahbāni – Zehavi
Dhib – Ze'evi
Ghiyāt – Yeshū'a
Ḥaddād – Barzilai, Peled
Ḥamāmi – Yonati
Manajjim – Ḥozeh, Kokhavi
Mas'ud – Oshiri
Maṭraqah – Paṭṭishi
Mu'allim – Melammed
Muqari – Melammed
Mishriqi – Mizraḥi, Qedem, Qedmi, Qadmon
Qa'ah– Arṣi
Qaḥm – Arye
Qa'īdah – Qedar
Qaṭū' – Halaḥmi
Qū'dah – Qedar
Raḍa – Raṣon
Rizqān – Bar Mazal

62. Mithqa is the daughter of Prof. Yehudah Ratzaby, and her father gave her the name *Mithqa*, the name of one of the stations on the journeys of the children of Israel in the Sinai desert, since she was born about half a year after the 1956 Sinai Campaign, and it comes from the verse in Numbers (33:28): "And they camped in Mithqa."

63. Yohanan Arnon wrote two articles on this topic. See Yohanan Arnon, "*Shemot Mishpaḥah shelanu* Onomastica Judaica," *Haumah* 102 (1991): 198–209; idem, "*Ivrut Shemot ha-Mishpaḥah eṣel Yehudei Teiman ba-Shanim 1947–1957*," *Yeda Am* 26 (1995): 196–223.

Ḥanash – Naḥshon, Naḥshoni
Hārūni – Aharoni
Ḥūbārah – Ḥevroni, Ḥaver
'Inbi – Karmi
'Iṭwār – 'Atar
Jibli – Harari
Khayyaṭ – Ḥayyaṭ
Lūzi – Sheqeidi
Maḍmūn – Shamur, Shomron, Shimron
Maḥfūḍ – Meshūmar, Shamur, Shemer
Sāliḥ – Ṣadoq
Sayyagh – Ṣoref
Shā'er – Meshorer, Avizemer
Si'did – Azrieli
Ṭawīl – Arikha
Ṭaybi – Tuvi
Ṭayri – Ṣippor
Waḥsh – Aryeh
Wahb – Yahav
Yamani – Yemini
Zughayir –Ze'irah

Homophonous Names

Abdar – Avidor, Avidar
Abusit – Avishai
Abyaḍ – Avi'ad
'Adani – 'Eden, Adini
'Amr – 'Amīr
'Amran – 'Amiran
'Aqwa– Ya'aqobi
A'raj – Erez
'Arūsi – 'Arūsi
'Ashri – Oshri

'Athari – 'Aṭari
'Awaḍ – 'Ovadyah
'Awawi – Avivi
'Azāni – Ha'ṣni
Adū'ar– Eduard
Aḥsan – Ḥen
Aḥwāl – Aḥi'el
Asbaṭ – Shivṭi'el
Ashwal – Eshel; Ashbal
Bagdalan – Golan
Basal – Bezalel
Khawlāni – Golani
Kisar – Qesar
Kuḥlani – Kaḥol
Lūluwi – Lulu, Lulavi
Ma'bari – Ha'ivri, Bar 'Ami
Maḍmun – 'Admoni
Maḥbub – Ḥovav
Maḥzari – Mizraḥi
Ma'ṭūf – Ma Tov, Ki Tov
Ma'ūḍah – Me'oded; Me'adyah; 'Amihud
Maj'ar – Almagor
Malāḥi – Mal'akhi
Manṣūr – Ben Ṣur
Manṣūrah – Ben Ṣur
Moraḥi – Ma'or; Ma'or-Ḥai
Naddāf – Nadav; Yehonadav
Nehari – Nehorai
Qāfiḥ – Kefir
Qārāh – Qaro
Qarawāni – Yarqoni, Qarbani
Qarni – Qoren

Bashāri – Bashan
Ba 'zah – Boaz
Būṭa' – Avital
Da'rūr – Deror
Dō'ōs – Da'os
Ḍāhiri – Yitshari; Dehari
Ḍūr'ani — Durani; Ben-Or
Farḥi – Peraḥ
Fetayḥi – Petaḥyah
Ghabra – Gavrah
Ghaimāni – Rimoni
Gharāma – Garmi
Ghiyat – Gat
Ḥaddad – Hadar
Ḥadri – Ḥetsroni
Ḥarāzi – 'Arazi
Ḥasan – Ḥason
Ḥaser – Ḥasid
Hashāsh – Shemesh
Ḥatrush – Tirosh
Hīlal – Hillel; Halali
Hiqri – Yaqir
Ḥirfuf – Ḥefer
Ḥubārah – Ḥevron
Ḥūdayfi – Ḥofi
Ja'di – Giladi
Ja'rani – Goren
Jamāl – Gamli'el, Gamli'eli
Jamīl – Gamli'el
Jimazah – Gamzo
Jishhush – Goshen
Jūbāri – Gov Ari
Qa'ṭabi – Katabi
Qeha' – Qehati
Qōrēni – Gorni
Quraysh – Gur 'Esh
Ray'āni – Ra'anan
Ramaḍān – Ramati
Raḥbi – Reḥavyah
Ṣafar – Ṣippor
Sanḥani – Ṣanḥani
Ṣārum – Ṣur
Saybhi – Zehavi
Sayyāni – Ṣiyyoni
Shā'ir – Shai
Sham'ah – Shim'i; Shammai
Shamūkh – Qame'aḥ
Shar'abi – Sar Avi; Shavit; Sharon, Shai
Sha'tāl – She'alti'el
Shḥib – Shevaḥ
Shiryān – Sharon; Shiryon
Shubayli – Shovali, Shoval
Sirri – Serayah; Sahar
Sisalūmi – Shlomi'el
Tan'ami – Ten 'Ami
'Umaysi – 'Amos
'Ūqabi – Ya'aqobi
'Ūrqabi – Argov
'Uzayri – 'Oz Ari, Bar 'Oz
Waḥshan – Naḥshon
Wanneh – Yonah
Wawah – Avivi
Yaf'i – Yafeh
Yana'i – Yanai
Zārib – Ze'ev

Transformations in Yemenite names began with their *aliyah* to Israel. While still in the Ge'ulah transit camp in Aden, they already were concerned with changing their Arabic names to Hebrew ones. Even in Israel and the Diaspora they behaved like their brethren, deciding not to preserve their Diaspora name.[64] As for family names in their natural environment, among their acquaintances, the Yemenite immigrants continued to act according to their previous custom of combining their name with that of the father or husband. This custom completely disappeared with the next generation.

4. NAMES AMONG THE LAST IMMIGRANTS FROM YEMEN

After the vast majority of the Yemenite diaspora came to Israel in 1950, only a few hundred Jews remained in northern Yemen. The old customs continued. Yosef Zārib, who immigrated in 1999, related that usually the father gave the names to the sons and the mother to the daughters, though the final decision was the father's. The names were the names of the parents, the grandparents, or other relatives. A daughter was named in the first few days after birth, without any special ceremony.[65] Mori Se'īd Ṣabari, who left the village of Raidah in northern Yemen in 2009, told me that the husband usually picked the names of the children and that he had chosen the names for his ten children. Naming of girls generally took place on the day they were born.[66]

Mori Faiz Jeraydi is a rabbinic figure among the remnant of Jews in Yemen, and, before emigrating from Raidah in 2007, he had been their leader on behalf of the government in Ṣan'a. He relates that the father named the boys in consultation with his father, while the mother usually gave the girls their names. Names were chosen also on the basis of the weekly Torah and Haftarah readings. For example, Mori Faiz called his son Elisha', a name expressing salvation, and it comes from the Haftarah of *parashat* Pinḥas that mentions the prophet Elisha'. Similarly, 'Imrān Jeraydi, Faiz's uncle, named his son Yesh'ayah from the Haf-

64. For a discussion about the names of Jews in Ereṣ Israel, see Sascha Veitman, "*Shemot Peratiyyim ke-Meimadim Tarbutiyyim: Megamot be-Zehutam ha-Le'umit shel Yisra'elim*, 1882–1980," in *Nequdot Taṣpit: Tarbut ve-Ḥevrah be-Ereṣ Yisrae'el*, ed. N. Graetz (Tel Aviv, 1988), pp. 141–51.

65. Interview conducted by Shelomo Jarafi of Gedera.

66. The meeting with Mori Se'īd Ṣabari took place in the Monsey synagogue in New York in November 2010.

tarah of *parashat* Mas'ei, which begins with the words *Ḥazon Yesha'yahu ben Amoṣ* (Isa. 1:1). Sometimes a name was given because of an event. For example, Mori Faiz's wife was named Simḥah, which expressed the family's joy at the grandfather Mori Ya'ish having been released from prison in Yemen.[67]

On some occasions a name was introduced from a verse alluding to the event. Moshe Ḥale', who left Raidah in 2005, called his daughter, who was born in Yemen, Neḥamah, for the verse beginning the Haftarah for the week when she was born, ענייה סערה לא נחמה ("*aniyya so'arah lo nuḥama*"; "unhappy, storm-tossed one, uncomforted"). The name also alluded to the consolation he had from the distress he had experienced.[68]

In 1990, Mori Ṣemaḥ Yiṣḥaq Halevi Qāḍi prepared a list of names of the Jews who were then living in northern Yemen as provided by the village leaders. The register lists 721 individuals, most of the Jewish population still remaining in Yemen, according to place of residence and family name. The following is a frequency list of 659 of those names.[69]

Men

Yiḥye' (including one occurrence as Zekharyah)—43. Yosef—41. Se'īd—34. Sālem—29. Slaymān (including one occurrence Shlomo)—24. Musa' (including Moshe)—22. Da'ūd—13. Ya'ish—9. Ya'aqūb.

7 times—Harūn. Lewi. Shim'on.

6 times—Ḥayim. Yehudah. Yiṣḥaq. Yisra'el. Mas'ūd.

5 times—Menaḥem. 'Iḍa'.

4 times—Avraham. Efrayim. Jamīl. Me'ir. Menashe. Ezra.

3 times—Binyamin. Khūrṣān. 'Azri. 'Amr. 'Imrān. Ṣāliḥ.

67. The meeting with Mori Fa'iz Jeraydi took place in Dec 2010. I wish to thank Mori Shim'on Jaraydi of New York for his assistance with this. *Fa'iz* is an Arabic name meaning 'Victor', but Mori Fa'iz derived his name from Jewish sources: as the initials of פותח את ידיך (Ps. 145:16), with the addition of the letter ז (*zayin*) for the seven words comprising that verse.

68. I received the information from Moshe Ḥale'. On the family of Moshe Ḥala, see below.

69. I wish to thank R. Yiṣḥaq Halevi (Qāḍi), who made the list of his father, Mori Ṣemaḥ, available to me. A few of the Jews were not listed by their personal name but noted as wife of X or son/daughter of X.

2 times—Banin. Bakhar. Maḥbūb. Sha'ul. Shukr.
1 time—Jarādi. Zāhir. Zāreb. Ṭabīb. Ya'beṣ. Yissakhar. Māreb. Maṭrūd. 'Abdāllah. 'Awāḍ. 'Alān. Fā'iz. Pinḥas. Ṣughayer. Re'uven. Refa'el. Shemu'el.

Women

Ni'meh—21. Lawzah—14. Sham'ah—13. Hadiyyah—12. Miryam—12. Ḥamāmah—10. Mazal—9. Sa'dah—9. Se'idah—9. 'Āfiye—9. Ṣiniyye—9. Kādhiyye—8.
7 times—Malkah. Naḍrah. Simḥah. Yosefe. Zihre.
6 times—Tūrkiyye.
5 times—Ghuṣna. Ḥannah. Lūluwah. Nakhlah.
4 times—'Aden. Berakhah. Ḍobyah. Hawidah. Le'ah. Rūmah. Sūrya. Wardah.
3 times—Amriqa. Banayyah. Fākhah. Fār'ah. Ghane'. Ḥāliyah. Khaḍrah. Jamālah. Raḥel. Ṣan'a'. Wāllah.
2 times—Badrah. Bardaqūshah. Far'ah. Fuḍah'. Ghusnah. Ḥikmah. Jāmilah. Mas'ūdah. Mikhal. Rivqah. Ṣālḥah. Shōshan. Tamniyyah.
1 time— Almanya [= Germany], 'Azah. Bilqīs [= the traditional Arabic name for the Queen of Sheba],[70] Fa'izah. Farashe. Fransa [= France]. Funūn. Gafriyah. Ghazāl, Ghirse. Ghuṣūn. Ḥabībah. Jamīlah. Lambah. Lundun. Libya. Liḥdah. Liyyah. Rafu'o. Ṣadīqah. Salāmeh. Shoni. Ṣubaḥ [= morning]. Sūwadah.

In 1992, immigrants from Yemen began to arrive in Israel. The names given below are taken from the data of the Absorption Ministry for Yemenite immigrants in the period 1992–1995. They include 447 names, and we can reasonably assume that the list is incomplete. Here are the names by frequency:

Men

Yiḥye'—26. Sālem—23. Yosef—22. Musa'—16. Slaymān—13. Ya'aqov—9. Da'ūd—8. Se'īd—8. Lewi—6.
5 times—Avraham. Shim'on.

70. The kingdom of Sheba was in South Arabia. The queen of Sheba is mentioned by the name Balqis in Arab tradition. A Muslim sheikh who falls in love with a young Jewish woman calls her by this name. See Nissim Binyamin Gamlieli, "*Ha-Aravim she-be-Qirbam Ḥayu Yehudei Teiman, Kitot ha-Islam ve-ha-Yaḥasim beinam le-vein 'Aṣman u-venan le-vein ha-Yehudim,*" in *Yahadut Teiman—Pirqei Meḥqar ve-'Iyyun*, ed. Y. Yeshayahu, J. Tobi (Jerusalem, 1976), p. 187.

4 times—Efrayim. Harūn. Mas'ud. Me'ir. Menaḥem. Menashe. Reuven. Ṣāliḥ. Ya'ish. Yehudah. Yisra'el.
3 times—Ezra. Yiṣḥaq.
2 times—'Ayḏah. Ḥayim. 'Iḏa'. Khūrsān. Yeḥi'el.
1 time— 'Amram. Barukh. Binyamin. Pinḥas. Ṣemaḥ. Sha'ul. Yiga'el. Zekharyah.

[B] Women
Ni'meh—14. Miryam—11. Hadiyyah—9. Mazal—9. Ḥamāmah—8. Lawzah—8. Se'īdah—8. Sham'ah—8. Jumlah—7. Simḥah—7.
6 times—Nakhlah. Naḏrah. Zihre.
5 times—'Āfiyya. Hawidah. Malkah. Rūmah. Sa'dah. Ṣīniyyah.
4 times— Ghuṣna. Ḥannah. Mikhal. Ṣiyyonah. Wardah.
3 times— 'Aden. Banayyah. Bardaqushah. Ḍobyah. Fār'ah. Kādhiyyah. Khaḏra'. Lūlūwah. Raḥel. Surya.
2 times—Esther. Fuḏah. Ghazāl. Ḥikmah. Hindah. Libiya [= Libya]. Ṣadīqah. Ṣālḥah. Shoshanah. Ṭovah. Tūrkiyyah. Yosefah.
1 time—'Adīna. Almanya [= Germany]. Amriqa. Osnat. Bilqīs [= the traditional name of the Queen of Sheba]. Bargelaḥ. Berakhah. Besorah. Devorah. Fa'izah. Faqhah. Fransa [= France]. Gafriyah. Ḥabībah. Ḥāliyah. Lambah. Le'ah. Lundun. Mas'ūdah. No'omi. Qādiyyah. Qaylah [= party]. Ṣana'. Ṣubaḥ [= morning]. Rivqah. Rizqah. Shōshan. Tamniyyah. Zilka.

An examination of the names, both of the Jewish communities in Yemen and of those who immigrated to Israel in 1992–1995 shows that alongside the names prevalent in northern Yemen, new women's names were used that had been previously unknown among Yemenite Jewry. For the men, most of the names are from Hebrew sources, while most of the women's names are Arabic. A number of them are names of countries and cities: America, Germany, Libya, London, Syria.

Below are data on the names of a number of families among the emigrants from Yemen at the end of the twentieth and in the early twenty-first centuries.

All of Mori Se'īd Ṣabari's children were born in Yemen. The boys' names are Yosef, Lewi, Yiḥye', Ḥayim, Yehudah, and Ya'ish, and the girls' names are Hawīdah, Naḏrah, Shfa', Lūlūwah, Nakhlah, and Ḥamāmah. The children were named after members of the extended family. The name Shfa (meaning 'health') is rare in Yemen. Mori Se'īd had been severely burned and was hospitalized in Ṣa'dah. Hospital in Arabic is *mustashafa*, and so the father named his daughter in gratitude for the hospital care he had received.[71] All the names remained what they had been in Yemen, except for two: Yiḥye' was shortened to Yoḥi and Ḥamāmah was translated into Yona (dove).

Yiḥye' and Rashushah Jarādi left Raidah in northern Yemen in 2009 and now live in New York. All their children were born in Yemen. The boys' names are Fa'īz, Musa', Da'ūd, Hārūn, and Slaymān. The girls' names are Ṣīniyyah, Le'ah, and Miriam. The boys names were translated into Hebrew: Musa' – Moshe, Da'ūd – David, Hārūn – Aharon, Slaymān – Shelomo. The daughter Ṣīniyyah's name was changed to Ṣiyyona, similar in sound to her original name.[72]

Shukr and Ḥamāmah Qarni emigrated from Raidah in 2010 and now live in New York. All their children were born in Yemen except for one daughter. The boys' names are Binyamin, Zevulun, Yissakhar, Slaymān; the girls' names are Hadiyyah, Tamniyyah and Dina (born in the United States). Among the boys' names, Slaymān was translated into Shelomo. As for the daughters, the one born in the United States was given a Hebrew name, Dinah, while the others were given names with an "American ring": Hadiyyah – Hudi, Tamniyyah – Tammy.[73]

The names of the children of Mori Fa'iz Jeraydi who were born in Yemen are Elisha', Rivqah, and Berakhah, while the daughter born in New York is Tova.[74]

Moshe Ḥale's family left Raidah for the United States in 2005. The names of the children born in Yemen are Neḥamah and Aryeh; the children born in New York are Yehudah, Ya'aqov, and Dan.[75]

R. Yissakhar Kūbāni says that his father, Binyamin, who immigrated to London, gave one of his sons two names: Yosef David. These were for the grandfathers: Yosef for his father's father, who died and was buried in London; David, for his mothers's father, who died and was buried in Yemen.[76]

Mori Fa'iz Jeraydi told me that some changed the name Yiḥye' to Yeḥi'el; Māreb (boy's name after a place in Yemen) became Me'ir;

71. In a meeting with him in Nov 2010.
72. I received the information from the son, Shelomo Jeraydi.
73. I heard this information from the son, Yissakhar Qarni.
74. The meeting with Mori Fa'iz Jeraydi took place in Dec 2010.
75. This information was related by Moshe Ḥale'.
76. I received this information from Mr. Yissakhar Kubaniin July 2009.

Sūriya, which had been given to a girl, was replaced by Sarit. He further related that the Yemenite Jews still call the daughter of Ḥayim Qarni, Ḥamāmah, by her original name, while in the Ḥasidic school they called her Ṭoybi, which is the Yiddish translation of her name (Dove).[77]

Some were named for well-known personalities, such as Ṣiyyon, for the Yemenite singer Zion Golan; Ḥayim for Mori Ḥayim Ya'aqubi, who had been active on behalf of the remnant of Jewry in Yemen; and Zalman for Shne'ur Zalman, who had been involved in aiding the Jews of Yemen; Yosef Ba'ka, for Yosef Bachar, the activist who paid numerous visits to Yemen from 1979 on and helped the community by distributing ritual objects; Ṣemaḥ for Mori Ṣemaḥ Yiṣḥaq Halewi (Qāḍi), who visited Yemen in the 1980s and helped the Jews in northern Yemen. Jamīl Shaghdari named his first son Asher for Mori Asher Jeraydi, who visited Yemen in the 1990s; and Yo'el for R. Yo'el Teitelbaum, the Satmar rebbe. After Jamīl immigrated to Israel, he was impressed by the character of Prime Minister Binyamin Netanyahu and so named his second son Netanyahu. But after leaving Israel for a Satmar community in New York, under their influence, he changed the boy's name to Aharon.[78]

As for the family names of the recent emigrés, they remained as they had been in Yemen, perhaps because there was no reason to Hebraicize them. For example in Monsey, New York, the family names are Jeraydi, Zārib, Ṣabari or 'Amār, Qārni, Qfari, and Shaghdari. The family names of the immigrants to London are Ḥamdi, Khūbāni, Fa'īz, and Qarni. The family names of those who went to Israel are 'Amr, 'Arji, 'Aṣār, Boni, Dahari, Fa'iz, Ghiyat, Ḥalle', Jamīl, Jarādi, Kūbāni, Nehari, N'aṭi, Qarni, Qa'ṭabi, Ṣabari, Slaymān, Zārib, and Zindani.

5. CHARACTERISTICS AMONG YEMENITE JEWS IN THE DIASPORA

Some of the Yemenites arriving in New York before the 1950s often used biblical names that could integrate well with the general population, such as Natan who was called Nathan, Mikha'el who was called Michael, and Ḥannah who was called Anna. They also changed Yiḥye' to Yeḥi'el. As for the children of Yemenites in New York, most of them tend to give two names: a Hebrew name and a corresponding American

77. The meeting with Mori Fa'iz Jeraydi took place in Dec 2010.

78. The meeting with Mori Fa'iz Jeraydi took place in Dec 2010. I wish to thank Mori Shim'on Jaraydi for his help in arranging it.

name, for example Yiṣḥaq Isaac, Ya'aqov Jack. Although most families did not change their family name out of pride for their roots, there were a few who did. For example, the name Ṣafira became Shapira to be more acceptable among the other Jews, and Jibli turned into Gable, a more American name.[79] Yemenite emigrés usually choose names for their children that will be easy to pronounce as well as common to the general population. As examples are the boys' names Adam, Ben, Binyamin, Guy and the girls' names Dana, Talya, and Daniel[le] as a name for both boys and girls.

R. Ovadyah Melammed, who lived in Yemen, then Israel, the United States, and now back in Israel, wrote about the phenomenon:

> Many of the Israelis who left their country tried to blur their identity and to come closer to the inhabitants of the country such as in America by obscuring their personal name, so Ya'aqov became Jacob and Shim'on turned into Simon; or they changed their name completely and called themselves by names that have no connection to Hebrew. The generation of the immigrants' offspring went one step further in blurring their identity so as to be like their friends in school or college to become part of the foreign society among which they lived ... Noteworthy is that if an Israeli immigrant married a local, American woman, this obscuring of the family's identity took place even faster, and the children they had were already given definitely American names.[80]

On the personal and family aspect, he wrote:

> If I take the example of my family, the Melammed family, who immigrated to New York about four decades ago, did not blur their Jewish identity for the dominant language within the family is Hebrew. The names of the boys and girls remained Israeli, even if born in the American *galut*. All of this is due to preserving a special Jewish Israeli framework, not only family but community-wide. So the names among my children and grandchildren are Or'el, 'Adi'el, Sari'el, Eitan'el,[81] 'Irit, Nir, and so on.

He also ascribes the firm maintenance of the tradition of Hebrew names in his family to the close connection that he and his family has

79. In an interview I conducted with R. Eliyahu Yiṣḥaq Halevi (Qaḍi).

80. In a personal correspondence dated 26 Jan 2011.

81. The children of his son Ronen. Ronen Melammed and his wife, Yif'at, were born in Israel to parents who came from Yemen.

with Israel. He further wrote about an acquaintance who also had come from Yemen:

> In the time we have lived in New York, we came to know a family with an Israeli Yemenite father who grew up in New York and his wife, who was Canadian, and they gave their children American names. In time, we used to visit each other on Shabbat and holidays, and suddenly their Hebrew names came to the fore, and they asked us to use their Hebrew name, when they did not know even one word of Hebrew, while English was their language from birth.

6. EPILOGUE

Until their immigration to Israel, the Yemenite Jews were known as being very conservative, preserving their ancient traditions more other Jewish immigrant groups. Assuredly, in part, this was the result of their having been geographically removed from other Jewish communities and their general lack of interaction with the gentile population.

This study of the names of Yemenite Jewry attests to the maintenance of these traditions. For example, the ethical will of R. Yehudah Heḥasid set down rules or guidelines on naming, which Jews throughout the Diaspora observed. In contrast, the Yemenite Jews, even though they were familiar with this will, were not influenced at all by the statements of R. Yehudah Heḥasid. They continued to follow their own tradition, which was based on ancient sources. The custom of Yemenite Jews to name their sons after themselves, such that the father and sons names were identical, and their custom of giving the same name to two brothers, while adding bynames to identical ones, exemplifies the continuity of their own traditions. This continuance of age-old traditions is borne out in S. D. Goitein's observation on the similarity in naming conventions between the names in the Cairo geniza and those of the Jews of Yemen.

In contrast to the situation among the Jews of Eastern European Ashkenaz in the eighteenth and nineteenth centuries, who were required by the governments to take family names, the authorities in Yemen made no such demand. In Ṣan'a and the other large communities, family names that were used derived from a variety of spheres, such as personal names, place names, occupations, plants, animals, and physical characteristics. In Ṣan'a, bynames were given to make identification easier. In the smaller communities, in which the majority of Yemenite Jews lived, they were identified mainly by the combination of their personal name with that of their father and sometimes also the grandfather.

With their immigration to Israel in the first half of the twentieth century, overall changes occurred in the life of Yemenite Jews. Social life in Yemen was conducted within an extended family framework. Residences included the extended family, and a married woman lived in her father-in-law's house. This family unit included the parents, their children, and their offspring. After coming to Israel, however, the old family model was undermined. From dwelling within the extended family it shifted to living within the nuclear family, which yielded a new type of life style. Moving from a traditional society to a secular, western one created a new reality.

In the sphere of naming there were changes, too, which began with the immigration to Israel. Whoever did not have a family name was required by the government to add one to make identification easier. Still, when among their old acquaintances, the Yemenite immigrants continued to be called in the previous manner of combining the personal name with the name of the father or the husband. But this custom, as well as the giving of the names traditional to the Jews of Yemen, disappeared almost completely in the next generation as the result of the social structure and community life in Israel. In school, a family name became an inseparable part of a person's identity, as it did in the workplace or when interacting with the state bureaucracy. Some, who had a family name in Yemen, changed it to conform to their Hebrew-speaking environment.

Through the prism of names, both personal and surnames, I have attempted to illuminate the history and social structure of Yemenite Jewry moving from a traditional way of life into the modern period. My sources are the written documents recording birth, marriage, and death of lay people, as well as rabbinic discussions regarding local nomenclature. In addition, these texts are supplemented by a great variety of contemporary oral and written testimony that I have collected and preserved reflecting the naming customs found in the cities and towns from which Yemenite Jewry came.

SOURCES

1. BIBLIOGRAPHY

DOCUMENTS AND ARCHIVAL MATERIAL

1,506 photographs of *ketubbot* in author's possession, 16th–20th century
175 photographs of *gittin* in author's possession, 16th–20th century
684 colophons of Yemenite manuscripts, 12th–20th century
Pinqas of the Ṣan'a Bet Din, 18th–19th century
Pinqas of the emissary Rabbi Shelomo Naddaf, 20th century
List of immigrants to Israel from the end of the 20th century, Rabbi Ṣemaḥ Yiṣḥaq Halevi (Qaḍi)

MANUSCRIPTS

Diwan, MS Tel Aviv, Bill Gross 160 (IMHM 46202)
Halakhah and Midrash, MS London 10738 (Gaster 1382)
Halakhah and Midrash, MS New York, JTS 693 (IMHM 41433)
Halakhah and Midrash, MS New York, JTS 290
Halakhah and Midrash, MS New York, JTS 328
Halakhah and Midrash, MS San Francisco Sutro (Brinner 115)
Halakhah and Midrash, MS San Francisco Sutro 75
Ḥen Tov le-R' Yiḥye Badiḥi, MS Jerusalem, Mosad Harav Kook 943 (IMHM 26427)
Mada'im u-Refuah, MS London 14059 (IMHM 7928)
Maḥberet ha-Tijān in Arabic, MS Jerusalem, JNUL, Yah. MS Heb. 5
Maimonides' Mishnah Commentary, MS Berlin, Staatsbibliotheque OR. Qu 574 (IMHM 1793)
Menorat ha-Ma'or, MS in the possession of David ben Shalom Qafiḥ, Jerusalem

Meqor Ḥayim le-R' Yiḥye ben Ya'aqov Ṣāliḥ, MS Chicago, Spertus College B 5 (IMHM 40230)
Midrash ha-Gadol le'R' David 'Adani, MS Tel Aviv, Yehuda Raṣhabi [5] (IMHM 39664)
Midrash ha-Ḥefeṣ le-R' Zekharya ha-Rofe, MS London 2381
Midrash ha-Ḥefeṣ le-R' Zekharya ha-Rofe, MS Sassoon 262 (IMHM 9753)
Mishnah Neziqin, MS in the possession of Mordekhai Yiṣhari, Rosh haAyin
Mishneh Torah of Maimonides, MS Jerusalem, JNUL Yah. MS Heb. 2
Mishneh Torah of Maimonides, MS Sassoon 1012 (IMHM 4743)
Mishneh Torah of Maimonides, MS Sassoon 1011 (IMHM 9800)
More Nevukhim, MS London, British Library Arabic MS I.O. 3379 (IMHM 49332)
Nevi'im Rishonim, MS in the possession of Rabbi Yosef Qafiḥ, Jerusalem
Or Torah, MS Rabbi Itamar Ḥayim Kohen, Bnei Brak
Pardes Rimmonim le-R' Moshe Cordovero, MS Munich, Bayerischen Staatsbibliothek HEBR 924
Pirqei Rabbi Eliezer, MS Ramat Gan, Bar-Ilan University 496 (IMHM 37015)
Qeri'ei Mo'ed, MS Jerusalem, issue [5] (IMHM 40441)
Qoveṣ be-Hilkhot Sheḥita, MS Bill Gross, Tel Aviv, no. 190 (IMHM 47250)
Qoveṣ be-Hilkhot Sheḥita, MS Jerusalem, Menahem Feldman 113 (IMHM 42715)
Qoveṣ be-Qabbalah, MS JTS, New York, Mic. 1767/8 (IMHM 10865).
Qoveṣ be-Qabbalah, manuscript in the possession of Shimon.
Qoveṣ be-Qabbalah, MS Jerusalem, JNUL, Manuscript Department 8^0 2428.
Rashi's Commentary, MS Yehudah Levi Naḥum, Mif'al Ḥasifat Ginze Teiman 64.
Rashi's Commentary, MS Jerusalem, Mosad Harav Kook 731 (IMHM 10233)
Sefer Haftariyyot, MS in the possession of Nissim Binyamin Gamlieli, Ramle
Sefer Hafṭariyyot, MS in the possession of Raṣon Halevi, Tel Aviv.
Seder ha-Yom by Moses ben Makhir, MS Rabbi Shim'on Ṣālih, Bnei Brak
Sefer ha-Kavvanot le-ha-Ari, MS in the possession of Rabbi Yosef Qafiḥ, Jerusalem
Sefer ha-Miṣvot by Maimonides, MS Moscow Ginsburg 1014 (IMH 48303)
Sha'arei Qedusha le-R' Yiḥye Ṣāliḥ, MS Tel Aviv, Bill Gross 3 (IMHM 37726)

Shabazi Collection, MS in the possession of Rabbi Assaf Haetzni, Elad
Shalosh Megillot, MS in the possession of Nissim 'Advi, Holon
Shalosh Megillot, MS in the possession of Shelomo Yiṣḥaq Halevi, Bnei Brak
Shulḥan 'Arukh, MS in the possession of Yehuda Mu'allem, Ahihud
Shulḥan 'Arukh, MS Chicago, Spertus College (IMHM 40226)
Shulḥan 'Arukh, MS New York, Public Library Heb. MS 109 (IMHM 31111)
Shulḥan 'Arukh, MS New York Public Library Heb. MS 111 (IMHM 31113)
Shulḥan 'Arukh, MS New York Public Library Heb. MS 112 (IMHM 31114)
Siddur, MS England, Leeds Roth 75 (IMHM 15307)
Siddur, MS Sassoon 339–340
Taj, MS in possession of Zekharya Samina, Elyakhin
Taj, MS in possession of Shimon Ṣadoq, Ma'aleh Shomron
Taj, MS Cambridge, England
Tiklal, MS Jerusalem, JNUL, Manuscript Dept. 949 4^0
Tiklal, MS London 2227 (IMHM 6061)
Tiklal, MS Schocken Library 12824 (IMHM 45361)
Tiklal, MS Ramat Gan, Bar-Ilan University 398 (IMHM 36881)
Tiklal Eṣ Ḥaim, MS in the possession of Rabbi Eliyahu Yiṣḥak Halevi (Qaḍi), New York
Tola'at Ya'aqov, MS Sassoon 1137
Tola'at Ya'aqov le-R' Meir Gabbai, MS Sassoon 568 (IMHM 9789)
Torah, MS Cambridge 1728 (IMHM 17483)
Torah, MS Jerusalem, JNUL, 1133 4^0 Heb
Torah, MS London, 2370 (IMHM 6036)
Torah, MS London 88
Torah, MS New York, JTS 136
Torah, MS San Francisco Sutro 74
Torah, MS Philadelphia 304
Torah, MS Yehuda Levi Naḥum, Mif'al Ḥasifat Ginze Teiman 7
Zera ha-Shalom, MS Yehudah Levi Naḥum, Mif'al Ḥasifat Ginze Teiman
Zohar, MS Jerusalem, Menaḥem Feldman 52 (IMHM 42662)

BOOKS AND ARTICLES

Aharoni, Reuven. *Yehudei 'Aden*: *Qehila she-Hayeta* [The Jews of Aden: A Community That Was]. Tel Aviv, 1991.

Ben David, Aharon. *"Shemot Yehudim bi-Ṣefon Teiman al pi ha-Sefer 'Beit ha-Even'"* [Jewish names in northern Yemen according to the book *Beit ha-Even*], *Mesora le-Yosef* 6 (2009); 441–62.

Ben Shimon, Mas'ud. *Shem Ḥadash.* Jerusalem, 1991.

Brauer, Erich. *Ethnologie der Jemenitischen Juden.* Heidelberg 1934.

Emden, R. Ya'aqov. *Sefer Birat Migdal Oz.* Warsaw 1882.

Feinstein, R. Moshe. *Igrot Moshe, Even ha-'Ezer,* part 3. New York, 1973.

Gagin, R. Shem Tov. *Keter Shem Tov: Yalquṭ Minhagei Qehilot ha-Sefardim u-Meqoroteihem* [*Keter Shem Tov: A Collection of Customs of Sephardi Congregations and Their Sources*], vols. 1–2. Jerusalem, 1998.

Gaimani, Aharon. *"Ha'ataqah Qedumah mi-Teiman le-*Moreh Nevukhim *le-ha-Rambam"* [An ancient copy from Yemen of *Guide for the Perplexed* of Maimonides], *Tehuda* 14 (1994): 15–20.

———. *"Ha-Hanhaga ha-Yehudit be-Ṣan'a, 'im Ḥissul Golat Teiman"* (Sanaa's Jewish Leadership and Communal Self-Liquidation), Miqqedem Umiyyam 7 (2000): 185–216.

———. *Temurot be-Moreshet Yahadut Teiman: be-Hashpa'at ha-Sulhan 'Arukh ve-Qabalat ha-Ari* [Changes in the Heritage of Yemenite Jews under the Influence of the Shulḥan 'Arukh and the Mysticism of the Ari], Ramat Gan: Bar-Ilan University, 2005.

Gamliel, R. Shalom. *Pequdei Teiman: Mas he-Ḥasut be-Teiman.* Jerusalem, 1982.

Gavra, Moshe. *Enṣiqlopedya le-Qehilot ha-Yehudiyyot be-Teiman* [*Encyclopedia of the Jewish Communities of Yemen*], 1–2. Bnei Brak 2005.

Goitein, Shlomo Dov. *A Mediterranean Society,* vol. 3, Berkeley, Calif., 1978

———. *Ha-Teimanim—Mivhar Mehqarim* [The Yemenites: Selected Studies]. Jerusalem, 1983.

———. *Sidrei Ḥinnukh bi-Ymei ha-Ge'onim u-Bet ha-Rambam: Meqorot Ḥadashim min ha-Genizah* [Educational Arrangements in the Time of the Geonim and of Maimonides]. Jerusalem, 1962.

———. *"Yahadut Teiman ve-Saḥar Hodu ha-Yehudi,"* in *Ha-Teimanim—Mivhar Mehqarim.* Jerusalem, 1983. Pp. 33–52.

Halberstam, R. Yehezkel Shraga. *Divrei Yeḥezqel he-Ḥadash.* Ramat Gan 1986.

Hamburger, R. Binyamin Shlomo. *Shorshei Minhag Ashkenaz,* 1. Bnei Brak, 1995.

Ha-Tiklal ha-Mevu'ar. Ed. and proofread under the direction of Rabbi Pinas Qoraḥ. Bnei Brak, 5766.

Ḥozeh, R. Sa'adya. *Toledot ha-Rav Shalom Shabazi u-Minhagei Yahadut*

Shar'ab be-Teiman [History of Rabbi Shalom Shabazi and the Customs of Shar'ab Jewry in Yemen]. vol. 1. Jerusalem 1973; vol. 2. Jerusalem 1982.
Idelsohn, Avraham Zevi and N. H. Torczyner, *Shirei Teiman [Poetry of the Yemenite Jews*]. Cincinnati, 1931.
Munitz, Sarah. *"Shemot Bnei Adam—Minhag ve-Halakhah"* [People's Names: Custom and Halakhah]. MA diss., Bar-Ilan University, 1989.
Naḥum, Yehuda Levi. *Ḥasifat Genuzim mi-Teiman* [Yemen's Treasures Revealed]. Holon 1971.
———. *Mi-Ṣefunot Teiman* [Yemen's Hidden Treasures]. Tel Aviv, 1987.
———. *Mi-Yeṣirot Sifrutiyyot mi-Teiman* [Some of Yemen's Literary Treasures]. Holon 1981.
———. *Ṣohar le-Ḥasifat Ginzei Teiman [A Window to the Treasures of Yemen*]. Tel Aviv 1986.
Oppenheimer, Yosef Hakohen. *Va-Yiqra Shemo be-Yisra'el* [Let his name be called in Israel]. Buenos Aires, 5735 [1975].
Oṣar Kitve Yad Ivriyyim mi-Ymei ha-Beinayim, 1, Descriptions, Jerusalem–Paris, 1980; 3, Descriptions, Jerusalem–Paris, 1986.
Qafiḥ, Yosef. *Halikhot Teiman* [Yemenite Customs], Jerusalem 1961.
———. *Ketavim* [Collected writings], 3 vol. Jerusalem, 1989.
Qoraḥ, Amram. *Sa'arat Teiman* [The Tempest of Yemen]. Jerusalem, 1954.
Raṣabi, R. Yiṣḥaq. *Shulḥan 'Arukh ha-Mequṣar* [Abridged Shulḥan Arukh], vol. 5, Bnei Brak 1989.
Ratzaby, Yehuda. *Be-Ma'agalot Teiman* [On Jewish life and customs in Yemen]. Tel Aviv, 1948.
———. *"Darda'im (Minhagim ve-Takkanot)"* [Darda'im: Customs and Regulations], *Edot* 1 (1946): 165–80.
———. *"Ezra ha-Sofer ve-Golei Teiman"* [Ezra the scribe and the Yemenite exiles], in his *Be-Ma'agalot Teiman*, pp. 1–5.
———. *Oṣar Leshon ha-Qodesh she-li-Vnei Teiman* [A thesaurus of the Holy Tongue of Yemenite Jews]. Tel Aviv, 1978.
———. *Shirei R' Shalom Shabazi—Bibliography*. Tel Aviv 2003.
———. *Toratan she-li-Vnei Teiman* [The Teachings of the Yemenites]. Qiryat Ono 1994.
Ratzaby, Yehuda (ed.). *Bo'i Teiman: Meḥkarim u-Te'udot be-Tarbut Yehudei Teiman*, ed. Yehuda Ratzaby. Tel Aviv, 1967.
Rut, Avraham Naftali Sevi. *"Al ha-Ho"l Qraysh"* [On the secular name Qraysh], *Yeda Am* 7 [1962]: 68–74.
Ṣan'a u-Sevivatah be-Ṣilumei Yeḥiel Ḥaybi. Ed. Yosef Sha'ar, published by

Ruma Haybi. Tel Aviv 1985.
Sappir, R. Yaacov. *Even Sappir* 1. Lyck 1866.
———. *Even Sappir* 2. Mainz 1874.
———. *Massa Teiman* [A Trip to Yemen], ed. A. Yaari. Jerusalem 1945.
Sassoon, D. S. *Ohel Dawid: Descriptive Catalogue of the Hebrew and Samaritan Manuscripts in the Sassoon Library*. Oxford 5692, 1932
Ṣubayri, R. Yosef. *Siddur Keneset ha-Gedolah* [The siddur Keneset ha-Gedolah], vol. 1. Tel Aviv–Jerusalem 1976; vol. 4, Jerusalem 1996.
———. *Va-yiṣbor Yosef Bar* [And Joseph laid up corn], vol. 4. Jerusalem, 2000.
Teherani, Avishai, *Keter Shem Ṭov* [A good reputation], 1–2. Jerusalem 2000.
Tobi, Joseph. *'Iyyunim bi-Megillat Teiman* [Studies in the Jews of Yemen]. Jerusalem 1986.
Tsuri'eli, Yosef, *Temurot ba-Ḥinukh be-Teiman (5663–5708; 1903–1948)*. Jerusalem 1990.
Weisberg, Yosef David. *Oṣar ha-Berit, Enṣiklopeya le-Inyanei Milah* [Circumcision Compendium, an Encyclopedia on Brit Milah], vols. 1–2. Jerusalem 1993.
Yosef, R. Ovadia. *Shut Yabi'a Omer*, pt. 2, *Even ha-Ezer*, Jerusalem, 1986; part 5 Jerusalem, 1969.
Zadok, Yosef. *Be-Se'arot Teiman* [In the Tempests of Yemen]. Tel Aviv 1956.

2. RESPONSA BY THE SAGES OF YEMEN

Rabbi Almog Shelomo Akhlufi, Jerusalem
Rabbi Raṣon Arusi, chief rabbi of Qiryat Ono
Rabbi Avraham Arye, rabbi of the Beit Midrash Torah ve-Hora'ah, Bnei Brak
Rabbi 'Azaryah Basis, chief rabbi of Rosh haAyin
Rabbi Aharon Ben David, chairman of the Ahavat Teiman Association, Qiryat Eqron
Rabbi Aviran Yiṣḥaq Halevi, a *dayyan* of the Tel Aviv Rabbinical Court
Rabbi Itamar Ḥayim Kohen, chairman, Or Israel Institute, Bnei Brak
Rabbi Shelomo Maḥfud, president of the Badatz Yoreh De'ah and neighborhood rabbi in Bnei Brak
Rabbi Pinḥas Qoraḥ, Rabbi, Bet ha-Midrah Sha'arei Halakhah, Bnei Brak
Rabbi Shelomo Qoraḥ, chief rabbi of Bnei Brak.

Rabbi Yiṣḥaq Raṣabi, head of Kolel Pe'ulat Ṣaddiq, Bnei Brak
Rabbi Ya'aqov Shar'abi, Jerusalem
Rabbi Ovadya Ya'beṣ, chief rabbi of Qiryat Eqron

3. INTERVIEWERS AND INFORMANTS

Abhar, Rumiyya, Ashqelon
'Adani, Shelomo, Bnei Brak
Aharon, Sa'ida, Rosh haAyin
Alsheikh, Sarah, Jerusalem
'Aṣmi, Zekharyah, Moshav Tarum
Atari, Ezra, Rosh haAyin
Atari, Yosi, Rosh haAyin
Badiḥi, Michal, Givatayim
Bashaḥ, Einat, Yavneh
Bashaḥ, Shoshana, Yavneh
Bin Nun, Adam, Bnei Brak
Bora, Beracha, Bat Yam
Dhahabani, Shimon, Qiryat Ono
Gafni, Sara, Yavneh
Himoff, Aviva, New York
Ḥofi, Ḥannah, Rosh haAyin
Ḥofi, Shemuel, New York
Ḥasid, Ilanit, Sha'ar Efrayim
Idan, Yehuda, Petah Tikvah
'Itwar, Yirmiyahu, Rishon Lezion
'Itwar, Zekharya, Rishon Lezion
Jerafi, Aviḥai, Pardes Hannah
Jeraydi, Fa'iz, New York
Jeraydi, Shimon, New York
Kohen, Aharon, Bnei Brak
Kubani, Yissakhar, London
Lahav, Shalom, Sede Ya'aqov
Levi, Yehonatan, Rosh haAyin
Maḥfud, Naomi, Givatyayin
Maḥfud, Shelomi, Einav
Maḥfud, Shimon and Raḥel, Netanya
Malakhi, Shimon, Kfar Saba
Nissim, Sara, Moshav Naḥam
Oshri, Yoel, Tel Aviv
Qa 'atabi, Na'ama, Gedera

Portuguez, Omri, Nes Ziona
Rada'i, Neḥemyah, Bnei Brak
Raṣhabi, Shelomo, Moshav Tenuvot
Sa'ad, Shalom, Rosh haAyin
Shar'abi, Ṣefanya, Modi'in
Shunem, Yair, Rosh haAyin
Shunem, Yocheved, Ra'anana
Ṣuberi, Menashe, Ramat haSharon
Ṣabari, Sa'id, New York
Ṣadoq, Gilad, Bnei Brak
Ṣadoq, Shimon and Ruma, Qiryat Ono
Ṣadoq, Tov, Qiryat Ono
Ta 'asa, 'Amiel, Qiryat Ono
Tov, Osheri, Hod haSharon
Yehuda, Aharon, Rosh haAyin
Yonati, Vardit, Qiryat Ono
Zehavi, Idit, Rehovot
Zindani, Lirit, Rehovot

INDEX

Male Personal Names

'Abdallah 111, 115, 164, 176, 178, 379. *See also* 'Ovadyah
'Ābiṣ 164
Abū S'ūd/Abūs'ūd 115, 141, 175, 178, 364
Abūrūs/Aburus 115, 175, 178
Adam 164, 383
Adi'el 383
Adīb 164
Aḥiya 108
Aḥsan 115. 175, 178
'Alān 379
'Amiel 164
Amiḥai 363
'Amr/'Amar/'Ammar 140, 176, 178, 263, 305, 378
'Amrān/'Amran/'Amram 58, 115, 165, 176, 178, 201, 364, 380
Aryeh 381
Asher 382
'Ashūra 108
Avigad 115, 141, 175, 178, 364. *See also* Abu Su'ūd
Avishai 363
Avraham/Ibrāhim/Ibrāhīm/Ibrahīm//Ībrahim/Brahīm/Brāhim/Bīrhīm/Barhūn 15, 18, 41, 57, 68, 72, 96, 109, 114, 175, 178, 200, 201, 253, 254, 263, 316, 378, 379
Avshalom 108, 165
'Awaḍ/'Awwaḍ/'Awāḍ/'Awūḍ/'Awwād/'Awād 57, 68, 108, 110, 114, 115, 144, 145, 178, 255, 262, 263, 364, 379. *See also* 'Oded; 'Ovadyah

Female Personal Names

Family and Male Bynames

Zaqen 219
Zaydi 67
Zekharyah/Zekharya' 145, 146

FAMILY NAMES

Place Names

Synagogue Names